Henrietta Maria of France and Navarre

James II, King of England, Scotland, and Ireland
~ Arabella Churchill

Henrietta FitzJames
= Henry Waldegrave, 1st Baron Waldegrave

Lady Anne Lennox
= William Anne Keppel, 2nd Earl of Albemarle

James Waldegrave, 1st Earl Waldegrave
= Mary Webb

Lady Elizabeth Keppel
= Francis Russell, Marquess of Tavistock

James Waldegrave, 2nd Earl Waldegrave
= Maria Walpole

John Russell, 6th Duke of Bedford
= Lady Georgiana Gordon

Lady Anne Horatia Waldegrave
= Vice Admiral Lord Hugh Seymour
(see left)

Lady Louisa Jane Russell
= James Hamilton, 1st Duke of Abercorn

James Hamilton, 2nd Duke of Abercorn
= Lady Mary Anna Curzon-Howe

Lady Rosalind Cecilia Caroline Bingham = James Albert Edward Hamilton, 3rd Duke of Abercorn

Four Lines of Descent from
CHARLES I, KING OF ENGLAND, SCOTLAND, AND IRELAND
to DIANA, PRINCESS OF WALES

THE ANCESTRY OF

PRINCESS OF WALES

THE ANCESTRY OF

Diana

PRINCESS OF WALES

for Twelve Generations

RICHARD K. EVANS

NEW ENGLAND HISTORIC GENEALOGICAL SOCIETY

Boston, Massachusetts

2007

ISBN-10: 0-88082-208-2
ISBN-13: 978-0-88082-208-4
Library of Congress Control Number: 2007927891

Design by Stephen Bridges, Bridges Design, *bridgesdesign@comcast.net*
Page layout by Anne Lenihan Rolland
Endpaper chart developed by Scott C. Steward and
rendered by Maria T. Sas, NuGraphic Design
Printed by Sheridan Books, Ann Arbor, Michigan

Jacket image: Diana, Princess of Wales, wearing the Spencer
family tiara during her 1983 tour of Australia. "Diana Australia,"
Tim Graham/Getty Images.

NEW ENGLAND HISTORIC GENEALOGICAL SOCIETY®
101 Newbury Street, Boston, MA 02116
www.NewEnglandAncestors.org

FIRST EDITION
Manufactured in the United States of America

To my dear wife Sherry,
who let me visit,
without losing her patience,
countless libraries across the United States
and Western Europe.

CONTENTS

PREFACE

I began compiling this ancestry of Lady Diana Spencer when she became engaged to the Prince of Wales in 1981. Yet one could say that the book had its real beginnings nearly twenty years earlier, when as a teenager I discovered a well-worn copy of *The Plantagenet Ancestry* by Lieutenant-Colonel William Harry Turton at the Newberry Library in Chicago. Turton's hand-drawn charts in that 1928 publication traced the known ancestors of Princess Elizabeth of York, wife of Henry VII, King of England. My interest in genealogy ignited, I was soon drawing similar charts detailing the forebears of Queen Elizabeth II and Prince Philip. A second inspiration, undocumented but extending through eighteen generations, was Gerald Paget's 1977 two-volume study, *The Lineage and Ancestry of Prince Charles, Prince of Wales,* which could be considered the "spousal companion" of this book. Paget deserves much credit as the first person to produce and publish a "stand-alone" ancestral study of the current British royal family.

My guiding principle has always been to identify as many of the late Princess's ancestors within twelve generations as possible. I have presented them in the classic genealogical format of an *ahnentafel,* or "ancestor table," whose numbering system offers a clear way to present successive generations. I have also included short profiles of approximately thirty of Diana's more noteworthy forebears.

To compile this book, I have relied heavily upon printed historical, biographical, and genealogical sources to reduce the number of blank spaces that often appear in multi-generation ancestral studies. In addition, I used parish registers, bishops' transcripts, court records, wills, and other documents containing data not often found in printed books. I have included at least one source citation for each ancestor, and I hope the many references and comprehensive bibliography at the end of the book will both document this work and facilitate future research.

As one might expect, the brilliant marriages of the Spencer family bring the Princess many descents from distinguished peers of the realm from the sixteenth through twentieth centuries. Notable eighteenth- and nineteenth-century peers include Lord Revelstoke of the Baring banking family and two famous field marshals, the Earl of Lucan (of the Crimean War) and the Marquess of Anglesey (who fought at Waterloo). Admiral the Earl Howe was victor of the Battle of the Glorious First of June in 1794, and nearly a century earlier the celebrated John Churchill, 1st Duke of Marlborough, resoundingly defeated the French at the battle of Blenheim; another ancestor, the 3rd Earl of Peterborough, drove the French from Spain. Diana also descends from two

British prime ministers (Sir Robert Walpole and the 2nd Earl Grey), from several hundred members of the House of Commons, and from some of the great merchants of London and Amsterdam. Her ancestry displays a liberal infusion of Royalist army officers who supported the King's cause during the English civil wars, as well as the King himself (Charles I) and his two sons, Charles II and James II. On Parliament's side, Diana counted among her ancestors General Lord Fairfax (whose son was Captain-General of the New Model Army), a Regicide colonel (Sir Hardress Waller), and an aunt of the Protector Oliver Cromwell. Lady Dorothy Sidney, later the wife of the 1st Earl of Sunderland, rejected the advances of Diana's poet ancestor Edmund Waller and was memorialized in verse as "Sacharissa." The 3rd Earl of Southampton was Shakespeare's preeminent patron, while another ancestor, the 2nd Earl of Rochester, wrote poetry of a more salacious nature.

Diana's paternal grandmother was a daughter of the 3rd Duke of Abercorn, who gives the Princess an infusion of noble Scottish ancestry. As was often the case with Scottish peers in the eighteenth and nineteenth centuries, the Duke's wife and mother were English. The Princess descends twice from the handsome 4th Duke of Gordon and his wife, Jane Maxwell, known for her vivacity and wit, and famous for raising the Gordon Highlanders from her husband's estates. Another Scots forebear was Archibald Campbell, 9th Earl of Argyll, general of the forces that invaded Scotland in support of Monmouth's rebellion in 1685. As a result, Argyll lost his head at the same place where his father, the 1st Marquess of Argyll, was decapitated for changing sides one time too many during the Civil War.

Yet another of Diana's ancestors, Arnold Joost van Keppel — a page in William of Orange's service — followed his master to England, where he was rewarded with an earldom. Through the Keppels, Diana descends from several dozen members of the knighthood of the seven provinces that are now The Netherlands. In addition to the Keppel family, Diana has other Dutch connections through the 1st Earl Cadogan's wife — Cecilia, daughter of Jan Munter, alderman of Amsterdam — and from the 1st Earl of Arlington's wife, a great-granddaughter of William "the Silent."

Moving farther east in Europe, Diana has several ancestors who provide a gateway to German princely and lesser nobility alike. King James I of England's daughter Elizabeth married Elector Friedrich V of the Palatinate, who accepted the Bohemian crown but ruled only a year before being deposed.* The eldest

---

*The youngest daughter of Elector Friedrich V was Sophia of the Palatinate, heir to the throne of Great Britain under the 1701 Act of Settlement, which placed Sophia ahead of 50 Roman Catholic (or otherwise debarred) heirs with better claims. Sophia was the wife of Elector Ernst August of Hanover and mother of Queen Anne's successor, Elector Georg Ludwig, who reigned in Great Britain as King George I. Since Diana descends from Sophia's elder brother and (probably) from Elector Ernst August, the Princess's ancestry — save for Electress Sophia herself — fully absorbs that of the first Hanoverian King of Great Britain.

surviving son of this marriage, Elector Karl Ludwig, regained possession of his ancestral Palatine lands but detested his wife and married, probably bigamously, one of her ladies-in-waiting. This morganatic marriage produced thirteen children, one of whom, the Duchess of Schomberg, figures in Diana's ancestry. Another German descent is derived through the wife of the 2nd Viscount Howe, a daughter of Sophia Charlotte von Platen-Hallermund, Countess of Leinster and Darlington. In addition to Hanoverian ancestry, this match provided Diana with a gateway into the Danish nobility through the prolific Ahlefeldt and Rantzau families.

Diana descends from several French and Swiss Huguenot families who settled in England, but her most famous Huguenot ancestor was French King Henri IV, who converted to Catholicism to end the French wars of religion in 1593. Most of Diana's forebears in the twelfth generation were born in the late sixteenth or early seventeenth centuries, but several made their mark during the later years of Queen Elizabeth I's reign. One in particular was the Queen's favourite, Robert Devereux, 2nd Earl of Essex, whose overweening ambition displeased his sovereign and ultimately led him to the chopping block. Diana is also descended from three of the four favourites of King James VI and I of Scotland and England. (Only the 1st Earl of Somerset is included in this volume, but the Princess was descended several times over from the siblings of another favourite, George Villiers, 1st Duke of Buckingham.) Queen Anne's intimate confidante, Sarah, Duchess of Marlborough, is one of Diana's most prominent female ancestors.

One of Diana's maternal great-grandfathers was an Irish peer who married an American "dollar princess," daughter of millionaire Wall Street broker Frank Work. This alliance was typical of many nineteenth-century transatlantic marriages, bringing infusions of American capital to the cash-starved European and British nobility. The marriage gives Diana more than one hundred American ancestors, some twenty-five of whom were among the early settlers of New England. One of her more prominent American forebears was Joseph Strong, a respected Philadelphia surgeon and first cousin of Revolutionary War hero Nathan Hale. Through her maternal grandfather, Lord Fermoy, Diana descends as well from several notable families of Cork, including the Hennessys and an ancestor shared with the statesman Edmund Burke.

Through her musically gifted maternal grandmother, Diana is descended from a large cross-section of middle-class Scots, primarily in the County and City of Aberdeen. This group includes paint manufacturers, an architect, printers, scholars, prosperous farmers, judges, soldiers, and a variety of merchants, but also more than a few baronets, lairds and their ladies, a King's "fool," a sprinkling of Scots peers and one Scottish primate, the Archbishop of St. Andrews.

In almost any study of this type, difficulty arises when there is an historical or legal dispute over a child's parentage. One notable case is that of Mary Crofts (daughter of Lucy Walter), whom King Charles II never accepted as one of his children. The currently accepted theory is that Mary Crofts was the daughter of the 1st Earl of Carlingford, an opinion I have accepted for the purposes of this study. (Lucy Walter's elder child, the Duke of Monmouth, was accepted by Charles II as his first illegitimate son, but Monmouth is not one of Diana's ancestors.) Other rumors of illegitimacy among Diana's ancestors of lower social standing have kept the research intriguing. In all these cases, I have researched the alternative lineage of the putative parents, but for the purposes of this work, only the most likely parent appears in the ancestor table.

The ancestry of Diana, Princess of Wales, suggests the social breadth of British — and American and continental European — history. These forebears will in all likelihood be shared by future monarchs of the United Kingdom; in any case, the Princess's ancestry is surely interesting in its own right, and this work is my tribute to her memory.

Richard K. Evans
June 2007

ACKNOWLEDGMENTS

I would like to thank my esteemed editorial colleagues, Gary Boyd Roberts and Scott C. Steward of the New England Historic Genealogical Society, for tirelessly reading and reviewing many drafts of this book, always making helpful suggestions, corrections, and additions. Both have also located materials that were not readily accessible to me. Without their help, this volume would still lie on a dusty shelf in manuscript form, never to be seen by anyone else. (In addition to editorial assistance, Gary also gave me the notes used to compile *American Ancestors and Cousins of The Princess of Wales,* the book he coauthored in 1984 with William Addams Reitwiesner.)

I also thank Penelope L. Stratton, Jerome E. Anderson, Elizabeth Petty Bentley, Stephen Bridges, David March, Rollins Maxwell, Anne Rolland, and Maria Sas for their assistance in matters of style, design, layout, and consistency, and for their help in bringing the book to press-ready form; Michael J. Wood, for contributing information on several ancestors he shares with the Princess of Wales; and Kimball G. Everingham for his research in Salt Lake City. The following institutions provided access to almost all the printed material referenced herein: Family History Library and University of Utah Library (Salt Lake City), Society of Genealogists and British Library (London), Edinburgh Public Library, Centraal Bureau voor Genealogie (The Hague), Bibliothèque Nationale (Paris), Library of Congress (Washington, D.C.), Atlanta Public Library and Emory University Library (Atlanta), Chicago Public Library, University of Chicago Library, and Newberry Library (Chicago), New England Historic Genealogical Society (Boston), Stanford University Library (Palo Alto), University of California at Berkeley Library, Fort Wayne Public Library, and Cleveland Public Library. In the United Kingdom, the Public Record Office at Kew (now part of the National Archives), the National Archives of Scotland (Edinburgh), the Wiltshire Archaeological and Natural History Society (Devizes), the Essex Record Office (Chelmsford), and the Surrey Archaeological Society (Guildford) have all been helpful in my search for original documents and manuscripts.

I gratefully acknowledge the following organizations for permission to publish images from their collections: Getty Images; The Image Works (Woodstock, Vermont); the Museum of the City of New York; the National Portrait Gallery, London; the New-York Historical Society; and the Tate Gallery, London.

R.K.E.

ABOUT THE FORMAT

In an *ahnentafel,* each person is assigned a number, with the subject (in this case, Lady Diana Frances Spencer) assigned the number 1. The subject's father is always number 2 and the mother number 3; paternal grandparents are 4 and 5, maternal grandparents 6 and 7, etc. In every father-mother pair, the father has an even number (n) and the mother an odd number ($n + 1$). The father's number is always double the child's number ($2n$), and the mother is always double the child's number plus one ($2n + 1$).

Thus the line from any ancestor in the *ahnentafel* can be determined mathematically, as the identity of father and child may be found by halving, or doubling, the number. For example, the line to one of the late Princess's great-great-grandmothers from King Charles II can be shown as follows:

16. Frederick Spencer, 4th Earl Spencer
17. Adelaide Horatia Elizabeth Seymour

34. Colonel Sir Horace Beauchamp Seymour
35. Elizabeth Malet Palk

68. Vice Admiral Lord Hugh Seymour
69. Lady Anne Horatia Waldegrave

136. Francis Seymour-Conway, 1st Marquess of Hertford
137. Lady Isabella Fitzroy

274. Charles Fitzroy, 2nd Duke of Grafton
275. Lady Henrietta Somerset

548. Henry Fitzroy, 1st Duke of Grafton
549. Isabella Bennet, Countess of Arlington in her own right

1096. HM King Charles II, King of England, Scotland, and Ireland
1097. Barbara Villiers, Duchess of Cleveland for life

With this kind of numbering system, of course, numbers cannot be skipped, even when an ancestor is unknown. Thus the reader will sometimes encounter numbers followed by blank lines to denote unknown names.

NOTES ON NUMBERING

As with most multi-generation ancestries, Diana has multiple lines of descent from some individuals or couples. For instance, she was descended in four ways from Henry Wriothesley, 3rd Earl of Southampton, and his wife, Elizabeth Vernon. Full biographical information is given the first time this couple appears, as numbers 4098 and 4099. At their subsequent mentions as Nos. 4910–4911, 5252–5253, and (outside the parameters of this work) 10156–10157, the reader will find only their names, along with numbers to show their respective places in the *ahnentafel*. For instance:

5252. HENRY WRIOTHESLEY, 3RD EARL OF SOUTHAMPTON = 4098 = 4910
5253. ELIZABETH VERNON = 4099 = 4911

Although the last numbered person in the twelfth generation, an unknown matrilineal ancestress, is number 8191, the reader will occasionally encounter forebears with higher numbers within some of the biographical information. These higher-numbered people are parents of someone already listed. For instance, in biographical material for George Feilding, 1st Earl of Desmond [No. 5276], we see mention of his father, William Feilding, 1st Earl of Denbigh, whose number is 5276 x 2, or 10552. Sometimes we can discern multiple lines of descent through these higher numbers. When we encounter the 1st Earl of Denbigh again, in the biographical material for his daughter, Lady Margaret Feilding [No. 5983], we see his number is still 10552. If the only line of ancestry between Denbigh and Diana was through Lady Margaret, her father would be 5983 x 2, or 11966. Halving the 10552 tells us that there is another line, and sends us back to No. 5276.

GLOSSARY

Bt.	Baronet
C.B.	Companion of the Most Honourable Order of the Bath
D.B.E.	Dame Commander of the Most Excellent Order of the British Empire
D.C.V.O.	Dame Commander of the Royal Victorian Order
G.C.V.O.	Knight Grand Cross of the Royal Victorian Order
F.R.S.	Fellow of the Royal Society
G.C.B.	Knight Grand Cross of the Most Honourable Order of the Bath
G.C.H.	Knight Grand Cross of the Royal Guelphic Order (Hanover)
HH	His or Her Highness
HIH	His or Her Imperial Highness
HM	His or Her Majesty
Hon.	Honourable
HRH	His or Her Royal Highness
HSH	His or Her Serene Highness
K.B.	Knight of the Most Honourable Order of the Bath
K.C.B.	Knight Commander of the Most Honourable Order of the Bath
K.C.H.	Knight Commander of the Royal Guelphic Order (Hanover)
K.G.	Knight Companion of the Most Noble Order of the Garter
K.P.	Knight of the Most Illustrious Order of St. Patrick
K.T.	Knight of the Most Ancient and Most Noble Order of the Thistle
M.C.	Military Cross
Most Rev.	Most Reverend
M.P.	Member of Parliament
M.V.O.	Member of the Royal Victorian Order
O.B.E.	[Member of the Most Excellent] Order of the British Empire
O.M.	[Member of the] Order of Merit
P.C.	Privy Councilor
Right Hon.	Right Honourable
Right Rev.	Right Reverend
TH	Their Highnesses
TM	Their Majesties
TRH	Their Royal Highnesses
V.A.	[Member of the] Royal Order of Victoria and Albert
Ven.	Venerable

Diana, Princess of Wales

---

1. LADY DIANA FRANCES SPENCER [from 28 Aug. 1996, Diana, Princess of Wales], born at Park House, Sandringham, Norfolk 1 July 1961 and died at Paris 31 Aug. 1997. She married at St. Paul's Cathedral, London 29 July 1981 (marriage dissolved by divorce 28 Aug. 1996), **HRH THE PRINCE CHARLES PHILIP ARTHUR GEORGE, PRINCE OF WALES, K.G. (1968), K.T. (1977), G.C.B. (1974), O.M. (2002), P.C. (1977),** born at Buckingham Palace, London 14 Nov. 1948, son of HRH The Prince Philip, Duke of Edinburgh, K.G., and HM Queen Elizabeth II Alexandra Mary, Queen of Great Britain and Northern Ireland. He married, 2nd, at the Guildhall, Windsor, Berkshire 9 April 2005, Camilla Rosemary Shand [from 9 April 2005, HRH The Duchess of Cornwall], born at King's College Hospital, London 17 July 1947, formerly wife of Brigadier General Andrew Henry Parker-Bowles, O.B.E., and daughter of Major Bruce Middleton Hope Shand, M.C., and Hon. Rosalind Maud Cubitt, daughter of Roland Calvert Cubitt, 3rd Baron Ashcombe.

Children:

    i. **HRH PRINCE WILLIAM ARTHUR PHILIP LOUIS OF WALES,** born at St. Mary's National Health Hospital, Paddington, London 21 June 1982.

    ii. **HRH PRINCE HENRY CHARLES ALBERT DAVID OF WALES,** born at St. Mary's National Health Hospital, Paddington, London 15 Sept. 1984.

Lady Diana Frances Spencer
Born at Sandringham, Norfolk 1 July 1961
Died at Paris 31 August 1997

Born into an aristocratic, landed family, the Hon. Diana Spencer's formative years were spent in comfortable circumstances. When their parents divorced, the Spencer children remained with their father, then Viscount Althorp. The divorce was a painful one for all parties involved, and for Diana it had a lasting impact. When she was thirteen, with the death of Diana's grandfather, Lord Althorp succeeded as Earl Spencer and moved his family to Althorp House, the Spencers' ancestral home in Northamptonshire. Now styled Lady Diana Spencer, Lord Spencer's youngest daughter attended a girls' school near Sevenoaks in Kent. She excelled at sports but was an otherwise average student. In 1977, Diana met Prince Charles at Althorp, where he had been invited by her elder sister Sarah. The next winter, Diana spent three months at a Swiss finishing school, where she learned to ski; skiing would remain a lifelong passion. When she returned to England she worked briefly as a nanny, and the following year her mother bought her a flat in South Kensington, which Diana shared with several roommates. Her developing interest in child care led to a job as an assistant in a kindergarten in Pimlico. She continued to work there until her engagement to the Prince of Wales was announced on 24 February 1981, a year after the couple had begun dating.

On the day of her wedding, the streets of London overflowed with people trying to get a glimpse of the beautiful young Princess. Outside Britain the ceremony was estimated to have reached an audience of a billion television viewers. The fairy-tale wedding, which the twenty-year-old Princess later described as one of the happiest days of her life, did not presage the troublesome marital problems of the years to come. Her newfound celebrity meant that she was photographed and documented wherever she went. She had to learn the roles and responsibilities of her new position as Princess of Wales, and she had to deal with an increasingly intrusive press corps. Diana was also determined to rear her two boys without heavy reliance on the network of surrogates typically employed in British royal households. She wanted to provide her sons with a normal, well-adjusted upbringing, which included keeping them sheltered from the prying eyes of the press.

The Princess of Wales used her influence and position to campaign for causes in which she believed, supporting more than 100 charitable organizations. Among her favorite causes were helping the young homeless; providing treatment for leprosy sufferers in many Third World countries; working with HIV and AIDS patients; providing support to children's hospitals; and the English National Ballet, as dance was another of her passions. The last cause that she supported, perhaps the one with which she will be most associated, was the campaign to ban the use of land mines.

Diana knew that her involvement with a charity would attract worldwide media attention, and that this sponsorship would make a major contribution. The Princess had become very astute at "working" the press. She learned how to use her beauty and the mystique of her position to obtain public sympathy or support. This skill was evident in the accounts of her dissolving marriage that appeared in the press or in televised interviews. In the battle for the hearts and minds of the people of Britain, Princess Diana emerged as the "people's princess," while the Royal Family's public relations effort to improve the Prince of Wales' standing failed to make much headway. By comparison, the Royal Family appeared out of touch, particularly in the late '90s. And so Diana's untimely death, and the funeral procession that followed, garnered even more press coverage and global viewership than had her wedding ceremony in 1981.

HRH The Prince Charles Philip Arthur George, Prince of Wales
Born at London 14 November 1948
Married, 2nd, at Windsor, Berkshire 9 April 2005
Camilla Rosemary (Shand) Parker-Bowles

As heir to the British throne, Prince Charles (as he is generally known) is the 21st Prince of Wales. His education began in the nursery, and at age nine he attended Hill House, a preparatory school in West London. He was then sent to Cheam School in Berkshire and afterwards to Gordonstoun in Morayshire, following his father to both schools. Prince Charles entered Trinity College, Cambridge, in 1967, where he read Archaeology and Anthropology and, for his last two years, History. In 1969, he spent a summer term in Aberystwyth at the University of Wales in preparation for his investiture as Prince of Wales. He graduated from Cambridge with a B.A. (Honours) degree in May 1970, the first heir to the throne to earn a degree.

In 1971, he spent five months at the Royal Air Force College at Cranwell learning to fly jet aircraft and obtaining his RAF wings. Later that year the Prince entered the Royal Navy, encouraged by his great-uncle, Earl Mountbatten. The Prince of Wales served as a sub-lieutenant on the destroyer *HMS Norfolk* and on two frigates, then joined the 845 Naval Air Squadron. In early 1976, he took command of the coastal minehunter *HMS Bronington,* leaving the Royal Navy at the end of the same year. He currently holds the rank of Vice-Admiral in the Royal Navy, Lieutenant-General in the Army, and Air Marshal in the Royal Air Force.

The Prince of Wales takes his official responsibilities very seriously and is associated as a patron or president with around 200 organizations that cover a broad range of interests and activities: young people, the unemployed, the disabled, the elderly, problems of the inner cities, education, medicine, the arts, conservation, national heritage, environment, architecture, and sports.

In 2005, Prince Charles married Camilla Rosemary (Shand), the former wife of Andrew Henry Parker-Bowles. Charles and Camilla share a passion for country pursuits, notably hunting and horseback-riding. Their romance began in 1970, although both ultimately married others. After their wedding, Mrs. Parker-Bowles became known as HRH The Duchess of Cornwall. When the Prince of Wales ascends the throne, she will be known as HRH The Princess Consort.

First Generation

---

2. Edward John Spencer, 8th Earl Spencer, M.V.O. (1954), Equerry to TM King George VI 1950-52 and Queen Elizabeth II 1952-54, Acting Master of the (Royal) Household 1954, born at 24 Sussex Square, London 24 Jan. 1924 and died at the Humana Wellington Hospital, St. John's Wood, London 29 March 1992. He married, 2nd, at Caxton Hall, London 14 July 1976, Raine McCorquodale, born at 6 Culross Street, Park Lane, London 9 Sept. 1929, formerly wife of Gerald Humphrey Legge, 9th Earl of Dartmouth, and daughter of Captain Alexander George McCorquodale and Dame Mary Barbara Hamilton Cartland, D.B.E. He married, 1st, at Westminster Abbey, London 1 June 1954 (marriage dissolved by divorce at London 15 April 1969),

    3. Hon. Frances Ruth Burke Roche, born at Park House, Sandringham, Norfolk 20 Jan. 1936 and died at Seil, Argyllshire 3 June 2004. She married, 2nd, at the Westminster Register Office, London 2 May 1969 (marriage dissolved by divorce in 1990), Peter Shand Kydd, born at "Waratah," Highgate, London 23 April 1925 and died 23 March, buried at Aldeburgh, Suffolk 6 April 2006, son of Norman Shand Kydd.

Edward John Spencer, 8th Earl Spencer
Born at London 24 January 1924
Died at London 29 March 1992
Married, 2nd, at London 14 July 1976
Raine (McCorquodale), Countess of Dartmouth

Hon. Frances Ruth Burke Roche
Born at Sandringham, Norfolk 20 January 1936
Died at Seil, Argyllshire 3 June 2004
Married, 2nd, at London 2 May 1969 (divorced in 1990)
Peter Shand Kydd

Educated at Eton and Sandhurst, "Johnnie" Althorp did not get along well with his father, the 7th Earl Spencer, although his father was pleased

---

by his choice of a bride. Soon after Viscount Althorp's betrothal to Hon. Frances Burke Roche, they were separated for six months when his duties as Equerry required him to attend the Queen and Prince Philip on their post-coronation Commonwealth tour. The couple exchanged letters daily during Johnnie's absence, and a life-size painting of Frances hung in Althorp's cabin aboard *HMS Gothic*. On the return leg of the tour the Queen gave Johnnie permission to disembark at Tobruk, and he flew home to prepare for his marriage. The Queen also gave her permission for the wedding to be held in Westminster Abbey. The press described the ceremony as the wedding of the year.

The couple first lived with Frances' recently widowed mother, Lady Fermoy, at Park House, Sandringham. A curious alliance developed between Johnnie and his mother-in-law, a friendship that made it impossible for Frances to confide in her mother. Lady Althorp found her marriage unfulfilling, and her relationship with Lord Althorp began to unravel. Frances often made trips into London to shop and dine, and on one such trip with Johnnie, she met Peter and Janet Shand Kydd. When, ultimately, Johnnie divorced her the details of her affair with the married Shand Kydd were used in the custody battle for the children. (When the divorce petition was heard, Lady Fermoy testified against her daughter.) Shortly after her divorce was finalized, Frances married Peter Shand Kydd, and later settled in Scotland, on the Isle of Seil.

Johnnie succeeded to the earldom in 1975 and moved his children to Althorp House in Brington. The following year he married the recently divorced Countess of Dartmouth, with whom he had worked in the European Heritage Year in 1975. Although Raine Spencer cared deeply for her husband, her Spencer stepchildren found her hard to tolerate. The 8th Earl Spencer is perhaps best remembered escorting his youngest daughter, Diana, up the aisle of St. Paul's Cathedral in 1981, during her marriage to the Prince of Wales. Lord Spencer had only recently recovered from a severe stroke; he died in 1992.

Frances Shand Kydd's second marriage ended in divorce. She later converted to the Roman Catholic faith, and lived quietly on Seil until her death in 2004.

Second Generation

---

4. ALBERT EDWARD JOHN SPENCER, 7TH EARL SPENCER, Lord Lieutenant of Northamptonshire 1952-67, born at London 23 May 1892 and died at St. Matthew's Nursing Home, Northampton 9 June 1975. He married at St. James's Church, Piccadilly, London 26 Feb. 1919,

5. LADY CYNTHIA ELINOR BEATRIX HAMILTON, D.C.V.O. (1953), O.B.E. (1943), Lady of the Bedchamber to HM Queen Elizabeth (later HM Queen Elizabeth The Queen Mother) 1937-72, born at 111 Park Street, London 16 Aug. 1897 and died at Althorp House, Brington, Northamptonshire 4 Dec. 1972.

6. EDMUND MAURICE BURKE ROCHE, 4TH BARON FERMOY, M.P. [as Lord Fermoy] 1924-35 and 1943-45, Mayor of King's Lynn 1931-32, twin, born at Chelsea, London 15 May 1885 and died at King's Lynn, Norfolk 8 July 1955. He married at St. Devenick's Church, Bielside, Aberdeenshire 17 Sept. 1931,

7. DAME RUTH SYLVIA GILL, D.C.V.O. (1966), O.B.E. (1952), Extra Lady of the Bedchamber to HM Queen Elizabeth The Queen Mother 1956-60, Lady of the Bedchamber to HM from 1960, an accomplished pianist, born at Dalhebity, Bielside 2 Oct. 1908 and died at 36 Eaton Square, London 6 July 1993.

Edmund Maurice Burke Roche, 4th Baron Fermoy
Born at London 15 May 1885
Died at King's Lynn, Norfolk 8 July 1955

Dame Ruth Sylvia Gill, D.C.V.O.
Born at Bielside, Aberdeenshire 2 October 1908
Died at London 6 July 1993

Early in 1921, the American-bred 4th Baron Fermoy arrived in England, wealthy, titled, and a graduate of Harvard. He soon became a great friend of the Duke of York (later George VI). As a favour to his second son, King George V granted Lord Fermoy the lease of Park

House, an enormous place originally built to handle the overflow of visitors at Sandringham House in Norfolk. Fermoy was an excellent shot, and as a neighbour and tenant spent much time with the Royal Family. Having built a good reputation locally, he was able to win the 1924 parliamentary election as candidate for King's Lynn, and was re-elected with growing majorities in the next two elections.

He then met the musically talented Ruth Gill, who had been sent to Paris in the 1920s to study under the renowned French pianist Alfred Cortot at the Paris Conservatory. The high point of her musical career was her performance before the Royal Family at the Royal Festival Hall, but following her marriage, with many responsibilities as the wife of an M.P., she stopped practicing the piano so conscientiously. Lady Fermoy eventually found her musical niche as founder of the King's Lynn Festival, an annual cultural event featuring music, plays, films and poetry readings. She chaired the festival for a quarter century and then served as its president for another fourteen years. Her contribution to music was recognized by the University of East Anglia, which gave her an honorary doctorate in 1975. After her husband's death, Lady Fermoy often came to London, where she kept a flat in Eaton Square. In 1956, Queen Elizabeth The Queen Mother appointed her Extra Woman of the Bedchamber, and promoted her in 1960 to Woman of the Bedchamber. Lady Fermoy was, with Lady Hambleden and Lady Elizabeth Basset, one of the Queen Mother's closest friends.

Third Generation

8. **Charles Robert Spencer, 6th Earl Spencer, K.G. (1913), G.C.V.O. (1911), P.C. (1892), M.P.** [as Hon. Charles Spencer] 1880-95 and 1900-5, Lord Chamberlain of the (Royal) Household 1905-12, Lord Lieutenant of Northamptonshire 1908-22, born at London 30 Oct. 1857 and died at Spencer House, St. James's Place, London 26 Sept. 1922. He married at St. James's Church, Piccadilly, London 25 July 1887,

9. **Hon. Margaret Baring,** born at London 14 Dec. 1868 and died there 4 July 1906.

10. **James Albert Edward Hamilton, 3rd Duke of Abercorn, K.G. (1928), K.P. (1922), P.C. (Northern Ireland) (1922) and (Great Britain) (1945), M.P.** [as Marquess of Hamilton] 1900-13, Governor of Northern Ireland 1922-45, born at Hamilton Place, Piccadilly, London 30 Nov. 1869 and died at London 12 Sept. 1953. He married at St. Paul's Church, Knightsbridge, London 1 Nov. 1894,

11. **Lady Rosalind Cecilia Caroline Bingham, D.B.E. (1936),** born at London 26 Feb. 1869 and died there 18 Jan. 1958.

12. **James Boothby Burke Roche, 3rd Baron Fermoy, M.P.** [as Hon. James Burke Roche] 1896-1900, born at Twyford Abbey, Middlesex 28 July 1851 and died at Artillery Mansions, Westminster, London 30 Oct. 1920. He married at Christ Church, New York 22 Sept. 1880 (marriage dissolved by divorce at Wilmington, Delaware 3 March 1891),

13. **Frances Eleanor Work,** born at New York 27 Oct. 1857 and died at 1020 Fifth Avenue, New York 26 Jan. 1947. She married, 2nd, at the Hotel Empire, New York 9 Aug. 1905 (marriage dissolved by divorce 5 Nov. 1909), Aurel Batonyi.

14. COLONEL WILLIAM SMITH GILL, C.B. (1919), varnish manufacturer, born at Rosemount Terrace, Aberdeen 16 Feb. 1865 and died at Dalhebity, Bielside, Aberdeenshire 25 Dec. 1957. He married at Queen's Cross Free Church, Aberdeen 30 June 1898,

15. RUTH LITTLEJOHN, born at Cotton Lodge, Woodside, near Aberdeen 4 Dec. 1879 and died at Dalhebity 24 Aug. 1964.

Fourth Generation

---

16. FREDERICK SPENCER, 4TH EARL SPENCER, K.G. (1849), P.C. (1846), M.P. [as Hon. Frederick Spencer] 1831-34 and 1837-41, Equerry to HRH The Duchess of Kent 1840-45, Lord Chamberlain of the (Royal) Household 1846-48 and Lord Steward 1854-57, Vice Admiral 1857, born at Admiralty House, Whitehall, London 14 April 1798 and died at Althorp House, Brington, Northamptonshire 27 Dec. 1857. He married, 1st, at St. George's Church, Hanover Square, London 23 Feb. 1830, his 2nd cousin Georgiana Elizabeth Poyntz, born 27 March, baptized at Easebourne, Sussex 26 June 1799 and died at St. Leonards-on-Sea, Sussex 10 April 1851, daughter of William Stephen Poyntz and Hon. Elizabeth Mary Browne, daughter of Anthony Joseph Browne, 7th Viscount Montagu. He married, 2nd, at St. James's Church, Westminster, London 9 Aug. 1854,

17. ADELAIDE HORATIA ELIZABETH SEYMOUR, born at London 27 Jan. 1825 and died at Guilsborough, Northamptonshire 29 Oct. 1877.

18. EDWARD CHARLES BARING, 1ST BARON REVELSTOKE, international banker, senior partner of Baring Brothers 1873-90, a Director of the Bank of England 1879-91, born at Felbrigg, Norfolk 13 April 1828 and died at 37 Charles Street, Berkeley Square, London 17 July 1897. He married at St. Paul's Church, Knightsbridge, London 30 April 1861,

19. LOUISA EMILY CHARLOTTE BULTEEL, born at London 18 June 1839 and died at Membland Hall, Noss Mayo, Devonshire 16 Oct. 1892.

20. JAMES HAMILTON, 2ND DUKE OF ABERCORN, K.G. (1892), M.P. [as Viscount Hamilton and Marquess of Hamilton] 1860-80, Lord of the Bedchamber to HRH The Prince of Wales (later HM King Edward VII) 1866-85, special envoy to Denmark, Sweden, Norway, France, and Saxony to announce the accession of King Edward VII 1902, born at Brighton, Sussex 24 Aug. 1838 and died at Hampden House, Green Street, London 3 Jan. 1913. He married at St. George's Church, Hanover Square, London 7 Jan. 1869,

21. Lady Mary Anna Curzon-Howe, Lady of the Bedchamber to HM Queen Alexandra, born at London 23 July 1848 and died at 115 Park Street, London 10 May 1929.

22. George Bingham, 4th Earl of Lucan, K.P. (1899), M.P. [as Lord Bingham] 1865-74, Irish representative peer from 1889, bore the Sceptre and Dove at the coronation of HM King Edward VII 1902, Lord Lieutenant of Mayo 1901, born at London 8 May 1830 and died at Laleham House, Staines, Middlesex 5 June 1914. He married at St. George's Church, Hanover Square, London 17 Nov. 1859,

Edward Charles Baring, 1st Baron Revelstoke

Born at Felbrigg, Norfolk 13 April 1828
Died at London 17 July 1897
Married at London 30 April 1861
Louisa Emily Charlotte Bulteel

Edward Charles Baring entered his family's merchant banking business as a clerk in 1850. He soon became a full partner in Baring Brothers and, after his cousin Thomas' death in 1873, Edward was named senior partner along with Russell Sturgis. By 1883, Baring was the undisputed leader of the firm. In recognition of his importance as an international banker, he was created Baron Revelstoke in 1885. Under his leadership, Barings initiated issues for British businesses such as Whitbreads, the Manchester Ship Canal, and Guinness, all extremely profitable investments.

Under Lord Revelstoke's direction in 1888 Barings made a £10 million issue for the Buenos Aires Water Supply and Drainage Company, which was inadequately underwritten and poorly subscribed, and which ultimately caused a liquidity crisis for the firm. With Barings near collapse the Governor of the Bank of England moved to avert a worldwide crisis, persuading the British government to put additional resources at the bank's disposal. Additional capital was obtained by purchasing gold from the Bank of France and the Russian government to strengthen Barings' reserve, and a guarantee fund was created for the firm's liabilities. Revelstoke retired in disgrace in 1890; although he was forced to liquidate many of his assets to meet Barings' obligations, his integrity was never doubted.

23. LADY CECILIA CATHERINE GORDON-LENNOX, born at Portland Place, London 13 April 1838 and died at Laleham House 5 Oct. 1910.

24. EDMUND BURKE ROCHE, 1ST BARON FERMOY, M.P. [as Lord Fermoy] 1859-65, Lord Lieutenant of Cork 1865-74, born at Cork 9 Aug. 1815 and died at Trabolgan, Cork 17 Sept. 1874. He married at West Twyford, Middlesex 27 Aug. 1848,

25. ELIZABETH CAROLINE BOOTHBY, born at Everton Priory, Lancashire 9 Aug. 1821 and died at Torquay, Devonshire 26 April 1897.

26. FRANK WORK, stockbroker with Frank Work & Co., New York, and other firms, born at Chillicothe, Ohio 28 Feb. 1819 and died at 13 East Twenty-sixth Street, New York 16 March 1911. He married at New York 19 Feb. 1857,

27. ELLEN WOOD, born at Chillicothe 18 July 1831 and died at 13 East Twenty-sixth Street 22 Feb. 1877.

28. ALEXANDER OGSTON GILL, varnish manufacturer, baptized at St. Nicholas' Church, Aberdeen 13 Nov. 1832 and died at Fairfield, Aberdeenshire 8 April 1908. He married at Tarves, Aberdeenshire 3 Dec. 1862,

29. BARBARA SMITH MARR, born 14 Aug., baptized at Tarves 11 Sept. 1842 and died before 30 June 1898.

30. MAJOR DAVID LITTLEJOHN, deputy Lord Lieutenant of Aberdeenshire 1893, born at 91 Union Street, Aberdeen 3 April 1841 and died at 9 Rubislaw Terrace, Aberdeen 11 May 1924. He married, 1st, 16 Oct. 1867, Ellen Maria Taylor of Groigue, Tipperary, who died 15 Aug. 1869. He married, 2nd, at Gorval, New Machar, Aberdeenshire 29 March 1872,

31. JANE CROMBIE, born at Gorval 8 Nov. 1843 and died at 9 Rubislaw Terrace 19 Sept. 1917.

Frank Work

Born at Chillicothe, Ohio 28 February 1819
Died at New York 16 March 1911
Married at New York 19 February 1857
Ellen Wood

At the age of 15, Frank Work moved with his widowed mother to Columbus, Ohio; three years later, he went to New York City to work in a dry goods store, soon becoming a partner in the firm of Daily & Work. As the business prospered, Work took his profits and invested them in racehorses. He was a racing enthusiast and competed against the other amateur fast horse drivers he met in the city. One of those rivals was "Commodore" Cornelius Vanderbilt. After racing each other, young Work, Vanderbilt, and other sportsmen met in Burnham's roadhouse at Bloomingdale Road and 76th Street. During the panic of 1873, with the dry goods business of Daily & Work near bankruptcy, Work asked Vanderbilt for a loan, which the Commodore duly provided. After the firm was financially secure, Vanderbilt convinced Work to sell out and become his stockbroker. Vanderbilt furnished the capital Work needed for his margins, and Work soon made enough to start a banking firm. In this way Work was able to increase his fortune to an estimated $15 million.

Fifth Generation

---

32. GEORGE JOHN SPENCER, 2ND EARL SPENCER, K.G. (1801), P.C. (1794), F.R.S. (1780), M.P. [as Viscount Althorp] 1780-83, Lord Privy Seal and Ambassador to Vienna 1794, First Lord of the Admiralty 1794-1801, Home Secretary 1806-7, bibliophile, born at Wimbledon, Surrey 1 Sept. 1758 and died at Althorp House, Brington, Northamptonshire 10 Nov. 1834. He married at the Earl of Lucan's house, Charles Street, Berkeley Square, London 6 March 1781,

33. LADY LAVINIA BINGHAM, a leading London hostess (described by Gibbon as a "charming woman, who with sense and spirit has the simplicity and playfulness of a child"), born at Castlebar, Mayo 27 July 1762 and died at Spencer House, St. James's Place, London 8 June 1831.

34. COLONEL SIR HORACE BEAUCHAMP SEYMOUR, K.C.H. (1836), M.P. 1819-32 and 1841-51, Equerry to TM King William IV 1833-37 and Queen Victoria 1837, and Extra Equerry to HM Queen Adelaide 1838, born at London 22 Nov. 1791 and died at Brighton, Sussex 21 Nov. 1851. He married, 2nd, at St. James's Church, Westminster, London 9 July 1835, Frances Selina Isabella Poyntz, born at London in 1795 and died at 28 St. James's Place, London 29 Aug. 1875, widow of Robert Cotton St. John Trefusis, 18th Baron Clinton, and daughter of William Stephen Poyntz and Hon. Elizabeth Mary Browne, daughter of Anthony Joseph Browne, 7th Viscount Montagu. He married, 1st, at St. George's Church, Hanover Square, London 15 May 1818,

35. ELIZABETH MALET PALK, died at Hampton Court Palace, Middlesex 18 Jan. 1827.

36. HENRY BARING, M.P. 1806-7 and 1820-26, partner in Baring Brothers 1803-23, born 18 Jan. 1776 and died at London 13 April 1848. He married, 1st, at St. Pancras Old Church, London 19 April 1802 (marriage dissolved by divorce in 1825), Maria Matilda Bingham, formerly wife of Comte Alexandre de Tilly, and daughter of U.S. Senator William Bingham and Anne Willing. He married, 2nd, at Felbrigg, Norfolk 9 July 1825,

37. CECILIA ANNE WINDHAM, born at Felbrigg 16 Feb. 1803 and died at Richmond Hill, Surrey 2 Sept. 1874.

38. JOHN CROCKER BULTEEL, M.P. 1832-34, baptized at Yealmpton, Devonshire 15 May 1793 and died at London 10 Sept. 1843. He married at the Earl Grey's house, London 13 May 1826,

39. LADY ELIZABETH GREY, born 10 July, baptized at Essendon, Hertfordshire 12 Aug. 1798 and died 8 Nov. 1880.

George Canning (Prime Minister 1827) is credited with the following quatrain:

> *Tomorrow will shortly reveal*
> *What is kept a secret today:*
> *The marriage of Mr. Bulteel*
> *To the Lady Elizabeth Grey.*

40. JAMES HAMILTON, 1ST DUKE OF ABERCORN, K.G. (1844), P.C. (1846), Groom of the Stole to HRH The Prince Albert (later The Prince Consort) 1846-59, Lord Lieutenant [i.e., Viceroy] of Ireland 1866-68 and 1874, born at Seamore Place, Mayfair, London 21 Jan. 1811 and died at Barons Court, Newtown Stewart, Tyrone 31 Oct. 1885. He married at Fochabers, Banffshire 25 Oct. 1832,

41. LADY LOUISA JANE RUSSELL, V.A., born 8, baptized at Woburn, Bedfordshire 31 July 1811 and died at Coats Castle, Pulborough, Sussex 31 March 1905.

42. RICHARD WILLIAM PENN CURZON [FROM 1821 CURZON-HOWE], 1ST EARL HOWE, G.C.H. (1830), P.C. (1831), Lord of the Bedchamber to HM King George IV 1829-30, Lord Chamberlain to HM Queen Adelaide 1830-31 and 1834-49, born at Gopsall, Leicestershire 11 Dec. 1796 and died at Curzon House, Mayfair, London 12 May 1870. He married, 1st, at 36 Portman Square, London 19 March 1820, Lady Harriet Georgiana Brudenell, born 18 Dec. 1799 and died at Penn House, near Amersham, Buckinghamshire 25 Oct. 1836, daughter of Robert Brudenell, 6th Earl of Cardigan [No. 90], and Penelope Anne Cooke [No. 91]. He married, 2nd, at Great Witley, Worcestershire 9 Oct. 1845,

43. ANNE FRANCES GORE, Maid of Honour to HM Queen Adelaide, born at Bath, Somerset 8 March 1817 and died at Hillesley House, Wotton-under-Edge, Gloucestershire 23 July 1877.

Lady Louisa Jane Russell
Baptized at Woburn, Bedfordshire 31 July 1811
Died at Pulborough, Sussex 31 March 1905
Married at Fochabers, Banffshire 25 October 1832
James Hamilton, 1st Duke of Abercorn

At her death, the Duchess of Abercorn left 162 living descendants. Among her extensive progeny (partly through her seven daughters, all of whom married into the peerage) were Alexander Frederick Douglas-Home, 14th Earl of Home (Prime Minister 1963-64 as Sir Alec Douglas-Home, K.T., and later a Life Peer as Lord Home of The Hirsel); Lady Alice Christabel Montagu-Douglas-Scott (later HRH The Duchess of Gloucester); Sarah Margaret Ferguson (later HRH The Duchess of York, now Sarah, Duchess of York); and Lady Dorothy Evelyn Cavendish, wife of Maurice Harold Macmillan, 1st Earl of Stockton (Prime Minister 1957-63 as Harold Macmillan).

44. GEORGE CHARLES BINGHAM, 3RD EARL OF LUCAN, G.C.B. (1855), M.P. [as Lord Bingham] 1826-30, Field Marshal 1887, an Irish representative peer 1840-88, Lord Lieutenant of Mayo 1845-88, born at London 16 April 1800 and died at 12 South Street, Park Lane, London 10 Nov. 1888. He married at St. Mary's Church, Bryanston Square, London 21 Feb. 1829 (separated ca. 1851),

45. LADY ANNE BRUDENELL, born at Hambleden, Buckinghamshire 29 June 1809 and died at Syon House, Richmond, Surrey 2 April 1877.

46. CHARLES LENNOX [FROM 1836 GORDON-LENNOX], 5TH DUKE OF RICHMOND AND LENNOX, K.G. (1829), P.C. (1830), F.R.S. (1840), M.P. [as Earl of March] 1812-19, bore the Sceptre and Dove at the coronations of TM King William IV 1831 and Queen Victoria 1838, Postmaster-General 1830-34, Lord Lieutenant of Sussex 1835-60, born at Richmond House, Whitehall Gardens, London 3 Aug. 1791 and died at 51 Portland Place, London 21 Oct. 1860. He married at St. James's Church, Westminster, London 10 April 1817,

47. LADY CAROLINE PAGET, born at London 6 June 1796 and died at 51 Portland Place 12 March 1874.

George Charles Bingham, 3rd Earl of Lucan
Born at London 16 April 1800
Died at London 10 November 1888
Married at London 21 February 1829 (separated ca. 1851)
Lady Anne Brudenell

When war broke out in the Crimea in 1854, Major General the Earl of Lucan was appointed to the command of a Cavalry division consisting of a Heavy and a Light Brigade. The Light Brigade was under the command of Lucan's brother-in-law, the Earl of Cardigan. Unfortunately, the two men detested each other and were unable to work together. Lord Cardigan complained about Lucan's interference, and Lucan complained that Cardigan's ideas of independent leadership were encouraged by Lord Raglan, the expedition commander. Held in abeyance by Raglan, Lucan was blamed unfairly for "lack of initiative." At the battle of Balaclava in 1854, it was Lucan who sent the Light Brigade into the "Valley of Death" to prevent the enemy from seizing captured guns. The two Heavy regiments suffered seriously, and Lucan was wounded in the leg by a bullet. Lucan had received orders from Raglan, but these orders became a matter of intense dispute.

When they met, Lord Raglan told Lucan, "You have lost the Light Brigade!" In his dispatch to the government, Raglan stated that "from some misconception of the instruction to advance the lieutenant-general [Lucan] considered that he was bound to attack at all hazards." Lord Lucan protested the censure, but the government decided that he should be recalled, as it was essential that the commander of the Forces should be on good terms with the commander of his Cavalry. Lucan's active military service ended in 1855 but he was made a Lieutenant General in 1858, full General in 1865, and eventually Field Marshal a year before his death.

48. EDWARD ROCHE, born at Cork 13 July 1771 and died 21 March 1855. He married in 1805,

49. MARGARET HONORIA CURTAIN, born posthumously in 1786 and died at Cahiracon, Killadysert, Clare 21 Jan. 1862.

50. JAMES BROWNELL BOOTHBY, born at Sheffield 10 Feb. 1791 and died at Twyford, Middlesex 28 Oct. 1850. He married 1 Aug. 1816,

51. CHARLOTTE CUNNINGHAM, born at Melcombe Regis, Dorset 6 Nov. 1799 and died at Leamington, Warwickshire 22 Jan. 1893.

52. JOHN WORK, civil engineer, born at Plymouth, Devonshire 28 Oct. 1781 and died at Chillicothe, Ohio 16 April 1823. He married at Baltimore, Maryland (license dated 2 Feb. 1808),

53. SARAH DUNCAN BOUDE, born at Elkridge Landing, Maryland 15 Dec. 1790 and died at Columbus, Ohio 17 Dec. 1860.

54. JOHN WOOD, pork packer, born at Shepherdstown, Berkeley County, Virginia [now West Virginia] 29 July 1785 and died at Chillicothe, Ohio 29 Jan. 1848. He married at St. Paul's Church, Chillicothe 13 March 1823,

55. ELEANOR STRONG, baptized at Philadelphia, Pennyslvania 25 Aug. 1805 and died at New York 9 July 1863.

56. DAVID GILL, plumber and painter, baptized at St. Nicholas' Church, Aberdeen 16 Dec. 1796 and died at Caroline Place, Aberdeen 2 Oct. 1868. He married at St. Nicholas' Church 28 July 1825,

57. SARAH OGSTON, baptized at St. Nicholas' Church 26 Oct. 1797 and died at Aberdeen 10 Feb. 1872.

58. WILLIAM SMITH MARR, sheep breeder, born at Tarves, Aberdeenshire 27 Nov. 1810 and died at Uppermill, Tarves 13 Jan. 1898. He married, 2nd, at Tarves 10 Jan. 1858, Elizabeth Munroe, who was born at Belhevie, Aberdeenshire ca. 1815. He married, 1st,

59. HELEN BEAN, baptized at Tarves 21 Sept. 1814 and died 20 July 1852.

60. WILLIAM LITTLEJOHN, bank cashier, born at Littlejohn Street, Aberdeen 12 Aug. 1803 and died at Queen's Gardens, Aberdeen 8 July 1888. He married, 2nd, at St. Nicholas' Church, Aberdeen 3 May 1853, Margaret Jane Urquhart, daughter of the Rev. Alexander Urquhart and Margaret Forbes. He married, 1st, at St. Nicholas' Church 25 March 1830,

61. JANET BENTLEY, born at Aberdeen 26 Jan. 1811 and died there 1 Oct. 1848.

62. JAMES CROMBIE, woolen manufacturer, born at Farway, Aberdeenshire 13 Jan. 1810 and died at 17 Albert Street, Aberdeen 31 Jan. 1878. He married at St. Nicholas' Church, Aberdeen 30 March 1837,

63. KATHERINE SCOTT FORBES, born at Surat, India 1 Dec. 1812 and died at 16 Bon Accord Square, Aberdeen 10 April 1893.

Sixth Generation

64. **JOHN SPENCER, 1ST EARL SPENCER, M.P.** [as John Spencer] 1756-61, born at Althorp House, Brington, Northamptonshire 19 Dec. 1734 and died at Bath, Somerset 31 Oct. 1783. He married at Althorp 20 Dec. 1755,

65. **MARGARET GEORGIANA POYNTZ,** of whom Lady Stafford said "she, somehow, has the art of leading, drawing, or seducing people into right ways," born at Midgham House, Berkshire 27 April 1737 and died at St. Albans, Hertfordshire 18 March 1814.

66. **CHARLES BINGHAM, 1ST EARL OF LUCAN, M.P.** [as Sir Charles Bingham, Bt., and Baron Lucan] 1761-76 and 1782-84, born 22 Sept. 1735 and died at Charles Street, Berkeley Square, London 29 March 1799. He married at Bath, Somerset 25 Aug. 1760,

67. **MARGARET SMITH,** miniature painter, died at St. James's Place, London 27 Feb. 1814.

68. **VICE ADMIRAL LORD HUGH SEYMOUR-CONWAY [LATER SEYMOUR], M.P.** 1784-86 and 1788-1801, Master of the Robes and Keeper of the Privy Purse for HRH The Prince of Wales (later HM King George IV) 1787-95, a Lord of the Admiralty 1795-98, Commander of the Jamaica Station 1799-1801, born 29 April 1759 and died off Jamaica 11 Sept. 1801. He married at the Earl Waldegrave's house, London 3 April 1786,

69. **LADY ANNE HORATIA WALDEGRAVE,** born 8 Nov. 1762 and died 12 June 1801.

70. **SIR LAWRENCE PALK, 2ND BARONET, M.P.** 1787-1812, baptized at Holme House, Madras, India 6 March 1766 and died at Bruton Street, Berkeley Square, London 20 June 1813. He married, 1st, at the Countess of Darnley's house, Berkeley Square 7 Aug. 1789, Lady Mary Bligh, who died 4

March 1791, daughter of John Bligh, 3rd Earl of Darnley, and Mary Stoyte. He married, 2nd, at the Earl of Lisburne's house, London 15 May 1792,

71. LADY DOROTHY ELIZABETH VAUGHAN, born 13 May 1764, baptized at Mamhead, Devonshire 6 Jan. 1765 and died at Bruton Street 15 Feb. 1849.

72. SIR FRANCIS BARING, 1ST BARONET, M.P. 1784-90 and 1794-1806, London partner of Baring Brothers from 1763, Chairman of the East India Company 1792-93, born at Loxbear, Devonshire 18 April 1740 and died at Lee, Kent 12 Sept. 1810. He married at Croydon, Surrey 12 May 1767,

73. HARRIET HERRING, born at Lambeth Palace, Surrey 18 May 1750 and died at Bath, Somerset 4 Dec. 1804.

74. VICE ADMIRAL WILLIAM LUKIN [FROM 1824 WINDHAM], born 20 Sept., baptized at Metton, Norfolk 20 Oct. 1768 and died 12 Jan. 1833. He married at Plaistow, Kent 24 June 1801,

75. ANNE THELLUSSON, born 25 Sept., baptized at the Church of St. Andrew Hubbard, London 19 Oct. 1774 and died 4 Jan. 1849.

Sir Francis Baring, 1st Baronet

Born at Loxbear, Devonshire 18 April 1740
Died at Lee, Kent 12 September 1810
Married at Croydon, Surrey 12 May 1767
Harriet Herring

Francis Baring was sent to London in his early teens to study business; although nearly deaf from his youth, he was notably adept at financial calculations. In 1755, he was accepted for a seven-year apprenticeship under a London merchant who charged his mother the huge sum of £800. Upon his release in 1762, Francis joined his two brothers in the interlocking partnerships of John and Francis Baring & Co. of London. (The other partnership was John and Charles Baring & Co. of Exeter, which was the larger of the two firms.) Barings' business profits were derived primarily from trade between Britain and western Europe, the Iberian peninsula, Italy, the West Indies, and – from the 1770s – with North America. Barings was hugely successful: Francis was worth £5,000 in 1763 and £500,000 forty years later, at which time he was considered the "first merchant of Europe." Pitt created him a baronet in 1793 as a reward for his tireless stewardship of the East India Company.

76. JOHN BULTEEL, born 14 Nov. 1763, baptized at Holbeton, Devonshire 12 Jan. 1765 and died 28 Jan. 1837. He married at Holbeton 29 April 1788,

77. ELIZABETH PERRING, baptized at the Church of St. Bartholomew Exchange, London 4 Aug. 1770 and died 13 Dec. 1834.

78. CHARLES GREY, 2ND EARL GREY, K.G. (1831), P.C. (1806), M.P. [as Charles Grey and Viscount Howick] 1786-1807, bearer of the Sword of State at the coronation of HM King William IV 1831, First Lord of the Admiralty 1806, Foreign Secretary and Leader of the House of Commons 1806-7, First Lord of the Treasury [i.e. **Prime Minister**] 1830-34, born at Falloden, Northumberland 13 March 1764 and died at Howick House, Northumberland 17 July 1845. He married at his mother's house, Hertford Street, London 18 Nov. 1794,

79. HON. MARY ELIZABETH PONSONBY, born 4 March 1776 and died at Eaton Square, London 26 Nov. 1861.

80. JAMES HAMILTON, VISCOUNT HAMILTON by courtesy, **M.P.** 1807-12, born at Petersham Lodge, Surrey 7 Oct. 1786 and died at Upper Brook Street, London 27 May 1814. He married at 7 Cumberland Place, London 25 Nov. 1809,

81. HARRIET DOUGLAS, born 8, baptized at the Church of St. Mary le Bone, Westminster, London 27 June 1792 and died at Argyll House, London 26 Aug. 1833. She married, 2nd, 8 July 1815, her brother-in-law George Gordon [from 1818 Hamilton-Gordon], 4th Earl of Aberdeen, K.G., **Prime Minister** 1852-55, born at Edinburgh 28 Jan. 1784 and died at Argyll House 14 Dec. 1860, son of George Gordon, Lord Haddo by courtesy, and Charlotte Baird.

82. JOHN RUSSELL, 6TH DUKE OF BEDFORD, K.G. (1830), P.C. (1806), M.P. [as Marquess of Tavistock] 1788-92 and 1802, Lord Lieutenant [i.e., Viceroy] of Ireland 1806-7, born at Bedford House, Bloomsbury, London 6 July 1766 and died at the Doune of Rothiemurchus, Perth 20 Oct. 1839. He married, 1st, at Brussels 21 March 1786, Hon. Georgiana Elizabeth Byng, who died at Bath, Somerset 11 Oct. 1801, daughter of George Byng, 4th Viscount Torrington, and Lady Lucy Boyle, daughter of John Boyle, 5th Earl of Cork and Orrery. He married, 2nd, by special license at Fife House, Whitehall, London 23 June 1803,

83. LADY GEORGIANA GORDON, born at Gordon Castle, Banffshire 18 July 1781 and died at Nice, Savoy [now France] 24 Feb. 1853.

Charles Grey, 2nd Earl Grey
Born at Falloden, Northumberland 13 March 1764
Died at Howick, Northumberland 17 July 1845
Married at London 18 November 1794
Hon. Mary Elizabeth Ponsonby

At the age of twenty-two, Charles Grey entered politics as an M.P. for Northumberland. Noted for his skill as a speaker, he soon became a follower of Charles James Fox, the leader of the Radical Whigs in the House of Commons. Like Fox, Grey was a consistent critic of William Pitt, the Prime Minister, attacking Pitt as an exploiter of the existing parliamentary system, noting that Pitt had created 30 new Tory peers who nominated or influenced the return of a total of 40 members of Parliament. William Pitt argued against reform, stating that it would provide additional encouragement to Radicals in Britain who were supporting the French Revolution.

After a three-year absence Grey returned to Westminster in 1800 to oppose the Act of Union with Ireland. In April 1803 Henry Addington offered Grey a place in his coalition government, but Grey refused, commenting that he would not take office without Fox. When Fox entered the Cabinet in January 1806, Grey joined him as First Lord of the Admiralty. After Fox died later that year, Grey became leader of the Whig section of the government. Grey became Foreign Secretary and leader of the House of Commons and was responsible for the act abolishing the African slave trade. When his father died he became 2nd Earl Grey and took his seat in the House of Lords. Although he was no longer in the House of Commons, Earl Grey continued to play an active role in politics. He took part in the campaign for Catholic emancipation and changes in the parliamentary system, but was unsuccessful in persuading Lord Liverpool and his Tory government to introduce other reforms.

In June 1830, Earl Grey made an impressive speech on the need for parliamentary reform. The Duke of Wellington, the prime minister and leader of the Tories in Parliament, replied that the "existing system of representation was as near perfection as possible." It was clear that the Tories would be unwilling to change the electoral system, and that if people wanted change they would have to give their support to the Whigs. In November, Wellington's government was defeated in a vote in the House of Commons. The new king, William IV, was more sympathetic to reform and invited Earl Grey to form a government. As soon as Grey became prime minister he formed a cabinet committee to put forth a plan for parliamentary reform. The resulting bill was passed by the House of Commons by a majority, but despite a powerful speech by Earl Grey, it was defeated in the House of Lords. After the defeat of the reform bill, riots took place in several British towns. Nottingham Castle was burnt down, and in Bristol the Mansion House was set on fire. In 1832, Earl Grey tried again but the House of Lords refused to pass the bill. Grey appealed to William IV for help. The King agreed to Grey's request to create a large number of new Whig peers. This promise was the impetus needed to gain agreement from the Lords to pass the Reform Act. On 7 June, the bill received the Royal Assent and large crowds celebrated in the streets of Britain.

Earl Grey now called another general election; in the new, reformed House of Commons, Grey had a large majority and the Whigs were now able to introduce and pass a series of reforming measures, including an act for the abolition of slavery in the colonies and the 1833 Factory Act. After passing the 1834 Poor Law, Earl Grey decided to resign from office.

84. LIEUT. COLONEL HON. PENN ASSHETON CURZON, M.P. 1784, 1790, and 1792, baptized at Hagley, Worcestershire 31 Jan. 1757 and died at Penn, Buckinghamshire 3 Sept. 1797. He married at Porter's Park, Shenley, Hertfordshire 31 July 1787,

85. SOPHIA CHARLOTTE HOWE, BARONESS HOWE in her own right, born at London 19 Feb. 1762 and died at Pope's Villa, Twickenham, Middlesex 3 Dec. 1835. She married, 2nd, at St. James's Church, Piccadilly, London 1 Oct. 1812, Sir Jonathan Wathen Phipps [from 1814 Waller], 1st Baronet, G.C.H., born 6 Oct. 1769 and died at 8 New Cavendish Street, London 1 Jan. 1852, son of Joshua Phipps and Mary Allen.

86. VICE ADMIRAL SIR JOHN GORE, K.C.B. (1815), Commander-in-Chief of the East Indies Fleet 1831-35, born at Kilkenny 9 Feb. 1772 and died at Datchett, Buckinghamshire 21 Aug. 1836. He married at St. George's Church, Hanover Square, London 15 Aug. 1808,

87. GEORGIANA MONTAGU, Lady of the Bedchamber to HM Queen Adelaide, born in 1786 and died at Wilcot Manor, Wiltshire 14 Nov. 1854.

88. RICHARD BINGHAM, 2ND EARL OF LUCAN, M.P. [as Hon. Richard Bingham, Lord Bingham, and Earl of Lucan] 1790-1800, an Irish representative peer 1801-39, born 4 Dec. 1764 and died at Serpentine Terrace, Knightsbridge, London 30 June 1839. He married by special license at London 26 May 1794 (separated in 1804),

89. LADY ELIZABETH BELASYSE, born at London 17 Jan. 1770 and died at Paris 24 March 1819. She married, 1st, at St. George's Church, Hanover Square, London 24 April 1789 (marriage dissolved by divorce in May 1794), Bernard Edward Howard [who succeeded his kinsman as 12th Duke of Norfolk in 1815], born at Sheffield 21 Nov. 1765 and died at Norfolk House, London 16 March 1842, son of Henry Howard and Juliana Molyneux.

90. ROBERT BRUDENELL, 6TH EARL OF CARDIGAN, born at London 25 April 1769 and died at Portman Square, London 14 Aug. 1837. He married at St. George's Church, Hanover Square, London 8 March 1794,

91. PENELOPE ANNE COOKE, Lady of the Bedchamber to HM Queen Charlotte 1818, born 14 Feb. 1770 and died at Gopsall, Nottinghamshire 2 Feb. 1826.

92. CHARLES LENNOX, 4TH DUKE OF RICHMOND AND LENNOX, K.G. (1812), P.C. (1807), M.P. [as Charles Lennox] 1790-1806, Governor-General of Canada 1818-19, General 1814, Lord Lieutenant of Sussex 1816-19, born 9 Sept. 1764 and died at Richmond, Upper Canada 28 Aug. 1819. He married at Gordon Castle, Banffshire 9 Sept. 1789,

93. LADY CHARLOTTE GORDON, born at Gordon Castle 20 Sept. 1768 and died at Upper Portland Street, London 5 May 1842.

94. HENRY WILLIAM PAGET, 1ST MARQUESS OF ANGLESEY, K.G. (1818), G.C.B. (1815), G.C.H. (1816), P.C. (1827), M.P. [as Lord Paget] 1790-1804 and 1806-10, Lord High Steward at the coronation of HM King George IV 1821, Master General of the Ordnance 1827-28 and 1846-52, Lord Lieutenant [i.e., Viceroy] of Ireland 1828-29 and 1830-33, Field Marshal 1846, commanded the cavalry at Waterloo [where he was wounded in, and subsequently lost, one of his legs], born at London 17 May 1768 and died at Uxbridge House, Old Burlington Street, London 29 April 1854. He married, 2nd, at Edinburgh 15 Nov. 1810, Lady Charlotte Cadogan, born at London 11 July 1781 and died at Uxbridge House 8 July 1853, formerly wife of Hon. Henry Wellesley [later 1st Baron Cowley], and daughter of Charles Sloane Cadogan, 1st Earl

Cadogan, and Mary Churchill. He married, 1st, at the Earl of Jersey's house, Grosvenor Square, London 25 July 1795 (divorced ca. Nov. 1810),

95. Lady Caroline Elizabeth Villiers, born 16 Dec. 1774 and died 16 June 1835; buried at All Souls' Cemetery, Kensal Green, Middlesex. She married, 2nd, at Edinburgh 29 Nov. 1810, George William Campbell, 6th Duke of Argyll, born at Argyll House, London 22 Sept. 1768 and died at Inverary Castle, Argyllshire 22 Oct. 1839, son of John Campbell, 5th Duke of Argyll, and Elizabeth Gunning, Baroness Hamilton in her own right.

96. Edmund Roche of Kildinan, Cork, died in 1823. He married in 1768,
97. Frances Coghlan of Ardoe, Waterford.

98. William Curtain, born ca. 1757 and died at Cork in 1785. He married 24 May 1785,
99. Margaret Deasy, born in 1761 and died 18 March 1847.

100. William Boothby, baptized at Bolingbroke, Lincolnshire 13 Jan. 1763 and died at Nottingham 17 Nov. 1845. He married at St. James's Church, Norton, Derbyshire 31 March 1790,
101. Ann Brownell, born at Rotherham, Yorkshire 15 March 1765 and died at Sheffield 23 Jan. 1814.

102. Alexander Cunningham, Chief Commissioner of Rio de Janeiro, born at London 20 June 1754 and died at Rio de Janeiro 13 April 1832. He married at the French Church, The Hague 18 Aug. 1783,
103. Susanne Charlotte Guinand, born 16 July, baptized at the Church of St. Helen Bishopsgate, London 10 Aug. 1761 and died at Puddletown, Dorset 2 Aug. 1804.

104. ? John Work, born at Stranraer, Wigtownshire ca. 1740. He married,
105. ? Sarah ——.

106. Joseph Boude, baptized at Christ Church, Philadelphia, Pennsylvania 29 Dec. 1740 and died after 1793. He married (license to marry in Baltimore County, Maryland dated 11 Dec. 1781),
107. Barbara Black of Anne Arundel County, Maryland.

108. ? GEORGE WOOD, died in Kentucky 23 Aug. 1803. He married in Berkeley County, Virginia 8 Oct. 1781,

109. ? ELIZABETH CONNER, midwife in Shepherdstown, Virginia [now West Virginia], born in 1766 and died in Franklin County, Ohio 13 Aug. 1818.

110. DR. JOSEPH STRONG, born at South Coventry, Connecticut 10 March 1770 and died at Philadelphia, Pennsylvania 24 April 1812. He married at the First Baptist Church, Philadelphia 8 Sept. 1796,

111. REBECCA YOUNG, born at Philadelphia 5 May 1779 and died at Piqua, Ohio 8 June 1862. She married, 2nd, between July 1816 and May 1817, Peter Gardiner, druggist.

112. JOHN GILL, ship owner, baptized at Old Machar, Aberdeenshire 30 Nov. 1766. He married at Elgin, Morayshire 11 June 1795,

113. ISABELLA NICOLL, born at Aberdeen 17 Dec. 1776.

114. ALEXANDER OGSTON, born 16, baptized at Tarves, Aberdeenshire 17 March 1766 and died 27 July 1838. He married at Fyvie, Aberdeenshire 14 June 1796,

115. HELEN MILNE, born 12 May, baptized at Fyvie 12 Nov. 1776 and died 20 Jan. 1842.

116. CAPTAIN JOHN MARR, baptized at Peterculter, Aberdeenshire 5 Sept. 1778 and died at Milbank, Udny, Aberdeenshire 12 March 1849. He married,

117. BARBARA SMITH, baptized at Tarves, Aberdeenshire 5 March 1790 and died at Milbank 27 Jan. 1873.

118. GEORGE BEAN of Tarves, Aberdeenshire, married,

119. ——.

120. JAMES LITTLEJOHN, architect, baptized at St. Nicholas' Church, Aberdeen 25 Dec. 1773 and died in 1819. He married at St. Nicholas' Church 9 Sept. 1802,

121. JEAN CHALMERS, baptized at St. Nicholas' Church 5 Sept. 1781 and died at Union Street, Aberdeen 8 June 1859.

Dr. Joseph Strong

Born at South Coventry, Connecticut 10 March 1770
Died at Philadelphia, Pennsylvania 24 April 1812
Married at Philadelphia 8 September 1796
Rebecca Young

Joseph Strong was a graduate of Yale College in 1788, and studied medicine under Dr. Lemuel Hopkins of Hartford 1788-90 and Dr. Benjamin Rush at the University of Pennsylvania's School of Medicine 1791-92. Although Strong did not go on to obtain his medical degree, an M.D. was not considered necessary to practice medicine in the 18th century. He first practiced at Middletown, Connecticut in 1792, and then enlisted as a surgeon's mate under General Anthony Wayne in the Ohio campaign against Native Americans 1792-96. During his military service, he was in charge of hospitals at several forts and military outposts on the Ohio frontier. After he resigned his commission he settled in Philadelphia, where he became a respected physician.

In addition to medicine, Strong was keenly interested in mechanical devices and enjoyed solving mechanical problems. He invented the axle tourniquet used in surgery to control bleeding, securing a patent for this device, and was a promoter of the Philadelphia Society for the Encouragement of Domestic Manufacturers.

122. JAMES BENTLEY, professor of Oriental languages at King's College, Aberdeen 1798–1846, born at Aberdeen 24 Nov. 1771 and died 7 Aug. 1846. He married at Blackrod, Lancashire 26 Oct. 1809,

123. ISOBEL DINGWALL FORDYCE, born at Aberdeen 4 March 1771 and died 16 July 1852.

124. JOHN CROMBIE, manufacturer, baptized at Garioch Chapel, Aberdeenshire 27 Sept. 1772 and died at the Old Manse, New Machar, Aberdeenshire 6 May 1858. He married at New Machar 8 Jan. 1809,

125. CATHERINE HARVEY, baptized at New Machar 18 Nov. 1786 and died at the Old Manse, Cothal Mills, Aberdeenshire 30 July 1864.

126. THEODORE FORBES, India merchant, baptized at Forgue, Aberdeenshire 3 Aug. 1788 and died at sea on board the *Blendon Hall* 24 Sept. 1820. He had issue by,

127. ELIZA KEWARK, an Armenian woman.

Seventh Generation

---

128. Hon. John Spencer, M.P. 1732-46, Ranger of Windsor Park 1744-46, principal heir of his maternal grandmother the Duchess of Marlborough, born at Althorp House, Brington, Northamptonshire 13 May 1708 and died at Wimbledon Park, Surrey 20 June 1746. He married at Lansdown, Gloucestershire 14 Feb. 1733/34,

129. Lady Georgiana Caroline Carteret, born at Lansdown 12 March 1715/16 and died at Richmond, Surrey 21 Aug. 1780. She married, 2nd, 1 May 1750, William Cowper [from 1762 Clavering-Cowper], 2nd Earl Cowper, born at Hertingfordbury, Hertfordshire 13 Aug. 1709 and died at Colne Green, Essex 18 Sept. 1764, son of William Cowper, 1st Earl Cowper, and Mary Clavering.

130. Right Hon. Stephen Poyntz, P.C. (1734/35), Joint Treasurer of Excise 1722, Commissioner of Excise 1723, Receiver-General of the Excise 1723-35, Ambassador to Sweden 1724-27 and to the Congress of Soissons 1728-29, Steward of the (Royal) Household 1731, called "the great light and ornament of his family," born 12, baptized at St. Michael's Church, Cornhill, London 22 Nov. 1685 and died at Midgham, Berkshire 17 Dec. 1750. He married in Feb. 1732/33,

131. Anna Maria Mordaunt, Maid of Honour to HM Queen Caroline, the subject of Samuel Croxall's poem "The Fair Circassian," died at Midgham 14 Nov. 1771.

132. Sir John Bingham, 5th Baronet, M.P. 1727-49, High Sheriff of Mayo 1721, born ca. 1690 and died 21 Sept. 1749; buried at Castlebar, Mayo. He married before 1730,

133. Anne Vesey, died in Feb. 1762.

134. James Smith, M.P. 1715-27, born ca. 1681 and died ca. 1734. He married,

135. Grace ——.

136. Francis Seymour-Conway, 1st Marquess of Hertford, K.G. (1757), P.C. (I.) (1749/50) and (G.B.) (1763), Lord of the Bedchamber to TM King George II and King George III 1751-64, Master of the Horse 1766, Lord Chamberlain of the (Royal) Household 1766-82 and 1783, Ambassador to France 1763-65, Lord Lieutenant [i.e. Viceroy] of Ireland 1765-66, born at Lindsey House, Chelsea, Middlesex 5 July 1718 and died at Putney, Surrey 17 June 1794. He married 29 May 1751,

137. Lady Isabella Fitzroy, born 19 July 1726 and died at Lower Grosvenor Street, London 10 Nov. 1782.

138. James Waldegrave, 2nd Earl Waldegrave, K.G. (1757), F.R.S. (1749), P.C. (1752), Lord of the Bedchamber to HM King George II 1743-52, Governor and Keeper of the Privy Purse to TRH The Prince of Wales (later HM King George III) and Prince Edward of Wales (later HRH The Duke of York and Albany), Lord Warden of the Stannaries 1751-63, born 4 March 1714/15 and died at London 8 April 1763. He married at Sir Edward Walpole's house in Pall Mall, London 15 May 1759,

139. Maria Walpole, baptized at St. James's Church, Westminster, London 10 July 1736 and died at Oxford Lodge, Brompton, Middlesex 22 Aug. 1807. She married, 2nd, privately at her father's house in Pall Mall 6 Sept. 1766 (the marriage declared in 1772), HRH The Prince William Henry, Duke of Gloucester and Edinburgh, K.G., born at Leicester House, London 14 Nov. 1743 and died at Gloucester House, Grosvenor Street, London 25 Aug. 1805, son of HRH The Prince Frederick Louis, Prince of Wales, and HSH Auguste Prinzessin von Sachsen-Gotha.

It was as a result of the private marriages of the Dukes of Gloucester and Cumberland that the Royal Marriages Act of 1772 was passed.

140. Sir Robert Palk, 1st Baronet, M.P. 1767-87, Governor of Madras 1763-67, born at Ambrooke, Devonshire 16 Dec. 1717 and died 29 April 1798. He married 11 Feb. 1761,

141. Anne Vansittart, born in 1737.

142. Wilmot Vaughan, 1st Earl of Lisburne, M.P. [as Hon. Wilmot Vaughan, Viscount Lisburne, and Earl of Lisburne] 1755-61 and 1765-96, a Lord of the Admiralty 1770-82, Lord Lieutenant of Cardiganshire 1762-1800, baptized at Berwick-upon-Tweed 9 Jan. 1728 and died at Mamhead House, Devonshire 6 Jan. 1800. He married, 1st, at St. George's Church, Hanover

Square, London 3 July 1754, Elizabeth Nightingale, who died 19 May 1755, daughter of Joseph Gascoigne Nightingale and Lady Elizabeth Shirley, daughter of Washington Shirley, 2nd Earl Ferrers. He married, 2nd, 19 April 1763,

143. DOROTHY SHAFTO, died at Mamhead House 12 Sept. 1805.

144. JOHN BARING, cloth manufacturer, born at Bremen 31 Jan. 1698 and died at Mount Radford, near Exeter 30 Oct. 1748. He married 15 Feb. 1728,

145. ELIZABETH VOWLER, "a woman of capacity and excellent understanding" who continued her husband's business after his death and nearly doubled its value in her lifetime, baptized at St. Petrock's Church, Exeter 30 April 1702 and buried at St. Leonard's Church, Exeter 16 April 1766.

146. WILLIAM HERRING, merchant of Croydon, Surrey, born ca. 1719 and died 28 Sept. 1801. He married at Silkstone, Yorkshire 18 May 1746,

147. MONTAGUE DOROTHY DAWSON, baptized at the Church of Holy Trinity Mickelgate, York 21 Sept. 1724 and died at Croydon 27 July 1789.

148. VERY REV. GEORGE WILLIAM LUKIN, DEAN OF WELLS (1799–1812), Prebendary of Westminster 1797, baptized at Braintree, Essex 26 Sept. 1739 and died at The Deanery, Wells, Somerset 27 Nov. 1812. He married at Hanworth, Norfolk 30 June 1767,

149. CATHERINE DOUGHTY, born at Hanworth Park 27 Feb. 1747/48 and died at 8 Stein Place, Brighton, Sussex 15 April 1814.

150. PETER THELLUSSON, merchant banker, born at Paris 27 June 1737 and died at Plaistow, Kent 21 July 1797. He married 6 Jan. 1761,

151. ANNE WOODFORD, born at Southampton 4 Jan. 1738/39 and died at Plaistow 18 Jan. 1805.

152. JOHN BULTEEL, born at Flete House, Holbeton, Devon 24 Aug. 1733 and died there 16 Sept. 1801. He married at St. Anne's Church, Soho, London 6 Nov. 1758,

153. HON. DIANA BELLENDEN, born 17 Dec. 1731, baptized at Westmill, Hertfordshire 9 Jan. 1731/32 and buried there 12 Feb. 1799.

154. THOMAS PERRING, merchant of London, baptized at Modbury, Devonshire 7 Feb. 1732 and died 30 Nov. 1791. He married,

155. ELIZABETH PAWLING, died before 30 Nov. 1791.

156. CHARLES GREY, 1ST EARL GREY, K.B. (1788), P.C. (1797), General 1796, Commander-in-Chief of British Forces in North America 1782-83 and in the West Indies 1793-94, born at Howick, Northumberland 23 Oct. 1729 and died there 14 Nov. 1807. He married at Southwick, Durham 8 June 1762,

157. ELIZABETH GREY, baptized at Whickham, Durham 10 May 1741 and died at Hertford Street, Mayfair, London 26 May 1822.

158. WILLIAM BRABAZON PONSONBY, 1ST BARON PONSONBY, P.C. (I.) (1784), M.P. [as William Ponsonby] 1764-1800 and 1801-6, Joint Postmaster-General (Ireland) 1784-89, born at Dublin 15 Sept. 1744 and died at Seymour Street, London 5 Nov. 1806. He married 26 Dec. 1769,

159. HON. LOUISA MOLESWORTH, born 23 Oct. 1749 and died 1 Sept. 1824. She married, 2nd, at Bishopscourt, Kildare 21 July 1823, William Wentworth-Fitzwilliam, 2nd Earl Fitzwilliam, born at Milton House, Northamptonshire 30 May 1748 and died there 8 Feb. 1833, son of William Wentworth-Fitzwilliam, 1st Earl Fitzwilliam, and Lady Anne Watson-Wentworth, daughter of Thomas Watson-Wentworth, 1st Marquess of Rockingham.

160. JOHN JAMES HAMILTON, 1ST MARQUESS OF ABERCORN, K.G. (1805), P.C. (I.) (1794), M.P. [as John James Hamilton] 1783-89, born in July 1756 and died at Bentley Priory, Stanmore, Middlesex 27 Jan. 1818. He married, 2nd, at Grosvenor Square, London 4 March 1792 (marriage dissolved by Act of Parliament in April 1799), his first cousin Lady Cecil Hamilton, raised to the rank of an earl's daughter 1789, born 15 March, baptized at Taplow, Buckinghamshire 3 May 1770 and died 19 June 1819, daughter of Rev. and Hon. George Hamilton and Elizabeth Onslow. He married, 3rd, at Dover Street, London 3 April 1800, Lady Anne Jane Gore, born in April 1773 and died at Naples, Sicily 8 May 1827, widow of Henry Hatton, and daughter of Arthur Saunders Gore, 2nd Earl of Arran, and Hon. Catherine Annesley, daughter of William Annesley, 1st Viscount Glerawley. He married, 1st, at the Church of St. Mary le Bone, London 20 June 1779,

161. CATHERINE COPLEY, died at Bentley Priory 13 Sept. 1791.

162. LIEUT. COLONEL HON. JOHN DOUGLAS, born 1 July 1756 and died at 7 Cumberland Place, London 1 May 1818. He married at St. George's Church, Hanover Square, London 4 Oct. 1784,

163. LADY FRANCES LASCELLES, born at Northallerton, Yorkshire 11 June 1762 and died at 7 Cumberland Place 31 March 1817.

164. FRANCIS RUSSELL, MARQUESS OF TAVISTOCK by courtesy, born 27 Sept., baptized at St. George's Church, Bloomsbury, London 25 Oct. 1739 and died at Houghton Park, Bedfordshire 22 March 1767. He married at Woburn Abbey, Bedfordshire 8 June 1764,

165. LADY ELIZABETH KEPPEL, born 17 Nov. 1739 and died at Lisbon 2 Nov. 1768.

166. ALEXANDER GORDON, 4TH DUKE OF GORDON, K.T. (1775), F.R.S. (1784), Keeper of the Great Seal of Scotland 1794-1806 and 1807-27, Scottish representative peer 1767-84, Lord Lieutenant of Aberdeenshire 1794-1808, born at Gordon Castle, Banffshire 18 June 1743 and died at Mount Street, Berkeley Square, London 17 June 1827. He married, 2nd, at Fochabers, Banffshire in July 1820, Jane Christie [who had long been his mistress, and with whom he had had four children], born ca. 1780. He married, 1st, at Ayton, Berwickshire 23 Oct. 1767,

167. JANE MAXWELL, the leading Tory hostess of her day ("with an open ruddy countenance, quick in repartee, and no one excelling her in performing the honors of the table, her society is generally courted"), born at Hyndford's Close, Edinburgh in 1748 and died at Pulteney's Hotel, Piccadilly, London 14 April 1812.

168. ASSHETON CURZON, 1ST VISCOUNT CURZON, M.P. [as Assheton Curzon] 1754-80 and 1792-94, born 2 Feb. 1729/30 and died at Lower Brook Street, London 21 March 1821. He married, 2nd, at St. George's Church, Hanover Square, London 6 Feb. 1766, Dorothy Grosvenor, who died 25 Feb. 1774, daughter of Sir Robert Grosvenor, 6th Baronet, and Jane Warre. He married, 3rd, at St. George's Church 17 April 1777, Anna Margaretta Meredith, who died 13 June 1804, widow of Barlow Trecothick, and daughter of Amos Meredith and Joanna Cholmondeley. He married, 1st, at St. George's Church, Queen Square, Bloomsbury, London 23 Feb. 1756,

169. ESTHER HANMER, born 10, baptized at St. George's Church, Queen Square 21 Sept. 1738 and died 21 July 1764.

170. RICHARD HOWE, 1ST EARL HOWE, K.G. (1797), P.C. (1765), M.P. [as Hon. Richard Howe] 1757-58, a Lord of Admiralty in 1763, Treasurer of the Navy 1765-70, Commander-in-Chief in the Mediterranean in 1770, in North America 1776-78, and in the Channel 1782-83 and 1793-97, First Lord of the Admiralty 1783-88, Admiral of the Fleet and General of the Marines 1796, born at London 19 March 1725/26 and died at Grafton Street, London 5 Aug. 1799. He married at Tamerton Foliott, Devonshire 10 March 1758,

171. MARY HARTOPP, baptized at Woodhouse, Leicestershire 20 July 1732 and died at Grafton Street 9 Aug. 1800.

172. COLONEL JOHN GORE, Lieutenant Governor of the Tower of London, born in 1724 and died in the Tower of London 5 March 1794. He married,

173. BELLAMIRA MUNBEE, died 17 June 1791; buried with her husband at the Church of St. Peter ad Vincula in the Tower of London.

174. ADMIRAL SIR GEORGE MONTAGU, G.C.B., Commander-in-Chief at Portsmouth 1803-8, born at Lackham, Wiltshire 12 Dec. 1750 and died 24 Dec. 1829; buried at Wilcot, Wiltshire. He married at Wilcot 9 Oct. 1783,

175. CHARLOTTE WROUGHTON, twin, born at Pierpont Street, Bath, Somerset 11 March 1757 and buried at Wilcot 1 Aug. 1839.

176. CHARLES BINGHAM, 1ST EARL OF LUCAN = 66.
177. MARGARET SMITH = 67.

178. HENRY BELASYSE, 2ND EARL OF FAUCONBERG, M.P. [as Lord Belasyse] 1768-74, Lord of the Bedchamber to HM King George III 1777-1802, Lord Lieutenant of the North Riding of Yorkshire 1777-1802, born at Yarm, Yorkshire 13 April 1743 and died at Coxwold, Yorkshire 23 March 1802. He married, 2nd, by special license at St. George's Chapel, Windsor Castle, Berkshire 5 April 1790, Jane Cheshyre, who died 4 April 1820, daughter of John Cheshyre. He married, 1st, at St. James's Church, Westminster, London 29 May 1766,

179. CHARLOTTE LAMB, born 1 Nov. 1743 and died 1 April 1790.

Richard Howe, 1st Earl Howe

Born at London 19 March 1725/26
Died at London 5 August 1799
Married at Tamerton Foliott, Devonshire 10 March 1758
Mary Hartopp

The Hon. Richard Howe entered the Navy in 1739. He was appointed to the *Dunkirk* (60 guns) in 1755, and his capture of the *Alcid* off the mouth of the St. Lawrence precipitated the Seven Years' War with France. As one of the most promising young captains, Howe spent almost the entire war in the Channel Fleet. He commanded the attack on Cherbourg in May 1758; in command of the *Magnanime*, he led the attack at Quiberon Bay in November 1759. While at sea, Captain Howe was returned unopposed for the government as M.P. for Dartmouth (in 1757), and he retained that seat for twenty-five years, even after he succeeded to his brother's Irish peerage. He was appointed a Lord of the Admiralty in 1763; two years later, he became Treasurer of the Navy in the Rockingham administration. He resigned this post at the end of April 1766, but Pitt recalled him three months later, and Howe remained in office until Pitt went into opposition in January 1770.

Viscount Howe was appointed Commander-in-Chief in the Mediterranean in 1770, but the mobilization of forces was short-lived. He was made a Vice-Admiral in 1775, immediately before the American War of Independence, and the following year was appointed Commander-in-Chief in North America as well as joint commissioner to treat with the colonists. Lord Howe wanted to conciliate the colonists and tried contacting George Washington, but Howe's arrival in New York in July 1776, immediately after the Declaration of Independence, left him no room for negotiation. During the War of Independence, Lord Howe conducted a brilliant defensive campaign off the American coast, blockading key ports and cooperating with his brother, Major-General Sir William Howe, who commanded the army against the colonists.

In September 1778, Lord Howe resigned his command and returned to England; discontented with the North ministry, he remained in retirement for three and a half years. He returned to service as Commander-in-Chief in the Channel in 1782, and was promoted to Admiral later that year. In October 1782, he relieved Gibraltar in the face of a greatly superior enemy and without loss of a ship. In 1788, he was given an earldom. His best known service was as Commander-in-Chief in the Channel 1793-97, where, with 20 ships, he defeated the fleet of 27 ships under the command of Admiral Villaret de Joyeuse in June 1794. In recognition of this feat, Earl Howe was made General of the Marines and Admiral of the Fleet (March 1796) and a Knight of the Garter in June 1797.

180. HON. ROBERT BRUDENELL, M.P. 1756-68, Groom of the Bedchamber to HM King George III, Deputy Governor of Windsor Castle 1752-68, born 20 Sept. 1726 and died in the Round Tower, Windsor Castle, Berkshire 20 Oct. 1768. He married at St. George's Church, Hanover Square, London 27 Jan. 1759,

181. ANNE BISHOPP, born in 1728 and died 8 Oct. 1803.

182. CAPTAIN GEORGE JOHN COOKE, M.P. 1768, buried at Harefield, Middlesex 29 May 1785. He married at Harefield 5 Aug. 1765,

183. PENELOPE BOWYER, died after 1816.

184. GENERAL LORD GEORGE HENRY LENNOX, M.P. 1761-90, Governor of Plymouth 1784-1805, born at Richmond House, Whitehall, London 29 Nov. 1737 and died at West Stoke, Sussex 22 March 1805. He married at the Marquess of Lothian's house, Berkeley Square, London 25 Dec. 1759,

185. LADY LOUISA MARY KERR, baptized at St. James's Church, Westminster, London 17 Nov. 1739 and died at Funtington, Sussex 25 Dec. 1830.

186. ALEXANDER GORDON, 4TH DUKE OF GORDON = 166.
187. JANE MAXWELL = 167.

188. HENRY BAYLY [FROM 1770 PAGET], 1ST EARL OF UXBRIDGE, Lord Lieutenant of Anglesey 1782 and Staffordshire 1801, born 18 June, baptized at St. George's Church, Hanover Square, London 16 July 1744 and died 13 March 1812. He married at Castle Forbes, Longford 11 April 1767,

189. JANE CHAMPAGNÉ, born ca. 1742 and died at Bolton Row, London 9 March 1817.

190. GEORGE BUSSY VILLIERS, 4TH EARL OF JERSEY, P.C. (1765), M.P. [as Viscount Villiers] 1756-69, Vice Chamberlain of the (Royal) Household 1765-69, Extra Lord of the Bedchamber to HM King George III 1769-77, Master of the Horse to HRH The Prince of Wales (later HM King George IV) 1795-99, a Lord of the Admiralty 1761-62, born 9 June, baptized at St. George's Church, Hanover Square, London 6 July 1735 and died at Tunbridge Wells, Kent 22 Aug. 1805. He married at General James Johnstone's house, London 26 March 1770,

191. FRANCES TWYSDEN, Lady of the Bedchamber to HRH The Princess of Wales (later HM Queen Caroline), one of the great London hostesses of her time, born at Raphoe, Donegal 25 Feb. 1753 and died at Cheltenham, Gloucestershire 23 July 1821.

192. EDMUND ROCHE of Trabolgan, Cork, died in 1750. He married in 1739,
193. BARBARA HENNESSY of Ballymacmoy, Cork.

194. GEORGE COUGHLAN of Ardoe, Waterford, married,
195. ——.

196. DANIEL CURTAIN, merchant of Cork, died in 1786. He married,
197. MARGARET NAGLE, died at Sullivan's Quay, Cork before 1 Nov. 1798.

198. TIMOTHY DEASY of Phale Court, Enniskeane, Cork, born ca. 1739 and died at Cork before 6 Jan. 1800. He married in 1759,
199. HONORIA O'DONOVAN, died in 1807.

200. WILLIAM BOOTHBY, born in 1730 and died in 1774. He married,
201. MARTHA HOBSON, born in 1736 and died in 1823.

202. JOHN BROWNELL married at Rotherham, Yorkshire 26 Dec. 1755,
203. ELIZABETH FORES, baptized at Rotherham 9 July 1732.

204-205. ——.

Frances Twysden

Born at Raphoe, Donegal 25 February 1753
Died at Cheltenham, Gloucestershire 23 July 1821
Married at London 26 March 1770
George Bussy Villiers, 4th Earl of Jersey

A crony of Georgiana, Duchess of Devonshire [sister of George John Spencer, 2nd Earl Spencer (No. 32)], the Countess of Jersey was satirized by Richard Brinsley Sheridan as "the venomous Lady Sneerwell" in *The School for Scandal* (1777). She was notorious for her many lovers, including Frederick Howard, 5th Earl of Carlisle; Georgiana's husband, the 5th Duke of Devonshire; and William Augustus Fawkener, Clerk of the Privy Council (said to be father of one of her daughters).

It was her affair with the Prince of Wales (later George IV) that earned the former Frances Twysden a place in history. Although Lady Jersey was nine years the Prince's senior, he preferred older women, especially witty and aloof ones. In 1794, Lady Jersey encouraged his marriage to Princess Caroline of Brunswick-Wolfenbüttel, presumably to weaken the Prince's ties to his great love (and secret wife), Mrs. Fitzherbert.

When the Princess of Wales learned of Frances' relationship with her husband, she tried to have her sacked as Lady of the Bedchamber, although it was a scandal over some purloined letters that ultimately forced Lady Jersey's resignation. It wasn't until the Prince began an affair with Elizabeth Fox that he decided to completely sever his relationship with Lady Jersey. By 1799, Lady Jersey had been dismissed as the Prince's mistress, and the Earl of Jersey lost the job of Master of the Horse. Despite her many lovers, Lady Jersey cherished her husband and was dutifully mournful when he died. By him she had three sons and six daughters (or seven, if one includes the daughter presumed to be Fawkener's).

206. HENRY GUINAND, India merchant, died before 23 July 1785; buried at Puttah, Bengal. He married,

207. ELISABETH YVONNET, born 27 Feb. 1732/33 and died 2 Nov. 1761.

208-211. ——.

212. THOMAS BOUDE, master bricklayer (a builder of Independence Hall, Philadelphia), born (probably at Perth Amboy, New Jersey) ca. 1700 and died at Philadelphia, Pennsylvania 11 Sept. 1781. He married ca. 1722,

213. SARAH NEWBOLD, born (probably at Springfield Township, Burlington County, New Jersey) 29 Nov. 1700 and buried at Christ Church, Philadelphia 11 April 1780.

214. WILLIAM BLACK of Anne Arundel County, Maryland, died between 8 Jan. and 21 April 1771. He married,

215. CATHERINE ——.

216–219. ——.

220. DEACON BENAJAH STRONG, member of the Connecticut General Assembly 1781, born at Coventry, Connecticut 13 Oct. 1740 and died there 25 Nov. 1809. He married, 2nd, 29 April 1784, Sarah Coleman, daughter of Ebenezer Coleman and Sarah Brown. He married, 1st, at Coventry 9 March 1769,

221. LUCY BISHOP, born at Norwich, Connecticut 21 Dec. 1747 and died at Coventry 27 Nov. 1783.

222. CAPTAIN PETER YOUNG, born ca. 1739 and died in the West Indies in Aug. 1784. He married (license dated in Gloucester County, New Jersey 30 Sept. 1761),

223. ELEANOR BEST, baptized as an adult 21 Dec. 1757 and died at Philadelphia, Pennsylvania 12 July 1816 aged 76.

224. DAVID GILL married at Old Machar, Aberdeenshire 11 June 1759,

225. MARGARET DAVIDSON.

226. ALEXANDER NICOLL married at St. Nicholas' Church, Aberdeen 17 June 1771,

227. JEAN WEMYSS.

228. ALEXANDER OGSTON, schoolmaster of Tarves, born ca. 1725 and died in 1774; buried at Footdee Churchyard, Aberdeen. He married at Tarves, Aberdeenshire 16 Oct. 1763,

229. ISABEL LIND, buried at Footdee Churchyard. She married, 1st, at Tarves 27 April 1749, James Paterson.

230. ALEXANDER MILNE married at St. Nicholas' Church, Aberdeen 4 May 1772,
231. JEAN KYNOCH.

232. WILLIAM MARR of Peterculter, Aberdeenshire, married,
233. ——.

234. WILLIAM SMITH of Tarves, Aberdeenshire, married,
235. ANNIE MAY.

236-239. ——.

240. WILLIAM LITTLEJOHN, builder and Baillie of Aberdeen, baptized at Old Meldrum, Aberdeenshire 8 July 1731 and died 13 June 1806. He married at St. Nicholas' Church, Aberdeen 22 Jan. 1759,
241. MARY DOWNIE, born in 1737 and died 28 May 1797.

242. JAMES CHALMERS, printer, born at Aberdeen 31 March 1742 and died there 17 June 1810. He married at St. James's Church, Westminster, London 22 March 1769,
243. MARGARET DOUGLAS, born 28 March, baptized at Swallow Street Scotch Church, Westminster 8 April 1749 and died 14 Aug. 1818.

244. JAMES BENTLEY, hosier of Leeds, born in 1712 and died in Aberdeen ca. 1776. He married, 1st, ——. He married, 2nd, at Bradford, Yorkshire 10 Nov. 1752,
245. RUTH POWELL, born in 1736 and died at Aberdeen ca. 1808.

246. Judge Arthur Dingwall Fordyce of the Consistorial Court in Aberdeen, born at Brucklay Castle, Aberdeenshire 28 Dec. 1745 and died at Arthur Seat, near Aberdeen 21 April 1834. He married at St. Nicholas' Church, Aberdeen 14 June 1770,

247. Janet Morison, born at Elsick, Aberdeenshire 23 Nov. 1747 and died at Arthur Seat 15 July 1831.

248. James Crombie married,
249. Margaret Coupland.

250. William Harvey, baptized at Old Machar, Aberdeenshire 20 March 1753 and died in 1834. He married at New Machar 10 Nov. 1781,

251. Jean Lumsden, baptized at Kintore, Aberdeenshire 29 July 1761 and died in 1837.

252. John Forbes of Upper Boyndlie, Aberdeenshire, born in 1758 and died 6 Dec. 1824. He married in 1783,

253. Katherine Morison, baptized at Forgue, Aberdeenshire 24 April 1757 and died 5 Jan. 1832.

254-255. ——.

Eighth Generation

256. **Charles Spencer, 3rd Earl of Sunderland, K.G. (1720), P.C. (1706), F.R.S. (1698), M.P.** [as Lord Spencer] 1695-1702, Groom of the Stole and First Lord of the Bedchamber to HM King George I 1719-22, Secretary of State for the South 1706-10 and the North 1717-18, Lord President of the Council 1718-19, First Lord of the Treasury 1718-21, a Lord Justice [i.e. Regent] 1719 and 1720, amassed the Sunderland Library, born 23 April 1675 and died at Sunderland House, Piccadilly, London 19 April 1722. He married, 1st, 12 Jan. 1694/95, Lady Arabella Cavendish, born 19 Aug. 1673 and died 4 June 1698, daughter of Henry Cavendish, 3rd Duke of Newcastle, and Frances Pierrepont. He married, 3rd, 5/16 Dec. 1717, Judith Tichborne, born ca. 1702 and died 17 May 1749, daughter of Benjamin Tichborne and Elizabeth Gibbs. He married, 2nd, at St. Albans, Hertfordshire 2 Jan. 1699/1700,

257. **Lady Anne Churchill,** Lady of the Bedchamber to HM Queen Anne 1702-12, known [from her height] as "the little Whig," born 27 Feb. 1682/83 and died 15 April 1716; buried at Brington, Northamptonshire.

258. **John Carteret, 2nd Earl Granville, K.G. (1750), P.C. (1720/21),** Lord of the Bedchamber to HM King George I 1714-21, Ambassador to Sweden 1719-20 and The Netherlands 1742, Secretary of State for the South 1721-24 and the North 1742-44 [when he was virtually **Prime Minister** under the nominal leadership of Spencer Compton, 1st Earl of Wilmington, and Hon. Henry Pelham] and 1745/46, Lord Lieutenant [i.e., Viceroy] of Ireland 1724-30, Lord President of the Council 1751-63, a Lord Justice [i.e. Regent] 1723, 1725, 1727, 1743, 1752, and 1755, Lord Lieutenant of Devonshire 1716-21, born 22 April 1690 and died at Bath, Somerset 2 Jan. 1763. He married, 2nd, 14 April 1744, Lady Sophia Fermor, born 29 May 1721 and died 7 Oct. 1745, daughter of Thomas Fermor, 1st Earl of Pomfret, and Hon. Henrietta Louisa Jeffreys, daughter of John Jeffreys, 2nd Baron Jeffreys. He married, 1st, at Longleat House, Wiltshire 17 Oct. 1710,

259. **Frances Worsley,** born 6 March 1693/94 and died in Hanover 20 June 1743.

Charles Spencer, 3rd Earl of Sunderland

Born 23 April 1675
Died at London 19 April 1722
Married, 1st, 12 January 1694/95
Lady Arabella Cavendish
Married, 2nd, at St. Albans, Hertfordshire
2 January 1699/1700
Lady Anne Churchill
Married, 3rd, 5/16 December 1717
Judith Tichborne

Lord Spencer was educated at home and (following his father's flight to Holland) in Utrecht. He was described by John Evelyn as a "youth of extraordinary hopes, very learned for his age and ingenious." Spencer entered politics as M.P. for Tiverton in 1695 and was an unwaveringly loyal Whig.

Upon his father's death in 1702, he became Earl of Sunderland. Lord Sunderland was seen by the leaders of the Whig party, all of whom sat in the House of Lords, as someone who could help them regain power. At the end of 1706, he was sworn to the Privy Council and appointed Secretary of State for the South. During the next four years Sunderland worked with the Whig party to mitigate the Jacobite threat, seize French territories, and secure a barrier treaty to protect the Dutch against invasion from the Spanish Netherlands. At the same time, Sunderland was at odds with Queen Anne, who sided with the Tories and took advice from Robert Harley (later 1st Earl of Oxford and Mortimer). Sunderland was dismissed as secretary and Privy Councilor in 1710 when the Tories came to power.

After the accession of George I, Sunderland gradually regained power, first obtaining reappointment to the Privy Council and then convincing the skeptical king that other leading ministers (Charles Townshend, 2nd Viscount Townshend, and Robert Walpole, later 1st Earl of Orford) were untrustworthy. Lord Sunderland was appointed Secretary of State for the North in 1717 and assumed the additional office of Lord President of the Council the following year. With Walpole's resignation in 1717, Sunderland succeeded as First Lord of the Treasury. He held that position for three years until he was forced to resign following the collapse of the South Sea Company. Sunderland built an incomparable library, although financial reverses caused him to mortgage it to his second wife's father in return for a loan.

His first marriage brought him a fortune of £25,000. His second marriage – to Lady Anne Churchill, daughter of the celebrated Duke and Duchess of Marlborough – gave Sunderland important political access as well as a fortune of £20,000. The second Countess of Sunderland was Lady of the Bedchamber to Queen Anne 1702-12, and, like her famous mother, a staunch Whig. After his second wife's death, Sunderland married Judith Tichborne, infuriating the Duchess of Marlborough, who rightly feared that Sunderland would impoverish Anne's children by giving the new Lady Sunderland the bulk of his estate.

260. WILLIAM POYNTZ, upholsterer of Cornhill, London, died in 1720. He married, 1st, Mary Avery, who was buried at Battersea, Surrey 3 Jan. 1679/80. He married, 2nd, 4 April 1681,

261. JANE MONTEAGE.

262. LIEUT. GENERAL HON. LEWIS MORDAUNT, born at Oxford 22 Dec. 1665 and died 2 Feb. 1712/13. He married, 1st, at the Church of St. Mary le Bone, Westminster, Middlesex 29 Oct. 1685, Anne Martin, daughter of Roger Martin. He married, 2nd,

263. MARY COLLYER, baptized at St Andrew's Church, Holborn, Middlesex 17 Nov. 1675 and died 7 April 1740.

264. SIR GEORGE BINGHAM, 4TH BARONET, died after 1727. He married, 2nd, after 1691, Phoebe Hawkins. He married, 1st, ca. 1688,

265. MARY SCOTT.

266. AGMONDESHAM VESEY, M.P. (I.) 1705-13, 1713-14, 1715-27 and 1727-39, born 21 Jan. 1677 and died at Lucan, Dublin 24 March 1739. He married, 2nd, Jane Pottinger, who died after 19 Feb. 1745, widow of i) John Reynolds and ii) Sir Thomas Butler, 3rd Baronet, and daughter of Captain Edward Pottinger. He married, 1st,

267. CHARLOTTE SARSFIELD of Lucan.

268. JAMES SMITH of Torrington, Devonshire, married,
269. ——.

270-271. ——.

272. FRANCIS SEYMOUR [FROM 1699 SEYMOUR-CONWAY], 1ST BARON CONWAY, P.C. (I.) 1727/28), M.P. [as Francis Seymour-Conway] 1701-3, born 28 May 1679 and died at Lisburn, Antrim 3 Feb. 1731/32. He married, 1st, 17 Feb. 1703/4, Lady Mary Hyde, who died at Northwicke, Blockley, Worcestershire 25 Jan. 1708/9, daughter of Laurence Hyde, 1st Earl of Rochester, and Lady Henrietta Boyle, daughter of Richard Boyle, 1st Earl of Burlington. He married, 2nd, in 1709, Jane Bowden of Drogheda, who died at Sandywell, Gloucestershire 13 Feb. 1715/16. He married, 3rd, in July 1716,
273. CHARLOTTE SHORTER, died 12 Feb. 1733/34; buried at Arrow, Warwickshire.

274. CHARLES FITZROY, 2ND DUKE OF GRAFTON, K.G. (1721), P.C. (1715), Lord of the Bedchamber to HM King George I 1714-17, Lord High Steward and bearer of St. Edward's Sword at the coronation of HM 1714, Lord Chamberlain of the (Royal) Household to TM King George I and King George II 1724-57, Lord Lieutenant [i.e. Viceroy] of Ireland 1720-24, a Lord Justice [i.e. Regent] 1720, 1723, 1725, 1727, 1740, 1743, 1745, 1748, 1750, 1752, and 1755, born at Arlington House, St. James's Park, London 25 Oct. 1683 and died 6 May 1757; buried at Euston, Suffolk. He married at Chelsea, Middlesex 30 April 1713,
275. LADY HENRIETTA SOMERSET, born 27 Aug. 1690 and died at Old Bond Street, London 9 Aug. 1726.

276. JAMES WALDEGRAVE, 1ST EARL WALDEGRAVE, K.G. (1737/38), P.C. (1734/35), Lord of the Bedchamber to TM King George I 1723 and King George II 1730-41, special envoy to Paris 1725 and 1727-28, Ambassador to Vienna 1728-30 and Paris 1730-40, born in 1684 and died at Navestock Hall, Essex 11 April 1741. He married in Gloucestershire ca. 20 May 1714,
277. MARY WEBB, born in 1695 and died at Bow Street, Covent Garden, London 22 Jan. 1718/19.

278. HON. SIR EDWARD WALPOLE, K.B. (1753), M.P. 1736, Chief
Secretary of Ireland 1737-39, baptized at the Church of St. Martin-in-the-Fields,
Westminster, London 19 Oct. 1706 and died 12 Jan. 1784. He had issue by,
279. DOROTHY CLEMENT, milliner, born ca. 1715 and died ca. 1739.

280. WALTER PALK of Lower Headborough, near Ashburton, Devonshire,
married in 1715,
281. FRANCES ABRAHAM, died 1 May 1793.

282. ARTHUR VANSITTART of Moat Park, Windsor, Berkshire, baptized at
the Church of St. Andrew Undershaft, London 23 Dec. 1691 and died 16 Sept.
1760. He married 23 May 1723,
283. MARTHA STONHOUSE, baptized at Radley, Berkshire 4 Feb. 1700/1
and died 13 June 1782.

284. HON. WILMOT VAUGHAN [SOMETIME 3RD VISCOUNT LISBURNE],
assumed the title **VISCOUNT FETHERS,** Lord Lieutenant of Cardiganshire
1744-60, died at Crosswood, Cardiganshire 4 Feb. 1766. He married at
Norham, Northumberland 16 March 1726,
285. ELIZABETH WATSON, baptized at Berwick-on-Tweed 18 March
1704/5 and died at Crosswood 19 Jan. 1764.

286. JOHN SHAFTO, M.P. 1730-42, baptized at St. Anne's Church, Soho,
London 16 March 1692 and died at London 3 April 1742. He married at the
Church of St. Michael Bassishaw, London 20 May 1731,
287. DOROTHY JACKSON, buried at Whitworth, Durham 14 Jan. 1768. She
married, 2nd, —— Wynne.

288. REV. DR. FRANZ BARING, Professor of Theology at Bremen 1691,
born at Bremen 21 Jan. 1656 and died there 3 Nov. 1697. He married at
Bremen 25 Sept. 1688,
289. REBECCA VAGD, died 27 June 1745.

290. JOHN VOWLER, grocer, buried at St. Petrock's Church, Exeter 24 May
1748. He married,
291. ELIZABETH TOWNSEND, buried at St. Petrock's Church 2 Nov. 1703.

292. Samuel Herring, merchant taylor of Lambeth, Surrey, and first cousin of the Most Rev. Dr. Thomas Herring, Archbishop of Canterbury, died between 19 Oct. 1756 and 13 Oct. 1757. He married, 2nd, at Lincoln's Inn Chapel, Holborn, Middlesex 24 Feb. 1727, Henrietta Pery, who died before 18 Oct. 1756. He married, 1st,
293. Elizabeth Watlington.

294. Samuel Dawson, Sheriff of York 1718, baptized at the Church of St. Martin Micklegate with St. Gregory, York 5 Jan. 1691 and died 24 June 1731. He married,
295. Sarah Watson. She married, 2nd, Captain Thomas Brown of Micklethorpe, Yorkshire.

296. Robert Lukin of Braintree, Essex, born in 1708 and died before 1744. He married at Sandon, Essex 8 June 1733,
297. Sarah Hicks, baptized at Panfield, Essex 19 March 1710/11 and died 12 March 1792. She married, 2nd, 13 Feb. 1750/51, Colonel William Windham, born in 1717 and died 30 Oct. 1761, son of Ashe Windham and Elizabeth Dobyns.

298. Robert Doughty of Hanworth Park, Norfolk, died 16 Dec. 1757. He married at St. Benet's Church, Paul's Wharf, London 22 May 1740,
299. Margaret Lee.

300. Isaac Thellusson, international banker, minister from the Republic of Geneva to France 1730-44, born at Geneva 14 Oct. 1690 and died at Champel, near Geneva 2 Sept. 1755. He married at the French Church, Leiden 11 Oct. 1722,
301. Sara Le Boullenger, born in 1700 and died 22 March 1769.

302. Matthew Woodford, baptized at All Saints' Church, Chichester, Sussex 20 Dec. 1706 and buried at St. Mary's Church, Southampton 11 Nov. 1767. He married at St. Mary's Church 1 Oct. 1733,
303. Mary Brideoak, born 10 Oct. 1704 and buried at St. Mary's Church 4 Oct. 1778.

304. JAMES BULTEEL, M.P. 1703-8 and 1711-15, born ca. 1676 and died between 21 Aug. and 2 Nov. 1757. He married at Yealmpton, Devonshire 1 Oct. 1718,

305. MARY CROCKER, baptized at Yealmpton 17 Oct. 1695 and died in 1741.

306. JOHN BELLENDEN, 3RD LORD BELLENDEN, born at Dalhousie Castle, Midlothianshire in 1685 and died at Westmill, Hertfordshire 16 March 1740/41. He married at Radwell, Hertfordshire 3 Sept. 1722,

307. MARY PARNELL, baptized at Baldock, Hertfordshire 26 June 1702 and died 23 Nov. 1792; buried at Westmill.

308. PHILIP PERRING, clothier, baptized at Modbury, Devonshire 13 April 1703 and died 3 June 1771. He married at Modbury 27 Dec. 1726,

309. ALICE LEGASSICK, baptized at Modbury 13 March 1701/2 and died 19 Aug. 1796.

310. MATTHIAS PAWLING of Lombard Street, London, married,

311. ——.

312. SIR HENRY GREY, 1ST BARONET, baptized at Howick, Northumberland 4 Dec. 1691 and buried there 6 May 1750. He married 19 April 1720,

313. HANNAH WOOD, buried at Howick 19 July 1764.

314. GEORGE GREY, born 4 Aug. 1713 and buried at St. Nicholas' Church, Durham 28 March 1747. He married at St. John's Church, Newcastle-upon-Tyne (marriage settlement dated 14 June 1740),

315. ELIZABETH OGLE, baptized at St. Nicholas' Church 29 June 1714 and died at Falloden, Northumberland before 6 April 1807.

316. RIGHT HON. JOHN PONSONBY, P.C. (I.) (1748, 1760, AND 1761-70), M.P. (I.) 1739-60 and 1761-89, Speaker of the Irish House of Commons 1756-69, born 29 March 1713 and died 12 Dec. 1789. He married at Edensor, Derbyshire 23 Sept. 1743,

317. LADY ELIZABETH CAVENDISH, born at Hardwick Hall, Derbyshire 24 April 1723 and died in 1796.

318. Richard Molesworth, 3rd Viscount Molesworth, P.C. (I.) (1733), F.R.S. (1721/22), M.P. [as Richard Molesworth and Hon. Richard Molesworth] 1715-26, Field Marshal 1757, born ca. 1680 and died 12 Oct. 1758. He married, 1st, Jane Lucas of Dublin, who died 1 April 1742. He married, 2nd, 7 Feb. 1743/44,

319. Mary Jenney Ussher, died at Upper Brook Street, London 6 May 1763.

320. Captain Hon. John Hamilton, born ca. 1714 and died at sea near Portsmouth 18 Dec. 1755. He married in Nov. 1749,

321. Harriet Craggs, born in 1712 and buried at St. Germans, Cornwall 1 Feb. 1769. She married, 1st, 4 March 1725/26, Richard Eliot, baptized at Port Eliot, Cornwall 12 Sept. 1706 and died 19 Nov. 1748, son of John Eliot and Frances May.

William Pitt the Elder apotheosized Harriet Eliot when she was 19, the mother of three small children, as follows:

> *Viewing that airy Mien, that lively face,*
> *Where youth and spirit shine easy grace,*
> *We form some sportive nymph of Phoebe's train,*
> *Some sprightly virgin of the sacred plain:*
> *But lo! a happy Progeny proclaim*
> *Love's garden shafts and Hymen's genial flame.*
> *So the gay orange, in some sylvan scene,*
> *Blooms fair and smiles with never-fading green,*
> *When flow'ry head, with vernal beauty crowned.*

322. Sir Joseph Moyle [from 1768 Copley], 1st Baronet, baptized at St. Paul's Church, Covent Garden, London 8 Jan. 1715 and died 11 or 15 April 1781. He married,

323. Mary Buller, baptized at Morval, Cornwall 18 Aug. 1726 and died 3 March 1787.

324. James Douglas, 14th Earl of Morton, K.T. (1738), F.R.S. (1733), Scottish representative peer 1739-68, born ca. 1702 and died at Chiswick, Middlesex 12 Oct. 1768. He married, 1st, before 1731, Agatha Halliburton, who died at Edinburgh 11 Dec. 1748, daughter of James Halliburton of Pictur, Forfarshire. He married, 2nd, at St. James's Church, Westminster, London 31 July 1755,

325. BRIDGET HEATHCOTE, born 18 Dec. 1723, baptized at the Church of St. Olave, Hart Street, London 9 Jan. 1723/24 and died at Lower Brook Street, London 2 March 1805.

326. EDWARD LASCELLES, 1ST EARL OF HAREWOOD, M.P. [as Edward Lascelles] 1761-74 and 1790-96, born in Barbados 7 Jan. 1739/40 and died at Harewood House, Yorkshire 3 April 1820. He married at St. George's Church, Hanover Square, London 12 May 1761,

327. ANNE CHALONER, baptized at Guisborough, Yorkshire 22 Sept. 1742 and died 23 Feb. 1805.

328. JOHN RUSSELL, 4TH DUKE OF BEDFORD, K.G. (1750), P.C. (1744), F.R.S. (1741/42), Lord High Constable at the coronation of HM King George III 1761, First Lord of the Admiralty 1744-48, Secretary of State for the South 1748-51, Lord Lieutenant [i.e. Viceroy] of Ireland 1756-61, Lord Privy Seal 1761-63, Ambassador to Paris 1762-63, Lord President of the Council 1763-65, a Lord Justice [i.e. Regent] 1745, born 30 Sept., baptized at Streatham, Surrey 20 Oct. 1710 and died at Bedford House, Bloomsbury, London 14 Jan. 1771. He married, 1st, 11 Oct. 1731, Lady Diana Spencer, who died at Southampton House, Holborn, Middlesex 27 Sept. 1735, daughter of Charles Spencer, 3rd Earl of Sunderland [No. 256], and Lady Anne Churchill [No. 257]. He married, 2nd, 2 April 1737,

329. LADY GERTRUDE LEVESON-GOWER, born 15 Feb. 1714/15 and died 1 July 1794; buried at Chenies, Buckinghamshire.

330. WILLIAM ANNE KEPPEL, 2ND EARL OF ALBEMARLE, K.G. (1750), K.B. (1725-49), P.C. (1751), Lord of the Bedchamber to HRH The Prince of Wales (later HM King George II) 1722-51, Groom of the Stole 1751-54, (absentee) Governor of Virginia 1737-54, Lieutenant General 1744/45, Commander-in-Chief in Scotland 1746-48, Ambassador to Paris 1749-54, a Lord Justice [i.e. Regent] 1752, born at Whitehall, London 5 June 1702 and died at Paris 22 Dec. 1754. He married at Caversham, Oxfordshire 21 Feb. 1722/23,

331. LADY ANNE LENNOX, Lady of the Bedchamber to HM Queen Caroline, born 24 June 1703 and died at New Street, Spring Gardens, London 20 Oct. 1789.

332. COSMO GEORGE GORDON, 3RD DUKE OF GORDON, K.T. (1747/48), Scottish representative peer 1747–52, born at Speymouth, Morayshire 27 April 1720 and died at Breteuil, near Amiens, France 5 Aug. 1752. He married (without her father's knowledge or consent) at Dunkeld, Perthshire 3 Sept. 1741,

333. LADY CATHERINE GORDON, born 20 Oct. 1718 and died at London 10 Dec. 1779. She married, 2nd (Faculty Office license dated 25 March 1756), General Staats Long Morris, M.P. 1774–84, born at New York 27 Aug. 1728 and died at Berrymead Lodge, Acton, Middlesex 2 April 1800, son of Lewis Morris and Catherine Staats.

334. SIR WILLIAM MAXWELL, 3RD BARONET, born ca. 1715 and died at Edinburgh 22 Aug. 1771. He married by 1748,

335. MAGDALENE BLAIR, born at Blair, Ayrshire 20 March 1725 and died 28 Jan. 1765.

336. SIR NATHANIEL CURZON, 3RD BARONET, M.P. 1713–15 and 1722–54, born ca. 1676 and died 16 Nov. 1758; buried at Kedleston, Derbyshire. He married at Middleton, Lancashire 19 Feb. 1716/17,

337. MARY ASSHETON, born in 1694 and died 18 March 1776; buried at Kedleston.

338. WILLIAM HANMER of Hanmer, Flintshire, died between 9 Feb. and 30 April 1754. He married,

339. ELIZABETH JENNENS, born in 1705 and died before 4 Nov. 1777.

340. EMMANUEL SCROPE HOWE, 2ND VISCOUNT HOWE, Governor of Barbados 1732–35, born ca. 1699 and died in Barbados 29 March 1735. He married at her mother's house, London 8 April 1719,

341. LADY MARIA SOPHIA CHARLOTTE VON KIELMANSEGG, born at Hanover 23 Sept. 1703 and died at Albemarle Street, London 13 June 1782.

342. MAJOR CHIVERTON HARTOPP, Deputy Governor of Plymouth 1745, born ca. 1696 and died 2 April 1759. He married at St. Mary's Church, Nottingham 14 Feb. 1726/27,

343. CATHERINE MANSFIELD, baptized at St. Nicholas' Church, Nottingham 13 Aug. 1701 and died in 1754.

344. WILLIAM GORE, M.P. (I.) 1727-47, Sheriff of Kilkenny 1730, died 18 Feb. 1747/48. He married in 1722,
345. DOROTHY MANLEY.

346. VALENTINE MUNBEE of Horringer, Suffolk, a member of the Legislative Council of Jamaica, born ca. 1695 and died 24 Sept. 1750. He married Bridget Beckford, who was born in 1705, daughter of Thomas Beckford and Mary Ballard. He had issue by,
347. ELIZABETH WARDEN, died after 1 Feb. 1750/51.

348. ADMIRAL JOHN MONTAGU, Commander-in-Chief in North America 1771-74 and Newfoundland 1776-79, Admiral of the Blue 1782, Commander-in-Chief at Portsmouth 1783-86, Admiral of the White 1787, born in 1719 and died at Fareham, Hampshire in Sept. 1795. He married 11 Dec. 1748,
349. SOPHIA WROUGHTON, died 14 April 1802.

350. GEORGE WROUGHTON, buried at Wilcot, Wiltshire 30 June 1779. He married,
351. SUSANNA MOYLE, baptized at Bodmin, Cornwall 1 March 1732/33 and buried at Wilcot 12 March 1816.

352. SIR JOHN BINGHAM, 5TH BARONET = 132.
353. ANNE VESEY = 133.

354. JAMES SMITH = 134.
355. GRACE —— = 135.

356. THOMAS BELASYSE, 1ST EARL OF FAUCONBERG, Lord of the Bedchamber to HM King George II 1738-60, born 27 April 1699 and died at Newborough Hall, Yorkshire 8 Feb. 1774. He married 5 Aug. 1726,
357. CATHERINE FOWLER, died at George Street, London 29 May 1760.

358. SIR MATTHEW LAMB, 1ST BARONET, M.P. 1741-68, born ca. 1705 and died 6 Nov. 1768; buried at Hatfield, Hertfordshire. He married at Stoke Poges, Buckinghamshire 29 April 1740,

359. CHARLOTTE COKE, born 26 Jan. 1718/19.

360. GEORGE BRUDENELL, 3RD EARL OF CARDIGAN, Master of the Buckhounds to TM Queen Anne and King George I 1712-15, born in 1685 and died at Maulden, Bedfordshire 5 July 1732. He married at the Church of St. Martin-in-the-Fields, Westminster, London 15 May 1707,

361. LADY ELIZABETH BRUCE, described by a contemporary as possessing "everything that can recommend a lady of quality," born ca. Jan. 1688/89 and died in Dec. 1745.

362. SIR CECIL BISHOPP, 6TH BARONET, M.P. 1727-34 and 1755-68, died 15 June 1778. He married in 1726,

363. HON. ANNE BOSCAWEN, born at Penkivel, Cornwall 17 Feb. 1703/4 and buried at Parham, Sussex 11 May 1749.

364. GEORGE COOKE, M.P. 1742-47 and 1750-68, Joint Paymaster-General of the Land Forces in Great Britain 1767-68, born ca. 1705 and died 5 June 1768; buried at Harefield, Middlesex. He married in July 1735,

365. CATHERINE TWYSDEN, born posthumously 7 Dec. 1712 and died at Bath, Somerset 8 Sept. 1765.

366. SIR WILLIAM BOWYER, 3RD BARONET, born ca. 1710 and died 12 July 1767. He married at Radley, Berkshire 20 Dec. 1733,

367. ANNE STONHOUSE, baptized at St. Anne's Church, Soho, London 12 July 1709 and died 22 May 1785.

368. CHARLES LENNOX, 2ND DUKE OF RICHMOND AND LENNOX, K.B. (1726), P.C. (1734), F.R.S. (1723/24), M.P. [as Earl of March] 1722-23, Lord of the Bedchamber to TM King George I and King George II 1725-35, Lord High Constable at the coronation of HM King George II 1727, General 1745, born at Goodwood, Sussex 18 May 1701 and died at Godalming, Surrey 8 Aug. 1750. He married at The Hague 4 Dec. 1719,

369. LADY SARAH CADOGAN, Lady of the Bedchamber to HM Queen Caroline, born at The Hague 18 Sept. 1706 and died 25 Aug. 1751.

370. WILLIAM HENRY KERR, 4TH MARQUESS OF LOTHIAN, K.T. (1768), M.P. [as Earl of Ancram] 1747-63, Scottish representative peer 1768-74, General 1770, born ca. 1713 and died at Bath, Somerset 12 Nov. 1775. He married at St. James's Church, Westminster, London 6 Nov. 1735,
371. LADY CAROLINE LOUISA DARCY, died 15 Nov. 1778.

372. COSMO GEORGE GORDON, 3RD DUKE OF GORDON = 332.
373. LADY CATHERINE GORDON = 333.

374. SIR WILLIAM MAXWELL, 3RD BARONET = 334.
375. MAGDALENE BLAIR = 335.

376. SIR NICHOLAS BAYLY, 2ND BARONET, M.P. 1734-41, 1747-61, and 1770-74, Lord Lieutenant of Anglesey 1763, born in Anglesey in 1709 and died at Bond Street, London 9 Dec. 1782. He married, 2nd, by special license from the Archbishop of Canterbury 18 Aug. 1775, Anne Hunter, who died 18 May 1818. He married, 1st, at St. George's Church, Hanover Square, London 19 April 1737,
377. CAROLINE PAGET, baptized at St. James's Church, Westminster, London 26 March 1716 and died at Plâs Newydd, Anglesey 7 Feb. 1766.

378. VERY REV. ARTHUR CHAMPAGNÉ, DEAN OF CLONMACNOIS (1761-1800), born ca. 1714 and died 20 Aug. 1800; buried at Portarlington, Leix. He married,
379. MARIANNE HAMON, died 21 Aug. 1784.

380. WILLIAM VILLIERS, 3RD EARL OF JERSEY, P.C. (1747), Lord of the Bedchamber to HRH The Prince of Wales 1733-38, an Extra Lord of the Bedchamber to HM King George II 1738, baptized at St. James's Church, Westminster, London 18 March 1707 and died 28 Aug. 1769; buried at Middleton Stoney, Oxfordshire. He married at St. James's Church 23 June 1733,
381. LADY ANNE EGERTON, baptized at St. James's Church 8 Jan. 1705 and died at Grosvenor Square, London 16 June 1762. She married, 1st, at Ashridge, Buckinghamshire 22 April 1725, Wriothesley Russell, 3rd Duke of Bedford, born 25 May 1708 and died at Corunna, Spain 23 Oct. 1732, son of Wriothesley Russell, 2nd Duke of Bedford [No. 656], and Elizabeth Howland [No. 657].

382. RIGHT REV. PHILIP TWYSDEN, BISHOP OF RAPHOE (1746-52), more known for his sporting interests than his piety, born at Roydon Hall, East Peckham, Kent ca. 1713 and died at Jermyn Street, London 2 Nov. 1752. He married, 1st, at St. Paul's Cathedral, London 2 March 1740/41, Mary (Wyvill) Purcell, who died at Crayford, Kent in 1743. He married, 2nd, 27 Feb. 1748/49,

383. FRANCES CARTER, born at Robertstown, Meath 11 May 1718. She married, 2nd, General James Johnstone.

384. EDWARD ROCHE of Trabolgan, Cork, died in 1696. He married in 1672,

385. CATHERINE LAVALLIN of Walterstown, Cork.

386. JAMES HENNESSY of Ballymacmoy, Cork, died in 1768. He married in 1718,

387. CATHERINE BARRETT, died in 1770.

388-393. ——.

394. GARRETT NAGLE of Cork married,

395. CECILY ——.

396. TIMOTHY DEASY of Aghmanister, Cork, married ca. 1735,

397. ANNE DONOVAN.

398. CORNELIUS O'DONOVAN, died in 1737. He married,

399. ——.

400. BENJAMIN BOOTHBY married,

401. ——.

402-405. ——.

406. WILLIAM FORES of Rotherham, Yorkshire, married,
407. ———.

408-411. ———.

412. JEAN HENRI GUINAND, merchant of London, baptized at Neuchâtel, Switzerland 29 Aug. 1686 and died 16 Dec. 1765; buried at the Church of St. Helen Bishopsgate, London. He married, 2nd, Elisabeth David, who died before 1 March 1757, sister of Suzanne David [No. 415], and, possibly, a third and a fourth time. He married, 1st,
413. ELISABETH MARIE HAMELOT, buried at the Church of St. Martin Outwich, London 24 Feb. 1732/33.

414. JOHN PAUL YVONNET, merchant of London, born 20 June 1704 and died 21 Dec. 1765. He married at Dulwich College Church, Dulwich, Surrey 31 Aug. 1725,
415. SUZANNE DAVID, died 19 Jan. 1761.

416-423. ———.

424. GRIMSTONE BOUDE, cordwainer of Boston, merchant of Perth Amboy, and innkeeper of Philadelphia, born ca. 1660 and died before 3 April 1716. He married, 1st, at Boston, Massachusetts ca. 1680, Elizabeth ———. He married, 2nd, by 1698,
425. MARY ———, buried at Christ Church, Philadelphia, Pennsylvania 15 June 1744. She married, 2nd, before May 1721, George Campion, brewer, born ca. 1691 and buried at Christ Church 6 Dec. 1731.

426. MICHAEL NEWBOLD, baptized at Eckington, Derbyshire 3 Oct. 1667 and died at Chesterfield Township, Burlington County, New Jersey 1 Dec. 1721. He married (probably at Chesterfield Township) 24 Feb. 1696/97,
427. RACHEL CLAYTON, born at Shrewsbury, Monmouth County, New Jersey 16 June 1677 and died in Burlington County shortly after 17 April 1712.

428-439. ———.

440. DEACON JOSEPH STRONG, farmer, member of the Connecticut General Assembly for nine sessions, born at Northampton, Massachusetts 25 July 1701 and died at Coventry, Connecticut 9 April 1773. He married at Coventry 12 May 1724,
   441. ELIZABETH STRONG, born at Northampton 27 Sept. 1704 and died at Coventry 1 May 1792.

442. CALEB BISHOP, born at Norwich, Connecticut 16 March 1714/15 and died at Guilford, Connecticut 16 Feb. 1785. He married at Norwich 19 April 1739,
   443. KEZIAH HIBBARD, born at Windham, Connecticut 19 May 1722.

444-445. ———.

446. SAMUEL BEST married at the First Presbyterian Church, Philadelphia, Pennsylvania 19 Nov. 1737,
   447. MARGARET ALBERT.

448-455. ———.

456. WILLIAM OGSTON, farmer of Ironhill, Coburty, Aberdeenshire, baptized at Aberdour, Aberdeenshire 12 Feb. 1706. He married at Tyrie, Aberdeenshire 30 April 1723,
   457. ELIZABETH RITCHIE.

458-479. ———.

480. PATRICK LITTLEJOHN, merchant of Old Meldrum, Aberdeenshire, died between 7 Jan. and 8 June 1738. He married,
   481. JEAN DAVIDSON. She married, 2nd, before 22 Feb. 1740, John Gillespie of Aberdeen.

482–483. ——.

484. JAMES CHALMERS, printer, baptized at Dyke, Morayshire 8 Jan. 1713 and died at Aberdeen 25 Aug. 1764. He married 14 March 1739,

485. SUSANNAH TRAIL, baptized at Montrose, Angus 28 April 1720 and died in 1791.

486. DAVID DOUGLAS married at the Church of St. Martin-in-the-Fields, Westminster, London 11 Jan. 1746/47,

487. CATHERINE FORBES, baptized at St. Nicholas' Church, Aberdeen 15 Oct. 1719.

488. JOSEPH BENTLEY, merchant, baptized at Rothwell, Yorkshire 10 Jan. 1671/72. He married,

489. —— **WAIT.**

490. RICHARD POWELL married at St. Peter's Church, Leeds 14 Oct. 1723,

491. RUTH WALKER.

492. WILLIAM DINGWALL of Culsh, Aberdeenshire, baptized 9 May 1712 and died after 1760. He married, 1st, ca. 1737, Lucretia Dingwall, daughter of William Dingwall and Anne Gordon. He married, 2nd, at Gask, Aberdeenshire 13 April 1744,

493. JEAN FORDYCE, baptized at Turriff, Aberdeenshire 8 March 1703/4 and died at Aberdeen 4 March 1778.

494. JAMES MORISON, Provost of Aberdeen 1744-45, born at Elsick House, Kincardineshire 25 April 1708 and died at Aberdeen 5 Jan. 1786. He married in 1735,

495. ISOBEL DYCE, baptized at St. Nicholas' Church, Aberdeen 10 Nov. 1716 and died 23 Jan. 1781.

496–499. ——.

500. JAMES HARVEY, farmer of Seaton, Bridge of Don, Aberdeenshire, married,

501. SUSAN FIDDES of Belhevie, Aberdeenshire.

502. JOHN LUMSDEN of Boghead, Kintore, Aberdeenshire, baptized at Kemnay, Aberdeenshire 31 March 1727. He married at New Machar, Aberdeenshire 22 Aug. 1751,

503. CHRISTIAN STEPHEN of Goval, Fintray, Aberdeenshire.

504. GEORGE FORBES of Upper Boyndlie, Aberdeenshire, baptized at St. Nicholas' Church, Aberdeen 22 Sept. 1715 and died in July 1794. He married, 2nd, at Tyrie, Aberdeenshire 22 Dec. 1765, Christian Ker. He married, 1st, at Old Deer, Aberdeenshire 22 Aug. 1754,

505. JANET KEITH, died in 1763.

506. ALEXANDER MORISON, baptized at Forgue, Aberdeenshire 13 Feb. 1724 and died 17 Sept. 1801. He married,

507. KATHERINE DUFF, born 14 March 1731/32 and died in 1803.

508-511. ——.

Ninth Generation

512. ROBERT SPENCER, 2ND EARL OF SUNDERLAND, K.G. (1687), P.C. (1674-81, 1682-89, AND 1697-1702), Lord of the Bedchamber to HM King Charles II 1673-79, Lord Chamberlain of the (Royal) Household to TM King William III and Queen Mary II 1693-97, Ambassador to Madrid 1671-72 and Paris 1672-73 and 1678, joint ambassador to the peace conference at Cologne 1673, Secretary of State for the North 1679-80 and 1683-84, Secretary of State for the South 1680-81 and 1684-88, Lord President of the Council 1685-88, of whom Macaulay noted that "in him the political morality of the age was personified in the most lively manner," born at Paris in 1641 and died at Althorp House, Brington, Northamptonshire 28 Sept. 1702. He married at St. Vedast's Church, Foster Lane, London 10 June 1665,

513. LADY ANNE DIGBY, whom Queen Anne called "the greatest jade that ever lived," born ca. 1646 and died 16 April 1715; buried at Brington.

514. JOHN CHURCHILL, 1ST DUKE OF MARLBOROUGH, K.G. (1701/2), P.C. (1689-92, 1698-1711, AND 1714-22), Gentleman of the Bedchamber to HRH The Duke of York (later HM King James II) 1673, Lord of the Bedchamber to HM 1685, Master of the Horse to and Governor of HRH The Duke of Gloucester 1698, Ambassador to Paris 1685 and The Hague 1701/2, Commander-in-Chief of the British forces in The Netherlands 1690-92 and 1698-1702, Generalissimo and Master General of the Ordnance 1702-11, Captain-General and Master General of the Ordnance 1714-22, a Lord Justice [i.e. Regent] 1698, 1699, and 1700, born at Ashe House, Devonshire 24 June 1650 and died at Cranbourne Lodge, Windsor, Berkshire 16 June 1722. Before his marriage he was the lover of Barbara Villiers, Duchess of Cleveland [No. 1097], by whom he (probably) had issue. He married 1 Oct. 1678,

515. SARAH JENNINGS, Maid of Honour to HRH The Duchess of York 1673, Woman and Lady of the Bedchamber of HRH The Princess Anne (later HM Queen Anne), Groom of the Stole to HRH 1685, Keeper of the Princess's Privy Purse, Mistress of the Robes to HM, born at Holywell, Hertfordshire 5 June 1660 and died at Marlborough House, London 18 Oct. 1744.

John Churchill, 1st Duke of Marlborough
Born at Ashe, Devonshire 24 June 1650
Died at Windsor, Berkshire 16 June 1722
Married 1 October 1678
Sarah Jennings

There have been many stories of John Churchill's amorous adventures as a young man, especially with the royal mistress, the Duchess of Cleveland, but these escapades came to an end when he fell in love with and married Sarah Jennings.

In February 1678, Churchill became colonel of a Regiment of Foot, and during the following year he was entrusted with many confidential missions by the heir presumptive, the Duke of York. When, in March 1679, the Duke was forced to leave England, Churchill and his wife followed him to The Hague. As a reward for his services to the Duke, he was created Lord Churchill of Eyemouth in Scotland in December 1682.

On the accession of the Duke of York as King James II, Churchill was appointed Ambassador to Paris, and later that year the King granted him the English title of Baron Churchill of Sandridge and appointed him Governor of the Hudson Bay Company, a position that Churchill held from 1685 until 1691. In spite of the King's generosity, Lord Churchill was one of the first to desert his benefactor in favor of the Prince and Princess of Orange. For his support of the future King and Queen, Churchill received the earldom of Marlborough two days before their coronation in April 1689. In 1690, Marlborough was appointed commander of the English forces in The Netherlands. Thereafter, a rift developed between the King and Marlborough: since Lord Marlborough was the leading British general, many officers looked to him for leadership and criticized the favor being shown the Dutch. As often happens in disputes between leaders, a subordinate is blamed for all the problems: in June 1692, Marlborough was sacked on suspicion of an intrigue with the exiled King James II. Queen Mary demanded that Princess Anne dismiss Lady Marlborough from her household, but the devoted Anne refused. When Sarah was forbidden at court, Princess Anne withdrew as well. The death of Queen Mary, at the end of 1694, altered the position of Princess Anne – now heiress presumptive – and improved Lord and Lady Marlborough's prospects. Finally, in 1698, Lord Marlborough was restored to favor and again appointed to the Privy Council, along with other important posts. He was also appointed Commander-in-Chief of the British and Dutch forces in the Netherlands. At the accession of Queen Anne, war was declared upon France and Spain, and Marlborough was appointed Generalissimo of the allied forces. He also received two additional titles: Marquess of Blandford and Duke of Marlborough.

In the following seven years, Marlborough established his reputation as one of Europe's greatest generals, leading British and allied armies to important victories over King Louis XIV of France, notably at Blenheim (13 August 1704), Tirlemont (18 June 1705), Ramillies (23 May 1706), Oudenaarde (11 July 1708), and Malplaquet (11 September 1709). The battle of Blenheim was the Duke of Marlborough's most famous victory: the French army's first major defeat in more than 50 years, it saved Vienna from a threatening Franco-Bavarian army; preserved the alliance of England, Austria, and the United Provinces against France; and removed Bavaria from the war. As reward for his victory at Blenheim, Marlborough was granted the manor of Woodstock and the Hundred of Wotton in Oxfordshire. Woodstock was to be the site of Blenheim Palace, designed by Sir John Vanbrugh and built (1705-24) by the English Parliament as a national gift to the Duke of Marlborough.

As a general, Marlborough was invincible, but he fared less well against political pressures in his own country. By 1706, the Duchess's relationship with the Queen was deteriorating. The Queen loathed the Whigs, but her cabinet thought military victory would be impossible without them. Marlborough, a political neutral, resolved to drive Secretary of State Robert Harley from the cabinet. The Duke demanded Harley's resignation, but the Queen fought to keep her favorite minister. Marlborough tendered his resignation, and the news that he had been dismissed paralyzed both Houses of Parliament. This struggle gave the Duke a temporary measure of power, but he had to a large extent lost the Queen and the moderate Tories. He now increasingly had to align himself with the Whigs, and consequently widened the breach with the Queen.

Against this backdrop, Marlborough began the campaign of 1708. At Oudenaarde, on the Scheldt, a quarter of the French army was destroyed or dispersed and 7,000 French prisoners were taken. With this victory, the Allies regained the initiative, and laid siege to Lille, which surrendered in October. Meanwhile, at home, the Whigs were triumphant, and Marlborough had to conform to the decisions of a Whig cabinet. Although he labored for peace, Marlborough could not bring Louis XIV to agree to all the terms demanded by the Whig government. With diplomacy at an impasse, the Allies began building a massive army for the campaign of 1709. With this strengthened allied army, Marlborough and Prince Eugene of Savoy began the siege of Tournai, which surrendered at the end of August. On 11 September, 110,000 allied troops assaulted the entrenchment near Malplaquet. Marlborough was deeply affected by the slaughter of this battle, and spoke of his misery at seeing so many old comrades killed when they thought themselves sure of peace. In England, the Whigs proclaimed victory, but the Tories accused them, and Marlborough, of having thrown away the chance for peace through fruitless carnage. The failure of peace negotiations created suspicions that Marlborough was promoting the war for his own interests.

Acting under Harley's advice, the Queen attacked Marlborough by giving the Lord Lieutenancy of the Tower to Lord Rivers without waiting for the usual recommendation of the Commander-in-Chief. She then offered a vacant regimental post to Colonel Jack Hill, brother of her new favorite, Abigail Masham. Marlborough protested against the latter appointment as diluting his influence in the army. Further rebuffs led Marlborough to the conclusion that he could no longer assume the support of the Queen. The great armies of Europe, even further enlarged, then faced each other in the campaigns of 1710 and 1711. The Duke returned home to find England in the control of his political foes and Lord Sunderland dismissed from office, but the ministry entreated Marlborough to restrain his resentment at the fall of his son-in-law and remain at the head of the army.

At the end of 1711 Marlborough was dismissed from all his offices after a commission of enquiry determined that he was taking bribes from contractors. Under threat of impeachment, the Duke and Duchess left for the Continent, where they were treated with much respect (rather more than they were accorded by the Tory government in England). After the accession of George I, Marlborough was restored to many of his former positions. In 1716, the Duke suffered two strokes, and although he was able to recover his faculties and discharge official duties, he was clearly declining. He spent his time at Blenheim, Windsor, and Holywell, where he played with his grandchildren and amused himself at cards.

Sarah Jennings

Born at Holywell, Hertfordshire 5 June 1660
Died at London 18 October 1744
Married 1 October 1678
John Churchill, 1st Duke of Marlborough

Sarah Jennings was appointed Maid of Honour to the Duchess of York in 1673. Soon afterwards, she was introduced to the Duke's younger surviving daughter, Anne, five years her junior. Attractive and intelligent, Sarah became Princess Anne's Lady of the Bedchamber and soon exerted much influence upon the princess. The relationship between Sarah and the princess was one of equals: Anne deeply loved Sarah and respected her opinion. Sarah was more seductive than beautiful; with an attractive figure, flaxen hair, and blue eyes, she was noted for her temper and self-confidence. Sarah became Anne's closest advisor as Groom of the Stole in 1685 and persuaded the Princess to side with her brother-in-law, the Prince of Orange, when he overthrew Anne's father, King James II, in 1688. The private advice of Sarah and her husband also convinced Princess Anne to surrender her right to succeed to the throne (the Act of Settlement) should Queen Mary predecease King William.

After Anne's accession, Sarah – now Duchess of Marlborough – obtained various positions at court, including Keeper of the Privy Purse, Mistress of the Robes, and Ranger of Windsor Park. With the salary she earned from three court posts, Sarah bought Wimbledon Manor in Surrey, Stene in Northamptonshire, and other large estates. Although her husband was neutral in politics, the Duchess was pro-Whig and, in the early decades of the 18th century, deeply concerned about the threat posed by the Jacobites. Feeling pity for her many poor relatives, Sarah obtained positions at court for several of them, one of whom, her first cousin, Abigail Hill, became the Queen's dresser. As the Duchess's relationship with Queen Anne cooled, Abigail (who became Mrs. Samuel Masham) supplanted Sarah as Anne's most trusted confidante. Sarah had further destroyed her friendship with the Queen by continually urging the appointment of Whig cabinet ministers when Anne's sympathies increasingly resided with the Tories. When Sarah suspected that the Queen was ignoring her counsel, the Duchess began spending more time away from the Court, retreating to her country estates with her daughters. Sarah also spent much of her time supervising the construction of Blenheim Palace. The influence of the Duchess of Marlborough over Queen Anne rapidly diminished after 1703, although the Duke remained commander of the British forces. When he was finally dismissed in 1711, Sarah was also removed from all her offices.

Other than a few remarks in Sarah's letters that hint at her husband's involvement with Hester Santlow, the Duke and Duchess had a very supportive relationship. Sarah survived the Duke by 22 years, and upon her death left a large portion of her estate to her favourite grandson, the Hon. John Spencer. As the principal beneficiary of his grandmother's will, Spencer inherited Holywell House, near St. Albans; the manor of Wimbledon; and Wimbledon Park, which Sarah had recently built on the latter estate.

516. GEORGE CARTERET, 1ST BARON CARTERET, born in July 1667 and died 22 Sept. 1695; buried at Hawnes, Bedfordshire. He married (Faculty Office license dated 15 March 1674/75),

517. GRACE GRANVILLE, COUNTESS GRANVILLE in her own right, born ca. 1667 and died 18 Oct. 1744; buried at Westminster Abbey, London.

518. SIR ROBERT WORSLEY, 4TH BARONET, M.P. 1715-22, baptized at St. Andrew's Church, Holborn, Middlesex 25 Sept. 1669 and died at New Burlington Street, London 29 July 1747. He married at Longbridge Deverill, Wiltshire (Faculty Office license dated 13 Aug. 1690),

519. HON. FRANCES THYNNE, born 31 Oct. 1673 and died 2 April 1750.

520. NEWDIGATE POYNTZ, baptized at Reigate, Surrey 16 Nov. 1608 and killed at Gainsborough, Lincolnshire 4 Aug. 1643. He married, 1st, Sarah Foxley, who was buried 31 May 1636, daughter of Francis Foxley and Mary Dryden. He married, 2nd, before 30 Jan. 1636/37, Ann Forest, living in June 1637, daughter of Miles Forest. He married, 3rd, at St. Margaret's Church, Westminster, Middlesex 21 Dec. 1637,

521. MARY PARKYNS, baptized at the Church of St. Botolph Bishopsgate, London 10 April 1614 and died by Dec. 1662. She married, 2nd, ca. 1649, Thomas Tedcastle, who died before 1657.

522. STEPHEN MONTEAGE, baptized at the Church of St. Giles Cripplegate, London 1 Feb. 1622 and died 21 Oct. 1687; buried at the Church of All Hallows-in-the-Wall, London. He married after 18 Feb. 1652,

523. JANE DEANE, buried at Buckingham, Buckinghamshire 21 Aug. 1670. She married, 1st, Drue Sparrow, who died 18 Feb. 1652, son of John Sparrow and Marian Hawley.

524. JOHN MORDAUNT, 1ST VISCOUNT MORDAUNT, Lord Lieutenant of Surrey 1660-75, born 18 June 1626 and died at Parson's Green, Middlesex 5 June 1675. He married ca. 1656,
525. ELIZABETH CAREY, born in March 1631/32 and died 5 April 1679.

526. COLONEL THOMAS COLLYER, Lieutenant Governor of Jersey 1685-1703, buried at St. Helier's Church, Jersey in July 1715. He married, 2nd, at the Church of St. Botolph Bishopsgate, London 15 Feb. 1693/94, Mary Marine. He married, 1st, at Waltham St. Lawrence, Berkshire 30 Nov. 1667,
527. MARY LUNSFORD.

528. SIR GEORGE BINGHAM, 2ND BARONET, M.P. 1661-66, born ca. 1625. He married, 1st, at St. Benet's Church, Paul's Wharf, London 21 April 1655, Mary Gould. He married, 2nd, at St. Benet's Church 6 June 1661, Anne (——) Pargiter, born ca. 1631 and died ca. Aug. 1661. He married, 3rd (Vicar-General's license dated 5 Dec. 1661),
529. REBECCA MIDDLETON, born ca. 1637.

530-531. ——.

532. MOST REV. DR. JOHN VESEY, ARCHBISHOP OF TUAM (1679-1716), P.C. (I.) (1679), Archdeacon of Armagh 1662-73, Bishop of Limerick 1673-79, a Lord Justice of Ireland 1713-15, born at Coleraine, Londonderry 10 March 1637/38 and died at Holymount, Mayo 28 March 1716. He married, 1st (license dated 1662), Rebecca Wilson. He married, 2nd, ca. 1670,
533. ANNE MUSCHAMP.

534. WILLIAM SARSFIELD of Lucan, Dublin, died before 1683. He married,
535. MARY CROFTS, born at The Hague 6 May 1651 and died in 1693. She married, 2nd, William Fanshaw.

536-543. ——.

544. RIGHT HON. SIR EDWARD SEYMOUR, 4TH BARONET, P.C. (1673), M.P. 1661-81, 1685, 1689, 1690, and 1695-1708, Comptroller of the (Royal) Household 1702-4, Speaker of the House of Commons 1673-79, Treasurer of the Navy 1673-81, born in 1633 and died at Maiden Bradley, Wiltshire 17 Feb. 1707/8. He married, 1st (Faculty Office license dated 7 Sept.), 7 Dec. 1661, Margaret Wale, who died before 1674, daughter of Sir William Wale and Margaret Sparke. He married, 2nd, in 1674,

545. LETITIA POPHAM, died 16 March 1713/14.

546. JOHN SHORTER, merchant of London, born ca. 1659 and died before 15 Feb. 1706/7. He married at the Church of St. Mary le Savoy, London (license dated 11 July 1681),

547. ELIZABETH PHILIPPS, born ca. 1662 and died 27 July 1728; buried at the Church of St. Giles-in-the-Fields, Holborn, Middlesex.

548. HENRY FITZROY, 1ST DUKE OF GRAFTON, K.G. (1680), born 2 Sept. 1663 and died 9 Oct. 1690. He married at Goring House, London 1 Aug. 1672 (and again 6 Nov. 1679),

549. ISABELLA BENNET, COUNTESS OF ARLINGTON in her own right, born in 1667 and died 7 Feb. 1722/23. She married, 2nd (Bishop of London's license to marry at Whitechapel dated 14 Oct. 1698), Sir Thomas Hanmer, 3rd Baronet, M.P. 1701-27, Speaker of the House of Commons 1713, born at Bettisfield, Flintshire 24 Sept. 1677 and died 5 May 1746, son of William Hanmer and Peregrina North.

550. CHARLES SOMERSET, MARQUESS OF WORCESTER by courtesy, **M.P.** 1677, 1679-80, 1681, 1685, and 1689-90, born at London in Dec. 1660 and died in Wales 13 July 1698. He married at Wanstead, Essex (Faculty Office license dated 29 May) 5 June 1682,

551. REBECCA CHILD, born in 1668 and died at Richmond, Surrey 17 July 1712. She married, 2nd (Faculty Office license dated 14), 15 April 1703, John Granville, 1st Baron Granville, born at London 12 April 1665 and died 3 Dec. 1707, son of John Granville, 1st Earl of Bath [No. 1034], and Jane Wyche [No. 1035].

552. HENRY WALDEGRAVE, 1ST BARON WALDEGRAVE, Comptroller of the (Royal) Household 1687-88 and [continuing in that office in exile with his father-in-law HM King James II] 1688-90, Lord Lieutenant of Somerset 1687-

88, born in 1661 and died at Saint-Germain, near Paris 24 Jan. 1689/90. He married 29 Nov. 1683,

553. Henrietta FitzJames, born ca. 1667 and died 3 April 1730; buried at Navestock, Essex. She married, 2nd (before 26 March 1695), Piers Butler, 3rd Viscount Galmoye, born ca. 1652 and died at Paris 18 June 1740, son of Edward Butler, 2nd Viscount Galmoye, and Eleanor White.

554. Sir John Webb, 3rd Baronet, died at Aix-la-Chapelle, France in Oct. 1745. He married, 2nd, Helen Moore, daughter of Sir Richard Moore, 3rd Baronet, and Anastasia Aylward. He married, 1st, before 1695,

555. Hon. Barbara Belasyse, died 28 March 1740.

556. Robert Walpole, 1st Earl of Orford, K.G. (1726), K.B. (1725), P.C. (1714), M.P. [as Robert Walpole and Sir Robert Walpole] 1701-12 and 1713-42, Secretary of War 1708-10, Treasurer of the Navy 1710-11, Paymaster of the Forces 1714-15 and 1720-21, Chancellor of the Exchequer and First Lord of the Treasury [i.e. **Prime Minister**] 1715-17 and 1721-42, born at Houghton, Norfolk 26 Aug. 1676 and died at Arlington Street, Piccadilly, London 18 March 1744/45. He married, 2nd, before 3 March 1737/38, Maria Skerrett, born 5 Oct. 1702 and died 4 June 1738, daughter of Thomas Skerrett and Esther ———. He married, 1st, at Knightsbridge Chapel, London 30 July 1700,

557. Katherine Shorter, born in 1682 and died at Chelsea, Middlesex 20 Aug. 1737.

558. Hammond Clement of Darlington, Durham, married,
559. Priscilla ———.

560. Walter Palk of Headboro, Ashburton, Devonshire, married,
561. Frances Ryder.

562. Robert Abraham, farmer of Gurrington, near Ashburton, Devonshire, married,
563. ———.

564. Peter van Sittart, London merchant, born 13 Jan. 1650/51 and died 8 March 1704/5. He married at St. Dionis Backchurch, London 3 Oct. 1678,
565. Susanna Sanderson, born ca. 1656 and died 25 March 1726.

Robert Walpole, 1st Earl of Orford

Born at Houghton, Norfolk 26 August 1676
Died at London 18 March 1744/45
Married, 1st, at London 30 July 1700
Katherine Shorter
Married, 2nd, before 3 March 1737/38
Maria Skerrett

Robert Walpole entered Parliament in 1701 as M.P. for Castle Rising. The following year he became member for King's Lynn, retaining that seat for 40 years. He was an excellent speaker, and rose rapidly within the Whig party, where he was recognized as a leader as early as 1703. A member of the Admiralty Board, Walpole was Secretary of War 1708-10, Treasurer of the Navy 1710-11, and leader of the Opposition against Robert Harley. However, the ruling Tories had Walpole tried in 1712 for accepting an illegal payment as Secretary of War, after which he was committed to the Tower for 6 months and expelled from the House of Commons until 1713.

On the accession of George I, with the Whigs back in power, Walpole was sworn Privy Councilor and made Paymaster of the Forces 1714-15. Walpole was soon promoted to the positions of Chancellor of the Exchequer and First Lord of the Treasury (in October 1715); during this period he devised the first general sinking fund. Walpole resigned amid party infighting in April 1717, splitting the Whigs in Parliament. In 1720, he returned to the government as Paymaster-General. Although Walpole opposed the Government's encouragement of the South Sea Company in 1720, he benefited from South Sea crisis in 1721, when thousands of people lost large amounts of money after the collapse of the investment scheme. As he had sold his shares early, Walpole was credited with great financial acumen, and he returned to the positions of Chancellor and First Lord of the Treasury in April 1721. He retained this position until 1742, although his power waxed and waned during this twenty-one-year period. After George I's death in 1727, Walpole was briefly superseded by the new King's favourite, Spencer Compton, but he returned to prominence by assiduously flattering the King.

Sir Robert Walpole was the first to give the post of First Lord of the Treasury the importance the position (now termed Prime Minister) has retained. He amassed power by winning the confidence and support of both King and Parliament. Walpole neutralized dangerous opponents, reduced the national debt, and stabilized prices and wages.

He also encouraged trade by removing duties on imported raw materials and many exports, cultivated friendship with France, and secured peace through the Treaty of Vienna in 1736. Walpole realized the importance of maintaining close ties with members in the House of Commons. Detractors alleged that he used bribery and corruption to retain the power he so relished. Walpole's position was threatened by a poor performance in the war against Spain of 1739, and his resignation was eventually forced by an election loss at Chippenham. When he retired from the premiership he was created Baron Walpole of Houghton, Norfolk, Viscount Walpole, and Earl of Orford in Suffolk. After his elevation to the House of Lords, Orford remained an influential parliamentarian. Poor health forced him to retire in 1744.

566. Right Hon. Sir John Stonhouse, 3rd Baronet, P.C. (1713), M.P. 1701-33, Comptroller of the (Royal) Household 1713-14, born ca. 1673 and died 10 Aug. 1733. He married, 2nd, **Penelope Dashwood [No. 735]**. He married, 1st,
567. Mary Mellish, died shortly before 29 Aug. 1706.

568. John Vaughan, 1st Viscount Lisburne, M.P. [as John Vaughan and Viscount Lisburne] 1694-98, Lord Lieutenant of Cardiganshire 1714, born 7, baptized at the Church of St. Andrew Undershaft, London 15 Dec. 1667 and died 20 March 1720/21; buried at Greenwich, Kent. He married at the Church of St. Giles-in-the-Fields, Holborn, Middlesex 18 Aug. 1692,
569. Lady Malet Wilmot, baptized at Adderbury, Oxfordshire 6 Jan. 1675/76 and died 13 Jan. 1708/9.

570. Thomas Watson, Mayor of Berwick 1733, 1735, and 1738, buried 1 Jan. 1739/40. He married at Berwick-upon-Tweed 17 Sept. 1700,
571. Margaret Clerk, buried 12 Jan. 1740/41.

572. Mark Shafto, born at Newcastle-upon-Tyne 8 April 1662 and died 28 Dec. 1723. He married at Ripley, Yorkshire 23 Oct. 1683,
573. Margaret Ingleby, baptized at Ripley 21 March 1662/63 and died 12 Sept. 1715; buried at Whitworth, Durham.

574. Thomas Jackson of Nunnington, Yorkshire, died 6 July 1737. He married,
575. ——.

576. Johann Baring, Postmaster of Bremen 1672, born at Bremen in 1620 and died there in 1676. He married 29 May 1649,
577. Anna Hildebrand.

578. Johann Vagd, serge merchant of Bremen, married,
579. Anna Stubbeman.

580. John Vowler, baptized at Westbury, Wiltshire 3 Sept. 1626. He married at Crediton, Devonshire 26 March 1666,
581. Mary Shute, baptized at Crediton 1 May 1634.

582. Thomas Townsend married at the Church of St. Mary Major, Exeter 17 Aug. 1669,
583. Elizabeth Skinner.

584. Gerard Herring, draper of Cambridge, died before 2 May 1704. He married,
585. Mary Linford, died between 15 Jan. 1714/15 and 24 May 1715.

586. Isaac Watlington, M.P. 1695-98, born ca. 1640 and died 24 Oct. 1700. He married, 1st, at Trumpington, Cambridgeshire 17 April 1677, Margaret Thompson, daughter of James Thompson and Sarah Greenwood. He married, 2nd, at St. Sepulchre's Church, Cambridge 29 July 1691,
587. Dorothy Dillingham, born ca. 1669 and died in 1744.

588. Thomas Dawson, Lord Mayor of York 1703, born ca. 1667 and died 17 Jan. 1703, buried at the Church of St. Martin Micklegate, York. He married,
589. Elizabeth Hutton, baptized at Poppleton, Yorkshire 28 May 1665 and buried at the Church of St. Martin Micklegate 13 Dec. 1731.

590. ROBERT WATSON of Whitby, Yorkshire, married,

591. DOROTHY BUSHELL, baptized at Whitby 25 May 1673.

592. ROBERT LUKIN, baptized at Good Easter, Essex 31 March 1683 and buried at Barnston, Essex 5 April 1716. He married (license dated 6 Nov. 1706),

593. DOROTHY LANE, died before 1744.

594. ROBERT HICKS, tobacconist of Braintree, Essex, died before 6 May 1752. He married at Rayne, Essex 6 May 1703,

595. SARAH GOLDSTONE, baptized at Panfield, Essex 15 Oct. 1677 and died before 22 March 1755.

596. GUYBON DOUGHTY, baptized at Oby, Norfolk 29 May 1678 and died 24 May 1740. He married,

597. ESTHER DOUGHTY, baptized at St. Giles' Church, Norwich 10 Feb. 1681/82 and died 14 Feb. 1726/27.

598. WEYMAN LEE, barrister, born at Tichmarsh, Northamptonshire 14 Oct. 1681 and died 12 Nov. 1765. He married, 2nd, at the Church of St. Martin-in-the-Fields, Westminster, London 17 Jan. 1729, Sarah Brumley. He married, 1st, at the Church of St. Martin-in-the-Fields 25 Sept. 1725,

599. MARY SHARP, died before 17 Jan. 1729.

600. THÉOPHILE THELLUSSON, born at Geneva 11 July 1646 and died there 16 Aug. 1705. He married at Lyon 27 Aug. 1679,

601. JEANNE GUIGUER, born at Lyon 2 May 1662 and died at Geneva 9 May 1712.

602. ABRAHAM LE BOULLENGER, SEIGNEUR DE RIDER, married, 2nd, 5 Nov. 1707, Jeanne de Robais of Abbeville, Ponthieu. He married, 1st, in 1699,

603. ANNE VAN DER HULST, died in 1702.

604. Rev. Matthew Woodford, baptized at Salisbury Cathedral 10 Oct. 1674 and died in Nov. 1719. He married at the Church of St. Peter the Great, Chichester, Sussex 7 Nov. 1704,

605. Anne Sherer, baptized at the Church of St. Peter the Great 9 Aug. 1685.

606. Rev. John Brideoak, Rector of Swerford, Oxfordshire, born at Isleworth, Middlesex ca. 1666 and died before 9 May 1727. He married at the Church of St. Mary Magdalene, Old Fish Street, London 17 July 1701,

607. Elizabeth Walker.

608. Samuel Bulteel, born ca. 1652 and buried at Tavistock, Devonshire 20 June 1682. He married,

609. Azarelle Condy, baptized at Tavistock 21 Sept. 1653.

610. Courtenay Crocker, M.P. 1695-1702, Governor of Dartmouth 1699-?1715, baptized at Yealmpton, Devonshire 13 June 1660 and died in 1740. He married, 2nd, at the Church of St. Thomas the Apostle, Exeter 16 March 1695/96, Katherine Tucker, daughter of John Tucker of Exeter. He married, 1st, ca. 1691,

611. Mary Hillersdon, baptized at Holbeton, Devonshire 21 Nov. 1671.

612. John Ker [from 1671 Bellenden], 2nd Lord Bellenden, died in March 1706/7. He married 10 April 1683,

613. Lady Mary Moore, died 17 March 1725/26. She married, 1st, William Ramsay, 3rd Earl of Dalhousie, who died in Nov. 1682, son of George Ramsay, 2nd Earl of Dalhousie, and Lady Janet Fleming, daughter of John Fleming, 2nd Earl of Wigtown. She married, 3rd, Dr. Samuel Collins.

614. John Parnell, buried at Baldock, Hertfordshire 26 Nov. 1738. He married at Ardeley, Hertfordshire 11 April 1700,

615. Mary Hodgson, baptized at Walkern, Hertfordshire 27 Aug. 1681.

616. Philip Perring of Modbury, Devonshire, died 23 April 1716. He married,

617. Elizabeth ——.

618. PASCOE LEGASSICK, born at Modbury, Devonshire 21 Jan. 1658. He married there 26 June 1682,
619. JOAN COVE.

620–623. ——.

624. JOHN GREY, baptized at Long Houghton, Northumberland 1 Feb. 1669/70 and buried at Howick, Northumberland 25 June 1710. He married in 1689,
625. MARGARET PEARSON, born ca. 1669 and buried at Howick 19 Jan. 1697/98.

626. THOMAS WOOD, baptized at Bamburgh, Northumberland 20 April 1675 and died after 3 July 1755. He married,
627. ——.

628. GEORGE GREY, born at Lawton, Cheshire 20 Oct. 1680 and buried at St. Nicholas' Church, Newcastle-upon-Tyne 24 May 1772. He married at Lanchester, Durham 13 Oct. 1712,
629. ALICE CLAVERING, baptized at All Saints' Church, Newcastle 20 Nov. 1681 and died 26 Dec. 1744.

630. DR. NATHANIEL OGLE, born in 1674 and buried at Ponteland, Northumberland 19 June 1739. He married at St. James's Church, Westminster, London 22 April 1708,
631. ELIZABETH NEWTON, died between 5 Oct. 1750 and 5 May 1751.

632. BRABAZON PONSONBY, 1ST EARL OF BESSBOROUGH, P.C. (I.) (1727), M.P. [as Brabazon Ponsonby and Hon. Brabazon Ponsonby] 1705-14 and 1715-24, born in 1679 and died at Bessborough, Kilkenny 4 July 1758. He married, 2nd, 28 Nov. 1733, Elizabeth Sankey, born in 1680 and died 17 July 1738, widow of i) Sir John King, 2nd Baronet, and ii) John Moore, 1st Baron Moore, and daughter of John Sankey and Eleanor Morgan. He married, 1st, before 1704,
633. SARAH MARGETSON, died 21 May 1733; buried at Fiddown, Kilkenny. She married, 1st, at St. James's Church, Westminster, Middlesex 4 July 1694, Hugh Colvill of Newtown, Downshire.

634. William Cavendish, 3rd Duke of Devonshire, K.G. (1733), P.C. (1731), F.R.S. (1747/48), M.P. [as Marquess of Hartington] 1721-29, Lord Steward of the (Royal) Household 1733-37 and 1745-49, Chief Governor [i.e. Lord Lieutenant] of Ireland 1737-45, Lord Justice [i.e. Regent] 1741, 1743, 1745, and 1748, born 26 Sept., baptized at the Church of St. Martin-in-the-Fields, Westminster, Middlesex 6 Oct. 1698 and died 5 Dec. 1755. He married at Oxted, Surrey 27 March 1718,

635. Catherine Hoskins, baptized at St. Andrew's Church, Holborn, Middlesex 17 Nov. 1698 and died 8 May 1777.

636. Robert Molesworth, 1st Viscount Molesworth, M.P. [as Robert Molesworth] 1695-99 and 1703-14, born posthumously at Dublin 7 Sept. 1656 and died 2 May 1725. He married 16 Aug. 1676,

637. Hon. Laetitia Coote, died at Brackenstown, Swords, Dublin 17 March 1729/30.

638. Ven. William Ussher, Archdeacon of Clonfert, baptized at St. Michan's Church, Dublin 12 May 1680 and died 18 Jan. 1743/44. He married,
639. Mary Jenney.

640. James Hamilton, 7th Earl of Abercorn, P.C. (E.) (1738) and (I.) (1739), F.R.S. (1715), born 22, baptized at the Church of St. Martin-in-the-Fields, Westminster, Middlesex 23 March 1685/86 and died at Cavendish Square, London 11 Jan. 1743/44. He married (Faculty Office license to marry at Widford, Hertfordshire dated 26 March 1711),

641. Anne Plumer, born 29 June, baptized at Ware, Hertfordshire 5 July 1690 and died at London 7 Aug. 1776.

642. Right Hon. James Craggs, P.C. (1718), M.P. 1713-21, Ambassador to Madrid 1711, Secretary of War 1717-18, Secretary of State for the South 1718, called "a showy, vaporing man," born at Westminster, Middlesex 9 April 1680 and died at Jermyn Street, Westminster 16 Feb. 1720/21. He had issue by,

643. Hester Santlow, an actress and dancer whose affair with John Churchill, 1st Duke of Marlborough [No. 514], roiled his marriage, born ca. 1690 and died at Great Russell Street, Bloomsbury, London 15 Jan. 1773. She married at Chipping Ongar, Essex 3 Aug. 1719, Barton Booth, an actor, born in 1681 and died at 4 Charles Square, Covent Garden, London 10 May 1733, son of John Booth.

644. JOSEPH MOYLE, M.P. 1705-8, born 4, baptized at St. Germans, Cornwall 11 Sept. 1679 and died 29 March 1742. He married in Oct. 1711,

645. CATHERINE COPLEY, died before 20 March 1775.

646. JOHN FRANCIS BULLER, baptized at Morval, Cornwall 11 April 1695 and died there 22 June 1751. He married at Trelawny Chapel, Pelynt, Cornwall 22 July 1716,

647. REBECCA TRELAWNY, baptized at Pelynt 5 Jan. 1695 and buried at Morval 6 Aug. 1743.

648. GEORGE DOUGLAS, 13TH EARL OF MORTON, M.P. [as Hon. George Douglas] 1702-7, 1708-13, and 1722-30, Scottish representative peer 1730-38, Lord Lieutenant of Orkney and Shetland 1725-38, born in 1662 and died at Edinburgh 4 Jan. 1737/38. He married, 1st, —— Muirhead, daughter of Alexander Muirhead of Linhouse, Edinburgh. He married, 2nd, at St. James's Church, Duke's Place, London 25 Dec. 1695,

649. FRANCES ADDERLEY, baptized at St. Andrew's Church, Holborn, Middlesex 26 Sept. 1669.

650. SIR JOHN HEATHCOTE, 2ND BARONET, M.P. 1715-22 and 1733-41, born 21 Aug., baptized at St. Swithin's Church, Stone Street, London 5 Sept. 1689 and died 5 Sept. 1759. He married 5 Aug. 1720,

651. BRIDGET WHITE, born ca. 1704 and died 5 May 1772.

652. EDWARD LASCELLES, baptized at Northallerton, Yorkshire 25 Feb. 1702/3 and died 31 Oct. 1747; buried at St. Michael's Church, Barbados. He married at St. Michael's Church 1 Jan. 1731/32,

653. FRANCES BALL, baptized in Barbados 2 March 1717/18 and died 18 May 1761. She married, 2nd, ca. 1750, Rear Admiral Francis Holburne, M.P. 1761-71, born in 1704 and died at Richmond, Surrey 15 July 1771, son of Sir James Holburne, 1st Baronet, and Jean Spittal.

654. WILLIAM CHALONER, born at Streatlam Castle, Durham 29 July 1714 and died 13 Feb. 1754; buried at Guisborough, Yorkshire. He married at Sedgefield, Durham 1 Oct. 1741,

655. MARY FINNEY of Finneyham, Staffordshire.

656. WRIOTHESLEY RUSSELL, 2ND DUKE OF BEDFORD, K.G. (1702/3), Lord of the Bedchamber to HM Queen Anne 1701-2, Lord High Constable at the coronation of HM 1702, Lord Lieutenant of Bedfordshire, Cambridgeshire, and Middlesex 1701-11, baptized at the Church of St. Giles-in-the-Fields, Holborn, Middlesex 1 Nov. 1680 and died 26 May 1711; buried at Chenies, Buckinghamshire. He married at Streatham, Surrey 23 May 1695,

657. ELIZABETH HOWLAND, born ca. 1682 and died at Streatham 29 July 1724.

658. JOHN LEVESON-GOWER, 1ST EARL GOWER, P.C. (1742), Lord Privy Seal 1742-43 and 1744-54, a Lord Justice [i.e. Regent] 1740, 1743, 1745, 1748, 1750, and 1752, Lord Lieutenant of Staffordshire 1742-54, born at London 10 Aug. 1694 and died at 6 Upper Brook Street, London 25 Dec. 1754. He married, 2nd, at the Church of St. George the Martyr, Queen Square, London 31 Oct. 1733, Penelope Stonhouse, born 9 May, baptized at St. Anne's Church, Soho, London 4 June 1707 and died at Trentham, Staffordshire 19 Aug. 1734, widow of Sir Henry Atkins, 4th Baronet, and daughter of Sir John Stonhouse, 3rd Baronet [No. 566], and Penelope Dashwood [No. 735]. He married, 3rd, 16 May 1736, Lady Mary Tufton, born 6 July 1701 and died at Bill Hill, Berkshire 12 Feb. 1785, widow of Anthony Grey, Earl of Harold by courtesy, and daughter of Thomas Tufton, 6th Earl of Thanet, and Lady Catherine Cavendish, daughter of Henry Cavendish, 2nd Duke of Newcastle. He married, 1st, at St. Anne's Church 13 March 1711/12,

659. LADY EVELYN PIERREPONT, born 6, baptized at St. Anne's Church 19 Sept. 1691 and died at Leicester Street, London 26 June 1727.

660. ARNOLD JOOST VAN KEPPEL, 1ST EARL OF ALBEMARLE, K.G. (1700), Page of Honour to HH The Prince of Orange (later HM King William III) 1688, Groom of the Bedchamber to HM 1691-95, Major General 1697, General of the Dutch forces [present in command at Ramillies (1706) and Oudenaarde (1708)], Governor of Tournai 1709, special ambassador for the States General to HM King George I on his accession in 1714, probably baptized at Zutphen, Gelderland 30 Jan. 1670 and died at The Hague 30 May 1718. He married at the English Church, The Hague 15 June 1701,

661. GEERTRUID JOHANNA QUIRINA VAN DER DUYN, baptized at The Hague 9 Dec. 1674 and died there in Dec. 1741.

Arnold Joost van Keppel, 1st Earl of Albemarle

Born ca. 1670
Died at The Hague 30 May 1718
Married at The Hague 15 June 1701
Geertruid Johanna Quirina van der Duyn

On his father's death, Keppel inherited a debt-ridden estate in Gelderland. The handsome young Dutch lord had an even temper and a quick – though not profound – understanding, and he soon obtained a position as Page of Honour to the Prince of Orange. Keppel became a favourite of the Prince – from 1689, King William III of England – who granted him an enormous amount of forfeited Irish lands and helped discharge his debts. Keppel's outgoing manner made him many friends, including the King's mistress, Elizabeth Villiers, and the favourite soon rose to become a leading representative of the younger generation at court. As such, William found him more useful than his other Dutch confidant, the Earl of Portland. Keppel became the King's closest aide after the death of Queen Mary, attending the King in several military campaigns, and having been admitted in 1692 into the knighthood of Zutphen and subsequently into that of Holland and West Friesland, he was given the English titles of Baron Ashford, Viscount Bury, and Earl of Albemarle in 1697.

In that year, Albemarle was also appointed a major general and colonel of the Life Guards. After the French seized barrier fortresses in the Spanish Netherlands, Lord Albemarle was sent to the Dutch States General to develop a strategy against France. He accomplished this mission and befriended the Duke of Marlborough. In 1702, having returned to England from The Hague, Albemarle was present at the death of William III, who bequeathed him 200,000 guilders. Afterwards he retired to Holland and took his seat among the nobles of the States General. The Earl was appointed General of the Dutch forces and was in command at Ramillies in 1706 and Oudenaarde in 1708; Marlborough entrusted Albemarle with thirty squadrons of cavalry to cover the supply lines to the siege being waged upon Liège later that year. Lord Albemarle was made Governor of Tournai in 1709. On the death of Queen Anne in 1714, the States General sent him to George I bearing congratulations upon the Elector's accession to the throne of Great Britain.

662. Charles Lennox, 1st Duke of Richmond and Lennox, K.G. (1681), P.C. (I.) (1715), Master of the Horse 1681-85, Lord High Admiral 1694, bore the Sceptre with the Dove at the coronation of HM Queen Anne 1702, born at London 29 July 1672 and died at Goodwood, Sussex 27 May 1723. He married ca. 8 Jan. 1692/93,

663. Hon. Anne Brudenell, born ca. 1672 and died at Whitehall, London 9 Dec. 1722. She married, 1st, Henry Belasyse, 2nd Baron Belasyse, who died before 26 Aug. 1691, son of Hon. Sir Henry Belasyse, K.B., and Susan Armyne, Baroness Belasyse for life.

664. Alexander Gordon, 2nd Duke of Gordon, born ca. 1678 and died at Gordon Castle, Banffshire 28 Nov. 1728. He married (contracts dated 7 Oct. 1706 and 5 Feb. 1706/7),

665. Lady Henrietta Mordaunt, born ca. 1682 and died at Prestonhall, Edinburgh 11 Oct. 1760.

666. William Gordon, 2nd Earl of Aberdeen, Scottish representative peer 1721-22, baptized at Methlic, Aberdeenshire 22 Dec. 1679 and died at Edinburgh 30 March 1745. He married, 1st, before 12 Oct. 1708, Lady Mary Leslie, born in July 1692 and buried at Methlic 29 Jan. 1709/10, daughter of David Leslie, 5th Earl of Leven, and Lady Anne Wemyss, daughter of Margaret Wemyss, Countess of Wemyss in her own right. He married, 3rd, at Bellie Parish Church, Fochabers, Banffshire 9 Dec. 1729, Lady Anne Gordon, born ca. 1714 and died at Edinburgh 26 June 1791, daughter of Alexander Gordon, 2nd Duke of Gordon [No. 664], and Lady Henrietta Mordaunt [No. 665]. He married, 2nd, at Huntingtower, Perthshire 25 April 1716,

667. Lady Susan Murray, born at Huntingtower 15 April 1699 and died 22 June 1725.

668. Sir Alexander Maxwell, 2nd Baronet, M.P. 1713-15, died 23 May 1730. He married 29 Dec. 1711,

669. Lady Jean Montgomerie, died at Edinburgh 20 Feb. 1744/45.

670. William Scott [later Blair], born 9 Aug. 1682. He married, 1st, Magdalene Blair, daughter of William Blair and Magdalene Campbell. He married, 2nd,

671. Catherine Tait, died 22 July 1767.

672. SIR NATHANIEL CURZON, 2ND BARONET, born 17, baptized at Kedleston, Derbyshire 25 Jan. 1635/36 and died 4 March 1718/19; buried at Kedleston. He married (Vicar-General's license to marry at the Church of St. Mary le Savoy, London dated 5 July 1671),

673. SARAH PENN, born ca. 1655 and died at Great George Street, London 4 Jan. 1727/28.

674. SIR RALPH ASSHETON, 2ND BARONET, M.P. 1677-79 and 1694-98, born at Middleton, Lancashire 11 Feb. 1651/52 and died 3 May 1716. He married, 2nd, at Denton, Lancashire 30 July 1696, Mary Hyde, who died at London 16 June 1721, daughter of Robert Hyde and Mary Jackson. He married, 1st, at Burley, Yorkshire in 1680,

675. MARY VAVASOUR, born in 1663 and died 11 Nov. 1694.

676. WILLIAM HANMER, baptized at Ludford, Shropshire 5 July 1674 and buried at Hanmer, Flintshire 2 May 1724. He married at Aston, Warwickshire 25 Nov. 1701,

677. ESTHER JENNENS, baptized at Aston 24 Dec. 1670 and died before 2 Aug. 1770.

678. REV. CHARLES JENNENS, Rector of Darley, Derbyshire, baptized at St. Martin's Church, Birmingham 28 July 1662 and died 4 July 1747; buried at Nether Whitacre, Warwickshire. He married, 1st, Mary ——. He married, 2nd, at Foremark, Derbyshire 11 Dec. 1689,

679. ELIZABETH BURDETT, baptized at Foremark 10 Dec. 1667 and buried at Nether Whitacre 10 Jan. 1707/8.

680. SCROPE HOWE, 1ST VISCOUNT HOWE, M.P. [as Sir Scrope Howe] 1673-86, 1689-98, and 1710-13, born in Nov. 1648 and died at Langar, Nottinghamshire 26 Jan. 1712/13. He married, 1st, at Selston, Nottinghamshire 20 April 1672, Lady Anne Manners, baptized at the Church of St. Martin-in-the-Fields, Westminster, Middlesex 3 July 1653, daughter of John Manners, 8th Earl of Rutland [No. 5268], and Hon. Frances Montagu [No. 5269]. He married, 2nd (Faculty Office license dated 15 July 1698),

681. HON. JULIANA ALINGTON, baptized at Horseheath, Cambridgeshire 30 Oct. 1665 and died 10 Sept. 1747; buried at Langar.

682. JOHANN ADOLF VON KIELMANSEGG, Master of the Horse to HH The Elector of Hanover (later HM King George I), born 30 Sept. 1668 and died 15 Nov. 1717. He married in 1701,

683. SOPHIA CHARLOTTE REICHSGRÄFIN VON PLATEN-HALLERMUND, COUNTESS OF LEINSTER AND DARLINGTON for life, an important figure in the court of [her likely half-brother] HM King George I [whom contemporaries judged her lover], born (probably at Osnabrück, Hanover) ca. 1675 and died at London 20 April 1725.

684. COLONEL THOMAS HARTOPP of Quorndon, Barrow-upon-Soar, Leicestershire, born ca. 1655 and died 17 Sept. 1727. He married,

685. ANNE BENNETT of Welby, Leicestershire.

686. THOMAS MANSFIELD, baptized at West Leake, Nottinghamshire 14 May 1664 and buried there 29 Jan. 1705/6. He married at Arnold, Nottinghamshire 27 Aug. 1685,

687. REBECCA CHADWICK, born ca. 1668.

688. RALPH GORE of Barrow Mount, Kilkenny, born ca. 1653 and died 12 Dec. 1721. He married,

689. HANNAH GORE of Manor Gore, Donegal.

690. ISAAC MANLEY, M.P. 1705-13 and 1715-36, Postmaster-General of Ireland 1703-36, born ca. 1658 and died at Dublin 30 Dec. 1736. He married at St. Peter's Church, Cornhill, London 20 May 1678,

691. MARY NEWLAND, baptized at St. Paul's Church, Covent Garden, near London 6 Dec. 1659.

692. VALENTINE MUNBEE of Clarendon Parish, Jamaica, member of the Council of Jamaica 1716, married,

693. ——.

694-695. ——.

696. JAMES MONTAGU, M.P. 1702-5, baptized 31 Jan. 1672/73 and buried at Lacock, Wiltshire 4 Aug. 1747. He married before 8 Aug. 1710,

697. ELIZABETH EYLES, buried at Lacock 3 Dec. 1741.

Sophia Charlotte Reichsgräfin von Platen-Hallermund, Countess of Leinster and Darlington

Born ca. 1675
Died at London 20 April 1725
Married in 1701
Johann Adolf von Kielmansegg

Sophia Charlotte Reichsgräfin von Platen-Hallermund was the daughter of Clara Elisabeth von Meysenbug, mistress of Ernst August, Elector of Hanover. Sophia's father was perhaps Franz Ernst Reichsgraf von Platen-Hallermund, her mother's husband, but the Elector was also a candidate. Sophia Charlotte was accepted in the Electoral family circle as Ernst August's daughter, and thus treated as a half-sister of his legitimate children. Sophia Charlotte established a very close relationship with her half-brother Georg Ludwig (after 1714 King George I of Great Britain), but George's mother stated that "to her certain knowledge" Sophia Charlotte was not her son's mistress. In 1701, Sophia married her half-brother the Elector's deputy Master of the Horse, Johann Adolf von Kielmansegg.

Madame von Kielmansegg followed King George I to London in 1714, where she became an important courtier, wielding considerable influence over the new monarch. Sophia Charlotte competed for the King's favor with Melusine von der Schulenburg, who was indeed the King's mistress. The two women were called the maypole (Melusine) and the elephant (Sophia Charlotte). With such access to the king, Madame von Kielmansegg had ample opportunity to accept bribes; one of them, a large number of shares in the South Sea Company, made her a fortune. (She used her influence at court to conceal her part in the scandal after the stock collapsed.)

In September 1721, Sophia Charlotte was created Countess of Leinster for life; six months later, she received further titles for life: Baroness Brentford of Brentford, Middlesex, and Countess of Darlington in Durham. Sophia Charlotte's coat of arms included those of the House of Brunswick with a bend sinister. Contemporary wags were emphatic that George I and Madame Kielmansegg were lover and mistress, but they overlooked the possibility that she was George's half-sister.

698. JAMES WROUGHTON, buried at Wilcot, Wiltshire 20 July 1745. He married before 7 Aug. 1718,
699. ANNE EYRE, born ca. 1699 and buried at Wilcot 30 April 1761.

700. JAMES WROUGHTON = 698.
701. ANNE EYRE = 699.

702. JOHN MOYLE, baptized at Plymouth, Devonshire 15 Dec. 1693 and buried at St. Germans, Cornwall 25 May 1743. He married, 1st, at St. Germans 21 Sept. 1715, Susanna Horndon. He married, 2nd, at Lanivet, Cornwall 2 May 1731,
703. SUSANNA BULLOCK, born ca. 1700 and buried at St. Germans 4 March 1760.

704. SIR GEORGE BINGHAM, 4TH BARONET = 264.
705. MARY SCOTT = 265.

706. AGMONDESHAM VESEY = 266.
707. CHARLOTTE SARSFIELD = 267.

708. JAMES SMITH = 268.
709. = 269.

710-711. = 270-271.

712. THOMAS BELASYSE, 1ST VISCOUNT FAUCONBERG, baptized at the Church of St. Michael-le-Belfry, York 11 March 1663 and died at Brussels 26 Nov. 1718. He married before July 1698,
713. BRIDGET GAGE, died 18 Nov. 1732; buried at Coxwold, Yorkshire.

714. JOHN BETHAM [LATER FOWLER], born 5 Oct. 1670 and buried at Baswich, Staffordshire 23 Nov. 1719. He married,
715. CATHERINE CASEY, buried 17 Sept. 1725.

716. Matthew Lamb, attorney and land agent of Southwell, Nottinghamshire, died in Feb. 1735/36. He married,

717. ——.

718. Right Hon. Thomas Coke, P.C. (1708), M.P. 1698-1700 and 1701-15, Vice Chamberlain of the (Royal) Household to TM Queen Anne and King George I 1706-27, baptized at Melbourne, Derbyshire 19 Feb. 1673/74 and died at Melbourne Hall 17 May 1727. He married, 1st, ca. June 1698, Lady Mary Stanhope, who died 11 Jan. 1703/4, daughter of Philip Stanhope, 2nd Earl of Chesterfield, and Lady Elizabeth Dormer, daughter of Charles Dormer, 2nd Earl of Carnarvon. He married, 2nd, 14 Oct. 1709,

719. Mary Hale, Maid of Honour to HM Queen Anne 1708-9, died in Jan. 1723/24.

720. Francis Brudenell, Lord Brudenell by courtesy, born in 1645 and died before 18 Aug. 1698. He married ca. 1 June 1668,

721. Lady Frances Savile, died in Sussex 6 June 1695.

722. Thomas Bruce, 3rd Earl of Elgin and 2nd Earl of Ailesbury, M.P. [as Lord Kinloss] 1679-81 and 1685, Page of Honour at the coronation of HM King James II 1685, Lord of the Bedchamber to HM 1685-88, Lord Lieutenant of Bedfordshire and Huntingdonshire 1685-88, born (probably at Ampthill, Bedfordshire) 26 Sept. 1656 and died at Brussels 16 Dec. 1741. He married, 2nd, at Brussels 27 April 1700, Charlotte Jacqueline Louise Thérèse d'Argenteau, Comtesse d'Essneux in her own right, born posthumously at Brussels 18 Oct. 1678 and died there 23 July 1710, daughter of Louis Conrad d'Argenteau, Comte d'Essneux, and Marie Gilberte de Locquenghien de Melsbroeck. He married, 1st, 31 Aug. 1676,

723. Lady Elizabeth Seymour, raised to the rank of a duke's daughter 1672, born in 1655 and died at the Tower of London 12 Jan. 1696/97.

724. Sir Cecil Bishopp, 5th Baronet, died 25 Oct. 1725. He married ca. Aug. 1698,

725. Elizabeth Dunch, died ca. 1751.

726. HUGH BOSCAWEN, 1ST VISCOUNT FALMOUTH, P.C. (1714), M.P. [as Hugh Boscawen] 1702-20, Groom of the Bedchamber to HRH The Duke of Gloucester 1698-1700 and HRH Prince George of Denmark 1702-8, Comptroller of the (Royal) Household 1714-20, Warden of the Stannaries 1708-10, Joint Treasurer of Ireland 1717-34, born ca. 1680 and died at Trefusis, Cornwall 25 Oct. 1734. He married at Westminster Abbey, London 23 April 1700,

727. CHARLOTTE GODFREY, born in 1679 and died 22 March 1754.

728. SIR GEORGE COOKE, Chief Prothonotary of the Court of Common Pleas, born ca. 1675 and died 4 Nov. 1740; buried at Hayes, Middlesex. He married at St. Paul's Cathedral, London 6 July 1700,

729. ANNE JENNINGS, born ca. 1681 and died 5 March 1735/36; buried at Hayes.

730. SIR THOMAS TWYSDEN, 4TH BARONET, born in 1676 and died 10 Oct. 1712. He married in 1710,

731. CATHERINE WYTHENS, died in April 1730. She married, 2nd, at Maidstone, Kent 14 Nov. 1713, Brigadier General George Jocelyn, who died in Nov. 1727.

732. CECIL BOWYER of Denham, Buckinghamshire, born ca. 1684 and died 5 Dec. 1720. He married at St. Paul's Cathedral, London 22 July 1707,

733. JULIANA PARKER of Hedsor, Buckinghamshire, died before 7 Sept. 1750.

734. SIR JOHN STONHOUSE, 3RD BARONET = 566. He married, 2nd, at Kirtlington, Oxfordshire 29 Aug. 1706,

735. PENELOPE DASHWOOD, baptized at St. John's Church, Hackney, Middlesex 29 Aug. 1686.

736. CHARLES LENNOX, 1ST DUKE OF RICHMOND AND LENNOX = 662.
737. HON. ANNE BRUDENELL = 663.

738. WILLIAM CADOGAN, 1ST EARL CADOGAN, K.T. (1716), P.C. (1717), M.P. [as William Cadogan] 1705-16, Master of the Robes to HM King George I 1714-26, Ambassador to Hanover 1706 and The Hague 1707-10 and 1714-22,

General 1717, Commander-in-Chief of the forces in Scotland 1716, Master General of the Ordnance 1722-25, a Lord Justice [i.e. Regent] 1723, Governor of the Isle of Wight 1715-26, born at Liscarton, Meath in 1672 and died at Kensington, Middlesex 17 July 1726. He married at The Hague in April 1704,

739. Margaretta Cecilia van Munter van Zanen-Raaphorst, born at The Hague 27 July 1675 and died there 2 Nov. 1749.

740. William Kerr, 3rd Marquess of Lothian, K.T. (1733/34), Scottish representative peer 1731-61, born ca. 1690 and died at Lothian House, Cannongate, Edinburgh 28 July 1767. He married, 2nd, 1 Oct. 1760, his 1st cousin Jean Janet Kerr, born ca. 1721 and died at Lothian House 26 Dec. 1787, daughter of Lord Charles Kerr and Janet Murray. He married, 1st (contract dated 7 and 8 Dec. 1711),

741. Margaret Nicolson, died at Newbattle Abbey, Edinburgh 30 Sept. 1759.

742. Robert Darcy, 3rd Earl of Holdernesse, P.C. (1717/18), Lord of the Bedchamber to HM King George I 1719-22, Lord Lieutenant of the North Riding of Yorkshire 1714-22, born at London 24 Nov. 1681 and died at Bath, Somerset 20 Jan. 1721/22. He married at Hillingdon, Middlesex 26 May 1715,

743. Frederica Susanna von Schomberg, Countess of Mertola in her own right, born at Berlin ca. 1688 and died 7 Aug. 1751; buried at Chelmsford, Essex. She married, 2nd, at St. James's Church, Westminster, Middlesex 18 June 1724, Benjamin Mildmay, 1st Earl Fitzwalter, baptized at Chelmsford 27 Dec. 1672 and died at London 29 Feb. 1756, son of Benjamin Mildmay, 14th Baron Fitzwalter, and Hon. Catherine Fairfax, daughter of William Fairfax, 3rd Viscount Fairfax.

744. Alexander Gordon, 2nd Duke of Gordon = 664.
745. Lady Henrietta Mordaunt = 665.

746. William Gordon, 2nd Earl of Aberdeen = 666.
747. Lady Susan Murray = 667.

748. Sir Alexander Maxwell, 2nd Baronet = 668.
749. Lady Jean Montgomerie = 669.

750. WILLIAM BLAIR = 670.

751. CATHERINE TAIT = 671.

752. SIR EDWARD BAYLY, 1ST BARONET, M.P. 1705-14, Sheriff of Downshire 1730, born 20 Feb. 1684 and died 28 Sept. 1741; buried at Delgany, Wicklow. He married (license dated 28 Aug. 1708),

753. DOROTHY LAMBART, died 16 Aug. 1745; buried at Delgany.

754. BRIGADIER GENERAL THOMAS PAGET, M.P. 1722-27, Groom of the Bedchamber 1714-41, deputy Governor of Minorca 1741, born ca. 1685 and died at Minorca 28 May 1741. He married,

755. MARY WHITCOMBE, died 15 Feb. 1740/41.

756. MAJOR JOSIAS CHAMPAGNÉ, born at Champagné, Saintonge 13 March 1673 and died 2 May 1737; buried at the French Church, Portarlington, Leix. He married,

757. LADY JANE FORBES, died at Lumville, Leix 11 Oct. 1760.

758. LIEUT. COLONEL ISAAC HAMON of Paris, died 9 Jan. 1755; buried at the French Church, Portarlington, Leix. He married,

759. DEBORAH ——.

760. WILLIAM VILLIERS, 2ND EARL OF JERSEY, M.P. [as Viscount Villiers] 1705-8, born ca. 1682 and died at Castlethorpe, Buckinghamshire 13 July 1721. He married at Hampstead, Middlesex 22 March 1704/5,

761. JUDITH HERNE, died 22 July 1735; buried at St. Bride's Church, London.

762. SCROOP EGERTON, 1ST DUKE OF BRIDGEWATER, Lord of the Bedchamber to HRH Prince George of Denmark 1703-5 and Master of the Horse to HRH 1705-8, Lord Chamberlain to HRH The Princess of Wales (later HM Queen Caroline) 1714-17, Lord of the Bedchamber to HM King George I 1719-27, Lord Lieutenant of Buckinghamshire 1702-11 and 1714-28, born 11, baptized at the Church of St. Giles Cripplegate, London 14 Aug. 1681 and died 11 Jan. 1744/45. He married, 2nd, 4 Aug. 1722, Lady Rachel

Russell, who died 22 May 1777, daughter of Wriothesley Russell, 2nd Duke of Bedford [No. 656], and Elizabeth Howland [No. 657]. He married, 1st, 9 Feb. 1702/3,

763. LADY ELIZABETH CHURCHILL, born 15 March 1686/87 and died 22 March 1713/14; buried at Little Gaddesden, Hertfordshire.

764. SIR WILLIAM TWYSDEN, 5TH BARONET, of Roydon Hall, East Peckham, Kent, born 14 Aug. 1677 and died 20 Aug. 1751. He married 7 May 1706,

765. JANE TWYSDEN, born ca. 1682 and died ca. 1756.

766. RIGHT HON. THOMAS CARTER, P.C. (I.) (1732), M.P. 1719-61, Master of the Rolls 1731-54, Secretary of State (Ireland) 1755-56, born at Hollybrook, Dublin in 1690 and died at Rathnally House, Meath 3 Sept. 1763. He married at Dublin in 1719,

767. MARY CLAXTON, born ca. 1700 and died in 1780.

768. FRANCIS ROCHE, High Sheriff of Cork 1641, died in 1669. He married,

769. JANE [OR KATHERINE] COPPINGER of Ballyvolane, Cork.

770. JAMES LAVALLIN of Walterstown, Cork, died in June or July 1681. He married,

771. —— MACCARTHY.

772. GEORGE HENNESSY of Ballymacmoy, Cork, married,

773. MARY O'PHELAN of Tipperary.

774-795. ——.

796. COLONEL DANIEL O'DONOVAN ("THE O'DONOVAN"), M.P. (I.) 1689, died in 1705. He married, 1st, Victoria Coppinger. He married, 2nd, in 1689,

797. ELIZABETH TONSON.

798–799. ——.

800. THOMAS BOOTHBY, born ca. 1662. He married,
801. SUSANNA —— of Moor House, Rearsby, Lincolnshire.

802–823. ——.

824. JACQUES GUINAND, master mason of Neuchâtel, died 11 Sept. 1726. He married,
825. SUZANNE HUMBERT-DROZ, died at Neuchâtel 15 March 1725.

826. DAVID HAMELOT married,
827. ——.

828. JEAN YVONNET of London, born 18 Dec. 1645 and died before 11 July 1716. He married 24 Oct. 1702,
829. MARIE YVONNET, born 14 Nov. 1663.

830–847. ——.

848. ? JOSEPH BOUDE, innkeeper of Boston, Massachusetts, married before 20 Aug. 1657,
849. ? ELIZABETH ——, died at Marblehead, Massachusetts in 1670.

850–851. ——.

852. MICHAEL NEWBOLD, born at Hansworth Woodhouse, Yorkshire 1 July 1623 and died before 25 Feb. 1692/93; will proved in Burlington County, New Jersey. He married,
853. ANNE ——.

854. JOHN CLAYTON, died before 2 June 1704; will proved in Burlington County, New Jersey. He married at Swarthmoor, Lancashire 11 10th mo. 1661,

855. Alice Myres, perhaps related to the Myres family of Beakcliffe, Adingham, Lancashire, died in New Jersey after 1678.

856-879. ——.

880. Joseph Strong, member of the Connecticut General Assembly 1721-62, born at Northampton, Massachusetts 2 Dec. 1672 and died at Coventry, Connecticut 23 Dec. 1763. He married, 2nd, 15 Sept. 1724, Ruth ——, who died at Glastonbury, Connecticut 14 Feb. 1768. He married, 1st, at Northampton in 1694,
881. Sarah Allen, born at Northampton 22 Aug. 1672 and died before 15 Sept. 1724.

882. Preserved Strong, born at Northampton, Massachusetts 29 March 1680 and died at Coventry, Connecticut 26 Sept. 1765. He married at Northampton 23 Oct. 1701,
883. Tabitha Lee, born at Farmington, Connecticut ca. 1677 and died at Coventry 23 June 1750.

884. Captain Samuel Bishop, born at Ipswich, Massachusetts in Feb. 1678/79 and died at Norwich, Connecticut 18 Nov. 1760. He married at Norwich 2 Jan. 1705/6,
885. Sarah Fobes, born at Norwich 24 June 1684 and died there 11 March 1759.

886. Ebenezer Hibbard, born at Wenham, Massachusetts in May 1682 and died at Windham, Connecticut in Oct. 1732. He married at Windham 10 March 1708/9,
887. Margaret Morgan, born at Preston, Connecticut 28 July 1686.

888-911. ——.

912. James Ogston, farmer of Urinell, Coburty, Aberdeenshire. He married at Aberdour, Fife 26 July 1702,
913. Margaret Forbes of Urinell.

914-959. ——.

960. PATRICK LITTLEJOHN married,
961. ——.

962-967. ——.

968. REV. JAMES CHALMER, minister of Grayfriars Parish, Aberdeen 1728, professor of divinity at Marischall College, Aberdeen 1728-44, baptized at Marnoch, Banffshire 16 April 1686 and died in 1744. He married at St. Nicholas' Church, Aberdeen 29 Aug. 1710,
969. JEAN CHALMER.

970. REV. JAMES TRAIL, minister of Montrose 1709, born at Ballindrait, Clonleigh, Donegal in 1681 and died in 1723. He married at St. Nicholas' Church, Aberdeen 26 Nov. 1714,
971. CHRISTIAN ALLARDES, baptized at St. Nicholas' Church 1 Feb. 1690 and died 9 Sept. 1747; buried at St. Nicholas' Church.

972-973. ——.

974. WILLIAM FORBES, merchant of Aberdeen, baptized at Echt, Aberdeenshire 9 Oct. 1688 and died in 1743. He married at St. Nicholas' Church, Aberdeen 27 Oct. 1713,
975. ELSPETH PYPER, baptized at St. Nicholas' Church 18 Aug. 1692.

976. THOMAS BENTLEY, farmer, baptized at Methley, Yorkshire 4 July 1637 and buried at Rothwell, Yorkshire 22 April 1675. He married, 1st, Alice Knowles. He married, 2nd, in 1661,
977. SARAH WILLIE, baptized at Rothwell 3 July 1642 and died ca. 1684.

978-983. ——.

984. ARTHUR DINGWALL, baptized at Monquhitter, Aberdeenshire 9 July 1678 and died in 1728. He married, 2nd, in 1721, Jean Chalmers, who died before 8 Feb. 1750, daughter of James Chalmers, merchant of Aberdeen. He married, 1st, at Monquhitter 14 June 1707,

985. SARAH MURRAY of Inverury, Aberdeenshire, died in 1720.

986. JOHN FORDYCE, merchant of Turriff, Aberdeenshire, died ca. 1730. He married at New Deer, Aberdeenshire 7 March 1692/93,

987. ISOBEL LINDSAY of Culsh, Aberdeenshire.

988. JAMES MORISON, Provost of Aberdeen 1730-31, born in 1665 and buried at St. Nicholas' Church, Aberdeen 8 March 1747/48. He married at Old Aberdeen 29 March 1692,

989. ANN LOW, born ca. 1672 and died 4 April 1713; buried at St. Nicholas' Church.

990. JAMES DYCE, merchant of Aberdeen, born at Disblair, Aberdeenshire 17 Oct. 1687 and died there 10 Jan. 1750/51. He married at Aberdeen 25 Jan. 1715/16,

991. AGNES BAXTER of Old Aberdeen.

992-1003. ———.

1004. ALEXANDER LUMSDEN of Boghead of Kintore, Aberdeenshire, married,

1005. ISOBEL SETON of Coull, Aberdeenshire.

1006. ALEXANDER STEPHEN of Goval, Fintry, Aberdeenshire, married,

1007. ———.

1008. JOHN FORBES, merchant of Glasgow, born 7 Feb. 1679/80 and died in the North Sea ca. Nov. 1716. He married 27 April 1704,

1009. SUSANNA MORISON, born at Frendraught, Banffshire 22 Dec. 1680.

1010. WILLIAM KEITH of Bruxie, Aberdeenshire, married 11 Sept. 1712,
1011. HELEN FORBES of Blackton, Aberdeenshire.

1012. THEODORE MORISON of Frendraught, Banffshire, born ca. 1685 and died at Bognie, Aberdeenshire 4 June 1766. He married at Edinburgh 14 April 1717,
1013. CATHERINE MAITLAND of Pitrichie, Aberdeenshire, died in 1748.

1014. JOHN DUFF of Cowbin [Culbin], Morayshire, ruined in trade with North America, died in 1743. He married, 1st, in 1701, Mary Gordon of Ellon, Aberdeenshire, who died 22 June 1727. He married, 2nd, ca. 1729,
1015. HELEN GORDON of Park, Banffshire, died in 1767.

1016-1023. ——.

Tenth Generation

1024. HENRY SPENCER, 1ST EARL OF SUNDERLAND, baptized at Brington, Northamptonshire 23 Nov. 1620 and killed in attendance on HM King Charles I at the battle of Newbury 20 Sept. 1643. He married at Penshurst, Kent 20 Sept. 1639,

1025. LADY DOROTHY SIDNEY, "Sacharissa" in the poems by Edmund Waller [No. 5806], baptized at Islesworth, Middlesex 5 Oct. 1617 and buried at Brington 25 Feb. 1683/84. She married, 2nd, at Penshurst 8 July 1652, Robert Smythe, born in 1613 and died after June 1665, son of Sir John Smythe and Lady Isabella Rich, daughter of Robert Rich, 1st Earl of Warwick.

Waller's "Of the Lady Who Can Sleep When She Pleases" begins:

> *No wonder sleep from careful lovers flies,*
> *To bathe himself in Saccharissa's eyes.*
> *As fair Astraæ once from earth to heaven,*
> *By strife and loud impiety was driven;*
> *So with our plaints offended, and our tears,*
> *Wise Somnus to that paradise repairs;*
> *Waits on her will, and wretches does forsake,*
> *To court the nymph for whom those wretches wake.*

1026. GEORGE DIGBY, 2ND EARL OF BRISTOL, K.G. (1661), P.C. (1643), M.P. [as Lord Digby] 1640-41, summoned to Parliament in his father's barony of Digby 1641, Secretary of State 1643-45, Governor of Nottingham 1642, Lieutenant General (north of the River Trent) 1645, Lieutenant General in France 1651, born at Madrid in Oct. 1612 and died at Chelsea, Middlesex 20 March 1676/77. He married ca. 1636,

1027. LADY ANNE RUSSELL, died 26 Jan. 1696/97; buried at Chenies, Buckinghamshire.

1028. Sir Winston Churchill, M.P. 1661 and 1685, baptized 18 April 1620 and died at London 26 March 1688; buried at the Church of St. Martin-in-the-Fields, Westminster, Middlesex. He married at St. Peter's Church, Paul's Wharf, London 26 May 1648,

1029. Elizabeth Drake, born ca. 1622 and died in 1698.

1030. Richard Jennings, M.P. 1642, 1659, 1660, and 1661-68, born ca. 1616 and buried at St. Albans, Hertfordshire 8 May 1668. He married (Bishop of London's license dated 18 Dec. 1643),

1031. Frances Thornhurst, born posthumously ca. 1628 and died 27 July 1693.

1032. Sir Philip Carteret, born ca. 1641 and died in the sea off Southwold Bay, Suffolk 28 May 1672. He married (Faculty Office license to marry at Deptford, Kent, or elsewhere in the Diocese of London) 31 July 1665,

1033. Lady Jemima Montagu, born 18 Feb. 1645/46 and died in 1671.

1034. John Granville, 1st Earl of Bath, P.C. (1663), Gentleman of the Bedchamber to HRH The Prince of Wales (later HM King Charles II) 1645 [following HM into exile and serving as a mediator between the King and Parliament 1660], Warden of the Stannaries 1660-1701, Keeper of St. James's Palace 1660, Groom of the Stole 1660-85, Governor of Plymouth 1661-96, (absentee) Lord Lieutenant [i.e., Viceroy] of Ireland 1665, born 29 Aug., baptized at Kilkhampton, Cornwall 16 Sept. 1628 and died at St. James's Palace, London 22 Aug. 1701. He married ca. Oct. 1652,

1035. Jane Wyche, born in 1630 and died 3 Feb. 1691/92; buried at the Church of St. Clement Danes, London.

1036. Sir Robert Worsley, 3rd Baronet, M.P. 1666-75, born ca. 1643 and died 19 Dec. 1675. He married at the Church of St. Andrew Undershaft, London 17 Aug. 1668,

1037. Mary Herbert, born ca. 1648 and died 6 April 1693; buried at Great Mintern, Dorset. She married, 2nd, at St. James's Church, Duke's Place, London 23 April 1683, Edward Noel, 1st Earl of Gainsborough, born before 27 Jan. 1640/41 and died in Jan. 1688/89, son of Baptist Noel, 3rd Viscount Campden [No. 2726], and Hon. Hester Wotton [No. 2727].

1038. Thomas Thynne, 1st Viscount Weymouth, P.C. (1702-7 and 1712-14), F.R.S. (1664), M.P. [as Thomas Thynne] 1674-79, Groom of the Bedchamber to HRH The Duke of York (later HM King James II), Ambassador to Sweden 1666-69, with the Earl of Pembroke carried the invitation to HH The Prince of Orange to succeed King James II 1688, First Lord of Trade and Foreign Plantations 1702-7, baptized at St. Margaret's Church, Westminster, Middlesex 8 Sept. 1640 and died at London 28 July 1714. He married (by 1673),

1039. Lady Frances Finch, baptized at Eastwell, Kent 2 April 1650 and died 17 April 1712; buried at Longbridge Deverell, Wiltshire.

1040. John Poyntz, baptized at Reigate, Surrey 8 Dec. 1577 and died after 1607. He married at Reigate 27 July 1598 (marriage dissolved by divorce),

1041. Anne Sydenham of Nympsfield, Gloucestershire.

1042. Aden Parkyns, baptized at Bunny, Nottinghamshire 22 July 1582. He married, 1st, at St. Mary's Church, Nottingham 10 Sept. 1604, Elizabeth Sprentall, daughter of Christopher Sprentall. He married, 2nd, at the Church of St. Michael Bassishaw, London 6 April 1613,

1043. Mary Silvester.

1044. Stephen Monteage, buried at St. Bartholomew's Church, London 8 Jan. 1657/58. He married,

1045. ———.

1046. Edward Deane of Temple Guiting and Pinnock, Gloucestershire, died in 1633. He married,

1047. Anne Wace, baptized at the Church of St. Michael le Quern, London 11 Dec. 1594 and died in 1670.

1048. John Mordaunt, 1st Earl of Peterborough, K.B. (1616), Lord Lieutenant of Northamptonshire 1640-42, baptized at Lowick, Northamptonshire 18 Jan. 1598/99 and died 19 June 1643; buried at Turvey, Bedfordshire. He married (settlement dated 31 March 1611),

1049. Hon. Elizabeth Howard, born at Arundel House, London 19 Jan. 1602/3 and buried at Chelsea, Middlesex 18 Nov. 1671.

1050. HON. THOMAS CAREY, Groom of the Bedchamber to HM King Charles I, baptized at Berwick-on-Tweed 16 Sept. 1597 and died at Whitehall, near London 9 April 1634. He married,
1051. MARGARET SMITH of Abingdon, Berkshire.

1052-1053. ——.

1054. SIR THOMAS LUNSFORD, member of the Council and Lieutenant General of Virginia 1651, born ca. 1610 and died in Virginia before 1 Dec. 1656. He married, 1st, Anne Hudson of Peckham, Surrey, who was buried at East Hoathly, Sussex 28 Nov. 1638. He married, 3rd, in Virginia, Elizabeth Wormeley, widow of Richard Kempe, and daughter of Henry Wormeley and Margaret Conset. He married, 2nd, at Binfield, Berkshire 1 June 1640,
1055. KATHERINE NEVILLE, died in Virginia ca. Oct. 1650.

1056. SIR HENRY BINGHAM, 1ST BARONET, M.P. 1634-35 and 1639-48, baptized at Milton Abbas, Dorset in 1573. He married before 1625,
1057. CATHERINE BYRNE of Ballinclough, Wicklow.

1058. SIR WILLIAM MIDDLETON, 2ND BARONET, M.P. 1630 and 1647, baptized at the Church of St. Matthew Friday Street, London 10 April 1603 and died before 26 March 1652. He married ca. 1632,
1059. ELEANOR HARRIS, died before 12 May 1651.

1060-1063. ——.

1064. VEN. THOMAS VESEY, ARCHDEACON OF ARMAGH (1661-62 AND 1663-69), born ca. 1605 and died in 1669. He married,
1065. —— WALKER of Londonderry.

1066. COLONEL AGMONDESHAM MUSCHAMP of Buttevant, Cork, born in 1621 and buried 22 July 1648. He married,
1067. ——.

1068. Patrick Sarsfield of Lucan, Dublin, married,

1069. Anne O'More of Ballina, Cadamstown, Kildare, died at Saint-Germain-en-Laye, near Paris 29 Jan. 1700/1.

1070. Theobald Taaffe, 1st Earl of Carlingford, M.P. [as Hon. Theobald Taaffe] 1639, Governor of Munster 1644-46, died 31 Dec. 1677. He married, 1st, Mary White, daughter of Sir Nicholas White and Hon. Ursula Moore, daughter of Garret Moore, 1st Viscount Moore [No. 4904]. He married, 2nd, Ann Pershall, who died before May 1711, daughter of Sir William Pershall and Hon. Frances Aston, daughter of Walter Aston, 1st Lord Aston [No. 5726]. He was most likely the father of Mary Crofts by,

1071. Lucy Walter, described by Evelyn as a "brown, beautiful, bold but insipid creature," born at Roch Castle, near Haverfordwest, Pembrokeshire in 1630 and died at Paris in Sept./Oct. 1658.

1072-1087. ———.

1088. Sir Edward Seymour, 3rd Baronet, M.P. 1640-44, 1660, and 1661-87, baptized at Berry Pomeroy, Devonshire 10 Sept. 1610 and died 7 Dec. 1688. He married after 29 Nov. 1630,

1089. Anne Portman, baptized 10 Nov. 1611 and died before 22 Nov. 1695; buried at Berry Pomeroy.

1090. Colonel Alexander Popham, M.P. 1640-55, 1656 [when Cromwell assigned him a seat in the Upper House], 1660, and 1661-69, born ca. 1605 and buried at Chilton Foliot, Wiltshire 8 Dec. 1669. He married, 1st, 29 Oct. 1635, Dorothy Cole, born ca. 1617 and died 2 April 1643, daughter of Richard Cole and Anne Hopton. He married, 2nd, ca. 1644,

1091. Laetitia Kerr, buried at Stoke Newington, Middlesex 27 April 1660.

1092. Sir John Shorter, Lord Mayor of London 1687-88, born ca. 1625 and died at Newgate, London 4 Sept. 1688. He married,

1093. Isabella Birkett, baptized at Crosthwaite, Cumberland 5 Jan. 1632/33 and died in Jan. 1703/4.

Lucy Walter (Mrs. Barlow)
Born at Roch, Pembrokeshire in 1630
Died at Paris in September/October 1658

Lucy Walter came from a landed Welsh family. When her parents separated in 1640 she went with her mother to live in London, where Lucy's first lover was the Parliamentarian Algernon Sidney. When he was ordered away to Ireland with his regiment she was probably taken to The Hague via Paris by her kinsman, the Earl of Carbery. Lucy had a brief affair with Algernon's younger brother, Robert Sidney, and then, during the summer of 1648, she captivated the young Prince of Wales. The Prince was only eighteen, and she was considered his first mistress, although he had had at least one affair several years earlier. At about this time, she became pregnant with her first child. Long after Lucy's death, and after the Prince had become King Charles II, Charles and Lucy were said to have been secretly married. Most people were skeptical of this suggestion, and Charles stated absolutely that there was no marriage. However, the suggestion benefited the Whigs by giving them another reason – a legitimate son of Charles II – to exclude the Duke of York from the succession.

Lucy had two children. Her first child, a son named James, was accepted by King Charles II as his son and created Duke of Monmouth. The intimacy between Charles and Lucy Walter – who chose to be known as Mrs. Barlow (Barlo) – lasted with intervals until late 1649. After Charles embarked for Scotland in June 1650, Lucy "intrigued" with Henry Bennet (later 1st Earl of Arlington), and upon the King's return to The Hague the relationship ended. Mrs. Barlow thereupon became the mistress of Theobald, 2nd Viscount Taaffe. It was during this period that her daughter, Mary Crofts, was born, in May 1651. (The child's surname derived from her later guardian, Lord Crofts.) Even though Lucy insisted Mary was his child, Charles never acknowledged Lucy's daughter, as she was born a full eleven months after Charles and Lucy had separated.

1094. Sir Erasmus Philipps, 3rd Baronet, M.P. 1654-55 and 1659, born ca. 1623 and died 18 Jan. 1696/97. He married, 1st, Lady Cicely Finch, daughter of Thomas Finch, 2nd Earl of Winchilsea [No. 4156], and Cicely Wentworth [No. 4157]. He married, 2nd (Faculty Office license to marry at the Church of St. Clement Danes, London, or Islington, Middlesex 1 Sept. 1660),

1095. CATHERINE DARCY, baptized at St. Anne's Church, Blackfriars, London 9 April 1641 and died 15 Nov. 1713.

1096. HM KING CHARLES II, KING OF ENGLAND, SCOTLAND, AND IRELAND, born at St. James's Palace, London 29 May 1630 and died at Whitehall Palace, London 6 Feb. 1684/85. He married at Winchester 21 May 1662, HRH Infanta Doña Catarina Henriqueta de Bragança, Regent of Portugal 1704-5, born at Villa Viçosa, Lisbon 25 Nov. 1638 and died at Bemposta Palace, Lisbon 31 Dec. 1705, daughter of HM Dom João IV de Bragança, King of Portugal, and Doña Luisa Maria Francisca de Guzmán. He was almost certainly not the father of Mary Crofts [No. 535], but he acknowledged as his sons Henry Fitzroy, 1st Duke of Grafton [No. 548], and Charles Lennox, 1st Duke of Richmond and Lennox [No. 662]. He had issue by,

1097. BARBARA VILLIERS, DUCHESS OF CLEVELAND for life, Lady of the Bedchamber to [her rival] HM Queen Catherine 1662-68, for ten years Charles II's mistress [it is thought that John Churchill, 1st Duke of Marlborough (No. 514), was the father of a child she passed off as the King's], baptized at St. Margaret's Church, Westminster, Middlesex 27 Nov. 1640 and died at Chiswick, Middlesex 9 Oct. 1709. She married, 1st, at the Church of St. Gregory by St. Paul's, London 14 April 1659 [but from whom she separated almost immediately], Roger Palmer, 1st Earl of Castlemaine, baptized at Dorney, Buckinghamshire 4 Sept. 1634 and died at Oswestry, Shropshire 28 July 1705, son of Sir James Palmer and Lady Katherine Herbert [No. 5167]. She married, 2nd, 25 Nov. 1705 (marriage declared null 23 May 1707), Colonel Robert "Beau" Fielding, who died 12 May 1712.

1098. HENRY BENNET, 1ST EARL OF ARLINGTON, K.G. (1672), P.C. (1662), M.P. [as Sir Henry Bennet] 1661-65, Secretary to HRH The Duke of York (later HM King James II) 1649-58, Keeper of the Privy Purse 1661, Lord Chamberlain of the (Royal) Household 1674-85, Secretary of State 1662-74, Postmaster-General 1665-85, one of the five members of "the Cabal" [which name derived from its members' initials] in 1670, Lord Lieutenant of Suffolk 1681-84, baptized at Little Saxham, Suffolk 6 Sept. 1618 and died at Arlington House, St. James's Park, London 28 July 1685. He is sometimes identified as the father of Mary Crofts [No. 535]. He married 16 April 1666,

1099. ISABELLA VAN NASSAU-LEK-BEVERWEERD, Groom of the Stole to HM Queen Catherine 1681, baptized at The Hague 28 Dec. 1633 and died at Arlington House 18 Jan. 1717/18.

HM King Charles II,
King of England, Scotland, and Ireland
Born at London 29 May 1630
Died at London 6 February 1684/85
Married at Winchester 21 May 1662
HRH Infanta Doña Catarina Henriqueta de Bragança

The education of the Prince of Wales was entrusted to William Cavendish, 1st Duke of Newcastle, as his Governor and to Dr. Brian Duppa as his tutor. Newcastle's influence was lasting, as he introduced the Prince to the appreciation of women, dancing, fencing, and other appealing aspects of life. At the outset of the Civil War, Prince Charles was at his father's side when the Royalist war standard was raised in Nottingham. The future King was also present at the Battle of Edgehill, where he and his brother, the Duke of York, both narrowly escaped capture. In 1645, Charles was appointed nominal General of the Western Association, under the council of Sir Edward Hyde, Sir Arthur Capell, and Lord Hopton. It was at this time that the Prince renewed an acquaintance with his former wet-nurse, Mrs. Christabella Wyndham, wife of the Governor of Bridgwater. She has the possible distinction of being his first sexual conquest, and Hyde – who viewed it as a distraction – wrote about the affair in his *History*.

Charles joined his mother's court in exile at Saint-Germain in June 1646, where he benefited from good tutors. Thomas Hobbes, John Earle, and Dr. Duppa all spent time with Charles and his boyhood friend, the 2nd Duke of Buckingham, while they were in France. After two fruitless years spent trying to obtain French aid, the Prince of Wales and his Council began to explore the possibility of Dutch support. Charles' brother-in-law, the Prince of Orange, was amenable to providing some financial backing, and the rebellion of a part of the Parliamentary fleet raised their hopes. In the summer of 1648, Charles set sail with his fleet of eleven ships heading to Scotland to join the army of the Engagers, but he was not able to arrive in time to help his friends, who had already marched off to their resounding defeat by Oliver Cromwell's army at the Battle of Preston.

Charles returned to Holland, where he spent the winter. It was there that he learned of his father's execution. Initially, Jersey was the sole English dominion where Charles II was proclaimed King, on 16 February 1648/49. In order to obtain the support of the Scots, Charles was obliged to take the oath of the Covenant. This act was deemed politically expedient since no other options for military support had materialized, and so he journeyed to Scotland in July 1650. Once there, Charles assembled a formidable army. Cromwell's military skills were never more in evidence than at Dunbar (September 1650), where his heavily outnumbered forces decisively defeated the Scots. Nonetheless, Charles was crowned at Scone, 1 January 1650/51. It was believed that a campaign on English soil would muster Royalist support, and in August 1651 Charles led a Scottish force of 10,000 into England, where he suffered a more devastating defeat at Worcester in early September. The King barely escaped, remaining a fugitive for six weeks until he engineered passage to France in mid-October. The next eight years were spent as an impoverished exile: first in France, living on his mother's pension until he found himself expelled (with a small exit pension granted to remove him as an obstacle to a Franco-Commonwealth alliance); then at Spa in Germany; after that, briefly in Brussels and Bruges, where he set up his court before being invited back to England as the Commonwealth dissolved.

King Charles II arrived in London on his 30th birthday. He was extremely tolerant of those who had condemned his father to death: only nine of the conspirators were executed. He had developed a shrewd sense of political realism, displayed in the Declaration of Breda (1660), in which he offered something to everyone in his terms for resuming government. A general pardon would be issued, a tolerant religious settlement would be sought, and security for private property would be assured. Charles left the specifics of his policies to the Convention Parliament (1660), composed of members of the competing religious and political parties contending for power. The Convention declared the restoration of the King and lords, disbanded the army, established a fixed income for the King, and returned to the crown and the bishops their confiscated estates. It made no headway on a religious settlement. Despite Charles' promise of a limited toleration and his desire to accept Presbyterians, as detailed in the Worcester House Declaration (1660), radicals from both sides made compromise impossible.

The King's desire to find a broad church settlement was not a guiding principle of the Cavalier Parliament, which instead passed repressive acts to compel conformity. In the central government the King relied upon men of diverse political backgrounds and religious beliefs. The Earl of Clarendon, who had lived with the King in exile, was his chief political advisor, and Charles' brother James, Duke of York, was his closest confidant and entrusted with the vital post of Lord Admiral. Monck, who had enabled the restoration, was created Duke of

Albemarle and continued to hold military authority over the small standing army that, for the first time in English history, the King maintained. Colonial trade was an important source of royal revenue, and Charles II continued Cromwell's policy of restricting trade to English ships and imposing duties on imports and exports. Charles' foreign policy precipitated a series of wars with the Dutch. In military terms the Dutch Wars (1665-67 and 1672-74) resulted in a stalemate, but they helped English trade expand, and the American colonies were consolidated by the capture of Nieuw Amsterdam in 1664.

In the long run Charles II's aggressive foreign policy solved the crown's fiscal crises, but the immediate impact was perceived as negative. The London plague (1665) and fire (1666) were interpreted as divine judgments against a sinful nation. These catastrophes were compounded when the Dutch burned a large portion of the English fleet in 1667, which led to Clarendon's dismissal and exile. The crown's debts led to the Stop of the Exchequer (1672), by which Charles suspended payment of his bills. The King now ruled through a group of ministers known as the Cabal, an anagram of the first letters of their names or titles (Clifford, Arlington, Buckingham, Ashley-Cooper, and Lauderdale). None of the five was Anglican; two were Roman Catholic. This moment was a turning point in English political history, as Parliament maintained a superior position to that of the King, and the modern concept of political parties evolved. The Cavaliers transformed into the Tory Party, Royalists intent on preserving the King's authority over Parliament, while the Roundheads became the Whig Party, men of property dedicated to expanding trade abroad and maintaining Parliament's political supremacy.

During the 1670s, Charles II forged a new alliance with France against the Dutch. French support was based on the promise that Charles would reintroduce Catholicism in England at a convenient time, but Charles did nothing to bring England under the Catholic umbrella, although he made a deathbed conversion to the Roman faith. The Whigs used Catholicism to undermine Charles during yet another wave of anti-Catholic feeling, employing this paranoia in an attempt to prevent the heir presumptive, Charles' Catholic brother James, from succeeding to the throne. Titus Oates, a defrocked Anglican minister, stoked the fires of anti-Catholicism by accusing the Queen and her favourites of attempting to murder Charles. Many accused Anthony Ashley-Cooper now Earl of Shaftesbury and founder of the Whig Party, of inciting the anti-Catholic violence of 1679-80. The Whig-dominated Parliament tried to push through an Exclusion Bill barring Catholics from holding public office (and keeping the Duke of York from the throne), but Charles was struck down by a fever and opinion swayed to his side. His last years were occupied with securing his brother's claim to the throne and consolidating Tory support.

Barbara Villiers, Duchess of Cleveland

Baptized at Westminster, Middlesex 27 November 1640
Died at Chiswick, Middlesex 9 October 1709
Married, 1st, at London 14 April 1659
Roger Palmer, 1st Earl of Castlemaine
Married, 2nd, 25 November 1705 (marriage declared null 23 May 1707)
Robert Fielding

Barbara Villiers, a great-niece of the 1st Duke of Buckingham, married Roger Palmer in 1659, but she soon afterwards became the mistress of King Charles II. From 1661, Barbara lived apart from her husband, who was created Earl of Castlemaine with remainder to his children by her – although it was believed that Castlemaine was likely the father of only the eldest daughter, Lady Anne Palmer or Fitzroy.

Lady Castlemaine exercised an almost uncontrolled influence over the King for the first decade of his rule. She became Lady of the Bedchamber to the Queen Consort in August 1662, despite the Queen's protests. She then took up residence in apartments in Whitehall over Holbein's Gatehouse, where many courtiers sought admission to gain favor. Lady Castlemaine sought the destruction of Lord Chancellor Clarendon, and it is likely that she hastened his downfall in 1667. In 1668, her residence at the Palace came to an end, but she was propitiated for her loss of royal favor by being created Duchess of Cleveland. The Duchess secured grants of lands and pensions for herself and her bastards. Ultimately she was replaced as the King's mistress by Louise de Kéroualle. When the Duchess was in her 65th year, four months before the death of her lawful husband, she bigamously married Robert Fielding, often called Colonel or Major General, but best known as Beau Fielding; though cash-strapped and dissolute, he was very handsome. The marriage was later annulled.

1100. HENRY SOMERSET, 1ST DUKE OF BEAUFORT, K.G. (1672), P.C. (1672), M.P. [as Lord Herbert] 1654 and 1660-64, carried the Queen's crown at the coronation of TM King James II and Queen Mary 1685, a Lord of the Bedchamber 1685-88, one of the twelve commoners sent to Breda to invite the King's return 1660, Lord Lieutenant of Gloucestershire, Herefordshire, and Monmouthshire 1660-90, born at Raglan Castle, Monmouthshire in 1629 and died at Badminton House, Gloucestershire 21 Jan. 1699/1700. He married at Badminton 17 Aug. 1657,

1101. HON. MARY CAPELL, baptized at Hadham Parva, Hertfordshire 16 Dec. 1630 and died at Chelsea, Middlesex 7 Jan. 1714/15. She married, 1st, **HENRY SEYMOUR, LORD BEAUCHAMP [No. 1446].**

1102. SIR JOSIAH CHILD, 1ST BARONET, M.P. 1658-59, 1673, and 1685, Governor of the East India Company 1681-83 and 1686-88, baptized at the Church of St. Bartholomew-by-the-Exchange, London 21 Feb. 1631 and died at Wanstead, Essex 22 June 1699. He married, 1st, **HANNAH BOATE [No. 2631].** He married, 3rd (Faculty Office license dated 8 Aug. 1676), Emma Barnard, baptized at the Church of St. Dunstan-in-the-East, London 27 Aug. 1644, widow of Francis Willoughby, F.R.S., and daughter of Sir Henry Barnard and Emma Charlton. He married, 2nd (Faculty Office license dated 14 July 1663),

1103. MARY ATWOOD, born in 1643 and died before 8 Aug. 1676. She married, 1st, Thomas Stone.

1104. SIR CHARLES WALDEGRAVE, 3RD BARONET, died after 26 May 1684. He married at Wotton Basset, Wiltshire 7 Oct. 1656,

1105. HELEN ENGLEFIELD, died 12 Jan. 1693/94.

1106. HM KING JAMES II, KING OF ENGLAND, SCOTLAND, AND IRELAND, born at St. James's Palace, London 14 Oct. 1633 and died at Saint-Germain-en-Laye, near Paris 6 Sept. 1701. He married, 1st, at Worcester House, London 3 Sept. 1660, Lady Anne Hyde, born at Cranbourne Lodge, Windsor, Berkshire 22 March 1637/38 and died at St. James's Palace 31 March 1671, daughter of Edward Hyde, 1st Earl of Clarendon, and Frances Aylesbury. He married, 2nd, at Dover 21 Nov. 1673, HH Princess Maria Beatrice Eleanora Anna Margherita Isabella d'Este, born at Modena 5 Oct. 1658 and died at St. Germain-en-Laye 7 May 1718, daughter of HH Alfonso IV d'Este, Duke of Modena, and Laura Martinozzi. He had issue by,

1107. ARABELLA CHURCHILL, Maid of Honour to HRH The Duchess of York 1665, born at Ashe House, Devonshire 28 Feb. 1648/49 and died at London 4 May 1730. She married ca. 1679, **CHARLES GODFREY [No. 1454].**

HM King James II,
King of England, Scotland, and Ireland
Born at London 14 October 1633
Died at Saint-Germain-en-Laye, near Paris 6 September 1701
Married, 1st, at London 3 September 1660
Lady Anne Hyde
Married, 2nd, at Dover 21 November 1673
HH Princess Maria Beatrice Eleanora Anna Margherita Isabella d'Este

At the restoration of King Charles II, his brother and heir-presumptive, the Duke of York, was given command of the Navy as Lord High Admiral. It was on James' initiative that Nieuw Amsterdam was seized from the Dutch in 1664; the town was renamed New York in his honour. In 1665, the Duke defeated the Dutch off Lowestoft. During the Third Dutch War he was surprised by De Ruyter at Solebay [Southwold Bay] in May 1672, fighting an intense battle in which both sides suffered heavy losses. In politics he was a strong supporter of the Earl of Clarendon, whose daughter Anne he married in 1660. Although the Duke was fond of his wife, marriage did not stop his philandering.

In 1669, he was admitted to the Roman Catholic Church, but at his brother's insistence, the Duke's daughters were raised in the Protestant faith. James' conversion did not affect his political views: for much of his life, York was more favorable to the Anglican Church than was his Protestant brother. As a consequence of the Test Act (1672), the Duke of York was compelled to resign all his offices because he abstained from the Anglican sacrament. After his wife Anne died, his marriage to a Roman Catholic princess compounded the fear of Popery. By 1678, James' Roman Catholicism had fueled rumors of a "popish plot" to assassinate Charles II and put the Duke on the throne. Three successive Parliaments tried to exclude York from the succession, but the exclusionists were ultimately defeated. In 1682, James resumed the leadership of the Anglican Tories, whose power in local government was increasing. By 1684, James' influence on state policy was at its peak, and when he finally came to the throne in February 1685, there was very little overt opposition or protest. And although much of his career was served as a military leader, he had more governing experience than most newly minted monarchs.

The new English Parliament that assembled in May voted King James II a large income and was seemingly favorable towards him. But the subsequent unsuccessful rebellions led by the Duke of Monmouth in England and the Earl of Argyll in Scotland were turning points for the

King. The rebellions were put down quickly, and the army was expanded. Catholics were admitted to the Privy Council, to the high offices of state, and to leadership positions in the two universities. In 1687, the King intensified his Roman Catholic policy, and to ensure his right to appoint Catholic army officers he dismissed six judges. In April, he issued the Declaration of Indulgence suspending the laws against Roman Catholics and Protestant dissenters. James II never clearly articulated his intentions about religious toleration or whether he planned the establishment of Roman Catholicism as the dominant or even exclusive state religion. Had King Louis XIV not revoked the Edict of Nantes, removing French Protestants' protection, suspicion of James' unspoken motives might not have reached a crisis.

In late 1687, the news that the Queen was pregnant – foreshadowing a Roman Catholic succession – further inflamed English Protestants. The policy of "remodeling" lord lieutenancies, deputy lieutenancies, and magistracies that winter alienated the majority of the nobility and gentry. When James reissued his Declaration of Indulgence in 1688 and on 4 May ordered it to be read in the churches, the clergy were pushed to their limits. The Archbishop of Canterbury and six of his bishops petitioned James to withdraw the order. To make matters worse, their petition was published, and James sought the prosecution of its authors for seditious libel. Crowds cheered when the bishops were all acquitted, and the next day an appeal signed by seven prominent English aristocrats was sent inviting William of Orange to intervene in the protection of English liberties. By September William's military intentions were obvious. James was confident in the ability of his forces to repel invasion, and he declined Louis XIV's offer of assistance. Unfortunately he overestimated his Protestant officers' loyalty. William evaded the English fleet and landed at Torbay in November 1688. In the subsequent campaign, James' Protestant officers deserted to the enemy in such large numbers that he was fearful of committing his army to battle. He attempted to flee to France and was intercepted briefly in Kent, but then made his escape. On 12 February 1688/89, the Convention Parliament declared that James had abdicated and next day offered the crown to William and Mary. In March, James landed in Ireland, where a parliament summoned in Dublin acknowledged him as King. Meanwhile the Scots Parliament declared for William and Mary in May. Although James had support in Ireland, his Irish-French army was defeated by King William at the Battle of the Boyne 11 July 1690, and James fled back to France. There he established a court in exile, and fell increasingly under the influence of his pietistic wife, becoming absorbed in his devotions.

Arabella Churchill

Born at Ashe, Devonshire 28 February 1648/49
Died at London 4 May 1730
Married ca. 1679
Colonel Charles Godfrey

Arabella Churchill was at sixteen appointed one of the Duchess of York's Maids of Honour through the influence of her mother and their cousin, Lady Castlemaine. She was tall and thin with a pale complexion. The Duke was infatuated with her but no one at court could understand why, since her face was so plain. James' liaison with Arabella was not one of his numerous casual affairs; it was his longest lasting extramarital affair, perhaps enduring ten or twelve years and producing four children. When offspring began to arrive, James moved Arabella out of Whitehall and to a house in St. James's Square, next door to Moll Davis (one of King Charles' mistresses).

The liaison ceased with the beginning of James' affair with Catherine Sedley. At about the time Arabella got a pass to go abroad with two of her children, in April 1679, she sold her house in St. James's Square for £8,000, a large profit, and was granted a pension of £1,000 per year. Her wealth and relative youth made her an appealing marriage prospect for Colonel Charles Godfrey, who had been a fellow officer with her brother, later the 1st Duke of Marlborough. Her marriage to Godfrey allowed Arabella to take her place in polite London society. As her elder children grew older, the Duke of York took them from her to provide for their upbringing, education, and introduction at Court. Arabella and her husband had a family of their own to raise, and after the Revolution, her pensions were confirmed and enlarged by William III.

1108. SIR JOHN WEBB, 2ND BARONET, died 29 Oct. 1700. He married after 12 May 1662,

1109. MARY BLOMER, died 27 March 1709; buried at Hatherop, Gloucestershire. She married, 1st, Richard Draycott, born 5 Nov. 1630 and died 12 May 1662, son of Philip Draycott and Lady Frances Weston, daughter of Richard Weston, 1st Earl of Portland.

1110. JOHN BELASYSE, 1ST BARON BELASYSE, P.C. (1686-89), M.P. [as Hon. John Belasyse] 1640-42, General of the Royal forces in Africa and

Governor of Tangiers 1664-66, First Lord Commissioner of the Treasury 1687-88, Lord Lieutenant of the East Riding of Yorkshire 1660-73, born at Newborough, Yorkshire 24 June 1614 and died 10 Sept. 1689; buried at the Church of St. Giles-in-the-Fields, Holborn, Middlesex. He married, 1st, at Coxwold, Yorkshire 7 March 1636, Jane Boteler, baptized at Aston, Hertfordshire 20 Jan. 1620/21 and died before 12 Dec. 1657, daughter of Sir Robert Boteler and Frances Drury. He married, 2nd, at St. Vedast's Church, Foster Lane, London after 24 July 1659, Anne Crane, who died 11 Aug. 1662, widow of Sir William Armyne, 2nd Baronet, and daughter of Sir Robert Crane, 1st Baronet [No. 4450], and Susan Alington [No. 4451]. He married, 3rd, after 11 Aug. 1662,

1111. LADY ANNE PAULET, buried at the Church of St. Giles-in-the-Fields 11 Sept. 1694.

1112. ROBERT WALPOLE, M.P. 1689, 1690, 1695, and 1698-1700, born 18 Nov. 1650 and died at Houghton, Norfolk 18 Nov. 1700. He married at Rougham, Suffolk 25 April 1671,

1113. MARY BURWELL, baptized at Rougham 23 Oct. 1653 and died 15 March 1710/11.

1114. JOHN SHORTER = 546.
1115. ELIZABETH PHILIPPS = 547.

1116-1119. ——.

1120. WALTER PALK, died in 1705. He married,
1121. ——.

1122-1127. ——.

1128. WILLEM VAN SITTART of Danzig, born 13 Dec. 1622 and died in Feb. 1675. He married 18 Sept. 1646,
1129. AEFJE JUNCKER, died in July 1676.

1130. ROBERT SANDERSON married,
1131. ——.

1132. Sir John Stonhouse, 2nd Baronet, M.P. 1675, 1679, 1681, 1685, and 1690, born ca. 1639 and died before 27 May 1700. He married (Vicar-General's license dated 10 Oct. 1668),

1133. Martha Brigges, died before 5 Feb. 1711/12. She married, 1st, at St. Dionis Backchurch, London 15 July 1656, Richard Spencer, merchant of London.

1134. Henry Mellish, baptized at All Hallows' Church, Bread Street, London 15 Jan. 1622/23 and buried at Sanderstead, Surrey 24 June 1677. He married at the Church of St. Bartholomew-the-Less, London 24 Dec. 1661,

1135. Elizabeth Goden, buried at Sanderstead 26 July 1707.

1136. Edward Vaughan, M.P. 1669, 1679, and 1681, born ca. 1635 and died 15 Feb. 1683/84. He married 23 March 1664/65,

1137. Letitia Hooker, died in 1716.

1138. John Wilmot, 2nd Earl of Rochester, Lord of the Bedchamber to HM King Charles II 1666-80, poet and patron of the theatre, born at Ditchley, Oxfordshire 10 April 1647 and died at the Ranger's Lodge, Woodstock, Oxfordshire 26 July 1680. He married 29 Jan. 1666/67 [having first attempted her abduction in May 1665],

1139. Elizabeth Malet, buried at Spelsbury, Oxfordshire 20 Aug. 1681.

1140. Robert Watson, buried 11 Dec. 1707. He married at Berwick-upon-Tweed 8 Nov. 1669,

1141. Elizabeth Webb, died before 21 April 1694.

1142-1143. ——.

1144. Sir Robert Shafto, Recorder of Newcastle 1660-85 and 1688, baptized at St. Nicholas' Church, Newcastle-upon-Tyne 13 May 1634 and died 21 May 1705. He married at St. Pancras' Church, London 18 July 1661,

1145. Catherine Widdrington, born in 1642 and died 31 Aug. 1676; buried at St. John's Church, Newcastle.

John Wilmot, 2nd Earl of Rochester

Born at Ditchley, Oxfordshire 10 April 1647
Died at Woodstock, Oxfordshire 26 July 1680
Married 29 January 1666/67
Elizabeth Malet

Raised in the exiled court of Queen Henrietta Maria, Lord Wilmot succeeded as 2nd Earl of Rochester at the age of ten. He entered Wadham College, Oxford, as a fellow commoner in 1660. Although Rochester was eager to learn, his Oxford tutor, Robert Whitehall, was a heavy drinker and greatly contributed to the debauchery of the thirteen-year-old student. Rochester was instructed in the art of poetry and became an M.A. in 1661. Earlier that year he had been granted a pension of £500 by the King, who in appreciation for his late father's military service made Rochester a foster son. The Earl then traveled at the expense of the crown with a small party of servants and retainers through France and Italy during the next four years. When he returned to England, the King encouraged him to propose to Elizabeth Malet, whom Charles suggested would make him a good wife. Elizabeth was a great beauty worth £2,500 per year, and Rochester ranked at the bottom of her list of eligible suitors. Lord Rochester promptly abducted his quarry, but before long he was apprehended and confined in the Tower of London. Rochester petitioned the King for his release and was discharged, volunteering to serve in the Navy; he was one of the few survivors of the deadly Four Days Battle in 1666. Eighteen months after her failed abduction, Elizabeth consented to the proposed marriage.

With King Charles as his patron, it is not surprising Rochester spent a good deal of time indulging his appetites. Rochester's main interest after wine and women was the theatre. He patronized playwrights such as John Dryden, Elkanah Settle, Nathaniel Lee, John Crowne, Sir Francis Fane, and Thomas Otway. His social position did not permit him to go on the stage himself, but he could coach actresses to improve their performances. He seduced Sarah Cooke, who though quite beautiful was the "worst actress in the realm," and then had a protracted affair with the actress Elizabeth Barry, whose performances afterwards were quite successful. He also wrote poetry, which has been disparaged by many critics although it is still widely read. One example refers admiringly to King Charles II (and somewhat uncharitably to the future King James II):

. . . The easiest King and best bred man alive.
Him no ambition moves to get reknown
Like the French fool, that wanders up and down
Starving his people, hazarding his crown.
Peace is his aim, his gentleness is such,
And love he loves, for he loves ——ing much.
Nor are his high desires above his strength:
His scepter and his —— are of a length
And she may sway the one who plays with th' other,
And make him little wiser than his brother.

While the 33-year old Rochester lay dying of syphilis at the Ranger's Lodge in Woodstock, he turned to the Bible and repented. He also ordered that all his profane writings and drawings be burned.

1146. Sir William Ingleby, 2nd Baronet, baptized at Ripley, Yorkshire 13 March 1620/21 and died 6 Nov. 1682. He married at Methley, Yorkshire 5 April 1660,

1147. Margaret Savile, baptized at St. Margaret's Church, Westminster, Middlesex 23 Feb. 1638 and died 9 Nov. 1697; buried at Ripley.

1148-1151. ——.

1152. Rev. Franz Baring, Pastor of Wassenhorst, near Bremen 1600-27, born at Lauenburg, Saxony 28 July 1570 and died in the River Weser near Wassenhorst 19 Sept. 1627. He married, 1st, Margarete Meiers, who died at Wassenhorst 18 March 1614. He married, 2nd, 29 Aug. 1615,

1153. Margarete Erasmus. She married, 2nd, in 1627, Rev. Johann Klavens of Wassenhorst.

1154. Rev. Dr. Hermann Hildebrand, Rector of St. Stephen's Church, Bremen 1620, born at Bremen in 1590 and died there 11 Dec. 1649. He married,

1155. Anna Seekamp.

1156-1159. ——.

1160. JOHN VOWLER married,
1161. ——.

1162. ROBERT SHUTE married at Crediton, Devonshire 14 Jan. 1628,
1163. AGNES SAUNDERS.

1164-1167. ——.

1168. JOHN HERRING, draper of Cambridge, died between 17 Sept. and 13 Nov. 1674. He married,
1169. MARY BAINBRIGG.

1170-1171. ——.

1172. CHRISTOPHER WATLINGTON of Cambridge married,
1173. —— PASKE.

1174. THEOPHILUS DILLINGHAM, Master of Clare Hall, Cambridge 1654, born at Over Dean, Bedfordshire 18 Oct. 1613 and died at Cambridge 22 Nov. 1678. He married at St. Edward's Church, Cambridge 30 March 1661,
1175. ELIZABETH PASKE, baptized at Canterbury Cathedral, Kent 12 Feb. 1641/42.

1176. SAMUEL DAWSON, Lord Mayor of York 1690, died 18 June 1712. He married,
1177. MARY WILKINSON, born 1639 and died 13 Oct. 1692.

1178. THOMAS HUTTON of Poppleton, Yorkshire, born 18 March 1638 and buried at Poppleton 5 July 1704. He married,
1179. ANNE STRINGER of Sutton-cum-Lound, Nottinghamshire.

1180-1181. ——.

1182. ROBERT BUSHELL, shipowner, baptized at Whitby, Yorkshire 18 April 1624 and buried there 12 Nov. 1698. He married,

1183. ISABEL WIGGINER, baptized at Whitby 17 June 1632.

1184. WILLIAM LUKIN, buried at Mashbery, Essex 16 Aug. 1695. He married at Good Easter, Essex 7 Nov. 1670,

1185. DOROTHY WOOD, buried at Mashbery 19 March 1729/30.

1186. LIONEL LANE of Felstead, Essex, born in 1639 and died before 6 Nov. 1706. He married,

1187. MARY YOUNG, baptized at Little Dunmow, Essex 26 March 1658. She married, 2nd, Thomas Walford of Cocking, Essex.

1188-1189. ——.

1190. THOMAS GOLDSTONE, baptized at Panfield, Essex 13 Oct. 1639 and buried at Rayne, Essex 24 Sept. 1721. He married at Panfield 9 July 1668,

1191. ESTHER HOWCHIN, baptized at Panfield 18 April 1647 and buried at Rayne 29 March 1708.

1192. ROBERT DOUGHTY, baptized at Horstead, Norfolk 30 June 1640 and buried at Aylsham, Norfolk 27 Dec. 1716. He married at Oby, Norfolk 9 Oct. 1673,

1193. CATHERINE GUYBON, baptized at Oby 21 Oct. 1652 and buried at Aylsham 9 July 1725.

1194. ROBERT DOUGHTY, baptized at the Church of St. Michael-at-Plea, Norwich 30 April 1656 and died before 1742. He married at St. Giles' Church, Norwich 31 May 1677,

1195. ESTHER PAYNE, baptized at the Church of St. Peter Mancroft, Norwich 9 Jan. 1658/59.

1196. Rev. Henry Lee, Rector of Tichmarsh 1678-1713 and Brington, Huntingdonshire 1690-1713, buried at Tichmarsh, Northamptonshire 30 Nov. 1713. He married,
1197. ——.

1198-1199. ——.

1200. Théophile Thellusson, born at Geneva 17 June 1611 and died there 19 Sept. 1654. He married at Geneva 5 March 1637,
1201. Judith Tronchin, born in 1618 and died 23 July 1686.

1202. Léonard Guiguer, born at Lyon 18 Nov. 1632 and died at Geneva 11 Aug. 1710. He married at Annonay, Ardèche 30 Nov. 1659,
1203. Elisabeth Tourton, born at Annonay 24 Oct. 1641 and died at Geneva in 1724.

1204. Abraham Le Boullenger, buried at Leiden 7/14 Jan. 1696. He married,
1205. ——.

1206. Abraham van der Hulst married,
1207. ——.

1208. Matthew Woodford, born ca. 1643 and died before 12 May 1675. He married at St. Martin's Church, Salisbury 20 May 1669,
1209. Dorothy Langford, born 31 March 1644 and died 27 Dec. 1682.

1210. John Sherer, died after 31 Jan. 1706. He married at Oving, Sussex 28 Oct. 1680,
1211. Mary Henshaw.

1212. Right Rev. Dr. Ralph Brideoak, Bishop of Chichester (1675-78), Chaplain to HM King Charles II 1660, Dean of Salisbury 1667-

74, baptized at Manchester 31 Jan. 1612/13 and died 5 Oct. 1678; buried at St. George's Chapel, Windsor, Berkshire. He married ca. 1660,

1213. MARY SALTONSTALL.

1214-1215. ——.

1216. SAMUEL BULTEEL, baptized at Barnstaple, Devonshire 5 May 1616 and buried at Tavistock, Devonshire 11 June 1679. He married, 1st, at St. Andrew's Church, Plymouth 25 June 1635, Agnes Page. He married, 2nd, before 1652,

1217. JANE KEKEWICH, baptized at St. Germans, Cornwall 26 March 1620 and buried at Tavistock 5 July 1662.

1218. DANIEL CONDY married at Tavistock, Devonshire 17 Dec. 1652,

1219. JANE LARKHAM.

1220. JOHN CROCKER, born ca. 1610 and buried 3 Dec. 1684. He married at Colyton, Devonshire 28 Sept. 1657,

1221. JOAN POLE, baptized at Colyton 7 April 1625.

1222. RICHARD HILLERSDON, M.P. 1679, baptized at Holbeton, Devonshire 4 April 1638 and died in 1703. He married at the Church of St. Stephen by Saltash, Cornwall 11 May 1659,

1223. ANNE NOSWORTHY of Truro.

1224. WILLIAM DRUMMOND [LATER KER], 2ND EARL OF ROXBURGHE, P.C. (1661), died 2 July 1675. He married (contract dated 17 May 1655),

1225. HON. JEAN KER, buried at Bowden, Roxburghshire in May 1675.

1226. HENRY MOORE, 1ST EARL OF DROGHEDA, P.C. (I.) (1660), M.P. [as Hon. Henry Moore] 1640-43, Governor of Meath and Louth 1643 and Drogheda 1660, died 12 Jan. 1675/76; buried at Christ Church, Dublin. He married,

1227. HON. ALICE SPENCER, baptized at Brington, Northamptonshire 29 Dec. 1625 and died after 15 July 1696.

1228-1229. ——.

1230. Samuel Hodgson, baptized at Walkern, Hertfordshire 14 Dec. 1640 and buried there 28 March 1712. He married,
1231. Mary ——, buried at Walkern 23 Sept. 1689.

1232-1235. ——.

1236. Henry Legassick married at Modbury, Devonshire, 28 March 1653,
1237. [? Elizabeth] Rabidge.

1238-1247. ——.

1248. John Grey of Howick, Northumberland, died before 4 May 1681. He married,
1249. Dorothy Lisle of Acton, Northumberland.

1250-1251. ——.

1252. Thomas Wood, buried at Bamburgh, Northumberland 19 July 1683. He married,
1253. Mary Armorer, died before 26 Sept. 1698. She married, 1st, Francis Brandling of Hoppen, Northumberland.

1254-1255. ——.

1256. Rev. George Grey, Rector of Burniston 1682, born at Southwick, Durham 28 Feb. 1651/52 and died at Burniston, Yorkshire 12 June 1711. He married, 2nd, in 1691, Sarah Harrison, born in Jan. 1661/62 and died in July 1692, daughter of Thomas Harrison of Allerthorpe, Yorkshire. He married, 3rd, in June 1693, Hannah Bendlowes, who died before 24 May 1720, daughter of Thomas Bendlowes of Howgrave, Yorkshire. He married, 1st, 10 Sept. 1675,
1257. Elizabeth [or Helen] Cawdrey, born ca. 1653 and died 3 Aug. 1690.

1258. JAMES CLAVERING, baptized at Whickham, Durham 17 Sept. 1647 and buried at Lanchester, Northumberland 26 Jan. 1721/22. He married at All Saints' Church, Newcastle-upon-Tyne 1 Sept. 1674,

1259. JANE ELLISON, baptized at St. Nicholas' Church, Newcastle 16 April 1654 and buried at Lanchester 15 March 1718/19.

1260. RALPH OGLE, born ca. 1646 and buried at Ponteland, Northumberland 29 May 1705. He married at Bolam, Northumberland 16 Aug. 1670,

1261. MARTHA THOMPSON, died in 1687.

1262. JONATHAN NEWTON, born 9, baptized at St. John's Church, Newcastle-upon-Tyne 10 Aug. 1653 and died before 8 Oct. 1723. He married at St. John's Church 2 Oct. 1688,

1263. ISABEL JENISON, baptized at St. Nicholas' Church, Newcastle 30 Dec. 1664 and died after 3 June 1742.

1264. WILLIAM PONSONBY, 1ST VISCOUNT DUNCANNON, P.C. (I.) (1715), M.P. [as William Ponsonby] 1692-93, 1695-99, and 1703-21, born ca. 1659 and died 17 Nov. 1724; buried at Fiddown, Kilkenny. He married before 1679,

1265. MARY MOORE, born ca. 1661 and died 26 May 1713.

1266. MAJOR JOHN MARGETSON of Bishopscourt, Kildare, twin, born at London ca. 1656 and killed at the siege of Limerick in 1690 or 1691. He married,

1267. HON. ALICE CAULFIELD, born ca. 1660 and died at Bath, Somerset 7 Oct. 1731. She married, 2nd, at the Church of St. Edmund the King, London 23 Jan. 1693/94, George Carpenter, 1st Baron Carpenter, born at Pitcher's Ocull, Herefordshire 10 Feb. 1656/57 and died 10 Feb. 1731/32, son of Warncombe Carpenter and Eleanor Taylor.

1268. WILLIAM CAVENDISH, 2ND DUKE OF DEVONSHIRE, K.G. (1710), P.C. (1708 AND 1714-16), M.P. [as Marquess of Hartington] 1695-1701 and 1702-7, Lord Steward of the (Royal) Household 1707-10 and 1714-16, Lord President of the Council 1716-17 and 1725-29, a Lord Justice [i.e. Regent] 1714, Lord Lieutenant of Derbyshire 1707-10 and 1714-29, born ca. 1673 and died at Devonshire House, London 4 June 1729. He married at Southampton House, London 21 June 1688,

1269. HON. RACHEL RUSSELL, born in Jan. 1673/74 and died 28 Dec. 1725.

1270. JOHN HOSKINS, steward to the Duke of Bedford, born in 1640 and died in May 1717. He married 11 Dec. 1695,
1271. KATHERINE HALE, born 15, baptized at Kings Walden, Hertfordshire 18 Sept. 1673 and died 5 March 1704/5; buried at Kings Walden.

1272. ROBERT MOLESWORTH, merchant of Dublin, died 3 Sept. 1656. He married,
1273. JUDITH BYSSE of Brackentown, Swords, Dublin. She married, 2nd, Sir William Tichborne of Beaulieu, Louth.

1274. RICHARD COOTE, 1ST BARON COOTE, P.C. (I.) (1660), born in 1620 and died 10 July 1683; buried at Christ Church, Dublin. He married,
1275. MARY ST. GEORGE, died at Kilrush, Kilkenny 5 Nov. 1701.

1276. VEN. ADAM USSHER, ARCHDEACON OF CLONFERT, born at Dublin in 1650 and died in 1713. He married ca. 1676,
1277. REBECCA WYE, buried at Dublin 10 Aug. 1694.

1278. REV. CHRISTOPHILUS JENNEY married,
1279. ——.

1280. JAMES HAMILTON, 6TH EARL OF ABERCORN, P.C. (TEMP. JAMES II), M.P. [as James Hamilton (refusing to use his inherited title of baronet)] 1692 and 1695, Groom of the Bedchamber to HM King Charles II 1673, born ca. 1661 and died 28 Nov. 1734; buried at Westminster Abbey, London. He married (Faculty Office license dated 24 Jan. 1683/84),
1281. ELIZABETH READING, born in 1668 and died at Sackville Street, London 19 March 1754.

1282. COLONEL JOHN PLUMER, born ca. 1656 and died 11 March 1718/19; buried at Eastwick, Hertfordshire. He married at Kings Walden, Hertfordshire 27 Feb. 1677/78,

1283. MARY HALE, born 28 Oct., baptized at Kings Walden 2 Nov. 1660 and died 27 Dec. 1709.

1284. JAMES CRAGGS, M.P. 1702-13, Joint Postmaster-General 1715-20, deeply involved in the East India Company and the South Sea Company [in whose crash he was implicated], baptized at Wolsingham, Durham 10 June 1657 and died 16 March 1721/22; buried at Charlton, Kent. He married at St. Benet's Church, Paul's Wharf, London 3 Jan. 1683/84,
1285. ELIZABETH RICHARDS, born 17, baptized at the Church of St. Martin-in-the-Fields, Westminster, Middlesex 18 May 1662 and died 20 Jan. 1711/12; buried at Charlton.

1286. —— **SANTLOW** married,
1287. JANE ——, died in April 1724.

1288. SIR WALTER MOYLE, M.P. 1654-55, 1656-58, 1659-60, and 1689-90, baptized at St. Germans, Cornwall 9 March 1626/27 and died 19 Sept. 1701. He married at the Church of St. Martin-in-the-Fields, Westminster, Middlesex 11 Feb. 1663,
1289. THOMASINE MORICE, buried at St. Germans 22 March 1681/82.

1290. SIR GODFREY COPLEY, 2ND BARONET, F.R.S. (1691), M.P. 1679, 1681, and 1695-1709, born ca. 1653 and died at Red Lion Square, London 9 April 1709. He married, 2nd, at the Church of St. Mary-at-Hill, Lovat Lane, London 10 June 1700, Gertrude Carew, baptized at Antony, Cornwall 26 May 1682 and died 14 April 1736, daughter of Sir John Carew, 3rd Baronet, and Mary Morice. He married, 1st, at the Church of St. Martin-in-the-Fields, Westminster, Middlesex 15 Oct. 1681,
1291. KATHERINE PURCELL, born ca. 1657 and died in 1697.

1292. JOHN BULLER, M.P. 1701, baptized at Morval, Cornwall 15 Dec. 1668 and died 17 March 1700/1. He married at Buckland Monachorum, Devonshire 9 June 1691,
1293. MARY POLLEXFEN, died before 4 Dec. 1722.

1294. Right Rev. Sir Jonathan Trelawny, 3rd Baronet, Bishop of Winchester (1707-21), Bishop of Bristol 1685-89 [one of seven bishops committed to the Tower of London 1688] and Exeter 1689-1707, born 24 March 1649/50, baptized at Pelynt, Cornwall 26 April 1650 and died at Chelsea, Middlesex 19 July 1721. He married at Egg Buckland, Devonshire 31 March 1684,

1295. Rebecca Hele, baptized at Kingsteignton, Cornwall 11 Feb. 1670/71 and died 11 Feb. 1709/10.

Bishop Trelawny is the hero of the Cornish anthem "The Song of the Western Men" (by Robert Stephen Hawker, 1824), which has the refrain:

And shall Trelawny live?
And shall Trelawny die?
Here's twenty thousand Cornish men
Will know the reason why!

1296. James Douglas, 10th Earl of Morton, Gentleman of the Privy Chamber to HM King Charles I, died 25 Aug. 1686. He married at Peebles 20 Feb. 1648/49,

1297. Anne Hay, buried 17 Feb. 1699/1700.

1298. William Adderley, M.P. 1690-93, buried at East Burnham, Buckinghamshire 28 June 1693. He married before 1666,

1299. Sarah ———.

1300. Sir Gilbert Heathcote, 1st Baronet, M.P. 1701-10 and 1715-33, Lord Mayor of London 1710, a founder of the Bank of England (Governor 1708), born at Chesterfield, Derbyshire 2 Jan. 1651/52 and died at St. Swithin's Lane, London 25 Jan. 1732/33. He married (Faculty Office license to marry at All Hallows, Barking, or St. Stephen's Church, Colman Street, London dated 30 May 1682),

1301. Hester Rayner, baptized at All Hallows' Church, Bread Street, London 21 Dec. 1658 and died 27 Sept. 1714.

1302. Thomas White, M.P. 1701, 1702, 1708-11, and 1715-30, born in Aug. 1667 and died at Tuxford, Nottinghamshire 24 Feb. 1729/30. He married 28 July 1698,

1303. Bridget Taylor, died 7 Jan. 1761.

1304. Daniel Lascelles, M.P. 1702, born 6 Nov. 1655 and died 5 Sept. 1734. He married, 1st, at Northallerton, Yorkshire 22 Aug. 1672, Margaret Metcalfe, who was buried at Northallerton 20 Dec. 1690, daughter of William Metcalfe and Anna Marwood. He married, 2nd, at the Church of St. Christopher-le-Stocks, London 23 April 1702,

1305. Mary Lascelles, born ca. 1662 and died 28 Oct. 1734; buried at Northallerton. She married, 1st, at the Church of St. Peter-le-Poer, London 21 May 1694, Thomas Osbourn, who died before 5 March 1699.

1306. Guy Ball, merchant and member of the Council in Barbados, born ca. 1674 and died before 21 April 1722. He married before 8 June 1704,

1307. Catherine Duboys, born ca. 1688.

1308. Edward Chaloner, born 11, baptized at Ingleby Greenhow, Yorkshire 17 July 1683 and buried at Guisborough, Yorkshire 8 Oct. 1737. He married at Barnard Castle, Durham 11 June 1713,

1309. Anne Bowes, baptized at Barnard Castle 27 Oct. 1695 and buried there 6 Nov. 1734.

1310. James Finney of Finneyham, Staffordshire, born 26 April 1687 and died ca. 1742. He married at Ryton, Durham 5 April 1719,

1311. Thomasine Burdon.

1312. William Russell, Lord Russell by courtesy, **P.C. (1679–80), M.P.** [as Hon. William Russell and Lord Russell] 1660-81, born 29 Sept. 1639 and executed at Lincoln's Inn Fields, London 21 July 1683; his attainder [for high treason] was reversed by Act of Parliament 16 March 1688/89. He married (Faculty Office license to marry at Titchfield, Hampshire dated 31 July 1669),

1313. Lady Rachel Wriothesley, baptized at Titchfield 19 Sept. 1637 and died at Southampton House, Bloomsbury, London 29 Sept. 1723. She married, 1st, at Walton-upon-Thames, Surrey 5 Oct. 1654, Francis Vaughan, Lord Vaughan by courtesy, who died 7 March 1667/68, son of Richard Vaughan, 2nd Earl of Carbery, and Frances Altham.

1314. John Howland, baptized at St. Dionis Backchurch, London 11 Jan. 1648/49 and buried at St. Leonard's Church, Streatham, Surrey 2 Sept. 1686. He married (Faculty Office license to marry at Streatham or . . . 19 July 1681),

1315. ELIZABETH CHILD, born ca. 1661 and died at Streatham 18 April 1719.

1316. JOHN LEVESON-GOWER, 1ST BARON GOWER, P.C. (1702-7), M.P. [as Sir John Leveson-Gower, Bt.] 1692-1703, born at Trentham Hall, Staffordshire 7 Jan. 1674/75 and died at Belvoir Castle, Leicestershire 31 Aug. 1709. He married in Sept. 1692,
1317. LADY CATHERINE MANNERS, born 19, baptized at Branston, Leicestershire 23 May 1675 and died at Great Russell Street, Bloomsbury, London 7 March 1722/23.

1318. EVELYN PIERREPONT, 1ST DUKE OF KINGSTON-UPON-HULL, K.G. (1719), P.C. (1708), M.P. [as Hon. Evelyn Pierrepont] 1689-90, presented the address of condolence to HM Queen Anne on the death of her husband 1708, Lord Privy Seal 1716-18 and 1720-26, Lord President of the Council 1719-20, a Lord Justice [i.e. Regent] 1719, 1720, 1723, and 1725-26, Lord Lieutenant of Wiltshire 1711-26, baptized 27 Feb. 1666/67 and died at Arlington Street, London 5 March 1725/26. He married, 2nd, 2 Aug. 1714, Lady Isabella Bentinck, born 4 May 1688 and died at Paris 23 Feb. 1727/28, daughter of Hans Willem Bentinck, 1st Earl of Portland, and Anne Villiers. He married, 1st (Faculty Office license to marry at Ealing, Acton, or Thistlethwaite, Middlesex dated 27 June 1687),
1319. LADY MARY FEILDING, born ca. 1668 and buried at Holme Pierrepont, Nottinghamshire 20 Dec. 1697.

1320. OSEWOLT VAN KEPPEL, HEER TOT VOORST, died 11 Oct. 1685; buried at Warnsveld, Gelderland. He married at Zutphen, Gelderland 17 April 1658,
1321. REINIERA ANNA GEERTRUID VAN LINTELO, baptized at Zutphen 5 Dec. 1638 and died 26 May 1700; buried at Warnsveld.

1322. ADAM VAN DER DUYN, HEER VAN RIJSWIJK 'SGRAVENMOER, Master of the Buckhounds to HH The Prince of Orange (later HM King William III), Governor of Bergen 1690, Lieutenant General 1691, born at Den Burgh (Rijswijk), Gelderland 2 Feb. 1639 and died at Mechelen, near Antwerp 18 Dec. 1693. He married at The Hague 12 March 1673,
1322. GEERTRUID PIETERSEN, born 27 Feb., baptized at the Great Church, The Hague 30 Nov. 1653 and died at The Hague 24 Feb. 1703.

1324. HM King Charles II, King of England, Scotland, and Ireland = 1096. He had issue by,

1325. Louise Renée de Penancoët de Kéroualle, Duchess of Portsmouth for life, Maid of Honour to HRH The Duchess of Orléans 1668-70 and HM Queen Catherine 1670, the King's mistress 1671-85, born at Kéroualle, Brittany in Sept. 1649 and died at Paris 14 Nov. 1734.

1326. Francis Brudenell, Lord Brudenell = 720.

1327. Lady Frances Savile = 721.

1328. George Gordon, 1st Duke of Gordon, K.T. (1687), P.C. (S.) (1686), born in 1649 and died at Leith 7 Dec. 1716. He married in Oct. 1676 (separated in 1707),

1329. Lady Elizabeth Howard, died at Abbey Hill, Edinburgh 16 July 1732.

1330. Charles Mordaunt, 3rd Earl of Peterborough, K.G. (1713), P.C. (1689-97), Lord of the Bedchamber to HM King William III 1689-97, (absentee) Governor of Jamaica 1702, General of the Allied Forces in Spain and joint Admiral of the Fleet 1705, Ambassador to HIH Archduke Charles (the Spanish pretender) 1706-7, to Vienna and Turin 1710-11, and to HM The King of Sicily 1713-14, Governor of Minorca 1714, commanding General of the Marines 1722, Lord Lieutenant of Northamptonshire 1689-97 and 1702-15, born ca. Dec. 1658 and died at Lisbon 25 Oct. 1735. He married, 2nd, ca. 1735, Anastasia Robinson, singer and actress [for many years his mistress], who was buried at Bath Abbey, Somerset 1 May 1755, daughter of Thomas Robinson. He married, 1st, privately ca. 1678,

1331. Carey Fraser, Maid of Honour to HM Queen Catherine 1674-80, Groom of the Stole to HRH The Princess of Orange (later HM Queen Mary II) 1687, born ca. 1658 and died 13 May 1709; buried at Turvey, Bedfordshire.

1332. George Gordon, 1st Earl of Aberdeen, P.C. (1678), M.P. [as Sir George Gordon, Bt.] 1669-74, 1678, and 1681-82, professor at Marischal College, Aberdeen, High Chancellor of Scotland 1682, born 3 Oct. 1637 and died at Kellie, Fife 20 April 1720. He married (contract dated 1671),

1333. Anne Lockhart, buried at Methlic, Aberdeenshire 19 July 1707.

Louise Renée de Penancoët de Kéroualle, Duchess of Portsmouth

Born at Kéroualle, Brittany in September 1649
Died at Paris 14 November 1734

In 1668, Louise Renée de Penancoët de Kéroualle was appointed Maid of Honour to Henriette-Anne, Duchess of Orléans (sister of Charles II), whom she accompanied on her visit to England in June 1670. After the duchess died later that year, Louise was taken into the service of Charles II's queen, Catherine of Braganza. She arrived in September or October 1670 to take her new position and was soon noticed at court by the King. For a year Louise resisted the King's advances, but in October 1671, Lady Arlington invited the French ambassador to bring her to stay at Euston, Suffolk, while the King was at Newmarket. Charles visited her frequently, and she became his mistress there. At some point before the birth of her son, she was given apartments of her own in Whitehall at the end of the Matted Gallery, which she gradually extended until they included 24 rooms.

She was naturalized and created Duchess of Portsmouth in August 1673, and later that year at Charles' request Louis XIV gave her the fief of Aubigny in Berry. The Duchess was active in court politics, where she was associated with the Earls of Danby and Sunderland. In 1676, Louise's pension from Charles II was established as an annuity, and with other payments in the last four years of the reign she appears to have collected about £20,000 a year, making her undoubtedly the most expensive of Charles' mistresses. She remained the King's mistress until his death, using her influence to keep him dependent on Louis XIV. She visited France from March to June 1682, traveling in great style and meeting with Louis XIV. Then from Paris she went to Brittany and purchased the family estates of Kéroualle and Mesnouales, which her father had been forced to sell.

On his deathbed Charles II asked his brother to be kind to all his mistresses, especially the Duchess of Portsmouth. After the king's death, she lost all her influence at court. The Duchess lived mostly in England until the end of July 1688, when she retired to France, and for the rest of her long life she lived chiefly on her estate in Aubigny, where she founded a convent. In 1704, the Estates of Brittany were forced to pay her compensation for the expropriation of her father's manor, which had been taken by the army. Although Louise received a pension from the King of France, she was in chronic financial difficulties until 1718, when her French pension was greatly increased and then turned into a life annuity in 1721. She made several return trips to England, where she tried in vain to reclaim her English pensions.

1334. John Murray, 1st Duke of Atholl, K.T. (1703/4), P.C. (1702 and 1712-14), Secretary of State (Scotland) 1696, Keeper of the Privy Seal (Scotland) 1703 and 1713-14, Scottish representative peer 1710 and 1713, Lord Lieutenant of Perthshire 1715-24, born at Knowsley House, Lancashire 24 Feb. 1659/60 and died at Huntingtower, Perthshire 14 Nov. 1724. He married, 2nd (contract dated 26 June 1710), Hon. Mary Ross, born 18 July 1687 and died at Huntingtower 17 Jan. 1767, daughter of William Ross, 12th Lord Ross, and Agnes Wilkie. He married, 1st (contract dated 24 April 1683),

1335. Lady Katherine Douglas-Hamilton, baptized at Hamilton, Lanarkshire 24 Oct. 1662 and buried there 17 Jan. 1706/7.

1336. Sir William Maxwell, 1st Baronet, born ca. 1635 and died in April 1709. He married, 1st, in Oct. 1685, Joanna MacDouall, daughter of Patrick MacDouall of Logan, Ayrshire. He married, 2nd,

1337. Elizabeth Hay.

1338. Alexander Montgomerie, 9th Earl of Eglinton, P.C. (S.), Scottish representative peer 1710-14, born ca. 1660 and died at Eglinton, Ayrshire 18 Feb. 1728/29. He married, 2nd, ca. 1695, Lady Anne Gordon, baptized at Methlic, Aberdeenshire 18 July 1675 and buried 16 Dec. 1708, daughter of George Gordon, 1st Earl of Aberdeen [No. 1332], and Anne Lockhart [No. 1333]. He married, 3rd (proclaimed 5, 12, and 19 June 1709), Susanna Kennedy, born ca. 1689 and died at Auchans, Ayrshire 18 March 1780, daughter of Sir Archibald Kennedy, 1st Baronet, and Hon. Elizabeth Leslie, daughter of David Leslie, 1st Lord Newark. He married, 1st (contract dated 7/16 Dec. 1676),

1339. Hon. Margaret Cochrane.

1340. John Scott of Malleny, Midlothianshire, died in 1709. He married,

1341. Anne Nicholson of Cockburnspath, Berwickshire.

1342. Alexander Tait, merchant of Edinburgh, died in Nov. 1713. He married,

1343. Katherine Brown, died before 23 March 1716.

1344. SIR JOHN CURZON, 1ST BARONET, M.P. 1627/28 and 1640/41, born 3 Nov. 1598 and died 13 Dec. 1686. He married at Kedleston, Derbyshire 26 Aug. 1623,
    1345. PATIENCE CREWE, died 30 Aug. 1642.

1346. WILLIAM PENN, Sheriff of Buckinghamshire 1656, born 28 Oct. 1628 and died in 1693. He married at St. Mary Colechurch, London 31 July 1651,
    1347. SARAH SHALLCROSS, born at Fulham, Middlesex ca. 1634 and died between 5 Dec. 1698 and 10 Jan. 1698/99.

1348. SIR RALPH ASSHETON, 1ST BARONET, born at Denby Grange, Yorkshire 9 July 1626 and died 23 April 1665; buried at Middleton, Lancashire. He married ca. 1647,
    1349. ANNE ASSHETON, born in 1624 and died 27 Oct. 1684; buried at Middleton.

1350. THOMAS VAVASOUR of Spaldington, Yorkshire, baptized at Bubwith, Yorkshire 15 June 1636 and died in 1679. He married (license dated 20 Jan. 1660/61),
    1351. DOROTHY LEIGH of Middleton, Lancashire.

1352. THOMAS HANMER, M.P. 1690, born ca. 1648 and buried at Hanmer, Flintshire 8 Aug. 1701. He married (settlement dated 25 May 1674),
    1353. JANE CHARLTON, baptized at the Church of St. Dunstan-in-the-East, London 27 Dec. 1646 and died in 1680.

1354. HUMPHREY JENNENS, baptized at St. Martin's Church, Birmingham 23 Aug. 1629 and died at Erdington Hall, Birmingham 6 July 1690. He married (banns published at St. Martin's Church 9, 16, and 23 Aug.) 16 Dec. 1657,
    1355. MARY MILWARD, born in 1636 and buried at Nether Whitacre, Warwickshire 27 Aug. 1708.

1356. HUMPHREY JENNENS = 1354.
1357. MARY MILWARD = 1355.

1358. SIR ROBERT BURDETT, 3RD BARONET, M.P. 1679-81, 1689, 1690, and 1695, born 11 Jan. 1639/40 and died 18 Jan. 1715/16. He married, 2nd, in 1676, Magdalen Aston, who died ca. 1694, daughter of Sir Thomas Aston, 1st Baronet, and Anne Willoughby. He married, 3rd, Mary Brome, who died in 1742, daughter of Thomas Brome of Croxhall, Derbyshire. He married, 1st (license dated at Nottingham 20 Nov. 1665),

1359. MARY PIGOT, born ca. 1641 and died 31 Aug. 1668.

1360. JOHN HOWE [LATER GROBHAM HOWE], M.P. 1654, 1656, 1659, and 1661, born 25 Jan. 1624/25 and buried at Langar, Nottinghamshire 27 May 1679. He married by 1648,

1361. LADY ANNABELLA SCROPE, legitimated at the Restoration, born in 1629 and died 21 March 1703/4.

1362. WILLIAM ALINGTON, 3RD BARON ALINGTON, M.P. [as Hon. William Alington] 1664, 1679, and 1681, Major General 1678, Constable of the Tower of London 1679-85, Lord Lieutenant of Cambridgeshire 1681-85, born ca. 1634 and died at the Tower of London 1 Feb. 1684/85. He married, 1st, Lady Catherine Stanhope, who died 19 Nov. 1662, daughter of Henry Stanhope, Lord Stanhope by courtesy, and Katherine Wotton, Countess of Chesterfield in her own right. He married, 3rd, at Hackney, Middlesex 15 July 1675, Lady Diana Russell, who died at Kensington, Middlesex 13 Dec. 1701, widow of Sir Greville Verney, and daughter of William Russell, 1st Duke of Bedford [No. 2624], and Lady Anne Carr [No. 2625]. He married, 2nd (Faculty Office license dated 30 July 1664),

1363. HON. JULIANA NOEL, baptized at Kensington 4 Feb. 1646/47 and died 14 Sept. 1667; buried at Horseheath, Cambridgeshire.

1364. FRIEDRICH CHRISTIAN VON KIELMANSEGG, born at Schleswig 1 Feb. 1639 and died at Hamburg 25 Sept. 1714. He married in 1666,

1365. MARIE ELISABETH CHRISTINE VON AHLEFELDT, born in 1643 and died 23 Sept. 1709.

1366. HH ERNST AUGUST HERZOG VON BRAUNSCHWEIG UND LÜNEBURG, ELECTOR OF HANOVER, born at Schloss Herzberg am Harz 20 Nov. 1629 and died at Schloss Herrenhausen, Hanover 23 Jan. 1698. He married at Heidelberg 30 Sept. 1658, HRH Sophie Prinzessin von der Pfalz, Heiress Presumptive to the Throne of Great Britain 1702-14, born at The Hague 13 Oct.

1630 and died at Schloss Herrenhausen 8 June 1714, daughter of HM King Friedrich I von der Pfalz, King of Bohemia [No. 5948], and HRH Princess Elizabeth of England and Scotland [No. 5949]. He is presumed to have had issue by,

1367. CLARA ELISABETH VON MEYSENBUG, born 24 Jan. 1648 and died at Neu-Linden, Hanover 30 Jan. 1700. She married in Sept. 1673, Franz Ernst Reichsgraf von Platen-Hallermund, Governor of the Elector's sons, born in 1631 and died at Hanover 14 Jan. 1709, son of Erasmus von Platen auf Granskevitz and Margarete Katherina von Alvensleben.

1368. SIR WILLIAM HARTOPP, Gentleman of the Privy Chamber 1675-85, born ca. 1626 and died in 1692 or later. He married, 2nd (settlement dated 4 Dec. 1688), Hon. Elizabeth Poulett, widow of William Ashburnham, and daughter of John Poulett, 1st Baron Poulett, and Elizabeth Kenn. He married, 1st, 12 Aug. 1649,

1369. AGNES LISTER, born in Jan. 1629/30 and buried 26 June 1667.

1370. ST. JOHN BENNETT, High Sheriff of Leicestershire 1679 and 1692, born in 1651. He married in 1673,

1371. MARY MIDDLETON, buried at Melton Mowbray, Leicestershire 7 July 1690.

1372. RICHARD MANSFIELD, baptized at West Leake, Nottinghamshire 27 July 1628 and buried there 11 May 1702. He married,

1373. ELIZABETH RICHARDSON of Honingham, Norfolk.

1374-1375. ——.

1376. SIR JOHN GORE, M.P. 1677, baptized at the Church of St. Mary Magdalen, Milk Street, London 17 April 1621 and died 14 Sept. 1697; buried at Watton at Stone, Hertfordshire. He married ca. 1642,

1377. CATHERINE BOTELER, born ca. 1625 and died 22 April 1698.

1378. RIGHT HON. SIR WILLIAM GORE, 3RD BARONET, P.C., M.P. 1661-66, died before 12 May 1705. He married,

1379. HANNAH HAMILTON, born in 1651 and died at Dublin 16 May 1733.

1380. MAJOR JOHN MANLEY, M.P. 1659 and 1689, Postmaster-General 1653-55, born ca. 1622 and died at the Old Artillery Ground, London in Jan. 1698/99. He married, 2nd, Mary ——, who died in 1701. He married, 1st, ca. 1650,

1381. MARGARET DORISLAUS, buried at the Church of St. Stephen Walbrook, London 17 Dec. 1675.

1382. WILLIAM NEWLAND of Nusells, Hertfordshire, born ca. 1616. He married at St. Paul's Church, Covent Garden, near London 20 Feb. 1653/54,

1383. MARY BLAKE of Essington, Hampshire.

1384-1391. ——.

1392. JAMES MONTAGU, born ca. 1634 and died ca. 15 March 1675/76; buried at Lacock, Wiltshire. He married at Blackbourton, Oxfordshire 30 May 1671,

1393. DIANA HUNGERFORD, baptized at Blackbourton 19 Nov. 1648 and died 16 March 1734/35; buried at Lacock.

1394. SIR JOHN EYLES, M.P. 1679, Lord Mayor of London 1688, buried at St. Helen's Church, Bishopsgate, London 6 July 1703. He married,

1395. SARAH COWPER, buried at St. Helen's Church 14 Aug. 1705.

1396. GEORGE WROUGHTON of Shercott, Wiltshire, born ca. 1643 and buried at Wilcot, Wiltshire 19 Oct. 1696. He married (Vicar-General's license to marry at St. Margaret's Church, Westminster, Middlesex, or the Churches of St. Lawrence or St. Mary, Reading, Berkshire dated 28 Sept. 1668),

1397. ANN FARWELL, baptized at St. Ann's Church, Blackfriars, London 1 June 1645 and buried at Wilcot 6 Nov. 1724.

1398. ROBERT EYRE of Putney, Surrey, born in 1658 and died 25 Aug. 1718; buried at Bath Abbey, Somerset. He married at London 20 May 1682,

1399. ANNE BRISCOE, born in 1662 and buried at Bath Abbey 10 March 1744/45.

1400. GEORGE WROUGHTON = 1396.
1401. ANN FARWELL = 1397.

1402. ROBERT EYRE = 1398.
1403. ANNE BRISCOE = 1399.

1404-1407. ——.

1408. SIR GEORGE BINGHAM, 2ND BARONET = 528.
1409. REBECCA MIDDLETON = 529.

1410-1411. = 530-531.

1412. MOST REV. DR. JOHN VESEY, ARCHBISHOP OF TUAM = 532.
1413. ANNE MUSCHAMP = 533.

1414. WILLIAM SARSFIELD = 534.
1415. MARY CROFTS = 535.

1416-1423. = 536-543.

1424. SIR ROWLAND BELASYSE, K.B. (1661), baptized at Coxwold, Yorkshire 25 March 1632 and died at Sutton Court, Cheshire 16 Aug. 1699. He married,
1425. ANNE DAVENPORT, baptized at Macclesfield, Lancashire 27 Aug. 1640 and buried at Bolton, Lancashire 13 Nov. 1677.

1426. SIR JOHN GAGE, 4TH BARONET, Sheriff of Sussex 1687-88, born ca. 1642 and died 27 May 1699. He married, 2nd, Mary Stanley, daughter of Sir William Stanley, 1st Baronet, and Hon. Charlotte Molyneux, daughter of Richard Molyneux, 1st Viscount Molyneux. He married, 1st,
1427. MARY MIDDLEMORE, died 28 July 1686.

1428. Richard Betham of Rowington, Warwickshire, born ca. 1630 and living in 1682. He married,

1429. Mary Wollascott of Tidmarsh, Berkshire.

1430. —— Casey married,

1431. Magdalen Fowler, died before 6 Feb. 1694/95.

1432-1435. ——.

1436. Colonel John Coke, M.P. 1685-87 and 1688-90, Gentleman Usher to HM Queen Catherine 1685-89, born ca. 1653 and died at Geneva 7 Jan. 1691/92. He married 15 June 1672,

1437. Mary Leventhorpe, died at Melbourne, Derbyshire in 1680.

1438. Richard Hale, born 4, baptized at Kings Walden, Hertfordshire 9 Nov. 1659 and died 10 April 1689; buried at Kings Walden. He married there 3 April 1684,

1439. Elizabeth Meynell, died ca. 17 Dec. 1718. She married, 2nd (allegation to marry at the Church of St. Botolph Aldersgate, London dated 28 July 1690), Hon. Robert Cecil, M.P. 1701 and 1708, baptized at Hatfield, Hertfordshire 6 Nov. 1670 and died 23 Feb. 1715/16, son of James Cecil, 3rd Earl of Salisbury, and Lady Margaret Manners, daughter of John Manners, 8th Earl of Rutland [No. 5268].

1440. Robert Brudenell, 2nd Earl of Cardigan, born 5 March 1606/7 and died 16 July 1703. He married, 1st, Hon. Mary Constable, daughter of Henry Constable, 1st Viscount Dunbar, and Mary Tufton. He married, 2nd,

1441. Lady Anne Savage, died 16 June 1696.

1442. Thomas Savile, 1st Earl of Sussex, P.C. (1640/41 and 1643), M.P. [as Sir Thomas Savile] 1624-25 and 1628, Gentleman of the Privy Chamber to HM King Charles I 1626, Treasurer of the (Royal) Household 1641-45, Lord President of the Council of the North 1641, Commissioner of Regency 1641, Lord Lieutenant of Yorkshire 1641, Governor of York 1642 [and suspected by both the Royalists and Parliamentarians], baptized at

Doddington-Pigot, Lincolnshire 14 Sept. 1590 and died between 8 Nov. 1657 and 8 Oct. 1659. He married, 1st, Frances Sondes [No. 10531], who was living in 1634, widow of Sir John Leveson [No. 10530], and daughter of Thomas Sondes and Hon. Margaret Brooke, daughter of William Brooke, 10th Baron Cobham. He married, 2nd, at Sunbury, Middlesex 26 Jan. 1640/41,

1443. LADY ANNE VILLIERS, died before 1 July 1670. She married, 2nd, Richard Pelson.

1444. ROBERT BRUCE, 2ND EARL OF ELGIN AND 1ST EARL OF AILES-BURY, P.C. (1678), F.R.S. (1685), M.P. [as Lord Kinloss] 1661-63, one of the twelve commoners deputed to invite the return of HM King Charles II 1660, bore St. Edward's Staff at the coronation of HM King James II 1685, Lord Chamberlain of the (Royal) Household 1685, Lord Lieutenant of Bedfordshire 1660 and 1667, Huntingdonshire 1681 and 1685, and Cambridgeshire 1685, baptized at the Church of St. Bartholomew the Less, London 19 March 1626 and died at Houghton Park, Bedfordshire 20 Oct. 1685. He married at St. Alphage's Church, London Wall 16 Feb. 1645/46,

1445. LADY DIANA GREY, died 8 April 1689; buried at Maulden, Bedfordshire.

1446. HENRY SEYMOUR, LORD BEAUCHAMP by courtesy, a leading royalist in the West of England, born ca. 1626 and died at Tilsy, Great Bedwyn, Wiltshire 14 March 1653/54. He married at Little Hadham, Hertfordshire 26 June 1648,

1447. HON. MARY CAPELL = 1101.

1448. SIR CECIL BISHOPP, 4TH BARONET, M.P. 1662, died 3 June 1705; buried at Parham, Sussex. He married at Culham, Oxfordshire 17 June 1666,

1449. SARAH BURY, born at Culham 11 Sept. 1650 and buried there 12 March 1678/79.

1450. HON. HENRY DUNCH, baptized at the Church of St. Martin-in-the-Fields, Westminster, Middlesex 11 Oct. 1649 and died between 8 Oct. and 4 Nov. 1686; buried at Newington, Oxfordshire. He married,

1451. ANNE DORMER, born ca. 1656 and died 13 May 1690; buried at Newington.

1452. EDWARD BOSCAWEN, M.P. 1659, 1660, 1661, 1679, and 1681, baptized at St. Michael Penkivel, Cornwall 21 Nov. 1628 and died 28 Oct. 1685; buried at the Church of St. Mary Abbot, Kensington, Middlesex. He married at Breage, Cornwall 5 Jan. 1664/65,

1453. JAEL GODOLPHIN, born 5 June 1647 and buried 18 April 1730.

1454. COLONEL CHARLES GODFREY, M.P. 1689, 1691, 1695, 1701, 1702, 1708, and 1710, Master of the Jewels 1698-1704 [during his brother-in-law's ascendancy], born ca. 1648 and died near Bath, Somerset 23 Feb. 1714/15. He married ca. 1679,

1455. ARABELLA CHURCHILL = 1107.

1456. JOHN COOKE, Chief Prothonotary of the Court of Common Pleas, died between 6 April 1709 and 1 June 1711. He married,

1457. MARY WARREN, buried at Cranbrooke, Kent 19 Dec. 1691.

1458. EDWARD JENNINGS, M.P. 1713-15, Attorney-General of Carnarvonshire 1677-89 and Denbighshire and Montgomeryshire 1688-89, born ca. 1647 and died 12 June 1725; buried at the Inner Temple, London. He married (Faculty Office license dated 9 June 1666),

1459. ELIZABETH HORNE, baptized at the Church of St. Matthew Friday Street, London 20 Aug. 1648.

1460. SIR WILLIAM TWYSDEN, 3RD BARONET, M.P. 1685-87 and 1695-97, born 11, baptized at the Church of St. Giles Cripplegate, London 15 Dec. 1635 and died at London 27 Nov. 1697. He married (Faculty Office license to marry at St. Swithin's Church, London or Westminster Abbey, Middlesex dated 8 June 1665),

1461. FRANCES CROSS, baptized at the Church of St. Martin Ludgate, London 2 Sept. 1649 and died before Aug. 1731.

1462. SIR FRANCIS WYTHENS, M.P. 1679-80, Judge of the Court of the King's Bench 1683-87, baptized at St. Mary Cray, Kent 27 July 1633 and died at Southend, Kent 9 May 1704. He married at Westminster Abbey, Middlesex 21 May 1685,

1463. ELIZABETH TAYLOR, born in 1656 and buried at Aylesford, Kent 5 Feb. 1707/8. She married, 2nd, 23 Aug. 1704, her brother-in-law Sir Thomas Colepeper, 3rd Baronet, born in 1657 and died at Prestonhall, Aylesford 18 May 1723, son of Sir Richard Colepeper, 2nd Baronet, and Margaret Reynolds.

1464. SIR WILLIAM BOWYER, 2ND BARONET, born ca. 1639 and died 13 Feb. 1721/22; buried at Denham, Buckinghamshire. He married (Vicar-General's license to marry at the Churches of St. Martin-in-the-Fields, Westminster, Middlesex, or St. Clement Danes, London dated 24 Dec. 1679),
1465. HON. FRANCES CECIL, born ca. 1647 and died 15 June 1723.

1466. RICHARD PARKER, born ca. 1658 and buried at Hedsor, Buckinghamshire before 6 July 1730. He married,
1467. SARAH CHILCOT, born 12 Jan., baptized at the Church of St. Gregory by St. Paul, London 1 Feb. 1658 and died before 5 May 1738.

1468. SIR JOHN STONHOUSE, 2ND BARONET = 1132.
1469. MARTHA BRIGGES = 1133.

1470. SIR ROBERT DASHWOOD, 1ST BARONET, M.P. 1689, 1690, 1695, and 1699-1700, baptized at St. Margaret's Church, Westminster, Middlesex 6 Nov. 1662 and died 14 June 1734; buried at Kirtlington, Oxfordshire. He married (Vicar-General's license to marry at the Church of St. Giles-in-the-Fields, Holborn, Middlesex 9 June 1682),
1471. PENELOPE CHAMBERLAYNE, born ca. 1663 and buried at Kirtlington 22 Feb. 1734/35.

1472. HM KING CHARLES II, KING OF ENGLAND, SCOTLAND, AND IRELAND = 1096 = 1324.
1473. LOUISE RENÉE DE PENANCOËT DE KÉROUALLE, DUCHESS OF PORTSMOUTH = 1325.

1474. FRANCIS BRUDENELL, LORD BRUDENELL = 720 = 1326.
1475. LADY FRANCES SAVILE = 721 = 1327.

1476. HENRY CADOGAN, High Sheriff of Meath 1700, born at Dublin ca. 1642 and died there 13 Jan. 1714/15. He married (license dated 31 July 1671), **1477. BRIDGET WALLER,** died 23 Dec. 1721.

1478. JAN MUNTER, HEER VAN ZANEN EN RAAPHORST, born at Amsterdam 23 Aug. 1634 and died at The Hague 26 April 1713. He married at Sloten, near Amsterdam 4 Oct. 1674,
1479. MARGRIET TRIP, born at Amsterdam 26 Nov. 1637 and died at The Hague 25 May 1711. She married, 1st, 29 Jan. 1658, Jacob Trip, baptized at the Walloon Church, Amsterdam 9 July 1636 and died 15 Sept. 1664, son of Lodewyk Trip and Ermgard Hoefsleger.

1480. WILLIAM KERR, 2ND MARQUESS OF LOTHIAN, K.T. (1705), proposed the first bill for the Union of England and Scotland 1705, Lieutenant General 1707, Scottish representative peer 1708-9 and 1715-22, baptized at Newbattle House, Edinburgh 27 March 1661 and died at London 28 Feb. 1721/22. He married (contract dated 30 June 1685),
1481. LADY JEAN CAMPBELL, born ca. 1661 and died 31 July 1712; buried at Newbattle House.

1482. SIR THOMAS NICOLSON, 1ST BARONET, baptized at Edinburgh 26 July 1666 and died 31 Aug. 1728. He married at Edinburgh 17 July 1688,
1483. MARGARET NICOLSON. She married, 1st, James Hamilton of Ballencreiff, Lothianshire.

1484. COLONEL HON. JOHN DARCY, M.P. 1681 and 1685, baptized at Hornby, Yorkshire 5 Nov. 1659 and died at London 6 Jan. 1688/89. He married 5 Feb. 1673/74,
1485. HON. BRIDGET SUTTON, born ca. 1663 and died 18 July 1736.

1486. MEINHARDT VON SCHOMBERG, 3RD DUKE OF SCHOMBERG AND 1ST DUKE OF LEINSTER, K.G. (1703), P.C. (1695-1714), Marshal of France 1678, General of the Horse 1692, born at Cologne 30 June 1641 and died at Hillingdon, near Uxbridge, Middlesex 5 July 1719. He apparently married, 1st, at La Rochelle 3 Aug. 1667 (abandoned before 24 Nov. 1668), Barbara Luisa Rizzi, daughter of Giovanni Girolamo Rizzi and Maria Margarita Callovi. He apparently married, 3rd, in 1702, —— Box. He married, 2nd, 4 Jan. 1683,

1487. Karoline Elisabeth Raugräfin von der Pfalz, born at Schwetzingen, Württemburg 19 Nov. 1659 and died at Kensington, Middlesex 28 June 1696.

1488. George Gordon, 1st Duke of Gordon = 1328.
1489. Lady Elizabeth Howard = 1329.

1490. Charles Mordaunt, 3rd Earl of Peterborough = 1330.
1491. Carey Fraser = 1331.

1492. George Gordon, 1st Earl of Aberdeen = 1332.
1493. Anne Lockhart = 1333.

1494. John Murray, 1st Duke of Atholl = 1334.
1495. Lady Katherine Douglas-Hamilton = 1335.

1496. Sir William Maxwell, 1st Baronet = 1336.
1497. Elizabeth Hay = 1337.

1498. Alexander Montgomerie, 9th Earl of Eglinton = 1338.
1499. Hon. Margaret Cochrane = 1339.

1500. John Scott = 1340.
1501. Anne Nicholson = 1341.

1502. Alexander Tait = 1342.
1503. Katherine Brown = 1343.

1504. Colonel Nicholas Bayly, M.P. (I.) 1661-66, Gentleman of the Bedchamber to HM King Charles II, Governor of Galway and the Isle of Arran, married,
1505. Dorothy [or Anne] Hall, buried at St. Michael's Church, Dublin 5 March 1713/14.

1506. Hon. Oliver Lambart, M.P. (I.) 1661-66, 1692-93, and 1695-99, died 13 Dec. 1700. He married, 1st, ca. 1662, Catherine Bridges, daughter of John Bridges and Mary Beale. He married, 3rd (license dated 12 Dec. 1681), Dorothy Whitfield. He married, 4th, ca. 1688, Anne Tighe, who died before 27 Sept. 1734, widow of i) Theophilus Sansford of Moyglare, Meath, and ii) John Preston, Alderman of Dublin, daughter of Richard Tighe, Alderman of Dublin, and Mary Rooke. He married, 2nd (license dated 6 Sept. 1671),

1507. Eleanor Crane, died before 12 Dec. 1681.

1508. Hon. Henry Paget married, 1st, Mary Sandford, who was buried at St. Michan's Church, Dublin 19 Dec. 1683, daughter of Robert Sandford of Sandford, Shropshire, and Anne Daniels. He married, 2nd (license dated at Dublin 29 March 1684),

1509. Mary O'Rorke.

1510. Peter Whitcombe of Great Braxted, Essex, Turkey merchant, died between 2 and 12 Sept. 1704. He married, 2nd, at the Church of St. Giles Cripplegate, London 1 Dec. 1702, Hon. Gertrude Arundell, baptized at Newlyn, Cornwall 22 June 1676 and died 23 Sept. 1709, daughter of John Arundell, 2nd Baron Arundell, and Margaret Acland. He married, 1st,

1511. Elizabeth Sherard, baptized at North Witham, Essex 25 Oct. 1663 and died before 27 Nov. 1702.

1512. Josias de Robillard, Seigneur de Champagné, died at Belfast 28 Oct. 1689. He married,

1513. Marie de la Rochefoucauld de Fontpastour, died at Portarlington, Leix 14 Feb. 1729/30.

1514. Arthur Forbes, 2nd Earl of Granard, born ca. 1656 and died at Symon's Court, near Dublin 24 Aug. 1734. He married (articles date 21-22 Oct. 1678),

1515. Mary Rawdon, born 19, baptized at Guiseley, Yorkshire 20 Aug. 1660 and died 1 April 1724; buried at St. Mary's Church, Dublin.

1516. Pierre Hamon married,
1517. Charlotte ——.

1518-1519. ———.

1520. EDWARD VILLIERS, 1ST EARL OF JERSEY, P.C. (1697 AND 1699-1707), Master of the Horse to HM Queen Mary II 1689-95, Lord Chamberlain of the (Royal) Household to TM King William III and Queen Anne 1700-4, minister to The Hague 1695, Ambassador to The Hague 1697-98 and Paris 1698-99, Secretary of State for the South 1699-1700, appointed Lord Privy Seal 1711, Lord Justice [i.e. Regent] of Ireland 1697-99 and England 1699, 1700, and 1701, baptized at Bartlow, Cambridgeshire 18 Nov. 1655 and died 25 Aug. 1711; buried at Westminster Abbey, London. He married (Faculty Office license to marry at the Churches of St. Mary Woolnoth or St. Stephen Walbrook, London dated 8 Dec. 1681),

1521. BARBARA CHIFFINCH, born in 1663 and died at Paris 22 July 1735.

1522. FREDERICK HERNE, M.P. 1698-1714, Director of the East India Company 1709-14, born 3, baptized at St. Olave's Church, Hart Street, London 19 March 1665/66 and died at London 15 March 1713/14. He married at Brackley, Northamptonshire (Vicar-General's license dated 5) 16 June 1688,

1523. ELIZABETH LISLE, born ca. 1664.

1524. JOHN EGERTON, 3RD EARL OF BRIDGEWATER, K.B. (1661), P.C. (1691), M.P. [as Lord Brackley] 1685-86, First Lord of Trade 1695-99, Speaker of the House of Lords 1697 and 1700, Lord Justice [i.e. Regent] 1699 and 1700, First Lord of the Admiralty 1699-1701, Lord Lieutenant of Buckinghamshire 1686-87 and 1689-1701, born 9 Nov. 1646 and died 19 March 1700/1; buried at Little Gaddesden, Hertfordshire. He married, 1st, at Bridgewater House, Barbican, London 17 Nov. 1664, Lady Elizabeth Cranfield, born ca. 1648 and died 3 March 1669/70, daughter of James Cranfield, 2nd Earl of Middlesex, and Lady Anne Bourchier, daughter of Edward Bourchier, 4th Earl of Bath. He married, 2nd, at Charterhouse Chapel, London 2 April 1673,

1525. LADY JANE POWLETT, baptized at the Church of St. Martin-in-the-Fields, Westminster, Middlesex 12 Nov. 1655 and died 23 May 1716; buried at Little Gaddesden.

1526. JOHN CHURCHILL, 1ST DUKE OF MARLBOROUGH = 514.
1527. SARAH JENNINGS = 515.

1528. Sir William Twysden, 3rd Baronet = 1460.
1529. Frances Cross = 1461.

1530. Francis Twysden, born at East Peckham, Kent 22 Oct. 1648 and died 20 Nov. 1721; buried at the Church of St. Benet Fink, London. He married there 24 Aug. 1677,
1531. Rebecca Lemon, born ca. 1647 and died 15 April 1698. She married, 1st, Thomas Hale, who died before 24 Aug. 1677, son of Sir Matthew Hale, Lord Chief Justice of England.

1532. Thomas Carter, M.P. (I.) 1695-99 and 1705-13, baptized 17 April 1666 and died 19 Aug. 1726. He married, 2nd, 2 Aug. 1702, Isabel Boynton, born ca. 1654 and died in Sept. 1721, widow of Wentworth Dillon, 4th Earl of Roscommon, and daughter of Matthew Boynton and Isabel Stapleton. He married, 1st, at Robertstown, Meath 18 Dec. 1681,
1533. Margaret Houghton, born ca. 1660 and died in 1696.

1534. Thomas Claxton of Dublin married,
1535. Mary Pearce.

1536. Edward Roche, died in 1626. He married,
1537. ——.

1538. Thomas Coppinger, Mayor of Cork, born in 1578 and died at Cork 24 Dec. 1635. He married,
1539. Catherine Coppinger.

1540. Patrick Lavallin of Walterstown, Cork, born ca. 1600. He married,
1541. ——.

1542-1543. ——.

1544. James Hennessy of Ballymacmoy, Cork, married,
1545. Helen Nagle.

1546-1591. ——.

1592. Daniel O'Donovan, died in 1660. He married,
1593. Gyles O'Shaughnessy.

1594. Major Richard Tonson of Spanish Island, Cork, died in 1693. He married,
1595. Elizabeth Becher.

1596-1599. ——.

1600. Richard Boothby of Hunscote, Leicestershire, born ca. 1633. He married,
1601. Grisel Halford of Kilby, Leicestershire.

1602-1647. ——.

1648. David Guinand, died in 1682. He married,
1649. Suzanne Parel.

1650-1655. ——.

1656. Pierre Yvonnet of La Rochelle, born 21 Feb. 1612. He married,
1657. Judith Herely, born 16 Feb. 1618.

1658. Paul Yvonnet, born 14 Dec. 1631. He married,
1659. Marie Challes, born 21 Nov. 1632.

1660-1703. ——.

1704. Thomas Newbold of Hanworth Woodhouse, Norfolk, died in 1652. He married 18 Feb. 1615/16,
1705. Jane Syms, baptized 11 Feb. 1587/88 and died 10 Feb. 1624/25.

1706-1759. ———.

1760. Thomas Strong, born at Hingham, Massachusetts ca. 1637 and died at Northampton, Massachusetts 3 Oct. 1689. He married, 1st, 5 Dec. 1660, Mary Hewett, daughter of Ephraim Hewett of Wraxall, Warwickshire, and Windsor, Connecticut, and Isabel ———. He married, 2nd, at Northampton 10 Oct. 1671,
    1761. Rachel Holton, born at Hartford, Connecticut ca. 1650. She married, 2nd, at Northampton 16 May 1698, Nathan Bradley.

1762. Nehemiah Allen, born ca. 1634 and died at Northampton, Massachusetts 27 June 1684. He married at Northampton 21 Sept. 1664,
    1763. Sarah Woodford, baptized at Hartford, Connecticut 2 Sept. 1649 and died at Northampton 31 March 1712. She married, 2nd, at Northampton 1 Sept. 1687, Richard Burke. She married, 3rd, at Northampton 11 July 1706, Judah Wright, born at Springfield, Massachusetts 10 May 1642 and died at Northampton 26 Nov. 1725.

1764. Jedediah Strong, farmer, baptized at Taunton, Massachusetts 14 April 1639 and died at Coventry, Connecticut 22 May 1733. He married, 2nd, 19 Dec. 1681, Abigail Stebbins, born 6 Sept. 1660 and died 15 July 1689, daughter of John Stebbins and Abigail Bartlett. He married, 3rd, **Mary Hart [No. 1767].** He married, 1st, at Northampton 18 Nov. 1662,
    1765. Freedom Woodward, baptized at Dorchester, Massachusetts in July 1642 and died at Northampton 17 May 1681.

1766. John Lee, born ca. 1620 and died at Farmington, Connecticut 8 Aug. 1690. He married at Farmington in 1658,
    1767. Mary Hart, born ca. 1630 and died at South Hadley, Massachusetts 10 Oct. 1710. She married, 2nd, at Northampton, Massachusetts 5 Jan. 1691/92, **Jedediah Strong [No. 1764].**

1768. Samuel Bishop, born (probably at Ipswich, Massachusetts) ca. 1645 and died at Ipswich before 2 March 1686/87. He married there 10 Aug. 1675,
    1769. Hester Cogswell, born at Ipswich ca. 1656 and died there after 17 Jan. 1703/4. She married, 2nd, at Ipswich 16 Dec. 1689, Sergeant Thomas Burnham, born at Ipswich 19 Jan. 1646 and died there 21 Feb. 1728, son of Thomas Burnham and Mary Tuttle.

1770. DEACON CALEB FOBES, born at Bridgewater, Massachusetts ca. 1653 and died at Preston, Connecticut 25 Aug. 1710. He married, 2nd, after 1702, Mary Huntington, who was born at Norwich, Connecticut in Aug. 1657, daughter of Deacon Simon Huntington and Sarah Clarke. He married, 1st, at Norwich 30 June 1681,

1771. SARAH GAGER, born at New London, Connecticut in Feb. 1650/51 and died ca. 1702.

1772. ROBERT HIBBARD, twin, baptized at Salem, Massachusetts 7 May 1648 and died at Windham, Connecticut 29 April 1710. He married at Wenham, Massachusetts in 1673,

1773. MARY WALDEN, born at Wenham ca. 1655 and died at Windham 7 March 1735/36.

1774. JOSEPH MORGAN, baptized at Roxbury, Massachusetts 20 Oct. 1646 and died at Preston, Connecticut 5 April 1704. He married at New London, Connecticut 26 April 1670,

1775. DOROTHY PARKE, born at New London 6 March 1651/52.

1776-1823. ——.

1824. JOHN OGSTON, farmer of Urinell, Coburty, Aberdeenshire, married,
1825. ——.

1826-1935. ——.

1936. REV. HUGH CHALMER, minister of Marnoch, Banffshire, born ca. 1648 and died in 1707. He married,

1937. ELIZABETH INNES of Culquoich, Aberdeenshire.

1938. REV. GEORGE CHALMER, minister of Drumblade, Aberdeenshire 1687, died in 1702. He married, 1st, Elizabeth Gordon, daughter of Rev. James Gordon of Rothiemay, Banffshire. He married, 2nd,

1939. RACHEL FORBES.

1940. REV. WILLIAM TRAIL, minister of Lifford, Donegal 1671, Potomac, Maryland 1684, and Borthwick, Midlothianshire 1691, baptized at Elie, Fife 28 Sept. 1640 and died in 1714. He married in Downshire 25 March 1679,
1941. HELENOR TRAIL, born in 1659 and died 4 Jan. 1694/95.

1942. JOHN ALLARDES, Provost of Aberdeen 1697-99, baptized at St. Nicholas' Church, Aberdeen 16 July 1657 and died 25 May 1718. He married, 2nd, Jean Smart, born ca. 1678 and died 29 Nov. 1722. He married, 1st,
1943. AGNES MERCER, born ca. 1659 and died 21 Aug. 1700.

1944. DAVID DOUGLAS, writer, married at Banchory, Aberdeenshire 22 April 1676,
1945. MARGARET REID.

1946-1947. ——.

1948. ARTHUR FORBES, 12th of Echt, Aberdeenshire, died in 1728. He married, 2nd, in 1696, Katherine Melville. He married, 1st, 4 Oct. 1681,
1949. ELIZABETH INNES, died in 1695.

1950. ALEXANDER PYPER, merchant of Aberdeen, married,
1951. MARGARET PYPER.

1952. CAPTAIN JAMES BENTLEY, baptized at Heptonstall, Yorkshire 24 Aug. 1606 and died at Pontefract Castle, Yorkshire. He married at Methley, Yorkshire 17 July 1633,
1953. JANE CRABTREE, baptized at Methley 2 April 1609 and buried there 4 Sept. 1649.

1954. MAJOR RICHARD WILLIE, buried at Rothwell, Yorkshire 23 April 1684. He married,
1955. ANN ——, buried at Rothwell 25 June 1683.

1956-1967. ——.

1968. Arthur Dingwall of Brownhill, Aberdeenshire, born ca. 1620 and died in 1707. He married ca. 1675,

1969. Lucretia Irvine of Bruckley, New Deer, Aberdeenshire, died in 1717.

1970. Rev. William Murray, minister of Inverury, Aberdeenshire, born ca. 1645. He married,

1971. Magdalen Gellie.

1972. George Fordyce, died 6 May 1681; buried at Turiff, Aberdeenshire. He married,

1973. Barbara Thomson, died 9 Jan. 1694/95.

1974. William Lindsay, writer in Edinburgh, died at Culsh, New Deer, Aberdeenshire in Nov. 1694. He married, 2nd, Agnes Mercer, who died 1 March 1690/91, widow of Alexander Youngson. He married, 3rd (contract dated 12 July 1693), Barbara Guthrie, daughter of Sir Henry Guthrie, 1st Baronet. He married, 1st,

1975. Barbara Leith, died before 1678.

1976-1977. ——.

1978. Robert Low, merchant of Aberdeen, married,

1979. Christian Forbes.

1980. Andrew Dyce, merchant of Old Aberdeen, born at Belhevie, Aberdeenshire in 1657 and died 25 April 1731. He married at New Machar, Aberdeenshire 28 May 1686,

1981. Janet Gray.

1982. William Baxter, Baillie of Aberdeen, married,

1983. Isobel Brebner.

1984-2007. ——.

2008. WILLIAM LUMSDEN married at Kildrummy, Aberdeenshire 21 Aug. 1687,
2009. JEAN GORDON of Lowlands of Auchindour, Aberdeenshire.

2010-2015. ——.

2016. SIR JOHN FORBES, 3RD BARONET, born in 1640 and died 13 Jan. 1714/15. He married, 1st, **HON. MARGARET ARBUTHNOTT [No. 4055].** He married, 2nd, 21 Feb. 1672/73,
2017. BARBARA DALMAHOY.

2018. GEORGE MORISON of Frendraught, Banffshire, died before 1 Aug. 1699. He married after 22 Jan. 1674/75,
2019. CHRISTIAN URQUHART, died before 1 Aug. 1699. She married, 1st (contract dated 24 Feb. 1662/63), Thomas Rutherford, 2nd Lord Rutherford, who died 11 April 1668, son of John Rutherford and Hon. Alison Ker, daughter of Andrew Ker, 1st Lord Jedburgh. She married, 2nd, by July 1669, James Crichton, 2nd Viscount Frendraught, died before 22 Jan. 1674/75, son of James Crichton, 1st Viscount Frendraught, and Marion Irvine.

2020-2021. ——.

2022. ALEXANDER FORBES, 4th of Blackton, Aberdeenshire, born ca. 1650. He married after March 1683,
2023. ISOBEL HACKET. She married, 1st, Alexander Abernethy, who died in March 1683, son of Thomas Abernethy.

2024. GEORGE MORISON = 2018.
2025. CHRISTIAN URQUHART = 2019.

2026. SIR CHARLES MAITLAND, 3RD BARONET, M.P. 1685-86, died in 1700. He married, 2nd, in 1696, Nicola Young, widow of Sir Alexander Burnett, and daughter of Peter Young of Auldbar, Forfarshire. He married, 1st,
2027. JEAN FORBES.

2028. ALEXANDER DUFF, M.P. 1702-7 and 1708-10, born in 1657 and died 22 Aug. 1726. He married in 1684,

2029. KATHERINE DUFF, born ca. 1669 and died in 1758.

2030. SIR JAMES GORDON, 2ND BARONET, died 15 Dec. 1727. He married, 2nd, ca. 1720, Hon. Margaret Elphinstone, widow of George Leslie, Count Leslie of Balquhain, and daughter of John Elphinstone, 8th Lord Elphinstone, and Lady Isabel Maitland, daughter of Charles Maitland, 3rd Earl of Lauderdale. He married, 1st,

2031. HON. HELEN FRASER.

2032-2047. ———.

Eleventh Generation

2048. WILLIAM SPENCER, 2ND BARON SPENCER, K.B. (1616), M.P. [as Hon. William Spencer] 1614 and [as Hon. Sir William Spencer] 1619-22, 1624-25, and 1626, baptized at Brington, Northamptonshire 4 Jan. 1591/92 and died 19 Dec. 1636; buried at Brington. He married in 1615,

2049. LADY PENELOPE WRIOTHESLEY, born ca. 28 Nov. 1598 and died 16 July 1667.

2050. ROBERT SIDNEY, 2ND EARL OF LEICESTER, K.B. (1610), P.C. (1639 AND 1660), M.P. [as Sir Robert Sidney] 1614 and [as Viscount L'Isle] 1620-22 and 1624-25, Ambassador to Denmark and Holstein 1632 and Paris 1636-41, Chief Governor [i.e. Lord Lieutenant] and General of the Army of Ireland 1641-43, Speaker of the House of Lords 1642, born at Baynard's Castle, London 1 Dec. 1595 and died at Penshurst, Kent 2 Nov. 1677. He married secretly in Jan. 1614/15,

2051. LADY DOROTHY PERCY, baptized at Petworth, Sussex 20 Aug. 1598 and died at Penshurst 20 Aug. 1659.

2052. JOHN DIGBY, 1ST EARL OF BRISTOL, P.C. (1616-25 AND 1640/41), M.P. [as Sir John Digby] 1610-11, Gentleman of the Privy Chamber and Carver to HM King James I, Gentleman of the Privy Chamber to HRH The Prince of Wales (later HM King Charles I), Vice Chamberlain of the (Royal) Household 1616-25, Ambassador to Spain 1610-18 and 1622-24, The Netherlands 1619 and 1621, and Vienna 1621, baptized at Coleshill, Warwickshire 27 Feb. 1580 and died at Paris 21 Jan. 1652/53. He married at St. James's Church, Clerkenwell, Middlesex 31 May 1609,

2053. BEATRICE WALCOTT, baptized at North Lydbury, Shropshire 13 March 1574 and died 12 Sept. 1658; buried at Sherborne, Dorset. She married, 1st, at the Church of St. Mary-le-Bow, London 18 Jan. 1598/99, Sir John Dyve of Bromham, Bedfordshire.

2054. Francis Russell, 4th Earl of Bedford, P.C. (1641), Lord Lieutenant of Devonshire 1623-41, drained the Fens ("the Bedford level") in Northamptonshire, Cambridgeshire, Huntingdonshire, Norfolk, and Lincolnshire, born in 1593 and died 9 May 1641; buried at Chenies, Buckinghamshire. He married at the Church of St. Mary le Strand, London 26 Feb. 1608/9,

2055. Hon. Catherine Brydges, born in 1580 and died 29 Jan. 1656/57; buried at Chenies.

2056. John Churchill of Newton Montacute, Wootton Glanville, Dorset, a deputy Registrar of Chancery, born ca. 1587 and died 6 April 1659. He married, 2nd, in 1644, Mary ——, who died after 1677. He married, 1st, at the Church of St. Stephen Walbrook, London 30 Sept. 1618,

2057. Sarah Winston, died by 1644.

2058. Sir John Drake of Ashe, Devonshire, died 25 Aug. 1636. He married at the Church of St. Giles-in-the-Fields, Holborn, Middlesex 18 May 1616,

2059. Hon. Eleanor Boteler, died 2 Oct. 1666; buried at Holyrood Church, Southampton.

2060. Sir John Jennings, K.B. (1625/26), M.P. 1627/28 and 1640, died before 9 Aug. 1642. He married,

2061. Alice Spencer of Offley, Hertfordshire.

2062. Sir Gifford Thornhurst, 1st Baronet, died 16 Dec. 1627; buried at Allington, Kent. He married there 16 Sept. 1627,

2063. Susan Temple, Maid of Honour to HM Queen Anne, buried at Burwell, Lincolnshire in Nov. 1669. She married, 2nd, at St. Bride's Church, Fleet Street, London 9 Dec. 1633, **Sir Martin Lister [No. 2738].**

2064. Right Hon. Sir George de Carteret, 1st Baronet, P.C. (1660-79), M.P. 1661, Vice Chamberlain of the (Royal) Household 1660-80, Comptroller of the Navy 1641-42, Lieutenant Governor of Jersey 1643-51, Vice Admiral 1644-47, Treasurer of the Navy 1660-67, Lord Proprietor of Carolina 1663-80, a Lord of the Admiralty 1673-79, born at Broad Street, St. Helier, Jersey 6 May 1610 and died at Whitehall, London 14 Jan. 1679/80. He married 6 May 1640,

2065. ELIZABETH DE CARTERET, apparently granted the precedence of a peer's widow 14 Feb. 1680, will proved in Feb. 1700.

2066. EDWARD MONTAGU, 1ST EARL OF SANDWICH, K.G. (1661), P.C. (1657 AND 1660), M.P. [as Edward Montagu] 1645, 1653, 1654/55, 1656–57, and 1660, Master of the Great Wardrobe 1660–70, bore St. Edward's Staff at the coronation of HM King Charles II 1661, Lord President of the Council of State 1653, a Lord Commissioner of the Treasury 1654–59, joint General-at-Sea 1655/56 and 1659/60, summoned to Cromwell's "House of Lords" 1657, Admiral and Captain-General of the Narrow Seas 1660/61, ambassador extraordinary and plenipotentiary to Portugal to bring Queen Catherine to England and arrange for the surrender of Tangiers 1661, Admiral of the Blue 1664 and 1672, Commander-in-Chief 1665, Ambassador to Madrid 1666–68, born at Barnwell, Northamptonshire 27 July 1625 and died off Southwold Bay, Suffolk 28 May 1672. He married at St. Margaret's Church, Westminster, Middlesex 7 Nov. 1642,
2067. HON. JEMIMA CREW, born 17 July 1625 and died at Cotehele, Cornwall in 1674.

2068. GENERAL SIR BEVIL GRENVILLE, M.P. 1621/22, 1624/25, 1626, 1628/29, and 1640–42, born 23, baptized at Kilkhampton, Cornwall 25 March 1595 and killed at Lansdown, Somerset 5 July 1643. He married,
2069. GRACE SMYTHE, baptized at Heavitree, Devonshire 22 Feb. 1601 and buried at Kilkhampton 8 June 1647.

2070. RIGHT HON. SIR PETER WYCHE, P.C. (1641), Gentleman of the Privy Chamber 1628, Ambassador to the Porte 1627–40, Comptroller of the (Royal) Household 1641, died at Oxford 5 Dec. 1643. He married 17 April 1627,
2071. JANE MEREDITH, died 5 Dec. 1660.

2072. SIR HENRY WORSLEY, 2ND BARONET, M.P. 1640, 1660, and 1661–66, born 31 May 1613 and died at Compton, Hampshire 11 Sept. 1666. He married 4 June 1632,
2073. BRIDGET WALLOP, died before 1676.

2074. HON. JAMES HERBERT, M.P. 1646–48, 1659, 1660, and 1661–67, baptized at St. Andrew's Church, Enfield, Middlesex 12 Nov. 1623 and died

4 April 1677; buried at St. Mary's Church, Thame, Oxfordshire. He married at St. Peter's Church, Paul's Wharf, London 3 Aug. 1646,

2075. JANE SPILLER, baptized at the Church of St. Martin-in-the-Fields, Westminster, Middlesex 19 Feb. 1624/25 and died in 1695.

2076. SIR HENRY FREDERICK THYNNE, 1ST BARONET, born 1 March 1614/15 and died at Oxford 6 March 1679/80. He married,

2077. HON. MARY COVENTRY, baptized at St. Bride's Church, Fleet Street, London 1 March 1618.

2078. HENEAGE FINCH, 3RD EARL OF WINCHILSEA, Governor of Dover 1660, representative of the Levant Company in Constantinople [regarded as the English Ambassador] 1660-69, Lord Lieutenant of Kent 1660-62, 1667/68, 1673-87, and 1689, and Somerset 1675-83, born ca. 1627 and died 28 Aug. 1689; buried at Eastwell, Kent. He married, 1st, at Church of St. Giles-in-the-Fields, Holborn, Middlesex 21 May 1645, Hon. Diana Willoughby, who was buried at Eastwell 27 March 1648, daughter of Francis Willoughby, 5th Baron Willoughby, and Hon. Elizabeth Cecil, daughter of Edward Cecil, 1st Viscount Wimbledon. He married, 3rd, at St. Andrew's Church, Holborn 10 April 1673, Catherine Norcliff, who died shortly after Aug. 1678, formerly wife of i) Christopher Lister and widow of ii) Sir John Wentworth, and daughter of Sir Thomas Norcliff and Hon. Dorothy Fairfax, daughter of Thomas Fairfax, 1st Viscount Fairfax. He married, 4th (Vicar-General's license to marry at the Church of St. Catherine Colman, London dated 29 Oct. 1681), Elizabeth Ayres, born ca. 1661 and died 10 April 1745, daughter of John Ayres. He married, 2nd, by 1649,

2079. LADY MARY SEYMOUR, died at Eastwell 20 Nov. 1672.

2080. WILLIAM POYNTZ of Woodhatch, Reigate, Surrey, born posthumously ca. 1545 and died before 25 April 1601. He married at Reigate 23 May 1569,

2081. ELIZABETH NEWDIGATE of Wivelsfield, Sussex, died between 5 May 1601 and 17 June 1602.

2082. JOHN SYDENHAM of Nympsfield, Gloucestershire, died between 21 Nov. 1590 and 5 Jan. 1590/91. He married,

2083. MARY POYNTZ, buried at Iron Acton, Gloucestershire 7 Oct. 1591. She married, 1st, Francis Codrington, who died before 28 Oct. 1581.

2084. RICHARD PARKYNS, M.P. 1584, 1586, 1589, and 1593, died at Bunny, Nottinghamshire 3 July 1603. He married,

2085. ELIZABETH BERESFORD, died 8 April 1608. She married, 1st, Humphrey Barlow, who died in June 1570.

2086-2091. ——.

2092. WILLIAM DEANE of Guiting, Gloucestershire, married,

2093. MARGARET WYKHAM, buried at Guiting Power 3 June 1602.

2094. CHRISTOPHER WACE, goldsmith, buried at St. Vedast's Church, Foster Lane, London 1 Oct. 1605. He married at Bacton, Suffolk 21 Aug. 1580,

2095. ANNE PRETTYMAN, baptized at Bacton 20 Jan. 1562/63 and buried at Lavington, Lincolnshire 2 May 1619. She married, 2nd, at the Church of St. Augustine Farringdon Within, London 9 March 1606/7, Sir William Armine, born ca. May 1562 and died 22 Jan. 1620/21, son of Bartholomew Armine and Mary Sutton.

2096. HENRY MORDAUNT, 4TH BARON MORDAUNT, born ca. 1568 and died 13 Feb. 1608/9; buried at Turvey, Bedfordshire. He married before 1 Oct. 1593,

2097. HON. MARGARET COMPTON, died before 13 Feb. 1644/45.

2098. WILLIAM HOWARD, 3RD BARON HOWARD, M.P. [as Hon. William Howard and Hon. Sir William Howard] 1597 and [Lord Howard by courtesy] 1601, summoned to Parliament in his father's barony 1603/4, born at Reigate, Surrey 27 Dec. 1577 and died at Hampton, Middlesex 28 Nov. 1615. He married at Chelsea, Middlesex 7 Feb. 1596/97,

2099. HON. ANNE ST. JOHN, died at St. Bartholomew's Close, London 7 June 1638.

2100. ROBERT CAREY, 1ST EARL OF MONMOUTH, M.P. [as Hon. Robert Carey] 1586/87 and 1588/89 and [as Hon. Sir Robert Carey] 1593, 1597-98, 1601, and 1620-22, Gentleman of the Bedchamber to HM King James I 1603, Gentleman of the Privy Chamber to HM 1603, Master of the Household to HRH The Prince of Wales (later HM King Charles I), Master of the Robes to HRH 1611, Chamberlain to HRH 1617-25, envoy to the Duc d'Alençon 1581 and to Scotland 1583, 1588 [when he pacified HM King James VI after his mother's execution], and 1593, announced the death of HM Queen Elizabeth I to her successor 1603, born in 1560 and died at Moor Park, Hertfordshire 12 April 1639. He married at Berwick-on-Tweed 20 Aug. 1593,

2101. ELIZABETH TREVANION, died before July 1641; buried at Rickmansworth, Hertfordshire. She married, 1st, Sir Henry Widdrington, who died before 15 Feb. 1592/93, son of Sir John Widdrington and Agnes Metcalfe.

2102. THOMAS SMITH, M.P. 1588-89 and 1593, Master of Requests 1608-9, born ca. 1556 and died at Fulham, Middlesex 28 Nov. 1609. He married by 1604,

2103. HON. FRANCES BRYDGES, born in 1580 and died before 17 July 1663.

2104-2107. ——.

2108. THOMAS LUNSFORD, buried at East Hoathly, Sussex 4 Nov. 1637. He married at Bearsted, Kent 7 March 1602,

2109. KATHERINE FLUDD, baptized at Bearsted 5 Dec. 1579 and buried at East Hoathly 19 May 1642.

2110. SIR HENRY NEVILLE, M.P. 1614 and 1621/22, born ca. 1588 and died 29 June 1629. He married at the Church of St. Margaret Lothbury, London 2 May 1609,

2111. ELIZABETH SMYTHE, died in Sept. 1669. She married, 2nd, Sir John Thoroughgood, who was buried at Clerkenwell, Middlesex 31 Jan. 1656/57.

2112. SIR GEORGE BINGHAM, Governor of Sligo, died in June 1595. He married in 1569,

2113. CICELY MARTIN of Athelhampton, Dorset, died in 1598.

2114. JOHN BYRNE of Ballinclough, Wicklow, married,
2115. CECILIA O'BYRNE.

2116. SIR HUGH MIDDLETON, 1ST BARONET, M.P. 1604-11, 1614, 1621-22, 1624-25, 1626, and 1628-29, Governor of the New River Company, born at Galch Hill, Henllan, Denbighshire ca. 1560 and died at Basinghall Street, London 7 Dec. 1631. He married, 1st, Anne Collins, who died 11 Jan. 1596/97, widow of Richard Edwards, and daughter of Richard Collins. He married, 2nd, by 1598,

2117. ELIZABETH OLMSTEAD, born ca. 1580 and died at Bush Hill, Edmonton, Middlesex 19 Dec. 1643.

2118. SIR THOMAS HARRIS, 1ST BARONET, Sheriff of Shropshire 1618/19, buried at Baschurch, Shropshire 27 Jan. 1627/28. He married, 1st, Sarah Kyffin. He married, 2nd, at St. Alkmond's Church, Shrewsbury 31 Jan. 1592/93,

2119. SARAH JONES, buried at Baschurch 9 April 1641.

2120-2127. ——.

2128. WILLIAM VESEY, who fled to Scotland after killing a man in a duel, married ca. 1600,

2129. —— KER.

2130. REV. GERVAISE WALKER of Londonderry married,

2131. ——.

2132. WILLIAM MUSCHAMP, M.P. 1624-25, baptized at Shalford, Surrey 4 Nov. 1593 and buried 7 Nov. 1660. He married,

2133. FRANCES LISLE of Bridleford, Isle of Wight, buried 26 Feb. 1676/77.

2134-2135. ——.

2136. PETER SARSFIELD of Tully, Kildare, born ca. 1590 and died ca. 29 March 1661. He married,

2137. HON. ELEANOR O'DEMPSEY.

2138. COLONEL RORY O'MORE of Ballina, Cadamstown, Kildare, died 16 Feb. 1654/55. He married,

2139. JANE BARNEWALL of Turvey, Lusk, Dublin.

2140. JOHN TAAFFE, 1ST VISCOUNT TAAFFE, died shortly before 9 Jan. 1641/42; buried at Ballymote, Sligo. He married,
2141. HON. ANNE DILLON.

2142. WILLIAM WALTER of Roche Castle, Pembrokeshire, born in 1605 and died in Feb. 1649/50. He married (separated in 1640),
2143. ELIZABETH PROTHEROE, born in 1606 and died in 1652.

2144-2175. ——.

2176. SIR EDWARD SEYMOUR, 2ND BARONET, M.P. 1601, 1604-11, 1614, 1621-22, and 1624-25, Ambassador to Denmark 1603, Governor of Dartmouth 1613, born ca. 1580 and died at Berry Pomeroy, Devonshire 5 Oct. 1659. He married at the Church of St. Margaret Lothbury, London 15 Dec. 1600,
2177. DOROTHY KILLIGREW, buried at Berry Pomeroy 30 June 1643.

2178. SIR JOHN PORTMAN, 1ST BARONET, Sheriff of Somerset 1606, died 4 Dec. 1612. He married at Goathurst, Somerset 4 Jan. 1594/95,
2179. ANNE GIFFORD, died at Wellow, Somerset 11 Feb. 1637/38. She married, 2nd, at North Curry, Somerset in 1619, Edward Popham, born in 1582 and died before 7 March 1640/41, son of Alexander Popham and Dulcibella Bayly.

2180. SIR FRANCIS POPHAM, M.P. 1597, 1604, 1614, 1621, 1624, 1625, 1626, 1628, and 1640, member of the Virginia and New England Companies, born ca. 1570 and died 28 July 1644. He married,
2181. ANNE DUDLEY, born 12, baptized at St. Mary's Church, Stoke Newington, Middlesex 24 Feb. 1574/75.

2182. WILLIAM KERR of Linton, Roxburghshire, Groom of the Bedchamber to TM King James I and King Charles I, living in 1640. He married,
2183. ISABEL KERR of Littledean, Roxburghshire.

2184. JOHN SHORTER of Staines, Middlesex, died between 8 and 16 May 1634. He married,
2185. SUSAN FORBIS ALIAS FOREBANK of Senn, Surrey.

2186. JOHN BIRKETT, baptized at Crosthwaite, Cumberland 28 June 1600 and buried there 12 Oct. 1645. He married, 1st, at Crosthwaite 24 Jan. 1622/23, Frances Wilson. He married, 2nd, at Crosthwaite 23 April 1629,
2187. ELIZABETH ROBINSON.

2188. SIR RICHARD PHILIPPS, 2ND BARONET, Sheriff of Pembrokeshire 1632-33 and Carmarthenshire 1640-41, died before 7 Aug. 1648. He married, 2nd, Katherine Oxenbridge, widow of i) John Fowler and ii) George Henley, and daughter of Dr. Daniel Oxenbridge and Katherine Harby. He married, 1st,
2189. ELIZABETH DRYDEN.

2190. EDWARD DARCY, baptized at St. Anne's Church, Blackfriars, London 16 Feb. 1609. He married, 1st, at St. Anne's Church 24 Oct. 1632, Elizabeth Evelyn, born in 1614 and died 24 Dec. 1634, daughter of Richard Evelyn and Eleanor Stansfield. He married, 2nd,
2191. LADY ELIZABETH STANHOPE.

2192. HM KING CHARLES I, KING OF ENGLAND, SCOTLAND, AND IRELAND, born at Dunfermline Palace, Fife 19 Nov. 1600 and executed at Whitehall, London 30 Jan. 1648/49. He married at Canterbury, Kent 13 June 1625,
2193. HRH PRINCESSE HENRIETTE MARIE DE FRANCE ET NAVARRE, born at the Palais du Louvre, Paris 25 Nov. 1609 and died at Colombes, near Paris 10 Sept. 1669.

2194. WILLIAM VILLIERS, 2ND VISCOUNT GRANDISON, born in 1614 and died at Oxford 30 Sept. 1643, great-nephew and heir of Oliver St. John, 1st Viscount Grandison. He married at St. Margaret's Church, Westminster, Middlesex 31 Oct. 1639,
2195. HON. MARY BAYNING, baptized at St. Olave's Church, Hart Street, London 24 April 1624 and died before 26 Jan. 1671/72. She married, 2nd, at the Church of St. Bartholomew-the-Less, London 25 April 1648, Charles Villiers, 2nd Earl of Anglesey, born ca. 1627 and died 4 Feb. 1660/61, son of Christopher Villiers, 1st Earl of Anglesey [No. 2886], and Elizabeth Sheldon [No. 2887]. She married, 3rd, Arthur Gorges, who died 18 April 1668, son of Sir Arthur Gorges and Elizabeth Chauncy.

HM King Charles I,
King of England, Scotland, and Ireland
Born at Dunfermline, Fife 19 November 1600
Died at London 30 January 1648/49
Married at Canterbury, Kent 13 June 1625
HRH Princesse Henriette Marie de France et Navarre

Upon the death of his older brother Henry in 1612, Charles became heir apparent, and in November 1616 he was created Prince of Wales in an extravagant celebration at Whitehall. In 1623, the Prince secretly visited Spain to arrange a marriage with the Infanta María, daughter of King Philip III. The mission failed largely because of Spanish insistence that Charles become a Roman Catholic. He then joined the Duke of Buckingham, his father's favourite, in seeking war with Spain. In the meantime his marriage was arranged with Princess Henrietta Maria, sister of King Louis XIII of France.

On 27 March 1625, Charles succeeded his father as King of England, Scotland, and Ireland, faithfully following his father's deathbed advice to defend the church, protect his sister Elizabeth [the embattled "Winter Queen" of Bohemia], and remain loyal to Buckingham. In June, Charles married Henrietta Maria, a pious Roman Catholic who refused to abandon her religion. When the new King convened his first Parliament, some members complained that the commander chosen to lead the Spanish campaign – Buckingham, now Charles' favourite – was too inexperienced. A recalcitrant Parliament granted Charles two subsidies, far less than he needed for a campaign against Spain, and the subsequent failure of a naval expedition against Cádiz was the predictable outcome of inadequate funding.

The second Parliament of his reign was even more embattled. Buckingham was blamed for losses to the Spaniards; to avoid the Duke's impeachment for treason, Charles dissolved Parliament without the war funding he needed. Now in desperate straits, the King imposed a forced loan, moderately successful but widely unpopular. Before Charles' third Parliament Buckingham's expedition to aid French Protestants had been decisively repelled and the King's government was thoroughly discredited. The House of Commons passed resolutions condemning arbitrary taxation and imprisonment, then outlined its grievances in the Petition of Right. The King resisted this petition, but finally gave his formal consent in exchange for subsidies. By the fourth Parliament in January 1629, Buckingham had been assassinated. The

Commons now objected both to "popish practices" in the churches and levying tonnage and poundage (granted to every monarch since Henry VIII) without its consent. After three resolutions condemning his conduct, the King ordered Parliament's adjournment in March 1629. In order not to depend on parliamentary grants, Charles made peace with both France and Spain. With trade expanding, customs duties and traditional Crown dues produced annual revenues adequate in peacetime. Charles I relied heavily on Richard Weston (later 1st Earl of Portland), the Lord Treasurer, to rebuild the Crown's credit.

For eleven years, Charles was able to rule without recalling Parliament. These years were certainly the happiest of his life. Buckingham's death turned Charles inward and made him seek love and counsel from his wife. The birth of two healthy sons in 1630 and 1633 fulfilled a major obligation and allowed him to enjoy the peace and prosperity of that decade.

Charles was viewed as an absentee king by his Scottish subjects. In 1637, he intensified church reform there by imposing a liturgy based on the English Book of Common Prayer. Although approved by a committee of Scottish bishops, this liturgy met strong resistance among the lesser clergy and the laity. When many Scots signed a covenant to defend their Presbyterian religion, Charles interpreted these actions as undermining royal prerogatives. His army marched north to meet a well-organized Scottish Covenanting army. Before his generals reached York in March 1639 the first of the Bishops' Wars was already lost; Charles's army was unable to penetrate the Scottish defenses. On advice from his two closest advisors – William Laud, Archbishop of Canterbury, and Thomas Wentworth, 1st Earl of Strafford, Lord Deputy in Ireland – Charles summoned the Parliament of April 1640 to raise money for the war against Scotland. John Pym's opening speech in the Commons was a litany of grievances against the government, so Charles offered a compromise: subsidies for his Scottish war in return for the permanent abolition of ship money. Objections were raised, and Charles, convinced that his proposal would not be accepted, dissolved Parliament on 5 May. A Scottish army occupied Newcastle in August. Charles, disturbed by his inability to muster enough support to quell the Scots, convened a council of peers on whose advice he summoned another Parliament (the "Long Parliament"), which met at Westminster in November 1640.

The new Parliament proved more uncooperative than the last, passing a bill that abolished the sovereign's right to dissolve Parliament without its consent, condemning Charles's recent actions, and preparing to impeach Strafford and Laud. Charles made many concessions, agreeing to Parliament's meeting every three years, but expressed his resolve to save Strafford. Strafford, who had assembled a standing army in Ireland loyal to the King, was found guilty of treason, however, and beheaded on 12 May 1641. Charles also accepted bills declaring ship money and other arbitrary fiscal measures illegal, and condemning his government of the past eleven years. But Charles also visited Scotland in August to enlist anti-parliamentary support. During his visit he agreed to the full establishment of Presbyterianism in Scotland and allowed the Scottish estates to nominate royal officials.

In November 1641 Parliament learned of a rebellion in Ireland. The leaders of the Commons, fearing that an army raised to repress the Irish rebellion would be used against them, planned to make the King agree to a militia bill. When asked to surrender his command of the army, Charles refused. Fearing the impeachment (spearheaded by Pym) of his Catholic Queen, Charles ordered the arrest of one member of the House of Lords and five members in the Commons, including Pym. The members Charles sought escaped, however, and Parliament gained political and economic support in London. The King fled to the north of England in January 1641/42, while the Queen went to Holland in February to raise funds by pawning the crown jewels.

During the next two months Royalists and Parliamentarians mustered troops and collected arms. Charles settled in York in April, gradually joined by royalists of both houses. In June, the majority of members in London sent the King nineteen propositions, including demands that no ministers be appointed without parliamentary approval, that the army be put under parliamentary control, and that Parliament decide the future of the church. Charles realized that these proposals were an ultimatum. He formally raised the royal standard at Nottingham on 22 August 1642, and sporadic fighting soon spread throughout the kingdom. In September, the Earl of Essex, commanding Parliamentarian forces, left London for the midlands, while Charles moved to Shrewsbury. During a battle fought at Edgehill near Warwick on 23 October, Charles I proved a brave man but no general, and he was greatly disheartened by the slaughter on the battlefield.

The royal cause prospered during the next year, especially in Yorkshire and the southwest. At Oxford, where Charles moved his court and military headquarters, he was briefly joined by his Queen, who, having sold some jewels, bought a shipload of arms from Holland. In late summer, John Pym made a Parliamentary alliance with Scottish Covenanters, granting freedom for the Presbyterian Church in

Scotland. The entry of a Scottish army into England in January 1644 put the King's armies on the defensive. Charles lost the north at the battle of Marston Moor in July but held Oxford, the west, and the southwest. The King's forces had the upper hand for about a year, as Charles's nephew, Prince Rupert of the Rhine, undertook cavalry raids that captured Parliamentary strongholds. A short truce at the end of the year collapsed when Charles rejected Parliament's proposal for a new government; he was cheered by the reports of dissension among the Parliamentary ranks.

The following spring Charles sent his eldest son into the west, where the Prince escaped to France and joined his mother, Henrietta Maria. On 14 June 1645, the highly disciplined New Model Army – organized and commanded by Sir Thomas Fairfax, with Oliver Cromwell as second in command – defeated the King and Prince Rupert at the Battle of Naseby, the first in a series of Royalist defeats through the summer and fall. Charles returned to Oxford in November; by spring 1646 the city was surrounded. The King escaped in disguise late in April and arrived at the Scots Covenanters' camp at Newark on 5 May. But when the Covenanters made another alliance with Parliament in January 1647, they delivered King Charles to Parliamentary commissioners. Held in Northamptonshire, he hoped quarrels between the New Model Army and Parliament would allow him to ally with one side or the other to regain his power. In June, he was seized and taken to army headquarters at Newmarket. When the army reached London in August, the King was moved to Hampton Court.

Charles escaped in November, but plans to take him to France backfired and instead Charles landed on the Isle of Wight, where the governor, loyal to Parliament, kept him under house arrest at Carisbrooke Castle. There Charles conducted simultaneous negotiations with army leaders, Parliament, and the Scots. In a secret understanding of 26 December 1647, the Scots offered to support the King's restoration to power in return for acceptance of Presbyterianism in Scotland and its establishment in England. Charles refused terms offered by Parliament and was put under closer guard.

On 17 August 1648, the army of the Engagers, the King's Scottish supporters, was defeated at the Battle of Preston. Army leaders began to demand that the King be tried for treason. Until this time Parliament had been content to keep Charles in their custody, but the threat that Charles would continue trying to regain power was too much of a burden, and the King was brought to Hurst Castle in Hampshire at the end of 1648 and then transported to Windsor Castle. On 20 January

1648/49, he was brought before a specially constituted High Court of Justice in Westminster and charged with high treason and other crimes against the realm of England. His steadfast refusal to recognize the court's legality or to plead only hastened the sentence of death, pronounced on 27 January. Charles was taken to a scaffold across from the Banqueting Hall of Whitehall on the morning of Tuesday, 30 January 1648/49, where he bravely met his death. In 1660, the Restoration Parliament declared Charles a martyr, added his name to the calendar of Anglican saints, and ordered that prayers be said on each 30 January in his memory.

2196. SIR JOHN BENNET, born ca. 1589 and buried 16 Nov. 1658. He married at the Church of St. Peter-le-Poer, London 26 June 1615,
2197. DOROTHY CROFTS of Saxham Parva, Sussex.

2198. LODEWIJK VAN NASSAU, HEER VAN LEK EN BEVERWEERD, Governor of Bergen-op-Zoom 1643 and Den Bosch 1658, Dutch Ambassador to London 1660, born ca. 1602 and died at The Hague 28 Feb. 1665. He married ca. 7 April 1630,
2199. ELISABETH GRAVIN VAN HOORNES, buried at Ouderkerk on the Ijssel 7 May 1664.

2200. EDWARD SOMERSET, 2ND MARQUESS OF WORCESTER, Lieutenant General of South Wales and Monmouth 1643, signed the "Glamorgan Treaty" making concessions to the Catholics in Ireland 1645 [for which he was imprisoned], General of the forces in Munster 1646-47, born at Raglan Castle, Monmouthshire ca. 9 March 1602/3 and died at Worcester House in the Strand, near London 3 April 1667. He married, 2nd, in Aug. 1639, Lady Margaret O'Brien, who died 26 July 1681, daughter of Henry O'Brien, 5th Earl of Thomond, and Hon. Mary Brereton, daughter of William Brereton, 1st Baron Brereton. He married, 1st, ca. 1628,
2201. ELIZABETH DORMER, died at Worcester House 31 May 1635.

2202. ARTHUR CAPELL, 1ST BARON CAPELL, P.C. (1644/45), M.P. [as Arthur Capell] 1640-41, Lieutenant General of Shropshire, Cheshire, and North Wales, born at Hadham Parva, Hertfordshire 20 Feb. 1603/4 and executed [with James Hamilton, 1st Duke of Hamilton (No. 5342), and Henry

Rich, 1st Earl of Holland (No. 6034)] at Palace Yard, Westminster, Middlesex 9 March 1648/49. He married 28 Nov. 1627,

2203. ELIZABETH MORRISON, baptized at St. Mary's Church, Watford, Hertfordshire 12 March 1610 and died 26 Jan. 1660/61; buried at Hadham.

2204. RICHARD CHILD, merchant and weaver of London, died between 5 and 25 May 1639. He married,

2205. ELIZABETH ROYCROFT of Weston Wick, Shropshire.

2206. WILLIAM ATWOOD, merchant of Hackney, Middlesex, died between 27 Sept. 1689 and 21 March 1689/90. He married at the Church of St. Michael Bassishaw, London 26 Feb. 1636/37,

2207. MARY HAMPTON of Leigh, Essex.

2208. SIR HENRY WALDEGRAVE, 2ND BARONET, born in 1598 and died 10 Oct. 1658; buried at Cossey, Norfolk. He married, 2nd, Catherine Bacon, who died before 4 April 1695, daughter of Richard Bacon of Stiffkey, Norfolk. He married, 1st,

2209. ANNE PASTON of Appleton, Norfolk.

2210. SIR FRANCIS ENGLEFIELD, 2ND BARONET, died at Englefield, Berkshire 1 May 1656. He married,

2211. WINIFRED BROOKSBY, died 25 June 1672.

2212. HM KING CHARLES I, KING OF ENGLAND, SCOTLAND, AND IRELAND = 2192.
2213. HRH PRINCESSE HENRIETTE MARIE DE FRANCE ET NAVARRE = 2193.

2214. SIR WINSTON CHURCHILL = 1028.
2215. ELIZABETH DRAKE = 1029.

2216. SIR JOHN WEBB, 1ST BARONET, died before 6 May 1681; buried at Odstock, Wiltshire. He married,
2217. MARY CARYLL, died in 1661.

2218. JOHN BLOMER, died 28 Dec. 1638; buried at Hatherop, Gloucestershire. He married,
2219. HON. FRANCES BROWNE, died in 1657.

2220. THOMAS BELASYSE, 1ST VISCOUNT FAUCONBERG, M.P. [as Thomas Belasyse] 1597/98 and [as Sir Thomas Belasyse] 1614, 1621, and 1624, born in 1577 and died 18 April 1653; buried at Coxwold, Yorkshire. He married ca. 1600,
2221. BARBARA CHOLMLEY, died 28 Feb. 1618/19; buried at Coxwold.

2222. JOHN PAULET, 5TH MARQUESS OF WINCHESTER, M.P. [as Lord John Paulet and Lord St. John] 1621-24, summoned to Parliament in his father's barony of St. John 1623/24, held Basing House 1643-45 [when Cromwell's New Model Army burned the house, and some of its inhabitants, to the ground], born ca. 1598 and died 5 March 1674/75; buried at Englefield, Berkshire. He married, 1st, **LADY JANE SAVAGE [No. 6101].** He married, 3rd, before 30 April 1669, Lady Isabella Theresa Lucy Howard, born in 1644 and died 2 Sept. 1691, daughter of Willliam Howard, 1st Viscount Stafford, and Mary Stafford, Countess of Stafford for life. He married, 2nd, ca. 4 Oct. 1633,
2223. LADY HONORA DE BURGH, born 19 Aug. 1610 and died 10 March 1661/62.

2224. LIEUT. COLONEL SIR EDWARD WALPOLE, K.B. (1661), M.P. 1660 and 1661-68, baptized 16 Nov. 1621 and died 18 March 1667/68. He married ca. 1649,
2225. SUSAN CRANE, born 26 May 1630 and died 7 July 1667; buried at Houghton, Norfolk.

2226. SIR GEOFFREY BURWELL, baptized at Woodbridge, Suffolk 20 July 1606 and died 6 July 1684; buried at Rougham, Suffolk. He married,
2227. ELIZABETH DEREHAUGH, born 25 March 1614 and died 24 Oct. 1678; buried at Rougham.

2228. SIR JOHN SHORTER = 1092.
2229. ISABELLA BIRKETT = 1093.

2230. SIR ERASMUS PHILIPPS, 3RD BARONET = 1094.
2231. CATHERINE DARCY = 1095.

2232-2239. ——.

2240. WALTER PALK married,
2241. ——.

2242-2255. ——.

2256. JOHANN WILHELM VAN SITTART, born in 1582 and died in Jan. 1631. He married in 1616,
2257. ANNE ROBOAN of Danzig, died in May 1655. She married, 2nd, in 1634, Stephen Kayser.

2258. WINHOLT JUNCKER married,
2259. ——.

2260-2263. ——.

2264. SIR GEORGE STONHOUSE, 3RD BARONET, M.P. 1640-44 and 1660-75, baptized at Radley, Berkshire 28 Aug. 1603 and died 31 March 1675; buried at Radley. He married (Archdeacon of Berkshire's license to marry at Hurley dated 22 April 1633),
2265. HON. MARGARET LOVELACE, died before 1693.

2266. ROBERT BRIGGES, merchant, buried at Shiffnal, Shropshire 27 Jan. 1701/2. He married,
2267. SARAH MORETON, baptized at Sheriff Hales, Shropshire 30 May 1624 and buried at Shiffnal 30 March 1699.

2268. GEORGE MELLISH, merchant taylor and draper, buried at Sander-stead, Surrey 10 May 1654. He married, 1st, Catherine Clarke, daughter of Richard Clarke. He married, 2nd, ca. 1617,

2269. MARY KYNNERSLEY. She married, 1st, at the Church of St. Dunstan-in-the-East, London 6 Feb. 1614/15, William Baker of Swindon, Wiltshire.

2270. JOHN GODEN of London married,
2271. ——.

2272. SIR JOHN VAUGHAN, M.P. 1628, 1640-45, and 1661-68, Chief Justice of the Common Pleas 1668, born at Trawscoed, Cardiganshire 14 Sept. 1603 and died at Serjeant's Inn, London 10 Dec. 1674. He married ca. 1624,
2273. JANE STEDMAN, died in 1680.

2274. SIR WILLIAM HOOKER, Lord Mayor of London 1673/74, Master of the Grocers' Company 1679-80, born in 1612 and died 10 July 1697. He married, 2nd, at St. James's Church, Clerkenwell, Middlesex 14 Oct. 1673, Susan Bendish, daughter of Sir Thomas Bendish and Anne Baker. He married, 1st, at the Church of St. Margaret Lothbury, London 10 Nov. 1640,
2275. LETTICE COPINGER, baptized at St. Dunstan's Church, Stepney, Middlesex 26 April 1609 and died before 14 Oct. 1673. She married, 1st, Paul Barneby.

2276. HENRY WILMOT, 1ST EARL OF ROCHESTER, P.C. (1650), M.P. [as Hon. Henry Wilmot] 1640, Lord of the Bedchamber to HM King Charles II 1649, Lieutenant General 1643, Lord President of Connaught 1644, envoy to the Duc de Lorraine 1652, the Diet of the Empire 1652, the Elector of Brandenburg 1654, and Denmark 1655, baptized at the Church of St. Martin-in-the-Fields, Westminster, Middlesex 26 Oct. 1613 and died at Ghent 19 Feb. 1657/58. He married, 1st, at Chelsea, Middlesex 21 Aug. 1633, Frances Morton, born in 1600 and died before 7 Jan. 1643/44, daughter of Sir George Morton and Catherine Hopton. He married, 2nd, ca. 1644,
2277. ANNE ST. JOHN, born 5 Nov. 1614 and buried at Spelsbury, Oxfordshire 18 March 1695/96. She married, 1st, at Battersea, Surrey 2 Oct. 1632, Sir Henry Francis Lee, 2nd Baronet, baptized at Spelsbury 3 March 1615/16 and died 23 July 1639, son of Sir Henry Lee, 1st Baronet, and Eleanor Wortley.

2278. JOHN MALET of Enmore, Somerset, died in 1656. He married,
2279. HON. UNTON HAWLEY, died 12 Nov. 1698. She married, 2nd, ca. 1658, Sir John Warre, M.P. 1665-69, born 25 Dec. 1636 and died before 19 Oct. 1669, son of Roger Warre and Anne Wyndham.

2280. THOMAS WATSON, Mayor of Berwick 1649, 1650/51, 1666, and 1668–71, buried 8 Jan. 1693/94. He married at Berwick 31 July 1642,
2281. ELIZABETH SMITH.

2282. WILLIAM WEBB, Burgess of Berwick, married,
2283. ——.

2284–2287. ——.

2288. MARK SHAFTO, M.P. 1659, baptized at St. Nicholas' Church, Newcastle-upon-Tyne 25 March 1601 and died 25 Feb. 1659/60. He married at All Saints' Church, Newcastle 7 March 1630/31,
2289. MARY LEDGER, baptized at St. Nicholas' Church 17 Jan. 1614/15.

2290. SIR THOMAS WIDDRINGTON, M.P. 1640-61, Speaker of the House of Commons 1656-58, born at Stamfordham, Northumberland ca. 1600 and died 13 May 1664; buried at the Church of St. Giles-in-the-Fields, Holborn, Middlesex. He married at Holme-upon-Spalding-Moor, Yorkshire 13 Oct. 1634,
2291. HON. FRANCES FAIRFAX, born at Denton, Yorkshire 13 Dec. 1612 and died 4 May 1649.

2292. SIR WILLIAM INGLEBY, 1ST BARONET, born ca. 1603 and died 22 Jan. 1651/52; buried at Ripley, Yorkshire. He married at Heversham, Westmorland 15 May 1616,
2293. ANNE BELLINGHAM, died in 1640.

2294. JOHN SAVILE, High Sheriff of Yorkshire 1647, baptized at Elland, Yorkshire 13 Oct. 1588 and buried at Methley, Yorkshire 23 March 1658/59. He married, 1st, at Methley 7 Nov. 1626, Mary Robinson, who was buried there 7 May 1636, daughter of John Robinson and Susan Holden. He married, 2nd, at the Church of St. Peter-le-Poer, Broad Street, London 16 March 1636/37,
2295. MARGARET GARWAY, baptized at the Church of St. Peter-le-Poer 21 May 1615 and buried at Methley 9 April 1648.

2296–2303. ——.

2304. REV. FRANZ BARING, Superintendent General [i.e. Bishop] of Lauenberg 1565, born at Venlo, Limburg 1 Feb. 1522 and died at Lütau, near Lauenberg in 1589. He married, 1st, Magdalena Tuchters, who died at Krempe, Holstein in 1552, daughter of Johannes Tuchters of Neufkirchen, near Geldern, Rheinland. He married, 2nd, 17 Jan. 1554,

2305. MARGARETE BURGSTEDE of Buxtehude, Saxony.

2306. REV. JOHANN ERASMUS of Hude, Saxony, married,
2307. ——.

2308-2343. ——.

2344. CHRISTOPHER WATLINGTON, born posthumously after 10 Nov. 1558. He married,
2345. JOAN SHERWOOD.

2346-2347. ——.

2348. REV. THOMAS DILLINGHAM, buried at Over Dean, Bedfordshire 10 Dec. 1647. He married,
2349. ——.

2350. REV. DR. THOMAS PASKE, Master of Clare Hall, Cambridge 1621-45, died between 12 Sept. and 19 Nov. 1662. He married,
2351. ANNE ——.

2352-2355. ——.

2356. RICHARD HUTTON, baptized at Poppleton, Yorkshire 5 April 1613 and died 8 April 1648. He married, 1st, at St. Martin's Church, Coney Street, York 9 Jan. 1634, Ursula Sheffield, who died in 1634, daughter of Hon. Sir Edmund Sheffield. He married, 2nd,

2357. HON. DOROTHY FAIRFAX, born at Steeton, Yorkshire 4 June 1617 and died 7 June 1687.

2358. NICHOLAS STRINGER of Sutton-cum-Lound, Nottinghamshire, died in 1647. He married at Kelstern, Lincolnshire 5 March 1630/31,
2359. ALICE SOUTH, baptized at Kelstern 3 May 1608.

2360-2363. ——.

2364. RICHARD BUSHELL of Whitby, Yorkshire, died in 1644. He married at St. Cuthbert's Church, York 4 Aug. 1618,
2365. ISABEL ELLIS, died 4 March 1656/57.

2366. WILLIAM WIGGINER married at Whitby, Yorkshire 22 Nov. 1619,
2367. MARY URPWITH.

2368. HENRY LUKIN of Much Baddow, Essex, born in 1586 and died in 1630. He married, 1st, at Worksop, Nottinghamshire 22 Dec. 1618, Catherine D'Oyley, widow of Wortley Jessop and daughter of Dr. Thomas D'Oyley. He married, 2nd,
2369. HANNAH ——.

2370. ROBERT WOOD of Barnston, Boughton, and Parkers, Essex, married,
2371. ——.

2372. VICE ADMIRAL LIONEL LANE of Beccles, Suffolk, baptized at Thuxton, Norfolk in 1617 and died between 23 May and 18 Oct. 1654. He married,
2373. DOROTHEA BOHUN, baptized at Westhall, Suffolk 19 May 1618 and living in Dec. 1660.

2374. ROBERT YOUNG, baptized at Rayne, Essex 18 April 1634 and died after 7 March 1699/1700. He married at Little Dunmow, Essex 21 June 1655,
2375. MARY THURBAND of Barnston, Essex.

2376-2379. ——.

2380. EDWARD GOLDSTONE of Panfield, Essex, married before 15 Feb. 1627/28,
2381. MARY ——.

2382. ROBERT HOWCHIN, baptized at Panfield, Essex 3 Dec. 1618 and buried there 16 Feb. 1691/92. He married at Panfield 2 Dec. 1639,
2383. ESTHER ALLYN.

2384. ROBERT DOUGHTY of Aylsham, Norfolk, died before 22 April 1679. He married at the Church of St. Michael-at-Plea, Norwich 13 Aug. 1639,
2385. KATHERINE TOWNSHEND, buried at Aylsham 11 April 1661.

2386. CLIPSBY GUYBON, baptized at Oby, Norfolk 25 Jan. 1629/30 and living in 1694. He married 5 Sept. 1651,
2387. BRIDGET BLOFELD, buried at Oby 28 Aug. 1682.

2388. WILLIAM DOUGHTY of Hanworth, Norfolk, born ca. 1630 and died 8 March 1672/73. He married,
2389. BETHIA ——.

2390. ADRIAN PAYNE, Sheriff of Norwich 1670, baptized at the Church of St. Peter Mancroft, Norwich 18 May 1630 and buried at St. Giles' Church, Norwich 4 May 1686. He married at the Church of St. Mary-in-the-Marsh, Norwich 10 Oct. 1650,
2391. KATHERINE OSBORNE, buried at St. Giles' Church 5 Nov. 1720.

2392. REV. WILLIAM LEE, Rector of Fletton, Huntingdonshire 1635-52, married,
2393. ——.

2394-2399. ——.

2400. JEAN FRANÇOIS THELLUSSON, SEIGNEUR DE FLÉCHÈRES, born at Lyon 23 Aug. 1572 and died at Geneva 10 March 1648. He married at Geneva 8 Aug. 1598,

2401. Marie de Tudert de Mazières.

2402. Rev. Théodore Tronchin, born at Geneva 17 April 1582 and died there 17 Nov. 1657. He married at Choully, Switzerland 21 June 1607,
2403. Théodora Rocca, baptized 25 July 1591 and died 5 March 1674.

2404. Léonard Guiguer, merchant taylor, born at St. Gall, Bürglen in 1593 and died at Lyon 24 Sept. 1643. He married at Lyon in 1615,
2405. Marie Penin, born at Lyon 26 Nov. 1599 and died at Croix Rousse, Lyon 21 March 1679.

2406. Louis Tourton, notary, born at Boulieu-lès-Annonay, Ardèche 5 April 1612 and died at Annonay 16 Oct. 1674. He married before Oct. 1639,
2407. Jeanne Rancon, born at Annonay 23 Jan. 1613 and died at Geneva 12 Nov. 1693.

2408-2415. ——.

2416. John Woodford of Salisbury, died 6 Sept. 1670. He married,
2417. Mary Banks, living 26 Sept. 1674.

2418. Henry Langford of The Close, Salisbury, married,
2419. Mary ——.

2420-2423. ——.

2424. Richard Brideoak of Cheetham Hill, Manchester, married,
2425. Cicely Boardman.

2426. Sir Richard Saltonstall, born ca. 1596 and died 25 Feb. 1649/50; buried at South Ockendon, Essex. He married, 1st, at St. Leonard's Church, Shoreditch, Middlesex 18 June 1617, Elizabeth Bassano, born 8 June 1600 and died 21 April 1630, daughter of Jeronimo Bassano — court musician to TM Queen Elizabeth I, King James I, and King Charles I — and Dorothy Symonds. He married, 2nd,

2427. MARY PARKER, died before 21 May 1662.

2428–2431. ——.

2432. JAMES BULTEEL, Mayor of Barnstaple 1617, born at London in 1578 and died there in Oct. 1632. He married at Barnstaple, Devonshire 26 Oct. 1613,

2433. JULIAN PEARD, baptized at Barnstaple 30 March 1592 and buried there 6 Jan. 1630/31.

2434. WILLIAM KEKEWICH, baptized at St. Germans, Cornwall 20 Nov. 1595 and buried there 15 April 1634. He married at Morval, Cornwall 27 Jan. 1612/13,

2435. JANE COODE, buried at St. Germans 7 Dec. 1668.

2436–2439. ——.

2440. JOHN CROCKER of Lineham, Devonshire, born ca. 1587 and died before 16 Nov. 1646. He married, 2nd, at Broad Winsor, Dorset 11 Aug. 1613, Elizabeth Champernowne, daughter of Arthur Champernowne and Amy Crewkerne. He married, 1st,

2441. JOAN LEIGH, died before 15 Jan. 1633/34. She married, 1st, —— Webber alias Gilbert.

2442. SIR JOHN POLE, 1ST BARONET, M.P. 1626, Sheriff of Devonshire 1638–39, died at Bromley St. Leonard's, Middlesex 16 April 1658. He married, 2nd, after 1625, Mary ——. He married, 1st, at Shute, Devonshire 5 Jan. 1613/14,

2443. ELIZABETH HOW.

2444. RICHARD HILLERSDON of Membland, Devonshire, born ca. 1602 and died before 21 March 1658/59. He married (license dated at Exeter 11 June 1625),

2445. BRIDGET HARRIS of Lanrest, Cornwall.

2446. EDWARD NOSWORTHY, M.P. 1660, 1661, 1665, and 1679, baptized at Truro, Cornwall 18 Nov. 1610 and buried at St. Mary's Church, Truro 22 May 1686. He married 10 Sept. 1632,

2447. FRANCES HILL, baptized at Truro 13 July 1615 and died in 1663.

2448. JOHN DRUMMOND, 2ND EARL OF PERTH, P.C. (S.) (1616 AND 1625), born ca. 1584 and died 11 June 1662. He married (contract dated 4 and 28 Aug. 1613),

2449. LADY JEAN KER, died in Oct. 1622.

2450. HENRY KER, LORD KER by courtesy, died at Edinburgh 1 Feb. 1642/43. He married at Glamis, Angus 4 Feb. 1637/38,

2451. LADY MARGARET HAY, buried at the Church of St. Martin-in-the-Fields, Westminster, Middlesex 22 April 1695. She married, 2nd (contract dated 20 Feb. 1643/44), **JOHN KENNEDY, 6TH EARL OF CASSILIS [No. 5358].**

2452. CHARLES MOORE, 2ND VISCOUNT MOORE, P.C. (I.) (1627/28), Governor of Louth 1642, born in 1603 and died at Portlester, Meath 7 Aug. 1643. He married before 21 June 1626,

2453. HON. ALICE LOFTUS, died 13 June 1649; buried at St. Peter's Church, Drogheda.

2454. WILLIAM SPENCER, 2ND BARON SPENCER = 2048.
2455. LADY PENELOPE WRIOTHESLEY = 2049.

2456-2459. ——.

2460. ROWLAND HODGSON of Walkern, Hertfordshire, married,
2461. JOAN ——.

2462-2495. ——.

2496. EDWARD GREY of Howick, Nortumberland, died in 1653. He married,
2497. —— FENWICK of Butterley, Northumberland.

2498. EDWARD LISLE, born ca. 1599 and buried at Felton, Northumberland 18 May 1676. He married after 8 Aug. 1629,
2499. MARY FORSTER, buried at Felton 17 Dec. 1665.

2500-2503. ———.

2504. THOMAS WOOD of Burton, Bamburgh, Northumberland, buried 2 July 1669. He married,
2505. ELIZABETH GRAY.

2506-2511. ———.

2512. CAPTAIN GEORGE GREY, born in 1617 and died at Southwick, Durham 13 Sept. 1702. He married, 2nd, in 1673, Philadelphia (———) Kirkbridge, who died in April 1681. He married, 1st, 20 July 1647,
2513. FRANCES ROBINSON, born ca. 1627 and died 19 July 1661.

2514. REV. ZACHARY CAWDREY, Rector of Barthomley 1649-84, baptized at Melton Mowbray, Leicestershire 23 Aug. 1618 and died 21 Dec. 1684; buried at Barthomley, Cheshire. He married,
2515. HELEN ———, buried at Barthomley.

2516. SIR JAMES CLAVERING, 1ST BARONET, M.P. 1656-58, Sheriff of Durham 1649-50 and 1673-74, baptized at St. Nicholas' Church, Newcastle-upon-Tyne 3 Feb. 1618/19 and buried at Whickham, Durham 24 March 1701/2. He married at St. Nicholas' Church 23 April 1640,
2517. JANE MADDISON, baptized at St. Nicholas' Church 18 May 1619 and buried at Whickham 1 July 1688.

2518. BENJAMIN ELLISON, merchant adventurer, baptized at St. Nicholas' Church, Newcastle-upon-Tyne 23 March 1618/19 and died 25 June 1676; buried at St. Nicholas' Church. He married,
2519. ISABEL LILBURN, died 25 Feb. 1697/98; buried at St. Nicholas' Church.

2520. JOHN OGLE, merchant adventurer, born 30 Nov. 1617 and buried at Ponteland, Northumberland 6 July 1699. He married 25 Nov. 1645,

2521. ELIZABETH FOWLER, perhaps the Elizabeth Ogle, widow, buried at St. Peter's Church, Bywell, Northumberland 31 Dec. 1708.

2522. REV. JOHN THOMPSON, Rector of Bothal, Northumberland 1662. He married ca. 29 July 1650,

2523. KATHERINE WILSON of Amble, Northumberland.

2524. MATTHEW NEWTON of Coldcoats, Ponteland, Northumberland, died 28 Nov. 1668. He married,

2525. MARGARET ———.

2526. THOMAS JENISON, merchant and alderman, baptized at St. Nicholas' Church, Newcastle-upon-Tyne 10 May 1636 and died 17 Dec. 1676; buried at St. Nicholas' Church. He married there 15 June 1658,

2527. ALICE EMERSON, died after 5 Sept. 1702.

2528. COLONEL SIR JOHN PONSONBY, M.P. 1661-66, Sheriff of Wicklow and Kildare 1654, born at Hale, Cumberland in 1608 and died ca. 1678. He married, 1st, Dorothy Briscoe, daughter of John Briscoe and Mary Braithwaite. He married, 2nd, before 1655,

2529. HON. ELIZABETH FOLLIOTT. She married, 1st, 7 May 1640, Richard Wingfield, M.P. 1639, who died ca. 1645, son of Sir Edward Wingfield and Hon. Anne Cromwell, daughter of Edward Cromwell, 3rd Baron Cromwell. She married, 2nd, 12 April 1646, Edward Trevor, son of Right Hon. Edward Trevor, P.C., and Rose Ussher.

2530. HON. RANDLE MOORE, attainted 7 May 1689. He married, 2nd, Priscilla Armitage. He married, 1st,

2531. LADY JANE BRABAZON.

2532. MOST REV. DR. JAMES MARGETSON, ARCHBISHOP OF ARMAGH (1663-78), P.C. (I.) (1660), Dean of Waterford 1635-38, Derry 1638-39, and Christ Church, Dublin 1639-47, Bishop of Glendalough 1661-63, Archbishop of Dublin 1661-63, born at Drighlington, Yorkshire in 1600 and died at Dublin

28 Aug. 1678. He married, 1st, Ann ——, who was buried at Thornton Watlass, Yorkshire 20 March 1626/27. He married, 2nd, ——. He married, 3rd (probably at London),

2533. ANNE BONNETT.

2534. WILLIAM CAULFIELD, 1ST VISCOUNT CHARLEMONT, P.C. (I.) (1660), born ca. 1625 and buried at Armagh Cathedral 25 May 1671. He married in 1653,

2535. HON. SARAH MOORE.

2536. WILLIAM CAVENDISH, 1ST DUKE OF DEVONSHIRE, K.G. (1689), P.C. (1679-80 AND 1689), F.R.S. (1663), M.P. [as Lord Cavendish] 1661, 1679, and 1681, bore the King's train at the coronation of HM King Charles II 1661, served as the Queen's cupbearer at the coronation of TM King James II and Queen Mary 1685, Lord Steward for the coronations of TM King William III and Queen Mary 1689 and HM Queen Anne 1702, Lord Steward of the (Royal) Household 1689-1707, one of the seven signatories inviting HH The Prince of Orange to assume the throne 1688, Lord Justice [i.e. Regent] 1695-1701, Lord Lieutenant of Derbyshire 1689-1707 and Nottinghamshire 1692-94, born 25 Jan. 1640/41 and died at Devonshire House, Piccadilly, London 18 Aug. 1707. He married at Kilkenny Castle, Tipperary 26 Oct. 1662,

2537. LADY MARY BUTLER, born in 1646 and died 31 July 1710; buried at Westminster Abbey, London.

2538. WILLIAM RUSSELL, LORD RUSSELL = 1312.
2539. LADY RACHEL WRIOTHESLEY = 1313.

2540. CHARLES HOSKINS, born in 1603 and died 28 or 29 Aug. 1657; buried at Oxted, Surrey. He married at Kings Walden, Hertfordshire 14 Dec. 1626,

2541. ANNE HALE, baptized at Kings Walden 25 June 1609 and died 2 Dec. 1651; buried at Oxted.

2542. LIEUT. COLONEL WILLIAM HALE, M.P. 1669, 1679, and 1681, born in 1633 and died 25 May 1688; buried at Kings Walden, Hertfordshire. He married before 19 July 1660,

2543. MARY ELWES, born in 1640 and died 28 July 1712.

2544. WILLIAM MOLESWORTH of Fotheringhay, Northamptonshire, married,
2545. MARY PALMES of Ashwell, Rutland.

2546. JOHN BYSSE, M.P. (I.) 1634 and 1640 [excluded from Cromwell's third Parliament in 1656], Chief Baron of the Exchequer 1660, died 28 Jan. 1679/80; buried at St. Audoen's Church, Dublin. He married,
2547. MARGARET EDGEWORTH, born in 1590 and died in 1676. She married, 1st, John King, son of Sir John King [No. 10138] and Catherine Drury [No. 10139].

2548. RIGHT HON. SIR CHARLES COOTE, 1ST BARONET, P.C. (1620/21), M.P. 1639-42, Sheriff of Cork 1606, died at Trim, Meath 7 May 1642. He married before 1610,
2549. DOROTHEA CUFFE.

2550. SIR GEORGE ST. GEORGE, born at Hatley St. George, Cambridgeshire 13 Jan. 1582/83 and died at Headford, Galway 5 Aug. 1660. He married,
2551. KATHERINE GIFFORD of Ballymagarett, Roscommon.

2552. SIR WILLIAM USSHER, M.P. 1661, born ca. 1610 and died 23 April 1671. He married, 1st, Elizabeth Parsons, who died 29 Nov. 1638, daughter of Sir William Parsons, 1st Baronet, Lord Justice of Ireland, and Elizabeth Lany. He married, 2nd, 14 May 1645,
2553. URSULA ST. BARBE.

2554. GILBERT WYE of Antrim married,
2555. ——.

2556-2559. ——.

2560. COLONEL JAMES HAMILTON, M.P. 1666, Groom of the Bedchamber to HM King Charles II 1664, died 6 June 1673; buried at Westminster Abbey, Middlesex. He married in 1661,
2561. HON. ELIZABETH COLEPEPER, baptized at Hollingbourne, Kent 4 Jan. 1637/38 and buried there 6 Feb. 1709/10.

2562. SIR ROBERT READING, 1ST BARONET, M.P. 1662-66, buried at Newark, Nottinghamshire 25 March 1689. He married ca. 1662,

2563. JANE HANNAY, buried at Westminster Abbey, Middlesex 18 Nov. 1684. She married, 1st, before May 1645, Charles Coote, 1st Earl of Mountrath, born ca. 1610 and died 18 Dec. 1661, son of Right Hon. Sir Charles Coote, 1st Baronet, P.C. [No. 2548], and Dorothea Cuffe [No. 2549].

2564. JOHN PLUMER, died between 15 March 1668 and 9 Oct. 1672; buried at New Windsor, Berkshire. He married, 2nd, after 30 March 1665, Mary ——. He married, 1st,

2565. ANNE GERARD.

2566. WILLIAM HALE = 2542.
2567. MARY ELWES = 2543.

2568. ANTHONY CRAGGS of Wolsingham, Durham, died ca. 1680. He married at Redmarshall, Durham 18 June 1654,

2569. ANNE MOORCROFT, baptized at Stanhope, Durham 28 Oct. 1628 and died 3 Sept. 1672; buried at Wolsingham.

2570. JACOB RICHARDS, corn chandler of Westminster, Middlesex, died between 5 Nov. and 17 Dec. 1675. He married,

2571. ANNE ——.

2572-2575. ——.

2576. JOHN MOYLE, M.P. 1649, Sheriff of Cornwall 1624, born ca. 1589 and died 9 Oct. 1661. He married at Farway, Devonshire 8 Sept. 1612,

2577. ADMONITION PRIDEAUX, died 29 Nov. 1675.

2578. COLONEL SIR WILLIAM MORICE, M.P. 1648, 1654, 1656, 1659, 1660, 1661, and 1676, Sheriff of Devonshire 1651/52, Governor of Plymouth 1660/61, born at Exeter 6 Nov. 1602 and died at Werrington, Devonshire 12 Dec. 1676. He married ca. 1627,

2579. ELIZABETH PRIDEAUX, died in Dec. 1663.

2580. MAJOR SIR GODFREY COPLEY, 1ST BARONET, born 21, baptized at Sprotborough, Yorkshire 23 Feb. 1622/23 and buried there 21 Feb. 1676/77. He married, 2nd, ca. 1663, Elizabeth Stanhope, who was buried at Sprotborough 22 Sept. 1682, daughter of William Stanhope and Ann Gawdy. He married, 1st, before 1653,

2581. ELEANOR WALMESLEY, buried at Sprotborough 18 Nov. 1659.

2582. JOHN PURCELL, M.P. 1660, Gentleman of the Privy Chamber 1661-65, died in 1665. He married,

2583. ELEANOR VAUGHAN.

2584. JOHN BULLER, M.P. 1656-58, 1659, 1660, 1661-81, 1689-90, and 1692-95, born ca. 1632 and died between 4 Nov. 1715 and 13 April 1716. He married, 2nd, Jane Langdon, daughter of Walter Langdon and Rhoda Martin. He married, 1st, at Morval, Cornwall 22 Dec. 1659,

2585. ANNE COODE, baptized at Morval 27 Nov. 1639.

2586. SIR HENRY POLLEXFEN, M.P. 1689, Lord Chief Justice of the Common Pleas, born ca. 1632 and died 15 June 1691; buried at Woodbury, Devonshire. He married (Faculty Office license dated 27 Sept. 1664)

2587. MARY DUNCOMBE, born ca. 1644 and died in Jan. 1694/95.

2588. COLONEL SIR JONATHAN TRELAWNY, 2ND BARONET, M.P. 1660, 1661, and 1679-81, Gentleman of the Privy Chamber to HM King Charles II 1660, Comptroller of the Household of HRH The Duke of York (later HM King James II) 1670-74, born ca. 1623 and buried at Pelynt, Cornwall 5 March 1680/81. He married at Berry Pomeroy, Devonshire 8 July 1645,

2589. MARY SEYMOUR, baptized at Berry Pomeroy 19 Dec. 1619.

2590. THOMAS HELE of Babcombe, Devonshire, born ca. 1619 and died 13 March 1672/73. He married at Egg Buckland, Devonshire 22 April 1670,

2591. ELIZABETH HALS, died 14 Nov. 1680.

2592. WILLIAM DOUGLAS, 7TH EARL OF MORTON, K.G. (1634), P.C. (E.) (1627), Lord of the Bedchamber in Scotland to HM King James VI 1621 and in England to HM King Charles I 1641, bore the Standard at the funeral of HM King James 1625, a member of the Prince [of Wales]'s Council 1624,

High Treasurer of Scotland 1630–36, nominated High Chancellor of Scotland 1640, alienated his family estates in return for the islands of Orkney and Shetland 1643, born ca. 1584 and died at Kirkwall, Orkney 7 Aug. 1648. He married in April 1604,

2593. LADY ANNE KEITH, died at Kirkwall 30 May 1649.

2594. SIR JAMES HAY, 1ST BARONET, M.P. 1628–33 and 1643, died after 19 Feb. 1654. He married Sidney Massey, who died after 19 Feb. 1654. He had issue by,

2595. ? —— BEAUMONT.

2596. WILLIAM ADDERLEY of Colney Hatch, Middlesex, died after 5 March 1663/64. He married,

2597. MARGARET EYRE of Burnham, Buckinghamshire.

2598-2599. ——.

2600. GILBERT HEATHCOTE, Mayor of Chesterfield, baptized at Chesterfield, Derbyshire 24 Aug. 1625 and died 24 April 1690; buried at Chesterfield. He married,

2601. ANNE DICKONS, born ca. 1630 and died at Low Leyton, Essex 29 Nov. 1705.

2602. CHRISTOPHER RAYNER, haberdasher, buried at All Hallows' Church, Bread Street, London 18 March 1663/64. He married,

2603. FRANCES BARON, died between 3 July and 4 Aug. 1681.

2604. JOHN WHITE, M.P. 1678–81, 1689–90, and 1691–98, born 3 Sept. 1634 and died at Ravensfield, Yorkshire 16 April 1713. He married 26 Nov. 1657,

2605. JANE WILLIAMSON of East Markham, Nottinghamshire.

2606. RICHARD TAYLOR, M.P. 1690–98, Sheriff of Nottinghamshire 1689/90, born ca. 1649 and died 20 April 1699; buried at Carlton, Nottinghamshire. He married (settlement dated 5 May 1677),

2607. BRIDGET KNIGHT, born ca. 1656 and died 13 June 1734; buried at Carlton.

2608. COLONEL FRANCIS LASCELLES, M.P. 1645, 1653, 1654, 1656, and 1660, one of Charles I's judges [although he refused to sign the death warrant] Jan. 1648/49, baptized at Sigston, Yorkshire 5 Aug. 1612 and buried there 28 Nov. 1667. He married in 1626,

2609. FRANCES ST. QUINTIN, buried at Kirby Sigston 30 Sept. 1658.

2610. EDWARD LASCELLES, grocer, baptized at Stainton in Cleveland, Yorkshire 21 Dec. 1630 and buried at the Church of St. Martin Outwich, London 19 Sept. 1700. He married, 2nd (Vicar-General's license to marry at Low Leyton or Ham, Essex, or Newington or Bow, Middlesex dated 3 Sept. 1673), Abigail (———) Felton, who was buried at the Church of St. Martin Outwich 18 May 1691. He married, 1st,

2611. MARY ———, buried at the Church of St. Martin Outwich 12 June 1671.

2612-2613. ———.

2614. THOMAS DUBOYS, merchant, died between 8 April and 15 Aug. 1699. He married at St. Michael Parish, Barbados 20 Sept. 1685,

2615. KATHERINE GILHAMPTON.

2616. WILLIAM CHALONER, baptized at Guisborough, Yorkshire 16 Oct. 1655 and buried there 18 Feb. 1715/16. He married at Ingleby Greenhow, Yorkshire 15 Aug. 1682,

2617. HONORA FOULIS, baptized at Ingleby Greenhow 29 Oct. 1663 and died at York 3 Oct. 1755.

2618. SIR WILLIAM BOWES, M.P. 1679-81, 1695-98, and 1702-7, baptized at Barnard Castle, Durham 6 Jan. 1657 and died at London 17 Jan. 1706/7. He married at Tanfield, Yorkshire 17 Aug. 1691,

2619. ELIZABETH BLAKISTON, buried at St. Mary's Church, Durham 5 July 1736.

2620. WILLIAM FYNNEY, born 5 Oct. 1647. He married at Leek, Staffordshire 3 March 1679/80,

2621. ELIZABETH MACHIN of Bucknall, Staffordshire.

2622-2623. ———.

2624. WILLIAM RUSSELL, 1ST DUKE OF BEDFORD, K.G. (1672), K.B. (1626), P.C. (1688/89), M.P. [as Lord Russell] 1640-41, carried the Sceptre of St. Edward at the coronation of HM King Charles II 1661 and the Queen's Sceptre at the coronation of TM King William III and Queen Mary II 1689, one of the 24 commoners who conferred with the House of Lords on a petition of grievances 1641, General 1642, Lord Lieutenant of Devonshire and Somerset 1642, Bedfordshire and Cambridgeshire 1689-1700, and Middlesex 1692-1700, born in Aug. 1616 and died at Bedford House in the Strand, near London 7 Sept. 1700. He married at St. Benet's Church, Paul's Wharf, London 11 July 1637,

2625. LADY ANNE CARR, born in the Tower of London 9 Dec. 1615 and died at Woburn, Bedfordshire 10 May 1684.

2626. THOMAS WRIOTHESLEY, 4TH EARL OF SOUTHAMPTON, K.G. (1661), P.C. (1641/42 AND 1660), Lord of the Bedchamber 1641/42, Lord High Treasurer 1660-67, Lord Lieutenant of Norfolk 1660-61, Hampshire 1660-67, Wiltshire 1661-67, Worcestershire 1662-63, and Kent 1662, joint Lord Lieutenant of Hampshire 1641, one of the four peers who attended the funeral of HM King Charles I Jan. 1648/49, baptized at Little Shelford, Cambridgeshire 2 April 1608 and died at Southampton House, Bloomsbury, London 16 May 1667. He married, 2nd (probably in London ca. 24 April 1642), Lady Elizabeth Leigh, who died after 14 June 1654, daughter of Francis Leigh, 1st Earl of Chichester, and Hon. Audrey Boteler, daughter of John Boteler, 1st Baron Boteler [No. 4118]. He married, 3rd (settlement dated 7 May 1659), Lady Frances Seymour, who was buried at Westminster Abbey, Middlesex 5 Jan. 1680/81, widow of Richard Molyneux, 2nd Viscount Molyneux, and daughter of William Seymour, 2nd Duke of Somerset [No. 2892], and Lady Frances Devereux [No. 2893]. He married, 1st, at Charenton, near Paris 18 Aug. 1634,

2627. RACHEL MASSÜE DE RUVIGNY, known as "la belle et vertueuse Huguenotte," born at Paris in 1603 and died at Tothill Street, Westminster, Middlesex 16 Feb. 1639/40. She married, 1st, Elysée de Beaujeu, Seigneur de la Maisonfort, who died ca. 1625.

2628. JEFFREY HOWLAND, Sheriff of Surrey 1658-60 and Suffolk 1667-68, baptized at Newport, Essex 29 July 1593 and buried at St. Leonard's Church, Streatham, Surrey 4 Sept. 1679. He married at St. Antholin's Church, Budge Row, London 4 May 1630,

2629. GRISOGON LANGLEY, baptized at St. Peter's Church, Cornhill, London 24 July 1608 and died between 24 Aug. and 7 Oct. 1680.

2630. SIR JOSIAH CHILD, 1ST BARONET = 1102. He married, 1st, at the Church of St. Thomas à Becket, Portsmouth 26 Dec. 1654,
2631. HANNAH BOATE, buried at Portsmouth 29 July 1662.

2632. SIR WILLIAM GOWER [LATER LEVESON-GOWER], 4TH BARONET, M.P. 1673, 1675-81, and 1689-91, born ca. 1647 and died 22 Dec. 1691. He married ca. 1669,
2633. LADY JANE GRANVILLE, baptized at Kilkhampton, Cornwall 23 Aug. 1653 and died 27 Feb. 1696/97.

2634. JOHN MANNERS, 1ST DUKE OF RUTLAND, M.P. [as Lord Roos] 1661-79, bore the Queen's Sceptre at the coronation of TM King James II and Queen Mary 1685, Lord Lieutenant of Leicestershire 1677-87, 1698-1703, and 1706, born at Boughton, Northamptonshire 29 May 1638 and died at Belvoir Castle, Leicestershire 10 Jan. 1710/11. He married, 1st (registered at Highgate and Hornsey, Middlesex 13 July 1658; marriage dissolved by Act of Parliament 11 April 1670 for her adultery), Lady Anne Pierrepont, baptized at St. Margaret's Church, Westminster, Middlesex 9 March 1630/31 and died before Jan. 1696/97, daughter of Henry Pierrepont, 1st Marquess of Dorchester, and Hon. Cecilia Bayning, daughter of Paul Bayning, 1st Viscount Bayning [No. 4390]. He married, 2nd, at Ampthill Park, Bedfordshire 10 Nov. 1671, Lady Diana Bruce, who died at Belvoir Castle 15 July 1672, widow of Sir Seymour Shirley, 5th Baronet, and daughter of Robert Bruce, 2nd Earl of Elgin and 1st Earl of Ailesbury [No. 1444], and Lady Diana Grey [No. 1445]. He married, 3rd, at Exton, Rutland 8 Jan. 1673/74,
2635. HON. KATHERINE NOEL, born at Campden House, Kensington, Middlesex 10 Aug. 1657 and died 24 Jan. 1732/33; buried at Bottesford, Leicestershire.

2636. ROBERT PIERREPONT, baptized at Tong, Shropshire 27 Sept. 1634 and died 26 April 1669. He married in Dec. 1658,
2637. ELIZABETH EVELYN, baptized at Everley, Wiltshire 20 Nov. 1639 and buried at West Dean, Wiltshire 4 Jan. 1698/99.

2638. WILLIAM FEILDING, 3RD EARL OF DENBIGH AND 2ND EARL OF DESMOND, Lord Lieutenant of Warwickshire 1683-85, born 29 Dec. 1640 and died at Canonbury House, Islington, Middlesex 23 Aug. 1685. He married, 2nd, after 12 Sept. 1669, Lady Mary Carey, who died 9 Dec. 1719, daughter of Henry Carey, 2nd Earl of Monmouth, and Lady Martha Cranfield, daughter of Lionel Cranfield, 1st Earl of Middlesex. He married, 1st, 11 April 1665,

2639. MARY KING, buried at St. Michan's Church, Dublin 12 Sept. 1669. She married, 1st, in Nov. 1655, Sir William Meredyth, 1st Baronet, born ca. 1620 and died at Kilcullen, Kildare before 14 Feb. 1664/65, son of Robert Meredyth and Anne Ussher.

2640. DIRK VAN KEPPEL, HEER TOT VOORST EN 'TVELDE, died 18 Sept. 1646; buried at Warnsveld, Gelderland. He married in 1635,

2641. THEODORA VAN SALLANDT, VROUWE TOT NYENHUIS, died 25 Sept. 1699; buried at Emmerik, Gelderland. She married, 2nd, Herman Jan de Rode van Hekeren van Tongerlo.

2642. JOHAN VAN LINTELO TOT DE MARSCH, born at de Marsch, near Zutphen 12 Nov. 1603 and died there 22 July 1652. He married at Weleveld, Overijssel 24 Feb. 1636,

2643. AGNES REINIERA SCHELE, died in May 1682.

2644. NICOLAAS VAN DER DUYN, HEER VAN RIJSWIJK 'SGRAVENMOER, died at Rijswijk, near The Hague 27 July 1649. He married, 1st, at The Hague 11 Oct. 1626, Tymana van Wassenaer, who died 16 Aug. 1627, daughter of Antony van Wassenaer and Machteld van der Duyn van Sanen. He married, 2nd, in 1633,

2645. BEATRIX VAN DER BOUCKHORST, died 20 Oct. 1642.

2646. COLONEL ANTHONY PIETERSEN, Mayor of The Hague 1669, born at The Hague 4 Jan. 1619 and died there 18 Feb. 1676. He married at the Abbey Church, The Hague 14 May 1644,

2647. CATHARINA COENEN, born 31 Aug. 1625 and died at The Hague 1 March 1660.

2648. HM KING CHARLES I, KING OF ENGLAND, SCOTLAND, AND IRELAND = 2192 = 2212.

**2649. HRH Princesse Henriette Marie de France et Navarre =
2193 = 2213.**

2650. Guillaume de Penancoët, Sieur de Kéroualle, died in 1690.
He married 27 Feb. 1645,
2651. Marie Anne de Plœuc, died in Jan. 1709.

2652. Robert Brudenell, 2nd Earl of Cardigan = 1440.
2653. Lady Anne Savage = 1441.

2654. Thomas Savile, 1st Earl of Sussex = 1442.
2655. Lady Anne Villiers = 1443.

2656. Lewis Gordon, 3rd Marquess of Huntly, died in Dec. 1653.
He married in Oct. 1644,
2657. Mary Grant, living 25 Dec. 1707. She married, 2nd (contract dated
31 Oct. 1668), **James Ogilvy, 2nd Earl of Airlie [No. 8122].**

2658. Henry Howard, 6th Duke of Norfolk, F.R.S. (1666), Earl
Marshal of England 1672, Ambassador to Morocco 1669-70, born at Arundel
House in the Strand, near London 12 July 1628 and died there 13 Jan.
1683/84. He married, 2nd, shortly before 23 Jan. 1677/78, Jane Bickerton,
born ca. 1644 and died at Rotherham, Yorkshire 28 Aug. 1693, daughter of
Robert Bickerton and Anne Hester. He married, 1st, shortly before 21 Oct.
1652,
2659. Lady Anne Somerset, born at Raglan Castle, Monmouthshire in
Oct. 1631 and died in 1662.

2660. John Mordaunt, 1st Viscount Mordaunt = 524.
2661. Elizabeth Carey = 525.

2662. Dr. Sir Alexander Fraser, 1st Baronet, F.R.S. (1663), Court
Physician in Ordinary to TM King Charles I and King Charles II, a founder of
the Royal Society, born ca. 1606 and died at Whitehall, near London 28 April
1681. He married, 1st, Elizabeth Dowchly. He married, 2nd, ca. 1658,

2663. MARY CAREY, Woman of the Bedchamber and Dresser to HM Queen Catherine 1662, buried at Fulham, Middlesex 22 Dec. 1695. She married, 1st, Dudley Wylde of Canterbury, Kent, who died between 15 July and 8 Sept. 1653, son of Sir John Wylde and Anne Honywood.

2664. SIR JOHN GORDON, 1ST BARONET, born early in 1610 and executed at Edinburgh 19 July 1644. He married in 1630,
2665. JANET [OR MARY] FORBES.

2666. GEORGE LOCKHART of Torbreck, Sutherland, died in Oct. 1658. He married ca. 1617,
2667. ANNE LOCKHART of Lee, Lanarkshire.

2668. JOHN MURRAY, 1ST MARQUESS OF ATHOLL, K.T. (1687), P.C. (1660), Keeper of the Privy Purse in Scotland 1672-89, born 2 May 1631 and died 6 May 1703; buried at Dunkeld, Perthshire. He married 5 May 1659,
2669. LADY AMELIA SOPHIA STANLEY, born in 1633 and died 22 Feb. 1702/3; buried at Dunkeld.

2670. WILLIAM DOUGLAS [LATER DOUGLAS-HAMILTON], 1ST DUKE OF HAMILTON, K.G. (1682), P.C. (S.) (1661-76 AND 1685) AND (E.) (1687 AND 1689), president of the convention at Edinburgh which declared the throne of Scotland vacant 1688/89, High Admiral of Scotland 1692-94, born (probably at Douglas Castle, Lanarkshire) 24 Dec. 1634 and died at Holyrood Abbey, Edinburgh 18 April 1694. He married at Corstorphine, near Edinburgh 29 April 1656,
2671. ANNE HAMILTON, DUCHESS OF HAMILTON in her own right, born at Wallingford House, Whitehall, London 16 Jan. 1631/32 and died at Hamilton Palace, Lanarkshire 17 Oct. 1716.

2672. WILLIAM MAXWELL of Monreith, Wigtownshire, died in April 1670. He married in 1632,
2673. MARGARET MACCULLOCH of Myreton, Wigtownshire.

2674. SIR THOMAS HAY, 1ST BARONET, married at Hamilton, Lanarkshire 1 Nov. 1661,
2675. MARION HAMILTON.

2676. ALEXANDER MONTGOMERIE, 8TH EARL OF EGLINTON, P.C. (S.) (1689), died at London at the end of 1701; buried at Kilwinning, Ayrshire. He married, 2nd, 2 Feb. 1678/79, Grace Popeley, who died after 18 April 1698, widow of Sir Thomas Wentworth, 1st Baronet, and daughter of Francis Popeley and Elizabeth Gomersal. He married, 3rd, at St. Bride's Church, London 6 Dec. 1698, Katherine St. Quintin, who was buried at Down, Kent 6 Aug. 1700, widow of i) Michael Wentworth, ii) Sir John Kaye, 1st Baronet, and iii) Henry Sandys of Down, and daughter of Sir William St. Quintin [No. 5218] and Mary Lacy [No. 5219]. He married, 1st, at the Church of St. Peter-le-Poer, London 9 Feb. 1657,

2677. LADY ELIZABETH CRICHTON, died 5 June 1675.

2678. WILLIAM COCHRANE, LORD COCHRANE by courtesy, **P.C. (S.) (BEFORE 1675),** died at Paisley, Renfrewshire 25 Aug. 1679. He married in 1653,

2679. LADY CATHERINE KENNEDY, buried at Greyfriars Churchyard, Edinburgh 15 Feb. 1699/1700.

2680. SIR WILLIAM SCOTT, a judge of the Court of Session as **LORD CLERKINGTON** 1649, died 28 Dec. 1659. He married, 1st, 4 Oct. 1621, Katherine Morison, daughter of John Morison. He married, 2nd, before 1642,

2681. BARBARA DALMAHOY.

2682. SIR THOMAS NICOLSON of Cockburnspath, Berwickshire, married,

2683. MARGARET SCOTT.

2684-2687. ——.

2688. JOHN CURZON, born ca. 1552 and buried at Kedleston, Derbyshire 6 May 1632. He married,

2689. MILLICENT SACHEVERELL, buried at Kedleston 22 Jan. 1618/19. She married, 1st, Thomas Gell of Hopton, Derbyshire.

2690. SIR THOMAS CREWE, M.P. 1604, 1614, and 1621-25, Speaker of the House of Commons 1623-25, born at Nantwich, Cheshire in 1566 and died at Stene, Northamptonshire 31 Jan. 1632/33. He married in 1596,

2691. TEMPERANCE BRAY, born in 1581 and died 25 Oct. 1619.

2692. JOHN PENN of Beaumond Manor, Buckinghamshire, died before 28 March 1639. He married,
2693. SARAH DRURY of Hedgerley, Buckinghamshire, died before 25 Feb. 1641.

2694. HUMPHREY SHALLCROSS, Sheriff of Hertfordshire 1653/54, born 15 Aug. 1595 and died 25 Aug. 1665. He married, 1st, Elizabeth Newgate. He married, 2nd, at the Church of St. Martin-in-the-Fields, Westminster, Middlesex 23 April 1629,
2695. ELIZA CATHARINA KEMP, born in 1605 and died 15 Feb. 1676/77.

2696. GENERAL RALPH ASSHETON, M.P. 1625 and 1640, Sheriff of Lancashire 1633, born 5, baptized at Middleton, Lancashire 18 Jan. 1595/96 and died 17 Feb. 1649/50; buried at Middleton. He married at Almondbury, Yorkshire 4 May 1623,
2697. ELIZABETH KAYE, baptized at Almondbury 19 Dec. 1608.

2698. SIR RALPH ASSHETON, 1ST BARONET, born ca. 1581 and died 18 Oct. 1644; buried at Whalley, Lancashire. He married, 2nd, at Padiham, Lancashire 18 April 1610, Eleanor Shuttleworth, who died in 1658, daughter of Thomas Shuttleworth and Anne Lever. He married, 1st (marriage settlement dated 19 Aug. 1604),
2699. DOROTHY BELLINGHAM.

2700. PETER VAVASOUR of Spaldington, Yorkshire, married ca. 1632,
2701. ANNE GOWER.

2702. COLONEL SIR FERDINANDO LEIGH, Gentleman of the Privy Chamber to HM King Charles I, died at Pontefract, Yorkshire 19 Jan. 1653/54. He married, 1st, Margery Cartwright, daughter of William Cartwright and Elizabeth Clay. He married, 2nd, Mary Pilkington, daughter of Thomas Pilkington and Catherine Rodes. He married, 3rd, Elizabeth Tyrwhit, who died on the Isle of Man in 1625, daughter of Robert Tyrwhit and Anne Bassett. He married, 4th,
2703. ANNE CLOUGH, buried 8 Nov. 1634.

2704. WILLIAM HANMER of Fenns, Flintshire, born ca. 1622 and died in 1669. He married, 2nd, Mary Sneyd, daughter of Colonel Ralph Sneyd and Jane Downes. He married, 1st,
2705. ELEANOR WARBURTON, died in 1649.

2706. SIR JOB CHARLTON, 1ST BARONET, M.P. 1659, 1660, and 1661-79, Speaker of the House of Commons 1673, born at London ca. 1615 and died at Ludford, Herefordshire 27 May 1697. He married, 2nd, 12 Nov. 1663, Lettice Waring, who died before 6 Dec. 1691, daughter of Walter Waring and Jane Robinson. He married, 1st, at Ludlow, Shropshire 31 March 1646,
2707. DOROTHY BLUNDEN, died 21 Feb. 1657/58; buried at Ludford.

2708. JOHN JENNENS, ironmaster, baptized at St. Martin's Church, Birmingham 8 April 1579 and died before 10 March 1652/53. He married, 1st, in 1602, his cousin Mary Jennens. He married, 2nd, before 1628,
2709. JOYCE WEAMAN.

2710. COLONEL JOHN MILWARD, M.P. 1665-70, Sheriff of Derbyshire 1635-37, born 28 Oct. 1599 and died 14 Sept. 1670. He married by 1633,
2711. ANNE WHITEHALGH, died in 1658.

2712. JOHN JENNENS = 2708.
2713. JOYCE WEAMAN = 2709.

2714. COLONEL JOHN MILWARD = 2710.
2715. ANNE WHITEHALGH = 2711.

2716. SIR FRANCIS BURDETT, 2ND BARONET, Sheriff of Derbyshire 1649-50, born 10 Sept. 1608 and died 30 Dec. 1696; buried at Repton, Derbyshire. He married in 1635,
2717. ELIZABETH WALTER, born in Sept. 1613 and died 17 April 1701; buried at Foremark, Derbyshire.

2718. GERVASE PIGOT, High Sheriff of Nottinghamshire 1668, born ca. 1616 and died 9 Aug. 1669. He married, 2nd, at Mortlake, Surrey 6 April 1647,

Elizabeth Edmonds, who died 28 Aug. 1649, daughter of Simon Edmonds and Mary Boothby. He married, 1st,

2719. MARY ST. ANDREW, born ca. 1624 and died 2 Feb. 1646/47.

2720. SIR JOHN HOWE, 1ST BARONET, M.P. 1654-55 and 1656-58, Sheriff of Gloucestershire 1650-51, born before 1 Sept. 1594 and died before 4 May 1675. He married 23 July 1620,

2721. BRIDGET RICH, born ca. 1596 and died 15 June 1642; buried at Withington, Gloucestershire.

2722. EMMANUEL SCROPE, 1ST EARL OF SUNDERLAND, Lord President of the Council of the North 1619-28, Lord Lieutenant of Yorkshire 1619-28, born 1, baptized at Hunsdon, Hertfordhire 16 Aug. 1584 and died 30 May 1630; buried at Langar, Nottinghamshire. He married before 29 Sept. 1609, Lady Elizabeth Manners, who was buried at Langar 16 March 1653/54, daughter of John Manners, 4th Earl of Rutland, and Elizabeth Charlton. He had issue by,

2723. MARTHA JONES of Twifield Heath, Buckinghamshire.

2724. WILLIAM ALINGTON, 1ST BARON ALINGTON, baptized at Horseheath, Cambridgeshire 14 March 1610/11 and buried there 25 Oct. 1648. He married (postnuptial settlement dated 1 Oct. 1631),

2725. ELIZABETH TOLLEMACHE, buried at Horseheath 14 April 1671. She married, 2nd, ca. 1651, Hon. Sir William Compton, who died 18 Oct. 1663, son of Spencer Compton, 2nd Earl of Northampton, and Mary Beaumont.

2726. BAPTIST NOEL, 3RD VISCOUNT CAMPDEN, M.P. [as Hon. Baptist Noel] 1640-43, born in 1612 and died 29 Oct. 1682; buried at Exton, Rutland. He married, 1st, 22 Dec. 1632, Lady Anne Feilding, who died 24 March 1635/36, daughter of William Feilding, 1st Earl of Denbigh [No. 10552], and Lady Susan Villiers [No. 10553]. He married, 2nd, ca. June 1638, Anne Lovet, who died before 25 Jan. 1638/39, widow of Edward Bourchier, 4th Earl of Bath, and daughter of Sir Robert Lovet and Anne Saunders. He married, 4th, **LADY ELIZABETH BERTIE [No. 5271].** He married, 3rd, at Boughton Malherbe, Kent 21 Dec. 1639,

2727. HON. HESTER WOTTON, baptized at Boughton Malherbe 11 Jan. 1615/16 and died ca. 1655.

2728. JOHANN ADOLF KIELMAN VON KIELMANSEGG, born 15 Nov. 1612 and died 8 July 1676. He married 2 Nov. 1635,

    2729. MARGARETE VON HATTEN, born 25 Aug. 1617 and died 12 Dec. 1656.

2730. MAJOR CLAUS VON AHLEFELDT-GJELTING, born in 1610 and died 31 Jan. 1674; buried at St. Nikolaus' Church, Kiel. He married at Kiel in June 1636,

    2731. HEDVIG RANTZAU-PUTLOS, born in 1618 and died 29 June 1695.

2732. HH GEORG, DUKE OF BRUNSWICK AND LÜNEBURG IN CALENBERG, born at Celle 17 Feb. 1582 and died at Hildesheim 2 April 1641. He married at Darmstadt 14 Dec. 1617,

    2733. HH ANNA ELEONORE LANDGRÄFIN VON HESSEN-DARMSTADT, born at Darmstadt 30 July 1601 and died at Herzberg 6 May 1659.

2734. GEORG PHILIPP VON MEYSENBUG, born at Schloss Eilhausen, Westphalia ca. 1600 and died in 1669. He married, 1st, Anna von Remmingen, who died in 1622. He married, 2nd, Catharina von Oyenhausen, who died in 1625. He married, 3rd, before 1647,

    2735. ANNA ELISABETH VON MEYSENBUG.

2736. SIR THOMAS HARTOPP, born in 1600 and died between 15 Oct. and 23 Nov. 1661; buried at Burton Lazars, Leicestershire. He married, 2nd, before 7 May 1649, Mary Hopton, born ca. 1600 and buried at Empringham 11 Feb. 1692/93, widow of Sir Henry Mackworth, 2nd Baronet, and daughter of Robert Hopton and Jane Kemeys. He married, 1st,

    2737. DOROTHY BENDISH.

2738. SIR MARTIN LISTER, M.P. 1640-48, born ca. 1603 and buried at Burwell, Lincolnshire 29 Aug. 1670. He married, 2nd, **SUSAN TEMPLE [No. 2063].** He married, 1st,

    2739. HON. MARY WENMAN, died before 9 Dec. 1633.

2740. GEORGE BENNETT of Welby, Leicestershire, born ca. 1629 and died between 1 and 14 March 1655/56. He married,

    2741. HON. ELIZABETH ST. JOHN.

2742. SIR THOMAS MIDDLETON, 1ST BARONET, M.P. 1646-48, 1660, and 1661-63, born 2 Nov. 1624 and died at Fleet Street, London 13 July 1663. He married, 2nd, after 1654, Jane Trevor, who died after July 1663, daughter of John Trevor and Margaret Jeffreys. He married, 1st, before 1650,
2743. MARY CHOLMONDELEY, baptized at Whitegate, Cheshire 11 Jan. 1628/29.

2744. THOMAS MANSFIELD, born ca. 1588 and buried at West Leake, Nottinghamshire 5 May 1638. He married, 1st, Joan Paget, daughter of Thomas Paget of Barwell, Lincolnshire. He married, 2nd,
2745. MILLICENT SACHEVERELL.

2746. SIR THOMAS RICHARDSON, born ca. 1597 and died 12 March 1642/43; buried at Honingham, Norfolk. He married, 2nd, in 1642, Mary Hanbury, who died ca. Jan. 1649/50, widow of Sir Miles Sandys, and daughter of Sir John Hanbury and Mary Whethill. He married, 1st, at the Church of St. Martin-in-the-Fields, Westminster, Middlesex 11 July 1626,
2747. ELIZABETH HEWITT, baptized at the Church of St. Lawrence Pountney, London 3 May 1607 and died 24 Jan. 1639/40; buried at the Church of St. Botolph Aldersgate, London.

2748-2751. ———.

2752. RALPH GORE, merchant taylor, buried at the Church of St. Mary Magdalen, Milk Street, London 8 Sept. 1637. He married there 21 Dec. 1618,
2753. AGNES YOUNG, buried at the Church of St. Mary Magdalen 25 April 1637. She married, 1st, Christopher Meyrick of Norcott, Middlesex, son of Richard Meyrick.

2754. SIR JOHN BOTELER, K.B. (1625/26), baptized at Watton, Hertfordshire 10 Dec. 1587 and buried there 10 Feb. 1652/53. He married at Offley, Hertfordshire 29 April 1624,
2755. ANNE SPENCER, buried at Watton 3 Dec. 1638.

2756. SIR RALPH GORE, 2ND BARONET, M.P. 1638/39, died before 1 Feb. 1661/62. He married (license dated 1640),

2757. HON. ANNE CAULFIELD. She married, 2nd, Sir Paul Harris. She married, 3rd, Sir John Wroth.

2758. JAMES HAMILTON of Manor Hamilton, Leitrim, died 27 Dec. 1652. He married in 1647 or 1648,

2759. HON. CATHERINE HAMILTON. She married, 2nd, before 29 March 1661, Owen Wynne of Lurganboy, Leitrim, who died in 1670. She married, 3rd, John Bingham of Castlebar, Mayo.

2760. CORNELIUS MANLEY of Erbistock, Denbighshire, died in 1623. He married,

2761. MARY LLOYD of Hardwick, Shropshire.

2762. JUDGE ISAAC DORISLAUS, lecturer at Cambridge University 1627 [but expelled for his republican principles], Parliamentary envoy to The Hague 1649, born at Alkmaar, The Netherlands in 1595 and assassinated at The Hague 2 May 1649; buried at Westminster Abbey, Middlesex. He married at St. Nicholas' Church, Colchester, Essex 23 Aug. 1621,

2763. ELIZABETH POPE, died in 1634.

2764-2765. ———.

2766. THOMAS BLAKE of Essington, Hampshire, married,

2767. DOROTHY MAYOWE.

2768-2783. ———.

2784. HON. JAMES MONTAGU, M.P. 1628/29, born ca. 1603 and died in Feb. 1664/65. He married at Lacock, Wiltshire 11 Nov. 1635,

2785. MARY BAYNARD, baptized at Lacock 26 March 1620 and died in 1665.

2786. ANTHONY HUNGERFORD, M.P. 1640-44, died 18 Aug. 1657; buried at Blackbourton, Oxfordshire. He married,

2787. RACHEL JONES.

2788. John Eyles, woolstapler of Devizes, Wiltshire, died between 17 June and 13 Nov. 1662. He married,

2789. Mary ———.

2790-2791. ———.

2792. Sir George Wroughton, baptized at Wilcot, Wiltshire 8 Oct. 1571 and buried there 23 Feb. 1649/50. He married, 1st, Anne Gibbes, who was buried at Wilcot 16 Oct. 1624, daughter of Robert Gibbes and Margaret Porter. He married, 2nd,

2793. Martha ———, buried at Wilcot 7 Feb. 1667/68.

2794. George Farewell of Hill-Bishops, Somerset, born ca. 1609 and died between 9 Feb. 1690 and 26 March 1691. He married in 1629,

2795. Anne Browne of Kent.

2796. Christopher Eyre of Maunden, Essex, born ca. 1620. He married,

2797. ———.

2798. John Briscoe, grocer, baptized at Aldenham, Hertfordshire 7 Feb. 1633/34 and buried at the Church of St. Stephen Walbrook, London 19 Jan. 1687/88. He married,

2799. Beatrix ———, buried at the Church of St. Stephen Walbrook 11 April 1719.

2800. Sir George Wroughton = 2792.
2801. Martha ——— = 2793.

2802. George Farewell = 2794
2803. Anne Browne = 2795.

2804. Christopher Eyre = 2796.
2805. = 2797.

2806. JOHN BRISCOE = 2798.
2807. BEATRIX —— = 2799.

2808-2815. ——.

2816. SIR HENRY BINGHAM, 1ST BARONET = 1056.
2817. CATHERINE BYRNE = 1057.

2818. SIR WILLIAM MIDDLETON, 2ND BARONET = 1058.
2819. ELEANOR HARRIS = 1059.

2820-2823. = 1060-1063.

2824. VEN. THOMAS VESEY, ARCHDEACON OF ARMAGH = 1064.
2825. —— WALKER = 1065.

2826. COLONEL AGMONDESHAM MUSCHAMP = 1066.
2827. = 1067.

2828. PATRICK SARSFIELD = 1068.
2829. ANNE O'MORE = 1069.

2830. THEOBALD TAAFFE, 1ST EARL OF CARLINGFORD = 1070.
2831. LUCY WALTER = 1071.

2832-2847. = 1072-1087.

2848. HON. HENRY BELASYSE, M.P. 1625-26, 1628/29, and 1640-42, baptized at Coxwold, Yorkshire 20 May 1604 and died 20 May 1647. He married,
2849. GRACE BARTON, died 7 Jan. 1658/59.

2850. JAMES DAVENPORT, baptized at Manchester 22 Sept. 1611 and buried at Macclesfield, Lancashire 1 March 1688/89. He married, 1st, Mary Moyle, who was buried at Macclesfield 14 May 1636, daughter of Thomas Moyle of Caversfield, Buckinghamshire. He married, 3rd, ——, who was buried [as the wife of James Davenport] at Macclesfield in Jan. 1677. He married, 2nd,
    2851. SARAH ROBINSON, buried at Macclesfield 2 Sept. 1640.

2852. SIR THOMAS GAGE, 2ND BARONET, born ca. 5 Dec. 1619 and died 2 July 1654; buried at Firle, Sussex. He married ca. 1635,
    2853. MARY CHAMBERLAIN, twin, died in 1694; buried at Burton, Sussex. She married, 2nd, before May 1661, Sir Henry Goring, 2nd Baronet, born ca. 1619 and died 8 June 1671, son of Sir William Goring, 1st Baronet, and Bridget [or Eleanor] Francis.

2854. ROBERT MIDDLEMORE of Edgbaston, Warwickshire, born ca. 1624 and died 4 March 1652. He married,
    2855. HENRIETTA MARIA DRUMMOND, buried 14 April 1694. She married, 2nd, ca. 1653, William Roper, born 12 Dec. 1623 and buried at St. Dunstan's Church, Canterbury, son of Thomas Roper and Susan Winchcombe.

2856. WALLISTON BETHAM of Rowington, Warwickshire, born ca. 1595 and died 3 Sept. 1667. He married,
    2857. EMMA MIDDLEMORE, died 6 Aug. 1665.

2858. THOMAS WOLLASCOT of Tidmarsh, Berkshire, born ca. 1601 and died ca. 1650. He married,
    2859. ELIZABETH FETTIPLACE of Swincombe, Oxfordshire.

2860-2861. ——.

2862. WALTER FOWLER, baptized at Baswich, Staffordshire 7 Oct. 1620 and buried there 10 March 1683/84. He married,
    2863. HON. CONSTANCE ASTON, buried at Baswich 29 March 1664.

2864-2871. ——.

2872. THOMAS COKE, M.P. 1640 and 1644, died in 1656. He married,
2873. MARY POPE, baptized at Whittington, Shropshire 27 Jan. 1629/30.

2874. SIR THOMAS LEVENTHORPE, 4TH BARONET, born at Sawbridge-worth, Hertfordshire 30 Nov. 1635 and died at Elvaston, Derby 27 July 1679. He married 2 Jan. 1654/55,
2875. MARY BEDELL, died at London 30 April 1683.

2876. WILLIAM HALE = 2542 = 2566.
2877. MARY ELWES = 2543 = 2567.

2878. ISAAC MEYNELL, goldsmith, born ca. 1636 and died between 2 Nov. 1675 and 1 July 1676. He married, 1st (Faculty Office license dated 6 June 1664), Elizabeth Dicer, born ca. 1643 and died before 5 Sept. 1668, daughter of Sir Robert Dicer, 1st Baronet, and Dorothy Styles. He married, 2nd (Vicar-General's license to marry at Cheshunt, Hertfordshire dated 5 Sept. 1668),
2879. ELIZABETH READE, born ca. 1649 and buried at the Church of St. Stephen Walbrook, London 1 March 1712/13. She married, 2nd (Faculty Office license dated 27 Aug. 1677), Nicholas Pollexfen, born ca. 1638 and buried at the Church of St. Stephen Walbrook 3 June 1682, son of Andrew Pollexfen [No. 5172] and Joan Woolcombe [No. 5173]. She married, 3rd (Faculty Office license dated 17 Dec. 1689), Sir William Norris, 1st Baronet, born in 1658 and died 10 Oct. 1702, son of Thomas Norris and Catherine Garway.

2880. THOMAS BRUDENELL, 1ST EARL OF CARDIGAN, received an earldom [promised by HM King Charles I and granted by HM King Charles II] for financing an uprising against the Parliamentarians, born ca. 1583 and died at Deene, Northamptonshire 16 Sept. 1663. He married in the summer of 1605,
2881. MARY TRESHAM, died 13 Oct. 1664.

2882. THOMAS SAVAGE, 1ST VISCOUNT SAVAGE, Chancellor to HM Queen Henrietta Maria 1628, born ca. 1586 and died at Tower Hill, London 20 Nov. 1635. He married 14 May 1602,
2883. ELIZABETH DARCY, COUNTESS RIVERS for life, Lady of the Bedchamber to HM, born in 1581 and died 9 March 1650/51; buried at Osyth, Essex.

2884. John Savile, 1st Baron Savile, P.C. (1626), M.P. [as John Savile] 1586-87, 1597/98, 1604-11 and 1614 and [as Sir John Savile, Bt.] 1624-26, vice president of the Council of the North 1626-28, born in 1556 and died at Howley Hall, Yorkshire 31 Aug. 1630. He married, 1st, Hon. Katherine Willoughby, daughter of Charles Willoughby, 2nd Baron Willoughby, and Lady Margaret Clinton, daughter of Edward Clinton, 1st Earl of Lincoln [No. 8222]. He married, 2nd, at Great Berkhamstead, Hertfordshire 20 Nov. 1586,
2885. Elizabeth Carey.

2886. Christopher Villiers, 1st Earl of Anglesey, Gentleman of the Bedchamber to HM King James I and HM's Master of the Robes 1617, died at Windsor Castle, Berkshire 3 April 1630. He married,
2887. Elizabeth Sheldon, died 12 April 1662; buried at Walton-on-Thames, Surrey. She married, 2nd, at Sunbury, Middlesex 5 Aug. 1641, Hon. Benjamin Weston, baptized at Roxwell, Essex 4 Aug. 1614 and died ca. 1673, son of Richard Weston, 1st Earl of Portland, and Frances Waldegrave.

2888. Thomas Bruce, 1st Earl of Elgin, born at Edinburgh 9 Dec. 1599 and died at Ampthill, Bedfordshire 21 Dec. 1663. He married, 2nd, 12 Nov. 1629, Lady Diana Cecil, born ca. 1596 and died 27 April 1654, widow of Henry de Vere, 18th Earl of Oxford, and daughter of William Cecil, 2nd Earl of Exeter [No. 5782], and Elizabeth Drury [No. 5783]. He married, 1st (Bishop of London's license dated 15 June 1622),
2889. Anne Chichester, born ca. 1603 and died 20 March 1627; buried at Exton, Rutland.

2890. Henry Grey, 1st Earl of Stamford, M.P. [although a peer] 1654/55, Lord Lieutenant of Leicestershire 1641/42, General and Parliamentary commander in chief of Herefordshire, Gloucestershire, Shropshire, and Worcestershire 1642, and Devonshire and Cornwall 1642/43, born at Bradgate, Leicestershire ca. 1599 and died 21 Aug. 1673; buried at Bradgate. He married (Bishop of London's license to marry at the Church of St. Bennet Sherehog dated 19 July 1620),
2891. Lady Anne Cecil, born ca. 1604 and died before 12 Oct. 1676.

2892. William Seymour, 2nd Duke of Somerset, K.G. (1660), K.B. (1616), P.C. (1640/41 and 1660), M.P. [as Lord Beauchamp] 1620-21,

Governor and Master of the Household of HRH The Prince of Wales (later HM King Charles II) 1641-43, Groom of the Stole to HM King Charles I 1643/44, Lord of the Bedchamber to HM King Charles II 1660, Lieutenant-General 1642, married in secret HM King James I's first cousin [for which he was imprisoned in the Tower of London 1610-11, when he escaped to The Netherlands and France, returning to England on his wife's death], one of the four peers who attended the funeral of Charles I in Jan. 1648/49, born 1 Sept. 1587 and died at Essex House, London 24 Oct. 1660. He married, 1st, at Greenwich Palace, Kent 22 June 1610, Lady Arabella Stuart, born ca. 1575 and died in the Tower of London 27 Sept. 1615 [having been imprisoned at Lambeth and the Tower since her marriage was discovered], daughter of Charles Stuart, 6th Earl of Lennox, and Elizabeth Cavendish. He married, 2nd, at Drayton Basset, Staffordshire 3 March 1616/17,

2893. LADY FRANCES DEVEREUX, born in Nov. 1599 and died 24 April 1674; buried at Great Bedwyn, Wiltshire.

2894. ARTHUR CAPELL, 1ST BARON CAPELL = 2202.
2895. ELIZABETH MORRISON = 2203.

2896. SIR EDWARD BISHOPP, 2ND BARONET, M.P. 1626 and 1640, Sheriff of Sussex 1636-37, born ca. 1601 and died in April 1649. He married ca. 1626,
2897. LADY MARY TUFTON, born in 1607 and died in 1663. She married, 2nd, at St. Bride's Church, Fleet Street, London 12 Aug. 1656, Percy Goring, who was buried at Burton, Sussex 17 Feb. 1697, son of Sir William Goring, 1st Baronet, and Bridget [or Eleanor] Francis.

2898. GEORGE BURY of Culham, Oxfordshire, born ca. 1623 and died in 1662. He married ca. Nov. 1649,
2899. SARAH DUNCOMBE, born ca. 1627 and died at Culham 22 Sept. 1650.

2900. EDMUND DUNCH, 1ST BARON BURNELL, M.P. [as Edmund Dunch] 1624, 1625, 1626, 1627, 1653, 1654/55, and 1656-58, Sheriff of Berkshire 1633-34 and Oxfordshire 1667/68, one of two peers created by [his cousin] the Protector, baptized at Little Wittenham, Berkshire 13 March 1602 and buried there 4 Aug. 1678. He married before 1639,
2901. BRIDGET HUNGERFORD, co-heiress of the feudal barony of Burnell.

2902. WILLIAM DORMER, High Sheriff of Oxfordshire 1666, died at Great Wycombe, Buckinghamshire 25 Sept. 1683. He married,

2903. ANNA MARIA WALLER, baptized at Beaconsfield, Buckinghamshire 23 Oct. 1634.

2904. HUGH BOSCAWEN, baptized at St. Michael Penkivel, Cornwall 28 April 1578 and buried there 9 Jan. 1640/41. He married at Petrockstowe, Devonshire 22 June 1622,

2905. MARGARET ROLLE, baptized at Petrockstowe 22 July 1600 and buried at St. Michael Penkivel 19 Dec. 1635.

2906. SIR FRANCIS GODOLPHIN, K.B. (1661), M.P. 1626, 1627/28, 1640-44, and 1660, to whom Hobbes dedicated "Leviathan," baptized at St. Margaret's Church, Westminster, Middlesex 27 Dec. 1605 and died before 21 May 1667. He married in 1631,

2907. DOROTHY BERKELEY, buried at Breage, Cornwall 23 Nov. 1668.

2908. LIEUT. COLONEL FRANCIS GODFREY of Little Chelsea, Middlesex, died 16 March 1687/88. He married,

2909. ——.

2910. SIR WINSTON CHURCHILL = 1028 = 2214.
2911. ELIZABETH DRAKE = 1029 = 2215.

2912-2915. ——.

2916. PHILIP JENNINGS of Duddleston Hall, Shropshire, born ca. 1623 and buried 27 Aug. 1670. He married,

2917. CHRISTIAN EYTON.

2918. JOHN HORNE, girdler, buried at St. Vedast's Church, Foster Lane, London 24 Sept. 1679. He married at All Hallows' Church, Bread Street, London 24 June 1641,

2919. ANNE SASCUTT, maidservant at the "Sprede Egle."

2920. SIR ROGER TWYSDEN, 2ND BARONET, M.P. 1625, 1626, and 1640, imprisoned [as was his wife] for seven years as a Royalist, born 21 Aug. 1597 and died 27 June 1672; buried at East Peckham, Kent. He married at Greenwich, Kent 1 June 1630,

2921. ISABELLA SAUNDERS, born ca. 1604 and died at Westminster, Middlesex 11 March 1656/57.

2922. JOSIAH CROSS of London and Southwark, died before 8 June 1665; buried at the Church of St. Nicholas Acon, London. He married,

2923. FRANCES GARRARD, died between 27 May 1710 and 3 Dec. 1711; buried at the Church of St. Nicholas Acon.

2924. WILLIAM WYTHENS, Gentleman of the Privy Chamber to HM King Charles I, baptized at Eltham, Kent 17 Sept. 1605 and died ca. 1647. He married,

2925. FRANCES KING of St. Mary Cray, Kent.

2926. SIR THOMAS TAYLOR, 1ST BARONET, born in 1630 and died after 18 Jan. 1664/65. He married before 1657,

2927. ELIZABETH HALL, died before 20 Aug. 1688. She married, 2nd (Faculty Office license dated 23 April 1667), Percy Goring, who was buried at Burton, Sussex 17 Feb. 1697, widower of Lady Mary Tufton [No. 2897], and son of Sir William Goring, 1st Baronet, and Bridget [or Eleanor] Francis.

2928. SIR WILLIAM BOWYER, 1ST BARONET, M.P. 1659/60 and 1661-79, Sheriff of Buckinghamshire 1646/47, Dryden's assistant in the translation of Virgil, baptized at St. Olave's Church, Hart Street, London 29 June 1612 and died 2 Oct. 1679. He married at St. Olave's Church, Old Jewry, London 29 May 1634,

2929. MARGARET WELD, died 8 Jan. 1677/78.

2930. CHARLES CECIL, VISCOUNT CRANBORNE by courtesy, **K.B. (1625/26), M.P.** 1640, baptized 15 July 1619 and died in Dec. 1660. He married at the Church of St. Martin-in-the-Fields, Westminster, Middlesex 2 April 1639,

2931. LADY DIANA MAXWELL, born in 1623 and died in June 1675.

2932. GEORGE PARKER, M.P. 1659 and 1660, born at Ratton, Sussex ca. 1619 and died 12 July 1673; buried at Willingdon, Sussex. He married by 1655,
2933. MARY NEWDIGATE, born 17 Aug. 1635.

2934. ROBERT CHILCOT ALIAS COMYN of Islesworth, Middlesex, merchant tailor of London, died between 21 July and 13 Nov. 1688. He married before 6 March 1650/51,
2935. MARY NEWMAN.

2936. SIR GEORGE STONHOUSE, 3RD BARONET = 2264.
2937. HON. MARGARET LOVELACE = 2265.

2938. ROBERT BRIGGES = 2266.
2939. SARAH MORETON = 2267.

2940. GEORGE DASHWOOD of Hackney, Middlesex, born ca. 1617 and died 8 March 1681/82; buried at the Church of St. Botolph Bishopsgate, London. He married,
2941. MARGARET PERRY, granted the precedence of a baronet's widow, buried at the Church of St. Botolph Bishopsgate 7 May 1714.

2942. SIR THOMAS CHAMBERLAYNE, 2ND BARONET, born ca. 1635 and died before 23 Nov. 1682. He married at St. Dionis Backchurch, London 8 April 1657,
2943. MARGARET PRIDEAUX, baptized at Ottery St. Mary, Devonshire 17 July 1639.

2944. HM KING CHARLES I, KING OF ENGLAND, SCOTLAND, AND IRELAND = 2192 = 2212 = 2648.
2945. HRH PRINCESSE HENRIETTE MARIE DE FRANCE ET NAVARRE = 2193 = 2213 = 2649.

2946. GUILLAUME DE PENANCOËT, SIEUR DE KÉROUALLE = 2650.
2947. MARIE ANNE DE PLŒUC = 2651.

2948. ROBERT BRUDENELL, 2ND EARL OF CARDIGAN = 1440 = 2652.
2949. LADY ANNE SAVAGE = 1441 = 2653.

2950. THOMAS SAVILE, 1ST EARL OF SUSSEX = 1442 = 2654.
2951. LADY ANNE VILLIERS = 1443 = 2655.

2952. MAJOR WILLIAM CADOGAN, M.P. 1639-40, High Sheriff of Meath 1658, born at Cardigan 5 Feb. 1600/1 and died at Dublin 14 March 1660/61. He married, 1st, Elizabeth Thring, who died 25 Jan. 1640/41. He married, 2nd,
2953. ELIZABETH ROBERTS, died 20 Feb. 1664/65.

2954. MAJOR GENERAL SIR HARDRESS WALLER, M.P. (I.) 1634 and 1640, Governor of Limerick 1651, one of the regicides who signed HM King Charles I's death warrant in Jan. 1648/49, born ca. 1604 and died at Mount Orgeuil Castle, Jersey ca. autumn 1666; he was attainted in 1660 but the sentence of execution was suspended. He married in Ireland in 1629,
2955. ELIZABETH DOWDALL, died 15 April 1658.

2956. JAN MUNTER, Mayor of Amsterdam 1670, 1674, 1676, 1680, 1682, and 1683, born at Amsterdam 26 Feb. 1611 and died there 9 March 1685. He married at the City Hall, Amsterdam 16 April 1630,
2957. MARGRIET GEELVINCK, born at Amsterdam 23 July 1612 and died there 22 July 1672.

2958. HENDRIK TRIPP, baptized at Dordrecht 14 Jan. 1607 and buried at Trippenhuys, Amsterdam 15 Nov. 1666. He married, 2nd, at Österby Castle, Sweden 14 June 1646, Jeanne de Geer, baptized at Liège 22 Feb. 1622 and died at Amsterdam 24 Nov. 1691, daughter of Matthias de Geer and Marguerite Gérard. He married, 1st, at the City Hall, Amsterdam 24 April 1633,
2959. CECILIA GODIN, born at Amsterdam in 1607 and buried at the Walloon Church, Amsterdam 8 Dec. 1637.

2960. ROBERT KERR, 1ST MARQUESS OF LOTHIAN, P.C. (1686), born at Newbattle House, Edinburgh 8 March 1635/36 and died at London 15 Feb. 1702/3. He married in Jan. 1660,
2961. LADY JEAN CAMPBELL, buried at Newbattle House 18 May 1700.

2962. ARCHIBALD CAMPBELL, 9TH EARL OF ARGYLL, P.C. (1664), F.R.S. (1663), restored to his father's earldom 1663, General of the Duke of Monmouth's forces in Scotland 1685, born at Dalkeith, Midlothianshire 26 Feb. 1628/29 and executed at the Cross of Edinburgh 30 June 1685 [having previously been attainted 1681]. He married, 2nd, 28 Jan. 1669/70, Lady Anne Mackenzie, buried at Balcarres, Fife 29 May 1707, widow of Alexander Lindsay, 1st Earl of Balcarres, and daughter of Colin Mackenzie, 1st Earl of Seaforth, and Lady Margaret Seton, daughter of Alexander Seton, 1st Earl of Dunfermline. He married, 1st, at Canongate, Edinburgh 13 May 1650,
2963. LADY MARY STEWART, died in May 1668.

2964. GEORGE NICOLSON, a Lord of Session as **LORD KEMNAY** 1682, died 8 Feb. 1710/11. He married 23 April 1663,
2965. MARGARET HALYBURTON, died 10 Aug. 1722.

2966. SIR THOMAS NICOLSON, 2ND BARONET, born 10 June 1628 and died 24 July 1664. He married,
2967. LADY MARGARET LIVINGSTON, died in 1674. She married, 2nd, in 1666, George Stirling of Keir, Stirlingshire, who died in 1667. She married, 3rd, in 1668, Sir John Stirling of Keir and Cawdor, Nairnshire, who died in 1684.

2968. CONYERS DARCY, 2ND EARL OF HOLDERNESSE, M.P. [as Hon. Conyers Darcy] 1660 and 1661-79, summoned to Parliament in his father's barony of Conyers 1680, baptized at the Church of St. Michael le Belfry, York 3 March 1621/22 and died at Aston, Yorkshire 13 Dec. 1692. He married, 1st, at Mereworth, Kent 14 May 1645, Lady Catherine Fane, buried at the Church of St. Bartholomew the Great, London 30 Aug. 1649, daughter of Francis Fane, 1st Earl of Westmorland, and Mary Mildmay. He married, 3rd, at St. Michael's Church, Coventry 19 May 1672, Lady Frances Seymour, who was buried at Westminster Abbey, Middlesex 5 Jan. 1680/81, widow of i) Richard Molyneux, 2nd Viscount Molyneux, and ii) Thomas Wriothesley, 4th Earl of Southampton [No. 2626], and daughter of William Seymour, 2nd Duke of Somerset [No. 2892], and Lady Frances Devereux [No. 2893]. He married, 4th, 8 Jan. 1684/85, Hon. Elizabeth Frescheville, born 1 Jan. 1634/35 and buried at Staveley, Derbyshire 9 March 1689/90, daughter of John Frescheville, 1st Baron Frescheville, and Sarah Harrington. He married, 2nd, at the Countess of Exeter's house, London 6 Feb. 1649/50,
2969. LADY FRANCES HOWARD, baptized at the Church of St. Martin-in-the-Fields, Westminster 19 Oct. 1623 and died at Hornby, Yorkshire 9 April 1670.

2970. ROBERT SUTTON, 1ST BARON LEXINGTON, M.P. [as Robert Sutton] 1624-25 and 1640-43, born at Averham, Nottinghamshire 21 Dec. 1594 and died 13 Oct. 1668; buried at Averham. He married, 1st, 14 April 1616, Elizabeth Manners, daughter of Sir George Manners and Grace Pierrepont. He married, 2nd, after 16 April 1635, Anne Palmes, living in 1649, widow of Sir Thomas Browne, 2nd Baronet, and daughter of Sir Guy Palmes and Anne Stafford. He married, 3rd, at St. James's Church, Clerkenwell, Middlesex 21 Feb. 1660/61,

2971. MARY ST. LEGER, died at Paris 3 Sept. 1669.

2972. FRIEDRICH HERMANN VON SCHOMBERG, 1ST DUKE OF SCHOMBERG, K.G. (1689), P.C. (1689), Gentleman of the Bedchamber to HH The Prince of Orange 1650, Commander-in-Chief of the Portuguese forces 1663 [when he was created Count of Mertola and a Grandee of Portugal], Marshal of France 1675-85, accompanied HM King William III to England 1688, Master General of the Ordnance 1689-90, Commander-in-Chief in Ireland 1689-90, born at Heidelberg 6 Dec. 1615 and killed at the Battle of the Boyne, near Drogheda 1 July 1690. He married, 2nd, 14 April 1669, Suzanne d'Aumale, who died at Dohna Palace, Berlin in July 1688, daughter of Daniel d'Aumale, Sieur d'Haucourt, and Françoise de Saint-Pol de Vaillières. He married, 1st, 30 April 1638,

2973. JOHANNA ELISABETH VON SCHÖNBURG, BURGGRÄFIN VON STARKENBURG, died at Geisenheim, Rheingau 21 March 1664.

2974. HRH KARL LUDWIG, ELECTOR PALATINE, born at Heidelberg 22 Dec. 1617/1 Jan. 1618 and died near Edingen 28 Aug./7 Sept. 1680. He married, 1st, at Cassel 12/22 Feb. 1650 (separated 14 April 1657), HH Charlotte Luise Landgräfin von Hessen-Cassel, born at Cassel 30 Nov. 1627 and died there 26 March 1686, daughter of HH Wilhelm, Landgrave of Hesse-Cassel, and Amalie Gräfin von Hanau-Münzenburg. He married, 3rd, at Schloß Friedrichsburg, Mannheim 11 Dec. 1679 [in the lifetime of his first wife], Elisabeth Holländer von Bernau, Raugräfin von der Pfalz, born at Schaffhausen in 1659 and died 8 March 1702, daughter of Tobias Holländer von Bernau and Margarete Moser. He married, 2nd, at Heidelberg 16 March 1657 [in the lifetime of his first wife],

2975. MARIA SUSANNA LUISE VON DEGENFELD, RAUGRÄFIN VON DER PFALZ, Lady in Waiting to [her predecessor] HRH The Electress Palatine, born at Strassburg 28 Nov. 1634 and died at Schloß Friedrichsburg 18 March 1677.

2976. Lewis Gordon, 3rd Marquess of Huntly = 2656.
2977. Mary Grant = 2657.

2978. Henry Howard, 6th Duke of Norfolk = 2658.
2979. Lady Anne Somerset = 2659.

2980. John Mordaunt, 1st Viscount Mordaunt = 524 = 2660.
2981. Elizabeth Carey = 525 = 2661.

2982. Dr. Sir Alexander Fraser, 1st Baronet = 2662.
2983. Mary Carey = 2663.

2984. Sir John Gordon, 1st Baronet = 2664.
2985. Janet [or Mary] Forbes = 2665.

2986. George Lockhart = 2666.
2987. Anne Lockhart = 2667.

2988. John Murray, 1st Marquess of Atholl = 2668.
2989. Lady Amelia Sophia Stanley = 2669.

2990. William Douglas-Hamilton, 1st Duke of Hamilton = 2670.
2991. Anne Hamilton, Duchess of Hamilton = 2671.

2992. William Maxwell = 2672.
2993. Margaret MacCulloch = 2673.

2994. Sir Thomas Hay, 1st Baronet = 2674.
2995. Marion Hamilton = 2675.

2996. Alexander Montgomerie, 8th Earl of Eglinton = 2676.
2997. Lady Elizabeth Crichton = 2677.

2998. William Cochrane, Lord Cochrane = 2678.
2999. Lady Catherine Kennedy = 2679.

3000. Sir William Scott = 2680.
3001. Barbara Dalmahoy = 2681.

3002. Sir Thomas Nicolson = 2682.
3003. Margaret Scott = 2683.

3004-3007. = 2684-2687.

3008. Right Rev. Lewis Bayly, Bishop of Bangor (1616-31), Chaplain to HM King James I, born in Carmarthenshire and died 16 Oct. 1631. He married,
3009. Anne Bagenall, died 11 Sept. 1633; buried at Chester Cathedral.

3010-3011. ——.

3012. Charles Lambart, 1st Earl of Cavan, P.C. (I.), M.P. [as Lord Lambart] 1626 and 1628-29, born in Ireland in March 1596/97 and died 25 June 1660; buried at St. Patrick's Cathedral, Dublin. He married before 30 June 1625,
3013. Hon. Jane Robartes, baptized at Truro, Cornwall 21 Dec. 1598 and died in 1655; buried at St. Patrick's Cathedral.

3014. Simon Crane of Dublin, died ca. 1685. He married,
3015. ——.

3016. William Paget, 6th Baron Paget, K.B. (1625/26), Lord Lieutenant of Buckinghamshire 1641, born 13 Sept. 1609 and died at Old Palace Yard, Westminster, Middlesex 19 Oct. 1672. He married at Kensington, Middlesex 28 June 1632,
3017. Lady Frances Rich, buried at West Drayton, Middlesex 12 Nov. 1672.

3018. COLONEL HUGH O'RORKE, Sheriff of Leitrim 1689, married,
3019. JOAN REYNOLDS of Loughscur, Kiltubbrid, Leitrim.

3020. PETER WHETCOMBE of Margaretting, Essex, baptized at St. Margaret's Church, Westminster, Middlesex 4 Nov. 1590 and died between 31 Jan. 1666/67 and 23 Nov. 1667. He married,
3021. JULIAN HYDE, died in 1666.

3022. RICHARD SHERARD, baptized at North Witham, Lincolnshire 16 Dec. 1616 and died 12 Sept. 1668. He married at the Church of St. Margaret Pattens, London 28 July 1658,
3023. MARGARET DEWE, baptized at Shobdon, Herefordshire 21 Jan. 1625/26 and buried at North Witham 3 Nov. 1680.

3024. DANIEL DE ROBILLARD married 10 April 1623,
3025. JUDITH POITEVIN.

3026. CASIMIR JEAN CHARLES DE LA ROCHEFOUCAULD, SEIGNEUR DE FONTPASTOUR, married,
3027. ? MARIE FRANÇOISE DE MAIZIÈRES.

3028. ARTHUR FORBES, 1ST EARL OF GRANARD, P.C. (I.) (1661, 1686, AND 1690), M.P. [as Sir Arthur Forbes, Bt.] 1661-66, Marshal of the Army in Ireland 1670-84, Lord Justice [i.e. Regent] in Ireland 1671, 1675-76, and 1684/85, born ca. 1623 and died at Castle Forbes, Longford 1 Nov. 1695. He married ca. 1655,
3029. CATHERINE NEWCOMEN, died at Dublin 8 Dec. 1714. She married, 1st, ca. 1648, Sir Alexander Stewart, 2nd Baronet, who was killed at Dunbar, Lothianshire 3 Sept. 1653, son of Sir William Stewart, 1st Baronet, and Frances Newcomen.

3030. RIGHT HON. SIR GEORGE RAWDON, 1ST BARONET, P.C. (I.) (1661), M.P. 1639/40, 1659, and 1661-66, Governor of Carrickfergus 1661, born at Rawdon, Yorkshire in 1604 and died 18 Aug. 1684; buried at Lisburn, Downshire. He married, 1st, in 1639, Ursula Stafford, who died at Brook Hill, Lisburn aged 30, widow of Francis Hill, and daughter of Sir Francis Stafford and Anne Grogan. He married, 2nd, in Sept. 1654,
3031. HON. DOROTHY CONWAY, died in 1676.

3032. ? Hector Hamon, died ca. 1741. He married,

3033. ? Marianne Mazik, born in 1684 and died in 1763.

3034-3039. ——.

3040. Colonel Sir Edward Villiers, Knight Marshal of the (Royal) Household 1678, baptized at Westminster Abbey, Middlesex 15 April 1620 and died in June 1689; buried at Westminster Abbey. He married, 2nd, 25 Feb. 1683/84, Martha Love, who died in 1738. He married, 1st (banns published at St. Paul's Church, Covent Garden, near London 3, 8, and 13 Nov. 1654),

3041. Lady Frances Howard, Governess to TRH Princesses Mary and Anne of York (later TM Queen Mary II and Queen Anne), buried at Westminster Abbey 7 Nov. 1677.

3042. William Chiffinch, M.P. 1685, Keeper of the Royal Closet [by which he made himself indispensable to TM King Charles II and King James II], buried at Bray, Berkshire 26 Nov. 1691. He married before 1662,

3043. Barbara Nunn.

3044. Sir Nathaniel Herne, M.P. 1679, Sheriff of London 1674/75, Governor of the East India Company 1674-76 and 1678-79, born in 1629 and died 10 Aug. 1679. He married at St. Olave's Church, Old Jewry, London 1 Sept. 1656,

3045. Judith Frederick, baptized at St. Olave's Church 7 Aug. 1639.

3046. Colonel William Lisle, M.P. 1659, 1660, 1679, and 1681, born ca. 1632 and died 12 July 1716; buried at Evenley, Northamptonshire. He married (Bishop of London's license to marry at St. Peter's Church, Paul's Wharf 9 Nov. 1661),

3047. Elizabeth Aylworth, died in 1687; buried at Evenley.

3048. John Egerton, 2nd Earl of Bridgewater, P.C. (1666/67), Lord Lieutenant of Buckinghamshire 1660-86, Cheshire and Lancashire 1670-76, and Hertfordshire 1681-86, born 29 May 1623 and died at Bridgewater House, Barbican, London 26 Oct. 1686. He married at St. James's Church, Clerkenwell, Middlesex 22 July 1641,

3049. LADY ELIZABETH CAVENDISH, born ca. 1626 and died at Black Rod's House, Westminster, Middlesex 14 June 1663.

3050. CHARLES POWLETT, 1ST DUKE OF BOLTON, P.C. (1679), M.P. [as Lord St. John] 1660 and 1661-75, Lord Lieutenant of Hampshire 1668-76 and 1689-99, of whom Burnet wrote that "though he was much hated, yet he carried matters before him with such authority and success, that he was in all respects the great riddle of the age," born ca. 1630 and died at Amport, Hampshire 27 Feb. 1698/99. He married, 1st, 28 Feb. 1651/52, Hon. Christian Frescheville, born 13 Dec. 1633 and died 22 May 1653, daughter of John Frescheville, 1st Baron Frescheville, and Sarah Harrington. He married, 2nd, at St. Dionis Backchurch, London 12 Feb. 1654/55,

3051. MARY SCROPE, died at Moulins, France 1 Nov. 1680. She married, 1st, Henry Carey, Lord Leffington by courtesy, who died in 1649, son of Henry Carey, 2nd Earl of Monmouth, and Lady Martha Cranfield, daughter of Lionel Cranfield, 1st Earl of Middlesex.

3052. SIR WINSTON CHURCHILL = 1028 = 2214 = 2910.
3053. ELIZABETH DRAKE = 1029 = 2215 = 2911.

3054. RICHARD JENNINGS = 1030.
3055. FRANCES THORNHURST = 1031.

3056. SIR ROGER TWYSDEN, 2ND BARONET = 2920.
3057. ISABELLA SAUNDERS = 2921.

3058. JOSIAH CROSS = 2922.
3059. FRANCES GARRARD = 2923.

3060. SIR THOMAS TWYSDEN, 1ST BARONET, M.P. 1647-48 and 1660, a Justice of the King's Bench 1660-83, born at Roydon Hall, Kent 8 Jan. 1601/2 and died at Bradburn, Kent 2 Jan. 1682/83. He married at Roydon Hall 26 Dec. 1639,

3061. JANE THOMLINSON, born ca. 1613 and died 24 Sept. 1702.

3062. PHILIP LEMON of Ditton, Surrey, married,
3063. ISABEL ——.

3064. ? WILLIAM CARTER of Dinton, Buckinghamshire, married in 1641,
3065. ? MARGARET THORPE.

3066-3069. ——.

3070. EDWARD PEARCE of Witlingham, Norfolk, died between 14 April and 10 Nov. 1683. He married,
3071. MARY CARLETON, died in 1728.

3072-3075. ——.

3076. STEPHEN COPPINGER, Mayor of Cork, died 2 July 1600. He married,
3077. ——.

3078. JOHN COPPINGER, Mayor of Cork 1616 and 1619, born ca. 1556 and died ca. 6 Dec. 1637. He married, 2nd, Catherine Roche, daughter of Richard Roche FitzPhilip of Kinsale. He married, 1st,
3079. JOAN MEAGH.

3080-3183. ——.

3184. DONEL O'DONOVAN, died ca. 1638. He married,
3185. JOANNA MacCARTHY.

3186. ROGER O'SHAUGHNESSY married,
3187. ELLIS LYNCH.

3188-3199. ——.

3200. RICHARD BOOTHBY, baptized at the Church of St. Lawrence Jewry, London 20 June 1596 and died at Potters Marston, Leicestershire 15 Aug. 1640. He married 14 Aug. 1630,

3201. ELEANOR CURZON, born 28 June 1597 and died before 7 July 1646; buried at Potters Marston.

3202. ANDREW HALFORD of Kilby, Leicestershire, born ca. 1603 and died in 1657. He married, 1st, Elizabeth Turpin, daughter of George Turpin of Knaptoft, Leicestershire. He married, 3rd, Mary Nichols, widow of Richard Orton, and daughter of William Nichols of Halsted, Essex. He married, 2nd, at Bourne, Lincolnshire 10 July 1636,

3203. MARY HACKET, born ca. July 1618.

3204-3295. ——.

3296. DAVID GUINAND, died ca. 1642. He married before 1615,
3297. MARIE PERRET-GENTIL.

3298. ABRAHAM PAREL married,
3299. ——.

3300-3311. ——.

3312. JEAN YVONNET, born 15 Oct. 1593. He married,
3313. JUDITH BOISBELET, born 12 Nov. 1594.

3314. JEAN YVONNET = 3312.
3315. JUDITH BOISBELET = 3313.

3316-3407. ——.

3408. JOHN NEWBOLD, yeoman of Hackenthorpe, Derbyshire, died 7 May 1610. He married,
3409. ISABEL ——, died in 1614.

3410. Matthew Syms married,
3411. ——.

3412-3519. ——.

3520. John Strong, born at or near Chard, Somerset ca. 1610 and died at Northampton, Massachusetts 14 April 1699. He married, 1st, ca. 1630, Margery Deane, who died after 22 July 1634, daughter of William Deane of Chard. He married, 2nd (perhaps at Dorchester, Massachusetts ca. 1636),
3521. Abigail Ford, baptized at Bridport, Dorset 8 Oct. 1619 and died at Northampton 6 July 1688.

3522. Deacon William Holton, possibly baptized at Nayland, Suffolk 20 Oct. 1610 and died at Northampton, Massachusetts 12 Aug. 1691. He married,
3523. Mary ——, died at Northampton 16 Nov. 1691.

3524. Samuel Allen, buried at Windsor, Connecticut 28 April 1648. He married,
3525. Ann ——, born ca. 1608 and died at Northampton, Massachusetts 13 Nov. 1687. She married, 2nd, before 1649, William Hulbird, born ca. 1606 and died at Northampton 17 April 1694.

3526. Thomas Woodford, born ca. 1614 and died at Northampton, Massachusetts 6 March 1666/67. He married (probably at Roxbury, Massachusetts before 1639),
3527. Mary Blott, baptized at Harrold, Bedfordshire 24 Dec. 1609 and died before 27 May 1662.

3528. John Strong = 3520.
3529. Abigail Ford = 3521.

3530. Henry Woodward, innkeeper, possibly baptized at Childwall, Much Woolton, Lancashire 22 March 1606/7 and died at Northampton, Massachusetts 7 April 1683. He married ca. 1640,
3531. Elizabeth ——, died at Northampton 13 Aug. 1690.

3532-3533. ———.

3534. STEPHEN HART, representative to the Connecticut General Court 1647–55 and 1660, possibly baptized at Ipswich, Suffolk 25 Jan. 1602/3 and died at Farmington, Connecticut between 16 March 1682/83 and 31 March 1683. He married, 2nd, Margaret ———, who died between 18 Feb. 1691/92 and 1 March 1693/94, widow of i) Arthur Smith and ii) Joseph Nash. He married, 1st, **3535. ———,** died at Farmington ca. 1678.

3536. THOMAS BISHOP, innkeeper, representative to the Massachusetts General Court 1666, died at Ipswich, Massachusetts 7 Feb. 1670/71. He married, **3537. MARGARET ———,** died at Ipswich before 29 March 1681.

3538. WILLIAM COGSWELL, baptized at Westbury Leigh, Wiltshire in March 1619/20 and died at Chebacco in Ipswich, Massachusetts 15 Dec. 1700. He married (probably at Lynn, Massachusetts ca. 1649), **3539. SUSANNA HAWKES,** twin, born at Charlestown, Massachusetts 13 Aug. 1633 and died at Ipswich before 5 Aug. 1696.

3540. JOHN FOBES, tailor, died at Bridgewater, Massachusetts in 1660. He married, **3541. CONSTANT MITCHELL.** She married, 2nd, in 1662, John Briggs of Portsmouth, Rhode Island, who died in 1690.

3542. JOHN GAGER, baptized at Little Waldingfield, Suffolk 5 May 1620 and died at Norwich, Connecticut 10 Dec. 1703. He married before Sept. 1647, **3543. ELIZABETH GORE,** born ca. 1627 and died after 10 Jan. 1703/4.

3544. ROBERT HIBBARD, salt maker and bricklayer, possibly baptized at St. Edmund's Church, Salisbury 13 March 1613 and died at Beverly, Massachusetts 7 May 1684. He married at Salem, Massachusetts ca. 1640, **3545. JOAN ? LUFF,** died at Beverly shortly before 6 April 1696.

3546. EDWARD WALDEN, born ca. 1625 and died at Wenham, Massachusetts before 25 June 1679. He married, **3547. THOMASINE ———,** living in June 1671.

3548. JAMES MORGAN, representative to the Connecticut General Court 1657, 1658, 1661, 1663, 1665, 1666, and 1670, born ca. 1607 and died at New London, Connecticut in 1685. He married at Roxbury, Massachusetts 6 Aug. 1640,
3549. MARGERY HILL.

3550. DEACON THOMAS PARKE, born at Hitcham, Suffolk in 1616 and died at Preston, Connecticut 30 July 1709. He married at Roxbury, Massachusetts before 28 Oct. 1644,
3551. DOROTHY THOMPSON, baptized at Preston Capes, Northamptonshire 5 July 1624 and died after 5 Sept. 1707.

3552-3871. ———.

3872. REV. GEORGE CHALMER of Rhynie, Aberdeenshire, died in 1660. He married in 1646,
3873. JEAN GORDON, died at Elgin, Morayshire 25 July 1691.

3874. ALEXANDER INNES of Culquoich, Aberdeenshire, married,
3875. ———.

3876. REV. GEORGE CHALMER = 3872.
3877. JEAN GORDON = 3873.

3878. ? SIR JOHN FORBES of Waterton, Aberdeenshire, born in 1638 and died in 1675. He married in 1663,
3879. ? JEAN GORDON of Haddo, Aberdeenshire, died in 1688.

3880. REV. ROBERT TRAIL, chaplain to Archibald Campbell, 1st Marquess of Argyll [No. 5922], refused to subscribe to the Oath of Allegiance to HM King Charles II 1662 [for which he was banished 1663-74], born in 1603 and died at Edinburgh in 1676. He married in 1639,
3881. JEAN ANNAND, died at Edinburgh in 1680.

3882. Lieut. Colonel James Trail, High Sheriff of Downshire 1655, born in 1600 and died at Tullochin, near Killyleagh, Downshire 18 May 1663. He married 21 March 1646/47,
3883. Mary Hamilton, died in 1686.

3884. John Allardes, Burgess of Aberdeen, born ca. 1600 and died 3 Dec. 1699. He married,
3885. Isobel Walker, born ca. 1617 and died 19 Feb. 1679/80.

3886-3887. ——.

3888. James Douglas of Inchmarlo, Kincardineshire, died in 1672. He married in 1642,
3889. Isobel Ramsay of Balmain, Kincardineshire.

3890-3895. ——.

3896. Thomas Forbes, 11th of Echt, Aberdeenshire, died in 1698. He married,
3897. Margaret Forbes of Wester Echt.

3898. Sir Robert Innes, 2nd Baronet, M.P. 1661-63 and 1678, married,
3899. Hon. Jean [or Margaret] Ross.

3900-3903. ——.

3904. Thomas Bentley married at Heptonstall, Yorkshire 29 Oct. 1605,
3905. Mary Mychell, buried at Heptonstall 19 June 1621.

3906. Joseph Crabtree, buried at Methley, Yorkshire 12 June 1634. He married at Methley 3 Feb. 1606/7,
3907. Julian Crabtree, baptized at Methley 11 June 1581 and buried there 17 March 1612/13.

3908-3935. ———.

3936. WILLIAM DINGWALL of Seilscruick, Monquhitter, Aberdeenshire, born ca. 1600. He married,
3937. BARBARA BARCLAY.

3938. JOHN IRVINE of Brucklaw, Aberdeenshire, died before 1679. He married, 2nd, Jean Johnstone. He married, 1st,
3939. MARGARET URQUHART of Cromartie, Ross-shire.

3940-3941. ———.

3942. JOHN GELLIE, died 4 Aug. 1683. He married,
3943. MARIA JEFFRAY, died 4 Feb. 1704/5.

3944-3947. ———.

3948. WILLIAM LINDSAY of Mill of Tollie, Fyvie, Aberdeenshire, married,
3949. ———.

3950. ALEXANDER LEITH married,
3951. CHRISTIAN HEPBURN.

3952-3959. ———.

3960. ANDREW DYCE, born at Belhevie, Aberdeenshire 14 March 1624/25. He married,
3961. ———.

3962-4015. ———.

4016. ROBERT LUMSDEN of Cushnie, Aberdeenshire, died before 1696. He married,
4017. AGNES LEITH of Bucharn, Aberdeenshire.

4018. ROBERT GORDON of Auchindour, Aberdeenshire, married,
4019. ——.

4020-4031. ——.

4032. SIR WILLIAM FORBES, 2ND BARONET, died in 1654. He married after 21 May 1632,
4033. JEAN BURNETT of Leys, Aberdeenshire, who persuaded James Graham, 1st Marquess of Montrose, to spare Monymusk House during the Scottish Civil War. She married, 2nd, Robert Cumyn of Altyre, Morayshire.

4034. JOHN DALMAHOY, died after 1 Dec. 1644. He married,
4035. RACHEL WILBRAHAM, born 7 March 1625/26.

4036. ALEXANDER MORISON of Bognie, Aberdeenshire. He married, 2nd, Katherine Gordon. He married, 1st,
4037. ELIZABETH GAIRDEN.

4038. ALEXANDER URQUHART of Cromartie, Ross-shire, born in 1613 and died in 1667. He married in 1637,
4039. HON. JEAN ELPHINSTONE.

4040-4043. ——.

4044. WALTER FORBES of Blackton, Aberdeenshire, born in 1625. He married,
4045. HELEN FORBES of Balfluig, Aberdeenshire.

4046. WALTER HACKET of Mayen, Morayshire, married,
4047. ——.

4048. ALEXANDER MORISON = 4036.
4049. ELIZABETH GAIRDEN = 4037.

4050. ALEXANDER URQUHART = 4038.
4051. HON. JEAN ELPHINSTONE = 4039.

4052. SIR RICHARD MAITLAND, 1ST BARONET, died 22 Feb. 1677/78. He married,
4053. MARGARET GORDON of Straloch, Aberdeenshire.

4054. SIR JOHN FORBES, 3RD BARONET = 2016. He married, 1st (contract dated 22 April 1657),
4055. HON. MARGARET ARBUTHNOTT.

4056. WILLIAM DUFF, Provost of Inverness 1692-95, 1699-1701, and 1703-6, born ca. 1632 and died in 1715. He married, 2nd, in 1666, Janet Lockhart of Inverness, who died in 1690. He married, 3rd, in 1691, Jean Fraser, widow of Rev. Alexander Clark. He married, 1st, at Inverness 9 Jan. 1654/55,
4057. CHRISTIAN DUFF, died ca. 1660.

4058. ADAM DUFF of Drummuir, Banffshire, died in 1682. He married, 2nd (contract dated 21 July 1679), Dorothy Lawson. He married, 1st (contract dated 30 Oct. 1667),
4059. ANNE ABERCROMBY, died ca. 1671.

4060. SIR JOHN GORDON, 1ST BARONET, died in Feb. 1712/13. He married, 1st, —— Graham. He married, 2nd, Jean Forbes of Tolquhoun, Aberdeenshire. He married, 3rd, Katherine Ogilvy of Kempcairn, Banffshire. He married, 4th (contract dated 3 March 1685/86),
4061. LADY HELEN OGILVY.

4062. William Fraser, 3rd Lord Saltoun, born 21 Nov. 1654 and died 18 March 1714/15. He married 11 Oct. 1683,

4063. Margaret Sharpe, born 8 Dec. 1664 and died at Edinburgh 29 Aug. 1734.

4064-4095. ——.

Twelfth Generation

4096. ROBERT SPENCER, 1ST BARON SPENCER, M.P. [as Robert Spencer] 1597-98, Ambassador to Württemburg 1603, created a peer, "as he said, for the report of his being the greatest moneyed man in England," born in 1570 and died at Wormleighton, Warwickshire 25 Oct. 1627. He married at Brington, Northamptonshire 15 Feb. 1587/88,

    4097. MARGARET WILLOUGHBY, died 17 Aug. 1597; buried at Brington.

4098. HENRY WRIOTHESLEY, 3RD EARL OF SOUTHAMPTON, K.G. (1603), Treasurer and Governor of the Virginia Company 1620-24, attainted for his role in Essex's rebellion and a prisoner in the Tower of London 1601-3 [after which he was pardoned and restored to all his honours], recognised by Shakespeare as his preeminent patron, born at Cowdray, Sussex 6 Oct. 1573 and died at Bergen-op-Zoom, The Netherlands 10 Nov. 1624. He married in secret shortly before 30 Aug. 1598,

    4099. ELIZABETH VERNON, Maid of Honour to HM Queen Elizabeth I, baptized at Hodnet, Shropshire 11 Jan. 1572/73 and died sometime after 23 Nov. 1655.

4100. ROBERT SIDNEY, 1ST EARL OF LEICESTER, K.G. (1616), M.P. [as Robert Sidney and Sir Robert Sidney] 1584-86, 1593, and 1597-98, Chamberlain to HM Queen Anne, born at Penshurst, Kent 19 Nov. 1563 and died there 13 July 1626. He married, 2nd, at Sutton at Hone, Kent 25 April 1625, Sarah Blount, who was buried there 12 March 1654/55, widow of Thomas Smythe, and daughter of William Blount and Anne Byrnand. He married, 1st, at St. Donat's, Glamorganshire 23 Sept. 1584,

    4101. BARBARA GAMAGE, born ca. 1559 and buried at Penshurst 26 May 1621.

4102. HENRY PERCY, 3RD EARL OF NORTHUMBERLAND, K.G. (1593), P.C. (1603), General 1599, joint Lord Lieutenant of Sussex 1604-5, arrested in "the Gunpowder plot" 1605 [imprisoned in the Tower of London 1605-21], born at Tynemouth Castle, Northumberland ca. 27 April 1564 and died at Petworth, Sussex 5 Nov. 1632. He married in 1594,

4103. LADY DOROTHY DEVEREUX, died 3 Aug. 1619, daughter of Walter Devereux, 1st Earl of Essex. She married, 1st, in July 1583, Sir Thomas Perrott, born in 1553 and died in Feb. 1593/94, son of Sir John Perrott and Anne Cheney.

4104. SIR GEORGE DIGBY, M.P. 1572 and 1584, Sheriff of Warwickshire 1580/81, born 4 Nov. 1550 and died in April 1587. He married,

4105. ABIGAIL HEVENINGHAM. She married, 2nd, Edward Cordell, who died 9 Dec. 1590, son of John Cordell and Emma Webb.

4106. CHARLES WALCOTT, M.P. 1586 and 1589, buried at North Lydbury, Shropshire 22 Aug. 1596. He married, 2nd, Margaret Isham, daughter of John Isham. He married, 1st, at Ludlow, Shropshire 19 Aug. 1566,

4107. BEATRICE GIRLING.

4108. WILLIAM RUSSELL, 1ST BARON RUSSELL, M.P. [as Hon. William Russell] 1572, Lieutenant General 1585, Chief Governor [as Lord Deputy] of Ireland 1594-97, born ca. 1553 and died at Northall, Buckinghamshire 9 Aug. 1613, son of Francis Russell, 2nd Earl of Bedford. He married at Watford, Hertfordshire (Bishop of London's license dated 13 Feb. 1584/85),

4109. ELIZABETH LONG, died 12 June 1611; buried at Watford.

4110. GILES BRYDGES, 3RD BARON CHANDOS, M.P. [as Hon. Giles Brydges] 1572-73, Lord Lieutenant of Gloucestershire 1586, born in 1548 and died 21 Feb. 1593/94, son of Edmund Brydges, 2nd Baron Chandos. He married before Sept. 1573,

4111. LADY FRANCES CLINTON, died at Woburn Abbey, Bedfordshire 12 Sept. 1623, daughter of Edward Clinton, 1st Earl of Lincoln.

4112. JASPER CHURCHILL of Bradford Peverell, Dorset, born ca. 1556 and died before 14 Aug. 1601. He married,

4113. ELIZABETH ——, living 14 Aug. 1601.

4114. Sir Henry Winston, born ca. 1561 and died in Feb. 1608/9. He married, 1st, Elizabeth Vaughan, daughter of Watkin Vaughan of Bredwardine, Herefordshire. He married, 2nd,

4115. Dionise Bond, baptized at the Church of St. Stephen Walbrook, London 3 July 1566 and died in March 1608/9, daughter of George Bond.

4116. John Drake, buried at Musbury, Devonshire 11 April 1628. He married,

4117. Dorothy Button, buried at Musbury 13 Dec. 1631.

4118. John Boteler, 1st Baron Boteler, born ca. 1565 and died at London 27 May 1637. He married ca. 1600,

4119. Elizabeth Villiers, daughter of Sir George Villiers [No. 5772] and half-sister of George Villiers, 1st Duke of Buckingham.

4120. Sir John Jennings, died before 22 Nov. 1611. He married, 2nd, Dorothy Bulbeck. He married, 1st,

4121. **Anne Brouncker** of Melksham, Wiltshire.

4122. Sir Richard Spencer, M.P. 1584, 1589, and 1604, born before 1553 and died 7 March 1623/24. He married in 1588,

4123. Helen Brockett, died 12 May 1614.

4124. Sir William Thornhurst, baptized at St. Peter's Church, Beaksbourne, Kent 18 Oct. 1575 and died 24 July 1606. He married,

4125. Hon. Anne Howard, buried at Bere Regis, Dorset 13 Nov. 1633, daughter of Thomas Howard, 1st Viscount Bindon. She married, 2nd, in 1608, John Turberville.

4126. Sir Alexander Temple, M.P. 1625/26, died in Dec. 1629; buried at Rochester Cathedral, Kent. He married, 1st, Mary Somer, widow of Thomas Peniston, and daughter of John Somer and Martina Ridge. He married, 2nd,

4127. Mary Beve of Bury St. Edmund, Suffolk.

4128. HELIER DE CARTERET, Attorney General of Jersey 1614, born ca. 1585 and died in 1634. He married at Sark 8 June 1608,
4129. ELIZABETH DUMARESQ, died ca. 1640.

4130. SIR PHILIP DE CARTERET, Lieutenant Governor of Jersey 1624 and 1634-43, born at Sark 18 Feb. 1583/84 and died at Elizabeth Castle, Jersey 23 Aug. 1643. He married before 1605,
4131. ANNE DOWSE, died 30 Jan. 1643/44.

4132. SIR SIDNEY MONTAGU, M.P. 1593, 1601, 1614, and 1640, Master of Requests 1618-44, born ca. 1571 and died 25 Sept. 1644. He married, 2nd, Anne Isham, baptized at Bugbrooke, Northamptontonshire 28 Jan. 1598/99 and died before 19 Dec. 1676, daughter of George Isham and Elizabeth Catlyn. He married, 1st, at All Saints' Church, Barnwell, Northamptonshire (license dated 21 Aug. 1619),
4133. PAULINA PEPYS, baptized at Cottenham, Cambridgeshire 17 Sept. 1581 and died 17 Feb. 1637/38.

4134. JOHN CREW, 1ST BARON CREW, M.P. [as John Crew] 1624-26, 1628-29, 1640-48, 1654-55, and 1660, one of the deputation to meet HM King Charles II at The Hague, born in 1598 and died 12 Dec. 1679, son of Sir Thomas Crewe [No. 2690]. He married at Lawford, Essex 24 Feb. 1621/22,
4135. JEMIMA WALDEGRAVE, baptized at Lawford 26 Oct. 1602 and died 14 Oct. 1675.

4136. SIR BERNARD GRENVILLE, M.P. 1620, Sheriff of Cornwall 1595/96, born ca. 1559 and died 16 June 1636; buried at Kilkhampton, Cornwall. He married at Withiel, Cornwall 10 July 1592,
4137. ELIZABETH BEVIL of Killygarth, Cornwall.

4138. SIR GEORGE SMYTHE of Madford, Heavitree, Devonshire, died in 1619. He married, 1st, at St. Martin's Church, Exeter 30 Sept. 1572, Joan Walker, daughter of James Walker. He married, 2nd (settlement dated 30 March 1598),
4139. GRACE VIELL, buried at Kilkhampton, Cornwall 16 Jan. 1644/45. She married, 1st, at St. Breock, Cornwall 6 Sept. 1591, Peter Bevil of Killygarth, Cornwall, son of John Bevil and Elizabeth Milliton.

4140. Richard Wyche, Master of the Skinners' Company, born in 1554 and died 20 Nov. 1621; buried at the Church of St. Dunstan-in-the-East, London. He married there 18 Feb. 1583/84,

4141. Elizabeth Saltonstall, buried at the Church of St. Dunstan-in-the-East 25 Jan. 1626/27, daughter of Sir Richard Saltonstall.

4142. Sir William Meredith, M.P. 1593, Paymaster of the forces in The Netherlands 1597, died after 25 July 1603. He married, 1st, before 12 Feb. 1565/66, Martha Long, daughter of Robert Long. He married, 2nd, after 1585,

4143. Jane Palmer. She married, 2nd, after 1604, John Vaughan, 1st Earl of Carbery, M.P. 1601 and 1620-22, Comptroller of the Household of HRH The Prince of Wales (later HM King Charles I) 1623, born ca. 1575 and died at Golden Grove, Carmarthenshire 6 May 1634, son of Walter Vaughan [No. 8574] and Mary Rice [No. 8575].

4144. Sir Richard Worsley, 1st Baronet, M.P. 1614 and 1620/21, Sheriff of Hampshire 1616/17, born ca. 1589 and died 27 June 1621; buried at Godshill, Isle of Wight. He married about 1610,

4145. Frances Neville, died between 18 Oct. 1659 and 27 May 1661, daughter of Sir Henry Neville [No. 4220].

4146. Sir Henry Wallop, Sheriff of Hampshire 1602/3 and Shropshire 1605/6, born 28 Oct. 1568 and died 16 Nov. 1642. He married before 1 June 1601,

4147. Elizabeth Corbet, died 5 Nov. 1624.

4148. Philip Herbert, 4th Earl of Pembroke and 1st Earl of Montgomery, K.G. (1608), K.B. (1603), M.P. [as Hon. Sir Philip Herbert] 1604-5 and [as Earl of Pembroke and Montgomery] 1648 [after the abolition of the House of Lords], Gentleman of the Privy Chamber to HM King James I 1603-25, bore the banner of the Union at the funeral of HRH The Prince Henry Frederick, Prince of Wales 1612 and the Great Banner at the funeral of HM Queen Anne 1619, served as assistant to the Chief Mourner at the funeral of HM King James I 1625, bore the Spurs at the coronation of HM King Charles I 1625/26, Lord Chamberlain of the (Royal) Household 1626-41, Captain General in the West 1642, Parliamentary Lord Lieutenant of Hampshire 1641/42, Monmouthshire, Glamorganshire, Brecknockshire, and Kent 1642, Somerset 1643, and Cardiganshire 1646, one of the "incomparable pair of brethren" to whom Shakespeare's First Folio was dedicated in 1623, born at Wilton House, Salisbury 10 Oct. 1584 and died at the Cockpit, Westminster, Middlesex 23 Jan. 1649/50. He married, 2nd, at Chenies, Buckinghamshire 3 June 1630, Anne Clifford, Baroness Clifford in her own right, born ca. 1588 and died at Brougham Castle, Westmorland 22 March 1675/76, widow of Richard Sackville, 3rd Earl of Dorset, and daughter of George Clifford, 3rd Earl of Cumberland, and Lady Margaret Russell, daughter of Francis Russell, 2nd Earl of Bedford [No. 8216]. He married, 1st, at Whitehall, near London 27 Dec. 1604,

4149. LADY SUSAN DE VERE, born 26 May 1587 and buried at Westminster Abbey, Middlesex 1 Feb. 1628/29, daughter of Edward de Vere, 17th Earl of Oxford.

4150. SIR ROBERT SPILLER, M.P. 1621-22 and 1624-25, born ca. 1591 and buried at Shepperton, Middlesex 21 May 1637. He married at the Church of St. Mary le Strand, London 11 Nov. 1615,

4151. DOROTHY DORMER of Haddenham, Buckinghamshire.

4152. SIR THOMAS THYNNE, M.P. 1601, 1604, 1621, 1624, 1625, 1626, and 1628, Sheriff of Wiltshire 1607-8, Gloucestershire 1621-22, Somerset 1629-30, and Shropshire 1633-34, born ca. 1578 and died 1 Aug. 1639. He married, 1st, ca. 1601, Hon. Mary Tuchet, daughter of George Tuchet, 11th Baron Audley, and Lucy Mervyn. He married, 2nd, ca. 1612,

4153. CATHERINE LYTE ALIAS HOWARD, died in 1650.

4154. THOMAS COVENTRY, 1ST BARON COVENTRY, P.C. (1625), M.P. [as Sir Thomas Coventry] 1620-21, Solicitor General 1617-21, Attorney General 1621-25, Lord Keeper of the Great Seal 1625-40, born at Croome Dabitot, Worcestershire in 1578 and died at Durham House in the Strand, near London 14 Jan. 1639/40. He married, 1st, before 1606, Sarah Sebright, who was baptized at Wolverley, Worcestershire 27 May 1583, daughter of John Sebright and Anne Bullingham. He married, 2nd, before 1610,

4155. ELIZABETH ALDERSEY, buried at St. Gregory's Church, London 25 May 1653. She married, 1st, William Pitchford, who died ca. 1609.

4156. THOMAS FINCH, 2ND EARL OF WINCHILSEA, M.P. [as Sir Thomas Finch, Bt.] 1621-22 and [as Viscount Maidstone] 1628-29, born at Heneage House, London 13 June 1578 and died at Charterhouse Yard, London 4 Nov.

1639, son of Sir Moyle Finch, 1st Baronet, and Elizabeth Heneage, Countess of Winchilsea in her own right. He married in 1609,

4157. Cicely Wentworth, died before 1 Dec. 1642; buried at Eastwell, Kent.

4158. William Seymour, 2nd Duke of Somerset = 2892.
4159. Lady Frances Devereux = 2893.

4160. John Poyntz, M.P. 1529, Sewer to HM Queen Catherine 1520, born ca. 1485 and died 29 Nov. 1544. He married, 1st, by 1528, Elizabeth Browne, daughter of Sir Matthew Browne and Fridiswide Guildford. He married, 2nd (settlement dated 1 May 1544),

4161. Margaret Saunders, died between 22 Sept. 1563 and 4 July 1564. She married, 2nd, James Skinner of Reigate, Surrey, who died 30 July 1558, son of John Skinner and Catherine ———.

4162. Thomas Newdigate, died at Wivelsfield, Sussex 16 Oct. 1559. He married after 1526,

4163. Katherine Hampden of Hampden, Buckinghamshire. She married, 1st, ca. 1523, Henry Ferrers, who died in 1526, son of Sir Edward Ferrers and Constance Brome.

4164. Sir John Sydenham, M.P. 1554, Sheriff of Somerset and Dorset 1546/47, born by 1493 and died 16 April 1557. He married by 1527,

4165. Ursula Brydges, died before Feb. 1575/76.

4166. Sir Nicholas Poyntz, M.P. 1559 and 1571, born ca. 1535 and died at Iron Acton, Gloucestershire 1 Sept. 1585. He married, 2nd, ca. 1569, Lady Margaret Stanley, who died before 3 June 1586, widow of John Jermyn, and daughter of Edward Stanley, 3rd Earl of Derby, and Margaret Barlow. He married, 1st (contract dated 12 May 1555),

4167. Anne Verney of Pendley, Hertfordshire.

4168. Richard Parkins of Ashby, Bottesford, Lincolnshire, died between 2 Oct. 1539 and 27 March 1541. He married,

4169. ——— Atkinson, died before 2 Oct. 1539.

4170. ADEN BERESFORD of Bentley, Derbsyhire, died in 1598. He married,
4171. URSULA ROLLESTON of The Lea, Derbyshire.

4172-4183. ——.

4184. GEORGE DEANE of Much Dunmow, Essex, married,
4185. ——.

4186. EDWARD WYKHAM of Swalcliffe, Oxfordshire, married,
4187. ISABEL PULTON of Desborough, Northamptonshire.

4188. JOHN WACE of Wickham, Buckinghamshire, married,
4189. OLIVE WELLS.

4190. WILLIAM PRETTYMAN, buried at Bacton, Suffolk 14 Sept. 1594. He married, 2nd, Katherine ——, who died ca. 1631. He married, 1st, at Bacton in Feb. 1561/62,
4191. ANNE HOWE, died before 20 April 1571.

4192. LEWIS MORDAUNT, 3RD BARON MORDAUNT, M.P. [as Hon. Lewis Mordaunt] 1563-67, attended the funeral of HM Queen Mary I Stewart 1587, a Lord in attendance on HM Queen Elizabeth I 1588 [when the Spanish Fleet threatened England] and 1589, born 21 Sept. 1538 and died at Drayton Manor, Northamptonshire 16 June 1601. He married,
4193. ELIZABETH DARCY, buried at Lowick, Northamptonshire 9 Sept. 1590.

4194. HENRY COMPTON, 1ST BARON COMPTON, K.B. (1566/67), M.P. [as Henry Compton and Sir Henry Compton] 1563-67, one of the four chief attendants at the funeral of HM Queen Mary I Stewart 1587, born 17 July 1544 and died 1 Nov. 1589; buried at Compton Wynyates, Warwickshire. He married, 2nd, after 1581, Anne Spencer, who died 22 Sept. 1618, daughter of Sir John Spencer and Catherine Kitson. He married, 1st,
4195. LADY FRANCES HASTINGS, died in 1574, daughter of Francis Hastings, 2nd Earl of Huntingdon.

4196. CHARLES HOWARD, 1ST EARL OF NOTTINGHAM, K.G. (1575), **M.P.** [as Hon. Charles Howard] 1563-67 and 1572-73, Gentleman of the Privy Chamber to HM Queen Elizabeth I 1558, General 1569, Lord High Admiral 1585-1619, born ca. 1536 and died at Haling House, near Croydon, Surrey 14 Dec. 1624. He married, 2nd, in Sept. 1603, Lady Margaret Stewart, who was buried at Chelsea, Middlesex 19 Aug. 1639, daughter of James Stewart, 2nd Earl of Moray [No. 15594], and Elizabeth Stewart, Countess of Moray in her own right [No. 15595]. He married, 1st, in July 1563,

4197. HON. KATHERINE CAREY, Lady of the Privy Chamber to HM Queen Elizabeth I, died at Arundel House in the Strand, near London 25 Feb. 1602/3, daughter of Henry Carey, 1st Baron Hunsdon [No. 4200].

4198. JOHN ST. JOHN, 2ND BARON ST. JOHN, M.P. [as John St. John] 1563-67, Lord Lieutenant of Huntingdonshire 1587-96, born in 1544 and died 12 Oct. 1596; buried at Bletso, Bedfordshire. He married after 28 Feb. 1574/75,

4199. CATHERINE DORMER, died 23 March 1614/15; buried at Westminster Abbey, Middlesex.

4200. HENRY CAREY, 1ST BARON HUNSDON, K.G. (1564), P.C. (1577), **M.P.** [as Henry Carey] 1547-52 and 1554-55, Master of the Queen's Hawks, Governor of Berwick 1568-70, Captain General 1581-96, Lord Chamberlain of the (Royal) Household 1585-96, co-heir [with his first cousin HM Queen Elizabeth I] to the earldom of Ormond, born 4 March 1525/26 and died at Somerset House in the Strand, near London 23 July 1596, son of William Carey [but possibly natural son of HM King Henry VIII]. He married (Faculty Office license dated 21 May 1545),

4201. ANNE MORGAN, died 19 Jan. 1606/7, daughter of Thomas Morgan of Arkeston, Herefordshire.

4202. SIR HUGH TREVANION, Sheriff of Cornwall 1564, born ca. 1522 and died 29 Dec. 1571. He married,

4203. SYBILLA MORGAN, buried at Fulham, Middlesex in 1595, daughter of Thomas Morgan [No. 8402].

4204. THOMAS SMITH married,
4205. JOAN JENNINGS.

4206. William Brydges, 4th Baron Chandos, M.P. [as Hon. William Brydges] 1572-83 and 1584-87, born after 1548 and died 18 Nov. 1602, son of Edmund Brydges, 2nd Baron Chandos [No. 8220]. He married,
4207. Mary Hopton, buried at Stepney, Middlesex 23 Oct. 1623.

4208-4215. ——.

4216. Sir John Lunsford, Sheriff of Sussex and Surrey 1611, born ca. 1551 and buried at East Hoathly, Sussex 5 May 1618. He married, 2nd, at Horsham, Sussex 2 Sept. 1577, Anna Apsley, baptized at Horsham 2 March 1557 and buried at East Hoathly 10 Sept. 1612, daughter of John Apsley and Mary Pelham. He married, 1st,
4217. Barbara Lewknor of Buckingham, Sussex, died before 2 Sept. 1577.

4218. Sir Thomas Lloyd alias Fludd, M.P. 1593, 1597, and 1601, died 30 May 1607; buried at Bearsted, Kent. He married, 2nd, Barbara ——. He married, 1st,
4219. Elizabeth Andrews of Willington, Somerset, died 25 Jan. 1590/91.

4220. Sir Henry Neville, M.P. 1584, 1586, 1589, 1593, 1597, 1604, and 1614, Ambassador to France 1596-1601, born in 1562 and died at London 10 July 1615. He married (Vicar-General's license dated 4 Dec. 1584),
4221. Anne Killigrew, died in 1632, daughter of Sir Henry Killigrew [No. 4354] and Katherine Cooke [No. 4355].

4222. John Smythe, M.P. 1584, 1586, 1589, and 1604, Sheriff of Kent 1600/1, baptized 16 Sept. 1557 and died 29 Nov. 1608; buried at Ashford, Kent. He married before Jan. 1577,
4223. Elizabeth Fyneux, died before 16 March 1607/8.

4224. Robert Bingham of Melcombe Bingham, Dorset, died in 1561. He married,
4225. Alice Coker of Mappowder, Dorset.

4226. Robert Martin of Athelhampton, Dorset, born in 1508 and died in 1548. He married,

4227. Elizabeth Kelloway of Rockborne, Wiltshire.

4228-4231. ——.

4232. Richard Middleton, M.P. 1542, Governor of Denbigh Castle temp. TM King Edward VI, Queen Mary I, and Queen Elizabeth I, born ca. 1508 and died 8 Feb. 1574/75; buried at St. Marcellus' Church, Whitchurch, Denbighshire. He married,

4233. Jane Dryhurst, born in 1525 and died 31 Dec. 1565.

4234. John Olmstead of Ingatestone, Essex, married,

4235. Elizabeth Davers.

4236. Roger Harris, draper, buried at St. Julian's Church, Shrewsbury 21 Sept. 1598. He married,

4237. Anne Gennowe, buried at St. Julian's Church 1 Jan. 1611/12.

4238. William Jones, alderman and draper of Shrewsbury, died 1 July 1614. He married,

4239. Eleanor Owen, buried 25 Feb. 1623/24.

4240-4263. ——.

4264. Agmondesham Muschamp of East Horsley, Surrey, buried 6 Dec. 1642. He married,

4265. Mary Bellingham, baptized at Newtimber, Surrey 14 Nov. 1568 and buried at East Horsley 31 July 1632.

4266. Thomas Lisley or Lisle of Bridleford, Isle of Wight, married,

4267. ——.

4268-4271. ——.

4272. Patrick Sarsfield of Tully, Kildare, died 9 Jan. 1629/30. He married,

4273. Cecily FitzHenry of Kilcavan, Wexford, died 9 June 1610.

4274. Terence O'Dempsey, 1st Viscount Clanmalier, Sheriff of Leix 1593, died before 8 Sept. 1638. He married, 2nd, Genet Finglass, who died 4 June 1617, widow of i) John Bathe, Chancellor of the Exchequer (Ireland), and ii) Sir William Warren, and daughter of Patrick Finglass. He married, 3rd, Margaret Whitley, widow of John Itchingham. He married, 1st,

4275. Mary FitzGerald, died 4 Jan. 1614.

4276. Callough O'More of Ballina, Cadamstown, Kildare, died 27 March 1618. He married,

4277. Margaret Scurlock, died 25 April 1615.

4278. Sir Patrick Barnewall of Turvey, Dublin, died 11 Jan. 1621/22. He married,

4279. Mary Bagenall.

4280. Sir William Taaffe of Smarmore and Ballymote, Sligo, died 9 Feb. 1630/31. He married, 1st, Margaret Brett. He married, 2nd,

4281. Ismay Bellew of Castletown, Louth, died before 1631.

4282. Theobald Dillon, 1st Viscount Dillon, died 15 March 1624. He married,

4283. Eleanor Tuite, died in Killinure, Westmeath 8 April 1638.

4284. Rowland Walter of Roche Castle, Pembrokeshire, died 15 Nov. 1645. He married,

4285. Frances Griffith.

4286. John Protheroe of Hawkesbrook, Carmarthenshire, died before 13 Dec. 1624. He married,

4287. Eleanor Vaughan of Golden Grove, Carmarthenshire.

4288-4351. ———.

4352. Sir Edward Seymour, 1st Baronet, M.P. 1590, 1601, and 1604-11, Sheriff of Devonshire 1595/96 and 1605/6, born ca. 1563 and buried at Berry Pomeroy, Devonshire 27 May 1613. He married at Dartington, Devonshire 30 Sept. 1576,
4353. Elizabeth Champernowne, living 6 Sept. 1613.

4354. Sir Henry Killigrew, M.P. 1553, 1563, 1571, and 1572, envoy to Germany 1558-59 and 1569, France 1559-60 and 1571-72, and Scotland 1560, 1572-73, 1574, and 1575, born ca. 1528 and died 2 March 1602/3. He married, 2nd, at the Church of St. Peter-le-Poer, London 7 Nov. 1590, Jael de Peigne, who died before 28 March 1632. He married, 1st, 4 Nov. 1565,
4355. Katherine Cooke, died in 1583.

4356. Henry Portman, died 25 Jan. 1590/91. He married at Orchard Portman, Somerset 1 Sept. 1549,
4357. Jane Michell of Cannington, Somerset.

4358. Henry Gifford, M.P. 1572, buried at East Tytherley, Hampshire 3 Nov. 1592. He married after 1570,
4359. Susan Brouncker. She married, 1st, Robert Halswell of Gotehurst, Somerset.

4360. Sir John Popham, M.P. 1558, 1571, and 1572, Speaker of the House of Commons 1581, Chief Justice of the Queen's Bench 1592-1603 and the King's Bench 1603-7, born at Huntworth, Somerset in 1533 and died at Wellington, Somerset 10 June 1607. He married before 18 Jan. 1549/50,
4361. Amy Adams, born ca. 1531 and died at Wellington in 1612.

4362. John Dudley, M.P. 1553 and 1563, born by 1526 and buried at Stoke Newington, Middlesex 17 Jan. 1580/81. He married after 1558,
4363. Elizabeth Gardiner, buried at Stoke Newington 17 June 1602. She married, 2nd (Bishop of London's license dated 17 Sept. 1582), Thomas Sutton, founder of the Charterhouse, born at Knaith, Lincolnshire ca. 1532 and died 12 Dec. 1611.

4364. William Kerr of Ancrum, Roxburghshire, assassinated 20 Dec. 1590 by Robert Ker, 1st Earl of Roxburghe [No. 4898]. He married,

4365. Margaret Dundas of Fingask, Perthshire. She married, 1st, Sir David Home of Fishwick, Berwickshire. She married, 3rd, after 20 Dec. 1590, George Douglas, Gentleman of the Bedchamber to HM King James VI, son of George Douglas and Mary Douglas.

4366. Sir John Kerr of Littledean, Roxburghshire, died before Aug. 1631. He married, 2nd, 5 March 1589/90, Margaret Whitelaw, formerly wife of Alexander Hamilton of Innerwick, Lothianshire, and daughter of Patrick Whitelaw of that Ilk. He married, 1st (contract dated 12 Jan. 1575/76, divorced 21 Feb. 1589 following his elopement with Margaret Whitelaw),

4367. Julian Home of Wedderburn, Berwickshire. She married, 2nd, after Dec. 1589, James Hop-Pringle of Whitelaw, Roxburghshire.

4368. John Shorter of Staines, Middlesex, died by 1614. He married,
4369. Elizabeth ——.

4370. Richard Forbis/Forbach of Send, Surrey, died between 19 Jan. 1619/20 and 19 June 1620. He married,
4371. Isabel ——.

4372. John Birkett married at Crosthwaite, Cumberland 16 July 1594,
4373. Isabel Birkett of Restwhait, Cumberland.

4374-4375. ——.

4376. Sir John Philipps, 1st Baronet, M.P. 1601, Sheriff of Pembrokeshire 1594-95 and 1610-11 and Carmarthenshire 1622-23, died at Clog-y-fran, Carmarthenshire 27 March 1629. He married, 2nd, Margaret Dennis, daughter of Sir Robert Dennis and Margaret Godolphin. He married, 1st,
4377. Anne Perrot of Haroldstone, Pembrokeshire.

4378. Sir Erasmus Dryden, 1st Baronet, M.P. 1624-25, Sheriff of Northamptonshire 1598/99 and 1619/20, born 29 Dec. 1553 and died 22 May 1632; buried at Canons Ashby, Northamptonshire. He married by 1580,

4379. FRANCES WILKES, died 16 Feb. 1630/31; buried at Canons Ashby.

4380. SIR ROBERT DARCY of Dartford Priory, Kent, Usher of the Privy Chamber to HRH The Prince Henry Frederick, Prince of Wales, born ca. 1582 and died by 1623. He married in 1610,
4381. GRACE REDDISH, born ca. 1588 and a widow in 1623.

4382. PHILIP STANHOPE, 1ST EARL OF CHESTERFIELD, born in 1584 and died 12 Sept. 1656; buried at the Church of St. Giles-in-the-Fields, Holborn, Middlesex. He married, 2nd, Anne Pakington, buried at the Church of St. Giles-in-the-Fields 13 Nov. 1667, widow of Sir Humphrey Ferrers, and daughter of Sir John Pakington and Dorothy Smith. He married, 1st, in 1605,
4383. HON. CATHERINE HASTINGS, died 28 Aug. 1636, daughter of Francis Hastings, Lord Hastings by courtesy.

4384. HM KING JAMES VI, KING OF SCOTLAND 1567-1625/KING JAMES I, KING OF ENGLAND AND IRELAND 1603-25, born at Edinburgh Castle 19 June 1566 and died at Theobalds, Hertfordshire 27 March 1625, son of Henry Stuart, Lord Darnley by courtesy, and HM Queen Mary I Stewart, Queen of Scotland. He married (by proxy at Kronborg, Zealand 20 Aug. and in person at Oslo 23 Nov. 1589),
4385. HRH PRINCESS ANNA AF DANMARK, born at Skanderborg Castle, Denmark 12 Oct. 1574 and died at Hampton Court Palace, Middlesex 2 March 1618/19, daughter of HM King Frederik II, King of Denmark.

4386. HM KING HENRI III, KING OF NAVARRE 1572-1610/KING HENRI IV, KING OF FRANCE 1589-1610, born at Pau, Béarn 14 Dec. 1553 and assassinated at Paris 14 May 1610, son of Antoine de Bourbon, Duc de Vendôme, and HM Queen Jeanne III d'Albret, Queen of Navarre. He married, 1st, at the Cathedral de Nôtre Dame, Paris 18 Aug. 1572 (marriage dissolved by divorce in 1599), HRH Princesse Marguerite de Valois, born at Saint-Germain-en-Laye, near Paris 14 May 1553 and died at Paris 27 March 1615, daughter of HM King Henri II, King of France, and Caterina de' Medici, Duchess of Urbino in her own right. He married, 2nd, at Lyon 27 Dec. 1600,
4387. PRINCESS MARIA DE' MEDICI, Queen Regent of France 1610-17, born at Florence 26 April 1573 and died at Cologne 3 July 1642, daughter of Francesco I de' Medici, Grand Duke of Tuscany.

HM King James I,
King of England, Scotland, and Ireland
Born at Edinburgh 19 June 1566
Died at Theobalds, Hertfordshire 27 March 1625
Married (by proxy at Kronborg, Zealand 20 August /
in person at Oslo 23 November 1589)
HRH Princess Anna af Danmark

King James was the only son and heir of Mary, Queen of Scots, by her
second husband, Henry Stuart, Lord Darnley, who was killed less than
eight months after James's birth. Upon his mother's defeat by rebel
Scottish lords, James became King of Scotland at his mother's abdication
(24 July 1567), and five days later was crowned in a Protestant ceremony
at Stirling. Four successive regents – the Earls of Moray (1567-70),
Lennox (1570-71), Mar (1571-72), and Morton (1572-78) – governed in
the young King's name. James, kept at Stirling Castle, studied languages,
mathematics, geography, history, and astronomy, tutored by the stern
humanist George Buchanan and the more kindly Peter Young.

James VI took the first step toward governing his kingdom after the
pro-English Earl of Morton was driven from the regency in March
1578. In 1579, James's witty and sophisticated cousin, Esmé Stuart,
Seigneur d'Aubigny, arrived from France: he soon became the King's
first favourite, and was created earl and then Duke of Lennox (in 1581).
James was kidnapped by the Earl of Gowrie in August 1582 and forced
to denounce Lennox, who fled back to France. The following year
James escaped from his Protestant captors, had Gowrie executed (2
May 1584), and began pursuing his own policies as king. His primary
goals were to subdue unruly Scottish factions and establish his claim to
succeed Queen Elizabeth I. To this latter end, in 1585-86 James concluded an alliance with England, and even Elizabeth's execution of his
mother in 1587 did not disrupt this relationship.

The king soon learned to play Protestant and Roman Catholic factions of the Scots nobility against each other. James instituted acts to
strengthen royal control and, with the help of Parliament, he made
himself head of the Presbyterian Church in Scotland in 1584, with the
power to appoint bishops. He was an extravagant spender, noted for
lavish ceremonies and festivities drawn on the coffers of his impoverished kingdom.

James became King of England on the death of Queen Elizabeth,
and was crowned with his consort at Westminster Abbey 25 July 1603.
He began his reign in England by trying to bring the English and the

Scots together in court and government. He also sought to broaden the Cecil-dominated English council of the late Elizabethan years by adding thirteen new members (doubling the council's size), only three of them Scots. James was unfamiliar with the dynamics of the English Parliament, and in his first address (1604) suggested the union of his two kingdoms. He proposed the title of King of Great Britain, but the Commons believed the name "England" essential to that kingdom's identity.

Many of James I's policies were laudable, and the opening years of his reign over the two kingdoms saw material prosperity in both. He speedily ended England's war with Spain in 1604, but was challenged by Parliament, which claimed increasing rights to shape public policy. The prerogative of levying taxes made Parliament's assent (and oversight) necessary, as the crown labored under ruinous debt from the protracted war with Spain. Although James had successfully divided Scottish assemblies, he wasn't able to manipulate the English Parliament. He was frustrated by not hearing parliamentary debate (he had regularly attended sessions in Scotland, but the bicameral English Parliament made Scottish practice impossible). Few privy councilors sat in the Commons, so independent M.P.s could seize the initiative. James's pedantic lecturing about royal prerogatives caused some members to draft the "Apology of the Commons" (1604), which sought to explain the proper relationship between king and Commons. In response, James prorogued Parliament. When that body was about to reassemble in November 1605, the Gunpowder Plot (to blow up Parliament and kill the Protestant King) was discovered and foiled. James then made some headway with his second Parliament, but was frustrated again in his attempt to promote Anglo-Scottish union. His British flag, the Union Jack (from Jacobus), would, however, be flown on ships.

When Parliament refused to grant a special subsidy, James tried to impose customs duties on merchants without Parliament's consent, then had his judges proclaim these actions law (1608). In four years of peace, James nearly doubled the crown debt. When James's chief minister, the Earl of Salisbury, tried in 1610-11 to replace the King's purveyances with a fixed annual sum, negotiations with Parliament stalled, and James once again prorogued and dissolved Parliament.

After Salisbury's death in 1612, James was never able to find someone equally experienced to serve as chief minister, and over the next ten years he summoned only the brief and ineffectual Addled Parliament (1614). Without grants, the crown was forced to adopt unpopular expedients, such as the sale of crown lands, monopolies, and baronetcies (a newly created rank). The King fell under the influence of his new favourite, Robert Carr, whom he created Earl of Somerset. Carr was succeeded by George Villiers, the most able of James's favourites, who rose rapidly, was knighted, ennobled, and then promoted to earl, marquess and finally Duke of Buckingham (in 1623). The King showed much affection for his favourites' wives and children, as he did his own family; although homosexual overtones have been suggested, favourites also served important political purposes.

The king forged peaceful relations with Spain as part of his foreign policy. He formed a close relationship with Spanish ambassador and bibliophile Diego Sarmiento de Acuña, Count of Gondomar. When Sir Walter Raleigh (in Guiana in search of gold) came into conflict with the Spaniards, Gondomar persuaded James to execute the famed explorer. James also planned to marry his son Charles to the Spanish Infanta María, and to join Spanish Habsburgs in mediating the Thirty Years' War in Germany. The latter plan had realistic goals, but disregarded the hard-line faction of English Protestants who wanted to support James's son-in-law, the Protestant Elector Palatine, whose lands were occupied by Imperial Habsburgs. James's third Parliament (1621), called to raise funds for his foreign policy, initially granted two subsidies, but then began an unproductive debate, finally saying that the Prince of Wales should marry a Protestant. In response to this challenge to his prerogative James tore the offending record from the House of Commons' journal and dissolved Parliament. Buckingham and Prince Charles traveled to Spain to secure the latter's marriage, but Spanish hard-liners added impossible religious demands and Charles and Buckingham then pressed for war with Spain. James pursued diplomacy instead.

The King suffered from kidney problems and arthritis, which worsened in September 1624, compounded by fever, a stroke, and dysentery in the winter of 1624/25. King James died at his country residence, Theobalds, in Hertfordshire. His rapid decline provoked rumors of poison.

A noted scholar, James wrote poetry and theological and philosophical tracts (plus one against tobacco), intellectual achievements unique among English kings. Political treatises of 1598 and 1599 expounded his views on the divine right of kings. James is perhaps best remembered, however, for his part in the 1611 publication of the King James version of the Bible, long influential in English literature and still much used today. In 1589, James married Anne, second daughter of King Frederik II of Denmark. Politically astute, Anne kept her Roman Catholicism quiet.

HM King Henri IV,
King of France and Navarre
Born at Pau, Béarn 14 December 1553
Died at Paris 14 May 1610
Married, 1st, at Paris 18 August 1572 (divorced in 1599)
HRH Princess Marguerite de Valois
Married, 2nd, at Lyon 27 December 1600
Princess Maria de' Medici

As a young Prince of the Blood Royal, Henri de Bourbon-Vendôme seemed unlikely to succeed to the throne of France – Queen Catherine de Médici had already borne three sons to the reigning French king, and would soon bear him a fourth. Henri, the Crown Prince of Navarre through his mother, spent much of his early childhood in Béarn. He entered the Collège de Navarre at Paris in 1561 and lived there with his second cousins, the children of the late King Henri II.

Religious turmoil between Roman Catholics and Calvinists (Huguenots) was intensifying as the leading nobility took sides in the conflict. Prince Henri's father, Antoine de Bourbon, Duc de Vendôme, temporarily allied himself with the Protestants but changed sides and was mortally wounded in battle against them. Henri's mother, Jeanne d'Albret, Queen of Navarre, announced her Calvinism in 1560. Henri was barely twelve when his mother brought him back to Béarn and introduced him to the strict principles of Protestantism. In the autumn of 1567, Henri served as nominal head of a victorious expedition against the rebellious Roman Catholic gentry of lower Navarre.

In 1568, the beginning of the third war of religion in France, the Prince's mother placed him under the charge of his uncle, Louis I de Bourbon, Prince de Condé, leader of the Protestant forces. The Protestants were surprised and defeated near Jarnac on 13 March 1569 by the Duc d'Anjou, and Condé was killed. Queen Jeanne sent her son to the new leader of the Protestant forces, Gaspard de Coligny, who gave the young prince a military education. Henri distinguished himself at the Battle of Arnay-le-Duc in June 1570, when he led the first charge of the Huguenot cavalry. The long campaign through the war-ravaged provinces, extending from Poitou to the heart of Burgundy, forged in Henri the martial spirit he would always retain. Peace was concluded in August 1570, and a liberal edict was granted the Protestants. Many persons, including Queen Catherine de Médici, hoped the civil war had come to an end. In order to strengthen the peace, a marriage was arranged between Prince Henri and Marguerite de Valois, Queen

Catherine's daughter. Meanwhile, upon his mother's death on 9 June 1572, Prince Henri became King of Navarre and sovereign Lord of Béarn. On 18 August 1572, he and Marguerite were married in Paris, but six days latter came the St. Bartholomew's Day Massacre, in which thousands of French Protestants were massacred by royal forces. The marriage was publicly styled the "scarlet nuptials" because of the bloodshed. The young King was ordered by his brother-in-law, Charles IX, to abjure his Protestant faith, but Henri's conversion to Roman Catholicism was of dubious sincerity, and he was therefore held captive for three-and-a-half years at the courts of the French kings Charles IX and Henri III. On 2 February 1576, he finally succeeded in escaping from the French court, whereupon he recanted and joined the combined forces of Protestants and Catholic rebels against Henri III. Once free, Henri of Navarre displayed his sharp intellect and political acumen in his role as protector of the Protestant churches.

Civil war began again at the end of 1576. The Huguenots fared badly, and the King of Navarre, evaluating the situation, persuaded his coreligionists to relinquish the struggle and accept the Treaty of Bergerac in September 1577, in spite of the sacrifices it entailed. As a result of disputes with his untrustworthy wife and her family, Henri of Navarre entered into the seventh war of religion, known as the War of Lovers, in which he seized Cahors. This war did not last long, ending when the King of Navarre and his mother-in-law, Queen Catherine, signed the Treaty of Nerac, followed by the Peace of Fleix on 26 November 1580.

With the death of the brother of King Henri III of France, Henri of Navarre became heir presumptive to the French throne. The militant Roman Catholics of the Holy League were unwilling to accept a Protestant king, however, and the pope excommunicated the King of Navarre. Headed by Henri, Duc de Guise, and his brothers, the Holy League claimed to be the defender of the ancestral faith of France, but relied increasingly on Spanish support. Henri III lacked the strength to contain the League's influence. Excluded from the succession by the Treaty of Nemours (1585) between Henri III and the League, Henri of Navarre fought the "war of the three Henrys," mainly in southwestern France. The outcome of the war hinged on the encounter between Henri of Navarre and Henri III, who had come increasingly under the League's influence. At the Battle of Coutras (20 October 1587), Henri of Navarre defeated the League's army, led by Anne, Duc de Joyeuse. The Holy League had accepted a Spanish proposal naming the daughter of King Felipe II of Spain and Elisabeth de Valois as the next ruler of France. Such a succession represented a clear threat to French independence, a danger which finally alarmed Henri III, who had the Duc de Guise assassinated in December 1588. The French king then reconciled with Henri of Navarre in order to recover Paris from the League's control. Their combined forces laid siege to Paris on 30 July 1589, but on 1 August, Henri III – the last monarch of the Valois dynasty – was stabbed in his headquarters at Saint-Cloud. He died the next day, after proclaiming Henri of Navarre as his successor to the French crown. Although Henri IV was now King of France, he waged a decade-long war with the Holy League and Spain to secure his kingdom. Many Roman Catholic gentry loyal to Henri III deserted his successor, and Henri IV was forced to withdraw from the outskirts of Paris, which remained the League's principal stronghold. King Henri won victories over Charles, Duc de Mayenne at Arques in September 1589 and at Ivry in March 1590, but his sieges of Paris in 1590 and Rouen in 1591-92 were less successful. He was able to capture Chartres and Noyon from the League, but the war continued and the King realized that his armies were exhausted.

After much consideration, Henri IV made a final conversion to Roman Catholicism in July 1593. Despite doubts about his sincerity, Henri's conversion removed any legitimate pretext for resistance, and important towns, notably Orléans and Lyon, submitted to him. On 22 March 1594, Paris finally surrendered. Whether or not he actually said "Paris is well worth a mass!," he marched, amongst cheering crowds, to hear a Te Deum at Nôtre Dame. Pope Clement VIII removed the ban of excommunication from Henri IV on 17 September 1595, but Spain continued to support the remaining resistance, chiefly in Brittany under the leadership of Philippe-Emmanuel, Duc de Mercoeur (younger brother of the late Duc de Guise). In order to smash the remaining resistance, Henri declared war on Felipe II of Spain in January 1595, defeating the Spanish army at Fontaine-Française in Burgundy (June 1595) and freeing Amiens from Spanish control in September 1597. Mercoeur came to terms with the King in March 1598, and the Peace of Vervins was signed between France and Spain on 2 May 1598.

A few weeks before, Henri had signed the Edict of Nantes, which confirmed Roman Catholicism as the state religion but granted religious freedom to Protestants (also given the right to hold public office and to retain their fortresses in certain cities). The Edict of Nantes ended nearly 40 years of religious and civil war that had left France on the verge of disintegration.

The rapidity with which Henri IV restored order was in large part a result of his personal policy, built upon broad experience acquired during the conquest of the kingdom. Henri IV is traditionally credited with having desired for every laborer *la poule au pot,* a chicken to eat, every Sunday. He used his persuasive manner to win obedience, although at times he exceeded his royal prerogatives, as when he raised taxes over the objection of the Estates General. Wealthy merchants and crown officials had contributed much to his success in acquiring his kingdom, and now he depended on them for its rebuilding and economic progress. He eliminated some redundant government offices and consolidated others. Officeholders could make their offices hereditary for a price. The immediate effect of this new policy was to restore an adequate income to the government, which helped rebuild the French economy. At first Henri controlled the Parlements (high courts) through the moderate Chancellor, Pomponne de Bellièvre, but gradually he asserted his personal authority, for this purpose utilizing Maximilien de Béthune, Duc de Sully. Among Henri's other formidable councilors were Nicolas Brulart de Sillery, Nicolas de Neufville, and Pierre Jeannin.

Henri's government eliminated the huge national debt and realized a reserve of 18 million livres. To revive the economy he undertook projects to develop agriculture and to drain the marshes of Saintonge. He introduced the silk industry to France and encouraged the manufacture of cloth, glassware, and tapestries, luxury items formerly imported from Holland or Italy. He took measures to prohibit importation of many goods that could be produced in France. Under Sully's direction, new highways and canals were constructed to aid commerce. A treaty was concluded with the Ottoman Sultan Ahmed I (1604), and commercial agreements were signed with England, Spain, and Holland. Samuel de Champlain's exploration of Canada was also supported. The French army was reorganized, a school of cadets formed, the artillery service reconstituted, and the frontier fortified. Henri also completed construction of the Tuileries as well as building the great gallery of the Louvre, the Pont Neuf, the Hôtel-de-Ville, and the Place Royale (now Place des Vosges).

Henri IV's foreign policy was designed to diminish Spanish influence in Europe. He forced Savoy to sign the Treaty of Lyons (1601), thereby acquiring Bresse, Bugey, and other territory on France's eastern border. He also concluded alliances with the German Protestant princes, Lorraine, the Swiss cantons, and Sweden. Pope Clement VIII's annulment of Henri's unhappy marriage to Marguerite de Valois allowed him to marry Marie de Médici, daughter of the Grand Duke of Tuscany. The new Queen gave birth on 27 September 1601 to a Dauphin, the future Louis XIII, followed in time by two additional sons and three daughters.

In March 1609, difficulties arose with the Holy Roman Emperor over the succession of Johann Wilhelm, Duke of Cleves-Jülich and Berg. Henri decided on a military expedition to expel the imperial troops from Jülich, but before the effort could begin, the King was assassinated in Paris on 14 May 1610 by a fanatical Roman Catholic named François Ravaillac. Henri IV was buried at Saint-Denis, where his widow joined him in 1642.

4388. SIR EDWARD VILLIERS, M.P. 1620-22 and 1624/25, Master of the Mint 1617-22 and 1624-26, Ambassador to the Elector Palatine 1620 [when he persuaded "The Winter King" to renounce the throne of Bohemia], Lord President of Munster 1625-26, born ca. 1585 and died at Youghal, Cork 7 Sept. 1626, son of Sir George Villiers [No. 5772] and half-brother of George Villiers, 1st Duke of Buckingham. He married ca. 1612,

4389. BARBARA ST. JOHN, buried at Westminster Abbey, Middlesex 16 Sept. 1672, daughter of Sir John St. John.

4390. PAUL BAYNING, 1ST VISCOUNT BAYNING, Sheriff of Essex 1617/18, baptized at St. Olave's Church, Hart Street, London 28 April 1588 and died at Mark Lane, London 29 July 1629. He married ca. 1613,

4391. ANNE GLEMHAM, died at Westminster, Middlesex 10 Jan. 1638/39. She married, 2nd, Dudley Carleton, 1st Viscount Dorchester, born 10 March 1573/74 and died 15 Feb. 1631/32, son of Anthony Carleton and Joyce Goodwin.

4392. SIR JOHN BENNET, M.P. 1597, 1601, 1604, 1614, and 1621, born ca. 1553 and died at Warwick Lane, Newgate, London 15 Feb. 1626/27. He married, 2nd, Elizabeth Lowe, who died 12 May 1614, daughter of Sir Thomas Lowe and Anne Coulston. He married, 3rd, Leonora Vierandeels, who died in 1638, daughter of Adriaen Vierandeels of Antwerp. He married, 1st, 29 May 1586,

4393. ANNE WEEKS of Salisbury, died at York 9 Feb. 1601/2.

4394. SIR JOHN CROFTS, M.P. 1597, Sheriff of Bedfordshire 1600/1, born ca. 1562 and buried at Little Saxham, Suffolk 29 March 1628. He married ca. 1590,

4395. MARY SHIRLEY, died before 13 March 1648/49.

4396. HH MAURITS VAN NASSAU, PRINCE OF ORANGE, Stadtholder of Holland and Zeeland 1585-1625, Guelderland, Overijssel, and Utrecht 1590-1625, and Groningen and Drenthe 1620-25, Captain-General and Admiral 1587, the greatest general of the period, born at Dillenburg Castle, Hesse 13 Nov. 1567 and died at The Hague 23 April 1625, son of HH Willem I van Nassau ("the Silent"), Prince of Orange. He had issue by,

4397. MARGRIET JONKVRAUW VAN MECHELEN, born ca. 1581 and died at The Hague 17 May 1662, daughter of Cornelis van Mechelen.

4398. WILLEM ADRIAEN VAN HOORN, HEER VAN KESSEL, Governor of Heusden, General of the States General, died at Bommel 15 July 1625. He married, 2nd, in 1614, Theodora van Haeften, who died ca. 1630, widow of Floris van Brederode, and daughter of Johan van Haeften and Anna van Spangen. He married, 1st,

4399. ELISABETH VAN DER MEEREN, VROUWE VAN WESTWESSEL, daughter of Philip van der Meeren, Heer tot Saventhem.

4400. HENRY SOMERSET, 1ST MARQUESS OF WORCESTER, Lord Lieutenant of Glamorganshire and Monmouthshire 1628-31, joint Lord Lieutenant 1626, born in Herefordshire ca. 1576 and died at Black Rod's house, Covent Garden, near London 18 Dec. 1646. He married at the Church of St. Martin Ludgate, London 16 June 1600,

4401. HON. ANNE RUSSELL, died at Worcester House in the Strand, near London 8 April 1639, daughter of John Russell, Lord Russell by courtesy.

4402. HON. SIR WILLIAM DORMER, died at Wing, Buckinghamshire 22 Oct. 1616, son of Robert Dormer, 1st Baron Dormer. He married 21 Feb. 1609/10,

4403. ALICE MOLYNEUX, died 2 July 1650.

4404. SIR HENRY CAPELL of Hadham Parva, Hertfordshire, born before 3 May 1579 and died 29 April 1622. He married, 2nd, **DOROTHY ALDERSEY [No. 5081].** He married, 1st,

4405. THEODOSIA MONTAGU, baptized at Weekley, Northamptonshire 8 Nov. 1584 and died 16 Jan. 1614/15.

4406. SIR CHARLES MORRISON, 1ST BARONET, K.B. (1603), M.P. 1621/22, 1625/26, and 1628, born 18 April 1587 and died 20 Aug. 1628; buried at Watford, Hertfordshire. He married at Low Leyton, Essex 4 Dec. 1606,
  4407. HON. MARY HICKS, baptized at the Church of St. Mary Magdalen, Milk Street, London 11 Feb. 1587/88, daughter of Baptist Hicks, 1st Viscount Campden. She married, 2nd, Sir John Cooper, 1st Baronet, who died 23 March 1631, son of John Cooper and Martha Skutt. She married, 3rd, Sir Richard Alford.

4408-4411. ——.

4412. THOMAS ATWOOD of Stanford Rivers, Essex, married,
4413. MARY POOLE.

4414. WILLIAM HAMPTON of Leigh, Essex, married,
4415. ——.

4416. SIR EDWARD WALDEGRAVE, 1ST BARONET, born ca. 1568 and died before Dec. 1646. He married, 2nd, Frances Sanderson, who was buried 21 Oct. 1648, widow of Francis Copledike, and daughter of Sir Nicholas Sanderson. He married, 1st, in Oct. 1599,
  4417. ELEANOR LOVELL of Harling, Norfolk, died 12 Dec. 1604.

4418. EDWARD PASTON, died 8 March 1629/30; buried at Blofield, Norfolk. He married, 1st, Elizabeth Lambart. He married, 2nd, 10 Oct. 1586,
  4419. MARGARET BERNEY, born ca. 1566 and died before 6 March 1640/41; buried at Blofield.

4420. SIR FRANCIS ENGLEFIELD, 1ST BARONET, born 30 June 1562 and died 26 Oct. 1631; buried at Englefield, Berkshire. He married at the Church of St. Mary Somerset, London 12 May 1593,
  4421. JANE BROWNE, died before 17 Sept. 1650.

4422. William Brokesby, died 26 May 1606. He married,
4423. Dorothy Wiseman of Brodokes, Wimbish, Essex.

4424. HM King James VI and I, King of England, Scotland, and Ireland = 4384.
4425. HRH Princess Anna af Danmark = 4385.

4426. HM King Henri III and IV, King of France and Navarre = 4386.
4427. Princess Maria de' Medici = 4387.

4428. John Churchill = 2056.
4429. Sarah Winston = 2057.

4430. Sir John Drake = 2058.
4431. Hon. Eleanor Boteler = 2059.

4432. Sir John Webb, born ca. 1557 and died in Feb. 1625/26. He married, 1st, Edith Falconer, daughter of William Falconer of Laverstock, Wiltshire. He married, 2nd,
4433. Catherine Tresham, born at Rushton, Northamptonshire 28 Dec. 1576 and died in 1623.

4434. Sir John Caryll, born at Warnham, Sussex 27 Aug. 1583 and living 29 Sept. 1628. He married,
4435. Hon. Mary Dormer, daughter of Robert Dormer, 1st Baron Dormer [No. 8804].

4436. William Blomer, buried at Hatherop, Gloucestershire 14 April 1613. He married, 2nd, ——. He married, 1st,
4437. Martha Wellesbourne of Westhaney, Berkshire.

4438. Anthony Maria Browne, 2nd Viscount Montagu, born 1 Feb. 1573/74 and died 23 Oct. 1629; buried at Midhurst, Sussex. He married 3 Feb. 1590/91,

4439. LADY JANE SACKVILLE, died before 8 Jan. 1651/52, daughter of Thomas Sackville, 1st Earl of Dorset.

4440. SIR HENRY BELASYSE, 1ST BARONET, Sheriff of Yorkshire 1603/4, baptized at Coxwold, Yorkshire 14 June 1555 and buried at St. Saviour's Church, York 19 Aug. 1624. He married,

4441. URSULA FAIRFAX, died 25 Aug. 1633. She married, 2nd, Sir William Mallory.

4442. SIR HENRY CHOLMLEY, buried at St. John's Church, York 13 Jan. 1615/16. He married,

4443. MARGARET BABTHORPE, buried at St. John's Church 15 April 1628.

4444. WILLIAM PAULET, 4TH MARQUESS OF WINCHESTER, Lord Steward for the funeral of HM Queen Mary I Stewart 1587, died at Hackwood, near Basingstoke 4 Feb. 1628/29. He married at the Church of St. Martin-in-the-Fields, Westminster, Middlesex 28 Feb. 1586/87,

4445. LADY LUCY CECIL, born at Burghley, Northamptonshire 7 March 1567/68 and died 1 Oct. 1614, daughter of Thomas Cecil, 1st Earl of Exeter.

4446. RICHARD DE BURGH, 4TH EARL OF CLANRICARDE, P.C. (I.) (1625), Lord President of Connaught 1604-16, born in 1572 and died 12 Nov. 1635; buried at Tunbridge, Kent. He married before 8 April 1603,

4447. FRANCES WALSINGHAM, born ca. 1568 and buried at Tunbridge 17 Feb. 1631/32, daughter of Sir Francis Walsingham, Principal Secretary of State to HM Queen Elizabeth I. She married, 1st, in March 1582/83, Sir Philip Sidney, poet [author of "Astrophil and Stella" and "Old Arcadia"], born 30 Nov. 1554 and died at Arnhem, Holland 16 Oct. 1586, son of Sir Henry Sidney [No. 8200] and Lady Mary Dudley [No. 8201]. She married, 2nd, in 1590, **ROBERT DEVEREUX, 2ND EARL OF ESSEX [No. 5786].**

4448. ROBERT WALPOLE, born 23 Sept. 1593 and died 1 May 1663; buried at Houghton, Norfolk. He married,

4449. SUSAN BARKHAM, baptized at the Church of St. Lawrence Jewry, London 18 Jan. 1595/96 and buried at Houghton 9 Nov. 1622.

4450. SIR ROBERT CRANE, 1ST BARONET, M.P. 1614, 1621-22, 1624-25, 1626, 1628-29, and 1640-43, Sheriff of Suffolk 1631-32, born ca. 1584 and died at London 17 Feb. 1642/43. He married, 1st, at St. Anne's Church, Blackfriars, London 19 Jan. 1606/7, Dorothy Hobart, born 14 March 1591/92 and died at Chilton, Suffolk 11 April 1624, daughter of Sir Henry Hobart, 1st Baronet, and Dorothy Bell. He married, 2nd, at Chilton 21 Sept. 1624,

4451. SUSAN ALINGTON, baptized at Horseheath, Cambridgeshire 30 Sept. 1605 and died before 14 Sept. 1681, daughter of Sir Giles Alington [No. 5448] and Lady Dorothy Cecil [No. 5449].

4452. EDMUND BURWELL, baptized at St. Mary's Church, Woodbridge, Suffolk 18 Nov. 1574 and died at Rougham Hall, Suffolk in 1652. He married at Woodbridge 13 May 1605,

4453. MARY PITMAN, baptized at Woodbridge 10 Nov. 1586.

4454. THOMAS DEREHAUGH, born 29 Jan. 1590 and buried at Badingham, Suffolk 26 April 1619. He married at the Church of St. Lawrence Pountney, London 4 May 1611,

4455. MARY SHEPPARD of Kirby, Norfolk.

4456. JOHN SHORTER = 2184.
4457. SUSAN FORBIS ALIAS FOREBANK = 2185.

4458. JOHN BIRKETT = 2186.
4459. ELIZABETH ROBINSON = 2187.

4460. SIR RICHARD PHILIPPS, 2ND BARONET = 2188.
4461. ELIZABETH DRYDEN = 2189.

4462. EDWARD DARCY = 2190.
4463. LADY ELIZABETH STANHOPE = 2191.

4464-4479. ——.

4480. William Palk married,

4481. ——.

4482-4511. ——.

4512. Johan van Sittart, born in 1552 and died at Danzig in 1612. He married,

4513. ——.

4514-4527. ——.

4528. Sir William Stonhouse, 1st Baronet, born ca. 1556 and died 5 Feb. 1631/32; buried at Radley, Berkshire. He married (Bishop of London's license dated 7 June 1592),

4529. Elizabeth Powell of Fulham, Middlesex, died ca. 1655.

4530. Richard Lovelace, 1st Baron Lovelace, M.P. [as Sir Richard Lovelace] 1601, 1604-11, and 1620-22, High Sheriff of Berkshire 1610-11 and Oxfordshire 1626/27, born ca. 1567 and died 22 April 1634. He married, 1st, after 30 Nov. 1598, Catherine Gill, widow of William Hyde, and daughter of George Gill and Gertrude Perient. He married, 2nd, in April 1608,

4531. Margaret Dodsworth, born 20 July 1588 and died between 1 Jan. 1651/52 and 4 May 1652.

4532. Sir Moreton Brigges, 1st Baronet, born ca. 1587 and died ca. 1650. He married ca. 1610,

4533. Grisogon Grey of Buildwas, Shropshire.

4534. Thomas Moreton, buried at Shiffnal, Shropshire 15 July 1634. He married,

4535. Elizabeth Moreton, buried at Shiffnal 24 June 1669.

4536. John Mellish of Willington, Lincolnshire, merchant taylor of London, died between 7 Aug. 1587 and 7 March 1587/88. He married,

4537. Bridget ——.

4538. HENRY KYNNERSLEY married at the Church of St. Mary Aldermary, London 16 Feb. 1597/98,
4539. MARGERY BUTLER.

4540-4543. ——.

4544. EDWARD VAUGHAN of Trawscoed, Cardiganshire, died in 1635. He married,
4545. LETTICE STEDMAN of Ystradffin, Cardiganshire.

4546. JOHN STEDMAN of Cilcennin, Cardiganshire, married,
4547. ANNE JONES of Abermarlais, Carmarthenshire.

4548. WILLIAM HOOKER of Berkhamstead, Hertfordshire, married,
4549. ——.

4550. SIR FRANCIS COPINGER, born in 1579 and died after 15 Oct. 1626. He married,
4551. HON. FRANCES BURGH, died before 24 Nov. 1619, daughter of Thomas Burgh, 5th Baron Burgh.

4552. CHARLES WILMOT, 1ST VISCOUNT WILMOT, P.C. (I.) (1607) AND (E.) (1628), M.P. [as Sir Charles Wilmot] 1614, Governor of Kerry 1605 and 1613 and Desmond 1605, Lord President of Connaught 1617-30, joint President 1630-1644, born in 1571 and died before April 1644. He married, 2nd, **MARY COLLEY [No. 4905].** He married, 1st, ca. 1605,
4553. SARAH ANDERSON, baptized at the Church of St. Olave Old Jewry, London 1 Sept. 1594 and buried at the Church of St. Martin-in-the-Fields, Westminster, Middlesex 8 Dec. 1615.

4554. SIR JOHN ST. JOHN, 1ST BARONET, M.P. 1624-25, died before 20 Sept. 1648; buried at Battersea, Surrey. He married, 2nd, in Oct. 1630, Margaret Whitmore, who died before 24 Nov. 1637, widow of Sir Richard Grubham, and daughter of William Whitmore and Anne Bond. He married, 1st, in 1611,
4555. ANNE LEIGHTON, died in 1628; buried at Liddiard Tregoze, Wiltshire.

4556. JOHN MALET, M.P. 1623-24, Sheriff of Somerset 1638-39, born ca. 1574 and buried at Bath Abbey, Somerset 10 April 1644. He married,

4557. HON. ANNE TRACY, daughter of John Tracy, 1st Viscount Tracy.

4558. FRANCIS HAWLEY, 1ST BARON HAWLEY, M.P. [as Lord Hawley] 1665-79, Lord of the Bedchamber to HRH The Duke of York (later HM King James II) 1673, born ca. 14 Jan. 1608/9 and died 22 Dec. 1684. He married,

4559. JANE GIBBES of Honington, Warwickshire.

4560-4575. ——.

4576. ROBERT SHAFTO, Sheriff of Northumberland 1607, buried at St. Nicholas' Church, Newcastle-upon-Tyne 12 Sept. 1623. He married 13 Jan. 1594/95,

4577. JANE EDEN, baptized 9 Nov. 1575 and buried 3 July 1658.

4578. ROBERT LEDGER, Sheriff of Newcastle 1622-23, buried at St. Nicholas' Church, Newcastle-upon-Tyne 21 April 1623. He married there 6 May 1611,

4579. JANE MITFORD, baptized 29 June 1575 and buried at St. Nicholas' Church 10 Aug. 1624. She married, 1st, there 4 Feb. 1593/94, Thomas Clarkson, buried at St. Nicholas' Church 10 Oct. 1605.

4580. LEWIS WIDDRINGTON, died at Cheesburn Grange, Northumberland 20 Aug. 1630. He married,

4581. CATHERINE LAWSON, born ca. 1578.

4582. FERDINANDO FAIRFAX, 2ND LORD FAIRFAX, M.P. [as Sir Ferdinando Fairfax] 1614, 1620-22, and 1624-26, [as Hon. Sir Ferdinando Fairfax] 1628-29, and [as Lord Fairfax] 1640, General 1642-45, Governor of York 1644-48, born at Denton, Yorkshire 29 March 1584 and died there 13 March 1646/47. He married, 2nd, at the Church of St. Giles-in-the-Fields, Holborn, Middlesex 16 Oct. 1646, Rhoda Chapman, who was buried at Aynho, Northamptonshire 11 Oct. 1686 aged 69, widow of Thomas Hussey and daughter of Thomas Chapman. He married, 1st, in 1607,

4583. LADY MARY SHEFFIELD, buried at Bolton Percy, Yorkshire 4 June 1619, daughter of Edmund Sheffield, 1st Earl of Mulgrave.

4584. SAMPSON INGLEBY, steward of the Earl of Northumberland, buried at Ripley, Yorkshire 18 July 1604. He married,
4585. JANE LAMBERT, buried 23 April 1628.

4586. SIR JAMES BELLINGHAM of Heslington, Westmorland, died in 1641. He married,
4587. AGNES CURWEN of Workington, Cumberland.

4588. JOHN SAVILE, M.P. 1572, born at Bradley, Yorkshire before 26 March 1546 and died at Serjeants' Inn, London 2 Feb. 1606/7. He married, 1st, 11 May 1574, Jane Garth, born in 1554 and died 11 Jan. 1585/86, daughter of Richard Garth of Morden, Surrey. He married, 3rd, at Altofts, Yorkshire 16 Jan. 1593/94, Hon. Dorothy Wentworth, who died 3 Jan. 1601/2, widow of i) Paul Wythypole and ii) Sir Martin Frobisher, and daughter of Thomas Wentworth, 1st Baron Wentworth, and Margaret Fortescue. He married, 4th, after 31 Dec. 1603, Margery Pert, widow of i) Sir Jerome Weston and ii) William Thwaites, and daughter of George Pert and Alice ———. He married, 2nd, 23 Dec. 1587,
4589. ELIZABETH WENTWORTH, died 7 Jan. 1591/92. She married, 1st, ca. 1578, Richard Tempest of Bowling and Bracewell, Yorkshire, born in 1534 and died before Sept. 1583, son of Nicholas Tempest and Beatrice Bradford.

4590. SIR HENRY GARWAY, Lord Mayor of London 1639-40, Sheriff of London 1627/28, Master of the Drapers' Company 1627/28 and 1639-40, Governor of the Levant Company 1635-43, the East India Company 1641-43, and the Russia Company 1643-44, baptized at the Church of St. Peter-le-Poer, Broad Street, London 17 April 1575 and buried there 24 July 1646. He married,
4591. MARGARET CLITHEROE, buried at the Church of St. Peter-le-Poer 26 June 1656.

4592-4607. ———.

4608. PETER BARING of Groningen, born ca. 1483 and died between 1532 and 1536. He married,
4609. EVERHARDA ——— of Groningen, died at Hamburg 1 Sept. 1558.

4610-4687. ——.

4688. John Watlington of Natley Scuers, Hampshire, died between 10 Nov. and 9 Dec. 1558. He married,
4689. Anne Folwell. She married, 2nd, ca. 9 Feb. 1559/60 —— Jaques.

4690-4711. ——.

4712. Thomas Hutton of Poppleton, Yorkshire, born in 1581 and died 23 Jan. 1620/21. He married,
4713. Anne Bennet, born ca. 1587 and died 18 Jan. 1650/51.

4714. Ferdinando Fairfax, 2nd Lord Fairfax = 4582.
4715. Lady Mary Sheffield = 4583.

4716. Nicholas Stringer of Eaton, Nottinghamshire, died 18 Dec. 1636. He married,
4717. Mary Hartopp.

4718. Francis South, Sheriff of Lincolnshire 1616, baptized at Keelby, Lincolnshire 30 July 1575 and buried at Kelstern, Lincolnshire 29 July 1632. He married, 1st, Elizabeth Meres, who died 1 June 1604, daughter of John Meres and Barbara Dalison. He married, 3rd, at Buckminster, Leicestershire 11 Aug. 1623, Anne Hartopp, daughter of William Hartopp and Eleanor Adcock. He married, 2nd, at Whaplode, Lincolnshire 9 June 1606,
4719. Anne Irby, baptized 3 Jan. 1584/85 and died 12 May 1620; buried at Kelstern.

4720-4727. ——.

4728. Leonard Bushell, buried at Whitby, Yorkshire 24 Oct. 1610. He married at St. Nicholas' Church, Newcastle-upon-Tyne 14 Oct. 1588,
4729. Jane Lambe, buried at Whitby 10 Aug. 1629.

4730. Robert Ellis married,
4731. ——.

4732-4735. ——.

4736. Thomas Lukin, buried at Mashbery, Essex 3 Nov. 1619. He married, 1st, at the Church of St. Botolph Bishopsgate, London 23 Aug. 1576, Mary Wood, daughter of John Wood of Baddow, Essex. He married, 2nd, before 1586,
4737. Joan Norris of Great Baddow, died after 15 Dec. 1619.

4738-4743. ——.

4744. Robert Lane, buried at Campsea Ash, Suffolk 20 June 1644. He married,
4745. Elizabeth Futter, baptized at Thuxton, Suffolk 30 Jan. 1591/92 and died after 1 April 1643.

4746. Edmund Bohun, baptized 17 May 1592 and buried at Westhall, Suffolk 16 Nov. 1658. He married 10 Jan. 1613/14,
4747. Dorothy Baxter of Mendham, Suffolk, buried 13 May 1661.

4748. Robert Young of Rayne, Essex, married,
4749. Elizabeth ——.

4750-4763. ——.

4764. Robert Howchin, buried at Panfield, Essex 23 Oct. 1647. He married,
4765. Margaret ——, buried at Panfield 19 Nov. 1666.

4766. ? John Allen, buried at Panfield, Essex 1 Feb. 1650/51. He married,
4767. ? Catherine ——, buried at Panfield 27 Dec. 1644.

4768. ROBERT DOUGHTY, died before 8 Sept. 1621. He married at Poringland, Norfolk 27 May 1617,

4769. SARAH BRANSBY, died after 8 Sept. 1621. She married 1st, —— Wrongrey.

4770. ROGER TOWNSHEND of Horstead, Norfolk, died ca. 1661. He married,

4771. ANNE MORYSON of Cadeny, Lincolnshire, died in 1657. She married, 1st, Gresham Hogaine of Hackney, Middlesex, who died after 1616.

4772. JOHN GUYBON, baptized at Oby, Norfolk in Sept. 1602 and buried there 19 Aug. 1650. He married at Rollesby, Norfolk 18 Oct. 1626,

4773. KATHERINE MAPES, buried at Oby 10 Feb. 1657/58.

4774. THOMAS BLOFELD of Sustead, Norfolk, born ca. 1564 and died before 30 April 1638. He married, 2nd, Elizabeth Mapes, daughter of Leonard Mapes of Beeston, Norfolk. He married, 1st,

4775. MARY WRIGHT of Sudthorp, Norfolk.

4776. WILLIAM DOUGHTY, born ca. 1592 and died before 21 Nov. 1654. He married, 1st, Elizabeth Browne, who died before 29 Oct. 1622, daughter of John Browne of Poringland, Norfolk. He married, 2nd, at Arminghall, Norfolk 29 Oct. 1622,

4777. FRANCES KEMP, buried at Hanworth, Norfolk 4 April 1667.

4778-4779. ——.

4780. ADRIAN PAYNE, born ca. 1600 and buried 16 Nov. 1648. He married at the Church of St. Peter Mancroft, Norwich 23 Feb. 1626/27,

4781. ELIZABETH GIRLING, died after 15 Dec. 1648.

4782. NICHOLAS OSBORNE of Norwich married,

4783. ——.

4784-4799. ——.

4800. SYMPHORIEN THELLUSSON, SEIGNEUR DE FLÉCHÈRES, born at Saint-Symphorien-le-Châtel, Lyon in April 1518 and died 9 May 1597. He married at Lyon ca. 1551,

4801. FRANÇOISE DE GASPARD DE PRAVINS, born at Villefranche-sur-Saône 1 Nov. 1532 and died at Geneva 26 Nov. 1613.

4802. JEAN TUDERT, SEIGNEUR DE MAZIÈRES, died ca. 1611. He married at Geneva 5 July 1574,

4803. MARIE BUISSON, born ca. 1552 and died 28 June 1626. She married, 1st, 11 April 1568, Antoine Pons, who died before 5 Sept. 1571. She married, 2nd, at Lyon 5 Sept. 1571, Jérôme Rully, who died before 5 July 1574.

4804. RÉMI TRONCHIN, born at Troyes in 1549 and died at Geneva 26 Nov. 1609. He married 5 June 1580,

4805. SARA MORIN, born in 1558 and died 4 Sept. 1623.

4806. JEAN BAPTISTE ROCCA, grocer, born ca. 1561 and died 29 Oct. 1619. He married 1 Dec. 1588,

4807. ANNE TARUFFO, died 30 March 1598.

4808. VINCENT GUIGUER, Mayor of St. Gall, Switzerland, married,

4809. ANNE PODEGGER.

4810. ABRAHAM PENIN, merchant of Lyon, born before 1583 and died before 1636. He married,

4811. JEANNE PELLOUTIER, born before 1586.

4812. ANDRÉ TOURTON of Boulieu-lès-Annonay, Ardèche, born before 1586. He married in 1602,

4813. JEANNE BOYRON, born before 1589.

4814. ISAAC RANCON, born before 1597 and died at Annonay, Ardèche 12 Jan. 1642. He married before Jan. 1613,

4815. ISABEAU CHAPUIS, died at Annonay 4 June 1650.

4816-4851. ——.

4852. SIR RICHARD SALTONSTALL of South Ockenden, Essex, died 11 Dec. 1619, son of Sir Richard Saltonstall [No. 8282]. He married,
4853. JANE BERNARD of Abington, Northamptonshire, died between 21 May and 4 June 1619.

4854. SIR CALTHORPE PARKER, M.P. 1601, died 5 Sept. 1618. He married,
4855. MERCY SOAME, buried at Erwarton, Suffolk 6 July 1636.

4856-4863. ——.

4864. GILES BULTEEL of Tournai, buried at the Church of St. Mary Woolnoth, London 7 May 1603. He married,
4865. MARIE BRONTIN of Hainault, died between 15 April and 28 June 1611.

4866. JOHN PEARD, Mayor of Barnstaple 1607, baptized at Barnstaple, Devonshire 1 Aug. 1565 and died between 20 Oct. 1631 and 20 Jan. 1632. He married at Barnstaple 23 Sept. 1589,
4867. JULYAN BEAPLE, baptized at Barnstaple 20 March 1570/71.

4868. GEORGE KEKEWICH, Sheriff of Cornwall 1592, baptized at Menheniot, Cornwall 14 Aug. 1556 and died 22 Dec. 1611; buried at St. Germans, Cornwall. He married, 2nd (antenuptial settlement dated 1 May 1601), Julian Viell, who died before 11 Jan. 1624/25, widow of George Grenville, and daughter of William Viell and Jane Arundell. He married, 1st, at Breage, Cornwall 3 Dec. 1584,
4869. BLANCHE GODOLPHIN, buried at St. Germans 11 Dec. 1597.

4870. WILLIAM COODE, M.P. 1639, Sheriff of Cornwall 1616, baptized 14 Nov. 1573 and buried at Morval, Cornwall 20 April 1655. He married, 2nd, Anne Stuckley, daughter of John Stuckley and Frances St. Leger. He married, 1st,
4871. LEODIA KENDALL, buried at Morval 2 June 1613.

4872-4879. ——.

4880. HUGH CROCKER of Lineham, Devonshire, died by 1614. He married,
4881. AGNES BONVILLE of Little Modbury, Devonshire.

4882-4883. ——.

4884. SIR WILLIAM POLE, M.P. 1586, Sheriff of Devonshire 1602-3, antiquary and genealogist, baptized at Shute, Devonshire 17 Aug. 1561 and died at
Colcombe, Devonshire 9 Feb. 1635/36. He married, 2nd, **JANE SYMES [No.
4887]**. He married, 1st, at Shobrook, Devonshire 20 July 1583,
4885. MARY PERIAM, born 30 April 1567 and buried 8 May 1606.

4886. ROGER HOW, mercer, buried at the Mercers' Chapel, London 16 Aug.
1606. He married,
4887. JANE SYMES, buried at Colyton, Devonshire 17 Jan. 1653/54. She
married, 2nd, after 16 Aug. 1606, **SIR WILLIAM POLE [No. 4884]**.

4888. RICHARD HILLERSDON of Memland, Devonshire, died before 16
June 1651. He married at St. Martin's Church, Exeter 30 April 1599,
4889. CATHERINE CHAMPERNOWNE, baptized at Dartington, Devonshire
26 May 1577, daughter of Gawyn Champernowne and Gabrielle Roberte de
Montgommery, daughter of Gabriel, Comte de Montgommery.

4890. JOHN HARRIS of Lanreste, Cornwall, born before 1564 and died 2
June 1623. He married,
4891. JOAN HARTE of Plimston in Stoke, Cornwall.

4892. FRANCIS NOSWORTHY of Chagord, Devonshire, died in 1640. He
married,
4893. JANE DANIELL of Truro, Cornwall.

4894. RICHARD HILL, born ca. 1592. He married at Truro, Cornwall 16
Nov. 1613,
4895. ANNE WHITE, born ca. 1594.

4896. PATRICK DRUMMOND, 3RD LORD DRUMMOND, born in 1550 and died ca. 1602. He married, 2nd, in 1588, Agnes Drummond, who died 21 Jan. 1589/90, widow of i) Sir Hugh Campbell and ii) Hugh Montgomerie, 3rd Earl of Eglinton, and daughter of Sir John Drummond and Lady Margaret Stewart, natural daughter of HM King James IV. He married, 1st, before 21 Oct. 1572,

4897. LADY ELIZABETH LINDSAY, died in May 1585, daughter of David Lindsay, 9th Earl of Crawford.

4898. ROBERT KER, 1ST EARL OF ROXBURGHE, P.C. (S.) (1599 AND 1609/10), Lord of the Bedchamber to HM King James VI 1607, Lord Privy Seal in Scotland 1637-50, assassinated William Kerr of Ancrum [No. 4364] in 1590, born ca. 1570 and died at Floors House, Roxburghshire 18 Jan. 1649/50. He married, 2nd, **HON. JEAN DRUMMOND [No. 4901].** He married, 3rd, Lady Isobel Douglas, who died 16 Dec. 1672, daughter of William Douglas, 7th Earl of Morton [No. 2592], and Lady Anne Keith [No. 2593]. He married, 1st, at Newbattle House, near Edinburgh 5 Dec. 1587,

4899. MARGARET MAITLAND, daughter of William Maitland of Lethington, Lothianshire, Secretary of State to HM Queen Mary I Stewart, and Hon. Mary Fleming, HM's Maid of Honour ("the flower of the Queen's Maries").

4900. ROBERT KER, 1ST EARL OF ROXBURGHE = 4898. He married, 2nd, at Somerset House in the Strand, near London 3 Feb. 1613/14,

4901. HON. JEAN DRUMMOND, Lady of the Bedchamber to HM Queen Anne and Preceptor of the Royal Children, died 7 Oct. 1643, daughter of Patrick Drummond, 3rd Lord Drummond [No. 4896], and Lady Elizabeth Lindsay [No. 4897].

4902. WILLIAM HAY, 10TH EARL OF ERROLL, Lord High Constable at the coronation of HM King Charles I in Scotland 1633, died at Erroll, Perthshire in Dec. 1636. He married (contract dated 2 and 9 Sept. 1618),

4903. LADY ANNE LYON, died at Erroll 8 Feb. 1636/37, daughter of Patrick Lyon, 1st Earl of Kinghorne.

4904. GARRET MOORE, 1ST VISCOUNT MOORE, P.C. (I.) (1604), M.P. [as Sir Garret Moore] 1613, Lord President of Munster 1615, born ca. 1564 and died at Drogheda 9 Nov. 1627. He married ca. 1590,

4905. Mary Colley, died 3 June 1654; buried at Drogheda. She married, 2nd, before 28 April 1630, **Charles Wilmot, 1st Viscount Wilmot [No. 4552].**

4906. Adam Loftus, 1st Viscount Loftus, P.C. (I.) (1608), M.P. [as Ven. Sir Adam Loftus] 1613-15, Archdeacon of Glendalough 1594-1643, Lord Chancellor of Ireland 1619 and 1625-38, a Chief Governor of Ireland 1622-25, 1629-33, and 1636, born in 1568 and died at Middleham, Yorkshire early in 1643. He married in 1597,
4907. Sarah Bathow, died 1 Aug. 1650. She married, 1st, the Right Rev. Richard Meredith, Bishop of Leighlin 1589-96, who died in 1596.

4908. Robert Spencer, 1st Baron Spencer = 4096.
4909. Margaret Willoughby = 4097.

4910. Henry Wriothesley, 3rd Earl of Southampton = 4098.
4911. Elizabeth Vernon = 4099.

4912-4991. ——.

4992. Philip Grey of Howick and Morpeth, Northumberland, died before 10 Feb. 1615/16. He married,
4993. Margaret Weetwood of Weetwood, Northumberland, died after 10 Jan. 1627/28.

4994. Martin Fenwick, Sheriff of Northumberland 1673/74, born ca. 1597 and died at Newcastle-upon-Tyne in 1680. He married (settlement dated 17 July 1609),
4995. Elizabeth Fenwick of Kenton, Northumberland, died ca. 1676.

4996. John Lisle of Acton, Northumberland, born ca. 1554 and died in April 1640. He married after 1594,
4997. Agnes Ogle, died after 1 Oct. 1601. She married, 1st, William Lorraine of Kirkharle, Northumberland, who died in 1594.

4998. Sir Matthew Forster, Sheriff of Durham 1620, living in 1631. He married,

4999. Catherine Grey of Chillingham, Northumberland.

5000-5023. ——.

5024. George Grey of Southwick, Durham, died ca. 1661. He married ca. 1616,

5025. Susan Amcotts, daughter of Matthew Amcotts of Wickenby, Lincolnshire, and Susanna Velez de Guevara [daughter of Francisco Velez de Guevara of Segusa, Biscay, who settled in England in the train of HM King Philip II in 1554].

5026. Colonel Thomas Robinson of Rokeby, Yorkshire, buried at Leeds 20 June 1643. He married,

5027. Frances Smelt of Fleetham, Yorkshire, born 30 Sept. 1604.

5028. Rev. Zachary Cawdrey, Vicar of Melton Mowbray 1613-59, born ca. 1578 and died 31 Dec. 1659. He married at Melton Mowbray, Leicestershire 14 May 1617,

5029. Anne Withers.

5030-5031. ——.

5032. John Clavering, Mayor of Newcastle 1629, baptized at St. Nicholas' Church, Newcastle-upon-Tyne 2 Dec. 1591 and died 4 May 1648. He married at St. Nicholas' Church 8 Sept. 1618,

5033. Ann Shafto, baptized at St. Nicholas' Church 8 Jan. 1597/98 and died 18 Nov. 1673, daughter of Robert Shafto [No. 4576].

5034. Henry Maddison, baptized at St. Nicholas' Church, Newcastle-upon-Tyne 30 Oct. 1574 and died 14 July 1634. He married 14 May 1594,

5035. Elizabeth Barker, born ca. 1574 and died 24 Sept. 1653.

5036. CUTHBERT ELLISON, merchant adventurer, baptized 31 Jan. 1579/80 and died in 1626. He married,

5037. JANE ILE, buried at St. Nicholas' Church, Newcastle-upon-Tyne 23 March 1618/19.

5038. GEORGE LILBURN, Mayor of Sunderland 1635-38 and 1640-42, baptized at Auckland St. Andrew, Durham 24 Aug. 1578 and buried at Bishop Wearmouth, Durham 1 Dec. 1676. He married, 1st, at Whitburn, Durham 8 Nov. 1620, Isabel Chamber, who was buried at Whitburn 8 Nov. 1627. He married, 2nd, at Whitburn 13 April 1629,

5039. ELEANOR HICKES, buried 23 Oct. 1677.

5040. CUTHBERT OGLE of Bothnal and Kirkley, Northumberland, born ca. 1569 and died 14 Jan. 1654/55. He married,

5041. DOROTHY FENWICK.

5042. RALPH FOWLER of Sandiford Stone House, Newcastle-upon-Tyne, died after 3 July 1658. He married,

5043. ISABEL ———.

5044-5045. ———.

5046. DIONIS WILSON of Pegsworth, Northumberland, died between 12 Aug. 1630 and 9 May 1632. He married, 2nd, ? Martha Short, died after 26 Feb. 1663. He married, 1st,

5047. ——— CLARK.

5048. MATTHEW NEWTON of Stocksfield Hall, Northumberland, married,

5049. BARBARA OGLE of Burradon, Northumberland.

5050-5051. ———.

5052. REV. DR. ROBERT JENISON, Vicar of St. Nicholas' Church, Newcastle-upon-Tyne 1642-52, baptized at St. Nicholas' Church 6 Jan. 1582/83 and buried there 8 Nov. 1652. He married, 1st, 22 June 1619, Anne Bonner, who was buried at Halifax 5 March 1624/25, daughter of William Bonner. He married, 2nd, at Halifax in 1625, Elizabeth Favour, who was buried 10 May 1634. He married, 3rd,

5053. BARBARA SANDERSON, baptized at Brancepeth, Northumberland 10 May 1615 and died 9 Aug. 1673. She married, 2nd, after 8 Nov. 1652, **JOHN EMERSON [No. 5054].**

5054. JOHN EMERSON, Mayor of Newcastle-upon-Tyne, died 9 Aug. 1673; buried at St. Nicholas' Church, Newcastle. He married, 2nd, **BARBARA SANDERSON [No. 5053].** He married, 1st, at St. Nicholas' Church 13 April 1630,

5055. ALICE SHAFTO, baptized at All Saints' Church, Newcastle 8 Oct. 1609, daughter of Robert Shafto [No. 4576].

5056. HENRY PONSONBY of Hale, Cumberland, married 14 May 1605,

5057. DOROTHY SANDS of Rottington, Cumberland.

5058. HENRY FOLLIOTT, 1ST BARON FOLLIOTT, M.P. [as Sir Henry Folliott] 1613-15, born ca. 1569 and died 10 Nov. 1622. He married before 1613,

5059. ANNE STRODE, died ca. 1652. She married, 2nd, before 1627, Robert Dillon, 2nd Earl of Roscommon, who died 27 Aug. 1642, son of James Dillon, 1st Earl of Roscommon, and Eleanor Barnewall.

5060. CHARLES MOORE, 2ND VISCOUNT MOORE = 2452.
5061. HON. ALICE LOFTUS = 2453.

5062. EDWARD BRABAZON, 2ND EARL OF MEATH, P.C. (I.) (1660-69), M.P. [as Lord Brabazon] 1634-35, born ca. 1610 and died near Holyhead in the Irish Sea 25 March 1675. He married in 1632,

5063. MARY CHAMBRE, buried at St. Catherine's Church, Dublin 14 Sept. 1685.

5064. JOHN MARGETSON married at Birstall, Yorkshire 9 Nov. 1589,
5065. MARY LAYTON.

5066-5067. ——.

5068. WILLIAM CAULFIELD, 2ND BARON CHARLEMONT, Sheriff of Tyrone 1620, Master-General of the Ordance (Ireland) 1627-34, baptized at the Church of St. Mary Magdalen, Oxford 8 Oct. 1587 and died 4 Dec. 1640; buried at Charlemont, Armagh. He married,

5069. MARY KING, died between 16 July and 15 Aug. 1663; buried at Mullaghbrack, Armagh.

5070. CHARLES MOORE, 2ND VISCOUNT MOORE = 2452 = 5060.
5071. HON. ALICE LOFTUS = 2453 = 5061.

5072. WILLIAM CAVENDISH, 3RD EARL OF DEVONSHIRE, F.R.S. (1663), Lord Lieutenant of Derbyshire 1638-42, born 10 Oct. 1617 and died at Roehampton House, Surrey 23 Nov. 1684. He married (Bishop of London's license dated 4 March 1638/39),

5073. LADY ELIZABETH CECIL, born ca. 1619 and died 19 Nov. 1689, daughter of William Cecil, 2nd Earl of Salisbury [No. 5860].

5074. JAMES BUTLER, 1ST DUKE OF ORMONDE, K.G. (1661), P.C. (I.) (1633/34), (E.) (CA. 1651), AND (S.) (1660/61), attended HM King Charles II in exile, Lord Steward of the (Royal) Household 1660, Lord of the Bedchamber 1660-66, Lord High Steward of England 1661 and 1685, Bearer of the Crown at the coronations of TM King Charles II 1661 and King James II 1685, Lieutenant General 1638 and 1640, Commander-in-Chief in Ireland 1641, Lord Lieutenant [i.e., Viceroy] of Ireland 1643-47, 1649-50, 1662-69, and 1677-85, born at Clerkenwell, Middlesex 19 Oct. 1610 and died at Kingston Hall, Dorset 21 July 1688, son of Thomas Butler, Viscount Thurles by courtesy. He married 25 Dec. 1629,

5075. ELIZABETH PRESTON, BARONESS DINGWALL in her own right, born 25 July 1615 and died at St. James's Square, London 21 July 1684, daughter of Richard Preston, 1st Earl of Desmond.

5076. WILLIAM RUSSELL, 1ST DUKE OF BEDFORD = 2624.
5077. LADY ANNE CARR = 2625.

5078. Thomas Wriothesley, 4th Earl of Southampton = 2626.
5079. Rachel Massüe de Ruvigny = 2627.

5080. Sir Thomas Hoskins of Oxted, Surrey, born in Sept. 1562 and died 14 Aug. 1605. He married,
5081. Dorothy Aldersey, born at Berden, Essex ca. 1585 and died 23 Dec. 1651. She married, 2nd, after 1615, **Sir Henry Capell [No. 4404].**

5082. William Hale, Sheriff of Hertfordshire 1621, born ca. 1568 and died 27 Aug. 1634; buried at Kings Walden, Hertfordshire. He married at the Church of St. Olave Old Jewry, London 23 Feb. 1595,
5083. Rose Bond, baptized at the Church of St. Stephen Walbrook, London 29 Jan. 1573/74 and died 31 July 1648, daughter of George Bond [No. 8230].

5084. Roland Hale, Sheriff of Hertfordshire 1647/48, born 8, baptized at Kings Walden, Hertfordshire 19 June 1600 and died 7 April 1669, son of William Hale [No. 5082]. He married at the Church of St. Peter-le-Poer, Broad Street, London 12 July 1631,
5085. Elizabeth Garway, baptized at the Church of St. Peter-le-Poer 16 Dec. 1610 and died 9 Jan. 1678/79, daughter of Sir Henry Garway [No. 4590].

5086. Jeremiah Elwes of Broxbourne, Hertfordshire, baptized at the Church of St. Mary Bothawe, London 15 Nov. 1584 and died before 31 Jan. 1653/54. He married after 13 July 1627,
5087. Mary Morley, born ca. 1604 and died 4 Dec. 1667; buried at Ayot St. Peter's, Hertfordshire.

5088. Anthony Molesworth of Fotheringhay, Northamptonshire, ruined by entertaining HM Queen Elizabeth I, died after 1618. He married,
5089. Cecily Hurland.

5090. Sir Francis Palmes, M.P. 1586, Sheriff of Hampshire 1601, born ca. 1534 and died 30 March 1613. He married,
5091. Mary Hadnall, died 21 March 1594/95.

5092. CHRISTOPHER BYSSE of Dublin, died ca. 1614. He married,
5093. MARGARET FORSTER, died 15 March 1639/40.

5094. FRANCIS EDGEWORTH of Cranalagh Castle, Longford, died in 1637. He married, 1st, —— O'Cavanagh, daughter of The O'Cavanagh. He married, 2nd,
5095. JANE TUITE of Sonnagh, Longford.

5096. SIR NICHOLAS COOTE of Barking, Essex, died 1 Sept. 1633. He married, 2nd, ——. He married, 1st,
5097. ANNE COOPER of Thurgarton, Nottinghamshire.

5098. HUGH CUFFE of Cuffe's Wood, Cork, married,
5099. ——.

5100. SIR RICHARD ST. GEORGE, Norroy King of Arms 1604-23, Clarenceux King of Arms 1623-35, born ca. 1554 and died at High Holborn, Middlesex 17 May 1635. He married in 1575,
5101. ELIZABETH ST. JOHN.

5102. CAPTAIN RICHARD GIFFORD of Ballymagarett, Roscommon, murdered in 1595. He married,
5103. MARY DUKE. She married, 2nd, Right Hon. Sir Francis Rush, P.C. (I.), who was baptized at Great Thornham, Suffolk 15 Aug. 1560 and died 18 June 1623, son of Anthony Rush and Eleanor Cutler. She married, 3rd, Right Hon. Sir John Jephson, P.C. (I.), who died 16 May 1638, son of William Jephson and Mary Darrell.

5104. ARTHUR USSHER of Donnybrook, Dublin, born ca. 1588 and died in the River Dodder 2 March 1627/28. He married,
5105. JUDITH NEWCOMEN, died in 1652.

5106. CAPTAIN GEORGE ST. BARBE, born ca. 1593. He married after 1623,
5107. MARY WARBURTON.

5108-5119. ———.

5120. Colonel Hon. Sir George Hamilton, 1st Baronet, born ca. 1607 and died in 1679, son of James Hamilton, 1st Earl of Abercorn. He married (contract dated 2 June 1629),

5121. Hon. Mary Butler, died in Aug. 1680, daughter of Thomas Butler, Viscount Thurles [No. 10148].

5122. John Colepeper, 1st Baron Colepeper, P.C. (1641/42), M.P. [as Sir John Colepeper] 1640-44, Chancellor of the Exchequer 1642-43, member of the Council of the Prince of Wales (later HM King Charles II) 1645-46, baptized at Salehurst, Kent 17 Aug. 1600 and died 11 July 1660; buried at Hollingbourne, Kent. He married, 1st, at the Church of St. Botolph Bishopsgate, London 29 Oct. 1628, Philippa Snelling, who was buried at Hollingbourne 16 Sept. 1630, daughter of Sir John Snelling of West Grinstead, Sussex. He married, 2nd (license dated at Canterbury 12 Jan. 1630/31),

5123. Judith Colepeper, baptized at Hollingbourne 1 June 1606 and probably buried there 21 Nov. 1691.

5124-5125. ———.

5126. Sir Robert Hannay, 1st Baronet, died 8 Jan. 1657/58; buried at Dublin. He married,

5127. Jean Stewart, died 22 March 1661/62; buried at Christ Church, Dublin.

5128. John Plumer, buried at St. Swithin's Church, London in Sept. 1608. He married,

5129. Audrey Page of Harrow-on-the-Hill, Middlesex. She married, 2nd, Robert Benett of New Windsor, Berkshire, son of John Benett and Alice Barley.

5130. Philip Gerard, Reader of Gray's Inn, London 1611, died between 27 March 1635 and 27 Feb. 1636/37. He married,

5131. Frances Page of Wembley, Middlesex.

5132. Roland Hale = 5084.
5133. Elizabeth Garway = 5085.

5134. Jeremiah Elwes = 5086.
5135. Mary Morley = 5087.

5136. Thomas Craggs of Landrew, Durham, born ca. 1592. He married 6 Dec. 1630,
5137. Cecilia Garthorne, buried at Wolsingham, Durham 15 Dec. 1665.

5138. Rev. Ferdinando Moorcroft, Rector of Stanhope, Durham 1608 and Heighington, Durham 1625, died after 15 Dec. 1640. He married,
5139. Margaret James, died after 23 April 1656.

5140. Jacob Richards married,
5141. ———.

5142-5151. ———.

5152. Robert Moyle, born in 1558 and buried at St. Germans, Cornwall 9 May 1604. He married,
5153. Anne Locke, buried at St. Germans 12 April 1604.

5154. Sir Edmund Prideaux, 1st Baronet, born ca. 1555 and died at Netherton, Devonshire 28 Feb. 1628/29. He married, 2nd, ca. 1596, Catherine Edgcombe, daughter of Piers Edgcombe and Margaret Luttrell. He married, 3rd, at Ugborough, Devonshire 22 July 1606, Mary Reynell, who died between 30 July 1630 and 16 Jan. 1630/31, widow of Arthur Fowell, and daughter of Richard Reynell and Agnes Southcott. He married, 1st, before 1590,
5155. Bridget Chichester.

5156. Evan Morice, died in 1605. He married,
5157. Mary Castell, died 2 Oct. 1647. She married, 2nd (license dated 26 Sept. 1611), Sir Nicholas Prideaux of Soldon, Devonshire.

The Princess's parents, then Viscount and Viscountess Althorp, following their marriage ceremony at Westminster Abbey in what was dubbed the "wedding of the year," 1 June 1954. © *Topham / The Image Works*

The Princess's grandfather, Viscount Althorp [later 7th Earl Spencer], by Lafayette Studio, 1921. *V&A Images/Victoria and Albert Museum*

A family gathering for the golden wedding anniversary of the 7th Earl and Countess Spencer, 1969. The group includes (*center, rear*) Lord and Lady Spencer, and (*right, rear*) Viscount Althorp. The Hon. Diana Spencer stands in front of her grandfather. © *Topham / The Image Works*

The Princess's maternal grandparents, Lord and Lady Fermoy, leaving the reception given by Lord and Lady Londonderry on the eve of the opening of Parliament, 1 February 1932. © *Topham / The Image Works*

Lord and Lady Fermoy with their daughters, Mary (*left, rear*) and Frances (*right, rear*), at the girls' debutante ball at Londonderry House, 23 May 1953. © *Topham / The Image Works*

The Duchess of Abercorn and Child, oil on copper by Sir Edwin Henry Landseer, ca. 1834–36. The sitter [No. 41] was actually Marchioness of Abercorn at the time this portrait was painted. Her daughter, Lady Harriet Hamilton, later became Countess of Lichfield. *Tate, London 2007*

Detail of *Charles Gordon-Lennox, 5th Duke of Richmond and Lennox,* by Thomas Heaphy, 1813–14. At the time this portrait was painted, the sitter [No. 46] was Earl of March. *National Portrait Gallery, London*

Mrs. James Boothby Burke Roche (née Frances Eleanor Work) [No. 13], watercolor on ivory by Carl and Fredrika Weidner, ca. 1895. *Collection of The New-York Historical Society, accession no. 1905.213*

Frank Work Driving a Fast Team of Trotters, oil on canvas by John J. McAuliffe, 1892. Born in Ohio, Work [No. 26] was a racing enthusiast. *Museum of the City of New York, the J. Clarence Davies Collection*

Charles Grey, 2nd Earl Grey, attributed to Thomas Phillips, ca. 1829. Earl Grey [No. 78] was Prime Minister under King William IV. *National Portrait Gallery, London*

Robert Walpole, 1st Earl of Orford, by Arthur Pond, 1742. Walpole [No. 556] served both King George I and King George II as First Lord of the Treasury, a position now known as Prime Minister. *National Portrait Gallery, London*

Barbara Palmer (née Villiers), Duchess of Cleveland, with her son, Charles Fitzroy, as Madonna and Child, by Sir Peter Lely, ca. 1664. The Duchess [No. 1097] was Lady of the Bedchamber to Queen Catherine and mistress to the Queen's husband, King Charles II. Charles Palmer or Fitzroy, Lord Limerick, later became Duke of Cleveland and Southampton. *National Portrait Gallery, London*

King James II, by Sir Peter Lely, ca. 1665–70. The Roman Catholic brother of and successor to Charles II, James II [No. 1106] was forced to abdicate in favor of William and Mary. *National Portrait Gallery, London*

John Wilmot, 2nd Earl of Rochester, by an unknown artist, ca. 1665–70. Samuel Johnson wrote that Rochester [No. 1138], a poet and Lord of the Bedchamber to King Charles II, "lived worthless and useless, and blazed out his youth and health in lavish voluptuousness." *National Portrait Gallery, London*

Robert Devereux, 2nd Earl of Essex, attributed to Nicholas Hilliard, ca. 1587. A longtime favourite of Queen Elizabeth I, Essex [No. 5786] incurred her displeasure when he wed Frances Walsingham, widow of Sir Philip Sidney. The hapless Essex was later executed after leading a failed coup. *National Portrait Gallery, London*

5158. HUMPHREY PRIDEAUX of Soldon, Devonshire, born ca. 1573 and died 31 March 1617. He married at East Allington, Devonshire 30 March 1600,
5159. HONOR FORTESCUE, baptized 11 May 1584 and died 17 Dec. 1663. She married, 2nd (license dated 14 Sept. 1618), Shilston Calmady.

5160. WILLIAM COPLEY of Sprotsborough, Yorkshire, died in 1644. He married,
5161. DOROTHY ROOTH of Romley, Derbyshire, died before 7 Sept. 1638.

5162. THOMAS WALMESLEY, died at Blackburn, Lancashire 13 July 1637. He married at Blackburn 2 Feb. 1616/17,
5163. JULIA MOLYNEUX, died in Oct. 1688.

5164. EDWARD PURCELL, Sheriff of Montgomeryshire 1625, died after 1646. He married,
5165. MARY PRICE of Goggerdan, Montgomeryshire.

5166. SIR ROBERT VAUGHAN of Llwydiarth and Llangedwyn, Montgomeryshire, died before 1625. He married,
5167. LADY KATHERINE HERBERT, born in 1600 and died at Windsor, Berkshire in 1666, daughter of William Herbert, 1st Earl of Powis. She married, 2nd, in 1625, Sir James Palmer, Gentleman of the Bedchamber to HM King James I and Gentleman Usher of the Privy Chamber to HM King Charles I, born in 1584 and died 15 March 1656/57, son of Thomas Palmer and Margaret Poley.

5168. FRANCIS BULLER, M.P. 1640, born ca. 1603 and died between 12 June and 22 Nov. 1677. He married at St. Stephen's by Saltash, Cornwall 21 Nov. 1625,
5169. THOMASINE HONYWOOD, died between 3 Dec. 1677 and 17 Jan. 1677/78, daughter of Sir Thomas Honywood.

5170. JOHN COODE, baptized at Morval, Cornwall 1 Feb. 1597/98 and died after 25 June 1651. He married, 1st, 29 Sept. 1622, Grace Langford, who was buried 9 July 1627, daughter of John Langford of Coxworthy, Devonshire. He married, 2nd, before 25 June 1651,
5171. MARY BASTARD of Westnorth, Duloe, Cornwall.

5172. ANDREW POLLEXFEN of Sherford, Devonshire, died in 1670. He married,
5173. JOAN WOOLCOMBE of Pitton, Yealmpton, Devonshire, born ca. 1607.

5174. GEORGE DUNCOMBE, perhaps **M.P.** 1656-58, born ca. 1605 and died 29 Oct. 1674. He married,
5175. CHARITY MUSCOTT, died in 1677.

5176. SIR JOHN TRELAWNY, 1ST BARONET, Sheriff of Cornwall 1630/31, born at Hall, Cornwall 24 April 1592 and buried at Pelynt, Cornwall 16 or 26 Feb. 1663/64. He married, 2nd, after Jan. 1639, Douglas Gorges, baptized at St. Budeaux, Devonshire 13 Sept. 1586 and died before 1 Oct. 1660, widow of Sir William Courtenay, and daughter of Tristram Gorges and Elizabeth Cole. He married, 1st, ca. 1617,
5177. ELIZABETH MOHUN, baptized at St. Pinnock, Cornwall 10 Feb. 1592/93 and died after Jan. 1639.

5178. SIR EDWARD SEYMOUR, 2ND BARONET = 2176.
5179. DOROTHY KILLIGREW = 2177.

5180. LEWIS HELE of Babcombe, Devonshire, born ca. 1579 and died 7 Jan. 1656/57. He married,
5181. ———.

5182. MATTHEW HALS, buried at Egg Buckland, Devonshire 25 Feb. 1675/76. He married,
5183. REBECCA SPECCOTT, buried at Egg Buckland 21 Nov. 1684.

5184. ROBERT DOUGLAS, younger of Lochleven, died in March 1584/85. He married (contract dated 19 March 1582/83),
5185. HON. JEAN LYON, died before March 1609/10, daughter of John Lyon, 8th Lord Glamis. She married, 2nd (contract dated 29 July 1587), Archibald Douglas, 8th Earl of Angus, born ca. 1555 and died 4 Aug. 1588, son of David Douglas, 7th Earl of Angus, and Margaret Hamilton. She married, 3rd (before 31) May 1590, Alexander Lindsay, 1st Lord Spynie, born ca. 1564 and died 16 June 1607, son of David Lindsay, 10th Earl of Crawford, and Margaret Beaton.

5186. George Keith, 4th Earl Marischal, P.C. (S.) (1585), Gentleman of the Bedchamber in Ordinary to HM King James VI 1580, envoy to Denmark to arrange the marriage of HM and Princess Anna of Denmark 1589, born in 1553 and died at Dunottar Castle, Aberdeenshire 2 April 1623. He married, 2nd, before 17 Dec. 1612, Hon. Margaret Ogilvy, who died after 20 Jan. 1624, daughter of James Ogilvy, 5th Lord Ogilvy, and Hon. Jean Forbes, daughter of William Forbes, 7th Lord Forbes. He married, 1st (contract dated 4-25 Feb. 1580/81),

5187. Hon. Margaret Home, born before 5 Dec. 1565 and died in May 1598, daughter of Alexander Home, 5th Lord Home.

5188. John Hay of Smithfield, Peeblesshire, died in 1628. He married,
5189. ——.

5190-5193. ——.

5194. Edmund Eyre, born ca. 1578 and died in Dec. 1650. He married (Bishop of London's license to marry at Great Yeldham, Essex dated 9 March 1603/4),
5195. Margaret Symonds, born ca. 1584

5196-5199. ——.

5200. Gilbert Heathcote of Chesterfield, Derbyshire, died before 30 Jan. 1634/35. He married,
5201. Elizabeth Owtrem.

5202. George Dickons of Chesterfield, Derbyshire, married,
5203. ——.

5204-5207. ——.

5208. Thomas White of Tuxford, Nottinghamshire, died 29 April 1638. He married,
5209. Anne Hartopp.

5210. Sir Thomas Williamson, 1st Baronet, Sheriff of Nottinghamshire 1639-40, baptized at East Markham, Nottinghamshire 14 May 1609 and died 14 Oct. 1657; buried at East Markham. He married, 2nd, at the Church of St. Bartholomew-the-Less, London 5 May 1647, Dionise Hale, baptized at Kings Walden, Hertfordshire 31 March 1611 and died before Feb. 1685, daughter of William Hale [No. 5082] and Rose Bond [No. 5083]. He married, 1st, at Honington, Lincolnshire 27 Aug. 1633,

5211. Jane Hussey, baptized at Honington 27 Jan. 1611/12 and buried at East Markham 22 Aug. 1643.

5212. Major Samuel Taylor, Mayor of Tangiers, born ca. 1624 and died 29 March 1679. He married, 1st, Barbara Gee of Retford, Nottinghamshire. He married, 2nd,

5213. Elizabeth Arlush, died at Oldcotes, Nottinghamshire ca. 1660.

5214. Colonel Sir Ralph Knight, M.P. 1659 and 1660, born ca. 1619 and died 21 April 1691; buried at Firbeck, Yorkshire. He married, 2nd (license dated 17 May 1687), Elizabeth ——, widow of John Rolleston of Sookholme, Nottinghamshire. He married, 1st, at Rotherham, Yorkshire 23 June 1646,

5215. Faith Dickenson, baptized at Sessay, Yorkshire 16 April 1627 and died 18 April 1671.

5216. William Lascelles alias Jackson, buried at Sigston, Yorkshire 16 Nov. 1624. He married,

5217. Elizabeth Wadeson of Yafforth, Yorkshire.

5218. Sir William St. Quintin, 1st Baronet, Sheriff of Yorkshire 1648/49, born ca. 1579 and buried at Harpham, Yorkshire 8 Oct. 1649. He married ca. 1605,

5219. Mary Lacy, died at St. Mary's Church, Beverley, Yorkshire 4 May 1649.

5220. Philip Lascelles of Thorneby, near Stockton in Cleveland, Yorkshire, died ca. 1662. He married,

5221. —— Bradley of Scarborough.

5222-5231. ——.

5232. Sir Edward Chaloner, born ca. 1625 and buried at Guisborough, Yorkshire 13 March 1679/80. He married,

5233. Anne Ingoldsby, born in 1626 and buried at Guisborough 28 Nov. 1704. She married, 2nd, at Guisborough 28 Feb. 1689/90, Edward Trotter.

5234. Colonel Sir David Foulis, 3rd Baronet, M.P. 1685-88, baptized at Ingleby, Yorkshire 14 March 1632/33 and died 13 March 1694/95; buried at Ingleby. He married (banns published at St. Paul's Church, Covent Garden, near London 16, 18, and 25 June 1655),

5235. Catherine Watkins, baptized at Chalfont St. Giles, Buckinghamshire 2 Oct. 1631 and died after 18 Aug. 1716.

5236. Thomas Bowes, baptized at Richmond, Yorkshire 23 Dec. 1607 and buried at Barnard Castle, Durham 9 Sept. 1661. He married,

5237. Anne Maxton, buried at Barnard Castle 31 Dec. 1705.

5238. Sir Francis Blakiston, 3rd Baronet, died 8 Oct. 1713; buried at Whickham, Durham. He married at Wolsingham, Durham 22 July 1656,

5239. Anne Bowes, buried at Whickham 26 Jan. 1700/1.

5240. William Fynney of Fynney, Staffordshire, born 16 July 1626 and died 4 Dec. 1688. He married 5 Nov. 1646,

5241. Mary Bateman, died 11 June 1683.

5242. Richard Machin of Bucknall, Staffordshire, married,

5243. ——.

5244-5247. ——.

5248. Francis Russell, 4th Earl of Bedford = 2054.

5249. Hon. Catherine Brydges = 2055.

5250. Robert Carr, 1st Earl of Somerset, K.G. (1611), P.C. (E.) (1612) and (S.) (1613), Gentleman of the Bedchamber to HM King James I 1607, Lord Chamberlain of the (Royal) Household 1613, Secretary of State

1612-14, the king's favourite from 1607 [until he and his wife were charged with the murder of Sir Thomas Overbury, Somerset's mentor, who had opposed the annulment of Lady Essex's first marriage; the Somersets were tried, found guilty, imprisoned 1615-22, and pardoned in 1624], born ca. 1587 and buried at St. Paul's Church, Covent Garden, near London 17 July 1645. He married at the Chapel Royal, Whitehall, near London 26 Dec. 1613,

5251. LADY FRANCES HOWARD, born 31 May 1590 and died at Chiswick, Middlesex 23 Aug. 1632, daughter of Thomas Howard, 1st Earl of Suffolk. She married, 1st, 5 Jan. 1605/6 (dissolved by decree of nullity 25 Sept. 1613), Robert Devereux, 3rd Earl of Essex, baptized at St. Olave's Church, Hart Street, London 22 Jan. 1590/91 and died at Essex House in the Strand, near London 14 Sept. 1646, son of Robert Devereux, 2nd Earl of Essex [No. 5786], and Frances Walsingham [No. 4447].

5252. HENRY WRIOTHESLEY, 3RD EARL OF SOUTHAMPTON = 4098 = 4910.
5253. ELIZABETH VERNON = 4099 = 4911.

5254. DANIEL MASSÜE, SEIGNEUR DE RUVIGNY, Governor of the Bastille, died in 1611. He married before 1603,
5255. MADELEINE PINOT, DAME DE LA CAILLEMOTTE, died in 1636. She married, 1st, Jean Pinot, Seigneur de Fontaine.

5256. JOHN HOWLAND, yeoman, buried at Newport, Essex 19 April 1593. He married there 15 July 1576,
5257. BLANCHE NIGHTINGALE, died 13 Oct. 1624.

5258. JOHN LANGLEY, linen draper of London, buried at St. Peter's Church, Cornhill, London 11 July 1639. He married,
5259. MARTHA JENOUR, born ca. 1585 and buried 1 July 1641. She married, 1st, John Hethersoll of Gray's Inn, London.

5260. RICHARD CHILD = 2204.
5261. ELIZABETH ROYCROFT = 2205.

5262. EDWARD BOATE, master shipwright of Portsmouth, born ca. 1589 and died between 29 March and 10 June 1650. He married, 2nd (Bishop of

London's license to marry at the Churches of St. Magnus or St. Mary Magdalen, New Fish Street, dated 30 July 1639), Rebecca (——) Holt, who was born ca. 1604. He married, 1st,

5263. ——.

5264. Sir Thomas Gower, 2nd Baronet, M.P. 1661-72, Sheriff of Yorkshire 1641-42 and 1662-63, Governor of York 1663-72, born ca. 1605 and died at Stittenham Manor, Yorkshire 3 Sept. 1672, son of Sir Thomas Gower, 1st Baronet [No. 5402]. He married, 1st, Elizabeth Howard, daughter of Sir William Howard and Hon. Mary Eure, daughter of William Eure, 4th Baron Eure. He married, 2nd (settlement dated 29 Sept. 1631),

5265. Frances Leveson, born in 1614 and died in 1661, daughter of Sir John Leveson.

5266. John Granville, 1st Earl of Bath = 1034.
5267. Jane Wyche = 1035.

5268. John Manners, 8th Earl of Rutland, M.P. [as John Manners] 1625/26 and 1640, High Sheriff of Derbyshire 1632, Lord Lieutenant of Derbyshire 1641/42 and Leicestershire 1667-77, born at Aylestone, Leicestershire 10 June 1604 and died at Nether Haddon, Derbyshire 29 Sept. 1679. He married at Barnwell Castle, Northamptonshire in 1628,

5269. Hon. Frances Montagu, baptized at Weekley, Northamptonshire 8 Aug. 1613 and died 19 May 1671, daughter of Edward Montagu, 1st Baron Montagu.

5270. Baptist Noel, 3rd Viscount Campden = 2726. He married, 4th, 6 July 1655 (published at St. Margaret's Church, Westminster, Middlesex),

5271. Lady Elizabeth Bertie, died ca. 20 July 1683, daughter of Montagu Bertie, 2nd Earl of Lindsey.

5272. Hon. William Pierrepont, M.P. 1640, 1654, and 1660, Sheriff of Shropshire 1637/38, born ca. 1608 and died 17 July 1678, son of Robert Pierrepont, 1st Earl of Kingston-upon-Hull. He married,

5273. Elizabeth Harris.

5274. SIR JOHN EVELYN, M.P. 1625-26, 1640-42, 1655, and 1660, born at Kingston, Surrey 11 Aug. 1601 and died 26 June 1685. He married at St. Bride's Church, London 2 April 1622,

5275. ELIZABETH COXE, buried at St. Mary Woolchurch-Haw, London 10 May 1658.

5276. GEORGE FEILDING, 1ST EARL OF DESMOND, K.B. (1625/26), born in 1614 and died 31 Jan. 1665/66, son of William Feilding, 1st Earl of Denbigh, and Lady Susan Villiers, daughter of Mary Beaumont, Countess of Buckingham for life [No. 5773], and sister of George Villiers, 1st Duke of Buckingham. He married at St. Peter's Church, Cornhill, London 17 April 1630,

5277. BRIDGET STANHOPE, baptized at Lady Bartlett's house, Kensington, Middlesex 19 Feb. 1615/16, spurned daughter of Sir Michael Stanhope.

5278. SIR ROBERT KING, M.P. 1634 and 1640, died at Cecil House in the Strand, near London between 13 April and 18 June 1657. He married, 2nd, after 16 Nov. 1638, Sophia Zouche, born ca. 1618 and died 12 Nov. 1691, widow of Edward Cecil, 1st Viscount Wimbledon, and daughter of Sir Edward Zouche and Dorothea Silking. He married, 1st,

5279. HON. FRANCES FOLLIOTT, died 13 March 1637/38, daughter of Henry Folliott, 1st Baron Folliott [No. 5058].

5280. OSEWOLT VAN KEPPEL, HEER IN DE VOORST, died ca. 24 Feb. 1621. He married, 2nd, in 1611, Wilhelmina de Ruyter, who died in 1633, daughter of Hendrik de Ruyter and Geertruid van der Hell. He married, 1st, before 29 May 1602,

5281. MECHTILD VAN DER CAPELLEN, died in 1610.

5282. COLONEL WIJNAND VAN SALLANDT, living in 1618; buried at Bennekom, Gelderland. He married, 1st, Anna toe Boecop, who died 16 Sept. 1612, daughter of Johan toe Boecop tot Harsselo and Elisabeth van Arnhem. He married, 2nd, in 1614,

5283. GEERTRUID VAN LYNDEN, died 12 Sept. 1666.

5284. EVERT VAN LINTELO TOT DE MARSCH, member of the States General 1610-26, died 16/26 Feb. 1637. He married, 1st (contract dated 31 March 1593), Nomina Beninga. He married, 2nd (contract dated 27 Dec. 1594),

5285. Arnolda van Hoemen, died at de Marsch 15 Dec. 1652.

5286. Sweder von Schele, Heer tot Welvelde, born at Haus Welvelde, Overijssel 2 Sept. 1569 and died at Haus Welbergen, Münster 28 May 1639. He married, 2nd (contract dated 23 Jan. 1615), Anna Brauwe, Vrouwe tot Camp en Dijckhuis, who died 9 May 1644, daughter of Herman Brauwe and Elske Schade. He married, 1st, at Den Ham 27 Oct. 1601,
5287. Sophia Reiniera van Coeverden, died 2 Dec. 1613.

5288. Adam van der Duyn, Heer van 'sGravenmoer, died 16 Oct. 1629. He married in 1581,
5289. Margriet Suys, Vrouwe van Rijswijck en den Burgh, died 10 April 1606.

5290. Nicolaas van der Bouckhorst, Heer van Wimmenum en Noordwijk, Dutch Ambassador to France 1621, born ca. 1581 and died in Oct. 1640. He married 15 Aug. 1606,
5291. Wilhelmina van der Noot.

5292. Colonel Adriaan Pietersen, Mayor of Zierikzee 1609 and 1613, born at Zierikzee, Zeeland in 1574 and died at The Hague 5 Feb. 1634. He married at Zierikzee 24 Dec. 1600,
5293. Quirina de Jonge, born at Zierikzee in 1579 and died at The Hague 20 April 1663.

5294. Pieter Coenen, secretary to TH Maurits van Nassau, Prince of Orange [No. 4396], and Prince Frederik Henrik of Nassau-Orange, born 16 Nov. 1586 and died at The Hague 19 Dec. 1637. He married at The Hague 25 Dec. 1622,
5295. Hester van Sijpesteyn, died at The Hague 9 May 1640.

5296. HM King James VI and I, King of England, Scotland, and Ireland = 4384 = 4424.
5297. HRH Princess Anna af Danmark = 4385 = 4425.

5298. HM KING HENRI III AND IV, KING OF FRANCE AND NAVARRE = 4386 = 4426.

5299. PRINCESS MARIA DE' MEDICI = 4387 = 4427.

5300. RENÉ DE PENANCOËT, SEIGNEUR DE KÉROUALLE, married, 2nd, 27 Sept. 1625, Françoise Laurens, Dame de Kerleguy, daughter of Jacques Laurens, Seigneur de la Mothe, and Jeanne de Kerloaguen. He married, 1st (contract dated 12 Oct. 1612),

5301. JULIENNE EMERY DU PONT-L'ABBÉ, DAME DU CHEF-DU-BOIS.

5302. SÉBASTIEN DE PLŒUC, MARQUIS DE TIMEUR, died after 1644. He married 8 Jan. 1617,

5303. MARIE DE RIEUX D'OIXANT, died in 1628, daughter of René de Rieux, Marquis d'Oixant.

5304. THOMAS BRUDENELL, 1ST EARL OF CARDIGAN = 2880.

5305. MARY TRESHAM = 2881.

5306. THOMAS SAVAGE, 1ST VISCOUNT SAVAGE = 2882.

5307. ELIZABETH DARCY, COUNTESS RIVERS = 2883.

5308. JOHN SAVILE, 1ST BARON SAVILE = 2884.

5309. ELIZABETH CAREY = 2885.

5310. CHRISTOPHER VILLIERS, 1ST EARL OF ANGLESEY = 2886.

5311. ELIZABETH SHELDON = 2887.

5312. GEORGE GORDON, 2ND MARQUESS OF HUNTLY, K.B. (1610), P.C. (1616), General 1623, HM King Charles I's Lieutenant in the North 1644, executed at Edinburgh 22 March 1648/49. He married (contract dated Feb. 1607),

5313. LADY ANNE CAMPBELL, born in 1594 and died at Aberdeen 14 June 1638, daughter of Archibald Campbell, 7th Earl of Argyll.

5314. Sir John Grant, born 17 Aug. 1596 and died 1 April 1637; buried at Holyrood Abbey, Edinburgh. He married (contract dated 11 Dec. 1613),

5315. Hon. Mary Ogilvy, died ca. 1647, daughter of Walter Ogilvy, 1st Lord Ogilvy.

5316. Henry Frederick Howard, 22nd Earl of Arundel and 2nd Earl of Norfolk, K.B. (1616), P.C. (1634), M.P. [as Lord Mowbray] 1628-29, 1634, and 1639/40, summoned to Parliament in his father's barony of Mowbray 1639/40, born 15 Aug. 1608 and died at Arundel House in the Strand, near London 17 April 1652. He married 7 March 1625/26,

5317. Lady Elizabeth Stuart, born 17 June 1610 and died 23 Jan. 1673/74, daughter of Esmé Stuart, 3rd Duke of Lennox.

5318. Edward Somerset, 2nd Marquess of Worcester = 2200.
5319. Elizabeth Dormer = 2201.

5320. John Mordaunt, 1st Earl of Peterborough = 1048.
5321. Hon. Elizabeth Howard = 1049.

5322. Hon. Thomas Carey = 1050.
5323. Margaret Smith = 1051.

5324. Adam Fraser of Finzeauch, Aberdeenshire, married,
5325. Margaret Duff of Drummuir, Banffshire.

5326. Sir Ferdinando Carey, born before 1 Feb. 1590/91 and died before 25 May 1638. He married,
5327. Philippa Throckmorton.

5328. George Gordon of Haddo, Aberdeenshire, died in his father's life-time. He married (contract dated 24 Jan. 1605/6),
5329. Margaret Bannerman of Waterton, Aberdeenshire. She married, 2nd, Sir William Keith of Ludquharn, Aberdeenshire, son of Gilbert Keith and Margaret Gordon.

5330. WILLIAM FORBES, 8th of Tolquhoun, Aberdeenshire, died before 1641. He married,

5331. JANET OGILVY of Dunlugas, Aberdeenshire.

5332. ALLAN LOCKHART, 5th of Cleghorn, Lanarkshire, died 15 Aug. 1623. He married, 2nd, ca. 1597, Christian Livingston. He married, 3rd, ca. 1612, Grizel Bannatyne. He married, 1st (contract dated 27 Nov. 1582),

5333. HON. ELIZABETH ROSS, died 16 July 1594, daughter of James Ross, 4th Lord Ross.

5334. RIGHT HON. SIR JAMES LOCKHART, P.C. (1661), Gentleman of the Privy Chamber to HM King Charles I 1629, born in 1596 and died 10 March 1674. He married, 1st, in 1617, Elizabeth Fairlie. He married, 2nd, in 1619,

5335. MARTHA DOUGLAS, born ca. 1598.

5336. JOHN MURRAY, 1ST EARL OF ATHOLL, died in June 1642. He married 6 June 1630,

5337. JEAN CAMPBELL of Glenorchy, Argyllshire.

5338. JAMES STANLEY, 7TH EARL OF DERBY, K.B. (1625/26), M.P. [as Lord Strange] 1625, summoned to Parliament in his father's barony of Strange 1628, Lord Lieutenant of North Wales 1642 and Cheshire and Lancashire 1642-47 [joint Lord Lieutenant with his father 1626-42], born at Knowsley, Lancashire 31 Jan. 1606/7 and executed at Bolton, Lancashire 15 Oct. 1651 [where his last words were "I die for God, the King, and the Laws, and this makes me not be ashamed of my life, nor afraid of my death"]. He married at The Hague 26 June 1626,

5339. CHARLOTTE DE LA TRÉMOÏLLE, who famously sustained the siege of Lathom House, Lancashire, in 1644, born at the Château de Thouars, Poitou in Dec. 1599 and died at Chester 21 March 1662/63, daughter of Claude de la Trémoïlle, Duc de Thouars, and Charlotte Brabantine van Nassau-Orange, daughter of HH Willem I van Nassau ("the Silent"), Prince of Orange [No. 8792].

5340. WILLIAM DOUGLAS, 1ST MARQUESS OF DOUGLAS, born in 1589 and died 19 Feb. 1659/60, son of William Douglas, 10th Earl of Angus. He married, 1st (contract dated 11 July 1601), Hon. Margaret Hamilton, born ca.

1585 and died 11 Sept. 1623, daughter of Claud Hamilton, 1st Lord Paisley, and Hon. Margaret Seton, daughter of George Seton, 5th Lord Seton. He married, 2nd, at Bellie, Elginshire 15 Sept. 1632,

5341. LADY MARY GORDON, born ca. 1610 and died in 1674, daughter of George Gordon, 1st Marquess of Huntly [No. 10624].

5342. JAMES HAMILTON, 1ST DUKE OF HAMILTON, K.G. (1630), P.C. (1632/33), bearer of the Sword at the coronation of HM King Charles I 1625/26, Lord of the Bedchamber 1628, Master of the Horse to HM 1628-44, born at Hamilton, Lanarkshire 19 June 1606 and executed [with Arthur Capell, 1st Baron Capell (No. 2202), and Henry Rich, 1st Earl of Holland (No. 6034)] at Palace Yard, Westminster, Middlesex 9 March 1648/49. He married in 1620,

5343. LADY MARGARET FEILDING, Lady of the Bedchamber to HM Queen Henrietta Maria, born in 1613 and died at Wallingford House, Charing Cross, near London 10 May 1638, daughter of William Feilding, 1st Earl of Denbigh [No. 10552].

5344. JOHN MAXWELL of Monreith, Wigtownshire, died in Jan. 1629/30. He married,

5345. CATHERINE MAXWELL of Garrerie, Wigtownshire.

5346. JOHN MACCULLOCH of Myreton, Clackmannanshire, died before 14 Sept. 1664. He married before July 1621,

5347. MARGARET COUPER of Edinburgh.

5348. SIR THOMAS HAY, 4th of Park, Wigtownshire, married,

5349. JEAN HAMILTON of Lettrick, Wigtownshire.

5350. JAMES HAMILTON, 1ST DUKE OF HAMILTON = 5342. He had issue by,

5351. ? EUPHEMIA HAMILTON.

5352. HUGH MONTGOMERIE, 7TH EARL OF EGLINTON, P.C. (1660/61), born 30 March 1613 and died at Eglinton, Ayrshire late in Feb. 1668/69. He married, 1st (contract dated 7-13 April 1631), Lady Anne Hamilton, who died at Struthers, Fife 16 Oct. 1632, daughter of James Hamilton, 2nd Marquess of

Hamilton [No. 10684], and Lady Anne Cunningham [No. 10685], daughter of James Cunningham, 7th Earl of Glencairn. He married, 2nd (contract dated 24 Dec. 1635),

5353. LADY MARY LESLIE, daughter of John Leslie, 6th Earl of Rothes.

5354. WILLIAM CRICHTON, 2ND EARL OF DUMFRIES, P.C. (S.) (1661), born after 1605 and died in 1691. He married 29 Aug. 1618,

5355. PENELOPE SWIFT, born after 1605.

5356. WILLIAM COCHRANE, 1ST EARL OF DUNDONALD, P.C. (S.) (1667), M.P. [in Scotland as Sir William Cochrane] 1644 and [in England as Lord Cochrane] 1656, born ca. 1605 and died in 1686; buried at Dundonald, Ayrshire. He married after 14 April 1633,

5357. EUPHEME SCOTT of Ardross, Fife.

5358. JOHN KENNEDY, 6TH EARL OF CASSILIS, P.C. (S.) (1660/61), known as "the grave and solemn Earl," born before 1607 and died in April 1668. He married, 2nd, **LADY MARGARET HAY [No. 2451].** He married, 1st, at Whitehall, near London 7 Jan. 1621/22,

5359. LADY JEAN HAMILTON, born at Edinburgh 5 Feb. 1606/7 and died shortly before 15 Dec. 1642, daughter of Thomas Hamilton, 1st Earl of Haddington.

5360. LAURENCE SCOTT of Harperrig, Midlothianshire, died in Dec. 1637. He married,

5361. ELIZABETH PRINGLE.

5362. SIR JOHN DALMAHOY of Dalmahoy, Midlothianshire, died in 1653. He married,

5363. BARBARA LINDSAY, died in Dec. 1656.

· **5364. JOHN NICOLSON** of Lasswade, Midlothianshire, died 5 March 1613/14. He married,

5365. JANET SWINTON.

5366-5375. ——.

5376. FRANCIS CURZON of Kedleston, Derbyshire, born ca. 1523 and died ca. 1592. He married,
5377. ELEANOR VERNON of Stokesay, Shropshire.

5378. RALPH SACHEVERELL of Staunton-by-Bridge, Derbyshire, born in 1532 and died 1 Sept. 1605. He married,
5379. EMMA DETHICK of Newhall, Derbyshire, died 30 April 1606.

5380. JOHN CREWE, born ca. 1524 and died in 1598; buried at Nantwich, Cheshire. He married,
5381. ALICE MAINWARING of Nantwich.

5382. REGINALD BRAY of Stene, Northamptonshire, born 1 May 1555 and died 28 Oct. 1583. He married,
5383. HON. ANNE VAUX, daughter of Thomas Vaux, 2nd Baron Vaux.

5384. WILLIAM PENN, Sheriff of Buckinghamshire 1624, died in Jan. 1638/39. He married,
5385. MARTHA PULTON of Bourton, Buckinghamshire.

5386. SIR HENRY DRURY of Hedgerley, Buckinghamshire, died in 1617. He married,
5387. SUSAN STEWKLEY, died before 25 Feb. 1640/41.

5388. HUMPHREY SHALLCROSS of Mayfield, Staffordshire, died before 1633. He married,
5389. JANE HORTON of Chester.

5390. FRANCIS KEMP of Fulham, Middlesex, died between 26 Jan. and 7 Feb. 1649/50. He married,
5391. BARBARA COCKS.

5392. RICHARD ASSHETON, died 7 Nov. 1618; buried at Middleton, Lancashire. He married,
5393. MARY VENABLES of Kinderton, Cheshire, died 24 Feb. 1643/44.

5394. JOHN KAYE, M.P. 1610/11, baptized at Almondbury, Yorkshire 26 Oct. 1578 and died 9 March 1640/41. He married at the Church of St. Michael-le-Belfry, York 18 Dec. 1603,
5395. ANNE FERNE, buried at Almondbury 9 March 1639/40.

5396. SIR RALPH ASSHETON, Sheriff of Lancashire 1594, died 8 May 1616. He married, 2nd, Anne Talbot, widow of James Assheton and daughter of Thomas Talbot. He married, 1st,
5397. JOANNA RADCLIFFE of Todmorden, Lancashire.

5398. SIR JAMES BELLINGHAM = 4586.
5399. AGNES CURWEN = 4587.

5400. SIR JOHN VAVASOUR of Spaldington, Yorkshire, died 17 Nov. 1641. He married,
5401. MARY GATES of Howden, Yorkshire.

5402. SIR THOMAS GOWER, 1ST BARONET, Sheriff of Yorkshire 1620/21, born in July 1584 and died after 12 Nov. 1652. He married 28 May 1604,
5403. ANNE DOYLEY, died 28 Oct. 1633; buried at the Church of St. Clement Danes, London.

5404. THOMAS LEIGH of Middleton, Yorkshire, buried 21 June 1594. He married,
5405. ELIZABETH STANLEY.

5406. EDMUND CLOUGH of Thorpe Stapleton, Yorkshire, died after 1625. He married, 1st, Margaret Lepton, daughter of Roger Lepton. He married, 2nd, in 1607,
5407. FRANCES VAVASOUR of Weston, Yorkshire.

5408. THOMAS HANMER of Fenns, Flintshire, died between 3 Feb. 1624/25 and 17 May 1625. He married,
5409. KATHERINE PULESTON.

5410. PETER WARBURTON of Crowley Lodge, Cheshire, born ca. 1585 and died 1 Jan. 1624/25. He married, 1st, ——. He married, 2nd, at Shocklach, Cheshire 10 June 1621,

5411. ELIZABETH EGERTON of Ridley, Cheshire.

5412. ROBERT CHARLTON of Whitton Court, Burford, Shropshire, goldsmith of London, died before 13 May 1670. He married, 2nd, before April 1625, Anne Wyche, baptized at the Church of St. Dunstan-in-the-East, London 8 Oct. 1599 and died before 12 May 1668, daughter of Richard Wyche [No. 4140] and Elizabeth Saltonstall [No. 4141]. He married, 1st,

5413. EMMA HARBY of Adstone, Northamptonshire, died 24 June 1622.

5414. WILLIAM BLUNDEN, M.P. 1625-26, died after 19 May 1641. He married,

5415. DOROTHY WARING, baptized at Albrighton, Shropshire 28 Sept. 1606.

5416. WILLIAM JENNENS of Moburne Mill, Duffield, Derbyshire, died between 26 Nov. 1602 and 9 Feb. 1602/3. He married at St. Martin's Church, Birmingham 28 Jan. 1559/60,

5417. JOANNA ELLIOTT, born ca. 1538 and died before 5 June 1622.

5418. WILLIAM WEAMAN, solicitor of Birmingham, died after 25 Feb. 1651. He married,

5419. ——.

5420. JOHN MILWARD of Bradley Ash, Derbyshire, born ca. 1551 and died before 20 May 1633. He married,

5421. MARY BLOUNT of Osbaldeston, Lancashire, died in 1651.

5422. JAMES WHITEHALGH of Whitehalgh, Ipstones, Staffordshire, died in 1620. He married,

5423. ANNE JACKSON of Pethills, Kniveton, Derbyshire.

5424. WILLIAM JENNENS = 5416.
5425. JOANNA ELLIOTT = 5417.

5426. William Weaman = 5418.
5427. = 5419.

5428. John Milward = 5420.
5429. Mary Blount = 5421.

5430. James Whitehalgh = 5422.
5431. Anne Jackson = 5423.

5432. Sir Thomas Burdett, 1st Baronet, Sheriff of Derbyshire 1610-11, born 3 Aug. 1585 and died before 22 May 1647. He married in 1602,
5433. Jane Francis of Foremark, Derbyshire, died in 1637.

5434. Sir John Walter, Attorney General to HRH The Prince of Wales (later HM King Charles I) 1613, Chief Baron of the Exchequer 1625, baptized at Ludlow, Shropshire 1 May 1565 and died at Serjeant's Inn, Fleet Street, London 18 Nov. 1630. He married, 2nd, 18 July 1622, Anne Wytham. He married, 1st, at the Church of St. Lawrence Pountney, London 24 Feb. 1600/1,
5435. Margaret Offley, baptized at the Church of St. Lawrence Pountney 19 Aug. 1582 and died ca. 1620.

5436. Gervase Pigot of Thrumpton, Nottinghamshire, died 8 Oct. 1618. He married, 1st, Margaret Hawford, who died 29 Jan. 1602/3, daughter of John Hawford of Kegworth, Leicestershire. He married, 2nd, Jane Bradshaw, who died 4 Feb. 1610/11, daughter of John Bradshaw of Burton-upon-Trent, Staffordshire. He married, 3rd,
5437. Frances Milward of Eaton, Derbyshire.

5438. John St. Andrew, born ca. 1601 and died before 30 Sept. 1631. He married (license dated 28 Sept. 1623),
5439. Elizabeth Bainbrigge, born in 1602. She married, 2nd, at Gotham, Nottinghamshire 6 Oct. 1631, John Bale.

5440. John Howe of Huntspill, Stogumber, Somerset, died after 13 Sept. 1630. He married before 15 April 1585,

5441. JOAN GRUBHAM of Bishop's Lydiard, Somerset, died after 13 Sept. 1630.

5442. THOMAS RICH of North Cerney, Gloucestershire, born ca. 1568 and died 27 Oct. 1647. He married,
5443. ANNE BOURCHIER of Barnesley, Gloucestershire.

5444. THOMAS SCROPE, 10TH BARON SCROPE, K.G. (1599), M.P. [as Hon. Sir Thomas Scrope] 1585 and 1588/89, born ca. 1567 and died at Langar, Nottinghamshire 2 Sept. 1609. He married ca. 1584,
5445. HON. PHILADELPHIA CAREY, Lady of the Bedchamber to TM Queen Elizabeth I 1595, 1596/97, and 1600, and Queen Anne 1603, died 3 Feb. 1626/27, daughter of Henry Carey, 1st Baron Hunsdon [No. 4200].

5446-5447. ———.

5448. SIR GILES ALINGTON, High Sheriff of Cambridgeshire and Huntingdonshire 1599, baptized at Horseheath, Cambridgeshire 18 Sept. 1572 and buried there 23 Dec. 1638. He married, 2nd, at West Wratting, Cambridgeshire 2 Dec. 1630, Dorothy Dalton, born in 1606 and died before 24 Sept. 1638, daughter of Michael Dalton and Mary Elrington. He married, 1st,
5449. LADY DOROTHY CECIL, baptized at St. Martin's Church, Stamford, Lincolnshire 11 Aug. 1577 and died 10 Nov. 1613, daughter of Thomas Cecil, 1st Earl of Exeter [No. 8890].

5450. RIGHT HON. SIR LIONEL TOLLEMACHE, 2ND BARONET, P.C. (BY 1625), M.P. 1621-22 and 1628-29, born 1, baptized at Helmingham, Suffolk 15 Aug. 1591 and died 6 Sept. 1640; buried at Helmingham. He married ca. 1620,
5451. HON. ELIZABETH STANHOPE, died ca. 1661, daughter of John Stanhope, 1st Baron Stanhope.

5452. EDWARD NOEL, 2ND VISCOUNT CAMPDEN, M.P. [as Edward Noel] 1601, Sheriff of Rutland 1608-9 and 1615-16, born in 1582 and died at Oxford 8 March 1642/43. He married at Leyton, Essex 20 Dec. 1605,

5453. Hon. Julian Hicks, died at Brooke, Rutland 25 Nov. 1680, daughter of Baptist Hicks, 1st Viscount Campden [No. 8814].

5454. Thomas Wotton, 2nd Baron Wotton, born in 1587 and died at Boughton Malherbe, Kent 2 April 1630. He married in 1608,
5455. Mary Throckmorton, died 25 April 1658; buried at Boughton Malherbe.

5456. Friedrich Christian Kielman, Provost of Itzehoe, Holstein 1612, born ca. 1580 and died ca. 1620. He married,
5457. Anna von Runge.

5458. Heinrich von Hatten, steward to the Duke of Holstein-Gottorp, born in 1580 and died 12 June 1655. He married, 2nd, Elisabeth Reiche. He married, 1st,
5459. Margarete Wasmer.

5460. Claus von Ahlefeldt-Gjelting, born 19 June 1578 and died late in 1632. He married,
5461. Adelheid von Ahlefeldt-Stubbe.

5462. Joachim Rantzau-Putlos, born 6 Aug. 1576 and died 6 Dec. 1652. He married (license dated in Oct. 1611),
5463. Hedevig Pogwisch-Hagen, born in 1595 and died 11 Sept. 1669.

5464. HH Wilhelm, Duke of Brunswick and Lüneburg in Celle, born 4 July 1535 and died at Celle 20/29 Aug. 1592. He married there 12 Oct. 1561,
5465. HRH Princess Dorothea af Danmark, born at Kolding, Denmark 29 June 1546 and died at Winsen an der Luhe, Saxony 6/16 Jan. 1617, daughter of HM King Christian III, King of Denmark and Norway.

5466. HH Ludwig, Landgrave of Hesse-Darmstadt, born at Darmstadt 24 Sept. 1577 and died there 27 July 1626. He married at Berlin 5/14 June 1598,

5467. HH Magdalene Markgräfin von Brandenburg, born at Berlin 7/16 Jan. 1582 and died at Darmstadt 4/14 May 1616, daughter of HH Johann Georg, Elector of Brandenburg.

5468. Johann von Meysenbug, died in 1611. He married,
5469. Anna Elisabeth von Wallenstein, died after 1614.

5470. Wilhelm von Meysenbug, died after 20 April 1637. He married, 2nd, Anna von Griffte. He married, 1st, 21 Oct. 1604,
5471. Margarete von Dörnberg, born 4 Aug. 1584 and died 20 April 1637; buried at St. Martin's Church, Cassel.

5472. Sir William Hartopp of Burton Lazars, Leicestershire, died between 17 Jan. 1622/23 and 13 May 1623. He married,
5473. Mary Rolt of Milton Ernest, Bedfordshire, died in 1635.

5474. Sir Thomas Bendish, 1st Baronet, Sheriff of Essex 1618-19 and 1630-31, baptized at Steeple Bumstead, Essex 27 Jan. 1564/65 and died at Bower Hall, Steeple Bumstead 26 March 1636. He married,
5475. Dorothy Cutts, living in June 1635.

5476. Michael Lister of Frearhead, Craven, Yorkshire, died between 5 Aug. and 28 Oct. 1618. He married,
5477. Mary Kebell.

5478. Richard Wenman, 1st Viscount Wenman, M.P. [as Sir Richard Wenman] 1620-22 and 1625, Sheriff of Oxfordshire 1627, born ca. 1573 and died 3 April 1640; buried at Twyford, Buckinghamshire. He married, 2nd, at the Church of St. Bartholomew-the-Great, London 4 Nov. 1618, Anne ———, widow of i) Thomas Roland and ii) Robert Chamberlain. He married, 3rd, Elizabeth ———, who was buried at Twyford 27 April 1629. He married, 4th, Mary Keble, who was buried at Twyford 28 July 1638, daughter of Thomas Keble. He married, 1st, ca. 1595,
5479. Agnes Fermor, buried at Twyford 4 July 1617.

5480. GEORGE BENNETT, High Sheriff of Leicestershire 1623, died before 23 Nov. 1633. He married, 2nd, ——. He married, 1st, at the Church of St. Dionis Backchurch, London 30 Nov. 1626,
5481. SUSAN COTTON.

5482. OLIVER ST. JOHN, 5TH BARON ST. JOHN, K.B. (1625/26), M.P. [as Hon. Oliver St. John and Hon. Sir Oliver St. John] 1625-26 and 1628-29, summoned to Parliament in his father's barony 1641, died at Kingston, Warwickshire 23 Oct. 1642, son of Oliver St. John, 1st Earl of Bolingbroke. He married before March 1627/28,
5483. LADY ARABELLA EGERTON, died at Welby, Lincolnshire after 2 Jan. 1668/69, daughter of John Egerton, 1st Earl of Bridgewater [No. 6096].

5484. MAJOR GENERAL SIR THOMAS MIDDLETON, M.P. 1624-25, 1640, and 1660, baptized 10 July 1586 and died 11 Dec. 1666. He married, 1st, 29 July 1612, Margaret Savile, who died ca. 1615, daughter of George Savile and Elizabeth Ayscough. He married, 2nd, at Luton Hoo, Bedfordshire 18 Feb. 1616/17,
5485. MARY NAPIER, born at Luton Hoo 13 March 1597/98 and died in 1674.

5486. THOMAS CHOLMONDELEY, Sheriff of Cheshire 1638, born at Holford, Cheshire 2 March 1594/95 and died at Vale Royal, Cheshire 3 Jan. 1652/53. He married,
5487. ELIZABETH MINSHULL, buried at Minshull, Cheshire 25 Sept. 1661.

5488. RICHARD MANSFIELD of West Leake, Nottinghamshire, born ca. 1549 and died 11 Aug. 1624. He married,
5489. JOYCE PAGET of Barwell, Lincolnshire.

5490. WILLIAM SACHEVERELL of Barton, Derbyshire, born in 1555 and died in 1616. He married,
5491. TABITHA SPENCER of Alveston, Derbyshire. She married, 2nd, Thomas Harrington.

5492. SIR THOMAS RICHARDSON, M.P. 1620-22, Speaker of the House of Commons 1621-22, Chancellor to HM Queen Anne, Chief Justice of the

Court of Common Pleas 1626, Chief Justice of the Court of the King's Bench 1631-35, baptized at Hardwick, near Shelton, Norfolk 3 July 1569 and died at Chancery Lane, Holborn, Middlesex 4 Feb. 1634/35. He married, 2nd, at the Church of St. Giles-in-the-Fields, Holborn 14 Oct. 1626, Elizabeth Beaumont, Baroness Cramond for life, who died 3 April 1651, widow of Sir John Ashburnham, and daughter of Thomas Beaumont and Katherine Farnham. He married, 1st, at Barham, Suffolk 20 July 1595,

5493. URSULA SOUTHWELL, baptized at Barham 5 Oct. 1567 and buried at St. Andrew's Church, Holborn 13 June 1624.

5494. SIR WILLIAM HEWITT, buried at the Church of St. Martin-in-the-Fields, Westminster, Middlesex 19 Oct. 1637. He married,

5495. ELIZABETH WISEMAN, buried at the Church of St. Martin-in-the-Fields 19 Oct. 1646.

5496-5503. ——.

5504. GERARD GORE, Treasurer of the Merchant Taylors' Company 1567/68, born ca. 1516 and died 11 Dec. 1607; buried at the Church of St. Mary Magdalen, Milk Street, London. He married at All Hallows' Church, Bread Street, London 25 May 1550,

5505. HELEN DAVENANT, born ca. 1532 and died 13 Feb. 1607/8; buried at the Church of St. Mary Magdalen.

5506. RICHARD YOUNG, salter of London, married,
5507. ——.

5508. SIR PHILIP BOTELER, died before 27 Jan. 1591/92. He married after 30 June 1580,

5509. CATHERINE KNOLLYS, buried at Watton, Hertfordshire 30 Dec. 1632. She married, 1st, in Oct. 1578, Gerald FitzGerald, Lord Offaly by courtesy, born at Maynooth, Kildare 28 Dec. 1559 and buried at St. Alban's Abbey, Hertfordshire 30 June 1580, son of Gerald FitzGerald, 11th Earl of Kildare, and Mabel Browne.

5510. SIR RICHARD SPENCER = 4122.
5511. HELEN BROCKETT = 4123.

5512. CAPTAIN SIR PAUL GORE, 1ST BARONET, M.P. 1613-15, died in Sept. 1629. He married ca. 1607,
5513. ISABELLA WYCLIFFE.

5514. WILLIAM CAULFIELD, 2ND BARON CHARLEMONT = 5068.
5515. MARY KING = 5069.

5516. CAPTAIN SIR FREDERICK HAMILTON, Gentleman of the Privy Chamber to HM King James I, died 31 March 1646. He married, 2nd, Agnes ———. He married, 1st,
5517. SYDNEY VAUGHAN.

5518. CLAUD HAMILTON, 2ND LORD HAMILTON, born ca. 1606 and died 14 June 1638, son of James Hamilton, 1st Earl of Abercorn [No. 10240]. He married at Bellie, Elginshire 28 Nov. 1632,
5519. LADY JEAN GORDON, imprisoned by Sir Phelim O'Neill 1641, died after 9 April 1668, daughter of George Gordon, 1st Marquess of Huntly [No. 10624]. She married, 2nd, ca. 1649, Sir Phelim O'Neill, who was executed at Dublin 10 March 1652/53.

5520. JOHN MANLEY, died near Coton, Shropshire 20 Sept. 1595. He married, 1st, Thomasine Mainwaring, daughter of John Mainwaring and Joan Lacon. He married, 2nd, after 1580,
5521. ERMYNE BELLOTT of Morton, Cheshire, died after 20 Sept. 1595.

5522. FRANCIS LLOYD of Hardwick, Shropshire, married,
5523. ———.

5524. REV. LIEVEN DORESLAER, Minister of Hensboeck 1627 and Enkuizen 1628-52, born in 1555 and died at Enkuizen, The Netherlands in 1652. He married,
5525. ———.

5526-5531. ———.

5532. Thomas Blake of Easton Town, Hampshire, born ca. 1562 and buried at St. Paul's Church, Covent Garden, near London 19 Aug. 1660. He married,

5533. Eleanor Hall of Bradford, Wiltshire, perhaps buried at St. Paul's Church 3 Nov. 1668.

5534. John Mayowe of Dinton, Wiltshire, married,
5535. ——.

5536-5567. ——.

5568. Henry Montagu, 1st Earl of Manchester, P.C. (1620), M.P. [as Henry Montagu] 1593, 1597-98 and 1601 and [as Sir Henry Montagu] 1604-11 and 1614, Chief Justice of the King's Bench 1616-21, Lord High Treasurer 1620-21, Lord President of the Council 1621-28, Lord Privy Seal 1628-42, Speaker of the House of Lords 1628/29, 1641, and 1642, Lord Lieutenant of Huntingdonshire 1627, born at Boughton, Northamptonshire ca. 1563 and died 7 Nov. 1642; buried at Kimbolton, Huntingdonshire. He married, 2nd, at the Church of St. Michael Bassishaw, London 9 Nov. 1613, Anne Wincoll, who was buried at the Church of St. Botolph Aldersgate, London before 26 April 1620, widow of Sir Leonard Holliday, Lord Mayor of London, and daughter of William Wincoll of Langham, Suffolk. He married, 3rd, at Totteridge, Hertfordshire 26 April 1620, Margaret Crouch, who was buried there 29 Dec. 1653, widow of John Hare, and daughter of John Crouch and Jane Scott. He married, 1st, 1 June 1601,

5569. Catherine Spencer, died 7 Dec. 1612; buried at the Church of St. Botolph Aldersgate.

5570. Sir Robert Baynard, Sheriff of Wiltshire 1629, died 14 April 1636. He married,
5571. Ursula Stapleton, baptized at St. Luke's Church, Chelsea, Middlesex 10 July 1587 and buried at Lacock, Wiltshire 9 Nov. 1623.

5572. Sir Anthony Hungerford, M.P. 1593, 1597, 1601, and 1604, baptized at Great Bedwyn, Wiltshire 29 Oct. 1567 and died 27 June 1627; buried at Blackbourton, Oxfordshire. He married, 1st, Lucy Hungerford [No. 8779], who died 4 June 1598, widow of Sir John St. John [No. 8778], and daughter of Sir Walter Hungerford and Anne Dormer. He married, 2nd, at Blackbourton 3 May 1605,

5573. Sarah Crouch, buried at Blackbourton 14 April 1627. She married, 1st, William Wiseman of Woolstone, Berkshire.

5574. Rice Jones, buried at Asthall, Oxfordshire 7 June 1615. He married,

5575. Frances Hopton, buried at Asthall 10 Feb. 1641/42. She married, 2nd, ca. 1621, Sir Giles Fettiplace, who died at Poulton, Wiltshire after 3 March 1640/41, son of George Fettiplace and Cecily Poole.

5576–5583. ———.

5584. Sir Thomas Wroughton of Broadhenton, Wiltshire, died 4 June 1597. He married,

5585. Anne Berwick, buried at Wilcot, Wiltshire 13 Dec. 1610.

5586–5587. ———.

5588. Sir George Farewell of Hill Bishops, Somerset, born 23 Aug. 1579 and died 14 May 1647. He married,

5589. Mary Seymour, born in 1586 and died 13 Dec. 1660.

5590–5591. ———.

5592. Thomas Eyre, Mayor of Salisbury 1610, baptized at Salisbury 24 Aug. 1580 and died 21 June 1633. He married,

5593. Anne Jaye of Fittleton, Wiltshire, buried 27 April 1661.

5594–5595. ———.

5596. Thomas Briscoe, baptized at Aldenham, Hertfordshire 15 March 1600/1. He married,

5597. Elizabeth ———.

5598-5599. ——.

5600. Sir Thomas Wroughton = 5584.
5601. Anne Berwick = 5585.

5602-5603. = 5586-5587.

5604. Sir George Farewell = 5588.
5605. Mary Seymour = 5589.

5606-5607. = 5590-5591.

5608. Thomas Eyre = 5592.
5609. Anne Jaye = 5593.

5610-5611. = 5594-5595.

5612. Thomas Briscoe = 5596.
5613. Elizabeth —— = 5597.

5614-5615. = 5598-5599.

5616-5631. ——.

5632. Sir George Bingham = 2112.
5633. Cicely Martin = 2113.

5634. John Byrne = 2114.
5635. Cecilia O'Byrne = 2115.

5636. SIR HUGH MIDDLETON, 1ST BARONET = 2116.
5637. ELIZABETH OLMSTEAD = 2117.

5638. SIR THOMAS HARRIS, 1ST BARONET = 2118.
5639. SARAH JONES = 2119.

5640–5647. = 2120–2127.

5648. WILLIAM VESEY = 2128.
5649. —— KER = 2129.

5650. REV. GERVAISE WALKER = 2130.
5651. = 2131.

5652. WILLIAM MUSCHAMP = 2132.
5653. FRANCES LISLE = 2133.

5654–5655. = 2134–2135.

5656. PETER SARSFIELD = 2136.
5657. HON. ELEANOR O'DEMPSEY = 2137.

5658. COLONEL RORY O'MORE = 2138.
5659. JANE BARNEWALL = 2139.

5660. JOHN TAAFFE, 1ST VISCOUNT TAAFFE = 2140.
5661. HON. ANNE DILLON = 2141.

5662. WILLIAM WALTER = 2142.
5663. ELIZABETH PROTHEROE = 2143.

5664-5695. = 2144-2175.

5696. Thomas Belasyse, 1st Viscount Fauconberg = 2220.
5697. Barbara Cholmley = 2221.

5698. Sir Thomas Barton, died 17 July 1659; buried at Bolton, Lancashire. He married (marriage covenant dated 30 Sept. 1607),
5699. Christiana Cartwright of Ossington, Nottinghamshire.

5700. Sir Humphrey Davenport, Chief Baron of the Exchequer, born before 1566 and buried at Macclesfield, Lancashire 4 March 1644/45. He married,
5701. Mary Sutton, baptized at Macclesfield 27 Feb. 1572/73.

5702. ? Sir Henry Robinson, died after 1 April 1614. He married,
5703. ——.

5704. Sir John Gage, 1st Baronet, born in 1570 and died at West Firle, Sussex 3 Oct. 1633. He married 8 July 1611,
5705. Lady Penelope Darcy, died before 2 July 1661, daughter of Thomas Darcy, 1st Earl Rivers [No. 5766]. She married, 1st, 11 June 1610, Sir George Trenchard, born ca. 1575 and died shortly after 25 June 1610, son of Sir George Trenchard and Anne Speke. She married, 3rd, in 1642, Sir William Hervey, born 21 March 1581 and died 30 Sept. 1660, son of John Hervey and Frances Bocking.

5706. John Chamberlain of Shirburn Castle, Oxfordshire, born in 1590 and died in 1651. He married,
5707. Katherine Plowden of Shiplake, Oxfordshire.

5708. Richard Middlemore of Edgbaston, Warwickshire, born in 1585 and buried 15 April 1647. He married,
5709. Mary Morgan of Heyford, Northamptonshire.

5710. SIR MAURICE DRUMMOND, Usher of the King's Chamber, died between 20 April 1640 and 13 May 1642. He married,
5711. DOROTHY LOWER of Treventy, Carmarthenshire, born ca. 1608 and died between 17 Sept. and 16 Dec. 1677.

5712. THOMAS BETHAM of Rowington, Warwickshire, died ca. 1630. He married,
5713. MARGARET WALLISTON of Ruislip, Middlesex.

5714. ROBERT MIDDLEMORE, born in 1558 and died at Edgbaston, Warwickshire 16 March 1631/32. He married,
5715. PRISCILLA BROOKE of Maddeley Court, Shropshire.

5716. EDMUND WOLLASCOT of Tidmarsh, Berkshire, died after 1623. He married,
5717. MARY HULSE of Sutton, Berkshire.

5718. ALEXANDER FETTIPLACE, born ca. 1557 and buried at Swinbrook, Oxfordshire 27 Sept. 1616. He married,
5719. MARTHA SKINNER of Rowington, Warwickshire.

5720-5723. ——.

5724. EDWARD FOWLER, buried at Baswich, Staffordshire 28 Nov. 1623. He married, 2nd, Anne Waldegrave of Staningdale, Suffolk. He married, 1st,
5725. DOROTHY EYRE of Hassop, Derbyshire.

5726. WALTER ASTON, 1ST LORD ASTON, K.B. (1603), Gentleman of the Privy Chamber to HM King Charles I, Ambassador to Spain 1620-25 and 1635-38, baptized at Charlecote, Warwickshire 9 July 1584 and died 13 Aug. 1639; buried at St. Mary's Church, Stafford. He married ca. 1607,
5727. GERTRUDE SADLEIR, died after 3 June 1635.

5728-5743. ——.

5744. RIGHT HON. SIR JOHN COKE. P.C., M.P. 1621, 1624, 1625, 1626, and 1628, Joint Principal Secretary of State 1625-39, Lord Privy Seal 1625-28, born at London 5 March 1562/63 and died at Tottenham, Middlesex 8 Sept. 1644. He married, 2nd, in Nov. 1624, Joan Lee, who was buried at the Church of St. James Garlickhithe, London 2 Sept. 1658, widow of Sir William Gore, Sheriff of London, and daughter of Sir Robert Lee and Joanna Sutton. He married, 1st, in 1604,

5745. MARY POWELL, died in Feb. 1623/24.

5746. RICHARD POPE, baptized at St. Alkmond's Church, Shrewsbury 15 Feb. 1588/89 and died 14 Sept. 1636; buried at Woolstaston, Shropshire. He married at St. Chad's Church, Shrewsbury 20 April 1623,

5747. MARY HANMER, died 9 Jan. 1638/39.

5748. SIR THOMAS LEVENTHORPE, 2ND BARONET, baptized at Sawbridgeworth, Hertfordshire 18 May 1592 and died 30 April 1636; buried at Sawbridgeworth. He married at Horseheath, Cambridgeshire 29 March 1623,

5749. DOROTHY ALINGTON, baptized at Horseheath 9 Jan. 1603/4 and buried at Sawbridgeworth 26 Sept. 1643, daughter of Sir Giles Alington [No. 5448] and Lady Dorothy Cecil [No. 5449]. She married, 2nd, —— Halford.

5750. SIR CAPELL BEDELL, 1ST BARONET, M.P. 1626, 1628/29, and 1640, Sheriff of Cambridgeshire and Huntingdonshire 1632-33, baptized at Little Hadham, Hertfordshire 10 Oct. 1602 and buried at Hamerton, Huntingdonshire 14 Dec. 1643. He married in June 1619,

5751. ALICE FANSHAW, baptized at Dronfield, Derbyshire 3 June 1602 and buried at Hamerton 12 Jan. 1666/67.

5752. ROLAND HALE = 5084 = 5132.
5753. ELIZABETH GARWAY = 5085 = 5133.

5754. JEREMIAH ELWES = 5086 = 5134.
5755. MARY MORLEY = 5087 = 5135.

5756. GODFREY MEYNELL, died between 16 April and 20 Dec. 1667; buried at Langley, Derbyshire. He married,
5757. DOROTHY WHITEHALL of Whitehalgh, Derbyshire.

5758. ROBERT READE of Cheshunt, Hertfordshire, born ca. 1622 and died after 7 Sept. 1677. He married, 2nd (Vicar-General's license to marry at the Church of All Hallows-in-the-Wall, London dated 7 Sept. 1677), Elizabeth (———) Portman, who was born ca. 1648. He married, 1st,
5759. ———.

5760. ROBERT BRUDENELL, Sheriff of Cambridgeshire 1595/96, died 4 July 1599. He married at Rushton, Northamptonshire 25 May 1570,
5761. CATHERINE TAYLARD of Doddington, Cambridgeshire.

5762. SIR THOMAS TRESHAM of Rushton, Northamptonshire, born in 1544 and died 11 Sept. 1605. He married ca. 1566,
5763. MURIEL THROCKMORTON, died in 1615.

5764. SIR JOHN SAVAGE, 1ST BARONET, Sheriff of Cheshire 1606/7, buried at Macclesfield, Cheshire 14 July 1615. He married before 1582,
5765. MARY ALINGTON, born 5 Feb. 1556/57 and buried at Macclesfield 16 Dec. 1635.

5766. THOMAS DARCY, 1ST EARL RIVERS, born ca. 1565 and died at Winchester House, near Broad Street, London 21 Feb. 1639/40. He married (articles dated 16 April 1583),
5767. MARY KITSON, died between 7 May and 28 June 1644; buried at Trinity Church, Colchester, Essex.

5768. SIR ROBERT SAVILE ALIAS BARKSTON, Sheriff of Yorkshire 1572/73, buried at Batley, Yorkshire 8 Dec. 1585, natural son of Sir Henry Savile and Margaret Barkston. He married, 2nd, Isabel Copley, who was baptized at Batley 1 Oct. 1563, daughter of Alvery Copley and Grace Bradford. He married, 1st, 1 March 1554/55,
5769. ANNE HUSSEY, born before 1529 and died in 1562. She married, 1st, Matthew Thimbleby, who died ca. 1551.

5770. SIR EDWARD CAREY, M.P. 1572, Groom of the Privy Chamber 1563, Master of HM Queen Elizabeth I's Jewel House 1596, died 18 July 1618. He married after 1568,

5771. KATHERINE KNYVETT, died 20 Dec. 1622.

5772. SIR GEORGE VILLIERS, Sheriff of Leicestershire 1591, born in 1544 and died 4 Jan. 1605/6; buried at Westminster Abbey, Middlesex. He married, 1st, Audrey Saunders [No. 8239], who died 7 May 1587, daughter of William Saunders and Frances Zouche. He married, 2nd,

5773. MARY BEAUMONT, COUNTESS OF BUCKINGHAM for life, born ca. 1570 and died at the Gate House, Whitehall, near London 19 April 1632. She married, 2nd, at Goadby, Leicestershire 19 June 1606, Sir William Rayner of Orton Longueville, Huntingdonshire, who died in Oct. 1606. She married, 3rd, Hon. Sir Thomas Compton, who died in April 1626, son of Henry Compton, 1st Baron Compton [No. 4194], and Lady Frances Hastings [No. 4195].

5774. THOMAS SHELDON of Howby, Leicestershire, married,

5775. ———.

5776. EDWARD BRUCE, 1ST LORD BRUCE, P.C. (E.) (1603), Scottish Ambassador to England 1600, Master of the Rolls 1603-11, born in 1548 and died 14 Jan. 1610/11; buried at the Rolls Chapel, Chancery Lane, London. He married,

5777. MAGDALEN CLERK, died after 28 Dec. 1630. She married, 2nd, at Abbot's Langley, Hertfordshire 9 April 1616, Sir James Fullerton, First Gentleman of the Bedchamber, who was buried at Westminster Abbey, Middlesex 3 Jan. 1630/31.

5778. SIR ROBERT CHICHESTER, K.B. (1603), born in 1578 and died 24 April 1627; buried at Pilton, Devonshire. He married, 2nd, Mary Hill, daughter of Robert Hill and Ursula Southcott. He married, 1st,

5779. HON. FRANCES HARINGTON, baptized at Stepney, Middlesex 12 Dec. 1594, daughter of John Harington, 1st Baron Harington.

5780. SIR JOHN GREY, M.P. 1601, Gentleman of the Privy Chamber to HM King James I, buried at Broughton Astley, Leicestershire 7 Oct. 1611. He married,

5781. HON. ELIZABETH NEVILLE, died after 19 May 1648, daughter of Edward Neville, 6th Baron Bergavenny. She married, 2nd, in July 1617, Sir John Bingley.

5782. WILLIAM CECIL, 2ND EARL OF EXETER, K.G. (1630), P.C. (1626), M.P. [as William Cecil] 1586-87 and 1588-89, Lord Lieutenant of Northamptonshire 1623-40, born at Burghley, Northamptonshire in Jan. 1565/66 and died at Exeter House, Clerkenwell, Middlesex 6 July 1640, son of Thomas Cecil, 1st Earl of Exeter [No. 8890]. He married, 1st, at Newark Castle, Stoke, Nottinghamshire 13 Jan. 1588/89, Elizabeth Manners, Baroness Ros in her own right, born ca. Jan. 1575/76 and died at Barking, Essex 1 May 1591, daughter of Edward Manners, 3rd Earl of Rutland, and Isabel Holcroft. He married, 2nd,

5783. ELIZABETH DRURY, born 4 Jan. 1578/79 and died at Exeter House 26 Feb. 1653/54.

5784. EDWARD SEYMOUR, LORD BEAUCHAMP by courtesy, considered illegitimate 1561-1608 [when he won the right to inherit his father's earldom], born in the Tower of London 21 Sept. 1561 and died at Wick, Wiltshire 13 July 1612, son of Edward Seymour, 1st Earl of Hertford, and Lady Catherine Grey, daughter of Henry Grey, 1st Duke of Suffolk, and sister of Lady Jane Grey. He married before 1 July 1582,

5785. HONORA ROGERS, died after 28 Feb. 1607/8.

5786. ROBERT DEVEREUX, 2ND EARL OF ESSEX, K.G. (1588), P.C. (1592/93), Master of Horse 1587, General 1588, Master General of Ordnance and Earl Marshal 1597-1601, Lord Lieutenant [i.e., Viceroy] of Ireland 1599, born at Netherwood, Herefordshire 19 Nov. 1566 and executed [following a failed uprising] on Tower Hill, London 25 Feb. 1600/1, son of Walter Devereux, 1st Earl of Essex [No. 8206]. He married in 1590,

5787. FRANCES WALSINGHAM = 4447.

5788. SIR HENRY CAPELL = 4404.
5789. THEODOSIA MONTAGU = 4405.

5790. SIR CHARLES MORRISON, 1ST BARONET = 4406.
5791. HON. MARY HICKS = 4407.

Robert Devereux, 2nd Earl of Essex

Born at Netherwood, Herefordshire 19 November 1566
Died at London 25 February 1600/1
Married in 1590
Frances (Walsingham), Lady Sidney

At his father's death, the nine-year-old Earl of Essex was placed under the guardianship of Lord Burghley, but two years later his mother's marriage to the Earl of Leicester attached him to the Dudley family. Intellectually precocious, Essex was educated at Trinity College, Cambridge, and later at Oxford. His stepfather Leicester first introduced Essex at court in 1584, where he immediately earned Queen Elizabeth's favor, and he soon gained a reputation as a daring soldier, accompanying Leicester to the Netherlands in 1585-86, where he was knighted for his gallantry at the battle of Zutphen. (The poet and soldier Sir Philip Sidney perished during this campaign.) In 1587, the young earl was appointed to Leicester's former post of Master of Horse, the perfect official vehicle for the realization of a personal political vision. Essex was general of the horse at Tilbury Camp in 1588, and sailed with the Portugal expedition in 1589, but Elizabeth abruptly insisted that he return to England and to Court. In 1590, he angered the Queen by secretly marrying Sir Philip Sidney's widow Frances, daughter of the Queen's Secretary of State, Sir Francis Walsingham. The following year, Essex commanded a flamboyant but unsuccessful expedition in Normandy to help King Henri III of Navarre. Lord Essex returned home and, advised by Francis Bacon, entered politics in an effort to seize power from Burghley.

Leicester, the Queen's favourite, was now dead, and Burghley, her principal adviser, was growing old. Essex wanted to fill the place of both and dominate the court. A contest over the office of Secretary, which fell vacant in 1590, was the first trial of strength between the Cecils and Essex. Although Essex was appointed P.C. in 1593, Elizabeth left the secretary's post vacant until she gave it to Lord Burghley's son Robert Cecil [later 1st Earl of Salisbury] in 1596. Meanwhile, the rivalry between the two factions became intense. For every vacant office, Essex proposed a candidate whom he implored the Queen to accept. There were heated arguments between them and once Elizabeth boxed her favourite's ears. Essex became a national hero when he shared command (with Lord Howard of Effingham) of the expedition that captured Cadiz on 20 June 1596, but he failed the next year to intercept the Spanish treasure fleet off the Azores.

In March 1599, at his own insistence, he was appointed Lord Lieutenant of Ireland and sent there with a large force to quell the rebellion of the Earl of Tyrone. Failing completely to accomplish this mission, Essex made an unauthorized truce with Tyrone and returned to England in November 1599. He was confined by the Council, kept in seclusion for eight months, and it was not until June 1600 that Essex was brought to trial before a special court. No actual sentence beyond dismissal from his offices and imprisonment in his own house was recorded against Essex, and he was released from arrest in August, but he had finally lost the favor of the Queen. Still popular with the citizens of London, Essex planned a coup to oust the Queen's advisors and replace them with men of his choice. To this end he sought support from the army in Ireland and simultaneously opened negotiations with James VI in Scotland, but these efforts failed. His only real accomplice in this plot was Shakespeare's patron, the Earl of Southampton. In desperation, Essex made his attempt with a small body of personal followers on 8 February 1600/1. The Londoners failed to respond, the Queen's government was thoroughly prepared, and Essex and Southampton were arrested. Elizabeth, after some hesitation, signed the death warrant, and Essex was beheaded on Tower Hill 25 February 1600/1, and buried at the Church of St. Peter ad Vincula in the Tower.

5792. SIR THOMAS BISHOPP, 1ST BARONET, M.P. 1584, 1586, and 1610-11, Sheriff of Surrey and Sussex 1584/85 and 1601-2, born in 1553 and died before 14 Feb. 1626/27. He married, 1st, 19 Sept. 1577, Anne Cromer, daughter of William Cromer and Margaret Kempe. He married, 2nd, at Findon, Sussex 7 Aug. 1600,

5793. JANE WESTON.

5794. NICHOLAS TUFTON, 1ST EARL OF THANET, M.P. [as Nicholas Tufton] 1601 and [as Sir Nicholas Tufton] 1623, baptized at Terling, Essex 19 Jan. 1577/78 and died at Sapcote, Leicestershire 1 July 1631. He married before 3 Sept. 1602,

5795. LADY FRANCES CECIL, baptized at the Church of St. Martin-in-the-Fields, Westminster, Middlesex 28 Feb. 1580/81 and died at Rainham, Kent 12 June 1653, daughter of Thomas Cecil, 1st Earl of Exeter [No. 8890].

5796. William Bury of Culham, Oxfordshire, died 24 Dec. 1632. He married,

5797. Anne Sprignell of Highgate, Middlesex.

5798. Thomas Duncombe, born ca. 1588 and died between 10 and 17 May 1632; buried at Broughton, Buckinghamshire. He married,

5799. Sarah Draper, died between 14 Feb. 1653 and 26 Feb. 1654; buried at Broughton.

5800. Sir William Dunch, M.P. 1603, 1604, and 1611, born before 25 May 1578 and died 22 Jan. 1611/12. He married,

5801. Mary Cromwell, aunt of Oliver Cromwell, the Lord Protector, died before 26 May 1617.

5802. Sir Anthony Hungerford of Down Ampney, Gloucestershire, baptized at Hungerford, Berkshire 30 Dec. 1584 and died in 1645. He married, 2nd, Jane Ernley, daughter of Michael Ernley and Susan Hungerford. He married, 1st, in 1610,

5803. Elizabeth Lucy of Charlecote, Warwickshire.

5804. Robert Dormer, High Sheriff of Oxfordshire 1628, born ca. 1590 and died 12 May 1649. He married, 2nd, —— Hamond. He married, 1st,

5805. Mary Read of Barton Court, Berkshire, born in 1608.

5806. Edmund Waller, M.P. 1624, 1626, 1628, 1640-43, 1661, and 1685, sole survivor of "Waller's plot" in 1643 [his fellow conspirators all being executed], a poet whose lyrics variously extolled King Charles I, Oliver Cromwell, King Charles II, King James II, and the future King William III, born at Stocks Place, Coleshill, Hertfordshire 3 March 1605/6 and died at St. James's Street, Westminster, Middlesex 21 Oct. 1687. He married, 2nd, at the Tower of London in 1644, Mary Bracey of Thame, Oxfordshire, who was buried at Beaconsfield, Buckinghamshire 2 May 1677. He married, 1st, at St. Margaret's Church, Westmister 15 July 1631,

5807. Anne Banks, born ca. 1609 and died in Oct. 1634.

5808. NICHOLAS BOSCAWEN of Tregothnan, Cornwall, born ca. 1543 and buried at St. Michael Penkivel, Cornwall 10 May 1626. He married,
5809. ALICE TREVANION, buried at St. Michael Penkivel 18 Sept. 1580.

5810. ROBERT ROLLE, died 29 Aug. 1633; buried at Petrockstowe, Devonshire. He married,
5811. JANE HELE of Flete, Devonshire, died 17 Aug. 1634.

5812. SIR WILLIAM GODOLPHIN, born before 1568 and buried at Breage, Cornwall 5 Sept. 1613. He married,
5813. THOMASINE SIDNEY, buried at Tavistock, Devonshire 24 April 1612.

5814. SIR HENRY BERKELEY, M.P. 1625/26, 1627/28, and 1640, born ca. 1579 and died between 21 Sept. 1666 and 27 Sept. 1667. He married (settlement dated 12 Feb. 1609/10),
5815. ELIZABETH NEVILLE, died ca. 1656/57, daughter of Sir Henry Neville [No. 4220].

5816-5819. ———.

5820. JOHN CHURCHILL = 2056 = 4428.
5821. SARAH WINSTON = 2057 = 4429.

5822. SIR JOHN DRAKE = 2058 = 4430.
5823. HON. ELEANOR BOTELER = 2059 = 4431.

5824-5831. ———.

5832. THOMAS JENNINGS of Duddleston, Shropshire, died 28 May 1640. He married,
5833. ——— BURTON.

5834. SIR GERARD EYTON of Eyton, Denbighshire, died between 14 Jan. 1650/51 and 23 May 1653. He married,
5835. ELIZABETH BROMFIELD, died 31 Oct. 1642.

5836–5839. ——.

5840. SIR WILLIAM TWYSDEN, 1ST BARONET, M.P. 1593, 1601, 1606–11, 1614, and 1626–28, born at Wye, Kent 4 April 1566 and died 8 Jan. 1627/28. He married at Heneage House, London 4 Oct. 1591,
5841. LADY ANNE FINCH, born 28 Feb. 1574/75 and died 14 Nov. 1638, daughter of Sir Moyle Finch, 1st Baronet [No. 8312], and Elizabeth Heneage, Countess of Winchilsea in her own right [No. 8313].

5842. SIR NICHOLAS SAUNDERS, M.P. 1593, 1604, and 1626, born ca. 1562 and died 9 Feb. 1648/49. He married before 1585, his stepsister
5843. ELIZABETH BLOUNT.

5844–5845. ——.

5846. SIR JOHN GARRARD, 1ST BARONET, born ca. 1590 and died between 25 May and 21 June 1637. He married, 2nd, at Westcombe, Kent 3 June 1636, Jane Lowe, baptized at the Church of St. Peter-le-Poer, London 16 March 1592/93 and buried there 22 Feb. 1672/73, widow of Sir Multon Lambarde, and daughter of Sir Thomas Lowe and Anne Coulston. He married, 1st, at the Church of St. Mary Aldermary, London 6 May 1611,
5847. ELIZABETH BARKHAM, born ca. 1594 and died 17 April 1632; buried at Wheathamstead, Hertfordshire.

5848. SIR WILLIAM WYTHENS, Sheriff of Kent 1610–11, buried at South-end, Eltham, Kent 2 Dec. 1631. He married,
5849. MARY GILBORNE, buried at Eltham 11 April 1632.

5850. ROBERT KING of St. Mary Cray, Kent, married,
5851. ——.

5852. THOMAS TAYLOR of Shadockhurst, Linstead, Kent, born in 1595 and died in 1631. He married, 1st, Catherine Honywood, who died in 1625, daughter of Sir Thomas Honywood [No. 10338] and Jane Hales [No. 10339]. He married, 2nd, in 1629,

5853. ANNE HENDLEY of Corshorne, Cranbrook, Kent, born in 1604.

5854. GEORGE HALL of Maidstone, Kent, married,

5855. ———.

5856. SIR HENRY BOWYER, born ca. 1590 and buried at Denham, Buckinghamshire 27 Dec. 1613. He married at St. Olave's Church, Hart Street, London 4 Dec. 1609,

5857. ANNE SALTER, baptized at the Church of St. Mary Aldermanbury, London 27 April 1595. She married, 2nd, at St. Olave's Church 31 Jan. 1614, Sir Arthur Harris of Creeksea, Essex, who was born ca. 1584, son of Sir William Harris and Alice Smythe.

5858. SIR JOHN WELD, buried at Arnold Chapel, Southgate, Middlesex 21 Feb. 1622/23. He married before 1608,

5859. FRANCES WHITMORE, died at London between 22 May 1656 and 6 Feb. 1656/57.

5860. WILLIAM CECIL, 2ND EARL OF SALISBURY, K.G. (1625), K.B. (1604/5), P.C. (1626), M.P. [as Viscount Cranborne] 1610-11 and [as Earl of Salisbury] 1649-53, 1654-55, and 1656-58, bore the train of HRH The Prince Henry Frederick, Prince of Wales, at HRH's installation 1610, bore the Sceptre with the Cross at the coronation of HM King Charles I 1625/26, Lord Lieutenant of Hertfordshire 1612, born at Westminster, Middlesex 28 March 1591 and died at Hatfield, Hertfordshire 3 Dec. 1668. He married privately 1 Dec. 1608,

5861. LADY CATHERINE HOWARD, buried at Hatfield 27 Jan. 1672/73, daughter of Thomas Howard, 1st Earl of Suffolk [No. 10502].

5862. JAMES MAXWELL, 1ST EARL OF DIRLETON, died at Holyrood, Edinburgh 19 April 1650. He married before April 1622,

5863. ELISABETH BUSSON DE PODOLSKO, buried at the Church of St. Martin-in-the-Fields, Westminster, Middlesex 26 April 1659.

5864. Sir Thomas Parker, M.P. 1642, born ca. 1594 and died 31 May 1663. He married at the Church of St. Giles Cripplegate, London 1 Dec. 1618,

5865. Hon. Philadelphia Lennard, born ca. 1597 and buried at Ratton, Sussex 20 Jan. 1660/61, daughter of Henry Lennard, 12th Baron Dacre.

5866. Sir Richard Newdigate, 1st Baronet, M.P. 1660, Chief Justice of the Upper Bench 1660, born at Arbury Hall, Warwickshire 17 Sept. 1602 and died 14 Oct. 1678; buried at Harefield, Middlesex. He married at the Church of St. Bartholomew-the-Great, West Smithfield, near London 2 Feb. 1631/32,

5867. Juliana Leigh, baptized at St. Margaret's Church, Westminster, Middlesex 10 March 1610 and died at Harefield 9 Dec. 1685.

5868. Robert Comyn alias Chilcot, died 25 Aug. 1609; buried at the Church of St. Andrew Undershaft, London. He married,

5869. Anne Cade. She married, 2nd, John Parker, merchant of London, who died between 12 Feb. and 5 April 1627.

5870. Robert Newman, merchant taylor of London, died between 6 March 1650/51 and 3 April 1651. He married,

5871. Anne Monnox.

5872. Sir William Stonhouse, 1st Baronet = 4528.
5873. Elizabeth Powell = 4529.

5874. Richard Lovelace, 1st Baron Lovelace = 4530.
5875. Margaret Dodsworth = 4531.

5876. Sir Moreton Brigges, 1st Baronet = 4532.
5877. Grisogon Grey = 4533.

5878. Thomas Moreton = 4534.
5879. Elizabeth Moreton = 4535.

5880. SAMUEL DASHWOOD of Rowden, Stogumber, Somerset, died between 9 July and 31 Dec. 1638. He married, 1st, 2 Sept. 1600, Elizabeth Sweeting. He married, 2nd, before 1617,
5881. ELIZABETH ——.

5882. WILLIAM PERRY of Thorpe, Surrey, married,
5883. ——.

5884. SIR THOMAS CHAMBERLAIN, 1ST BARONET, Sheriff of Oxfordshire 1643, born in 1613 and died 6 Oct. 1643. He married, 1st, —— Acland of Acland, Devonshire. He married, 2nd,
5885. ANNE CHAMBERLAIN of Temple House, Warwickshire.

5886. SIR EDMUND PRIDEAUX, 1ST BARONET, M.P. 1640-59, Solicitor General 1648, Attorney General 1649-58, baptized at Farway, Devonshire 27 Sept. 1601 and died 8 Aug. 1659; buried at Ford Abbey, Thornecombe, Devonshire. He married, 1st, 23 Aug. 1627, Jane Collyns, who was buried at Ottery St. Mary, Devonshire 16 Nov. 1629, daughter of Henry Collyns and Joan Farant. He married, 2nd, shortly after 16 Nov. 1629,
5887. MARGARET EVERY, born ca. 1608 and died 25 April 1683; buried at Ford Abbey.

5888. HM KING JAMES VI AND I, KING OF ENGLAND, SCOTLAND, AND IRELAND = 4384 = 4424 = 5296.
5889. HRH PRINCESS ANNA AF DANMARK = 4385 = 4425 = 5297.

5890. HM KING HENRI III AND IV, KING OF FRANCE AND NAVARRE = 4386 = 4426 = 5298.
5891. PRINCESS MARIA DE' MEDICI = 4387 = 4427 = 5299.

5892. RENÉ DE PENANCOËT, SEIGNEUR DE KÉROUALLE = 5300.
5893. JULIENNE EMERY DU PONT-L'ABBÉ, DAME DU CHEF-DU-BOIS = 5301.

5894. SÉBASTIEN DE PLŒUC, MARQUIS DE TIMEUR = 5302.
5895. MARIE DE RIEUX D'OIXANT = 5303.

5896. Thomas Brudenell, 1st Earl of Cardigan = 2880 = 5304.
5897. Mary Tresham = 2881 = 5305.

5898. Thomas Savage, 1st Viscount Savage = 2882 = 5306.
5899. Elizabeth Darcy, Countess Rivers = 2883 = 5307.

5900. John Savile, 1st Baron Savile = 2884 = 5308.
5901. Elizabeth Carey = 2885 = 5309.

5902. Christopher Villiers, 1st Earl of Anglesey = 2886 = 5310.
5903. Elizabeth Sheldon = 2887 = 5311.

5904. Henry Cadogan of Trostney, Pembrokshire, married,
5905. Catherine Stradling of Merthyr Mawr, Glamorganshire.

5906-5907. ———.

5908. George Waller of Groombridge, Kent, died before 1622. He married, 1st, Elizabeth Sondes, daughter of Michael Sondes and Mary Finch. He married, 2nd,
5909. Mary Hardress of Hardres, Kent, died in 1622.

5910. Sir John Dowdall of Castletown, Limerick, married,
5911. Elizabeth Southwell of Polylong, Cork.

5912. Jan Munter, born at Harlingen, Friesland in 1570 and buried at the New Church, Amsterdam 4 Sept. 1617. He married at Amsterdam 17 May 1596,
5913. Sara van Tongerloo, born at Amsterdam in 1578 and died there 11 April 1642.

5914. Jan Corneliszoon Geelvinck, Mayor of Amsterdam 1626, 1628, 1629, 1634, 1636, 1637, 1639, 1641, 1643, 1644, 1646, and 1647, born at

Amsterdam 11 June 1579 and died there 9 Nov. 1651. He married, 1st, 9 Sept. 1601, Margriet Wuytiers, born in 1582 and died 5 Oct. 1601, daughter of Gouvert Wuytiers and Dieuwertje Benningh. He married, 2nd, at Amsterdam 3 Feb. 1608,

5915. Aechtje de Vlaming van Oudtshoorn, born at Amsterdam in 1585 and died there 9 Sept. 1666.

5916. Jacob Trip, merchant, born at Zaltbommel, Gelderland ca. 1576 and died at Dordrecht 8 May 1661. He married at Dordrecht 9 Feb. 1603,

5917. Marguerite de Geer, born at Liège 10 Nov. 1583 and died at Dordrecht in 1672.

5918. Samuel Godin, director of the West Indies and North Seas companies, born in 1561 and buried at the Walloon Church, Amsterdam 29 Sept. 1633. He married,

5919. Anna Anselmo, born ca. 1583 and buried at the Walloon Church 22 Aug. 1630.

5920. William Kerr, 1st Earl of Lothian, P.C. (1641), Lieutenant General in Ireland 1642 and 1645, Joint Secretary of State in Scotland 1649-52, born ca. 1605 and died at Newbattle Abbey, Edinburgh in Oct. 1675, son of Robert Kerr, 1st Earl of Ancrum. He married 9 Dec. 1630,

5921. Anne Kerr, Countess of Lothian in her own right, died at Newbattle Abbey 26 March 1667, daughter of Robert Kerr, 2nd Earl of Lothian.

5922. Archibald Campbell, 1st Marquess of Argyll, P.C. (1628), M.P. [as Marquess of Argyll] 1658-59, Extraordinary Lord of Session as **Lord Lorn** 1638, remarkable for his skill at changing sides, born at Inveraray Castle, Argyllshire ca. 1606 and [having been attainted] executed at the Cross of Edinburgh 27 May 1661. He married shortly before 6 Aug. 1626,

5923. Lady Margaret Douglas, born in 1610 and died 13 March 1677/78, daughter of William Douglas, 7th Earl of Morton [No. 2592].

5924. Archibald Campbell, 1st Marquess of Argyll = 5922.
5925. Lady Margaret Douglas = 5923.

5926. James Stewart, 4th Earl of Moray, P.C. (1637/38), died 4 March 1652/53; buried at Dyke, Morayshire. He married (contract dated 18 Oct. 1627),

5927. Lady Margaret Home, died between March and May 1683, daughter of Alexander Home, 1st Earl of Home.

5928. Thomas Nicolson of Pitmedden, Aberdeenshire, died after 1640. He married,

5929. Elizabeth Abercromby.

5930-5931. ——.

5932. Sir Thomas Nicolson, 1st Baronet, died 8 Jan. 1645/46. He married,

5933. Isabel Henderson of Granton, Midlothianshire, died before 10 June 1668.

5934. Alexander Livingston, 2nd Earl of Linlithgow, P.C. (S.) (1623/24), Extraordinary Lord of Session 1610-26, Lord High Admiral of Scotland 1627, died between 11 June and 20 Dec. 1648. He married, 1st (contract dated at Huntly, Aberdeenshire 29 April and at Callendar, Perthshire 4 May 1611), Lady Elizabeth Gordon, who died at Edinburgh in July 1616, daughter of George Gordon, 1st Marquess of Huntly [No. 10624] and Lady Henrietta Stuart [No. 10625]. He married, 2nd (contract dated 17 Oct. 1620),

5935. Lady Mary Douglas, daughter of William Douglas, 10th Earl of Angus [No. 10680].

5936. Conyers Darcy, 1st Earl of Holdernesse, Constable of Middleham Castle 1660-71, baptized at Kirkby Fleetham, Yorkshire 24 Jan. 1598/99 and died at Hornby, Yorkshire 14 June 1689. He married at Wentworth, Yorkshire 14 Oct. 1616,

5937. Grace Rokeby, buried at Hornby 4 Jan. 1657/58.

5938. Thomas Howard, 1st Earl of Berkshire, K.G. (1625), K.B. (1604/5), P.C. (1639 and 1660), M.P. [as Hon. Sir Thomas Howard] 1605-11, 1614, and 1620-22, Master of the Horse to HRH The Prince of Wales (later

HM King Charles I) 1614, Governor to HRH The Prince of Wales (later HM King Charles II) 1643-46, Lord of the Bedchamber to HM 1661-69, Lord Lieutenant of Oxfordshire 1632-42, born ca. 1590 and died 16 July 1669, son of Thomas Howard, 1st Earl of Suffolk [No. 10502]. He married 26 May 1614,

5939. LADY ELIZABETH CECIL, buried at Westminster Abbey, Middlesex 24 Aug. 1672, daughter of William Cecil, 2nd Earl of Exeter [No. 5782], and Elizabeth Drury [No. 5783].

5940. SIR WILLIAM SUTTON, born ca. 1559 and buried at Averham, Nottinghamshire in Oct. 1611. He married at Bassingthorpe, Lincolnshire 10 Nov. 1584,

5941. SUSAN CONY, baptized at Bassingthorpe 1 May 1568.

5942. SIR ANTHONY ST. LEGER, Warden of the Mint ca. 1648, 1660, and 1672-80, died in 1680. He married, 1st, Mary Norwood. He married, 2nd, at St. Peter's Church, Cornhill, London 30 Dec. 1630, Barbara Shirley, who was born ca. 1588, widow of Sir Thomas Thornhurst, and daughter of Thomas Shirley and Philippa Caryll. He married, 3rd,

5943. BRIDGET MAYNY of Linton, Kent, died in 1639.

5944. HANS MEINHARDT VON SCHÖNBURG, Court Marshal to HH The Elector Palatine (later HM King Friedrich I von der Pfalz [No. 5948]), Palatine Ambassador to England 1612, 1613, and 1616, born at Bacharach, Pfalz 28 Aug. 1582 and died at Heidelberg 3 Aug. 1616. He married 22 March 1614/15,

5945. HON. ANNE SUTTON, Lady in Waiting to HRH The Electress Palatine [who wrote that "both in her life, and when dying, she testified the respect and friendship she bore me, and her sincere fidelity"], died at Heidelberg 8 Dec. 1615, daughter of Edward Sutton, 5th Baron Dudley.

5946. HEINRICH DIETRICH VON SCHÖNBURG, BURGGRAF VON STARKENBURG, died in 1621. He married,

5947. ELISABETH KETTELER ZU MELRICH.

5948. HM KING FRIEDRICH I VON DER PFALZ, KING OF BOHEMIA 1619-20, ELECTOR PALATINE 1610-23, born at Jagdschloss Deinschwang, Pfalz 16 Aug. 1596 and died at Mainz 29 Nov. 1632. He married at Whitehall Palace, London 14 Feb. 1612/13,

5949. HRH Princess Elizabeth of England and Scotland, born at Dunfermline Palace, Fife 19 Aug. 1596 and died at Leicester House, London 13 Feb. 1661/62, daughter of HM King James VI and I, King of England and Scotland [No. 4384].

5950. Christof Martin Reichsfreiherr von Degenfeld, General of the Republic of Venice, born at Hohen-Eybach bei Geislingen, Württemberg in Nov. 1599 and died at Dürnau bei Göppingen, Württemberg 13 Oct. 1653. He married at Dürnau 22 April 1628,
5951. Anna Maria Adelmann von Adelmannsfelden, born in 1610 and died in 1651.

5952. George Gordon, 2nd Marquess of Huntly = 5312.
5953. Lady Anne Campbell = 5313.

5954. Sir John Grant = 5314.
5955. Hon. Mary Ogilvy = 5315.

5956. Henry Frederick Howard, 22nd Earl of Arundel and 2nd Earl of Norfolk = 5316.
5957. Lady Elizabeth Stuart = 5317.

5958. Edward Somerset, 2nd Marquess of Worcester = 2200 = 5318.
5959. Elizabeth Dormer = 2201 = 5319.

5960. John Mordaunt, 1st Earl of Peterborough = 1048 = 5320.
5961. Hon. Elizabeth Howard = 1049 = 5321.

5962. Hon. Thomas Carey = 1050 = 5322.
5963. Margaret Smith = 1051 = 5323.

5964. Adam Fraser = 5324.
5965. Margaret Duff = 5325.

HM King Friedrich I von der Pfalz, King of Bohemia

Born at Deinschwang, Pfalz 16 August 1596
Died at Mainz 29 November 1632
Married at London 14 February 1612/13
HRH Princess Elizabeth of England and Scotland

After receiving a French education at the Huguenot enclave of Sedan, Friedrich succeeded his father, the Elector Friedrich IV, on 9 September 1610. Early in 1612 a search was conducted to find a suitable match for the eldest daughter of King James I of England. Friedrich was not the ideal choice for a husband of the English princess, but King James saw the benefit of having an elector of the Holy Roman Empire as his son-in-law. Friedrich sent his steward, Hans Meinhardt von Schönburg and the steward of the Palatinate, Johann Albrecht Graf von Solms, to prepare the groundwork for his marriage. Two months after the wedding, Friedrich returned to Heidelberg. When the Protestant Bohemian estates revolted against the Catholic Holy Roman Emperor Ferdinand II and offered the crown to the young Elector Palatine, Friedrich, on the advice of his counselors, accepted, even though this step meant declaring war against the Emperor. Friedrich's father-in-law threatened to disown him, as the Elector was disrupting King James's diplomatic plans for Europe.

Abandoned by many of his allies, Friedrich was routed in the Battle of the White Mountain, near Prague, in November 1620, by the armies of the Catholic League under Johann Tserclaes Graf von Tilly. Two Protestant armies, raised by Ernst Graf von Mansfeld and Christian Herzog von Braunschweig, fought for Friedrich's cause in western Germany, but were defeated within two years. The situation deteriorated when Spanish and Bavarian troops occupied the Palatinate and Friedrich's electoral dignities were transferred to Maximilian I of Bavaria (1623). As more Protestant princes entered the widening conflict, one of their aims was the Elector Palatine's restoration, but this goal was never achieved. Friedrich fled to The Hague in 1622 via Breslau, Küstrin, Berlin, and Wolfenbüttel. Once in The Hague, he and his family maintained a court in exile, living extravagantly and dependent on money from the Dutch and English.

In 1628 Bavaria annexed the Upper Palatinate. Friedrich hoped that his brother-in-law, King Charles I, could defeat the Spanish and thereby help the Elector regain his dominions as well as his electoral dignity. However, the Treaty of Madrid in 1630 ended the war between

Spain and England without Friedrich's restoration. When Sweden joined the anti-Habsburg coalition and liberated the Palatinate, Friedrich followed King Gustaf II Adolf in his march across Germany (1631-32), dying at Mainz before reaching the Palatinate.

5966. SIR FERDINANDO CAREY = 5326.
5967. PHILIPPA THROCKMORTON = 5327.

5968. GEORGE GORDON = 5328.
5969. MARGARET BANNERMAN = 5329.

5970. WILLIAM FORBES = 5330.
5971. JANET OGILVY = 5331.

5972. ALLAN LOCKHART = 5332.
5973. HON. ELIZABETH ROSS = 5333.

5974. SIR JAMES LOCKHART = 5334.
5975. MARTHA DOUGLAS = 5335.

5976. JOHN MURRAY, 1ST EARL OF ATHOLL = 5336.
5977. JEAN CAMPBELL = 5337.

5978. JAMES STANLEY, 7TH EARL OF DERBY = 5338.
5979. CHARLOTTE DE LA TRÉMOÏLLE = 5339.

5980. WILLIAM DOUGLAS, 1ST MARQUESS OF DOUGLAS = 5340.
5981. LADY MARY GORDON = 5341.

5982. JAMES HAMILTON, 1ST DUKE OF HAMILTON = 5342 = 5350.
5983. LADY MARGARET FEILDING = 5343.

5984. JOHN MAXWELL = 5344.
5985. CATHERINE MAXWELL = 5345.

5986. JOHN MACCULLOCH = 5346.
5987. MARGARET COUPER = 5347.

5988. SIR THOMAS HAY = 5348.
5989. JEAN HAMILTON = 5349.

5990. JAMES HAMILTON, 1ST DUKE OF HAMILTON = 5342 = 5350 = 5982.
5991. ? EUPHEMIA HAMILTON = 5351.

5992. HUGH MONTGOMERIE, 7TH EARL OF EGLINTON = 5352.
5993. LADY MARY LESLIE = 5353.

5994. WILLIAM CRICHTON, 2ND EARL OF DUMFRIES = 5354.
5995. PENELOPE SWIFT = 5355.

5996. WILLIAM COCHRANE, 1ST EARL OF DUNDONALD = 5356.
5997. EUPHEME SCOTT = 5357.

5998. JOHN KENNEDY, 6TH EARL OF CASSILIS = 5358.
5999. LADY JEAN HAMILTON = 5359.

6000. LAURENCE SCOTT = 5360.
6001. ELIZABETH PRINGLE = 5361.

6002. SIR JOHN DALMAHOY = 5362.
6003. BARBARA LINDSAY = 5363.

6004. JOHN NICOLSON = 5364.
6005. JANET SWINTON = 5365.

6006-6015. = 5366-5375.

6016-6017. ——.

6018. Sir Henry Bagenall, M.P. 1586, born in 1556 and killed at Blackwater, Armagh 14 Aug. 1598. He married in 1577,
6019. Eleanor Savage, born in 1557 and died after 1604.

6020-6023. ——.

6024. Oliver Lambart, 1st Baron Cavan, P.C. (I.) (1603), M.P. [as Sir Oliver Lambart] 1613-15, Governor of Connaught 1601, buried at Westminster Abbey, Middlesex 10 June 1618. He married before 3 Jan. 1598/99,
6025. Hester Fleetwood, died 12 March 1638/39; buried at St. Patrick's Church, Dublin.

6026. Richard Robartes, 1st Baron Robartes, Sheriff of Cornwall 1614, died 19 April 1634; buried Lanhydrock, Cornwall. He married (settlement dated 5 Jan. 1598),
6027. Frances Hender, buried at Lanhydrock 12 Aug. 1626.

6028-6031. ——.

6032. William Paget, 5th Baron Paget, member of the council of the Virginia Company 1611/12, born in 1572 and died 29 Aug. 1628; buried at West Drayton, Middlesex. He married before 19 June 1602,
6033. Lettice Knollys, died in 1655; buried at West Drayton.

6034. Henry Rich, 1st Earl of Holland, K.G. (1625), K.B. (1610), P.C. (1625), M.P. [as Hon. Sir Henry Rich] 1610-11 and 1614, Lord of the Bedchamber 1626, Master of the Horse 1628, High Steward to HM Queen Henrietta Maria 1629-48, Groom of the Stole 1636-42, Ambassador to Paris 1624 and joint Ambassador 1624-26, General 1639, Lord Lieutenant of

Middlesex and Berkshire 1642-43, baptized at Stratford-le-Bow, Middlesex 19 Aug. 1590 and executed [with Arthur Capell, 1st Baron Capell (No. 2202), and James Hamilton, 1st Duke of Hamilton (No. 5342)] at Palace Yard, Westminster, Middlesex 9 March 1648/49. He married ca. 1616,

6035. ISABEL COPE, died 30 Aug. 1655; buried at Kensington, Middlesex.

6036-6037. ——.

6038. HUMPHREY REYNOLDS of Loughscur, Leitrim, married,
6039. RUSSELL WARE.

6040. PETER WHETCOMBE of Writtle, Essex, died after 1634. He married at St. Margaret's Church, Westminster, Middlesex 11 Aug. 1585,
6041. MARGARET DODDINGTON of Bremer, Hampshire.

6042. JOHN HYDE of Wallingford, Berkshire, married,
6043. HELEN SANDERSON. She married, 2nd, James Altham, a Baron of the Exchequer, who died 21 Feb. 1616/17, son of James Altham and Elizabeth Blanck.

6044. JOHN SHERARD, born ca. 1584 and buried at North Witham, Lincolnshire 7 March 1661/62. He married, 1st, at North Witham 13 Nov. 1610, Rose Sherard, born in 1591 and died 22 May 1612, daughter of Francis Sherard and Anne Moore. He married, 2nd, before 1615,
6045. ELIZABETH BROWNLOW, died 6 Feb. 1657/58.

6046. LUMLEY DEWE married at Shobdon, Herefordshire 25 Dec. 1612,
6047. MARY WIGMORE, born 31 Aug., baptized at Shobdon 5 Sept. 1599.

6048. CHRISTOPHE DE ROBILLARD, died before 18 May 1619. He married,
6049. JUDITH BOURSICOT, died before 18 May 1619.

6050-6051. ——.

6052. Charles de la Rochefoucauld, Seigneur de la Renaudie et de la Rigaudière, died after 1641. He married in June 1608,

6053. Sara de Verrières, Dame de Fontpastour.

6054. ? Daniel de Maizières, Seigneur du Passage, married,

6055. ? Elisabeth de Sainte-Hermine.

6056. Colonel Sir Arthur Forbes, 1st Baronet, born ca. 1569 and killed in a duel at Hamburg 14 April 1632. He married after 12 Feb. 1617/18,

6057. Jane Lauder, who after a long siege surrendered Castle Forbes, Longford, in Aug. 1642. She married, 1st, Sir Claud Hamilton of Clonyn, Cavan.

6058. Sir Robert Newcomen, 4th Baronet, M.P. (I.) 1646-49 and 1661-66, died 12 Aug. 1677; buried at St. Catherine's Church, Dublin. He married, 2nd, 31 March 1650, Katherine Verschoyle. He married, 1st,

6059. Anne Boleyn, "consanguinea Elizabethae Reginae Angliae," died before 31 March 1650.

6060. Francis Rawdon of Rawdon, Yorkshire, born ca. 1582 and died 25 April 1668; buried at Guiseley, Yorkshire. He married in 1603,

6061. Dorothy Aldborough of Aldborough, Yorkshire, died in 1660.

6062. Edward Conway, 2nd Viscount Conway, P.C. (I.) (1639/40), M.P. [as Hon. Sir Edward Conway] 1624-25 and 1626, summoned to Parliament in his father's barony 1628, Marshal of the Army in Ireland 1639/40, baptized at Arrow, Warwickshire 10 Aug. 1594 and died at Lyon, France 26 June 1655. He married ca. Oct. 1621,

6063. Frances Popham, born ca. 1597 and died 7 May 1671; buried at Arrow.

6064-6079. ——.

6080. Sir Edward Villiers = 4388.
6081. Barbara St. John = 4389.

6082. THEOPHILUS HOWARD, 2ND EARL OF SUFFOLK, K.G. (1628), P.C. (1626), M.P. [as Lord Walden] 1605-10, summoned to Parliament in his father's barony of Howard of Walden 1609/10, Lord Warden of the Cinque Ports 1628-40, joint Lord Lieutenant of Cumberland, Westmorland and Northumberland 1614-39, Lord Lieutenant of Cambridgeshire, Suffolk and Dorset 1626-40, baptized at Walden, Essex 13 Aug. 1584 and died at Suffolk House, Charing Cross, London 3 June 1640, son of Thomas Howard, 1st Earl of Suffolk [No. 10502]. He married (contract dated 17 Nov. 1606) in March 1611/12,

6083. LADY ELIZABETH HOME, born ca. 1599 and died at Greenwich Park, Kent 19 Aug. 1633, daughter of George Home, 1st Earl of Dunbar.

6084. THOMAS CHIFFINCH, innkeeper of Salisbury, married,
6085. ——.

6086-6087. ——.

6088. NICHOLAS HERNE of the "Blue Anchor," Cheapside, merchant taylor, died in 1642; buried at Hendon, Middlesex. He married, 1st (Bishop of London's license to marry at Hendon dated 13 Aug. 1613), Elizabeth Hooker, daughter of Nicholas Hooker. He married, 2nd, ca. 1627,

6089. SARAH IRONSIDE of Rickmansworth, Hertfordshire.

6090. SIR JOHN FREDERICK, M.P. 1660 and 1663-69, Lord Mayor of London 1661/62, Sheriff of London 1655/56, baptized at the Church of St. Olave Old Jewry, London 25 Oct. 1601 and buried there 19 March 1684/85. He married at the Church of St. Helen Bishopsgate, London 10 Jan. 1635/36,

6091. MARY ROUSE, buried at St. Olave's Church 19 Dec. 1689.

6092. TOBIAS LISLE, grocer and woollen draper, born ca. 1594 and died at Saffron Hill, Middlesex 22 March 1658/59. He married,

6093. SUSANNA TRYST, baptized at Maidford, Northamptonshire 10 May 1607 and died in 1691; buried at Evenly, Northamptonshire.

6094. JOHN AYLWORTH, barrister of the Middle Temple, baptized at St. Andrew's Church, Holborn, Middlesex 21 Feb. 1584/55. He married,

6095. ——.

6096. John Egerton, 1st Earl of Bridgewater, K.B. (1603), P.C. (1626), M.P. [as Hon. John Egerton] 1597-98 and [as Hon. Sir John Egerton] 1601, Lord President of Wales and Lord Lieutenant of Shropshire, Worcestershire, Herefordshire and Monmouthshire 1632-42, born in 1579 and died 4 Dec. 1649; buried at Little Gaddesden, Hertfordshire. He married before 24 March 1602/3, his stepsister

6097. Lady Frances Stanley, born in May 1583 and died 11 March 1635/36, daughter of Ferdinando Stanley, 5th Earl of Derby.

6098. William Cavendish, 1st Duke of Newcastle-upon-Tyne, K.G. (1661), K.B. (1610), P.C. (1639 and 1650), M.P. [as Sir William Cavendish] 1614, Lord of the Bedchamber to HRH The Prince of Wales (later HM King Charles II) 1637/38 and HRH's Governor 1638, Lord of the Bedchamber to HM 1660-76, raised the Royal Standard in the North 1642, King Charles' envoy to Denmark 1650, Lord Lieutenant of Nottinghamshire 1626-42 and 1660-76, Derbyshire 1628-38, and Northumberland 1670-76, a noted horseman known as "the Loyal Duke," baptized at Handsworth, Yorkshire 16 Dec. 1593 and died at Welbeck Abbey, Nottinghamshire 25 Dec. 1676. He married, 2nd, at Paris ca. Dec. 1645, Margaret Lucas, Maid of Honour to HM Queen Henrietta Maria, a prolific author of plays and poetry, born in 1617 and died at Welbeck Abbey 15 Dec. 1673, daughter of Thomas Lucas and Elizabeth Leighton. He married, 1st, shortly before 24 Oct. 1618,

6099. Elizabeth Basset, born in 1599 and died at Bolsover, Derbyshire 17 April 1643, daughter of William Basset and Judith Austin [No. 6401]. She married, 1st, Hon. Henry Howard, who died 3 Oct. 1616, son of Thomas Howard, 1st Earl of Suffolk [No. 10502], and Catherine Knyvett [No. 10503].

6100. John Paulet, 5th Marquess of Winchester = 2222. He married, 1st (Bishop of London's license dated 18 Dec. 1622),

6101. Lady Jane Savage, died before 16 April 1631, daughter of Thomas Savage, 1st Viscount Savage [No. 2882], and Elizabeth Darcy, Countess Rivers [No. 2883].

6102. Emmanuel Scrope, 1st Earl of Sunderland = 2722.
6103. Martha Jones = 2723.

6104. John Churchill = 2056 = 4428 = 5820.
6105. Sarah Winston = 2057 = 4429 = 5821.

6106. Sir John Drake = 2058 = 4430 = 5822.
6107. Hon. Eleanor Boteler = 2059 = 4431 = 5823.

6108. Sir John Jennings = 2060.
6109. Alice Spencer = 2061.

6110. Sir Gifford Thornhurst, 1st Baronet = 2062.
6111. Susan Temple = 2063.

6112. Sir William Twysden, 1st Baronet = 5840.
6113. Lady Anne Finch = 5841.

6114. Sir Nicholas Saunders = 5842.
6115. Elizabeth Blount = 5843.

6116-6117. = 5844-5845.

6118. Sir John Garrard = 5846.
6119. Elizabeth Barkham = 5847.

6120. Sir William Twysden, 1st Baronet = 5840 = 6112.
6121. Lady Anne Finch = 5841 = 6113.

6122. John Thomlinson, buried at the Church of St. Michael-le-Belfry, York 3 Aug. 1617. He married at the Church of the Holy Trinity, Goodramgate, York 17 Aug. 1608,
6123. Eleanor Dodsworth. She married, 2nd, at the Church of the Holy Trinity 21 Sept. 1626, Thomas Coventry.

6124. William Lemon of Beccles, Suffolk, married,
6125. Alice Bourne.

6126-6139. ——.

6140. Edward Pearce married at the Church of St. Bartholomew the Less, London 15 Aug. 1613,
6141. Mary Bishop.

6142. Sir Dudley Carleton, born ca. 1601 and buried at St. James's Church, Clerkenwell, Middlesex 9 March 1653/54. He married, 1st, in 1625, Barbara van Duyck. He married, 2nd (Faculty Office license to marry at the Churches of St. Peter, St. Martin, or St. Nicholas, Hereford dated 8 Feb. 1632/33),
6143. Lucy Croft, born ca. 1606 and died in 1648.

6144–6157. ——.

6158. Justice John Meagh of the Munster Presidency Court married,
6159. ——.

6160–6367. ——.

6368. Donel O'Donovan, died in 1584. He married,
6369. ——.

6370. Sir Owen MacCarthy Reagh of Carbery, Cork, died in 1593. He married,
6371. Ellen O'Callaghan.

6372.–6399. ——.

6400. William Boothby of Marchington, Staffordshire, merchant taylor of London, buried at the Church of St. Lawrence Old Jewry, London 14 July 1597. He married ca. 1585,
6401. Judith Austin, baptized at Bushbury, Staffordshire 16 May 1566 and buried at Blore, Staffordshire 28 Aug. 1640. She married, 2nd, William Basset [No. 12198], born 18 Aug. 1551 and died at Blore 9 Dec. 1601, son of William Basset and Elizabeth FitzHerbert. She married, 3rd, Sir Richard Corbet, born

ca. 1545 and died at Moreton Corbet, Shropshire before 29 Sept. 1606, son of Sir Andrew Corbet and Jane Needham.

6402. JOHN CURZON = 2688.
6403. MILLICENT SACHEVERELL = 2689.

6404. SIR RICHARD HALFORD, Sheriff of Rutland 1619/20 and 1631/32 and Leicestershire 1621/22, born ca. 1580 and died 30 Aug. 1658; buried at Wistow, Leicestershire. He married, 2nd, Joan Archer, who died in 1665, widow of i) —— Leaver and ii) Thomas Adams. He married, 1st, ca. 1602,
6405. ISABEL BOWMAN of Malbourn, Leicestershire.

6406. HUMPHREY HACKET of Creeton, Lincolnshire, born ca. 1593 and died 11 June 1629. He married (license dated 9 Oct. 1616),
6407. AUDREY LISTER, born in 1596. She married, 2nd, Matthew Clerk, who was buried at Bourne, Lincolnshire 21 Dec. 1636.

6408-6591. ——.

6592. JACQUES GUINAND married in 1567,
6593. PERRENON PEQUEGNOT.

6594. JACQUES PERRET-GENTIL married,
6595. ——.

6596-6515. ——.

6816. THOMAS NEWBOLD of Hackenthorpe, Derbyshire, died in 1562/63. He married,
6817. ——.

6818-7039. ——.

7040. John Strong of Chard, Somerset, born ca. 1585 and died before 26 Nov. 1627 [perhaps the John Strong buried at Chard 14 July 1613]. He married in 1609,

7041. ——, died before 24 April 1654. She married, 2nd, William Cogan of Chard.

7042. Thomas Ford, deputy to the Connecticut General Court 1637, 1638, 1639, 1640, 1641, 1644, and 1654, born ca. 1591 and died at Northampton, Massachusetts 28 Nov. 1676. He married, 2nd, at Hartford, Connecticut 7 Nov. 1644, Ann ——, who died at Northampton 5 May 1675, widow of Thomas Scott. He married, 1st, at Bridport, Dorset 19 June 1616,

7043. Elizabeth Charde, died at Windsor, Connecticut 18 April 1643. She married, 1st, at Thorncombe, Devonshire 2 Sept. 1610, Aaron Cooke, who died before 19 June 1616.

7044. ? Edward Holton of Holt St. Mary, Suffolk, married,
7045. ——.

7046–7053. ——.

7054. Robert Blott, born ca. 1584 and died between 27 March and 22 Aug. 1665. He married at Harrold, Bedfordshire 31 Aug. 1609,
7055. Susanna Selbee, died at Boston, Massachusetts 20 Jan. 1659/60.

7056. John Strong = 7040.
7057. = 7041.

7058. Thomas Ford = 7042.
7059. Elizabeth Charde = 7043.

7060. ? Thomas Woodward of Much Woolton, Lancashire, married 23 May 1592,
7061. ? Elizabeth Tynen.

7062-7067. ——.

7068. ? STEPHEN HART of Ipswich, Suffolk, married,
7069. ——.

7070-7075. ——.

7076. JOHN COGSWELL, baptized at Westbury Leigh, Wiltshire 2 April 1592 and died at Ipswich, Massachusetts 29 Nov. 1669. He married at Westbury Leigh 10 Sept. 1615,
7077. ELIZABETH THOMPSON, died at Ipswich 2 June 1676.

7078. ADAM HAWKES, baptized at Hingham, Norfolk 26 Jan. 1604/5 and died at Lynn, Massachusetts 13 March 1671/72. He married, 2nd, in June 1670, Sarah Hooper, born at Reading, Massachusetts 7 Dec. 1650, daughter of William Hooper and Elizabeth ——. He married, 1st, ca. 1631,
7079. ANNE ——, born ca. 1595 and died at Lynn 4 Dec. 1669. She married, 1st, Thomas Hutchinson.

7080-7081. ——.

7082. ? THOMAS MITCHELL of Cambridge and Leyden, born ca. 1566. He married, 1st, Maria Tromdin. He married, 2nd, at Amsterdam 9 May 1606,
7083. ? MARGARET WILLIAMS. She married, 1st, Christopher Stocking.

7084. DR. WILLIAM GAGER, baptized at Little Waldingfield, Suffolk 15 June 1592 and died at Boston, Massachusetts 20 Sept. 1630. He married before 6 Aug. 1618,
7085. ——, died at Boston before 29 Nov. 1630.

7086. SAMUEL GORE, grocer of London, died before 19 May 1643. He married 18 Jan. 1625/26,
7087. ELIZABETH HILL of Rotherhithe, Surrey.

7088. ? John Hibbard of Salisbury married,
7089. ——.

7090. ? John Luff, weaver, died at Salem, Massachusetts ca. 1678. He married,
7091. ? Bridget ——, born ca. 1587 and living in 1671.

7092-7099. ——.

7100. Robert Parke, deputy to the Connecticut General Court 1642, baptized at Postingford, Suffolk 3 June 1580 and died at Mystic (Stonington), Connecticut 14 March 1664/65. He married, 2nd, **Alice Freeman [No. 7103].** He married, 1st, at Semer, Suffolk 9 Feb. 1601/2, his 1st cousin
7101. Martha Chaplin, baptized at Semer 4 Feb. 1583/84 and died before 1643.

7102. John Thompson of Little Preston, Northamptonshire, died at London 6 Nov. 1626. He married, 1st, ——. He married, 2nd, before 1 May 1616,
7103. Alice Freeman of Cranford, Northamptonshire. She married, 2nd, after 30 May 1644, **Robert Parke [No. 7100].**

7104-7743. ——.

7744. Rev. George Chalmer, minister of Gartly, Aberdeenshire 1607-14 and Kintore, Aberdeenshire 1614, born in 1572 and died in 1626. He married in 1604,
7745. Marion Lawson.

7746-7751. ——.

7752. Rev. George Chalmer = 7744.
7753. Marion Lawson = 7745.

7754-7755. ——.

7756. ? THOMAS FORBES of Waterton, Aberdeenshire, died 11 June 1652. He married,
7757. ? JEAN RAMSAY of Balmain, Kincardineshire.

7758. ? SIR JOHN GORDON, 1ST BARONET = 2664.
7759. ? JANET FORBES = 2665.

7760. JAMES TRAIL, Gentleman of the Privy Chamber to HRH The Prince Henry Frederick, Prince of Wales, born ca. 1555 and died in 1635. He married, 2nd, Grizel Myrton, daughter of William Myrton of Randerston, Fife. He married, 1st, in 1595,
7761. MATILDA MELVILLE of Cambee, Fife, died 23 Nov. 1608.

7762. ALEXANDER ANNAND of Auchterallan, Aberdeenshire, married,
7763. MARGARET CHEYNE of Esselmont, Aberdeenshire.

7764. JAMES TRAIL = 7760.
7765. MATILDA MELVILLE = 7761.

7766. JOHN HAMILTON, M.P. (I.) 1613 and 1634, died 16 Sept. 1639. He married in 1617,
7767. SARAH BRABAZON of Ballynasloe, Galway, died in 1633.

7768-7775. ——.

7776. JOHN DOUGLAS of Tilwhilly, Aberdeenshire, born ca. 1577. He married at Holyrood House, Edinburgh in 1594,
7777. MARY YOUNG, born ca. 1579, daughter of Sir Peter Young, Almoner to HM King James VI, and Elizabeth Gib, daughter of Robert Gib, jester to HM King James V.

7778. David Ramsay, M.P. 1612, 1625, and 1630, died in 1636. He married,

7779. Margaret Ogilvy of Ogilvy, Angus.

7780-7791. ——.

7792. Robert Forbes of Echt, Aberdeenshire, married,

7793. —— Burnett of Leys, Kincardineshire.

7794. Patrick Forbes of Wester Echt, Aberdeenshire, married,

7795. ——.

7796. Sir Robert Innes, 1st Baronet, P.C. (S.), M.P. 1639-41 and 1648, died between 1649 and 1660. He married,

7797. Lady Grizel Stewart, daughter of James Stewart, 2nd Earl of Moray.

7798. James Ross, 6th Lord Ross, died 17 Dec. 1633; buried at Renfrew, Renfrewshire. He married (contract dated 19 Dec. 1614 and 30 Jan. 1614/15),

7799. Hon. Margaret Scott, died at Hull 3 Oct. 1651 [where her 2nd husband was then a prisoner], daughter of Walter Scott, 1st Lord Scott. She married, 2nd, between Nov. 1642 and March 1643/44, Alexander Seton [afterwards Montgomerie], 6th Earl of Eglinton [No. 10704], born in 1588 and died at Eglinton, Ayrshire 7 Jan. 1660/61, son of Robert Seton, 1st Earl of Winton, and Lady Margaret Montgomerie, daughter of Hugh Montgomerie, 3rd Earl of Eglinton.

7800-7813. ——.

7814. John Crabtree, buried at Methley, Yorkshire 29 Oct. 1607. He married,

7815. Joan ——, buried at Methley 11 Nov. 1587.

7816-7875. ——.

7876. James Irvine of Brucklaw, Aberdeenshire, married his 1st cousin,
7877. Lucretia Irvine, daughter of Gilbert [or George] Irvine of Cullerly, Aberdeenshire.

7878. Sir Thomas Urquhart of Cromartie, Ross-shire, born in 1586 and died in 1642. He married,
7879. Hon. Christian Elphinstone, born 19 Dec. 1590, daughter of Alexander Elphinstone, 4th Lord Elphinstone.

7880-7895. ——.

7896. James Lindsay of Cushnie, Auchterless, Aberdeenshire, married,
7897. ——.

7898-7919. ——.

7920. William Dyce of Belhevie, Aberdeenshire, born in 1590. He married,
7921. ——.

7922-8031. ——.

8032. Alexander Lumsden of Cushnie, Aberdeenshire, died before 1626. He married,
8033. Christian Irvine of Kingscausie, Aberdeenshire.

8034. Alexander Leith of Bucharn, Aberdeenshire, married,
8035. ——.

8036-8063. ——.

8064. SIR WILLIAM FORBES, 1ST BARONET, died before July 1661. He married,

8065. ELIZABETH WISHART of Balisycht, Kincardineshire, died in 1628.

8066. SIR THOMAS BURNETT, 1ST BARONET, died 27 June 1653. He married, 2nd (contract dated 9 Aug. 1621), Jane Moncrieffe, widow of Sir Simon Fraser, and daughter of Sir John Moncrieffe, 1st Baronet, and Lady Mary Murray, daughter of William Murray, 2nd Earl of Tullibardine. He married, 1st, in 1610,

8067. MARGARET DOUGLAS of Glenbervie, Stirlingshire.

8068. SIR JOHN DALMAHOY = 5362 = 6002.
8069. BARBARA LINDSAY = 5363 = 6003.

8070. THOMAS WILBRAHAM of Nantwich, Cheshire, born 25 June 1589. He married 24 March 1618/19,

8071. RACHEL CLIVE of Huxley, Cheshire, died ca. 5 April 1657.

8072-8075. ———.

8076. SIR THOMAS URQUHART = 7878.
8077. HON. CHRISTIAN ELPHINSTONE = 7879.

8078. ALEXANDER ELPHINSTONE, 6TH LORD ELPHINSTONE, died 26 Oct. 1654. He married (contract dated 14 Nov. 1645), his 1st cousin

8079. HON. LILIAS ELPHINSTONE, born 6 June 1613 and died in Nov. 1675, daughter of Alexander Elphinstone, 5th Lord Elphinstone.

8080-8087. ———.

8088. JAMES FORBES of Blackton, Aberdeenshire, died before 1647. He married 12 Sept. 1622,

8089. MAGDALENE FRASER of Philorth, Aberdeenshire.

8090. JOHN FORBES of Balfluig and Corsendae, Aberdeenshire, died before 22 April 1658. He married,
8091. MARGARET FRASER of Durris, Aberdeenshire.

8092-8095. ——.

8096-8099. = 8072-8075.

8100. SIR THOMAS URQUHART = 7878 = 8076.
8101. HON. CHRISTIAN ELPHINSTONE = 7879 = 8077.

8102. ALEXANDER ELPHINSTONE, 6TH LORD ELPHINSTONE = 8078.
8103. HON. LILIAS ELPHINSTONE = 8079.

8104. SIR PATRICK MAITLAND of Pitrichie, Aberdeenshire, married (contract at Crathes, Aberdeenshire dated 27 Sept. 1607),
8105. KATHERINE BURNETT of Leys, Kincardineshire.

8106. ROBERT GORDON, geographer, born at Kinmundy, Aberdeenshire 14 Sept. 1580 and died 18 Aug. 1661. He married in 1608,
8107. KATHERINE IRVINE of Lenturk, Aberdeenshire, died 3 Aug. 1662.

8108. SIR WILLIAM FORBES, 2ND BARONET = 4032.
8109. JEAN BURNETT = 4033.

8110. ROBERT ARBUTHNOTT, 1ST VISCOUNT ARBUTHNOTT, P.C. (1649), born ca. 1618 and died 10 Oct. 1655. He married, 2nd, 30 June 1653, Hon. Katherine Fraser, born in 1619 and died 18 Oct. 1663, widow of Sir John Sinclair, and daughter of Hugh Fraser, 7th Lord Lovat, and Isabel Wemyss. He married, 1st, at Arbuthnott, Kincardineshire before 1639,
8111. LADY MARJORY CARNEGIE, died 22 Dec. 1651, daughter of David Carnegie, 1st Earl of Southesk. She married, 1st, William Halliburton of Pictur, Forfarshire.

8112. ADAM DUFF of Archindoun, Lanarkshire, born in 1590 and died in April 1674. He married, 1st, —— Murray of Milegen, Galway. He married, 2nd,

8113. BEATRIX GORDON of Cairnburrow, Aberdeenshire, born ca. 1608.

8114. ALEXANDER DUFF, town clerk of Inverness, married,

8115. ——.

8116. ROBERT DUFF of Invermarkie and Towiemore, Banffshire, killed at Alford, Banffshire 2 July 1645. He married,

8117. EUPHEME LYON. She married, 2nd, William McPherson.

8118. JOHN ABERCROMBY of Glasshaugh, Aberdeenshire, married,

8119. KATHERINE GORDON of Lesmoir, Aberdeenshire.

8120. SIR JOHN GORDON of Park, Banffshire, died in 1672. He married in 1631,

8121. HELEN SIBBALD of Rankeilor, Fife.

8122. JAMES OGILVY, 2ND EARL OF AIRLIE, P.C., born ca. 1615 and died in 1703, son of James Ogilvy, 1st Earl of Airlie, and Lady Isabel Hamilton, daughter of Thomas Hamilton, 1st Earl of Haddington [No. 10718]. He married, 2nd, **MARY GRANT [No. 2657].** He married, 1st (contract dated 20 March 1628/29),

8123. HON. HELEN OGILVY, died after Feb. 1663/64, daughter of George Ogilvy, 1st Lord Banff.

8124. HON. ALEXANDER FRASER, MASTER OF SALTOUN, born ca. 1630 and died in Nov. 1682, son of Alexander Fraser, 10th Lord Saltoun. He married, 2nd, 29 Oct. 1660, Lady Marion Cunningham, who died at Holyrood, Edinburgh in Jan. 1660/61, widow of James Ogilvie, 1st Earl of Findlater, and daughter of William Cunningham, 8th Earl of Glencairn, and Lady Janet Kerr, daughter of Mark Kerr, 1st Earl of Lothian. He married, 3rd, 5 Aug. 1663, Hon. Sophia Erskine, daughter of Alexander Erskine, Viscount Fentoun by courtesy, and Lady Anne Seton, daughter of Alexander Seton, 1st Earl of Dunfermline. He married, 1st (contract dated 11 Jan. 1651/52),

8125. Lady Anne Kerr, died 30 Aug. 1658, daughter of William Kerr, 1st Earl of Lothian [No. 5920].

8126. Most Rev. James Sharpe, Archbishop of St. Andrews (1661-79), born at Banff Castle 4 May 1618 and assassinated on Magus Moor, near St. Andrews 3 May 1679. He married in April 1653,

8127. Helen Moncrieffe of Randerston, Fife.

8128-8191. ——.

NOTES

Lady Diana Frances Spencer

1 Charles Mosley, ed., *Burke's Genealogical and Heraldic History of the Peerage and Baronetage*, 2 vols. (1999), 2: 2674; Charles Spencer, Earl Spencer, *The Spencer Family: A Personal History of an English Family* (2003); Andrew Morton, *Diana: Her True Story* (1998); *Time*, 20 April 1981, 68; *The New York Times*, 15 Nov. 1948, 1, 15 Dec. 1948, 1, 30 July 1981, A1, A11, 29 Aug. 1996, A9, and 1 Sept. 1997, A8; Rebecca Tyrrel, *Camilla: An Intimate Portrait* (2004), 17, 86; *www.royal.gov.uk/output/Page5571.asp, accessed 16 Feb. 2007; http://en.wikipedia.org/wiki/List_of_titles_and_honours_of_Charles%2C_Prince_of_Wales,* accessed 21 April 2007.

First Generation

2-3 George E. Cokayne et al., *The Complete Peerage*, 14 vols. in 15 (1910-98), 14: 238, 589; Peter Townend, ed., *Burke's Genealogical and Heraldic History of the Peerage, Baronetage and Knightage* (1970), 1689-90; Charles Mosley, ed., *Burke's Genealogical and Heraldic History of the Peerage and Baronetage*, 2 vols. (1999), 2: 2674; *The New York Times*, 7 Feb. 1936, 16, 13 March 1936, 20, 2 June 1954, 36; *The Times,* London, 28 April 1925, 1, 10 Sept. 1929, 1, 30 March 1992, 1, 17, and 3 June 2004, 1, 17; *The Sunday Times*, London, 11 July 1993, 24; Charles Spencer, Earl Spencer, *The Spencer Family: A Personal History of an English Family* (2003); Max Riddington and Gavan Naden, *Frances: The Remarkable Story of Princess Diana's Mother* (2004); *http://announcements.telegraph.co.uk/deaths/30-Mar-2006/30-Mar-2006/Peter~Shand~Kydd/1/results.aspx,* accessed 29 Jan. 2007; *http://en.wikipedia.org/wiki/Peter_Shand_Kydd,* accessed 21 April 2007.

Second Generation

4-5 *The Times*, London, 18 Aug. 1897, 1; David Williamson, "The Ancestry of Lady Diana Spencer," *The Genealogists' Magazine: Official Organ of the Society of Genealogists* 20 [1980-82]: 194; George E. Cokayne et al., *The Complete Peerage*, 14 vols. in 15 (1910-98), 13: 39; *Obituaries from The* Times *1971–1975* (1976), 503; M. G. Dauglish and P. G. Stephenson, eds., *Harrow School Register 1800–1911* (1911), 861; Charles Spencer, Earl Spencer, *The Spencer Family: A Personal History of an English Family* (2003), 146; Charles Mosley, ed., *Burke's Genealogical and Heraldic History of the Peerage and Baronetage*, 2 vols. (1999), 1: 6; *http://en.wikipedia.org/wiki/Lord_Lieutenant_of_Northamptonshire,* accessed 21 April 2007.

6-7 *The Complete Peerage*, 14: 319; *Burke's Genealogical and Heraldic History of the Peerage and Baronetage* (1999), 1: 1049; *The New York Times*, 18 Sept. 1931, 26, 9 July 1955, 15, and 8 July 1993, D19; *The Times*, London, 8 July 1993, 4, 19; Gary Boyd Roberts and William Addams Reitwiesner, *American Ancestors and Cousins of The Princess of Wales* (1984), 24-25; "The Ancestry of Lady Diana Spencer," 194; *Who's Who* (1980), 837.

Third Generation

8-9 Charles Spencer, Earl Spencer, *The Spencer Family: A Personal History of an English Family* (2003), 143; David Williamson, "The Ancestry of Lady Diana Spencer," *The Genealogists' Magazine: Official Organ of the Society of Genealogists* 20 [1980-82]: 194; John Venn and John Archibald Venn, *Alumni Cantabrigienses: A biographical list of all known students, graduates and holders of office at the University of Cambridge, from the earliest times to 1900,* 10 vols. (1922-54), 5: 603; George E. Cokayne et al., *The Complete Peerage,* 14 vols. in 15 (1910-98), 13: 39; *The Times,* London, 27 Sept. 1922, 12; *http://en.wikipedia.org/wiki/Lord_Lieutenant_of_ Northamptonshire,* accessed 21 April 2007.

10-11 Leslie G. Pine, *Burke's Genealogical and Heraldic History of the Peerage and Baronetage* (1953), 2; Charles Mosley, ed., *Burke's Genealogical and Heraldic History of the Peerage and Baronetage,* 2 vols. (1999), 1: 6; *The Times,* London, 14 Sept. 1953, 10; *The Complete Peerage,* 1: 10, 14: 2; "The Ancestry of Lady Diana Spencer," 194; Sir James Balfour Paul, *The Scots Peerage,* 9 vols. (1904-14), 1: 72-73.

12-13 *The Complete Peerage,* 14: 319; Gary Boyd Roberts and William Addams Reitwiesner, *American Ancestors and Cousins of The Princess of Wales* (1984), 24; "The Ancestry of Lady Diana Spencer," 194; *Alumni Cantabrigienses,* 5: 338; *The New York Times,* 26 Sept. 1880, 7, 4 March 1891, 1, 16 July 1906, 7, 17 July 1906, 3, 2 Nov. 1906, 11 (where Aurel Batonyi's original surname is given as Kohn), and 27 Jan. 1947, 23; *The Oakland Tribune,* 8 Sept. 1907, 17-18.

14-15 "The Ancestry of Lady Diana Spencer," 194; *Who was Who 1951–60* (1961), 421.

Fourth Generation

16-17 *Oxford Dictionary of National Biography,* 60 vols. (2004), 51: 892-93; George E. Cokayne et al., *The Complete Peerage,* 14 vols. in 15 (1910-98), 12: 1: 157; *Publications of the Northamptonshire Record Society,* vol. 31, Peter Gordon, ed., *The Red Earl: The Papers of the Fifth Earl Spencer 1885–1910,* 2-3; John Venn and John Archibald Venn, *Alumni Cantabrigienses: A biographical list of all known students, graduates and holders of office at the University of Cambridge, from the earliest times to 1900,* 10 vols. (1922-54), 5: 603; *Parish registers of Easebourne, 1538–1901* Family History Library film 0918,250; 1871 England Census, RG10, Folio 57: 47.

18-19 *Oxford Dictionary of National Biography,* 3: 819-20; *The Complete Peerage,* 10: 769; David Williamson, "The Ancestry of Lady Diana Spencer," *The Genealogists' Magazine: Official Organ of the Society of Genealogists* 20 [1980-82]: 194, 281.

20-21 *Oxford Dictionary of National Biography,* 24: 859-60; *The Complete Peerage,* 1: 9-10, 14: 2; "The Ancestry of Lady Diana Spencer," 194; M. G. Dauglish and P. G. Stephenson, eds., *Harrow School Register 1800–1911* (1911), 247; Sir James Balfour Paul, *The Scots Peerage,* 9 vols. (1904-14), 1: 72; Joseph Foster, *Alumni Oxonienses: The members of the University of Oxford, 1715–1886: their parentage, birthplace, and year of birth, with a record of their degrees. Being the matriculation register of the University, alphabetically arranged, revised and annotated,* 4 vols. (1887-88), 1-2: 594.

22-23 *The Complete Peerage,* 8: 240.

24-25 *The Complete Peerage,* 5: 302-3.

26-27 Gary Boyd Roberts and William Addams Reitwiesner, *American Ancestors and Cousins of The Princess of Wales* (1984), 92; *The New York Times,* 17 March 1911, 9.

28-29   "The Ancestry of Lady Diana Spencer," 194; *St. Nicholas Aberdeen, Baptisms,* Family History Library film 0991,199; *Parish registers 1695–1854 Tarves parish, Aberdeen,* Family History Library film 0993,301.

30-31   "The Ancestry of Lady Diana Spencer," 195; *The Times,* London, 14 May 1924, 1; Alexander Dingwall Fordyce, *Family Records of the Name of Dingwall Fordyce in Aberdeenshire* (1885), 188; Peter John Anderson, ed., *Fasti Academiae Mariscallanae* (1889), 577.

Fifth Generation

32-33   *Oxford Dictionary of National Biography,* 60 vols. (2004), 51: 841-44; Sir Lewis Namier and John Brooke, *The House of Commons 1754–1790,* 3 vols. (1964; reprinted 1985), 3: 459-60; George E. Cokayne et al., *The Complete Peerage,* 14 vols. in 15 (1910-98), 12: 1: 154-55; John Venn and John Archibald Venn, *Alumni Cantabrigienses: A biographical list of all known students, graduates and holders of office at the University of Cambridge, from the earliest times to 1900,* 10 vols. (1922-54), 5: 604; *The Dictionary of National Biography, founded in 1882 by George Smith, edited by Sir Leslie Stephen and Sir Sidney Lee,* 2nd ed., 22 vols. (1885–1901; reprinted 1908-9), 18: 763-64; *Publications of the Harleian Society, Register Series,* vol. 11, John H. Chapman, ed., *The Register Book of Marriages Belonging to the Parish of St. George, Hanover Square, in the County of Middlesex, 1725 to 1837,* 320.

34-35   R. G. Thorne, *The History of Parliament: the House of Commons 1790–1820,* 5 vols. (1986), 5: 122-23; David Williamson, "The Ancestry of Lady Diana Spencer," *The Genealogists' Magazine: Official Organ of the Society of Genealogists* 20 [1980-82]: 194, 281; *The Complete Peerage,* 3: 322; Michael Stenton, *Who's Who of British Members of Parliament, Volume 1: 1832–1885* (1976), 346; Leslie G. Pine, *Burke's Genealogical and Heraldic History of the Peerage and Baronetage* (1953), 1048; M. G. Dauglish and P. G. Stephenson, eds., *Harrow School Register 1800–1911* (1911), 30; *The Register Book of Marriages Belonging to the Parish of St. George, Hanover Square, in the County of Middlesex, 1725 to 1837,* 22: 161; 1851 England Census, HO107, Folio 187: 22; *Parish Registers for St. James's Church, Westminster 1685–1881* Family History Library film 1042,320.

36-37   Roger Owen, *Lord Cromer: Victorian Imperialist, Edwardian Proconsul* (2004), 9; *The House of Commons 1790–1820,* 3: 141-42; "The Ancestry of Lady Diana Spencer," 195, 281; Joseph Jackson Howard et al., eds., *Visitation of England and Wales,* 21 vols. (1893-1921), 7: 41; *The Complete Peerage,* 10: 769, note a; *Burke's Genealogical and Heraldic History of the Peerage and Baronetage* (1953), 1579; *Parish registers of St. Pancras Old Church, Marriages, 1794–1811* Family History Library film 0598,179; *Deutsches Geschlechterbuch (Genealogisches Handbuch Bürgerlicher Familien),* vol. 102, "Baring, v. Baring, Baring v. Wallerode: Freiherr v. Baring, Baring-Gould, Baring Baronet of Larkbear, Baring Baronet of Nubia House, Baring Baron of Hillburton, Baring Baron Viscount und Earl of Cromer, Viscount Errington, Baring Baron Viscount und Earl of Northbrook, Baring Baron Revelstoke, aus Groningen in Friesland," 118-19 (which states that Cecilia Anne Windham died 21 Oct. 1874); 1871 England Census, RG10, Folio 64: 18.

38-39   Charles Edward Pitman, *History and pedigree of the family of Pitman of Dunchideock, Exeter, and their collaterals, and of the Pitmans of Alphington, Norfolk and Edinburgh: with part pedigrees and acccounts of families connected by marriage* (1920), 57; Leslie G. Pine, ed., *Burke's Genealogical and Heraldic History of the Landed Gentry including American Families with British Ancestry* (1939), 282; *Parish register transcripts of Yealmpton, 1600–1850,* Family History Library film 0917,560; Joseph Foster, *Alumni Oxonienses: The members of the University of Oxford, 1715–1886: their parentage, birthplace, and year of birth, with a record of their degrees. Being the matriculation register of the University, alphabetically arranged, revised and annotated,* 4 vols. (1887-

88), 1-2: 190; *The Register Book of Marriages Belonging to the Parish of St. George, Hanover Square, in the County of Middlesex, 1725 to 1837*, 24: 50; *Bishops' transcripts, 1604–1869 Parish of Essendon, Hertfordshire,* Family History Library film 0569,718; Vivien Allen, *The Bulteels: The Story of a Huguenot Family* (2004), 60-69, 166; Will of John Crocker Bulteel of Flete, Devon 19 June 1842, Proved at London P.C.C. 5 Dec. 1843 PROB 11/1989.

40-41 *Oxford Dictionary of National Biography*, 24: 857-88; *The Complete Peerage*, 1: 8-9; *Harrow School Register 1800–1911*, 105; Sir James Balfour Paul, *The Scots Peerage*, 9 vols. (1904-14), 1: 68-70; *Alumni Oxonienses: The members of the University of Oxford, 1715–1886*, 1-2: 594; F. G. Emmison, *Bedfordshire Parish Registers*, 43 vols. (1931-52), 3: 108 (most accounts of the Duchess of Abercorn state that she was born in 1812, but the Woburn parish register records that she was born and baptized in 1811); Gary Boyd Roberts, "The Leveson-Gower Progeny: Our 'Whig Cousinage,'" *NEHGS NEXUS* 14 [1997]: 70-73.

42-43 *The Complete Peerage,* 6: 601-2; *Parish Registers of Great Witley 1538–1968* Family History Library film 0596,845.

44-45 *Oxford Dictionary of National Biography*, 5: 753-56; *The Complete Peerage*, 8: 239; *The Dictionary of National Biography*, Supplement 1: 196-97; G. F. Russell Barker and Alan H. Stenning, *The Record of Old Westminsters…*, 2 vols. (1928), 1: 89; 1871 England Census, RG10, Folio 38: 27.

46-47 *Oxford Dictionary of National Biography*, 33: 366-68; *The Complete Peerage*, 10: 844-45; *The Record of Old Westminsters*, 2: 570-71; George Dames Burtchaell and Thomas Ulick Sadleir, eds., *Alumni Dublinenses; a register of the students, graduates, professors and provosts of Trinity college in the University of Dublin (1593–1860)* (1935), 495; 1851 England Census, HO107, Folio 386: 27.

48-49 David Williamson, "The Ancestry of Lady Diana Spencer," *The Genealogists' Magazine* 20 [1980-82]: 195; *Burke's Genealogical and Heraldic History of the Peerage and Baronetage* (1953), 788; *Alumni Dublinenses*, 710.

50-51 "The Ancestry of Lady Diana Spencer," 195, 281; Henry Wagner, "Pedigree of Guinand," *Miscellanea Genealogica et Heraldica*, 4th series, 4 [1912]: 271.

52-53 Gary Boyd Roberts and William Addams Reitwiesner, *American Ancestors and Cousins of The Princess of Wales* (1984), 75; Francis James Dallett, "The Inter-Colonial Grimstone Boude and his family," *The Genealogist* 2 [1981]: 98-99.

54-55 *American Ancestors and Cousins of The Princess of Wales*, 22, 120; Francis James Dallett, "Captain Peter Young and Descendants: Further Philadelphia Roots of the Princess of Wales," *The Pennsylvania Genealogical Magazine* 33 [1984]: 196.

56-57 "The Ancestry of Lady Diana Spencer," 195-96, 281; *Parish registers, St. Nicholas, Aberdeen — Marriages vol. xxviii 1820–1831* Family History Library film 0991,201; 1851 Scotland Census, CSSCT1851_41, parish # 168B, E.D. # 6: 49; *Parish Registers of St. Nicholas, Aberdeen 1771–1820: Baptisms* Family History Library film 0991,137.

58-59 William Temple, *The Thanage of Fermartyn including the district commonly called Formartine, its proprietors: with genealogical deductions, its parishes, ministers, churches, churchyards, antiquities, &c* (1894), 405; "The Ancestry of Lady Diana Spencer," 196; 1851 Scotland Census, CSSCT1851_52, parish # 243, E.D. # 12, household # 54; 1861 Scotland Census, CSSCT1861_33, parish #243, E.D. # 11: 1; *Parish registers 1695–1854 Tarves parish, Aberdeen* Family History Library film 0993,301.

60-61 Alexander Dingwall Fordyce, *Family Records of the Name of Dingwall Fordyce in Aberdeenshire* (1885), 188; "The Ancestry of Lady Diana Spencer," 196; Peter John Anderson, ed., *Fasti Academiae Mariscallanae* (1889), 424; *Parish registers, St. Nicholas, Aberdeen — Marriages v. 28 1820–1831* Family History Library film 0991,201; *Parish Registers of St. Nicholas, Aberdeen: Marriages 1820–1854* Family History Library film 0991,202.

62-63 "The Ancestry of Lady Diana Spencer," 196, 282; *Family Records of the Name of Dingwall Fordyce in Aberdeenshire*, 40; *Fasti Academiae Mariscallanae*, 444; 1851 Scotland Census, CSSCT1851_49, parish # 227, E.D. # 3: 4; *Parish registers, St. Nicholas, Aberdeen — Marriages vol. xxviii 1820–1831* Family History Library film 0991,201.

Sixth Generation

64-65 *Oxford Dictionary of National Biography*, 60 vols. (2004), 51: 864-65, 845-46; Sir Lewis Namier and John Brooke, *The History of Parliament: The House of Commons 1754–1790*, 3 vols. (1964; reprinted 1985), 3: 460; George E. Cokayne et al., *The Complete Peerage*, 14 vols. in 15 (1910-98), 12: 1: 153-54.

66-67 *The History of Parliament 1754–1790*, 2: 93; *The Complete Peerage*, 8: 237-38; *Oxford Dictionary of National Biography*, 5: 760.

68-69 R. G. Thorne, *The History of Parliament: The House of Commons 1790–1820*, 5 vols. (1986), 5: 127-28; *The Complete Peerage*, 6: 514, 12: 2: 309, note b; *Publications of the Harleian Society, Register Series*, vol. 52, W. Bruce Bannerman et al., eds., *The Registers of Marriages of St. Mary le Bone, Middlesex, 1668–1812, and Oxford Chapel, Vere Street, St. Marylebone, 1736–1754*, 44.

70-71 *The History of Parliament 1790–1820*, 4: 711–12; *The History of Parliament 1754–1790*, 3: 245; George E. Cokayne, *The Complete Baronetage, 1611–1880*, 5 vols. (1900-1906), 5: 220; David Williamson, "The Ancestry of Lady Diana Spencer," *The Genealogists' Magazine: Official Organ of the Society of Genealogists* 20 [1980-82]: 196, 282; Joseph Foster, *Alumni Oxonienses: The members of the University of Oxford, 1715–1886: their parentage, birthplace, and year of birth, with a record of their degrees. Being the matriculation register of the University, alphabetically arranged, revised and annotated*, 4 vols. (1887-88), 3-4: 1059; *Publications of the Harleian Society, Register Series*, vol. 14, John H. Chapman, ed., *The Register Book of Marriages Belonging to the Parish of St. George, Hanover Square, in the County of Middlesex, 1725 to 1837*, 29; *The Registers of Marriages of St. Mary le Bone, Middlesex, 1668–1812, and Oxford Chapel, Vere Street, St. Marylebone, 1736–1754*, 53: 7; *Parish Church of Mamhead registers and bishops' transcripts, 1549–1837* Family History Library film 0916,857, item 1.

72-73 *Oxford Dictionary of National Biography*, 3: 829-35; *The History of Parliament 1790–1820*, 3: 140-41; Joseph Jackson Howard and Frederick Arthur Crisp, *Visitation of England and Wales, Notes*, 14 vols. (1896-1921), 5: 60; *The Complete Baronetage*, 5: 286; *Deutsches Geschlechterbuch (Genealogisches Handbuch Bürgerlicher Familien)*, vol. 102, "Baring, v. Baring, Baring v. Wallerode: Freiherr v. Baring, Baring-Gould, Baring Baronet of Larkbear, Baring Baronet of Nubia House, Baring Baron of Hillburton, Baring Baron Viscount und Earl of Cromer, Viscount Errington, Baring Baron Viscount und Earl of Northbrook, Baring Baron Revelstoke, aus Groningen in Friesland," 103-4 (which states that Sir Francis Baring, Bt., was married 12 May 1766 and died 21 Sept. 1810, and that Harriet Herring died 3 Oct. 1804).

74-75 *Visitation of England and Wales, Notes*, 7: 33, 40; *Parish registers of St. Andrew Hubbard Church, London, 1538–1846* Family History Library film 0374,407; Will of William Windham, Vice Admiral in His Majesty's Navy, of Felbrigg, Norfolk 9 Dec. 1832, Proved at London

P.C.C. 4 March 1833 PROB 11/1813; Will of Anne Windham, Widow of Leamington, Warwickshire 4 Dec. 1848, Proved at London P.C.C. 9 March 1849 PROB 11/2090.

76-77 Charles Edward Pitman, *History and pedigree of the family of Pitman of Dunchideock, Exeter, and their collaterals, and of the Pitmans of Alphington, Norfolk and Edinburgh: with part pedigrees and acccounts of families connected by marriage* (1920), 59-60; Sir Bernard Burke, *A Genealogical and Heraldic Dictionary of the Peerage and Baronetage* (1879), 962; *St. Bartholomew by the Exchange Parish Registers 1558–1840* Family History Library film 0374,424; *Bishops' transcripts, Parish Church of Holbeton 1620–1850* Family History Library film 0917,144; Vivien Allen, *The Bulteels: The Story of a Huguenot Family* (2004), 52-60; Will of John Bulteel of Fleet Damerell, Devon 20 June 1835, codicil 20 Dec. 1836, Proved at London 19 May 1837 PROB 11/1877.

78-79 *Oxford Dictionary of National Biography*, 23: 811-19; *The History of Parliament 1790–1820*, 4: 99-110; *The Complete Peerage*, 6: 120; *The Dictionary of National Biography, founded in 1882 by George Smith, edited by Sir Leslie Stephen and Sir Sidney Lee*, 2nd ed., 22 vols. (1885–1901; reprinted 1908-9), 8: 616-22; *The Register Book of Marriages Belonging to the Parish of St. George, Hanover Square, in the County of Middlesex, 1725 to 1837*, 14: 121.

80-81 *The Complete Peerage*, 1: 1, 8, 15-17; *The History of Parliament 1790–1820*, 4: 134-35; Sir James Balfour Paul, *The Scots Peerage*, 9 vols. (1904-14), 1: 66-67; *Parish registers of Marylebone: Baptisms 1782–1793* Family History Library film 0580,906; *The Registers of Marriages of St. Mary le Bone, Middlesex, 1668–1812, and Oxford Chapel, Vere Street, St. Marylebone, 1736–1754*, 57: 8.

82-83 *Oxford Dictionary of National Biography*, 48: 292-93; *The History of Parliament 1790–1820*, 5: 64-66; *The Complete Peerage*, 2: 85.

84-85 *The History of Parliament 1790–1820*, 3: 554; G. F. Russell Barker and Alan H. Stenning, *The Record of Old Westminsters…*, 2 vols. (1928), 1: 242; *Visitation of England and Wales, Notes*, 13: 100.

86-87 *Oxford Dictionary of National Biography*, 22: 982-83; Leslie G. Pine, *Burke's Genealogical and Heraldic History of the Peerage and Baronetage* (1953), 1386; *The Dictionary of National Biography*, 8: 238-39; "The Ancestry of Lady Diana Spencer," *The Genealogists' Magazine* 20 [1980-82]: 282; *The Register Book of Marriages Belonging to the Parish of St. George, Hanover Square, in the County of Middlesex, 1725 to 1837*, 14: 393.

88-89 *The History of Parliament 1790–1820*, 3: 207; *The Complete Peerage*, 8: 238-39; *The Registers of Marriages of St. Mary le Bone, Middlesex, 1668–1812, and Oxford Chapel, Vere Street, St. Marylebone, 1736–1754*, 53: 58; *The Register Book of Marriages Belonging to the Parish of St. George, Hanover Square, in the County of Middlesex, 1725 to 1837*, 14: 22.

90-91 *The Complete Peerage*, 3: 16; *The Register Book of Marriages Belonging to the Parish of St. George, Hanover Square, in the County of Middlesex, 1725 to 1837*, 14: 109.

92-93 *Oxford Dictionary of National Biography*, 33: 365-66; *The Complete Peerage*, 10: 842-44.

94-95 *Oxford Dictionary of National Biography*, 42: 355-59; *The History of Parliament 1790–1820*, 4: 709-10; Romney Sedgwick, *The History of Parliament: The House of Commons 1715–1754*, 2 vols. (1971), 1: 552; *The Complete Peerage*, 1: 138-40, 210-11; *The Register Book of Marriages Belonging to the Parish of St. George, Hanover Square, in the County of Middlesex, 1725 to 1837*, 14: 133; *Old Parochial Registers for Edinburgh 1595–1860* Family History Library film 1066,690; 1851 England Census, HO107, Folio 415: 13.

96-97 *Burke's Genealogical and Heraldic History of the Peerage and Baronetage* (1953), 788.

98-99 "The Ancestry of Lady Diana Spencer," *The Genealogists' Magazine* 20 [1980-82]: 197.

100-101 "The Ancestry of Lady Diana Spencer," 197, 282; *Bishops' transcripts of Bolingbroke, 1562–1831* Family History Library film 0421,928, item 1; W. P. W. Phillimore and Ll. Ll. Simpson, eds., *Derbyshire Parish Registers*, 15 vols. (1906-22), 5: 52; *Bishops' transcripts of Rotherham, 1600–1837* Family History Library film 0919,315; Peter Townend, ed., *Burke's Genealogical and Heraldic History of the Peerage, Baronetage and Knightage* (1970), 305.

102-103 "The Ancestry of Lady Diana Spencer," 197, 282; Henry Wagner, "Pedigree of Guinand," *Miscellanea Genealogica et Heraldica*, 4th series, 4 [1912]: 271; *Publications of the Harleian Society, Register Series*, vol. 31, W. Bruce Bannerman, *The Registers of St. Helen's, Bishopsgate, London, 1575 to 1837*, 88.

104-105 Gary Boyd Roberts and William Addams Reitwiesner, *American Ancestors and Cousins of The Princess of Wales* (1984), 75.

106-107 *American Ancestors and Cousins of The Princess of Wales*, 75; Francis James Dallett, "The Inter-Colonial Grimstone Boude and his family," *The Genealogist* 2 [1981]: 96-97.

108-109 *American Ancestors and Cousins of The Princess of Wales*, 22-23.

110-111 *American Ancestors and Cousins of The Princess of Wales*, 21; Francis James Dallett, "Captain Peter Young and Descendants: Further Philadelphia Roots of the Princess of Wales," *The Pennsylvania Genealogical Magazine* 33 [1984]: 188, 194; Lockwood Barr, "Biography of Dr. Joseph Strong," *Yale Journal of Biology and Medicine* 13 [1941]: 429-50.

112-113 "The Ancestry of Lady Diana Spencer," *The Genealogists' Magazine* 20 [1980-82]: 282; *Old Machar parish registers — Baptisms vol. iv 1763–1792* Family History Library film 0991,206.

114-115 William Temple, *The Thanage of Fermartyn including the district commonly called Formartine, its proprietors: with genealogical deductions, its parishes, ministers, churches, churchyards, antiquities, &c* (1894), 393; *Parish registers 1695–1854 Tarves parish, Aberdeen* Family History Library film 0993,301; *Parish Church of Fyvie 1685–1854* Family History Library film 0993,186.

116-117 *The Thanage of Fermartyn*, 404-5; *Parish Registers of Peterculter 1643–1854* Family History Library film 0993,352; *Parish registers 1695–1854 Tarves parish, Aberdeen* Family History Library film 0993,301; 1861 Scotland Census, CSSCT1861_33, parish # 249, E.D. # 4: 4.

118-119 *Parish registers 1695–1854 Tarves parish, Aberdeen* Family History Library film 0993,301.

120-121 Alexander Dingwall Fordyce, *Family Records of the Name of Dingwall Fordyce in Aberdeenshire* (1885), 186; "The Ancestry of Lady Diana Spencer," 282; *Parish Registers of St. Nicholas, Aberdeen 1771–1820: Baptisms* Family History Library film 0991,137.

122-123 *Family Records of the Name of Dingwall Fordyce in Aberdeenshire*, 15; Vere Langford Oliver, "Pedigree of the family of Dingwall of Brucklay," *Miscellanea Genealogica et Heraldica*, 4th series, 3 [1900]: 7; Peter John Anderson, ed., *Fasti Academiae Mariscallanae* (1889), 367; 1851 Scotland Census, CSSCT1851_80, parish # 387, E.D. # 5: 11.

124-125 "The Ancestry of Lady Diana Spencer," 197, 282; *Parish Registers of New Machar: vol. 1. Baptisms, 1676–1699, 1713–1819; marriages, 1676–1698, 1717–1819; burials, 1738–1820* Family History Library film 0993,349.

126-127 "The Ancestry of Lady Diana Spencer," 197, 282; *The Thanage of Fermartyn*, 155.

Seventh Generation

128-129 Charles Spencer, Earl Spencer, *The Spencer Family: A Personal History of an English Family* (2003); George E. Cokayne et al., *The Complete Peerage*, 14 vols. in 15 (1910-98), 12: 1: 153, note b, 3: 483-84; Sir Lewis Namier and John Brooke, *The History of Parliament: The House of Commons 1754–1790*, 3 vols. (1964; reprinted 1985), 2: 432-33.

130-131 John Maclean, *Historical and Genealogical Memoir of the Family of Poyntz, or, Eight Centuries of an English House* (1886), 208, 226; John Venn and John Archibald Venn, *Alumni Cantabrigienses; A biographical list of all known students, graduates and holders of office at the University of Cambridge, from the earliest times to 1900*, 10 vols. (1922-54), 3: 390; R. A. Austen-Leigh, *The Eton College Register 1698–1752* (1927), 278; *Oxford Dictionary of National Biography*, 60 vols. (2004), 45: 198-99; *Publications of the Harleian Society, Register Series*, vol. 7, Joseph Lemuel Chester, *The Parish Registers of St. Michael, Cornhill, London, 1546 to 1754*, 153.

132-133 George E. Cokayne, *The Complete Baronetage, 1611–1880*, 5 vols. (1900-6), 2: 399; Edith Mary Johnston-Liik, *History of the Irish Parliament 1692–1800: commons, constituencies and statutes*, 6 vols. (2002), 3: 186-87.

134-135 Romney Sedgwick, *The History of Parliament: The House of Commons 1715–1754*, 2 vols. (1971), 2: 427.

136-137 *Oxford Dictionary of National Biography*, 13: 49; *The Complete Peerage*, 6: 509-10.

138-139 *The Complete Peerage*, 12: 2: 308-9; *The Eton College Register 1698–1752*, 353.

140-141 *The Complete Baronetage*, 5: 220; Joseph Foster, *Alumni Oxonienses: The members of the University of Oxford, 1715–1886: their parentage, birthplace, and year of birth, with a record of their degrees. Being the matriculation register of the University, alphabetically arranged, revised and annotated*, 4 vols. (1887-88), 3-4: 1059; *The History of Parliament 1754–1790*, 3: 245; Charles Edward Pitman, *History and pedigree of the family of Pitman of Dunchideock, Exeter, and their collaterals, and of the Pitmans of Alphington, Norfolk and Edinburgh: with part pedigrees and acccounts of families connected by marriage* (1920), 120.

142-143 R. G. Thorne, *The History of Parliament: The House of Commons 1790–1820*, 5 vols. (1986), 5: 446-47; *The Complete Peerage*, 8: 36; Robert Surtees, *The History and Antiquities of the County Palatine of Durham: Compiled from Original Records, Preserved in Public Repositories and Private Collections, and Illustrated by Engravings of Architectural and Monumental Antiquities, Portraits of Eminent Persons &c., &c.* 4 vols. (1816-40), 3: 295; *Publications of the Harleian Society, Register Series*, vol. 11, John H. Chapman, ed., *The Register Book of Marriages Belonging to the Parish of St. George, Hanover Square, in the County of Middlesex, 1725 to 1837*, 53; *Berwick-upon-Tweed Parish Register Transcripts 1573–1812* Family History Library film 0094,988.

144-145 Joseph Jackson Howard and Frederick Arthur Crisp, *Visitation of England and Wales, Notes*, 14 vols. (1896-1921), 5: 59; *The Complete Peerage*, 10: 769, note a; Cokayne, *The Complete Baronetage*, 5: 286; *Exeter St. Petrock's Parish Register* 1538-1837 Family History Library film 0916,838; *Oxford Dictionary of National Biography*, 3: 820-21; *Deutsches Geschlechterbuch (Genealogisches Handbuch Bürgerlicher Familien)*, vol. 102, "Baring, v. Baring, Baring v. Wallerode: Freiherr v. Baring, Baring-Gould, Baring Baronet of Larkbear, Baring Baronet of Nubia House, Baring Baron of Hillburton, Baring Baron Viscount und Earl of Cromer, Viscount Errington, Baring Baron Viscount und Earl of Northbrook, Baring Baron Revelstoke, aus Groningen in Friesland," 101 (which states that John Baring was born 15 Nov. 1697 and married 15 Feb. 1729, and that his wife's given name was Anna Elizabeth Vowler).

146-147 George Steinman Steinman, *A history of Croydon* (1834), 204; *Parish register transcripts, Parish Church of Silkstone 1557–1784* Family History Library film 0098,538, item 2; *Publications of the Harleian Society, Visitation Series*, vol. 46, Sir George J. Armytage, Bart., ed., *Obituary Prior to 1800 (as far as relates to England, Scotland, and Ireland), Compiled by Sir William Musgrave, 6th Bart. Of Hayton Castle, co. Cumberland, and entitled by him "A General Nomenclator and Obituary, with reference to the books where the persons are mentioned, and where some account of their character is to be found,"* 201; *Bishops' Transcripts Holy Trinity Micklegate, York 1601–1864* Family History Library film 0990,869; *Deutsches Geschlechterbuch (Genealogisches Handbuch Bürgerlicher Familien)*, 102: 101; Will of William Herring of Croydon, Surrey 1 Feb. 1801, Proved at London P.C.C. 6 Nov. 1801 PROB 11/1365.

148-149 *Alumni Cantabrigienses 1752–1900*, 4: 233; *Visitations of England and Wales, Notes*, 5: 7; G. H. Holley, "Pedigrees compiled from the parish registers, wills, monumental inscriptions, court records, etc., Norfolk County England" (a 7 vol. manuscript at the Family History Library, Salt Lake City, Utah), 2: 110.

150-151 *Visitations of England and Wales, Notes*, 11: 110; *Oxford Dictionary of National Biography*, 54: 212-13; *St. Mary's, Southampton parish register transcripts, 1675–1837* Family History Library film 1595,861.

152-153 *History and pedigree of the family of Pitman*, 59; *Parish registers St. Anne's Soho, 1686–1931* Family History Library film 0918,609; *Parish registers of Westmill church, Herts, 1562–1947* Family History Library film 0991,401; Vivien Allen, *The Bulteels: The Story of a Huguenot Family* (2004), 48-50; *Alumni Oxonienses: The members of the University of Oxford, 1715–1886*, 1-2: 190; Will of John Bulteel of Fleet Damerell, Devon, Proved 7 Oct. 1801 PROB 11/1363.

154-155 Sir Bernard Burke, *A Genealogical and Heraldic Dictionary of the Peerage and Baronetage* (1879), 962; *The Gentleman's Magazine* 61 [1791]: 1161; *Modbury, Devon Parish register transcripts, Baptisms 1599–1837* Family History Library film 0916,861.

156-157 *Oxford Dictionary of National Biography*, 23: 809-11; *The Complete Peerage*, 6: 119-20.

158-159 *The History of Parliament 1790–1820*, 4: 866-67; *Alumni Cantabrigienses 1752–1900*, 5: 153; *The Complete Peerage*, 10: 576-77.

160-161 *The Complete Peerage*, 1: 7, 8; Sir James Balfour Paul, *The Scots Peerage*, 9 vols. (1904-14), 1: 66; *The Register Book of Marriages Belonging to the Parish of St. George, Hanover Square, in the County of Middlesex, 1725 to 1837*, 14: 217; *Publications of the Harleian Society, Register Series*, vol. 51, W. Bruce Bannerman et al., eds., *The Registers of Marriages of St. Mary le Bone, Middlesex, 1668–1812, and Oxford Chapel, Vere Street, St. Marylebone, 1736–1754*, 57; *Parish Church of Taplow (Buckinghamshire) 1710–1897* Family History Library film 0919,250.

162-163 *The Complete Peerage*, 9: 301; *The Scots Peerage*, 6: 382-83; *The Register Book of Marriages Belonging to the Parish of St. George, Hanover Square, in the County of Middlesex, 1725 to 1837*, 11: 365; Jean Goodman and David Williamson, *Debrett's Book of the Royal Engagement* (1986), 121.

164-165 *The Complete Peerage*, 2: 84; *Debrett's Book of the Royal Engagement*, 121.

166-167 *Oxford Dictionary of National Biography*, 22: 855-56, 922-23; *The Complete Peerage*, 6: 5-6.

168-169 G. F. Russell Barker and Alan H. Stenning, *The Record of Old Westminsters…*, 2 vols. (1928), 1: 241; *The Complete Peerage*, 3: 582-83; *Visitations of England and Wales, Notes*, 5: 98;

The Register Book of Marriages Belonging to the Parish of St. George, Hanover Square, in the County of Middlesex, 1725 to 1837, 11: 151, 275.

170-171   *Oxford Dictionary of National Biography*, 28: 480-88; *The Record of Old Westminsters*, 1: 488; *The Complete Peerage*, 6: 599-600; *Visitation of England and Wales, Notes*, 13:100.

172-173   "Annotations to the Heraldic Visitation of London, 1633. Gore," *Miscellanea Genealogica et Heraldica*, 2nd series, 3 [1890]: 151; James Ralfe, *The naval biography of Great Britain: consisting of historical memoirs of those officers of the British Navy who distinguished themselves during the reign of His Majesty George III*, 4 vols. (1828), 4: 460; *The Gentleman's Magazine* 64 [1794]: 283, 61 [1791]: 589.

174-175   *The Dictionary of National Biography, founded in 1882 by George Smith, edited by Sir Leslie Stephen and Sir Sidney Lee*, 2nd ed., 22 vols. (1885–1901; reprinted 1908-9), 13: 694-95; Leslie G. Pine, *Burke's Genealogical and Heraldic History of the Peerage and Baronetage* (1953), 1386; W. S. Sykes, "Notes on Wilcot and Families" (a manuscript at the Wiltshire Archaelogical Society, Devizes); *Parish registers of the Church of Wymering, 1653–1875* (including Widley parish) Family History Library film 0918,878; *Wiltshire Family History Society*, 1999-2000 vol., *The bishop's transcripts and parish registers of Wilcot, baptisms & burials, 1564–1837 and Huish, baptisms & burials, 1603–1837*, 39, 93; *The bishop's transcripts and parish registers of Wilcot, baptisms, marriages & burials, 1782–1812 & 1812–1842* Family History Library film 1279,437, items 22 and 23.

176-177   See 66-67.

178-179   *The History of Parliament 1754–1790*, 2: 79-80; *The Complete Peerage*, 5:266.

180-181   *The History of Parliament 1754–1790*, 2: 125; Joan Wake, *The Brudenells of Deene* (1953), 281-86; *The Register Book of Marriages Belonging to the Parish of St. George, Hanover Square, in the County of Middlesex, 1725 to 1837*, 11: 83; *The Complete Baronetage*, 1: 156; *Alumni Oxonienses: The members of the University of Oxford, 1715–1886*, 1-2: 179.

182-183   "Family of Cooke," "Pedigree of Cooke," *Miscellanea Genealogica et Heraldica*, 2nd series, 4 [1892]: 152.

184-185   *Oxford Dictionary of National Biography*, 33: 374-75; *The History of Parliament 1754–1790*, 3: 35; *Burke's Genealogical and Heraldic History of the Peerage and Baronetage* (1953), 1776; *The Record of Old Westminsters*, 2: 571; *The Register Book of Marriages Belonging to the Parish of St. George, Hanover Square, in the County of Middlesex, 1725 to 1837*, 11: 93; Will of the Right Hon. Lady Louisa Mary Lennox, Widow of Funtington 10 Sept. 1829, Proved 1 Feb. 1831 PROB 11/1781.

186-187   See 166-167.

188-189   *The Complete Peerage*, 10: 288-89; Gary Boyd Roberts, *Notable Kin: An Anthology of Columns First Published in the* NEHGS NEXUS, *1986–1995, Volume Two … with contributions by John Anderson Brayton and Richard E. Brenneman* (1999), 216, 219; Scott C. Steward, "Six Generations of the Anglo-American Ancestry of Sir Winston Churchill," *NEHGS NEXUS* 13 [1996]: 167-72, and "The Eighth-Generation Ancestry of Sir Winston Churchill," 14 [1997]: 65-68.

The Right Hon. Sir Winston Churchill, K.G., and Diana, Princess of Wales, both descend from this couple.

190-191   *The History of Parliament 1754–1790*, 3: 586; *The Complete Peerage*, 7: 90-91; *Oxford Dictionary of National Biography* 56: 486, 507.

192-195 *Burke's Genealogical and Heraldic History of the Peerage and Baronetage* (1953), 788.

196-197 *The Sunday Times Magazine*, 26 July 1981, 28; Thomas W. Copeland, ed., *The Correspondence of Edmund Burke*, 10 vols. (1958-69), 1: 125-26; *Hibernian Chronicle*, 1 Nov. 1798.

198-199 Hugh Montgomery-Massingberd, *Burke's Irish Family Records* (1976), 357; *Hibernian Chronicle*, 6 Jan. 1800.

200-201 Peter Townend, ed., *Burke's Genealogical and Heraldic History of the Peerage, Baronetage and Knightage* (1970), 305.

202-203 *Bishops' transcripts, 1600–1837, Parish Church of Rotherham* Family History Library film 0919,315.

206-207 Henry Wagner, "Pedigree of Guinand," *Miscellanea Genealogica et Heraldica*, 4th series, 4 [1912]: 271.

212-213 Francis James Dallett, "The Inter-Colonial Grimstone Boude and his family," *The Genealogist* 2 [1981]: 90-92.

214-215 "The Inter-Colonial Grimstone Boude and his family," 97.

220-221 Gary Boyd Roberts and William Addams Reitwiesner, *American Ancestors and Cousins of The Princess of Wales* (1984), 27; Benjamin W. Dwight, *The History of the Descendants of Elder John Strong of Northampton, Mass.*, 2 vols. (1871), 1: 414.

222-223 Francis James Dallett, "Captain Peter Young and Descendants: Further Philadelphia Roots of the Princess of Wales," *The Pennsylvania Genealogical Magazine* 33 [1984]: 181-83, 186.

224-225 *Old Machar parish registers — Marriages vol. vii, 1722–1783* Family History Library film 0991,141.

226-227 *Parish Registers of St. Nicholas, Aberdeen — Marriages vol. xiii 1695–1776* Family History Library film 0991,138.

228-229 William Temple, *The Thanage of Fermartyn including the district commonly called Formartine, its proprietors: with genealogical deductions, its parishes, ministers, churches, churchyards, antiquities, &c* (1894), 392; *Tarves Parish Registers vol. ii, marriages, 1762–1801* Family History Library film 0993,301.

230-231 *The Thanage of Fermartyn*, 393; *Parish Registers of St. Nicholas, Aberdeen — Marriages vol. xiii 1695–1776* Family History Library film 0991,138.

232-233 *Parish Registers of Peterculter 1643–1854* Family History Library film 0993,352.

234-235 *The Sunday Times Magazine*, 26 July 1981, 28.

240-241 Alexander Dingwall Fordyce, *Family Records of the Name of Dingwall Fordyce in Aberdeenshire* (1885), 188, 46; *Parish registers of Old Meldrum, Aberdeen 1713–1854* Family History Library film 0993,351; *Parish Registers of St. Nicholas, Aberdeen — Marriages vol. xiii 1695–1776* Family History Library film 0991,138.

242-243 *Oxford Dictionary of National Biography*, 10: 865; Charles John Guthrie, *Genealogy of the descendants of Reverend Thomas Guthrie, D. D., and Mrs. Anne Burns or Guthrie: connected chiefly with the families of Chalmers and Trail, to which Mrs. Guthrie belonged through her mother, Mrs. Christina Chalmers or Burns, and her great-grandmother, Mrs. Susannah Trail or Chalmers; also incidental references to the families of Guthrie and Burns* (1902), 26; *Family Records of the Name of*

Dingwall Fordyce in Aberdeenshire, 73; *Scotch Church, 1750–1840 St. James, Westminster* Family History Library film 0596,973.

244-245   *Family Records of the Name of Dingwall Fordyce in Aberdeenshire*, 14.

246-247   Vere Langford Oliver, "Pedigree of the family of Dingwall of Brucklay," *Miscellanea Genealogica et Heraldica*, 4th series, 3 [1900]: 7; *Family Records of the Name of Dingwall Fordyce in Aberdeenshire*, 122-24.

248-249   *The Sunday Times Magazine*, 26 July 1981, 28.

250-251   *The Sunday Times Magazine*, 26 July 1981, 28; *The Thanage of Fermartyn*, 643; *Parish Registers of Old Machar — Baptisms vol. iii 1721–1763* Family History Library film 0991,206; *Parish Church of Kintore 1717–1854* Family History Library film 0993,336.

252-253   A. Alistair N. Tayler and H. A. Henrietta Tayler, *The House of Forbes* (1937), pedigree opposite 304; *The Thanage of Fermartyn*, 155; *Parish Church of Forgue 1684–1854* Family History Library film 0993,183.

Eighth Generation

256-257   *Oxford Dictionary of National Biography*, 60 vols. (2004), 51: 825-32; Eveline Cruickshanks, Stuart Handley and David Hayton, *The History of Parliament: The House of Commons 1690–1715,* 5 vols. (2002), 5: 533-36; George E. Cokayne et al., *The Complete Peerage*, 14 vols. in 15 (1910-98), 12: 1: 487-89, 8: 497, note d; Ophelia Field, *Sarah Churchill, Duchess of Marlborough, The Queen's Favourite* (2003), 365.

258-259   *Oxford Dictionary of National Biography*, 10: 381-86; *The Complete Peerage*, 6: 89-90; *The Dictionary of National Biography, founded in 1882 by George Smith, edited by Sir Leslie Stephen and Sir Sidney Lee*, 2nd ed., 22 vols. (1885–1901; reprinted 1908-9), 3: 1119-24.

260-261   John Maclean, *Historical and Genealogical Memoir of the Family of Poyntz, or, Eight Centuries of an English House* (1886), 202.

262-263   Charles James Feret, *Fulham Old and New being an exhaustive history of the ancient parish of Fulham*, 3 vols. (1900), 2: 143; Egerton Brydges, *Collins's Peerage of England, Genealogical, Biographical, and Historical, Greatly Augmented, and Continued to the Present Time,* 9 vols. (1812), 3: 329; E.M. Boyle, *Sixty-Four "Quartiers" of Major Gerald Edmund Boyle, and his brothers and sister* (1882); *Publications of the Harleian Society, Register Series*, vol. 47, W. Bruce Bannerman et al., eds., *The Registers of Marriages of St. Mary le Bone, Middlesex, 1668–1812, and Oxford Chapel, Vere Street, St. Marylebone, 1736–1754*, 133; *St. Andrew, Holborn, Middlesex Parish registers, 1556–1934* Family History Library film 0374,349.

264-265   George E. Cokayne, *The Complete Baronetage, 1611–1880,* 5 vols. (1900-6), 2: 399.

266-267   Ashworth P. Burke, *A Genealogical and Heraldic History of the Landed Gentry of Ireland* (1899), 461; Sir Bernard Burke, *A Genealogical and Heraldic Dictionary of the Peerage and Baronetage* (1879), 363; *The Complete Baronetage*, 2: 258; Edith Mary Johnston-Liik, *History of the Irish Parliament 1692–1800: commons, constituencies and statutes,* 6 vols. (2002), 5: 468-69.

268-269   Romney Sedgwick, *The History of Parliament: The House of Commons 1715–1754,* 2 vols. (1971), 2: 427.

272-273   *The History of Parliament 1690–1715,* 3: 691; *The Complete Peerage*, 3: 402-3; *Publications of the Harleian Society, Visitation Series*, vol. 92, J. B. Whitmore, ed., *London Visitation Pedigrees, 1664* (1940), 124, and vol. 8, George W. Marshall, ed., *Le Neve's Pedigrees of the*

Knights made by King Charles II, King James II, King William III and Queen Mary, King William alone, and Queen Anne, 302.

274-275 *The Complete Peerage,* 6: 45.

276-277 *The Complete Peerage,* 12: 2: 306; *The Dictionary of National Biography,* 20: 473-75.

278-279 *The Yale Edition of Horace Walpole's Correspondence,* 48 vols. (1937-83), 25: 466; R. A. Austen-Leigh, *The Eton College Register 1698–1752* (1927), 355; William A. Shaw, *The Knights of England,* 2 vols. (1906), 1: 169; *The Complete Peerage,* 12: 2: 309, note a; *Parish Registers for St. Martin-in-the-Fields 1550–1926* Family History Library film 0560,372.

280-281 Sir Lewis Namier and John Brooke, *The History of Parliament: The House of Commons 1754–1790,* 3 vols. (1964; reprinted 1985), 3: 245; Charles Edward Pitman, *History and pedigree of the family of Pitman of Dunchideock, Exeter, and their collaterals, and of the Pitmans of Alphington, Norfolk and Edinburgh: with part pedigrees and acccounts of families connected by marriage* (1920), 120; *The Gentleman's Magazine* 63 [1793]: 482.

282-283 Leslie G. Pine, ed., *Burke's Genealogical and Heraldic History of the Peerage, Baronetage and Knightage* (1956), 2202; *St. Andrew Undershaft Church (London) Registers 1558–1901* Family History Library film 0374,408; *Parish Registers of Radley, Berkshire 1599–1837* Family History Library film 1040,564, item 8.

284-285 *The Complete Peerage,* 8: 35-36; James Raine, *The History and Antiquities of North Durham, as Subdivided into the Shires of Norham, Island and Bedlington, which from the Saxon Period until the Year 1844, Constituted Parcels of the County Palatine of Durham, but Are Now United to the County of Northumberland* (1852), 319; *Parish Church of Norham (Northumberland) Transcripts 1654–1812* Family History Library film 0090,787; *Berwick-upon-Tweed Parish Register Transcripts 1573–1812* Family History Library film 0094,988.

286-287 *The History of Parliament 1715–1754,* 2: 418; Robert Surtees, *The History and Antiquities of the County Palatine of Durham: Compiled from Original Records, Preserved in Public Repositories and Private Collections, and Illustrated by Engravings of Architectural and Monumental Antiquities, Portraits of Eminent Persons &c., &c.,* 4 vols. (1816-40), 3: 295; *St. Anne's Church (Soho, Westminster) Parish Registers 1686–1931* Family History Library film 0918,606; *Publications of the Harleian Society, Register Series,* vol. 73, A. W. Hughes Clarke, *The Registers of St. Mary Magdalen Milk Street, London and St. Michael Bassishaw, London, 1558 to 1892,* 87.

288-289 Thomas George Baring, Earl of Northbrook, et al., eds., *Journals and correspondence from 1808 to 1852, of Sir Francis Thornhill Baring afterwards Lord Northbrook, compiled and edited by his son Thomas George, Earl of Northbrook* (1905), 272, 274-75; *Deutsches Geschlechterbuch (Genealogisches Handbuch Bürgerlicher Familien),* vol. 102, "Baring, v. Baring, Baring v. Wallerode: Freiherr v. Baring, Baring-Gould, Baring Baronet of Larkbear, Baring Baronet of Nubia House, Baring Baron of Hillburton, Baring Baron Viscount und Earl of Cromer, Viscount Errington, Baring Baron Viscount und Earl of Northbrook, Baring Baron Revelstoke, aus Groningen in Friesland," 99-100.

290-291 *Exeter St. Petrock's Parish Register 1538–1837* Family History Library film 0916,838, item 3; Margery M. Rowe, *Exeter Freemen 1266–1967* (1973), 189, 210, 234; *Deutsches Geschlechterbuch (Genealogisches Handbuch Bürgerlicher Familien),* 102: 101; Will of John Vowler of Exeter, Devon 14 April 1747, Proved at London P.C.C. 4 June 1748 PROB 11/763.

292-293 *Parish Church of Lincoln's Inn Registers, 1695–1842* Family History Library film 0823,848, item 3; Will of Samuel Herring, Merchant Taylor of Lambeth 18 Oct. 1756, codicil 19 Oct. 1756, Proved at London P.C.C. 13 Oct. 1757 PROB 11/833; Will of Isaac Watlington of Cambridge 1 Jan. 1699, Proved at London P.C.C. 10 Feb. 1701 PROB 11/459.

294-295 *Bishops' Transcripts, Holy Trinity Micklegate, York 1601–1864* Family History Library film 0990,869; *Publications of the Harleian Society, Visitation Series*, vol. 94, J. W. Walker, ed., *Yorkshire Pedigrees*, 144; *Bishops' Transcripts of St. Martin-Micklegate-with-St. Gregory's Church, York* Family History Library film 0990,875.

296-297 Joseph Jackson Howard et al., eds., *Visitation of England and Wales*, 21 vols. (1893–1921), 7: 33; Joseph Jackson Howard and Frederick Arthur Crisp, *Visitation of England and Wales, Notes*, 14 vols. (1896–1921), 5: 6; R. Wyndham Ketton-Cremer, *Felbrigg, the Story of a House* (1962); Sir Algernon Tudor Tudor-Craig, *The romance of Melusine and de Lusignan: together with genealogical notes and pedigrees of Lovekyn of London, Lovekyn of Lovekynsmede, and of Luckyn of Little Waltham, and Lukyn of Mashbery, all in the county of Essex, and of Lukin of Felbrigg, co. Norfolk* (1932), 19; *Sandon, Essex, Christenings, Burials & Marriages, 1554–1740* Family History Library film 1472,680, item 24; *Panfield, Essex, Christenings, Burials & Marriages, 1569–1711* Family History Library film 1472,590, item 23.

298-299 *Visitation of England & Wales, Notes,* 7: 33; G. H. Holley, "Pedigrees compiled from the parish registers, wills, monumental inscriptions, court records, etc., Norfolk County England" (a 7 vol. manuscript at the Family History Library, Salt Lake City, Utah), 2: 110; "Fenns Manuscripts of Suffolk and Norfolk" (manuscripts in the Norman Collection, Salford, Lancashire), 85; *Publications of the Harleian Society, Register Series*, vol. 40, Willoughby Littledale, *The Registers of St. Bene't and St. Peter, Paul's Wharf, London, 1607 to 1837*, 110; *The Gentleman's Magazine* 27 [1757]: 578; Will of Robert Doughty of Hanworth 25 Sept. 1756, Proved at London P.C.C. 12 Jan. 1759 PROB 11/843.

300-301 Gabriel Girod de l'Ain, *Les Thellusson histoire d'une famille* (1977), 43; Herbert Lüthy, *La banque protestante en France, de la révocation de l'Édit de Nantes à la Révolution* (1959).

302-303 L. H. Bouwens and B. G. Bouwens, *A Thousand Ancestors* (1935), vii: 42; *Chichester: All Saints Parish Registers 1563–1812* Family History Library film 0504,430; *St. Mary's, Southampton parish register transcripts, 1675–1837* Family History Library film 1595,861.

304-305 *The History of Parliament 1690–1715*, 3: 402; J. L. Vivian, *The visitations of the county of Devon, comprising the heralds' visitations of 1531, 1564, & 1620* (1895), 466; "The family of Croker," *Herald & Genealogist* 8 [1874]: 380; *Parish register transcripts of Yealmpton (Devonshire), 1600–1850,* Family History Library film 0917,560; Vivien Allen, *The Bulteels: The Story of a Huguenot Family* (2004), 42–48; Will of James Bulteell or Bulteel of Fleet Damerel, Devon 11 July 1744, codicil 21 Aug. 1757, Proved at London P.C.C. 2 Nov. 1757 PROB 11/833.

306-307 *The Complete Peerage*, 2: 99; *Bishops' Transcripts, parish church of Ardeley, Herts: Marriages 1604–1850* Family History Library film 0569,700.

308-309 *A Genealogical and Heraldic Dictionary of the Peerage and Baronetage* (1879), 962; *Parish register transcripts Modbury, Devon, Marriages 1553–1565, 1601–1837* Family History Library film 0916,862; *Parish register transcripts, Modbury, Devon Baptisms 1599–1837* Family History Library film 0916,861; Will of Philip Perring, Clothier of Modbury 3 Feb. 1764, Proved at London P.C.C. 11 Sept. 1771 PROB 11/971.

310-311 *The Bulteels: The Story of a Huguenot Family*, 53.

312-313 *The Complete Baronetage*, 5: 89; Northumberland County History Commission, *A history of Northumberland*, 15 vols. (1893-1940), 2: 352, 1: 332; *Parish Church of Howick Register Transcripts, 1678–1812* Family History Library film 0094,970.

314-315 *The History and Antiquities of the County Palatine of Durham*, 2: 19; Henry A. Ogle, *Ogle and Bothal: Or, A History of the Baronies of Ogle, Bothal, and Hepple, and of the Families of Ogle and Bertram, Who Held Possession of Those Baronies and Other Property in the County of Northumberland and Elsewhere; Showing Also How the Property Descended into Other Hands: To Which Is Added Accounts of Several Branches of Families Bearing the Name of Ogle Settled in Other Counties and Countries; with Appendices and Illustrations Compiled from Ancient Records and Other Sources* (1902), 135-36; Will of Elizabeth Grey, Widow of Falloden 1 April 1801, codicil 25 March 1803, Proved at London P.C.C. 6 April 1807 PROB 11/1459.

316-317 *Oxford Dictionary of National Biography*, 44: 813-15; Leslie G. Pine, *Burke's Genealogical and Heraldic History of the Peerage and Baronetage* (1953), 196; *The Complete Peerage*, 10: 576 note d; Major-General Sir John Ponsonby, *The Ponsonby Family* (1929), 60-63; *Bishops' transcripts, 1662–1848 Parish registers of Edensor* Family History Library film 0428,909; *History of the Irish Parliament 1692–1800*, 6: 89-96.

318-319 *The Complete Peerage*, 9: 32-34.

320-321 *Oxford Dictionary of National Biography*, 24: 872; Sir James Balfour Paul, *The Scots Peerage*, 9 vols. (1904-14), 1: 63; Henry Holman Drake, *Hasted's history of Kent: corrected, enlarged and continued to the present time, from the manuscript collections of the late Rev. Thomas Streatfield and the late Rev. Lambert Blackwell Larking, the public records, and other sources. pt. 1. The hundred of Blackheath* (1886), 138.

322-323 *The Complete Baronetage*, 5: 200; Arthur Stephens Dyer, "Pedigree of Moyle of Bake, St. Germans, Cornwall," *Miscellanea Genealogica et Heraldica*, 5th series, 9 [1932]: 350; *The registers of St. Paul's Church, Covent Garden, London 1653–1837* Family History Library film 0845,241; *Parish Church of Morval (Cornwall) register transcripts 1538–1837* Family History Library film 0916,952; Will of Sir Joseph Copley heretofore Joseph Moyle and afterwards Joseph Copley of Southampton, Hampshire, Proved at London P.C.C. 27 April 1781 PROB 11/1076; Will of Dame Mary Copley, Widow of Princes Street, Cavendish Square, Middlesex, Proved at London P.C.C. 20 March 1787 PROB 11/1151.

324-325 *The Complete Peerage*, 9: 299-300; *The Scots Peerage*, 6: 381-82; *Registers of St. Olave's Hart Street, London: Baptisms, 1631–1812* Family History Library film 0557,012.

326-327 R. G. Thorne, *The History of Parliament: The House of Commons 1790–1820*, 5 vols. (1986), 5: 377-78; *The Complete Peerage*, 6: 311; John William Clay, ed., *Dugdale's Visitation of Yorkshire in 1665-6, with additions*, 3 vols. (1899-1917), 2: 234; *Publications of the Harleian Society, Register Series*, vol. 11, John H. Chapman, ed., *The Register Book of Marriages Belonging to the Parish of St. George, Hanover Square, in the County of Middlesex, 1725 to 1837*, 103.

328-329 *The Complete Peerage*, 2: 82-83.

330-331 *Oxford Dictionary of National Biography*, 31: 371-73; *The Complete Peerage*, 1: 93-94.
HRH The Duchess of Cornwall and Diana, Princess of Wales, both descend from this couple.

332-333 *The Complete Peerage*, 6: 4-5; *Parish Church of Speymouth (Morayshire) Registers, 1651–1854* Family History Library film 0990,811.

334-335 *The Complete Baronetage*, 4: 311.

336-337 *The History of Parliament 1690–1715*, 3: 814; *Visitations of England and Wales, Notes*, 5: 97; *The Complete Baronetage*, 2: 133; *Lancashire Parish Register Society*, vol. 18, Giles Shaw, trans., *The Registers of the Parish Church of Middleton in the County of Lancaster: Christenings, Burials, and Weddings 1653–1729*, 191.

338-339 Calvert Hanmer, *The Hanmers of Marton and Montford, Salop* (1916), 46; John Nichols, *The History and Antiquities of the County of Leicestershire: Compiled from the Best and Most Ancient Historians; Inquisitions Post Mortem, and Other Valuable Records; Including Also Mr. Burton's Description of the County, Published in 1622; and the Later Collections of Mr. Stavely, Mr. Carte, Mr. Peck, and Sir Thomas Cave*, 4 vols. in 8 (1795–1815), 4: 859; George Lipscomb, *The History and Antiquities of the County of Buckingham*, 4 vols. (1847), 4: 342; Will of William Hanmer of Fenns, Flintshire, 14 June 1746 (codicil – as of Iscoyd – 9 Feb. 1754), Proved at London P.C.C. 30 April 1754 PROB 11/808; Will of Elizabeth Hanmer of Iscoyd 16 Oct. 1773, Proved 4 Nov. 1777 PROB 11/1036.

340-341 *The History of Parliament 1715–1754*, 2: 154; *The Complete Peerage*, 6: 596-97; *Visitation of England and Wales, Notes*, 13: 99; Eduard Georg Ludwig William Howe Graf von Kielmansegg and Erich Friedrich Christian Ludwig Graf von Kielmansegg, *Familien-Chronik der Herren Freiherren und Grafen von Kielmansegg* (1872), Tafel III.

342-343 *The History and Antiquities of the County of Leicestershire*, 2: 1: 267; *The Index Library (British Record Society)*, vol. 60, Thomas Mathews Blagg and F. Arthur Wadsworth, eds., *Abstracts of Nottinghamshire marriage licences*, 255; W. P. W. Phillimore et al., eds., *Nottingham Parish Registers*, 22 vols. (1898-1938), 1: 163; *Bishops' transcripts St. Nicholas' Church Nottingham, 1601–1877* Family History Library film 0503,803.

344-345 Joseph Foster, *Peerage, baronetage, and knightage of the British empire* (1881), 30; *History of the Irish Parliament 1692–1800*, 4: 288-89.

346-347 *Suffolk Green Books*, vol. 4, S. H. A. H[ervey], ed., *Horringer Parish Registers. Baptisms, Marriages, and Burials, with appendixes and biographical notes (1558–1850)*, 215, 338; John Venn and John Archibald Venn, *Alumni Cantabrigienses; A biographical list of all known students, graduates and holders of office at the University of Cambridge, from the earliest times to 1900*, 10 vols. (1922-54), 4: 496; *The Eton College Register 1698–1752*, 244; John Burke, *A Genealogical and Heraldic History of the Commoners of Great Britain and Ireland Enjoying Territorial Possessions or High Official Rank but uninvested with Heritable Honours*, 4 vols. (1836-37), 2: 600; Frank Cundall, *The Governors of Jamaica in the First Half of the Eighteenth Century* (1937), 69; Will of Valentine Munbee of Horningsheath, Suffolk 14 Nov. 1741, Proved at London P.C.C. 1 Feb. 1750/51 PROB 11/786.

348-349 *The Dictionary of National Biography*, 13: 705-6; *Burke's Genealogical and Heraldic History of the Peerage and Baronetage* (1953), 1386; W.S. Sykes, "Notes on Wilcot and Families" (a manuscript at the Wiltshire Archaelogical Society, Devizes).

350-351 "Notes on Wilcot and Families"; *[The Victoria] History of Wiltshire*, 15 vols. in 16 (1953-), 10: 194; Reginald Morshead Glencross, ed., "Parish registers of Bodmin, Cornwall," 2 vols. in 4 (undated, unpaginated, at the Family History Library, Salt Lake City, Utah), 1: 2: 1, 2; *Wiltshire Family History Society*, 1999-2000 vol., *The Bishops' Transcripts and Parish Registers of Wilcot, baptisms & burials, 1564–1837 and Huish, baptisms & burials, 1603–1837*, 87, 92; Will of George Wroughton 16 June 1779, Proved at London P.C.C. 2 Aug. 1779 PROB 11/1056; Will of Susanna Wroughton, Widow of Wilcot House, Wiltshire 16 Dec. 1815, codicil 13 Jan. 1816, Proved at London P.C.C. 6 April 1816 PROB 11/1579.

352-355 See 132-135.

356-357 *The Complete Peerage*, 5: 266.

358-359 *Oxford Dictionary of National Biography*, 32: 275-76; *The History of Parliament 1754-1790*, 3: 17; *The Complete Baronetage*, 5:100; George Baker, *The History and Antiquities of the County of Northampton*, 2 vols. (1822-41), 1: 141; John Edwin Cussans, *History of Hertfordshire, Containing an Account of the Descents of the Various Manors, Pedigrees of Families Connected with the County, Antiquities, Local Customs, &c., &c.: Chiefly Compiled from Original Mss., in the Record Office and British Museum, Parochial Registers, Local Archives and Collections in the Possession of Private Families*, 8 parts in 3 vols. (1870-81), 1: 1: 101; *Parish Church of Stoke-Poges (Buckinghamshire) Registers 1563–1753* Family History Library film 0924,121.

360-361 *The Complete Peerage*, 3: 14; Joan Wake, *The Brudenells of Deene* (1953), 270-79.

362-363 *The History of Parliament 1715–1754*, 1: 463; *The Complete Baronetage*, 1: 156; *Registers of St. Michael, Penkivel, Cornwall: Christenings, 1547–1958* Family History Library film 0226,184.

364-365 *The History of Parliament 1754–1790*, 2: 249-50; "Family of Cooke," "Pedigree of Cooke," *Miscellanea Genealogica et Heraldica*, 2nd series, 4 [1892]: 152; Charles Humble Dudley Ward, *The family of Twysden and Twisden; their history and archives from an original by Sir John Ramskill Twisden, 12th baronet of Bradbourne* (1939), 297.

366-367 *The Complete Baronetage*, 3: 59; *Parish Registers of Radley, Berkshire 1599–1837* Family History Library film 1040,564; *St. Anne's Church (Soho, Westminster) Parish Registers 1686–1931* Family History Library film 0918,606.

368-369 *Oxford Dictionary of National Biography*, 33: 359-61; *The Complete Peerage*, 10: 838-39.

370-371 *Oxford Dictionary of National Biography*, 31: 430-31; *The Complete Peerage*, 8: 153; *The Scots Peerage*, 5: 480-81; *The Knights of England*, 1: 79; *Parish Registers for St. James's Church, Westminster, 1685–1881* Family History Library film 1042,313.

372-375 See 332-335.

376-377 *The History of Parliament 1754–1790*, 2: 68-69; *The Complete Baronetage*, 5: 352; *The Register Book of Marriages Belonging to the Parish of St. George, Hanover Square, in the County of Middlesex, 1725 to 1837*, 11: 18; *Publications of the Harleian Society, Register Series*, vol. 50, W. Bruce Bannerman et al., *The Registers of St. Stephen, Walbrook, and St. Benet Sherehog, London, 1716 to 1860*, 208-9; *Parish registers for St. James' Church, Westminster, 1685–1881* Family History Library film 1042,307, items 2-3; *The Gentleman's Magazine* 36 [1766]: 103.

378-379 David C. A. Agnew, *Protestant exiles from France in the reign of Louis XIV; or, The Huguenot refugees and their descendants in Great Britain and Ireland*, 3 vols. (1871-74), 2: 127; Mervyn Archdall, *The Peerage of Ireland; or, a genealogical history of the present nobility of that kingdom with Engravings of their Paternal Coats of Arms. Collected from public records, authentic Manuscripts, approved Historians, well-attested Pedigrees, and Personal Information, by John Lodge, 2nd edition. Revised, enlarged and continued to the Present Time*, 7 vols. (1789), 2: 148.

380-381 *The Complete Peerage*, 7: 90, 2: 82; *Parish registers for St. James' Church, Westminster, 1685–1881* Family History Library film 1042,307, items 2-3.

382-383 *The Family of Twysden and Twisden*, 299, 301, 303-5; *The Complete Baronetage*, 1: 75, note b; Sir Bernard Burke and Ashworth Peter Burke, *A Genealogical and Heraldic Dictionary of the Peerage and Baronetage* (1913), 1914; Hugh Montgomery-Massingberd, *Burke's Irish Family Records* (1976), 215; *Publications of the Harleian Society, Register Series*, vol. 26, John W. Clay, *The Registers of St. Paul's Cathedral, 1697 to 1899*, 136.

384-385 *Burke's Genealogical and Heraldic History of the Peerage and Baronetage* (1953), 788; *Journal of the Cork Historical & Archeological Society*, 2nd series, vol. 30, George Berkeley, "History of the Lavallins," pedigree facing 10, 14, 75.

386-387 *Burke's Irish Family Records*, 574; Louis M. Cullen, *The Irish Brandy Houses of Eighteenth-Century France* (2000), 71, 73; *Oxford Dictionary of National Biography*, 25: 386.

394-397 *Burke's Irish Family Records*, 357.

398-399 *Burke's Irish Family Records*, 906.

400-401 Peter Townend, ed., *Burke's Genealogical and Heraldic History of the Peerage, Baronetage and Knightage* (1970), 305.

406-407 *Bishops' transcripts, 1600–1837, Parish Church of Rotherham* Family History Library film 0919,315.

412-413 Henry Wagner, "Pedigree of Guinand," *Miscellanea Genealogica et Heraldica*, 4th series, 4 [1912]: 270; *Publications of the Harleian Society, Register Series*, vol. 32, W. Bruce Bannerman, *The Registers of St. Martin Outwich, London, 1670 to 1873*, 117.

414-415 Henry Wagner, "Huguenot Refugee family of Yvonnet," *The Genealogist: A Quarterly Magazine of Genealogical, Antiquarian, Topographical and Heraldic Research*, New Series 28 [1912]: 88; *Dulwich College Church (Camberwell [sic]) Parish register transcripts, 1616–1837* Family History Library film 0434,254.

424-425 Francis James Dallett, "The Inter-Colonial Grimstone Boude and his Family," *The Genealogist* 2 [1981]: 76-79.

426-427 Gary Boyd Roberts and William Addams Reitwiesner, *American Ancestors and Cousins of The Princess of Wales* (1984), 76; Helen Van Uxem Cubberley, *Newbold Family Notes* (1937), 18-22.

440-441 *American Ancestors and Cousins of The Princess of Wales*, 27; Benjamin W. Dwight, *The History of the Descendants of Elder John Strong of Northampton, Mass.*, 2 vols. (1871), 1: 330; 2: 986.

442-443 *American Ancestors and Cousins of The Princess of Wales*, 27; Ruby Parke Anderson and Elizabeth Miller Hunter Ruppert, *The Parke Scrapbook...*, 3 vols. (1965-66), 3: 14; *Vital Records of Norwich 1659–1848*, 2 vols. (1913), 1: 64.

446-447 Francis James Dallett, "Captain Peter Young and Descendants: Further Philadelphia Roots of the Princess of Wales," *The Pennsylvania Genealogical Magazine* 33 [1984]: 187.

456-457 William Temple, *The Thanage of Fermartyn including the district commonly called Formartine, its proprietors: with genealogical deductions, its parishes, ministers, churches, churchyards, antiquities, &c* (1894), 392; *Parish Church of Aberdour (Aberdeenshire) Registers, 1698–1854* Family History Library film 0091,252.

480-481 Alexander Dingwall Fordyce, *Family Records of the Name of Dingwall Fordyce in Aberdeenshire* (1885), 188; *Parish registers of Old Meldrum, Aberdeen 1713–1854* Family History

Library film 0993,351; Testament Testamentar and Inventory of Patrick Littlejohn, merchant of Old Meldrum 7 Jan. 1738, registered 8 June 1738, inventory 22 Feb. 1740 Aberdeen Commissary Court CC1/6/21.

484-485 *Oxford Dictionary of National Biography*, 10: 864; *The Thanage of Fermartyn*, 89–90; Charles John Guthrie, *Genealogy of the descendants of Reverend Thomas Guthrie, D.D., and Mrs. Anne Burns or Guthrie: connected chiefly with the families of Chalmers and Trail, to which Mrs. Guthrie belonged through her mother, Mrs. Christina Chalmers or Burns, and her great-grandmother, Mrs. Susannah Trail or Chalmers; also incidental references to the families of Guthrie and Burns* (1902), 27-28, 39; *Parish Registers of Montrose — Baptisms v. 3 1697–1732* Family History Library film 0993,496.

486-487 *Genealogy of the Descendants of Rev. Thomas Guthrie, D.D. and Mrs. Anne Burns*, 26; A. Dingwall-Fordyce, *Addenda to the Family Records of Dingwall-Fordyce* (1888), l; A. Alistair N. Tayler and H. A. Henrietta Tayler, *The House of Forbes* (1937), 462-63; *Parish registers of St. Nicholas, Aberdeen: Baptisms vol. vii 1704–1734* FHL film 0991,136; *Parish registers of St. Martin's-in-the-Fields, Westminster, Marriages 1658–1757* Family History Library film 0561,155.

488-489 *Family Records of the Name of Dingwall Fordyce in Aberdeenshire*, 17; *Parish registers of Rothwell, Yorkshire 1599–1780* Family History Library film 0990,764; *The Publications of the Yorkshire Parish Register Society*, vol. 27, George Denison Lumb, ed., *The Registers of the Parish Church of Rothwell, Co. York*, 312.

490-491 *Family Records of the Name of Dingwall Fordyce in Aberdeenshire*, 217; *The Registers of the parish church of Leeds* Family History Library film 0599,919.

492-493 Vere Langford Oliver, "Pedigree of the family of Dingwall of Brucklay," *Miscellanea Genealogica et Heraldica*, 4th series, 5 [1914]: 4; *Family Records of the Name of Dingwall Fordyce in Aberdeenshire*, 66; *Parish Church of Turriff (Aberdeenshire) Registers, 1696–1769* Family History Library film 0993,303.

494-495 Alexander MacDonald Munro, *Memorials of the Aldermen, Provosts and Lord Provosts of Aberdeen 1272–1895* (1897), 226-31; *Parish registers of St. Nicholas, Aberdeen: Baptisms vol. vii 1704–1734* Family History Library film 0991,136.

500-501 *The Thanage of Fermartyn*, 642; *Parish Registers of Old Machar — Baptisms vol. iii 1721–1763* Family History Library film 0991,206.

502-503 *The Thanage of Fermartyn*, 629; *Parish registers of Kemnay, 1660–1854* Family History Library film 0993,195; *Parish Registers of New Machar: vol. 1. Baptisms, 1676–1699, 1713–1819; marriages, 1676–1698, 1717–1819; burials, 1738–1820* Family History Library film 0993,349 .

504-505 *The House of Forbes*, 304; *The Thanage of Fermartyn*, 155, 341; *Parish registers of St. Nicholas, Aberdeen: Baptisms vol. vii 1704–1734* FHL film 0991,136; *Parish registers of Tyrie, 1710–1854* Family History Library film 0993,305; Testament Testamentar and Inventory of George Forbes of Upper Boyndlie 30 Dec. 1794 Aberdeen Commissary Court CC1/6/57.

506-507 *The Thanage of Fermartyn*, 157-59; A. Alistair N. Tayler and H. A. Henrietta Tayler, *The Book of the Duffs*, 2 vols. (1914), 1: 391; *Parish registers of Forgue, 1684–1854*, Family History Library film 0993,183; Testament Dative and Inventory of Alexander Morison of Bognie 30 May 1809 Aberdeen Commissary Court CC1/6/72.

Ninth Generation

512-513 George E. Cokayne et al., *The Complete Peerage*, 14 vols. in 15 (1910-98), 12: 1: 484-85; Charles Spencer, Earl Spencer, *The Spencer Family: A Personal History of an English Family* (2003); *Publications of the Harleian Society, Register Series*, vol. 30, Willoughby A. Littledale, *The Registers St. Vedast, Foster Lane, 1558 to 1836, and St. Michael Le Quern, 1558 to 1837*, 26; *Publications of the Harleian Society, Visitation Series*, vol. 23, Joseph Lemuel Chester and George J. Armytage, *Allegations for Marriage Licences issued by the Dean and Chapter of Westminster, 1558–1699; Also for those issued by the Vicar-General of the Archbishop of Canterbury, 1660–1679*, 107.

514-515 *The Complete Peerage*, 8: 491-97; Henry Steele Commager, arr., *Churchill's History of the English Speaking Peoples* (1995), 232-50; Winston Spencer Churchill, *Marlborough, his Life and Times*, 7 vols. (1933-38); *The Dictionary of National Biography, founded in 1882 by George Smith, edited by Sir Leslie Stephen and Sir Sidney Lee*, 2nd ed., 22 vols. (1885–1901; reprinted 1908-9), 4: 315-41; Ophelia Field, *Sarah Churchill, Duchess of Marlborough, The Queen's Favourite* (2003).

516-517 *The Complete Peerage*, 3: 67-68, 6: 89; J. L. Vivian, *The visitations of Cornwall, comprising the Heralds' visitations of 1530, 1573, & 1620* (1887), 195; Joseph Foster, *London Marriage Licences, 1521–1869* (1887), 249; *Publications of the Harleian Society, Visitation Series*, vol. 10, Joseph Lemuel Chester, ed., *The Marriage, Baptismal and Burial Registers of the Collegiate Church or Abbey of St. Peter, Westminster*, 367; *Parish Church of Kilkhampton (Cornwall) register, 1539–1839* Family History Library film 0897,356.

518-519 Romney Sedgwick, *The History of Parliament: The House of Commons 1715–1754*, 2 vols. (1971), 2: 554; *Publications of the Harleian Society, New Series*, vol. 10, G. D. Squibb, ed., *The Visitation of Hampshire and the Isle of Wight 1686 made by Sir Henry St. George, Knight, Clarenceux King of Arms*, 54; George E. Cokayne, *The Complete Baronetage, 1611–1880*, 5 vols. (1900-6), 1: 66; *St. Andrew, Holborn, Middlesex Parish registers, 1556–1934* Family History Library film 0374,349.

520-521 John Maclean, *Historical and Genealogical Memoir of the Family of Poyntz, or, Eight Centuries of an English House* (1886), 198; A. W. Cornelius Hallen, *The Registers of St. Botolph, Bishopsgate, London*, 3 vols. (1889-93), 1: 190; Gary Boyd Roberts, *The Royal Descents of 600 Immigrants to the American Colonies or the United States: Who Were Themselves Notable or Left Descendants Notable in American History* (2004; revised and reissued 2006), 321; Douglas Richardson, *Plantagenet Ancestry: A Study in Medieval and Colonial Families* (2004), 560.

By his first wife, Newdigate Poyntz was the maternal grandfather of Thomas Owsley of Virginia.

522-523 *Historical and Genealogical Memoir of the Family of Poyntz*, 202; *Publications of the Harleian Society, Visitation Series*, vol. 13, Walter C. Metcalfe, ed., *The Visitations of Essex by Hawley, 1552, Hervey 1558, Cooke 1570, Raven 1612 and Owen and Lilly, 1634, to which are added Miscellaneous Essex Pedigrees from various Harleian Manuscripts and an appendix containing Berry's Essex Pedigrees. Parts I & II*, 492; *St. Giles Cripplegate Church (London) Registers, 1559–1936* Family History Library film 0380,199; Will of Stephen Monteage, Merchant of All Hallows on the Wall, City of London, 26 June 1685, Proved at London P.C.C. 26 Nov. 1687 PROB 11/389.

524-525 *The Complete Peerage*, 9: 200-2.

526-527 Marguerite Syvret and Joan Stevens, *Balleine's History of Jersey* (1981), 163; E.M. Boyle, *Sixty-Four "Quartiers" of Major Gerald Edmund Boyle, and his brothers and sister* (1882); *Parish registers of Waltham-St. Lawrence, 1559–1845* Family History Library film 0088,466; A. W. Cornelius Hallen, *The Registers of St. Botolph, Bishopsgate, London,* 3 vols. (1889-93), 1: 504; Will of The Honorable Thomas Collier, Colonel of Jersey, 8 Feb. 1714/15, codicil 16 June 1715, Proved 2 Nov. 1715 PROB 11/5.

528-529 *The Complete Baronetage,* 2: 398; *Publications of the Harleian Society, Register Series,* vol. 39, Willoughby Littledale, *The Registers of St. Bene't and St. Peter, Paul's Wharf, London, 1607 to 1837,* 34, 45; *London Marriage Licences, 1521–1869,* 130.

532-533 *Oxford Dictionary of National Biography,* 60 vols. (2004), 56: 391-92; Peter Townend, ed., *Burke's Genealogical and Heraldic History of the Peerage, Baronetage and Knightage* (1970), 786.

534-535 *Journal of the County Kildare Archaeological Society,* vol. 4, Lord Walter FitzGerald, "Patrick Sarsfield, Earl of Lucan, with an account of his family and their connection with Lucan and Tully," 119; Antonia Fraser, *Royal Charles* (1979), 137; Lord George Scott, *Lucy Walter, Wife or Mistress* (1947), 189-200.

544-545 Eveline Cruickshanks, Stuart Handley and David Hayton, *The History of Parliament: The House of Commons 1690–1715,* 5 vols. (2002), 5: 409-41; B. D. Henning, *The History of Parliament: The House of Commons 1660–1690,* 3 vols. (1983), 3: 411-20; *Oxford Dictionary of National Biography,* 49: 871-75; *The Complete Baronetage,* 1: 34; *Publications of the Harleian Society, Visitation Series,* vol. 92, J. B. Whitmore, ed., *London Visitation Pedigrees, 1664,* 143; J. L. Vivian, *The visitations of the county of Devon, comprising the heralds' visitations of 1531, 1564, & 1620* (1895), 703.

546-547 *London Visitation Pedigrees, 1664,* 92: 124; *Publications of the Harleian Society, Visitation Series,* vol. 8, George W. Marshall, ed., *Le Neve's Pedigrees of the Knights made by King Charles II, King James II, King William III and Queen Mary, King William alone, and Queen Anne* (1873), 302, and vol. 48, Sir George J. Armytage, Bart., ed., *Obituary Prior to 1800 (as far as relates to England, Scotland, and Ireland), Compiled by Sir William Musgrave, 6th Bart. Of Hayton Castle, co. Cumberland, and entitled by him "A General Nomenclator and Obituary, with reference to the books where the persons are mentioned, and where some account of their character is to be found,"* 269; *London Marriage Licences, 1521–1869,* 1224; Will of John Shorter, Merchant of London 30 Dec. 1702, Proved at London P.C.C. 15 Feb. 1706/7 (also proved 10 June 1707) PROB 11/49.

548-549 *The Complete Peerage,* 6: 43-45, 1: 218; *The Complete Baronetage,* 1: 153; *The Dictionary of National Biography,* 7: 205.

550-551 *The History of Parliament 1660–1690,* 3: 453-54; *The Complete Peerage,* 2: 52, 6: 88.

552-553 *The Complete Peerage,* 12: 2: 306-7; Alison Weir, *Britain's Royal Families: The Complete Genealogy* (1989; revised 1996), 263; *The Complete Baronetage,* 2: 214; *The Dictionary of National Biography,* 20: 473.

554-555 *The Complete Baronetage,* 2: 221.

556-557 *The History of Parliament 1690–1715,* 5: 775-84; *The Complete Peerage,* 10: 81-84; John Venn and John Archibald Venn, *Alumni Cantabrigienses; A biographical list of all known students, graduates and holders of office at the University of Cambridge, from the earliest times to 1900,*

10 vols. (1922-54), 4: 325; *London Visitation Pedigrees, 1664,* 92: 124; *Le Neve's Pedigrees,* 8: 302; *The Registers of St. Bene't and St. Peter, Paul's Wharf, London, 1607 to 1837,* 38: 62.

558-559   *The Complete Peerage,* 12: 2: 309, note a.

560-561   William Betham, *The Baronetage of England, or, the History of the English Baronets, and Such Baronets of Scotland, as Are of English Families: With Genealogical Tables, and Engravings of Their Armorial Bearings; Collected from the Present Baronetages, Approved Historians, Public Records, Authentic Manuscripts, Well Attested Pedigrees, and Personal Information,* 5 vols. (1801-5), 4: 108.

562-563   Charles Edward Pitman, *History and pedigree of the family of Pitman of Dunchideock, Exeter, and their collaterals, and of the Pitmans of Alphington, Norfolk and Edinburgh: with part pedigrees and acccounts of families connected by marriage* (1920), 120.

564-565   Leslie G. Pine, ed., *Burke's Genealogical and Heraldic History of the Peerage, Baronetage and Knightage* (1956), 2202; *Publications of the Harleian Society, Register Series,* vol. 3, Joseph Lemuel Chester, *The Register Book of St. Dionis Backchurch Parish (City of London), 1538 to 1754,* 39; *Publications of the Harleian Society, Visitation Series,* vol. 34, George J. Armytage, *Allegations for Marriage Licences issued by the Vicar-General of the Archbishop of Canterbury,* 286; Will of Susanna Vansittart, Widow of Ormond Street, St. Andrew Holborn, Middlesex 13 April 1725, Proved at London P.C.C. 4 April 1726 PROB 11/608.

566-567   *The Complete Baronetage,* 4: 47; *Publications of the Harleian Society, Visitation Series,* vol. 39, John W. Clay, ed., *Familiae Minorum Gentium. Diligentiâ Josephi Hunter, Sheffieldiensis, S.A.S.,* 979.

568-569   *The History of Parliament 1690–1715,* 5: 721-22; *The Complete Peerage,* 8: 34-35; *St. Andrew Undershaft Church (London) Registers 1558–1901* Family History Library film 0374,408.

570-571   James Raine, *The History and Antiquities of North Durham, as Subdivided into the Shires of Norham, Island and Bedlington, which from the Saxon Period until the Year 1844, Constituted Parcels of the County Palatine of Durham, but Are Now United to the County of Northumberland* (1852), 319; *Parish Church of Berwick-upon-Tweed (Northumberland) Register Transcripts, 1573–1812* Family History Library film 0094,987.

572-573   Robert Surtees, *The History and Antiquities of the County Palatine of Durham: Compiled from Original Records, Preserved in Public Repositories and Private Collections, and Illustrated by Engravings of Architectural and Monumental Antiquities, Portraits of Eminent Persons &c., &c.,* 4 vols. (1816-40), 3: 295; *Alumni Cantabrigienses,* 4: 48; John William Clay, ed., *Dugdale's Visitation of Yorkshire in 1665–6, with additions,* 3 vols. (1899-1917), 2: 352.

574-575   *The History and Antiquities of the County Palatine of Durham,* 3: 295; *Musgrave's Obituary,* 46: 307.

576-577   Thomas George Baring, Earl of Northbrook, et al., eds., *Journals and correspondence from 1808 to 1852, of Sir Francis Thornhill Baring afterwards Lord Northbrook, compiled and edited by his son Thomas George, Earl of Northbrook* (1905), 272, 274; *Deutsches Geschlechterbuch (Genealogisches Handbuch Bürgerlicher Familien),* vol. 102, "Baring, v. Baring, Baring v. Wallerode: Freiherr v. Baring, Baring-Gould, Baring Baronet of Larkbear, Baring Baronet of Nubia House, Baring Baron of Hillburton, Baring Baron Viscount und Earl of Cromer, Viscount Errington, Baring Baron Viscount und Earl of Northbrook, Baring Baron Revelstoke, aus Groningen in Friesland," 97.

578-579 *Journals and correspondence from 1808 to 1852, of Sir Francis Thornhill Baring afterwards Lord Northbrook*, 274; *Deutsches Geschlechterbuch (Genealogisches Handbuch Bürgerlicher Familien)*, 102: 100.

580-581 *Parish register transcripts, Church of Crediton, Devon 1558–1843* Family History Library film 0917,184; *Registers of the Parish Church of Westbury Wiltshire* Family History Library film 1279,369.

582-583 *Oxford Dictionary of National Biography*, 3: 820; *Parish register transcripts, St. Mary Major Church (Exeter) 1561–1837* Family History Library film 0917,103.

584-585 Will of Gerrard Herring, Draper of Cambridge, Cambridgeshire 8 Aug. 1701, Proved at London P.C.C. 2 May 1704 PROB 11/476; Will of Mary Herring, Widow of Cambridge, Cambridgeshire 15 Jan. 1714/15, Proved at London P.C.C. 24 May 1715 PROB 11/546.

586-587 W. P. W. Phillimore et al., eds., *Cambridgeshire Parish Registers*, 8 vols. (1907-27), 2: 33; *The History of Parliament 1690–1715*, 5: 813; Will of Isaac Watlington of Cambridge, Cambridgeshire 1 Jan. 1699, Proved at London P.C.C. 10 Feb. 1701 PROB 11/459.

588-589 *Publications of the Harleian Society, Visitation Series*, vol. 94, J. W. Walker, ed., *Yorkshire Pedigrees*, 144; *Dugdale's Visitation of Yorkshire in 1665–6*, 1:284.

590-591 *Yorkshire Pedigrees*, 94: 144; *The parish registers of Whitby, 1600–1676* Family History Library film 0599,996, item 6.

592-593 Joseph Jackson Howard and Frederick Arthur Crisp, *Visitation of England and Wales, Notes*, 14 vols. (1896-1921), 5: 6; Algernon Tudor Craig, "Lane of Campsea Ash, co. Suffolk," *Miscellanea Genealogica et Heraldica*, 5th series, 2 [1918]: 59.

594-595 *Rayne, Essex, Christenings, Burials & Marriages, 1558–1664* Family History Library film 1472,666, item 20; *Panfield, Essex, Christenings, Burials & Marriages, 1569–1711* Family History Library film 1472,590, item 23; Will of Robert Hicks of Braintree, Essex 28 Sept. 1737, Proved at Chelmsford 6 May 1752 E.R.O. BR23/101; Will of Sarah Hicks, Widow of Rivenhall, Essex 19 Nov. 1754, Proved at P.C.C. 22 March 1755 PROB 11/814.

596-597 G. H. Holley, "Pedigrees compiled from the parish registers, wills, monumental inscriptions, court records, etc., Norfolk County England" (a 7 vol. manuscript at the Family History Library, Salt Lake City, Utah), 2: 107-9.

598-599 *Alumni Cantabrigienses*, 3: 66; *The Gentleman's Magazine* 35 [1765]: 539; *Parish registers of St. Martin's-in-the-Fields, Westminster, Marriages 1658–1757* Family History Library film 0561,155; "Fenns Manuscripts of Suffolk and Norfolk" (manuscripts in the Norman Collection, Salford, Lancashire), 85; *The Registers of St. Bene't and St. Peter, Paul's Wharf, London, 1607 to 1837*, 40: 110; Will of Weyman Lee of the Inner Temple, Middlesex 10 June 1765, Proved 26 Nov. 1765 PROB 11/913.

600-601 Gabriel Girod de l'Ain, *Les Thellusson histoire d'une famille* (1977), 34.

602-603 Ir. J. C. Deknatel, "le Boullenger-van Roubais," *De Nederlandsche Leeuw: Maandblad van het Koninklijk Nederlandsch Genootschap voor Geslacht- en Wapenkunde* 87 [1970]: 202.

604-605 L. H. Bouwens and B. G. Bouwens, *A Thousand Ancestors* (1935), viii: 83; Joseph Foster, *Alumni Oxonienses: The members of the University of Oxford, 1500–1714: their parentage, birthplace, and year of birth, with a record of their degrees. Being the matriculation register of the University, alphabetically arranged, revised and annotated*, 4 vols. (1891-92), 3-4: 1675; *Parish Registers of Chichester, St. Peter the Great: 1679–1812* Family History Library film 0504,431.

606–607 *A Thousand Ancestors*, viii: 84; *Alumni Oxonienses: The members of the University of Oxford, 1500–1714*, 1: 179; *Parish Registers of St. Mary Magdalen Old Fish Street Church: marriages, 1664–1754* Family History Library film 0374,490; Will of John Brideoake, Rector of Swerford in the diocese of Oxford 2 March 1724, Proved at London P.C.C. 9 May 1727 PROB 11/615; Will of Reverend Ralph Brideoake, Archdeacon of Winchester and Rector of the Church of St. Maries near Southampton of Hampshire 9 Nov. 1742, Proved 17 May 1743 PROB 11/726.

608–609 *History and pedigree of the family of Pitman*, 59; Vivien Allen, *The Bulteels: The Story of a Huguenot Family* (2004), 42-43; Will of Samuel Bulteel of Tavistock 8 June 1682, Proved in the registry of the Bishop of Exeter 17 Aug. 1682.

610–611 "The family of Croker," *Herald & Genealogist* 8 [1874]: 380; *The History of Parliament 1690–1715*, 3: 792; *Parish register transcripts of Yealmpton (Devonshire), 1600–1850* Family History Library film 0917,560; *Bishops' transcripts, Parish Church of Holbeton 1620–1850* Family History Library film 0917,144; *St. Thomas the Apostle's Church (Exeter) Register Transcripts, 1554–1837* Family History Library film 0916,843.

612–613 *The Complete Peerage*, 2: 99.

614–615 *Parish Register of Baldock, Herts: Baptisms and burials 1710–1792* Family History Library film 0991,305; *Registers of Walkern, Herts: Baptisms 1559–1812* Family History Library film 1040,799, items 6-9; *Bishops' Transcripts, parish church of Ardeley, Herts: Marriages 1604–1850* Family History Library film 0569,700.

616–617 Sir Bernard Burke, *A Genealogical and Heraldic Dictionary of the Peerage and Baronetage* (1879), 962; Sir Bernard Burke, *A Genealogical and Heraldic Dictionary of the Peerage and Baronetage* (1881), 1003; *Parish register transcripts Modbury, Devon, Marriages 1553–1565, 1601–1837* Family History Library film 0916,862.

618–619 *A Genealogical and Heraldic Dictionary of the Peerage and Baronetage* (1879), 962; *Parish register transcripts, Modbury, Devon, Baptisms 1599–1837* Family History Library film 0916,861; *Parish register transcripts Modbury, Devon, Marriages 1553–1565, 1601–1837* Family History Library film 0916,862.

624–625 Northumberland County History Commission, *A history of Northumberland*, 15 vols. (1893-1940), 2: 352.

626–627 *A history of Northumberland*, 1: 331.

628–629 *The History and Antiquities of the County Palatine of Durham*, 2: 15, 19; Percy W. Hedley, *Northumberland Families*, 2 vols. (1968), 1: 174; *Parish Church of Lanchester (Durhamshire) Register Transcripts* Family History Library film 0091,099; *All Saints Church (Newcastle-upon-Tyne, Northumberland) register transcripts, 1600–1720* Family History Library film 0095,005.

630–631 Henry A. Ogle, *Ogle and Bothal: Or, A History of the Baronies of Ogle, Bothal, and Hepple, and of the Families of Ogle and Bertram, Who Held Possession of Those Baronies and Other Property in the County of Northumberland and Elsewhere; Showing Also How the Property Descended into Other Hands: To Which Is Added Accounts of Several Branches of Families Bearing the Name of Ogle Settled in Other Counties and Countries; with Appendices and Illustrations Compiled from Ancient Records and Other Sources* (1902), 127-28; *The History and Antiquities of the County Palatine of Durham*, 3: 322; Will of Elizabeth Ogle, Widow of Kirkley, Northumberland 5 Oct. 1750, Proved P.C.C. 25 May 1751 PROB 11/788.

632-633 *The Complete Peerage*, 2: 170; Major-General Sir John Ponsonby, *The Ponsonby Family* (1929), 199; *Parish registers for St. James' Church, Westminster, 1685–1881* Family History Library film 1042,307, items 2-3.

634-635 *The Complete Peerage*, 4: 344; David Williamson, "The Ancestry of Lady Diana Spencer," *The Genealogists' Magazine: Official Organ of the Society of Genealogists* 20 [1980-82]: 192; *Parish Registers for St. Martin-in-the-Fields 1550–1926* Family History Library film 0560,371; *Parish registers of St. Andrew Holborn: Baptisms 1693–1704* Family History Library film 0374,351.

HRH The Prince of Wales and Diana, Princess of Wales, both descend from this couple.

636-637 *The Complete Peerage*, 9: 31; *The History of Parliament 1690–1715*, 4: 826-35; Gary Boyd Roberts, "Royal Descents and American Cousins of Sophie Helen Rhys-Jones," *NEHGS NEXUS* 16 [1999]: 116-19.

HRH The Countess of Wessex and Diana, Princess of Wales, both descend from this couple.

638-639 Hugh Montgomery-Massingberd, *Burke's Irish Family Records* (1976), 1158; *Parish Register Society of Dublin*, vol. 3, Henry F. Berry, *The Registers of the church of St. Michan, Dublin, 1636 to 1685*, 118; George Dames Burtchaell and Thomas Ulick Sadleir, eds., *Alumni Dublinenses; a register of the students, graduates, professors and provosts of Trinity college in the University of Dublin (1593–1860)* (1935), 834.

640-641 *The Complete Peerage*, 1: 6; Sir James Balfour Paul, *The Scots Peerage*, 9 vols. (1904-14), 1: 62-63; *London Marriage Licences, 1521–1869*, 613; *The Marriage, Baptismal and Burial Registers of the Collegiate Church or Abbey of St. Peter, Westminster Registers of the Collegiate Church or Abbey of St. Peter, Westminster*, 10: 365, 422; *Parish Registers for St. Martin-in-the-Fields 1550–1926* Family History Library film 0560,371.

642-643 *Oxford Dictionary of National Biography*, 6: 600-1, 620-21, 13: 927-28; *The History of Parliament 1690–1715*, 3: 782-84; Henry Holman Drake, *Hasted's history of Kent: corrected, enlarged and continued to the present time, from the manuscript collections of the late Rev. Thomas Streatfield and the late Rev. Lambert Blackwell Larking, the public records, and other sources. pt. 1. The hundred of Blackheath* (1886), 138; *The Dictionary of National Biography*, 12: 440-41; *The Marriage, Baptismal and Burial Registers of the Collegiate Church or Abbey of St. Peter, Westminster Registers of the Collegiate Church or Abbey of St. Peter, Westminster*, 10: 302; Sarah Churchill, *Duchess of Marlborough, The Queen's Favourite*, 321-22, 369.

644-645 Arthur Stephens Dyer, "Pedigree of Moyle of Bake, St. Germans, Cornwall," *Miscellanea Genealogica et Heraldica*, 5th series, 9 [1932]: 350; *The History of Parliament 1690–1715*, 4: 651; Will of Joseph Moyle of Southampton, Hampshire 13 April 1741, Proved at London P.C.C. 14 April 1742 PROB 11/717; Will of Catherine Moyle, Widow of Southampton, Hampshire 22 April 1748, Proved at London P.C.C. 20 March 1775 PROB.

646-647 *The visitations of Cornwall*, 58; *The History of Parliament 1714–1754*, 1: 506; Jean Goodman and David Williamson, *Debrett's Book of the Royal Engagement* (1986), 130; *Alumni Oxonienses: The members of the University of Oxford, 1500–1714*, 1-2: 208; *Parish Church of Pelynt (Cornwall) transcripts and bishops' transcripts 1641–1837* Family History Library film 0916,953; Will of John Francis Buller of Morval, Cornwall 4 Nov. 1745, Proved 1 Feb. 1751/52 PROB 11/792.

648-649 *The History of Parliament 1690–1715*, 3: 906-8; *The Complete Peerage*, 9: 299; *The Scots Peerage*, 6: 380-81; *St. Andrew, Holborn, Middlesex Parish registers, 1556–1934* Family

History Library film 0374,349; W. P. W. Phillimore and G. E. Cokayne, *London Parish registers, Marriages at St. James' Duke's Place*, 4 vols. (1900-2), 3: 242.

650-651 *The History of Parliament 1715–1754*, 5: 123; *Visitation of England and Wales, Notes*, 7: 144; *The Complete Baronetage*, 5: 74; *Registers of St. Swithin Stone Church London* Family History Library film 0375,020.

652-653 *Pedigrees of the County Families of Yorkshire, comp. by Joseph Foster and authenticated by the members of each family*, 2 vols. (1874), 1: Lascelles; *The Complete Baronetage*, 4: 438-39; *The History of Parliament 1754–1790*, 2: 629-30.

654-655 *Dugdale's Visitation of Yorkshire in 1665–6*, 2: 234; Llewellynn Frederick William Jewitt, ed., *The Reliquary and illustrated archæologist*, 34 vols. in 2 series (1860-94), 8: 48.

656-657 *The Complete Peerage*, 2: 81-82.

658-659 *Oxford Dictionary of National Biography*, 23: 130-31; *The Complete Peerage*, 6: 37-38; *St. Anne's Church (Soho, Westminster) Parish Registers 1686–1931* Family History Library film 0918,606.

See Gary Boyd Roberts, "Royally Descended Immigrant Kin and Presidential Cousins of Sir Winston Churchill," *NEHGS NEXUS* 13 [1996]: 205-6, and his "The Leveson-Gower Progeny: Our 'Whig Cousinage,'" 14 [1997]: 70-73, for a discussion of the 1st Earl Gower's notable progeny.

660-661 *Oxford Dictionary of National Biography*, 21: 360-61; *The Complete Peerage*, 1: 91-93.

662-663 *Oxford Dictionary of National Biography*, 33: 357-59; *The Complete Peerage*, 2: 89-91, 10: 836-38, 6: Appendix F; *The Scots Peerage*, 1: 30-32; *The Marriage, Baptismal and Burial Registers of the Collegiate Church or Abbey of St. Peter, Westminster*, 10: 308-9.

664-665 *The Complete Peerage*, 6: 4; *The Scots Peerage*, 4: 550-52.

666-667 *The History of Parliament 1690–1715*, 4: 42-44; *The Complete Peerage*, 1: 13; *The Scots Peerage*, 1: 90-93.

668-669 *The Complete Baronetage*, 4: 311.

670-671 Keith Stanley Malcolm Scott, *Scott 1118–1923: being a collection of "Scott" pedigrees containing all known male descendants from Buccleuch, Sinton, Harden, Balweary, etc.* (1923), 258; James Paterson, *History of the County of Ayr with a Genealogical Account of the families of Ayrshire*, 2 vols. (1847-52), 1: 416-17.

672-673 *Visitations of England and Wales, Notes*, 5: 97; *The Complete Baronetage*, 2: 133; *London Marriage Licences, 1521–1869*, 367; O. F. G. Hogg, *Further Light on the Ancestry of William Penn* (1964), pedigree.

674-675 *The History of Parliament 1690–1715*, 3: 82-83; *The Complete Baronetage*, 3: 113; *Chetham Society Series: Remains, Historical and Literary, Connected with the Palatine Counties of Lancaster and Chester*, vol. 84, *The Visitation of the County Palatine of Lancaster, Made in the Year 1664–5, by Sir William Dugdale, Knight, Norroy King of Arms*, 15; *Lancashire Parish Register Society*, vol. 18, Giles Shaw, trans., *The Registers of the Parish Church of Middleton in the County of Lancaster: Christenings, Burials, and Weddings 1653–1729*, 177.

676-677 John Nichols, *The History and Antiquities of the County of Leicestershire: Compiled from the Best and Most Ancient Historians; Inquisitions Post Mortem, and Other Valuable Records; Including Also Mr. Burton's Description of the County, Published in 1622; and the Later Collections of Mr. Stavely, Mr. Carte, Mr. Peck, and Sir Thomas Cave*, 4 vols. in 8 (1795–1815), 4: 859;

George Lipscomb, *The History and Antiquities of the County of Buckingham*, 4 vols. (1847), 4: 342; Joseph Foster, *Alumni Oxonienses: The members of the University of Oxford, 1500–1714*, 1-2: 645; *Parish Church of Ludford (Shropshire) register transcripts, 1643–1838* Family History Library film 0510,667; Will of Esther Hanmer, Widow of Bettisfield, Flintshire 2 Oct. 1754, Proved at London P.C.C. 2 Aug. 1770 PROB 11/959.

678-679   Caroline Robbins, *The diary of John Milward, esq., member of Parliament for Derbyshire, September 1666 to May 1668* (1938), xiii; *The History and Antiquities of the County of Leicestershire*, 4: 859; W. P. W. Phillimore et al., eds., *Derbyshire Parish Registers*, 15 vols. (1906-22), 4: 140.

680-681   *Visitation of England and Wales, Notes*, 13: 99; *The Dictionary of National Biography*, 28: 101; *The History of Parliament 1660–1690*, 2: 611-12; *The Complete Peerage*, 6: 596; *London Marriage Licences, 1521–1869*, 718; *Parish registers for St. Martin-in-the-Fields, 1550–1653* Family History Library film 0560,369.

682-683   *Oxford Dictionary of National Biography*, 41: 537-38; Nigel Cawthorne, *Sex Lives of the Kings and Queens of England* (1994), 93; Ragnhild Marie Hatton, *George I, elector and king* (1978), 23-24; Joyce Marlow, *The Life and Times of George I* (1973), 33-34; *The Complete Peerage*, 4: 80-81; Eduard Georg Ludwig William Howe Graf von Kielmansegg and Erich Friedrich Christian Ludwig Graf von Kielmansegg, *Familien-Chronik der Herren Freiherren und Grafen von Kielmansegg* (1872), 120-28; *The Marriage, Baptismal and Burial Registers of the Collegiate Church or Abbey of St. Peter, Westminster*, 10: 313.

684-685   *The History and Antiquities of the County of Leicestershire*, 2: 1: 267, 285.

686-687   *The Index Library (British Record Society)*, vol. 58, Thomas Mathews Blagg and F. Arthur Wadsworth, eds., *Abstracts of Nottinghamshire Marriage Licenses*, 385; W. P. W. Phillimore et al., eds., *Nottingham Parish Registers*, 22 vols. (1898-1938), 13: 9; *The History and Antiquities of the County of Leicestershire*, 3: 394; *West Leake Baptisms, Marriages & Burials 1622–1812* Family History Library film 0503,787; *Alumni Oxonienses: The members of the University of Oxford, 1500–1714*, 3-4: 968.

688-689   P. D. Vigors, "Gore," *Miscellanea Genealogica et Heraldica*, New Series, 4 [1884]: 244; Joseph Foster, *Peerage, baronetage, and knightage of the British empire for 1883*, 2 vols. (1883), 1: 30; *Le Neve's Pedigrees*, 8: 107.

690-691   *The History of Parliament 1660–1690*, 3: 14; *The Gentleman's Magazine* 6 [1736]: 55; *Publications of the Harleian Society, Register Series*, vol. 1, Granville Leveson-Gower, *The Registers of Christening, Burials and Weddings within the Parish of St. Peter's upon Cornhill, London, 1538 to 1666*, 55, and vol. 33, William H. Hunt, *The Registers of St. Paul's Church, Covent Garden, London, 1653 to 1853*, 13; Edith Mary Johnston-Liik, *History of the Irish Parliament 1692–1800: commons, constituencies and statutes*, 6 vols. (2002), 5: 190-91; *Allegations for Marriage Licences issued by the Vicar-General of the Archbishop of Canterbury*, 34: 222.

692-693   R. A. Austen-Leigh, *The Eton College Register 1698–1752* (1927), 244; Frank Cundall, *The Governors of Jamaica in the First Half of the Eighteenth Century* (1937), 69.

696-697   *The History of Parliament 1690–1715*, 4: 896; "Pedigree of Montagu, of Lackham," *Wiltshire Archeological and Natural History Magazine* 3 [1857]: between 86 and 87.

698-701   *Wiltshire Family History Society*, 1999-2000 vol., *The bishop's transcripts and parish registers of Wilcot, baptisms & burials, 1564–1837 and Huish, baptisms & burials, 1603–1837*, 82, 84; W.S. Sykes, "Notes on Wilcot and Families" (a manuscript at the Wiltshire Archaelogical

Society, Devizes); *[The Victoria] History of Wiltshire,* 15 vols. in 16 and index to date (1953–), 10: 194; Will of James Wroughton of Wilcot, Wiltshire 10 May 1745, codicil 26 June 1745; Proved at London P.C.C. 13 Jan. 1745/46 PROB 11/744; Will of Ann Wroughton, Widow of Bath, Somerset 14 May 1760, Proved at London P.C.C. 15 May 1761 PROB 11/866; Will of Robert Eyre, Citizen and Grocer of London 7 Aug. 1718, Proved at London P.C.C. 24 Sept. 1718 PROB 11/565.

702-703 *The visitations of Cornwall,* 335; Arthur Stephens Dyer, "Pedigree of Moyle of Bake, St. Germans, Cornwall," *Miscellanea Genealogica et Heraldica,* 5th series, 9 [1932]: 351; "St. Germans Parish Register, 1590-1837," 2 vols. (1938-39; unpaginated manuscript at the Devon and Cornwall Record Society, Exeter); Will of Susanna Moyle of Bath, Somerset 14 Feb. 1760, Proved at London P.C.C. 10 April 1760 PROB 11/855.

704-708 See 264-268.

712-713 *The Complete Peerage,* 5: 265-66; *The registers of St. Michael-le-Belfry, York, 1565–1778* Family History Library film 0496,806.

714-715 *Collections for a History of Staffordshire,* vol. 5, part 2, H. Sydney Grazebrook, ed., *The Heraldic Visitations of Staffordshire Made by Sir Richard St. George, Norroy, in 1614, and by Sir William Dugdale in the Years 1663 and 1664,* 137; G. Dashwood, *Pedigrees selected from the Visitation of the County of Warwick, begun by Thomas May, Chester, and Gregory King, Rouge Dragon, in Hillary Vacan n, 1682, etc., etc.* (1859), Betham.

716-717 George Baker, *The History and Antiquities of the County of Northampton,* 2 vols. (1822-41), 1: 141; *The Complete Baronetage,* 5: 100.

718-719 *Oxford Dictionary of National Biography,* 12: 471-72; *The History of Parliament 1690–1715,* 3: 640-45; *Alumni Oxonienses: The members of the University of Oxford, 1500–1714,* 1-2: 299; *The History and Antiquities of the County of Northampton,* 1: 141.

720-721 *The Complete Peerage,* 3: 14.

722-723 *Oxford Dictionary of National Biography,* 8: 328-29; *The History of Parliament 1660–1690,* 1: 739-40; Detlev Schwennicke, ed., *Europäische Stammtafeln: Stammtafeln zur Geschichte der Europäischen Staaten,* Neue Folge, 21 vols. (1978-2001), 18: 128; *The Complete Peerage,* 1: 59-61; Gary Boyd Roberts, *Notable Kin: An Anthology of Columns First Published in the* NEHGS NEXUS*, 1986–1995, Volume Two … with contributions by John Anderson Brayton and Richard E. Brenneman* (1999), 216-21.

Lady Marie Thérèse Charlotte Bruce, the only child of Thomas Bruce, 3rd Earl of Elgin and 2nd Earl of Ailsbury by his second wife, married Maximilian Emmanuel, Prince of Hornes, and was an ancestress of the Hohenzollern kings of Romania, recent kings of the Belgians, and the current Grand Duke of Luxembourg, as well as past queens of the Hellenes, Portugal, Italy, and Montenegro.

724-725 *The Complete Baronetage,* 1: 156; B. W. Greenfield, "Pedigree of Dunch of Little Wittenham, Berks.," *Miscellanea Genealogica et Heraldica,* 3rd series, 2 [1898]: 46.

726-727 *The Complete Peerage,* 5: 246; *The Marriage, Baptismal and Burial Registers of the Collegiate Church or Abbey of St. Peter, Westminster,* 10: 36.

728-729 "Family of Cooke," "Pedigree of Cooke," *Miscellanea Genealogica et Heraldica,* 2nd series, 4 [1892]: 152, 173; *Publications of the Harleian Society, Register Series,* vol. 26, John W. Clay, *The Registers of St. Paul's Cathedral, 1697 to 1899,* 8; William A. Shaw, *The Knights of England,* 2 vols. (1906), 2: 280.

730-731 *The Complete Baronetage*, 1: 75; *Hasted's history of Kent*, 1: 195; Charles Humble Dudley Ward, *The family of Twysden and Twisden; their history and archives from an original by Sir John Ramskill Twisden, 12th baronet of Bradbourne* (1939), 293-96.

732-733 *The Complete Baronetage*, 3: 59; *Alumni Oxonienses: The members of the University of Oxford, 1500–1714*, 1-2: 162; John Burke and John Bernard Burke. *A Genealogical and Heraldic History of the Extinct and Dormant Baronetcies of England, Ireland, and Scotland*, 2nd ed. (1844), 400; *The Registers of St. Paul's Cathedral, 1697 to 1899*, 26: 18; Will of Juliana Bowyer, Widow of Windsor Castle, Berkshire 26 Dec. 1746, Proved at London P.C.C. 7 Sept. 1750 PROB 11/782.

734-735 *The Complete Baronetage*, 4: 47; *St. John's Church (Hackney) Parish register transcripts, 1540–1812* Family History Library film 0569,924. See also 566-567.

736-737 See 662-663.

738-739 *The Complete Peerage*, 2: 460-61; *The Marriage, Baptismal and Burial Registers of the Collegiate Church or Abbey of St. Peter, Westminster*, 10: 318.

740-741 *The Complete Peerage*, 8: 152; *The Scots Peerage*, 5: 480.

742-743 *The Complete Peerage*, 6: 536-37, 5: 491-92; *Europäische Stammtafeln, Neue Folge*, 10: 28.

744-751 See 664-671.

752-753 John Edwards Griffith, *Pedigrees of Anglesey and Carnarvonshire families* (1914), 57; *The Complete Baronetage*, 5: 351; *History of the Irish Parliament 1692–1800*, 3: 147.

754-755 *The History of Parliament 1715–1754*, 3: 320; *Musgrave's* Obituary, 47: 343; *The Complete Baronetage*, 5: 352; *The Gentleman's Magazine* 11 [1741]: 332; Philip Morant, *The History and Antiquities of the County of Essex: Compiled from the Best and Most Ancient Historians: from Domesday-Book, Inquisitiones Post Mortem and Other the Most Valuable Records and Mss. &c, the Whole Digested, Improved, Perfected and Brought Down to the Present Time*, 2 vols. (1768), 1: 403.

756-757 David C. A. Agnew, *Protestant exiles from France in the reign of Louis XIV; or, The Huguenot refugees and their descendants in Great Britain and Ireland*, 3 vols. (1871-74), 2: 126-27; *Publications of the Huguenot Society of London*, vol. 19, Thomas Philip Le Fanu, ed., "Registers of the French Church of Portarlington, Ireland," 108; Mervyn Archdall, *The Peerage of Ireland; or, a genealogical history of the present nobility of that kingdom with Engravings of their Paternal Coats of Arms. Collected from public records, authentic Manuscripts, approved Historians, well-attested Pedigrees, and Personal Information, by John Lodge*, 2nd ed. Revised, enlarged and continued to the Present Time, 7 vols. (1789), 2: 148.

758-759 "Registers of the French Church of Portarlington, Ireland," 123, and *Publications of the Huguenot Society of London*, vol. 46, Thomas Philip Le Fanu et al., eds., "Dublin and Portarlington veterans: King William III's Huguenot army," 44; Sheelah Ruggles-Brise, "Spencer and Other Pedigrees," *Notes and Queries: A Medium of Inter-Communication for Literary Men, Artists, Antiquaries, Genealogists, etc.*, 186 [1944]: 22; Will of Isaac Hamon of Portarlington, Queen's County, Ireland 19 May 1753, codicil 12 Aug. 1754, Administration 4 April 1755 PROB 11/815.

760-761 *The History of Parliament 1690–1715*, 5: 751-52, 4: 342; *Alumni Cantabrigienses*, 4: 303; *The Complete Peerage*, 7: 89; *The East Anglian: or, Notes and queries on subjects connected with* *the counties of Suffolk, Cambridge, Essex and Norfolk,* vol. 4, George W. Marshall, "Pedigree of the Hernes, of Tibenham, co. Norfolk," 123.

762-763 *The Complete Peerage,* 2: 313-14, 8: 497, note d.

764-765 *The Family of Twysden and Twisden,* 285, 299-302; *The Complete Baronetage,* 1: 75.

766-767 *Oxford Dictionary of National Biography,* 10: 368-69; *Burke's Irish Family Records,* 215; *Alumni Dublinenses,* 139; *History of the Irish Parliament 1692–1800,* 3: 377-81.

768-769 Leslie G. Pine, *Burke's Genealogical and Heraldic History of the Peerage and Baronetage* (1953), 788; Walter Arthur Copinger, *History of the Copingers or Coppingers of the County of Cork, Ireland, and the Counties of Suffolk and Kent, England* (1884), 174.

770-771 *Journal of the Cork Historical & Archeological Society,* 2nd series, vol. 30, George Berkeley, "History of the Lavallins," pedigree facing 10, 77.

772-773 *Burke's Irish Family Records,* 574.

796-797 *Burke's Irish Family Records,* 906.

800-801 *Burke's Genealogical and Heraldic History of the Peerage, Baronetage and Knightage* (1970), 305.

824-825 Henry Wagner, "Pedigree of Guinand," *Miscellanea Genealogica et Heraldica,* 4th series, 4 [1912]: 270; Noel Currer-Briggs and Royston Gambier, *Huguenot Ancestry* (1985), pedigree.

826-827 "Pedigree of Guinand," 270.

828-829 Henry Wagner, "Huguenot Refugee family of Yvonnet," *The Genealogist: A Quarterly Magazine of Genealogical, Antiquarian, Topographical and Heraldic Research,* New series, 28 [1912]: 88.

848-849 Francis James Dallett, "The Inter-Colonial Grimstone Boude and his family," *The Genealogist* 2 [1981]: 79.

852-853 Gary Boyd Roberts and William Addams Reitwiesner, *American Ancestors and Cousins of The Princess of Wales* (1984), 76; Helen Van Uxem Cubberley, *Newbold Family Notes* (1937), 10-17.

854-855 *American Ancestors and Cousins of The Princess of Wales,* 76; Mary Ann Nicholson, "Recent Gleaning from English Quaker Records," *The American Genealogist* 58 [1982]: 115, and Gary Boyd Roberts, "Clayton of New Jersey to Prince William of Wales," 58: 242, 246.

880-881 *American Ancestors and Cousins of The Princess of Wales,* 28; Benjamin W. Dwight, *The History of the Descendants of Elder John Strong of Northampton, Mass.,* 2 vols. (1871), 1: 308.

882-883 *American Ancestors and Cousins of The Princess of Wales,* 28; *The History of the Descendants of Elder John Strong of Northampton, Mass.,* 2: 986.

884-885 *American Ancestors and Cousins of The Princess of Wales,* 28; Donald Lines Jacobus and Edgar Francis Waterman, *The Granberry Family and allied families: including the ancestry of Helen (Woodward) Granberry* (1945), 171-72, 218; *Vital Records of Norwich 1659–1848,* 2 vols. (1913), 1: 37, 64.

886-887 *American Ancestors and Cousins of The Princess of Wales,* 28; Augustus George Hibbard, *Genealogy of the Hibbard Family Who are Descendants of Robert Hibbard of Salem, Massachusetts* (1901), 26; *The Granberry Family and allied families,* 282-83.

912-913   William Temple, *The Thanage of Fermartyn including the district commonly called Formartine, its proprietors: with genealogical deductions, its parishes, ministers, churches, churchyards, antiquities, &c* (1894), 392.

960-961   Alexander Dingwall Fordyce, *Family Records of the Name of Dingwall Fordyce in Aberdeenshire* (1885), 188.

968-969   Charles John Guthrie, *Genealogy of the descendants of Reverend Thomas Guthrie, D. D., and Mrs. Anne Burns or Guthrie: connected chiefly with the families of Chalmers and Trail, to which Mrs. Guthrie belonged through her mother, Mrs. Christina Chalmers or Burns, and her great-grandmother, Mrs. Susannah Trail or Chalmers; also incidental references to the families of Guthrie and Burns* (1902), 29; *Parish Registers of Marnoch 1676–1854* Family History Library film 0990,988.

970-971   *Genealogy of the descendants of Reverend Thomas Guthrie, D. D., and Mrs. Anne Burns or Guthrie*, 40; *Parish Registers of St. Nicholas, Aberdeen — Marriages vol. xiii 1695–1776* Family History Library film 0991,138; *St. Nicholas, Aberdeen parish registers -Baptisms vol. vi 1688–1704* Family History Library film 0991,135; "St. Nicholas (Aberdeen) Churchyard Inscriptions," *Scottish Notes and Queries* 2 [1889]: 183.

972-973   A. Dingwall-Fordyce, *Addenda to the Family Records of Dingwall-Fordyce* (1888), l.
—— Douglas, father of David Douglas of Panton Street, London, is thought to be a son of David Douglas [No. 1944] and Margaret Reid [No. 1945].

974-975   A. Alistair N. Tayler and H. A. Henrietta Tayler, *The House of Forbes* (1937), 462-63; *Parish registers of Echt, Aberdeen 1648–1854* Family History Library film 0993,524; *Parish Registers of St. Nicholas, Aberdeen — Marriages vol. xiii 1695–1776* Family History Library film 0991,138; *St. Nicholas, Aberdeen parish registers -Baptisms vol. vi 1688–1704* Family History Library film 0991,135.

976-977   *Oxford Dictionary of National Biography*, 5: 291; *The Dictionary of National Biography*, 2: 306; *Family Records of the Name of Dingwall Fordyce in Aberdeenshire*, 17; *Methley, Yorkshire Bishops' transcripts, 1598–1845* Family History Library film 0990,707; *Parish registers of Rothwell, Yorkshire 1599–1780* Family History Library film 0990,764; *Publications of the Thoresby Society*, vol. 12, George Denison Lumb, ed., *The Registers of the Parish Church of Methley in the County of York, from 1560 to 1812*, 30; *The Publications of the Yorkshire Parish Register Society*, vol. 27, George Denison Lumb, ed., *The Registers of the Parish Church of Rothwell, Co. York*, 209, 363.

984-985   Vere Langford Oliver, "Pedigree of the family of Dingwall of Brucklay," *Miscellanea Genealogica et Heraldica*, 4th series, 5 [1914]: 3; *Parish register of Monquhitter, Aberdeenshire: vol. i. Baptisms, 1670–1771* Family History Library film 0993,345; Testament Testamentar and Inventory of Arthur Dingwall of Brownhill 18 Dec. 1729 Aberdeen Commissary Court CC1/6/10; Testament Testamentar and Inventory of Jean Chalmers, relict of Arthur Dingwall, sometime of Brownhill, 8 Feb. 1750 Aberdeen Commissary Court CC1/6/31A.

986-987   "Pedigree of the family of Dingwall of Brucklay," 4, 12; *Family Records of the Name of Dingwall Fordyce in Aberdeenshire*, 110.

988-989   Alexander MacDonald Munro, *Memorials of the Aldermen, Provosts and Lord Provosts of Aberdeen 1272–1895* (1897), 216-18.

990-991   *Memorials of the Aldermen, Provosts and Lord Provosts of Aberdeen 1272–1895*, 226; *The Thanage of Fermartyn*, 975; *Family Records of the Name of Dingwall Fordyce in Aberdeenshire*, 78-79.

1004-1007   *The Thanage of Fermartyn*, 629.

1008-1009   *The House of Forbes,* 302, 303; *The Thanage of Fermartyn,* 155-56.

1010-1011   *The House of Forbes,* 341.

1012-1013   *The Thanage of Fermartyn,* 156; *Old parochial registers for Edinburgh, 1595–1860* Family History Library film 1066,689.

1014-1015   A. Alistair N. Tayler and H. A. Henrietta Tayler, *The Book of the Duffs,* 2 vols. (1914), 1: 388-91; Testament Dative of John Duff of Culbin 29 Oct. 1747   Inverness Commissary Court CC11/1/5.

Tenth Generation

1024-1025   *Oxford Dictionary of National Biography,* 60 vols. (2004), 51: 849; George E. Cokayne et al., *The Complete Peerage,* 14 vols. in 15 (1910-98), 12: 1: 482-84; *Archæologia Cantiana: Being Transactions of the Kent Archæological Society,* vol. 20, John J. Stocker, "Pedigree of Smythe of Ostenhanger, Kent; of Smythe of Bidborough and Sutton-at-Hone, Kent; and of the Smythes, Viscounts of Strangford, of Dromore, Ireland," 77.

1026-1027   *Oxford Dictionary of National Biography,* 16: 143-46; *The Complete Peerage,* 1: 321-22.

1028-1029   *Oxford Dictionary of National Biography,* 11: 652-53; B. D. Henning, *The History of Parliament: The House of Commons 1660–1690,* 3 vols. (1983), 2: 70-73; A.L. Rowse, *The Churchills, The Story of a Family* (1956), 4-56; George E. Cokayne, *The Complete Baronetage, 1611–1880,* 5 vols. (1900-6), 3: 118; J. L. Vivian, *The visitations of the county of Devon, comprising the heralds' visitations of 1531, 1564, & 1620* (1895), 297; Robert Clutterbuck, *The History and Antiquities of the County of Hertford: Compiled from the Best Printed Authorities and Original Records, Preserved in Public Repositories and Private Collections: Embellished with Views of the Most Curious Monuments of Antiquity, and Illustrated with a Map of the County,* 3 vols. (1815-27), 1: 218, 2: 46-47; *Publications of the Harleian Society, Register Series,* vol. 40, Willoughby Littledale, *The Registers of St. Bene't and St. Peter, Paul's Wharf, London, 1607 to 1837,* 287; William A. Shaw, *The Knights of England,* 2 vols. (1906), 2: 239.

1030-1031   *The History of Parliament 1660–1690,* 2: 649-50; Ophelia Field, *Sarah Churchill, Duchess of Marlborough, The Queen's Favourite* (2003), 83; Herbert C. Andrews, "Notes on the Rowlett and Jennings families," *Miscellanea Genealogica et Heraldica,* 5th series, 8 [1932-34]: 107; *The Complete Baronetage,* 1: 212; *Publications of the Harleian Society, Visitation Series,* vol. 26, Joseph Lemuel Chester, *Allegations for Marriage Licences issued by the Bishop of London,* 727.

1032-1033   *The Complete Peerage,* 3: 67; Edwin Chappell, *Eight Generations of the Pepys Family 1500–1800* (1936), 59; *The Knights of England,* 2: 242; Joseph Foster, *London Marriage Licences, 1521–1869* (1887), 249.

1034-1035   *The Complete Peerage,* 2: 20-21; Charles George Young, "The Earldom of Glamorgan: Addendum for Dugdale," *Collectanea Topographica et Genealogica* 7 [1841]: 193; John Horace Round, *Family Origins* (1930), 130-41.

1036-1037   *The History of Parliament 1660–1690,* 3: 758-59; *The Complete Baronetage,* 1: 66; *Publications of the Harleian Society, New Series,* vol. 10, G. D. Squibb, ed., *The Visitation of Hampshire and the Isle of Wight 1686 made by Sir Henry St. George, Knight, Clarenceux King of Arms,* 54; W. P. W. Phillimore and G. E. Cokayne, *London Parish registers, Marriages at St. James' Duke's Place,* 4 vols. (1900-2), 1: 292.

1038-1039 *The History of Parliament 1660–1690*, 3: 565; *The Complete Peerage*, 12: 2: 585-87; *The Complete Baronetage*, 2: 103; *Memorials of St. Margaret's church, Westminster: comprising the parish registers, 1539–1660* Family History Library film 0908,519, item 1.

1040-1041 John Maclean, *Historical and Genealogical Memoir of the Family of Poyntz, or, Eight Centuries of an English House* (1886), 156; Douglas Richardson and Kimball G. Everingham, *Plantagenet Ancestry: A Study in Medieval and Colonial Families* (2004), 560.

1042-1043 *Publications of the Harleian Society, Visitation Series*, vol. 4, George W. Marshall, ed., *The Visitations of the County of Nottingham in the years 1569 and 1614, with many other descents of the same County*, 160; *Publications of the Harleian Society, Register Series*, vol. 72, A. W. Hughes Clarke, *The Registers of St. Mary Magdalen Milk Street, London and St. Michael Bassishaw, London, 1558 to 1892*, 125; *The Index Library (British Record Society)*, vol. 58, Thomas Mathews Blagg and F. Arthur Wadsworth, eds., *Abstracts of Nottinghamshire marriage licences*, 23; W. P. W. Phillimore et al., eds., *Nottingham Parish Registers*, 22 vols. (1898-1938), 1: 25.

1044-1045 *Historical and Genealogical Memoir of the Family of Poyntz*, 202.

1046-1047 *Historical and Genealogical Memoir of the Family of Poyntz*, 202, 293; *Oxford Dictionary of National Biography*, 15: 638.

1048-1049 *The Complete Peerage*, 10: 496-97; *The Knights of England*, 1: 159.

1050-1051 Charles James Feret, *Fulham Old and New being an exhaustive history of the ancient parish of Fulham*, 3 vols. (1900), 2: 137-38; Joseph Foster, *Alumni Oxonienses: The members of the University of Oxford, 1500–1714: their parentage, birthplace, and year of birth, with a record of their degrees. Being the matriculation register of the University, alphabetically arranged, revised and annotated*, 4 vols. (1891-92), 1-2: 247.

1054-1055 *Oxford Dictionary of National Biography*, 34: 775-78; "Note: Sir Thomas Lunsford," *Virginia Magazine of History and Biography* 17 [1909]: 26-33; "Sir Thomas Lunsford," *William & Mary Quarterly*, 1st series, 8 [1900]: 183-86; *The Dictionary of National Biography, founded in 1882 by George Smith, edited by Sir Leslie Stephen and Sir Sidney Lee*, 2nd ed., 22 vols. (1885–1901; reprinted 1908-9), 12: 281-83; "Pedigree of the family of Lunsford, of Lunsford and Wilegh, co. Sussex," *Collectanea Topographica et Genealogica* 4 [1837]: 142; *The Knights of England*, 2: 211; *Publications of the Harleian Society, Visitation Series*, vol. 56, W. Harry Rylands, ed., *The Four Visitations of Berkshire Made and Taken by Thomas Benolte, Clarenceux, Anno 1532, By William Harvey, Clarenceux, Anno 1566, By Henry Chitting, Chester Herald, and John Philipott, Rouge Dragon, for William Camden, Clarenceux, Anno 1623, and by Elias Ashmole, Windsor Herald, for Sir Edward Bysshe, Clarenceux, Anno 1665–66*, 250; Gary Boyd Roberts, *The Royal Descents of 600 Immigrants to the American Colonies or the United States: Who Were Themselves Notable or Left Descendants Notable in American History* (2004; revised and reissued 2006), 359; *Plantagenet Ancestry*, 481.

1056-1057 *The Complete Baronetage*, 2: 398, 419; *Alumni Oxonienses: The members of the University of Oxford, 1500–1714*, 1-2: 124.

1058-1059 *The Complete Baronetage*, 1: 210; George Morris, *Shropshire Genealogies: Shewing the Descent of the principal landed proprietors of the County of Salop from the time of William the Conqueror to the present time; compiled from Heraldic Visitations, public records, chartularies, family documents, parish registers and other sources*, 8 vols. (ca. 1836), 5: 436.

1064-1065 *Oxford Dictionary of National Biography*, 56: 391; George Dames Burtchaell and Thomas Ulick Sadleir, eds., *Alumni Dublinenses; a register of the students, graduates, professors and* *provosts of Trinity college in the University of Dublin (1593–1860)* (1935), 840; Mervyn Archdall, *The Peerage of Ireland; or, a genealogical history of the present nobility of that kingdom with Engravings of their Paternal Coats of Arms. Collected from public records, authentic Manuscripts, approved Historians, well-attested Pedigrees, and Personal Information, by John Lodge*, 2nd ed. Revised, enlarged and continued to the Present Time, 7 vols. (1789), 6: 33.

1066-1067 Owen Manning and William Bray, *The History and Antiquities of the County of Surrey: Compiled from the Best and Most Authentic Historians, Valuable Records, and Manuscripts in the Public Offices and Libraries, and in Private Hands; with a Facsimile Copy of Domesday, Engraved on Thirteen Plates*, 3 vols. (1804–14), 3: 29; *The Peerage of Ireland*, 4: 263.

1068-1069 *Journal of the County Kildare Archaeological Society*, vol. 4, Lord Walter FitzGerald, "Patrick Sarsfield, Earl of Lucan, with an account of his family and their connection with Lucan and Tully," 118-19; *The Complete Peerage*, 8: 236, note a.

1070-1071 *The Complete Peerage*, 3: 28, 6: 706; *Oxford Dictionary of National Biography*, 57: 179; Antonia Fraser, *Royal Charles* (1979), 137; Lord George Scott, *Lucy Walter, Wife or Mistress* (1947), 189-200.

1088-1089 *The History of Parliament 1660–1690*, 3: 420-21; *The Complete Baronetage*, 1: 34; Joseph Jackson Howard and Frederick Arthur Crisp, *Visitation of England and Wales, Notes*, 14 vols. (1896-1921), 2: 167; *The visitations of the county of Devon*, 703.

1090-1091 *The History of Parliament 1660–1690*, 3: 263-64; *Alumni Oxonienses: The members of the University of Oxford, 1500–1714*, 3-4: 1181; *Publications of the Harleian Society, Visitation Series*, vol. 11, Frederic Thomas Colby, ed., *The Visitation of the County of Somerset in the year 1623*, 27; W. L. Rutton, "Pedigree of Hopton of Suffolk and Somerset," *Miscellanea Genealogica et Heraldica*, 3rd series, 3 [1898]: 12; "Kerr of Ancrum, Earl of Ancrum, Earl and Marquis of Lothian," *The Genealogist: A Quarterly Magazine of Genealogical, Antiquarian, Topographical and Heraldic Research Genealogist* 2 [1878]: 290.

1092-1093 John Roger Woodhead, *The rulers of London 1660–1689: a biographical record of the aldermen and common councilmen of the City of London* (1965), 149; *Publications of the Harleian Society, Visitation Series*, vol. 8, George W. Marshall, ed., *Le Neve's Pedigrees of the Knights made by King Charles II, King James II, King William III and Queen Mary, King William alone, and Queen Anne*, 302, and vol. 92, J. B. Whitmore, ed., *London Visitation Pedigrees, 1664*, 124; Henry Brierley, ed., *The Registers of Crosthwaite*, 2 vols. (1928-30), 2: 114.

1094-1095 *The Complete Baronetage*, 1: 176; *Dictionary of Welsh Biography Down to 1940* (1959), 753; *St. Ann Blackfriars Church (London) Parish registers, 1560–1849* Family History Library film 0374,416.

1096-1097 *Royal Charles*; Arthur Bryant, *King Charles II* (1931); *The Dictionary of National Biography*, 4: 84-108; William Dunn Macray, *The history of the rebellion and civil wars in England begun in the year 1641: by Edward, Earl of Clarendon; re-edited from a fresh collation of the original ms. in the Bodleian Library with marginal dates and occasional notes by W. Dunn Macray*, 6 vols. (1992), 4: 23; *Oxford Dictionary of National Biography*, 42: 476-81; *The Complete Peerage*, 3: 90-1, 280-82; Neil D. Thompson and Col. Charles M. Hansen, "A Medieval Heritage: The Ancestry of Charles II, King of England," *The Genealogist* 2 [1981]: 161. See also 1324-1325.

1098-1099 *The Complete Peerage*, 1: 216-18; Adriaan Willem Eliza Dek, *Van Het Vorstenhuis Nassau* (1970), 149; *The History of Parliament 1660–1690*, 1: 620-22; *Little Saxham parish registers, 1559–1850* Family History Library film 0496,951.

1100-1101   *Oxford Dictionary of National Biography*, 50: 590-92; *The History of Parliament 1660–1690*, 3: 454-56; *The Complete Peerage*, 2: 51-52.

1102-1103   *The History of Parliament 1660–1690*, 2: 57-58; *The Complete Baronetage*, 4: 106-7; *Oxford Dictionary of National Biography*, 11: 428-33.

1104-1105   *The Complete Baronetage*, 2: 213; *The Complete Peerage*, 12: 2: 306.

1106-1107   *The Complete Peerage*, 12: 2: 914-18; *The Dictionary of National Biography*, 10: 618-36; *Oxford Dictionary of National Biography*, 11: 587-90; *The Churchills*, 60-70; *Publications of the Harleian Society, Visitation Series*, vol. 10, Joseph Lemuel Chester, ed., *The Marriage, Baptismal and Burial Registers of the Collegiate Church or Abbey of St. Peter, Westminster*, 328; *The History and Antiquities of the County of Hertford*, 1: 218. See also 1454-1455.

1108-1109   *Collections for a History of Staffordshire*, 3rd series, vol. 25, W. Fowler Carter, "Notes on Staffordshire Families," 141-42; *The Complete Baronetage*, 2: 221.

1110-1111   *The Complete Peerage*, 2: 89-90; *The parish registers of Coxwold, 1583–1666* Family History Library film 0844,560, item 4.

1112-1113   Eveline Cruickshanks, Stuart Handley and David Hayton, *The History of Parliament: The House of Commons 1690–1715*, 5 vols. (2002), 5: 774-75; *The History of Parliament 1660–1690*, 3: 663; John Venn and John Archibald Venn, *Alumni Cantabrigienses; A biographical list of all known students, graduates and holders of office at the University of Cambridge, from the earliest times to 1900*, 10 vols. (1922-54), 4: 325; *The Complete Peerage*, 10: 81, note f; *Alumni Oxonienses: The members of the University of Oxford, 1500–1714*, 3-4: 1563; *Le Neve's Pedigrees*, 8: 166; George Henry Dashwood et al., eds., *The Visitation of Norfolk in the Year 1563, taken by William Harvey, Clarenceux King of Arms*, 2 vols. (1878-95), 1: 368; Francis Blomefield and Charles Parkin, *An Essay Towards a Topographical History of the County of Norfolk, a Description of the Towns, Villages, and Hamlets, with the Foundations of Monasteries, Churches, Chapels, Chantries, and Other Religious Buildings: Also an Account of the Ancient and Present State of All the Rectories, Vicarages, Donatives, and Impropriations, Their Former and Present Patrons and Incumbents, with Their Several Valuations in the King's Book, Whether Discharged or Not: Likewise an Historical Account of the Castles, Seats, and Manors, Their Present and Antient Owners, Together with the Most Remarkable Epitaphs, Inscriptions and Arms, in All the Parish Churches and Chapels; with Several Draughts of Churches, Monuments, Arms, Antient Ruins, and Other Relicts of Antiquity: Collected Out of Ledger-Books, Registers, Records, Evidences, Deeds, Court-Rolls, and Other Authentic Memorials*, 2nd ed., 11 vols. (1805-10), 7: 110; Robert Battle, "English Ancestry of Anne (Derehaugh) Stratton of Salem, Massachusetts," *The New England Historical and Genealogical Register* 156 [2002]: 44.

1114-1115   See 546-547.

1120-1121   William Betham, *The Baronetage of England, or, the History of the English Baronets, and Such Baronets of Scotland, as Are of English Families: With Genealogical Tables, and Engravings of Their Armorial Bearings; Collected from the Present Baronetages, Approved Historians, Public Records, Authentic Manuscripts, Well Attested Pedigrees, and Personal Information*, 5 vols. (1801-5), 4: 108.

1128-1131   Leslie G. Pine, ed., *Burke's Genealogical and Heraldic History of the Peerage, Baronetage and Knightage* (1956), 2202.

1132-1133   *The History of Parliament 1660–1690*, 3: 492-93; *The Complete Baronetage*, 4: 47; *Publications of the Harleian Society, Register Series*, vol. 3, Joseph Lemuel Chester, *The Register*

Book of St. Dionis Backchurch Parish (City of London), 1538 to 1754, 32; *Publications of the Harleian Society, Visitation Series*, vol. 23, Joseph Lemuel Chester and George J. Armytage, *Allegations for Marriage Licences issued by the Dean and Chapter of Westminster, 1558–1699; Also for those issued by the Vicar-General of the Archbishop of Canterbury, 1660–1679*, 157.

1134-1135 John William Clay, ed., *Dugdale's Visitation of Yorkshire in 1665–6, with additions*, 3 vols. (1899–1917), 3: 276; *Publications of the Harleian Society, Register Series*, vol. 43, W. Bruce Bannerman, *The Registers of Allhallows, Bread Street, 1538 to 1892, and St. John The Evangelist, Friday Street, London, 1653 to 1822*, 21; *Transcripts of parish registers of London, St. Bartholomew the Less, London, Marriages 1558–1706* Family History Library film 0416,713; *Publications of the Harleian Society, Visitation Series*, vol. 39, John W. Clay, ed., *Familiae Minorum Gentium. Diligentiâ Josephi Hunter, Sheffieldiensis, S.A.S.*, 978.

1136-1137 *The History of Parliament 1660–1690*, 3: 624-26.

1138-1139 *Oxford Dictionary of National Biography*, 59: 458-64; *The Complete Peerage*, 11: 47-48.

1140-1141 James Raine, *The History and Antiquities of North Durham, as Subdivided into the Shires of Norham, Island and Bedlington, which from the Saxon Period until the Year 1844, Constituted Parcels of the County Palatine of Durham, but Are Now United to the County of Northumberland* (1852), 186, 319; *Parish Church of Berwick-upon-Tweed (Northumberland) Register Transcripts, 1573–1812* Family History Library film 0094,987.

1144-1145 Robert Surtees, *The History and Antiquities of the County Palatine of Durham: Compiled from Original Records, Preserved in Public Repositories and Private Collections, and Illustrated by Engravings of Architectural and Monumental Antiquities, Portraits of Eminent Persons &c., &c.*, 4 vols. (1816-40), 3: 295; *Alumni Cantabrigienses*, 4: 48; *The Knights of England*, 2: 244; *St. Nicholas' Church (Newcastle-upon-Tyne) parish register transcripts, 1558–1837* Family History Library film 0095,017.

1146-1147 *Dugdale's Visitation of Yorkshire in 1665–6*, 2: 352; *The Complete Baronetage*, 2: 175; *The Registers of the Parish Church of Methley in the County of York, from 1560 to 1812*, 92; *Memorials of St. Margaret's church, Westminster: comprising the parish registers, 1539–1660* Family History Library film 0908,519, item 1.

1152-1153 Thomas George Baring, Earl of Northbrook, et al., eds., *Journals and correspondence from 1808 to 1852, of Sir Francis Thornhill Baring afterwards Lord Northbrook, compiled and edited by his son Thomas George, Earl of Northbrook* (1905), 272, 273; *Deutsches Geschlechterbuch (Genealogisches Handbuch Bürgerlicher Familien)*, vol. 102, "Baring, v. Baring, Baring v. Wallerode: Freiherr v. Baring, Baring-Gould, Baring Baronet of Larkbear, Baring Baronet of Nubia House, Baring Baron of Hillburton, Baring Baron Viscount und Earl of Cromer, Viscount Errington, Baring Baron Viscount und Earl of Northbrook, Baring Baron Revelstoke, aus Groningen in Friesland," 94.

1154-1155 *Journals and correspondence from 1808 to 1852, of Sir Francis Thornhill Baring afterwards Lord Northbrook*, 272, 274; *Deutsches Geschlechterbuch (Genealogisches Handbuch Bürgerlicher Familien)*, 102: 97.

1160-1161 *Registers of the Parish Church of Westbury, Wiltshire* Family History Library film 1279,369.

1162-1163 *Parish register transcripts, Church of Crediton, Devon 1558–1843* Family History Library film 0917,184.

1168-1169 Will of John Herring, Draper of Cambridge, Cambridgeshire 20 Aug. 1674, codicil 17 Sept. 1674, Proved 13 Nov. 1674 PROB 11/346.

1172-1173 *The History of Parliament 1690–1715,* 5: 813; William Berry, *County Genealogies: Pedigrees of Hertfordshire Families* (1837), 235; William Berry, *County Genealogies: Pedigrees of Berkshire Families* (1837), 83–84.

1174-1175 *Oxford Dictionary of National Biography,* 16: 196-97; W. P. W. Phillimore et al., eds., *Cambridgeshire Parish Registers,* 8 vols. (1907-27), 1: 53; John Nichols, *The History and Antiquities of the County of Leicestershire: Compiled from the Best and Most Ancient Historians; Inquisitions Post Mortem, and Other Valuable Records; Including Also Mr. Burton's Description of the County, Published in 1622; and the Later Collections of Mr. Stavely, Mr. Carte, Mr. Peck, and Sir Thomas Cave,* 4 vols. in 8 (1795–1815), 1: 615.

1176-1177 *Publications of the Harleian Society, Visitation Series,* vol. 94, J. W. Walker, ed., *Yorkshire Pedigrees,* 143.

1178-1179 *Dugdale's Visitation of Yorkshire in 1665–6,* 1: 284; *Publications of the Harleian Society, New Series,* vol. 5, G. D. Squibb, ed., *The Visitation of Nottinghamshire begun in 1662 and finished in 1664 made by William Dugdale, Norroy King of Arms,* 118; *Publications of the Harleian Society, Visitation Series,* vol. 88, J. W. Walker, ed., *Hunter's Pedigrees: A Continuation of Familiae Minorum Gentium, Diligentiâ Josephi Hunter, Sheffieldiensis, S.A.S.,* 138.

1182-1183 *Dugdale's Visitation of Yorkshire in 1665–6,* 3: 509; *Publications of the Surtees Society,* vol. 36, *Dugdale's Visitation of Yorkshire,* 82; *The parish register of Whitby, 1600–1676* Family History Library film 0599,996, item 6.

1184-1185 *Visitation of England and Wales, Notes,* 5: 5; Sir Algernon Tudor Tudor-Craig, *The romance of Melusine and de Lusignan: together with genealogical notes and pedigrees of Lovekyn of London, Lovekyn of Lovekynsmede, and of Luckyn of Little Waltham, and Lukyn of Mashbery, all in the county of Essex, and of Lukin of Felbrigg, co. Norfolk* (1932), 18; *Alumni Cantabrigienses,* 3: 115.

1186-1187 Algernon Tudor Craig, "Lane of Campsea Ash, co. Suffolk," *Miscellanea Genealogica et Heraldica,* 5th series, 2 [1918]: 59.

1190-1191 *Panfield, Essex, Christenings, Burials & Marriages, 1569–1711* Family History Library film 1472,590, item 23; *Rayne, Essex, Christenings, Burials & Marriages, 1558–1664* Family History Library film 1472,666, item 20.

1192-1193 G. H. Holley, "Pedigrees compiled from the parish registers, wills, monumental inscriptions, court records, etc., Norfolk County England" (a 7 vol. manuscript at the Family History Library, Salt Lake City, Utah), 2: 107, 3: 76.

1194-1195 "Pedigrees compiled from the parish registers, wills, monumental inscriptions, court records, etc., Norfolk County, England," 2: 106, 5: 25.

1196-1197 *Alumni Cantabrigienses,* 3: 62.

1200-1201 Gabriel Girod de l'Ain, *Les Thellusson histoire d'une famille* (1977), 32.

1202-1203 *Les Thellusson histoire d'une famille,* 34; *http://www.huguenots-france.org/english/lyon/lyon17/dat19.htm#17,* accessed 17 April 2007.

1204-1207 Ir. J. C. Deknatel, "le Boullenger-van Roubais," *De Nederlandsche Leeuw* 87 [1970]: 202.

1208-1209 L. H. Bouwens and B. G. Bouwens, *A Thousand Ancestors* (1935), viii: 83, 114;

Allegations for Marriage Licences issued by the Dean and Chapter of Westminster, 1558–1699; Also for those issued by the Vicar-General of the Archbishop of Canterbury, 1660–1679, 23: 164.

1210-1211 *A Thousand Ancestors*, viii: 83; *Parish Register of Oving, Sussex 1561–1876* Family History Library film 0918,463; Will of Thomas Sherer, Gentleman of Chichester, Sussex 31 Jan. 1706, Proved at London P.C.C. 8 Sept. 1707 PROB 11/496.

1212-1213 *Oxford Dictionary of National Biography*, 7: 549-50; *A Thousand Ancestors*, viii: 84; *Alumni Oxonienses: The members of the University of Oxford, 1500–1714*, 1-2: 179; P. Draper, *The House of Stanley* (1864), 202.

1216-1217 Charles Edward Pitman, *History and pedigree of the family of Pitman of Dunchideock, Exeter, and their collaterals, and of the Pitmans of Alphington, Norfolk and Edinburgh: with part pedigrees and acccounts of families connected by marriage* (1920), 59; *The visitations of Cornwall*, 254.

1218-1219 *History and pedigree of the family of Pitman*, 59.

1220-1221 "The family of Croker," *Herald & Genealogist* 8 [1874]: 380; *The visitations of the county of Devon*, 254.

1222-1223 *The History of Parliament 1660–1690*, 2: 551, 3: 164; "The family of Croker," 380; *The visitations of the county of Devon*, 447, 470; *Alumni Oxonienses: The members of the University of Oxford, 1500–1714*, 1-2: 714; *Bishops' transcripts, Parish Church of Holbeton 1620–1850* Family History Library film 0917,144.

1224-1225 *The Complete Peerage*, 11: 219-20; *The Scots Peerage*, 7: 50.

1226-1227 *The Complete Peerage*, 4: 463.

1230-1231 *Registers of Walkern, Herts: Baptisms 1559–1812* Family History Library film 1040,799.

1236-1237 *Parish register transcripts Modbury, Devon, Marriages 1553–1565, 1601–1837* Family History Library film 0916,862.

1248-1249 Northumberland County History Commission, *A history of Northumberland*, 15 vols. (1893-1940), 2: 352.

1252-1253 *A history of Northumberland*, 1: 331.

1256-1257 *The History and Antiquities of the County Palatine of Durham*, 2: 15, 19.

1258-1259 Percy W. Hedley, *Northumberland Families*, 2 vols. (1968), 1: 172; *The History and Antiquities of the County Palatine of Durham*, 2: 78.

1260-1261 Henry A. Ogle, *Ogle and Bothal: Or, A History of the Baronies of Ogle, Bothal, and Hepple, and of the Families of Ogle and Bertram, Who Held Possession of Those Baronies and Other Property in the County of Northumberland and Elsewhere; Showing Also How the Property Descended into Other Hands: To Which Is Added Accounts of Several Branches of Families Bearing the Name of Ogle Settled in Other Counties and Countries; with Appendices and Illustrations Compiled from Ancient Records and Other Sources* (1902), 123; *A history of Northumberland*, 5: 288.

1262-1263 *A history of Northumberland*, 6: 257; *The History and Antiquities of the County Palatine of Durham*, 3: 322; *St. John's Church (Newcastle-upon-Tyne, Northumberland) parish register transcripts, 1587–1812* Family History Library film 009,5014.

1264-1265 *The Complete Peerage*, 2: 169-70.

1266-1267 *The Complete Peerage*, 2: 170, note c, 3: 54; *The Dictionary of National Biography*, 36:157-58; H. Loftus Tottenham, "James Margetson, Archbishop of Armagh," *Notes and Queries: A Medium of Inter-Communication for Literary Men, Artists, Antiquaries, Genealogists, etc.*, 8th series, 6 [1894]: 1; Major-General Sir John Ponsonby, *The Ponsonby Family* (1929), 199; Edith Mary Johnston-Liik, *History of the Irish Parliament 1692–1800: commons, constituencies and statutes*, 6 vols. (2002), 6: 79, 81.

1268-1269 *The Complete Peerage*, 4: 343; *Publications of the Harleian Society, Visitation Series*, vol. 31, George J. Armytage, *Allegations for Marriage Licences issued by the Vicar-General of the Archbishop of Canterbury*, 67.

1270-1271 *The History and Antiquities of the County of Hertford*, 3: 132; *Le Neve's Pedigrees*, 8: 216; Will of John Hoskins of Oxted, Surrey 25 March 1713, Proved at London P.C.C. 3 June 1717 PROB 11/558.

1272-1273 *The History of Parliament 1690–1715*, 4: 826; Leslie G. Pine, *Burke's Genealogical and Heraldic History of the Peerage and Baronetage* (1953), 1469; *The Complete Peerage*, 5: 304.

1274-1275 *The Complete Peerage*, 3: 415-16; *The Royal Descents of 600 Immigrants to the American Colonies or the United States*, 263, 265-66.
Richard Coote, 1st Baron Coote, and Mary St. George were the parents of Richard Coote, 1st Earl of Bellomont, Governor of Massachusetts, New Hampshire, and New York.

1276-1277 Hugh Montgomery-Massingberd, *Burke's Irish Family Records* (1976), 1158; *Alumni Dublinenses*, 832.

1278-1279 *Burke's Irish Family Records*, 1158.

1280-1281 *The Complete Peerage*, 1: 6; *The Scots Peerage*, 1: 58-59; *London Marriage Licences, 1521–1869*, 613; *The Marriage, Baptismal and Burial Registers of the Collegiate Church or Abbey of St. Peter, Westminster*, 10: 365, 386.

1282-1283 *The History and Antiquities of the County of Hertford*, 3: 171; *Alumni Oxonienses: The members of the University of Oxford, 1500–1714*, 3-4: 1173; *The Four Visitations of Berkshire*, 56: 262; *Parish registers of Kings-Walden, 1557–1951 Hertfordshire Record Office: D/P 112 1/18–19* Family History Library film 0991,340; *Bishop's transcripts for Kings-Walden, 1604–1855* Family History Library film 0569,765.

1284-1285 *Oxford Dictionary of National Biography*, 13: 926-27; *The History of Parliament 1690–1715*, 3: 775-82; Sarah Churchill, Duchess of Marlborough, *The Queen's Favourite*, 374-76; *The Dictionary of National Biography*, 12: 439-40; Henry Holman Drake, *Hasted's history of Kent: corrected, enlarged and continued to the present time, from the manuscript collections of the late Rev. Thomas Streatfield and the late Rev. Lambert Blackwell Larking, the public records, and other sources. pt. 1. The hundred of Blackheath* (1886), 138; *The Marriage, Baptismal and Burial Registers of the Collegiate Church or Abbey of St. Peter, Westminster*, 10: 302; *The Registers of St. Bene't and St. Peter, Paul's Wharf, London, 1607 to 1837*, 39: 49.

1286-1287 *Oxford Dictionary of National Biography*, 6: 620.

1288-1289 *The History of Parliament 1660–1690*, 3: 114-15; Arthur Stephens Dyer, "Pedigree of Moyle of Bake, St. Germans, Cornwall," *Miscellanea Genealogica et Heraldica*, 5th series, 9 [1932]: 349; *Alumni Oxonienses: The members of the University of Oxford, 1500–1714*, 3-4: 1044; *The Knights of England*, 2: 239; *Parish registers of St. Martin's-in-the-Fields, Westminster, Marriages 1658–1757* Family History Library film 0561,155.

1290-1291 *Oxford Dictionary of National Biography*, 13: 344-45; *The History of Parliament 1660–1690*, 2: 127; *The Complete Baronetage*, 3: 212; *St. Mary at Hill's Church (London) parish registers 1560–1812* Family History Library film 0374,485; *Bishop's transcripts for Antony (Cornwall), 1677–1772* Family History Library film 0090,239.

1292-1293 *The History of Parliament 1690–1715*, 3: 400-1; *The visitations of the county of Devon*, 601; *The visitations of Cornwall*, 58; *Alumni Oxonienses: The members of the University of Oxford, 1500–1714*, 1-2: 208.

1294-1295 *Oxford Dictionary of National Biography*, 55: 279-82; *The Complete Baronetage*, 2: 44; *The visitations of the county of Devon*, 466; *Parish Church of Kingsteignton register transcripts, 1606–1837* Family History Library film 0916,852.

1296-1297 *The Complete Peerage*, 9: 297; *The Scots Peerage*, 6: 379-80; *The Knights of England*, 2: 203; *Parish registers for Peebles, 1622–1854* Family History Library film 1067,919.

1298-1299 *The History of Parliament 1690–1715*, 3: 10-11; *St. Andrew, Holborn, Middlesex Parish registers, 1556–1934* Family History Library film 0374,349.

1300-1301 *The History of Parliament 1690–1715*, 3: 309-16; Alfred Beaven, *The Aldermen of the City of London Temp. Henry III–1908 with Notes on the Parliamentary Representation of the City, the Aldermen and the Livery Companies, the Aldermanic Veto, Aldermanic Baronets and Knights, etc.*, 2 vols. (1908-13), 2: 120; *Visitation of England and Wales, Notes*, 7: 141; *London Marriage Licenses, 1521–1869*, 663; *The Registers of Allhallows, Bread Street, 1538 to 1892, and St. John The Evangelist, Friday Street, London, 1653 to 1822*, 43: 33.

1302-1303 *The History of Parliament 1690–1715*, 5: 850-51; Alfred T. Butler, *A Genealogical and Heraldic Dictionary of the Peerage and Baronetage* (1926), 2373; Joseph Foster, *Peerage, baronetage, and knightage of the British empire* (1881), 652.

1304-1305 *Pedigrees of the County Families of Yorkshire, comp. by Joseph Foster and authenticated by the members of each family*, 2 vols. (1874): Lascelles pedigree; *The History of Parliament 1690–1715*, 4: 589-90; *Parish Register of St. Peter-Le-Poer, London, Baptisms, marriages 1561–1904* Family History Library film 0374,993; Edwin Freshfield, *The register book of the parish of St. Christopher-le-Stocks, in the city of London*, 3 vols. (1882), 2: 13; C. J. Davison Ingledew, *The History and Antiquities of North Allerton, in the County of York* (1858), 195; Will of Edward Lascelles, Citizen and Grocer of London 5 March 1699, Proved at London P.C.C. 20 Sept. 1700 PROB 11/457.

1306-1307 James C. Brandow, *Genealogies of Barbados Families: from* Caribbeana *and* The Journal of the Barbados Museum and Historical Society (1983), 136, 138, 140, 144, 645-46; Joanne McRee Sanders, *Barbados Records: Marriages 1643–1800*, 2 vols. (1982), 1: 61.

1308-1309 *Dugdale's Visitation of Yorkshire in 1665–6*, 2: 233-34; *The register booke of Inglebye iuxta Grenhow since 1539* Family History Library film 0599,156.

1310-1311 Llewellynn Frederick William Jewitt, ed., *The Reliquary and illustrated archæologist*, 34 vols. in 2 series (1860-94), 8: 48; *The Publications of the Durham and Northumberland Parish Register Society*, vol. 6, Johnson Baily, *The registers of Ryton: marriages, 1581–1812*, 52.

1312-1313 *Oxford Dictionary of National Biography*, 48: 358-62; *The Complete Peerage*, 2: 80; *London Marriage Licences, 1521–1869*, 1169; *Parish registers for Walton-upon-Thames, 1639–1918* Family History Library film 1041,721.

1314-1315 Richard Evans, "Jeffrey Howland, Citizen and Grocer of London," *The New England Historical and Genealogical Register* 152 [1998]: 461.

1316-1317 *Oxford Dictionary of National Biography*, 23: 130; *The History of Parliament 1690–1715*, 4: 618-22; *The Complete Peerage*, 6: 36-37; *Parish Church of Branston (Leicestershire) registers, 1591–1975* Family History Library film 0811,942.

1318-1319 *Oxford Dictionary of National Biography*, 44: 259-60; *The History of Parliament 1660–1690*, 3: 241-42; *The Complete Peerage*, 7: 306-7; *London Marriage Licences, 1521–1869*, 1059; *Publications of the Harleian Society, Visitation Series*, vol. 62, W. Harry Rylands, ed., *The Visitation of the County of Warwick begun by Thomas May, Chester, and Gregory King, Rouge Dragon, in Hilary Vacation 1682. Reviewing them in the Trinity Vacation following, and Finished by Henry Dethick, Richmond, and the said Rouge Dragon Pursuivant in Trinity Vacation 1683, by virtue of several deputations from Sir Henry St. George, Clarenceux King of Arms*, 8.

1320-1321 W. J. Baron d'Ablaing van Giesenburg, *Bannerheeren en Ridderschap van Zutphen: van den aanvang der beroerten in de 16e eeuw tot het jaar 1795* (1877), 131, 149.

1322-1323 K. van de Sigtenhorst, "Lady Diana Spencer," *Gens Nostra: Ons Geslacht, Maanblad der Nederlandse Genealogische Vereniging* 36 [1981]: 226-27; *Nederland's Adelsboek 1913* (1913), 239.

1324-1325 *Oxford Dictionary of National Biography*, 31: 404-7; *The Complete Peerage*, 10: 607; Henri Forneron, *Louise de Kéroualle, duchesse de Portsmouth, 1649–1734: society in the court of Charles II. Compiled from state papers preserved in the archives of the French foreign office, by H. Forneron. With portraits, facsimile letter, etc., and a preface by Mrs. G.M. Crawford* (1888), 1, note 1; Anselm de Saint-Marie and M. du Fourny, *Histoire de la Maison Royale de France Anciens Barons du Royaume: et des Grands Officiers de la Couronne*, 3rd ed., 9 vols. (1726–33), 5: 918. See also 1096-1097.

1326-1327 See 720-721.

1328-1329 *The Complete Peerage*, 6: 3-4; *The Knights of England*, 1: 75.

1330-1331 *Oxford Dictionary of National Biography*, 39: 13-21; *The Complete Peerage*, 10: 499-503.

1332-1333 *The Complete Peerage*, 1: 14-15; *The Scots Peerage*, 1: 88-89.

1334-1335 *The Complete Peerage*, 1:316-17; *The Scots Peerage*, 1: 478-80.

1336-1337 *The Complete Baronetage*, 4: 311.

1338-1339 *The Complete Peerage*, 5: 23.

1340-1341 Keith Stanley Malcolm Scott, *Scott 1118–1923: being a collection of "Scott" pedigrees containing all known male descendants from Buccleuch, Sinton, Harden, Balweary, etc.* (1923), 255; *The Scottish antiquary, or, Northern notes and queries*, 17 vols. (1888-1903), 3: 51.

1342-1343 *Scott 1118–1923*, 255; Testament Dative and Inventory of Alexander Tait, Merchant in Edinburgh, residenter in South Leith 23 March 1716 Edinburgh Commissary Court CC8/8/86.

1344-1345 *Visitations of England and Wales, Notes*, 5: 96.

1346-1347 O. F. G. Hogg, *Further Light on the Ancestry of William Penn* (1964), pedigree; *The Victoria History of the County of Buckingham*, 4 vols. (1905–28), 3: 237; P. S. P. Conner, "The Descent of William Penn from the Penns of Penn, co. Bucks," *Notes and Queries*, 5th series, 1 [1874]: 266; W.H. Shawcross alias Shallcross, *Shallcross Pedigrees* (1908), LXI; *Publications of the Harleian Society, Visitation Series*, vol. 58, W. Harry Rylands, ed., *The Visitation of the County* of Buckingham Made in 1634 by John Philipot, Esq., Somerset Herald, and William Ryley, Bluemantle Pursuivant, Marshals and Deputies to Sir Richard St. George, Knight, Clarenceux, and Sir John Borough, Knight, Garter, who visited as Norroy by mutual agreement; Including the Church Notes then taken, together with Pedigrees from the Visitation Made In 1566 by William Harvey, Esq., Clarenceux and some Pedigrees from other sources, Being a Transcript of MS. Eng. Misc. CM in the Bodleian Library, Oxford, with additions, 98; Parish registers of St. Mildred Poultry's Church with St. Mary Colechurch, 1538–1871 Family History Library film 0374,989; Will of William Penn the younger of Penn Place, Buckinghamshire 8 July 1686, Proved at London P.C.C. 15 June 1696 PROB 11/432; Will of Sarah Penn, Widow of Penn, Buckinghamshire 5 Dec. 1698, Proved at London P.C.C. 10 Jan. 1698/99 PROB 11/449.

1348-1349 The Complete Baronetage, 3: 113; The History of Parliament 1660–1690, 1: 563; The Knights of England, 2: 230.

1350-1351 Pedigrees of the County Families of Yorkshire, Vavasour pedigree; Ralph Thoresby, Ducatus Leodiensis: or, the Topography of the Ancient and Populous Town and Parish of Leedes, and Parts Adjacent, in the West-Riding of the County of York, with the Pedigrees of Many of the Nobility and Gentry, and Other Matters Relating to those Parts; Extracted from Records, Original Evidence, and Manuscripts, 2nd ed., With notes and additions by Thomas Dunham Whitaker (1816), 225; The parish register of Bubwith, 1600–1753 Family History Library film 0599,998.

1352-1353 The History of Parliament 1690–1715, 4: 186-87; George Lipscomb, The History and Antiquities of the County of Buckingham, 4 vols. (1847), 4: 342; Hanmer Parish Registers, 8 vols. (1992-2000), 2: 2: 59; Alumni Oxonienses: The members of the University of Oxford, 1500–1714, 1-2: 644; Publications of the Harleian Society, Register Series, vol. 69, A.W. Hughes Clarke et al., Registers of St. Dunstan in the East, 1558 to 1766, 85.

1354-1357 The History and Antiquities of the County of Leicestershire, 4: 859; William Harrison, Thomas Harrison, and George Willis, The great Jennens case: being an epitome of the history of the Jennens family (1879); Caroline Robbins, The diary of John Milward, esq., member of Parliament for Derbyshire, September 1666 to May 1668 (1938), xii.

1358-1359 The History of Parliament 1660–1690, 1: 751; The Complete Baronetage, 1: 119; The History and Antiquities of the County of Leicestershire, 3: 352; Publications of the Harleian Society, New Series, vol. 5, G. D. Squibb, ed., The Visitation of Nottinghamshire begun in 1662 and finished in 1664 made by William Dugdale, Norroy King of Arms, 22.

1360-1361 The History of Parliament 1660–1690, 2: 607-8; Visitation of England and Wales, Notes, 13: 96; The History and Antiquities of the County of Hertford, 1: 479.

1362-1363 The History of Parliament 1660–1690, 1: 527-28; The Complete Peerage, 1: 108; London Marriage Licences, 1521–1869, 17.

1364-1365 Eduard Georg Ludwig William Howe Graf von Kielmansegg and Erich Friedrich Christian Ludwig Graf von Kielmansegg, Familien-Chronik der Herren Freiherren und Grafen von Kielmansegg (1872), Tafel III; Danmarks Adels Aarbog 1884 (1884), 620; Louis Bobé, Slaegten Ahlefeldts Historie, 6 vols. (1897-1912), 4: 53.

1366-1367 Ragnhild Marie Hatton, George I, elector and king (1978), 20-69; Detlev Schwennicke, ed., Europäische Stammtafeln: Stammtafeln zur Geschichte der Europäischen Staaten, Neue Folge, 21 vols. (1978-2001), 1: 1: 25; Ahnentafeln berühmter Deutscher, vol. 9, Ernst Freiherr von Obernitz, "256stellige Ahnentafel des Dichters August von Platen-Hallermund 1796-1835," 265.

1368-1369 *The History of Parliament 1660–1690*, 2: 503-4; *The History and Antiquities of the County of Leicestershire*, 2: 1: 267; Egerton Brydges, *Collins's Peerage of England, Genealogical, Biographical, and Historical, Greatly Augmented, and Continued to the Present Time*, 9 vols. (1812), 4: 12; *The Complete Peerage*, 1: 271, note b; *The Knights of England*, 2: 228.

1370-1371 *Alumni Oxonienses: The members of the University of Oxford, 1500–1714*, 1-2: 107; *The History and Antiquities of the County of Leicestershire*, 2: 1: 285; G. Milner-Gibson-Cullum, "Middleton or Myddelton of Chirk Castle, Denbigh, Stanstead Mountfichet, Essex, and other places," *Miscellanea Genealogica et Heraldica*, 3rd series, 2 [1888]: 228.

1372-1373 *The History and Antiquities of the County of Leicestershire*, 3: 394; *West Leake Baptisms, Marriages & Burials 1622–1812* Family History Library film 0503,787; *The Visitation of Nottinghamshire begun in 1662 and finished in 1664 made by William Dugdale, Norroy King of Arms*, 5: 89; *Archdeaconry wills for the deaneries of Nottingham & Bingham 1698–1712* Family History Library film 1278,629.

1376-1377 *The History of Parliament 1660–1690*, 2: 414-15; "Annotations to the Heraldic Visitation of London, 1633. Gore," *Miscellanea Genealogica et Heraldica*, 2nd series, 3 [1890]: 116; *The Knights of England*, 2: 231; *The Registers of St. Mary Magdalen Milk Street, London and St. Michael Bassishaw, London, 1558 to 1892*, 72: 27.

1378-1379 *The Complete Baronetage*, 1: 234; *The Scots Peerage*, 1: 45.

1380-1381 *Oxford Dictionary of National Biography*, 35: 425-27; *The History of Parliament 1660–1690*, 3: 13; *Publications of the Harleian Society, Register Series*, vol. 49, W. Bruce Bannerman et al., *The Registers of St. Stephen, Walbrook, and St. Benet Sherehog, London, 1716 to 1860*, 118, 106.

1382-1383 *Publications of the Harleian Society, New Series*, vol. 17, T. C. Wales et al., eds., *The Visitation of London begun in 1687*, 2: 523, 499; *Publications of the Harleian Society, Register Series*, vol. 35, William H. Hunt, *The Registers of St. Paul's Church, Covent Garden, London, 1653 to 1853*, 29; *Publications of the Harleian Society, Visitation Series*, vol. 66, W. Harry Rylands, ed., *Grantees of Arms Named in Docquets and Patents to the End of the Seventeenth Century, in the Manuscripts preserved in the British Museum, The Bodleian Library, Oxford, Queen's College, Oxford, Gonville and Caius College, Cambridge, and Elsewhere, alphabetically Arranged by The Late Joseph Foster and Contained in the Additional Ms. No. 37,147 in the British Museum*, 181; Henry Chauncy, *The Historical Antiquities of Hertfordshire: With the Original of Counties, Hundreds or Wapentakes, Boroughs, Corporations, Towns, Parishes, Villages, and Hamlets; the Foundation and Origin of Monasteries, Churches, Advowsons, Tythes, Rectories, Impropriations and Vicarages, in General; Describing Those of This County in Particular: As Also the Several Honors, Mannors, Castles, Seats, and Parks of the Nobility and Gentry; and the Succession of the Lords of Each Mannor Therein: Also the Characters of the Abbots of St. Albans, Faithfully Collected from Public Records, Leiger Books, Ancient Manuscripts, Charters, Evidences, and Other Select Authorities, Together with an Exact Transcript of Domesday-Book, so far as Concerns This Shire, and the Translation Thereof in English, to which are Added the Epitaphs and Memorable Inscriptions, in All the Parishes, and Likewise the Blazon of the Coats of Arms of the Several Noblemen, and Gentlemen, Proprietors in the Same, Illustrated with a Large Map of the County; a Prospect of Hertford; the Ichnography of St. Albans and Hitchin; and many Sculptures of Principal Edifices and Monuments* (1826), 203.

1392-1393 *Publications of the Harleian Society, Visitation Series*, vol. 5, William Henry Turner, ed., *The Visitations of the County of Oxford taken in the years 1566 by William Harvey, Clarencieux, 1574 by Richard Lee, Portcullis, Deputy of Robert Cooke, Clarencieux, and in 1634 by John Philipott, Somerset and William Ryley, Bluemantle, Deputies of Sir John Borough, Knt.,*

Garter and Richard St. George, knt., Clarencieux; Together with the gatherings of Oxfordshire Collected by Richard Lee in 1574, 259, and vol. 87, H. Isham Longden, ed., *The Visitation of the County of Northampton in the Year 1681,* 142; *Alumni Cantabrigienses,* 3: 201; "Pedigree of Montagu, of Lackham," *Wiltshire Archeological and Natural History Magazine* 3 [1857]: between 86 and 87.

1394-1395 *The History of Parliament 1660–90,* 2: 285-86; *The Knights of England,* 2: 263; *Publications of the Harleian Society, Register Series,* vol. 31, W. Bruce Bannerman, *The Registers of St. Helen's, Bishopsgate, London, 1575 to 1837,* 348, 349.

1396-1397 W.S. Sykes, "Notes on Wilcot and Families" (a manuscript at the Wiltshire Archaelogical Society, Devizes); *[The Victoria] History of Wiltshire,* 15 vols. in 16 (1953-), 10: 194; *Wiltshire Family History Society,* 1999-2000 vol., *The bishop's transcripts and parish registers of Wilcot, baptisms & burials, 1564–1837 and Huish, baptisms & burials, 1603–1837,* 77, 80; *Allegations for Marriage Licences issued by the Dean and Chapter of Westminster, 1558–1699; Also for those issued by the Vicar-General of the Archbishop of Canterbury, 1660–1679,* 23: 155; *St. Ann Blackfriars Church (London) Parish registers, 1560–1849* Family History Library film 0374,416; Will of George Wroughton of Shercott in the parish of Pewsey, Wiltshire 14 Nov. 1691, Proved at London P.C.C. 29 March 1698 PROB 11/444; Will of George Farewell of St. Margaret, Westminster, Middlesex 9 Feb. 1690, Proved at London P.C.C. 26 March 1691 PROB 11/404.

1398-1399 Peter Townend et al., eds., *Burke's Genealogical and Heraldic History of the Landed Gentry,* 3 vols. (1965-72), 3: 787; *Publications of the Harleian Society, Register Series,* vol. 28, Arthur J. Jewers, *The Registers of The Abbey Church of SS. Peter & Paul, Bath, 1569 to 1800,* 410, 434; Will of Robert Eyre, Citizen and Grocer of London 7 Aug. 1718, Proved at London P.C.C. 24 Sept. 1718 PROB 11/565.

1400-1403 See 1396-1399.

1408-1409 See 528-529.

1412-1415 See 532-535.

1424-1425 *The Complete Peerage,* 5: 265; *The Knights of England,* 1: 163; J. P. Earwaker, *East Cheshire, Past and Present, or, a History of the Hundred of Macclesfield in the County Palatine of Chester—from Original Records,* 2 vols. (1877-80), 2: 444.

1426-1427 *Publications of the Harleian Society, Visitation Series,* vol. 89, A. W. Hughes Clarke, ed., *The Visitation of Sussex Anno Domini 1662,* 51; *The Complete Baronetage,* 1: 193.

1428-1429 G. Dashwood, *Pedigrees selected from the Visitation of the County of Warwick, begun by Thomas May, Chester, and Gregory King, Rouge Dragon, in Hillary Vacac n, 1682, etc., etc.* (1859), Betham; *The Visitation of the County of Warwick begun by Thomas May, Chester, and Gregory King, Rouge Dragon, in Hilary Vacation 1682,* 62: 44; *The Four Visitations of Berkshire,* 56: 315; J. Renton Dunlop, "The Family of Fettiplace," *Miscellanea Genealogica et Heraldica,* 5th series, 2 [1918]: 242.

1430-1431 *Collections for a History of Staffordshire,* vol. 5, part 2, H. Sydney Grazebrook, ed., *The Heraldic Visitations of Staffordshire Made by Sir Richard St. George, Norroy, in 1614, and by Sir William Dugdale in the Years 1663 and 1664,* 137.

1436-1437 *The History of Parliament 1660–1690,* 2: 100-1; *Publications of the Harleian Society, New Series,* vol. 8, G. D. Squibb, ed., *The Visitation of Derbyshire begun in 1662 and finished in 1664 made by William Dugdale, Norroy King of Arms,* 116; John Edwin Cussans, *History of*

Hertfordshire, Containing an Account of the Descents of the Various Manors, Pedigrees of Families Connected with the County, Antiquities, Local Customs, &c., &c.: Chiefly Compiled from Original Mss., in the Record Office and British Museum, Parochial Registers, Local Archives and Collections in the Possession of Private Families, 8 parts in 3 vols. (1870-81), 1: 1: 101; *Alumni Oxonienses: The members of the University of Oxford, 1500–1714,* 1-2: 299.

1438-1439   *The History and Antiquities of the County of Hertford,* 3: 133; Duncan Warrand, *Hertfordshire Families* (1907), 118; Stephen Glover, *The History and gazetteer of the county of Derby: drawn up from actual observation and from the best authorities: containing a variety of geological, mineralogical, commercial and statistical information,* 2 vols. in 3 (1831-33), 2: 159; *Allegations for Marriage Licences issued by the Dean and Chapter of Westminster, 1558–1699; Also for those issued by the Vicar-General of the Archbishop of Canterbury, 1660–1679,* 23: 155.

1440-1441   *The Complete Peerage,* 3: 13-14; Joan Wake, *The Brudenells of Deene* (1953), 114, 174-78.

1442-1443   *Oxford Dictionary of National Biography,* 49: 124-27; *The Complete Peerage,* 12: 1: 531-33; *The Knights of England,* 2: 161; *Parish Church of Sunbury (Middlesex) registers, 1565–1875* Family History Library film 0577,573.

1444-1445   *Oxford Dictionary of National Biography,* 8: 324; *The History of Parliament 1660–1690,* 1: 737-39; *The Complete Peerage,* 1: 58-59.

1446-1447   *The Complete Peerage,* 12: 1: 74; Amy Audrey Locke, *The Seymour family, history and romance* (1911), 138. See also 1100-1101.

1448-1449   *The History of Parliament 1660–1690,* 1: 661; *The Complete Baronetage,* 1: 156; *The Visitation of the County of Buckingham Made in 1634,* 58: 48.

1450-1451   "Pedigree of Dunch of Little Wittenham, Berks.," *Miscellanea Genealogica et Heraldica,* 3rd Series, 2 [1898]: 46; *Alumni Oxonienses: The members of the University of Oxford, 1500–1714,* 1-2: 431; *Parish registers for St. Martin-in-the-Fields, 1550–1653* Family History Library film 0560,369; Will of Henry Dunch of Newington, Oxfordshire 8 Oct. 1686; Proved at London P.C.C. 4 Nov. 1686 PROB 11/385.

1452-1453   *The History of Parliament 1660–1690,* 1: 685-86; *The Complete Peerage,* 5: 246; *The visitations of Cornwall,* 47; *Parish registers for Breage, 1559–1995* Family History Library film 0254,175.

1454-1455   *The History of Parliament 1660–90,* 2: 402-3; *The Churchills, The Story of a Family,* 68-69; *The Marriage, Baptismal and Burial Registers of the Collegiate Church or Abbey of St. Peter, Westminster,* 10: 328. See also 1106-1107.

1456-1457   "Family of Cooke," "Pedigree of Cooke," *Miscellanea Genealogica et Heraldica,* 2nd series, 4 [1892]: 152.

1458-1459   *The History of Parliament 1690–1715,* 4: 495; Sir Lewis Namier and John Brooke, *The History of Parliament: The House of Commons 1754–1790,* 3 vols. (1964; reprinted 1985), 2: 177; *Musgrave's Obituary,* 46: 323; Abel Boyer et al., eds., *Political State of Great Britain,* 60 vols. (1711-40), 34: 198; *Historical Register Chronicle,* 3: 31; *Publications of the Harleian Society, New Series,* vol. 1, G. D. Squibb, ed., *The Register of the Temple Church, London Baptisms 1629–1853; Marriages 1628–1760,* 123-24; *Publications of the Harleian Society, Register Series,* vol. 63, W. Bruce Bannerman, *Registers of St. Matthew, Friday Street, London, 1538 to 1812, and the United Parishes of St. Matthew and St. Peter, Cheap, 1754 to 1812,* 22; *Publications of the Harleian Society, Visitation Series,* vol. 24, Joseph Lemuel Chester and George

J. Armytage, *Allegations for Marriage Licences issued by the Faculty Office of the Archbishop of Canterbury at London, 1543–1869,* 92-93.

1460-1461 *The History of Parliament 1660–1690,* 3: 616-17; Charles Humble Dudley Ward, *The family of Twysden and Twisden; their history and archives from an original by Sir John Ramskill Twisden, 12th baronet of Bradbourne* (1939), 181; *The Complete Baronetage,* 1: 75; *Allegations for Marriage Licences issued by the Faculty Office of the Archbishop of Canterbury at London, 1543–1869,* 24: 88; *Parish Registers, St. Martin Ludgate, London 1646–1654* Family History Library film 0374,476; *St. Giles Cripplegate Church (London) Registers, 1559–1936* Family History Library film 0380,199.

1462-1463 *The History of Parliament 1660–1690,* 3: 783-84; *The Dictionary of National Biography,* 21: 1191-93; *Hasted's history of Kent,* 1: 195; *The Knights of England,* 2: 254; *The Marriage, Baptismal and Burial Registers of the Collegiate Church or Abbey of St. Peter, Westminster,* 10: 24-25; *Parish registers of St. Mary Cray, 1579–1916* Family History Library film 1042,461.

1464-1465 *The Complete Baronetage,* 3: 59; *Allegations for Marriage Licences issued by the Vicar-General of the Archbishop of Canterbury,* 30: 16.

1466-1467 *Alumni Oxonienses: The members of the University of Oxford, 1500–1714,* 3-4: 1115; Joseph Foster, *The Visitation of Middlesex, began in the year 1663, by William Ryley, esq., Lancaster, and Henry Dethick, Rouge croix, marshalls and deputies to Sir Edward Bysshe, Clarencieux. As recorded in the College of arms, (D. 17.)* (1887), 2; John Burke and John Bernard Burke. *A Genealogical and Heraldic History of the Extinct and Dormant Baronetcies of England, Ireland, and Scotland,* 2nd ed. (1844), 400; *Parish registers of St. Gregory by St. Paul's Church, 1559–1853* Family History Library film 0375,028; Will of Sarah Parker, Widow of Denham, Buckinghamshire 6 July 1730, Proved 5 May 1738 PROB 11/689; Will of Robert Chilcott of Islesworth, Middlesex 21 July 1688, Proved at London P.C.C. 13 Nov. 1688 PROB 11/393.

1468-1469 See 1132-1133.

1470-1471 *The History of Parliament 1660–1690,* 2: 195; *The Complete Baronetage,* 4: 132, 2: 207, note a; *Publications of the Harleian Society, Register Series,* vol. 64, Herbert F. Westlake et al., *The Register of St. Margaret's, Westminster, 1660 to 1699,* 18; *Allegations for Marriage Licences issued by the Vicar-General of the Archbishop of Canterbury,* 30: 98.

1472-1473 See 1096-1097 and 1324-1325.

1474-1475 See 720-721.

1476-1477 *The Complete Peerage,* 2: 460; *Alumni Dublinenses,* 126.

1478-1479 "Lady Diana Spencer," *Gens Nostra* 36 [1981]: 230-31; Johan Engelbert Elias, *De Vroederschap van Amsterdam 1578-1795; met een inleidend woord van den archivaris der stad Amsterdam W. R. Veder,* 2 vols. (1903-5; reprinted in 1963), 2: 626, 548-49.

1480-1481 *Oxford Dictionary of National Biography,* 31: 429-30; *The Complete Peerage,* 8: 151; *The Scots Peerage,* 5: 478-79.

1482-1483 *The Complete Baronetage,* 4: 391-92; *Old parochial registers for Edinburgh, 1595–1860* Family History Library films 1066,663 and 1066,689.

1484-1485 *The History of Parliament 1660–1690,* 2: 191-92; *The Complete Peerage,* 6: 535-36; *The Marriage, Baptismal and Burial Registers of the Collegiate Church or Abbey of St. Peter, Westminster,* 10: 222; *Dugdale's Visitation of Yorkshire in 1665–6,* 2: 84.

1486-1487 *Oxford Dictionary of National Biography*, 49: 252-53; *Europäische Stammtafeln, Neue Folge*, 1: 1: 95; *The Complete Peerage*, 7: 573, 11: 527-29; *The Marriage, Baptismal and Burial Registers of the Collegiate Church or Abbey of St. Peter, Westminster*, 10: 296, 236.

1488-1502 See 1328-1342.

1504-1505 John Edwards Griffith, *Pedigrees of Anglesey and Carnarvonshire families* (1914), 57; Philip Henry Dudley Bagenal, *Vicissitudes of an Irish Family 1530–1800: a story of Irish romance and tragedy* (1925), 66; *The Complete Baronetage*, 5: 351.

1506-1507 *Burke's Genealogical and Heraldic History of the Peerage and Baronetage* (1953), 1213; *History of the Irish Parliament 1692–1800*, 5: 54-55; *The Baronetage of England*, 3: 193-94; Ashworth P. Burke, *A Genealogical and Heraldic History of the Landed Gentry of Ireland* (1899), 441.

1508-1509 *The Complete Baronetage*, 5: 352.

1510-1511 *Allegations for Marriage Licences issued by the Faculty Office of the Archbishop of Canterbury at London, 1543–1869*, 24: 243; *The visitations of Cornwall*, 14; Philip Morant, *The History and Antiquities of the County of Essex: Compiled from the Best and Most Ancient Historians: from Domesday-Book, Inquisitiones Post Mortem and Other the Most Valuable Records and Mss. &c, the Whole Digested, Improved, Perfected and Brought Down to the Present Time*, 2 vols. (1768), 2: 139; *North Witham Bishop's Transcripts* Family History Library film 0436,048, item 5; *The History and Antiquities of the County of Leicestershire*, 2: 1: 353; *St. Giles Cripplegate Church (London) Registers, 1559–1936* Family History Library film 0380,199; *Parish register transcripts for Newlyn (near St. Columb-Major), 1559–1837* Family History Library film 0916,981; Will of Peter Whitcomb or Whitcombe of Great Braxted, Essex 2 Sept. 1704, Proved at London P.C.C. 12 Sept. 1704 PROB 11/478.

1512-1513 David C. A. Agnew, *Protestant exiles from France in the reign of Louis XIV; or, The Huguenot refugees and their descendants in Great Britain and Ireland*, 3 vols. (1871-74), 2: 125-26; Charles E. Lart, *Huguenot Pedigrees*, 2 vols. (1924-25), 1: 75.

1514-1515 *The Complete Peerage*, 6: 55; *The Peerage of Ireland*, 2: 147; *A transcript of the early registers of the parish of Guiseley in the county of York, 1584–1720* Family History Library film 6035,726.

1516-1517 *Publications of the Huguenot Society of London*, vol. 41, Thomas Philip Le Fanu et al., eds., "Dublin and Portarlington veterans: King William III's Huguenot army," 44.

1520-1521 *Alumni Cantabrigienses*, 4: 302; *The Complete Peerage*, 7: 88-89; *London Marriage Licences, 1521–1869*, 1388; *The Marriage, Baptismal and Burial Registers of the Collegiate Church or Abbey of St. Peter, Westminster*, 10: 272-73; *Parish Church of Bartlow (Cambridgeshire) registers, 1573–1876* Family History Library film 1040,366.

1522-1523 *The History of Parliament 1690–1715*, 4: 341-43; *The East Anglian; or, Notes and queries on subjects connected with the counties of Suffolk, Cambridge, Essex and Norfolk*, vol. 4, George W. Marshall, "Pedigree of the Hernes, of Tibenham, co. Norfolk," 123; *The Visitation of the County of Northampton in the Year 1681*, 87: 123; *Publications of the Harleian Society, Register Series*, vol. 46, W. Bruce Bannerman, *The Registers of St. Olave, Hart Street, London, 1563 to 1700*, 74; *Allegations for Marriage Licences issued by the Vicar-General of the Archbishop of Canterbury*, 31: 65.

1524-1525 *The History of Parliament 1660–1690*, 2: 254-55; *The Complete Peerage*, 2: 313; *The Knights of England*, 1: 163; *Publications of the Harleian Society, Register Series*, vol. 18,

Francis Collins, *The Registers and Monumental Inscriptions of Charterhouse Chapel, 1671 to 1890,* 1; *Parish registers for St. Martin-in-the-Fields, 1550–1653* Family History Library film 0560,369.

1526-1527 See 514-515.

1528-1529 See 1460-1461.

1530-1531 *The Family of Twysden and Twisden,* 372-74.

1532-1533 *Oxford Dictionary of National Biography,* 10: 368-69; *Burke's Irish Family Records,* 215; *The Complete Peerage,* 9: 128; *History of the Irish Parliament 1692–1800,* 3: 376.

1534-1535 *Oxford Dictionary of National Biography,* 10: 368; *Burke's Irish Family Records,* 215.

1536-1537 *Burke's Genealogical and Heraldic History of the Peerage and Baronetage* (1953), 788.

1538-1539 Walter Arthur Copinger, *History of the Copingers or Coppingers of the County of Cork, Ireland, and the Counties of Suffolk and Kent, England* (1884), 174.

1540-1541 *Journal of the Cork Historical & Archeological Society,* 2nd series, vol. 30, George Berkeley, "History of the Lavallins," pedigree facing 10, 14.

1544-1545 *Burke's Irish Family Records,* 574.

1592-1593 *Burke's Irish Family Records,* 906.

1594-1595 Sir Bernard Burke, *A Genealogical History of the Dormant, Abeyant, Forfeited and Extinct Peerages of the British Empire* (1883), 534.

1600-1601 Peter Townend, ed., *Burke's Genealogical and Heraldic History of the Peerage, Baronetage and Knightage* (1970), 305; *The History and Antiquities of the County of Leicestershire,* 4: 177, 2: 2: 874.

1648-1649 Noel Currer-Briggs and Royston Gambier, *Huguenot Ancestry* (1985), pedigree.

1656-1659 Henry Wagner, "Huguenot Refugee family of Yvonnet," *The Genealogist,* New Series, 28 [1912]: 88.

1704-1705 Gary Boyd Roberts and William Addams Reitwiesner, *American Ancestors and Cousins of The Princess of Wales* (1984), 76.

1760-1761 *American Ancestors and Cousins of The Princess of Wales,* 28; Mary Lovering Holman and Winifred Lovering Holman, *Ancestry of Colonel John Harrington Stevens and his wife, Frances Helen Miller: compiled for Helen Pendleton (Winston) Pillsbury,* 2 vols. (1948-52), 1: 391; Benjamin W. Dwight, *The History of the Descendants of Elder John Strong of Northampton, Mass.,* 2 vols. (1871), 1: 228.

1762-1763 *American Ancestors and Cousins of The Princess of Wales,* 28; Donald Lines Jacobus and Edgar Francis Waterman, *Hale, House and related families: mainly of the Connecticut River Valley* (1952), 451.

1764-1765 *American Ancestors and Cousins of The Princess of Wales,* 28; *The History of the Descendants of Elder John Strong of Northampton, Mass.,* 2: 986. See also 1766-1767.

1766-1767 *American Ancestors and Cousins of The Princess of Wales,* 28; Leonard Lee and Sarah Fiske Lee, *John Lee of Farmington, Hartford co. Connecticut and His Descendants, 1634–1897: containing over 4,000 names, with much miscellaneous history of the family, brief notes of other Lee families of New England, biographical notices, valuable data collected by William Wallace Lee, military* *records, to which is added a "roll of honor" of two hundred who have served in the various wars of the country* (1897), 53-55. See also 1764-1765.

1768-1769 *American Ancestors and Cousins of The Princess of Wales*, 28; Donald Lines Jacobus and Edgar Francis Waterman, *The Granberry Family and allied families: including the ancestry of Helen (Woodward) Granberry* (1945), 170; John Langdon Sibley et al., *Biographical Sketches of Graduates of Harvard University in Cambridge, Massachusetts*, 18 vols. to date (1873-), 2: 189.

1770-1771 *American Ancestors and Cousins of The Princess of Wales*, 28; *The Granberry Family and allied families*, 218; W. M. Bollenbach, Jr., *The New England Ancestry of Alice Everett Johnson 1899–1986* (2003), 125, 166; *Vital Records of Norwich 1659–1848*, 2 vols. (1913), 1: 5, 37.

1772-1773 *American Ancestors and Cousins of The Princess of Wales*, 29; Augustus George Hibbard, *Genealogy of the Hibbard Family Who are Descendants of Robert Hibbard of Salem, Massachusetts* (1901), 12, 19; *The New England Ancestry of Alice Everett Johnson 1899–1986*, 185.

1774-1775 *American Ancestors and Cousins of The Princess of Wales*, 29; *The Granberry Family and allied families*, 282-83.

1824-1825 William Temple, *The Thanage of Fermartyn including the district commonly called Formartine, its proprietors: with genealogical deductions, its parishes, ministers, churches, churchyards, antiquities, &c* (1894), 392.

1936-1937 Charles John Guthrie, *Genealogy of the descendants of Reverend Thomas Guthrie, D.D., and Mrs. Anne Burns or Guthrie: connected chiefly with the families of Chalmers and Trail, to which Mrs. Guthrie belonged through her mother, Mrs. Christina Chalmers or Burns, and her great-grandmother, Mrs. Susannah Trail or Chalmers; also incidental references to the families of Guthrie and Burns* (1902), 30; *The Thanage of Fermartyn*, 88-89.

1938-1939 *The Thanage of Fermartyn*, 88.

1940-1941 *Genealogy of the descendants of Reverend Thomas Guthrie, D.D., and Mrs. Anne Burns or Guthrie*, 41.

1942-1943 Alexander MacDonald Munro, *Memorials of the Aldermen, Provosts and Lord Provosts of Aberdeen 1272–1895* (1897), 197; *St. Nicholas, Aberdeen parish registers — Baptisms vol. iv 1647–72* Family History Library film 0991,134.

1944-1945 A. Dingwall-Fordyce, *Addenda to the Family Records of Dingwall-Fordyce* (1888), 1; "Pedigree of Douglas of Tilquhilly or Tilwhilly, co. Kincardine," *The Genealogist* 5 [1881]: 195.

1948-1949 A. Alistair N. Tayler and H. A. Henrietta Tayler, *The House of Forbes* (1937), 462; G. F. Browne, *Echt-Forbes family charters 1345–1727, records of the Forest of Birse Notarial Signs 926–1786* (1923).

1950-1951 *St. Nicholas, Aberdeen parish registers — Baptisms vol. vi 1688–1704* Family History Library film 0991,135.

1952-1953 *Oxford Dictionary of National Biography*, 5: 291; *The Dictionary of National Biography*, 2: 306; *Publications of the Thoresby Society*, vol. 12, George Denison Lumb, ed., *The Registers of the Parish Church of Methley in the County of York, from 1560 to 1812*, 19, 48, 88; *The Publications of the Yorkshire Parish Register Society*, vol. 78, Edith Horsfall, ed., *The Parish Registers of Heptonstall, in the County of York, 1593–1660*, 141; *Methley, Yorkshire Bishop's transcripts, 1598–1845* Family History Library film 0990,707.

1954-1955   *The Dictionary of National Biography*, 2: 306; *The Publications of the Yorkshire Parish Register Society*, vol. 27, George Denison Lumb, ed., *The Registers of the Parish Church of Rothwell, Co. York*, 370, 371.

1968-1971   Vere Langford Oliver, "Pedigree of the family of Dingwall of Brucklay," *Miscellanea Genealogica et Heraldica*, 4th series, 5 [1914]: 3.

1972-1973   Alexander Dingwall Fordyce, *Family Records of the Name of Dingwall Fordyce in Aberdeenshire* (1885), 101.

1974-1975   "Pedigree of the family of Dingwall of Brucklay," 12; *Family Records of the Name of Dingwall Fordyce in Aberdeenshire*, 183; *The Complete Baronetage*, 2: 451.

1978-1979   *Memorials of the Aldermen, Provosts and Lord Provosts of Aberdeen 1272–1895*, 217.

1980-1983   *Family Records of the Name of Dingwall Fordyce in Aberdeenshire*, 78-79.

2008-2009   *The Thanage of Fermartyn*, 628; *Parish registers of Kildrummy 1678–1854* Family History Library film 0993,195.

2016-2017   *The House of Forbes*, 302; *The Complete Baronetage*, 2: 305; *Notes and Queries*, 3rd series, 9 [1866]: 389. See also 4054-4055.

2018-2019   *The Thanage of Fermartyn*, 154-55; *The Complete Peerage*, 5: 570, 9: 243.

2022-2023   *The House of Forbes*, 341; Alexander Fraser, 17th Lord Saltoun, *The Frasers of Philorth*, 3 vols. (1879), 2: 163.

2024-2025   See 2018-2019.

2026-2027   *The House of Forbes*, 302; *The Complete Baronetage*, 4: 289.

2028-2029   A. Alistair N. Tayler and H. A. Henrietta Tayler, *The Book of the Duffs*, 2 vols. (1914), 1: 366.

2030-2031   *The Complete Baronetage*, 4: 344.

Eleventh Generation

2048-2049   George E. Cokayne et al., *The Complete Peerage*, 14 vols. in 15 (1910-98), 12: 2: 260.

2050-2051   *Oxford Dictionary of National Biography*, 60 vols. (2004), 50: 572-75; *The Complete Peerage*, 7: 554-55.

2052-2053   *Oxford Dictionary of National Biography*, 16: 147; *The Complete Peerage*, 2: 320; John Paul Rylands et al., "Pedigrees from the Visitation of Dorset 1623. Walcot," *Miscellanea Genealogica et Heraldica*, 2nd series, 2 [1888]: 121; *Parish Church of Coleshill (Warwickshire) registers, 1538–1956* Family History Library film 0229,158; *Parish Church of North Lydbury registers, 1563–1812* Family History Library film 0510,668; *Publications of the Harleian Society, Register Series*, vol. 45, W. Bruce Bannerman, ed., *The Registers of St. Mary le Bowe, Cheapside, All Hallows, Honey Lane, and of St. Pancras, Soper Lane, London, 1538–1837*, 323.

2054-2055   *The Complete Peerage*, 2: 78-79.

2056-2057   P. N. Dawe, "The Dorset Churchills," *Notes & Queries for Somerset and Dorset* 27 [1958]: 191; *Publications of the Harleian Society, Register Series*, vol. 49, W. Bruce Bannerman et al., *The Registers of St. Stephen, Walbrook, and St. Benet Sherehog, London, 1716 to 1860*, 59; A.L. Rowse, *The Churchills, The Story of a Family* (1956), 2; *Oxford Dictionary of National Biography*, 11: 652.

2058-2059   George E. Cokayne, *The Complete Baronetage, 1611–1880,* 5 vols. (1900-6), 3: 118; *The Complete Peerage,* 2: 230; J. L. Vivian, *The visitations of the county of Devon, comprising the heralds' visitations of 1531, 1564, & 1620* (1895), 297; Robert Clutterbuck, *The History and Antiquities of the County of Hertford: Compiled from the Best Printed Authorities and Original Records, Preserved in Public Repositories and Private Collections: Embellished with Views of the Most Curious Monuments of Antiquity, and Illustrated with a Map of the County,* 3 vols. (1815-27), 1: 218, 2: 46-47; Will of Sir John Drake of Ash, Devon 8 Aug. 1636, Proved 26 Jan. 1636/37 PROB 11/173.

2060-2061   Herbert C. Andrews, "Notes on the Rowlett and Jennings families," *Miscellanea Genealogica et Heraldica,* 5th series, 8 [1932-34]: 90, 107; William A. Shaw, *The Knights of England,* 2 vols. (1906), 1: 163; B. D. Henning, *The History of Parliament: The House of Commons 1660–1690,* 3 vols. (1983), 2: 649; Will of Sir John Jennyns of St. Albans, Hertfordshire 21 March 1638/39, Proved at London P.C.C. 9 Aug. 1642 PROB 11/190.

2062-2063   *The Complete Baronetage,* 1: 212; *Publications of the Harleian Society, Visitation Series,* vol. 51, A. R. Maddison, *Lincolnshire Pedigrees,* 596; John Alexander Temple and Harald Markham Temple, *The Temple Memoirs: an account of this historic family and its demesnes; with biographical sketches, anecdotes & legends from Saxon times to the present day* (1925), 49; *Parish registers for St. Bride Fleet Street, 1274–1939* Family History Library film 0380,154. See also 2738-2739.

2064-2065   *The History of Parliament 1660–1690,* 2: 28-31; *The Complete Baronetage,* 2: 232-33.

2066-2067   *The History of Parliament 1660–1690,* 2: 82-83; Edwin Chappell, *Eight Generations of the Pepys Family 1500–1800* (1936), 44; *The Complete Peerage,* 11: 430-33; *Publications of the Harleian Society, Visitation Series,* vol. 10, Joseph Lemuel Chester, ed., *The Marriage, Baptismal and Burial Registers of the Collegiate Church or Abbey of St. Peter, Westminster,* 176.

2068-2069   *The visitations of the county of Devon,* 192; *The Complete Peerage,* 2: 20; Joseph Foster, *Alumni Oxonienses: The members of the University of Oxford, 1500–1714: their parentage, birthplace, and year of birth, with a record of their degrees. Being the matriculation register of the University, alphabetically arranged, revised and annotated,* 4 vols. (1891-92), 1-2: 604; *The Knights of England,* 2: 206; *Parish Church of Kilkhampton (Cornwall) register, 1539–1839* Family History Library film 0897,356; *Parish Church of Heavitree (Devonshire) register transcripts, 1653–1837* Family History Library film 0917,199.

2070-2071   *The Dictionary of National Biography, founded in 1882 by George Smith, edited by Sir Leslie Stephen and Sir Sidney Lee,* 2nd ed., 22 vols. (1885–1901; reprinted 1908-9), 21: 1108; Sir Richard Colt Hoare, Bt., *The History of Modern Wiltshire,* 14 parts in 6 vols. (1822-44), 5: 2: 29; *The Knights of England,* 2: 191.

2072-2073   *The History of Parliament 1660–1690,* 3: 758-59; *The Complete Baronetage,* 1: 66.

2074-2075   *The History of Parliament 1660–1690,* 2: 533-34; *Kwartierstatenboek: verzameling kwartierstaten bijeengebracht ter gelegenheid van de herdenking van het 100–jarig bestaan van het Koninklijk Nederlandsch Genootschap voor Geslacht-en Wapenkunde, 1883–1983* (1983), 71; *Publications of the Harleian Society, Register Series,* vol. 40, Willoughby Littledale, *The Registers of St. Bene't and St. Peter, Paul's Wharf, London, 1607 to 1837,* 285, and vol. 66, J.V. Kitto, *The Register of St. Martin-in-the-Fields, London 1619–1636,* 36; *Alumni Oxonienses: The members of the University of Oxford, 1500–1714,* 1-2: 695; *St. Andrew's Church (Enfield, Middlesex) registers, 1550–1928* Family History Library film 0585,397.

2076-2077 *The Complete Baronetage*, 2: 102-3; *Parish registers for St. Bride Fleet Street, 1274–1939* Family History Library film 0380,154.

2078-2079 *The Complete Peerage*, 12: 2: 777-79; *Publications of the Harleian Society, Visitation Series*, vol. 30, George J. Armytage, *Allegations for Marriage Licences issued by the Vicar-General of the Archbishop of Canterbury*, 77.

2080-2081 John Maclean, *Historical and Genealogical Memoir of the Family of Poyntz, or, Eight Centuries of an English House* (1886), 156; *Publications of the Harleian Society, Visitation Series*, vol. 43, W. Bruce Bannerman, ed., *The Visitations of the County of Surrey Made and Taken in the years 1530 by Thomas Benolte, Clarenceux King of Arms; 1572 by Robert Cooke, Clarenceux King of Arms; and 1623 by Samuel Thompson, Windsor Herald, and Augustin Vincent, Rouge Croix Pursuivant, marshals and deputies to William Camden, Clarenceux King of Arms*, 27; Douglas Richardson, *Plantagenet Ancestry: A Study in Medieval and Colonial Families* (2004), 560.

2082-2083 George F. Sydenham, *The History of the Sydenham Family: Collected from Family Documents, Pedigrees, Deeds, and Copious Memoranda* (1928), 133-35; *Historical and Genealogical Memoir of the Family of Poyntz*, 96; *Plantagenet Ancestry*, 699.

2084-2085 P. W. Hasler, *The History of Parliament: The House of Commons 1558–1603*, 3 vols. (1981), 3: 176-77; *Transactions of the Thoroton Society*, vol. 49, G. Ellis Flack, "Sir Thomas Parkyns of Bunny," 28-29.

2092-2093 *Historical and Genealogical Memoir of the Family of Poyntz*, 293.

2094-2095 Joseph James Muskett, *Suffolk Manorial Families: Being the County Visitations and Other Pedigrees*, 3 vols. (1900-8), 2: 312; *Lincolnshire Pedigrees*, 50: 40; *Publications of the Harleian Society, Register Series*, vol. 30, Willoughby A. Littledale, *The Registers St. Vedast, Foster Lane, 1558 to 1836, and St. Michael Le Quern, 1558 to 1837*, 149.

2096-2097 *The Complete Peerage*, 9: 197; Robert Halstead (Henry Mordaunt, Earl of Peterborough), *Succinct Genealogies of the Noble and Ancient Houses of Mordaunt of Turvey* (1685), 627-31.

2098-2099 *The History of Parliament 1558–1603*, 2: 347-48; *The Complete Peerage*, 5: 10-11; *The Marriage, Baptismal and Burial Registers of the Collegiate Church or Abbey of St. Peter, Westminster*, 10: 133.

2100-2101 *The History of Parliament 1558–1603*, 1: 550-51; *The Complete Peerage*, 9: 58-59; Percy W. Hedley, *Northumberland Families*, 2 vols. (1968), 2: 94-95.

2102-2103 *The History of Parliament 1558–1603*, 3: 399; Charles James Feret, *Fulham Old and New being an exhaustive history of the ancient parish of Fulham*, 3 vols. (1900), 2: 135-36; *Camden Society Series*, vol. 44, Sir Henry Ellis, *Obituary of Richard Smyth, secondary of the Poultry Compter, London: being a catalogue of all such persons as he knew in their life: Extending from A.D. 1627 to A.D. 1674*, xi, 7; *Publications of the Harleian Society, Visitation Series*, vol. 57, W. Harry Rylands, ed., *The Four Visitations of Berkshire Made and Taken by Thomas Benolte, Clarenceux, Anno 1532, By William Harvey, Clarenceux, Anno 1566, By Henry Chitting, Chester Herald, and John Philipott, Rouge Dragon, for William Camden, Clarenceux, Anno 1623, and by Elias Ashmole, Windsor Herald, for Sir Edward Bysshe, Clarenceux, Anno 1665–66*, 76.

2108-2109 "Pedigree of the family of Lunsford, of Lunsford and Wilegh, co. Sussex," *Collectanea Topographica et Genealogica* 4 [1837]: 141; *Publications of the Harleian Society, Visitation Series*, vol. 75, W. Bruce Bannerman, *The Visitations of Kent Taken in the Years 1530–1* *by Thomas Benolte, Clarenceux, and 1574 by Robert Cooke, Clarenceux, and 1592 by Robert Cooke, Clarenceux,* 99; *Plantagenet Ancestry,* 481.

2110-2111 *The Four Visitations of Berkshire,* 56: 250; *Alumni Oxonienses: The members of the University of Oxford, 1500–1714,* 3-4: 1058; *Archæologia Cantiana: Being Transactions of the Kent Archæological Society,* vol. 20, John J. Stocker, "Pedigree of Smythe of Ostenhanger, Kent; of Smythe of Bidborough and Sutton-at-Hone, Kent; and of the Smythes, Viscounts of Strangford, of Dromore, Ireland," 77; *Publications of the Harleian Society, Register Series,* vol. 17, Robert Hovenden, *A True Register of all the Christenings, Marriages and Burials in the Parish of St. James, Clerkenwell, 1551 to 1754,* 313.

2112-2113 John Hutchins, *The History and Antiquities of the County of Dorset: Compiled from the Best and Most Ancient Historians, Inquisitions Post Mortem, and Other Valuable Records and Mss. in the Public Offices and Libraries, and in Private Hands. With a Copy of Domesday Book and the Inquisitio Gheldi for the County: Interspersed with Some Remarkable Particulars of Natural History; and Adorned with a Correct Map of the County, and Views of Antiquities, Seats of the Nobility and Gentry, &c.,* 3rd ed., corrected, augmented and improved, 4 vols. (1861-70), 4: 374; *The Complete Baronetage,* 2: 398.

2114-2115 *The Complete Baronetage,* 2: 398.

2116-2117 *The Complete Baronetage,* 1: 209-10; *Publications of the Harleian Society, Register Series,* vol. 63, W. Bruce Bannerman, *Registers of St. Matthew, Friday Street, London, 1538 to 1812, and the United Parishes of St. Matthew and St. Peter, Cheap, 1754 to 1812,* 117, 123.

2118-2119 *The Complete Baronetage,* 1: 216; *Publications of the Harleian Society, Visitation Series,* vol. 28, George Grazebrook and John Paul Rylands, eds., *The Visitation of Shropshire Taken in the year 1623 by Robert Tresswell, Somerset Herald, and Augustine Vincent, Rouge Croix Pursuivant of Arms, Marshals and deputies to William Camden, Clarenceux King of Arms. With Additions from the Pedigrees of Shropshire Gentry Taken by the Heralds in the years 1569 and 1584, and other sources,* 281; George Morris, *Shropshire Genealogies: Shewing the Descent of the principal landed proprietors of the County of Salop from the time of William the Conqueror to the present time; compiled from Heraldic Visitations, public records, chartularies, family documents, parish registers and other sources,* 8 vols. (ca. 1836), 5: 436, 477.

2128-2129 Mervyn Archdall, *The Peerage of Ireland; or, a genealogical history of the present nobility of that kingdom with Engravings of their Paternal Coats of Arms. Collected from public records, authentic Manuscripts, approved Historians, well-attested Pedigrees, and Personal Information, by John Lodge,* 2nd ed. Revised, enlarged and continued to the Present Time, 7 vols. (1789), 6: 33.

2130-2131 *Oxford Dictionary of National Biography,* 56: 391.

2132-2133 Owen Manning and William Bray, *The History and Antiquities of the County of Surrey: Compiled from the Best and Most Authentic Historians, Valuable Records, and Manuscripts in the Public Offices and Libraries, and in Private Hands; with a Facsimile Copy of Domesday, Engraved on Thirteen Plates,* 3 vols. (1804-14), 3: 29; *Alumni Oxonienses: The members of the University of Oxford, 1500–1714,* 3-4: 1046; *The Visitations of the County of Surrey,* 43: 22.

2136-2137 *Journal of the County Kildare Archaeological Society,* vol. 4, Lord Walter FitzGerald, "Patrick Sarsfield, Earl of Lucan, with an account of his family and their connection with Lucan and Tully," 118.

2138-2139 *Journal of the County Kildare Archaeological Society,* vol. 6, Lord Walter FitzGerald, "Pedigree of the O'Mores of Leix, and of Ballina, co. Kildare," xii, pedigree c.

NOTES

2140-2141 *The Complete Peerage*, 12: 1: 595.

2142-2143 *Oxford Dictionary of National Biography*, 57: 179; Lord George Scott, *Lucy Walter, Wife or Mistress* (1947), 36.

2176-2177 *The History of Parliament 1558–1603*, 3: 369-70; *The Complete Baronetage*, 1: 34.

2178-2179 Joseph Jackson Howard and Frederick Arthur Crisp, *Visitation of England and Wales, Notes*, 14 vols. (1896-1921), 2: 165; *Publications of the Harleian Society, Visitation Series*, vol. 64, W. Harry Rylands, ed., *Pedigrees from the Visitation of Hampshire Made by Thomas Benolte, Clarenceulx, A⁰ 1530; Enlarged with the Vissitation of the same county made by Robert Cooke, Clarenceulx, Anno 1575, Both wch are continued wth the Visitation made by John Phillipott, Somersett (for William Camden, Clarenceux) in A⁰ 1622 most part then don(e) & finished in Ao 1634, as collected by Richard Mundy in Harleian MS. No. 1544*, 17.

2180-2181 *The History of Parliament 1558–1603*, 3: 234; *Alumni Oxonienses: The members of the University of Oxford, 1500–1714*, 3-4: 1181; *St. Mary's Church (Stoke-Newington) parish register transcripts, 1559–1812* Family History Library film 0094,717.

2182-2183 "Kerr of Ancrum, Earl of Ancrum, Earl and Marquis of Lothian," *The Genealogist: A Quarterly Magazine of Genealogical, Antiquarian, Topographical and Heraldic Research* 2 [1878]: 290.

2184-2185 *Publications of the Harleian Society, Visitation Series*, vol. 92, J. B. Whitmore, ed., *London Visitation Pedigrees, 1664*, 124; Will of John Shorter, Baker of Staines, Middlesex 8 May 1634, Proved at London P.C.C. 16 May 1634 PROB 11/165.

2186-2187 Henry Brierley, ed., *The Registers of Crosthwaite*, 2 vols. (1928-30), 2: 2, 213, 217, 309.

2188-2189 Leslie G. Pine, *Burke's Genealogical and Heraldic History of the Peerage and Baronetage* (1953), 1848; *Dictionary of Welsh Biography Down to 1940* (1959), 753; *The Complete Baronetage*, 1: 176; George Baker, *The History and Antiquities of the County of Northampton*, 2 vols. (1822-41), 2: 6; Henry Fitz-Gilbert Waters, "Genealogical Gleanings in England," *The New England Historical and Genealogical Register* 44 [1890]: 195 and note.

2190-2191 Donald Lines Jacobus, "The Darcy Ancestry of Mrs. John Sherman," *The American Genealogist* 21 [1945]: 175; *Alumni Oxonienses: The members of the University of Oxford, 1500–1714*, 1-2: 372; *The History and Antiquities of the County of Surrey*, 2: 150; *St. Ann Blackfriars Church (London) Parish registers, 1560–1849* Family History Library film 0374,416.

2192-2193 *Oxford Dictionary of National Biography*, 9: 96-122; Charles Carlton, *Charles I: The Personal Monarch* (1983); *The Dictionary of National Biography*, 4: 67-84; Neil D. Thompson and Col. Charles M. Hansen, "A Medieval Heritage: The Ancestry of Charles II, King of England," *The Genealogist* 2 [1981]: 161-62.

2194-2195 *The Complete Peerage*, 6: 75; John Hutchins, *The History and Antiquities of the County of Dorset: Compiled from the Best and Most Ancient Historians, Inquisitions Post Mortem, and Other Valuable Records and Mss. in the Public Offices and Libraries, and in Private Hands. With a Copy of Domesday Book and the Inquisitio Gheldi for the County: Interspersed with Some Remarkable Particulars of Natural History; and Adorned with a Correct Map of the County, and Views of Antiquities, Seats of the Nobility and Gentry, &c.*, 3rd ed., corrected, augmented and improved, 4 vols. (1861-70), 3: 342; *Publications of the Harleian Society, Register Series*, vol. 46, W. Bruce Bannerman, *The Registers of St. Olave, Hart Street, London, 1563 to 1700*, 36.

392

2196-2197 *The Complete Peerage*, 10: 190; *Alumni Oxonienses: The members of the University of Oxford, 1500–1714*, 1-2: 106; John Gage, *History of the Antiquities of Suffolk, Thingoe Hundred* (1838), 134; *The Knights of England*, 2: 158; *Parish Register of St. Peter-Le-Poer, London, Baptisms, marriages 1561–1904 Burials 1561–1853 Banns 1755–1817* Family History Library film 0374,993.

2198-2199 Adriaan Willem Eliza Dek, *Van Het Vorstenhuis Nassau* (1970), 149.

2200-2201 *Oxford Dictionary of National Biography*, 51: 577-81; *The Complete Peerage* , 12: 2: 859-63.

2202-2203 *The Complete Peerage*, 3: 5-6; *St. Mary's Church (Watford, Hertfordshire) parish registers and miscellaneous public records, 1539–1932* Family History Library film 0991,355.

2204-2205 *The History of Parliament 1660–1690*, 2: 57; M. E. Light, "Hedington and the Child family," *Wiltshire Notes & Queries* 2 [1897]: 210; *The Peerage of Ireland*, 2: 128; Will of Richard Childe or Child, Weaver of London 8 Sept. 1638, codicils 13 March 1638/39 and 5 May 1639, Proved 25 May 1639 PROB 11/180.

2206-2207 *London Visitation Pedigrees*, 92: 11; *Publications of the Harleian Society, New Series*, vol. 16, T. C. Wales et al., eds., *The Visitation of London begun in 1687*, 99; *Publications of the Harleian Society, Register Series*, vol. 72, A. W. Hughes Clarke, *The Registers of St. Mary Magdalen Milk Street, London and St. Michael Bassishaw, London, 1558 to 1892*, 55; Will of William Atwood, Merchant of Hackney, Middlesex 27 Sept. 1689, Proved at London P.C.C. 21 March 1690 PROB 11/398.

2208-2209 *The Complete Baronetage*, 2: 213; Henry Foley, *Records of the English Province of the Society of Jesus: historic facts illustrative of the labours and sufferings of its members in the sixteenth and seventeenth centuries*, 7 vols. in 8 (1877-83), 1: pedigree; Will of Dame Catherine Waldegrave Proved 4 April 1695 PROB 11/425.

2210-2211 *The Complete Baronetage*, 1: 91; John Nichols, *The History and Antiquities of the County of Leicestershire: Compiled from the Best and Most Ancient Historians; Inquisitions Post Mortem, and Other Valuable Records; Including Also Mr. Burton's Description of the County, Published in 1622; and the Later Collections of Mr. Stavely, Mr. Carte, Mr. Peck, and Sir Thomas Cave*, 4 vols. in 8 (1795-1815), 3: 406.

2212-2213 See 2192-2193.

2214-2215 See 1028-1029.

2216-2217 *The Complete Baronetage*, 2: 220; *The History and Antiquities of the County of Dorset*, 3: 298; *The History of Modern Wiltshire*, 3: 5: 20; Will of Sir John Webb of Odstock, Wiltshire, Baronet 8 June 1676, Proved 6 May 1681 PROB 11/366.

2218-2219 *The Victoria History of the County of Gloucester*, 7 vols. to date. (1907-), 7: 89; "Inquisitiones Post Mortem *temp.* Henry VIII to Charles I," *The Genealogist*, New Series, 10 [1894]: 57; *Publications of the Harleian Society, Visitation Series*, vol. 21, Sir John Maclean and W. C. Heane, *The Visitation of the County of Gloucester Taken in the year 1623, by Henry Chitty and John Phillipot as Deputies to William Camden, Clarenceaux King of Arms, with Pedigrees from the Herald's Visitations of 1569 and 1582-3, and Sundry Miscellaneous Pedigrees*, 21-22; William Berry, *County Genealogies: Pedigrees of the Families in the County of Sussex: Collected from the Heraldic Visitations and Other Authentic Manuscripts in the British Museum, and in the Possession of Private Individuals, and from the Information of the Present Resident Families* (1830), 355; Will of John Blomer of Hatherop, Gloucestershire Proved 27 May 1639 PROB 11/180.

2220-2221   *The Complete Peerage*, 5: 264.

2222-2223   *The Complete Peerage*, 12: 2: 767-69; *The Dictionary of National Biography*, 15: 535-37; Egerton Brydges, *Collins's Peerage of England, Genealogical, Biographical, and Historical, Greatly Augmented, and Continued to the Present Time*, 9 vols. (1812), 2: 376-80; *Publications of the Harleian Society, Visitation Series*, vol. 26, Joseph Lemuel Chester and George J. Armytage, *Allegations for Marriage Licences issued by the Bishop of London*, 118. See also 6100-6101.

2224-2225   *The History of Parliament 1660–1690*, 3: 662-63; George Henry Dashwood et al., eds., *The Visitation of Norfolk in the Year 1563, taken by William Harvey, Clarenceux King of Arms*, 2 vols. (1878-95), 1: 368.

2226-2227   John Venn and John Archibald Venn, *Alumni Cantabrigienses; A biographical list of all known students, graduates and holders of office at the University of Cambridge, from the earliest times to 1900*, 10 vols. (1922-54), 1: 269; *The Knights of England*, 2: 237; *Publications of the Harleian Society, Visitation Series*, vol. 8, George W. Marshall, ed., *Le Neve's Pedigrees of the Knights made by King Charles II, King James II, King William III and Queen Mary, King William alone, and Queen Anne*, 165, 166; Robert Battle, "English Ancestry of Anne (Derehaugh) Stratton of Salem, Massachusetts," *The New England Historical and Genealogical Register* 156 [2002]: 44; Walter C. Metcalfe, ed., *The Visitations of Suffolk made by Hervey, Clarenceux, 1561, Cooke, Clarenceux, 1577 and Raven, Richmond Herald, 1612 with notes and an appendix of Additional Suffolk Pedigrees* (1882), 189.

2228-2231   See 1092-1095.

2240-2241   *The Baronetage of England*, 4: 108.

2256-2259   Leslie G. Pine, ed., *Burke's Genealogical and Heraldic History of the Peerage, Baronetage and Knightage* (1956), 2202.

2264-2265   *The History of Parliament 1660–1690*, 3: 492; *The Complete Baronetage*, 2: 37, 4: 47.

2266-2267   *The History of Parliament 1660–1690*, 3: 492; "Pedigrees and heraldic notes of Gregory King: Briggs of Ernestree and Haughton, Salop," *Miscellanea Genealogica et Heraldica*, 5th series, 9 [1932]: 150; *Shropshire Genealogies* , 6: 282; *The Complete Baronetage*, 4: 47.

2268-2269   John William Clay, ed., *Dugdale's Visitation of Yorkshire in 1665–6, with additions*, 3 vols. (1899-1917), 3: 276; *Publications of the Harleian Society, Register Series*, vol. 43, W. Bruce Bannerman, *The Registers of Allhallows, Bread Street, 1538 to 1892, and St. John The Evangelist, Friday Street, London, 1653 to 1822*, 18, 19, 20, 21, 24, and vol. 69, A. W. Hughes Clarke et al., *Registers of St. Dunstan in the East, 1558 to 1766*, 108; *Publications of the Harleian Society, Visitation Series*, vol. 39, John W. Clay, ed., *Familiae Minorum Gentium. Diligentiâ Josephi Hunter, Sheffieldiensis, S.A.S.*, 978.

2270-2271   *Familiae Minorum Gentium*, 39: 978.

2272-2273   *The History of Parliament 1660–1690*, 3: 628-30; *The Dictionary of National Biography*, 20: 167-68; Edward Foss, *The Judges of England with Sketches of Their Lives and Miscellaneous Notices Connected with the Courts at Westminster, from the Time of the Conquest*, 9 vols. (1848-64), 7: 187-89.

2274-2275   John Roger Woodhead, *The rulers of London 1660–1689: a biographical record of the aldermen and common councilmen of the City of London* (1965), 92; Alfred Beaven, *The Aldermen of the City of London Temp. Henry III–1908 with Notes on the Parliamentary*

Representation of the City, the Aldermen and the Livery Companies, the Aldermanic Veto, Aldermanic Baronets and Knights, etc., 2 vols. (1908-13), 2: 96; Walter Arthur Copinger, *History of the Copingers or Coppingers of the County of Cork, Ireland, and the Counties of Suffolk and Kent, England* (1884), 4: pedigree; *Parish registers for St. Margaret Lothbury, London* Family History Library film 0374,471; *Parish Registers of the Stepney parish church, 1568–1929* Family History Library film 0595,417; *A True Register of all the Christenings, Marriages and Burials in the Parish of St. James, Clerkenwell, Registers of St. James, Clerkenwell, 1551 to 1754*, 13: 177.

2276-2277 *Oxford Dictionary of National Biography*, 59: 456-57; *The Complete Peerage*, 11: 45-47.

2278-2279 *The History of Parliament 1660–1690*, 3: 672; Arthur Malet, *Notices of an English branch of the Malet family* (1885), 48-49.

2280-2281 James Raine, *The History and Antiquities of North Durham, as Subdivided into the Shires of Norham, Island and Bedlington, which from the Saxon Period until the Year 1844, Constituted Parcels of the County Palatine of Durham, but Are Now United to the County of Northumberland* (1852), 186.

2282-2283 *The History and Antiquities of North Durham*, 319.

2288-2289 Northumberland County History Commission, *A history of Northumberland*, 15 vols. (1893-1940), 13: 223; *Publications of the Surtees Society*, vol. 142, H. M. Wood, ed., *Wills and Inventories from the Registry at Durham*, 177.

2290-2291 *Northumberland Families*, 2: 132; *The Knights of England*, 2: 206; *Pedigrees of the County Families of Yorkshire, comp. by Joseph Foster and authenticated by the members of each family*, 2 vols. (1874), 1: Fairfax; *Parish Church of Holme-upon-Spalding-Moor (Yorkshire) register transcripts, 1559–1650* Family History Library film 0098,534, item 3; Gary Boyd Roberts, *The Royal Descents of 600 Immigrants to the American Colonies or the United States: Who Were Themselves Notable or Left Descendants Notable in American History* (2004; revised and reissued 2006), 187-88.

Sir Thomas Widdrington and Hon. Frances Fairfax were the matrilineal great-grandparents of Samuel Ogle, Governor of Maryland.

2292-2293 *Dugdale's Visitation of Yorkshire in 1665–6*, 2: 350-51; Joseph Nicolson and Richard Burn. *The History and Antiquities of the Counties of Westmorland and Cumberland*, 2 vols. (1777), 1: 205; *The Complete Baronetage*, 2: 174-75.

2294-2295 *Dugdale's Visitation of Yorkshire in 1665–6*, 1: 335-36, 3: 413; *Familiae Minorum Gentium*, 38: 627; *Publications of the Thoresby Society*, vol. 12, George Denison Lumb, ed., *The Registers of the Parish Church of Methley in the County of York, from 1560 to 1812*, 47, 81, 87, 116; *Parish Register of St. Peter-Le-Poer, London, Baptisms, marriages 1561–1904 Burials 1561–1853 Banns 1755–1817* Family History Library film 0374,993.

2304-2305 Thomas George Baring, Earl of Northbrook, et al., eds., *Journals and correspondence from 1808 to 1852, of Sir Francis Thornhill Baring afterwards Lord Northbrook, compiled and edited by his son Thomas George, Earl of Northbrook* (1905), 271, 273; *Deutsches Geschlechterbuch (Genealogisches Handbuch Bürgerlicher Familien)*, vol. 102, "Baring, v. Baring, Baring v. Wallerode: Freiherr v. Baring, Baring-Gould, Baring Baronet of Larkbear, Baring Baronet of Nubia House, Baring Baron of Hillburton, Baring Baron Viscount und Earl of Cromer, Viscount Errington, Baring Baron Viscount und Earl of Northbrook, Baring Baron Revelstoke, aus Groningen in Friesland," 12-14.

2306-2307 *Deutsches Geschlechterbuch (Genealogisches Handbuch Bürgerlicher Familien)*, 102: 94.

2344-2345 William Berry, *County Genealogies: Pedigrees of Berkshire Families* (1837), 83; William Berry, *County Genealogies: Pedigrees of Hertfordshire Families* (1837), 235; Will of John Watlyngton or Watlington, Yeoman of Natley Scuers, Hampshire 10 Nov. 1558, Proved at London 9 Dec. 1558 PROB 11/42A.

2348-2349 *Alumni Cantabrigienses*, 2: 43; Will of Thomas Dillingham, Clerk of Over Dean, Bedfordshire 1 Dec. 1647, Proved at London P.C.C. 28 Jan. 1648 PROB 11/203.

2350-2351 *Oxford Dictionary of National Biography*, 42: 967-68; Will of Thomas Paske, Doctor in Divinity and Rector of Much Hadham, Hertfordshire 12 Sept. 1662, Proved at London P.C.C. 19 Nov. 1662 PROB 11/309.

2356-2357 *Dugdale's Visitation of Yorkshire in 1665–6*, 1: 283-84.

2358-2359 *Publications of the Harleian Society, New Series*, vol. 5, G. D. Squibb, ed., *The Visitation of Nottinghamshire begun in 1662 and finished in 1664 made by William Dugdale, Norroy King of Arms*, 118; *Publications of the Harleian Society, Visitation Series*, vol. 88, J. W. Walker, ed., *Hunter's Pedigrees: A Continuation of Familiae Minorum Gentium, Diligentiâ Josephi Hunter, Sheffieldiensis, S.A.S.*, 138; *Lincolnshire Pedigrees*, 52: 912.

2364-2365 *Publications of the Surtees Society*, vol. 36, Robert Davies, ed., *The Visitation of the County of Yorke, Began in Ao Dñi MDCLXV and Finished Ao Dñi MDCLXVI, by William Dugdale, Esqr, Norroy King of Armes*, 82; *Dugdale's Visitation of Yorkshire in 1665–6*, 3: 509.

2366-2367 *The Parish Register of Whitby, 1600–1676* Family History Library film 0599,996, item 6.

2368-2369 *Visitation of England and Wales, Notes*, 5: 4; Sir Algernon Tudor Tudor-Craig, *The romance of Melusine and de Lusignan: together with genealogical notes and pedigrees of Lovekyn of London, Lovekyn of Lovekynsmede, and of Luckyn of Little Waltham, and Lukyn of Mashbery, all in the county of Essex, and of Lukin of Felbrigg, co. Norfolk* (1932), 18.

2370-2371 *Visitation of England and Wales, Notes*, 5: 5.

2372-2373 A. T. Craig, "Lane of Campsea Ash, Norfolk," *Miscellanea Genealogica et Heraldica*, 5th series, 2 [1918]: 59; *Publications of the Navy Records Society*, vols. 13, Samuel Rawson Gardiner and C. T. Atkinson, *Letters and Papers relating to the First Dutch War 1652–1654*, 64, 30: 12, 147, 167-68, 37: 9, 21, 125, 211-15, 293, 41: 18, 46: 49, 107, 181-82; Will of Lyonell or Lionell Lane of Beccles, Suffolk 23 May 1654, Proved at Westminster P.C.C. 18 Oct. 1654 PROB 11/242.

2374-2375 *Baptisms, Parish Registers of Rayne, Essex, 1558–1663* Family History Library film 1472,666, item 20.

2380-2381 *Panfield, Essex, Christenings, Burials & Marriages, 1569–1711* Family History Library film 1472,590, item 23.

2382-2383 *Panfield, Essex, Christenings, Burials & Marriages, 1569–1711* Family History Library film 1472,590, item 23; Will of Robert Hutchin of Rayne, Essex 22 Jan. 1690/91, Proved 2 May 1692 E.R.O. D/A MR8/24.

2384-2385 G. H. Holley, "Pedigrees compiled from the parish registers, wills, monumental inscriptions, court records, etc., Norfolk County England" (a 7 vol. manuscript at the Family History Library, Salt Lake City, Utah), 2: 107; Percy Millican, *A History of Horstead and Stanninghall, Norfolk* (1937), 130.

2386-2387 "Pedigrees compiled from the parish registers, wills, monumental inscriptions, court records, etc., Norfolk County, England," 3: 76; *Publications of the Harleian Society, Visitation Series,* vol. 85, A. W. Hughes Clarke and Arthur Campling, *The Visitation of Norfolk Anno Domini 1664 made by Sir Edward Bysshe, Knt., Clarenceux King of Arms,* 27.

2388-2389 "Pedigrees compiled from the parish registers, wills, monumental inscriptions, court records, etc., Norfolk County, England," 2: 106.

2390-2391 "Pedigrees compiled from the parish registers, wills, monumental inscriptions, court records, etc., Norfolk County, England," 5: 24.

2392-2393 *Alumni Cantabrigienses,* 3: 66.

2400-2401 *Visitations of England and Wales, Notes,* 11: 107; Gabriel Girod de l'Ain, *Les Thellusson histoire d'une famille* (1977), 29-30.

2402-2403 *Les Thellusson histoire d'une famille,* 32; *http://www.huguenots-france.org/france/ lyon/lyon17/pag23.htm#24,* accessed 17 April 2007.

2404-2405 *http://www.huguenots-france.org/france/lyon/lyon17/pag17.htm#11,* accessed 17 April 2007.

2406-2407 *http://www.huguenots-france.org/france/lyon/lyon17/pag23.htm#20,* accessed 17 April 2007.

2416-2417 L. H. Bouwens and B. G. Bouwens, *A Thousand Ancestors* (1935), viii: 83, 114.

2418-2419 *A Thousand Ancestors,* viii: 83; *London Marriage Licences, 1521–1869,* 1502.

2424-2425 *Oxford Dictionary of National Biography,* 7: 549; *A Thousand Ancestors,* viii: 83.

2426-2427 Henry Fitz-Gilbert Waters, "Genealogical Gleanings in England," *The New England Historical and Genealogical Register* 48 [1894]: 506-9, 511, 49 [1895]: 107-8, 122; *Alumni Oxonienses: The members of the University of Oxford, 1500–1714,* 3-4: 1304; *Familiae Minorum Gentium,* 38: 639; Philip Morant, *The History and Antiquities of the County of Essex: Compiled from the Best and Most Ancient Historians: from Domesday-Book, Inquisitiones Post Mortem and Other the Most Valuable Records and Mss. &c, the Whole Digested, Improved, Perfected and Brought Down to the Present Time,* 2 vols. (1768), 1: 101; *The History and Antiquities of the County of Northampton,* 1: 527; *The Knights of England,* 2: 167; *South Ockendon Register 1538–1783* Family History Library film 1472,589, item 23; Will of Sir Richard Saltonstall of South Ockenden, Essex 16 Feb. 1649, Proved at London P.C.C. 6 March 1649/50 PROB 11/211; Will of Dame Mary Saltonstall of South Ockendon, Essex 11 Nov. 1651, Proved at London P.C.C. 21 May 1662 PROB 11/308.

2432-2433 Charles Edward Pitman, *History and pedigree of the family of Pitman of Dunchideock, Exeter, and their collaterals, and of the Pitmans of Alphington, Norfolk and Edinburgh: with part pedigrees and acccounts of families connected by marriage* (1920), 59; Vivien Allen, *The Bulteels: The Story of a Huguenot Family* (2004), 19-21, 35-36; Will of James Bulteel, Merchant of Barnstaple, Devon Aug. 1632, Proved at London P.C.C. 30 Oct. 1632 PROB 11/162.

2434-2435 J. L. Vivian, *The visitations of Cornwall, comprising the Heralds' visitations of 1530, 1573, & 1620* (1887), 254.

2440-2441 *The visitations of the county of Devon,* 254, 165, 471; "The family of Croker," *Herald & Genealogist* 8 [1874]: 380.

2442-2443 *The Complete Baronetage,* 2: 57-58.

2444-2445   *The visitations of the county of Devon*, 470, 447.

2446-2447   *The History of Parliament 1660–1690*, 3: 164-65; *The visitations of Cornwall*, 229.

2448-2449   *The Complete Peerage*, 10: 478-79; Sir James Balfour Paul, *The Scots Peerage*, 9 vols. (1904-14), 7: 48-50.

2450-2451   *The Complete Peerage*, 11: 219; *The Scots Peerage*, 7: 343-44. See also 5358-5359.

2452-2453   *Oxford Dictionary of National Biography*, 38: 915-16; *The Complete Peerage*, 4: 463; *The Knights of England*, 2: 181; *The Peerage of Ireland*, 2: 101-5.

2454-2455   See 2048-2049.

2460-2461   *Registers of Walkern, Herts: Baptisms 1559–1812* Family History Library film 1040,799.

2496-2497   *A history of Northumberland*, 2: 351, 363.

2498-2499   *A history of Northumberland*, 7: 258.

2504-2505   *A history of Northumberland*, 1: 331.

2512-2513   Robert Surtees, *The History and Antiquities of the County Palatine of Durham: Compiled from Original Records, Preserved in Public Repositories and Private Collections, and Illustrated by Engravings of Architectural and Monumental Antiquities, Portraits of Eminent Persons &c., &c.*, 4 vols. (1816-40), 2: 14, 19; *Dugdale's Visitation of Yorkshire in 1665–6*, 1: 286.

2514-2515   *The Dictionary of National Biography*, 3: 1286; *The History and Antiquities of the County of Leicestershire*, 2: 2: 259; *Alumni Cantabrigienses*, 1: 311; George Ormerod, *The History of the County Palatine and City of Chester: Compiled from Original Evidences in Public Offices, the Harleian and Cottonian Mss., Parochial Registers, Private Muniments, Unpublished Mss., Collections of Successive Cheshire Antiquaries, and a Personal Survey of Every Township in the County, Incorporated with a Republication of King's Vale Royal and Leycester's Cheshire Antiquities. Also known as: The King's Vale Royal, The Vale Royall of England and Cheshire Antiquities*, 2nd ed. Revised and enlarged by Thomas Helsby, 3 vols. in 6 (1882), 3: 303; *Melton Mowbray Parish Registers: Baptisms, marriages and burials 1547–1718* Family History Library film 0588,441.

2516-2517   *The Complete Baronetage*, 3: 204.

2518-2519   *Visitation of England and Wales, Notes*, 6: 197; *The History and Antiquities of the County Palatine of Durham*, 2: 78; *St. Nicholas' Church (Newcastle-upon-Tyne) parish register transcripts, 1558–1837* Family History Library film 0095,017.

2520-2521   Henry A. Ogle, *Ogle and Bothal: Or, A History of the Baronies of Ogle, Bothal, and Hepple, and of the Families of Ogle and Bertram, Who Held Possession of Those Baronies and Other Property in the County of Northumberland and Elsewhere; Showing Also How the Property Descended into Other Hands: To Which Is Added Accounts of Several Branches of Families Bearing the Name of Ogle Settled in Other Counties and Countries; with Appendices and Illustrations Compiled from Ancient Records and Other Sources* (1902), 120.

2522-2523   *Ogle and Bothal*, 123; *A history of Northumberland*, 5: 288.

2524-2525   *A history of Northumberland*, 6: 257.

2526-2527   *The History and Antiquities of the County Palatine of Durham*, 3: 322, 294; *St. Nicholas' Church (Newcastle-upon-Tyne) parish register transcripts, 1558–1837* Family History Library film 0095,017.

2528-2529 *Alumni Cantabrigienses*, 3: 377; *Burke's Genealogical and Heraldic History of the Peerage and Baronetage* (1953), 196; *The Complete Peerage*, 1: 169, note a, 10: 636, note f, 4: 535, note c; *The Knights of England*, 2: 233; Joseph Foster, *Pedigrees Recorded at the Heralds' Visitations of the Counties of Cumberland and Westmorland made by Richard St. George, Norroy King of Arms in 1615, and by William Dugdale, Norroy King of Arms in 1666* (1891), 21.

2530-2531 *The Peerage of Ireland*, 2: 105.

2532-2533 *Oxford Dictionary of National Biography*, 36: 657-58; *The Dictionary of National Biography*, 36: 157-58; H. Loftus Tottenham, "James Margetson, Archbishop of Armagh," *Notes and Queries: A Medium of Inter-Communication for Literary Men, Artists, Antiquaries, Genealogists, etc.*, 8th series, 6 [1894]: 1-2.

2534-2535 *The Complete Peerage*, 3: 136.

2536-2537 *The History of Parliament 1660–1690*, 2: 35-39; *The Complete Peerage*, 4: 341; *The Marriage, Baptismal and Burial Registers of the Collegiate Church or Abbey of St. Peter, Westminster*, 10: 269.

2538-2539 See 1312-1313.

2540-2541 *The History and Antiquities of the County of Hertford*, 3: 132; *Le Neve's Pedigrees*, 8: 215; Will of Charles Hoskins of Oxted, Surrey 8 July 1657, nuncupative codicil 26 Aug. 1657, Proved at London P.C.C. 6 Nov. 1657 PROB 11/269.

2542-2543 *The History of Parliament 1660–1690*, 2: 462-63; Oswald Barron, ed., *Northamptonshire Families* (1906), 75; *The History and Antiquities of the County of Hertford*, 3: 132; Will of William Hale of King's Walden, Hertfordshire Proved 4 July 1688 PROB 11/392.

2544-2545 *Burke's Genealogical and Heraldic History of the Peerage and Baronetage* (1953), 1469; *The Peerage of Ireland*, 5: 134.

2546-2547 Francis Elrington Ball, *The Judges in Ireland 1221–1921*, 2 vols. (1927), 1: 344; Eveline Cruickshanks, Stuart Handley and David Hayton, *The History of Parliament: The House of Commons 1690–1715*, 5 vols. (2002), 4: 826-27; *The Peerage of Ireland*, 5: 134; Leslie G. Pine, *Burke's Genealogical and Heraldic History of the Landed Gentry of Ireland* (1958), 252.

2548-2549 *The Complete Baronetage*, 1: 226-27; *The Peerage of Ireland*, 2: 63-68; *The Knights of England*, 2: 160.

2550-2551 Sir John St. George, "Pedigree of the family of St. George," *Miscellanea Genealogica et Heraldica*, New Series, 3 [1882]: 79; *The Knights of England*, 2: 192; *The Complete Baronetage*, 3: 120.

2552-2553 Hugh Montgomery-Massingberd, *Burke's Irish Family Records* (1976), 1158; *The Knights of England*, 2: 204.

2554-2555 *Burke's Irish Family Records*, 1158.

2560-2561 *The Scots Peerage*, 1: 56-57; *Sussex Archeological Collections: Illustrating the History and Antiquities of the County*, vol. 47, F. W. T. Attree and J. H. L. Booker, "The Sussex Colepepers," pedigree; *The Marriage, Baptismal and Burial Registers of the Collegiate Church or Abbey of St. Peter, Westminster*, 10: 180.

2562-2563 *The Complete Baronetage*, 4: 208; *The Marriage, Baptismal and Burial Registers of the Collegiate Church or Abbey of St. Peter, Westminster*, 10: 211; *The Complete Peerage*, 9: 357-59.

2564-2565 *The History and Antiquities of the County of Hertford,* 3: 171; *The Four Visitations of Berkshire,* 56: 262; John Edwin Cussans, *History of Hertfordshire, Containing an Account of the Descents of the Various Manors, Pedigrees of Families Connected with the County, Antiquities, Local Customs, &c., &c.: Chiefly Compiled from Original Mss., in the Record Office and British Museum, Parochial Registers, Local Archives and Collections in the Possession of Private Families,* 8 parts in 3 vols. (1870-81), 1: 1: 141; Will of John Plumer, Gentleman of New Windsor, Berkshire 15 March 1668, Proved at London P.C.C. 9 Oct. 1672 PROB 11/340.

2566-2567 See 2542-2543.

2568-2569 Henry Holman Drake, *Hasted's history of Kent: corrected, enlarged and continued to the present time, from the manuscript collections of the late Rev. Thomas Streatfield and the late Rev. Lambert Blackwell Larking, the public records, and other sources. pt. 1. The hundred of Blackheath* (1886), 1: 138; Albert W. Woods, "Report on the Pedigree of the family of the Right Honourable James Craggs, Postmaster General, the father of the Right Honourable James Craggs, secretary of state in the reign of King George the First," *Miscellanea Genealogica et Heraldica* 2 [1876]: 34; *The History and Antiquities of the County Palatine of Durham,* 3: 415.

2570-2571 "Report on the Pedigree of the family of the Right Honourable James Craggs," 2: 34; Will of Jacob Richards, Salter of London 5 Nov. 1675, Proved P.C.C. 17 Dec. 1675 P.C.C. PROB 11/349.

2576-2577 Arthur Stephens Dyer, "Pedigree of Moyle of Bake, St. Germans, Cornwall," *Miscellanea Genealogica et Heraldica,* 5th series, 9 [1932]: 348.

2578-2579 *Oxford Dictionary of National Biography,* 39: 170-71; *The History of Parliament 1660–1690,* 3: 101-3; *Alumni Oxonienses: The members of the University of Oxford, 1500–1714,* 3-4: 1036; *The Knights of England,* 2: 226.

2580-2581 *The Complete Baronetage,* 3: 211; Stephen Glover, *The History and gazetteer of the county of Derby: drawn up from actual observation and from the best authorities: containing a variety of geological, mineralogical, commercial and statistical information,* 2 vols. in 3 (1831-33), 2: 191.

2582-2583 *The History of Parliament 1660–1690,* 3: 304; William Valentine Lloyd, *The Sheriffs of Montgomeryshire: with their armorial bearings, and notices, genealogical & biographical, of their families from 1540 to 1639* (1876), 489; "The Pedigree of the Ancient Family of the Palmers of Sussex, 1672," *Miscellanea Genealogica et Heraldica* 1 [1868]: 109.

2584-2585 *The History of Parliament 1690–1715,* 3: 400; *The visitations of Cornwall,* 57; Will of John Buller of Morval, Cornwall 21 Nov. 1714, codicils 24 Jan. 1714/15, 1 Sept. 1715, and 4 Nov. 1715, Proved at London P.C.C. 13 April 1716 PROB 11/552.

2586-2587 *The History of Parliament 1660–1690,* 3: 259-61; *The visitations of the county of Devon,* 601; *The History and Antiquities of the County of Surrey,* 2: pedigree facing 127; *The Knights of England,* 2: 264; *Publications of the Harleian Society, Visitation Series,* vol. 24, Joseph Lemuel Chester and George J. Armytage, *Allegations for Marriage Licences issued by the Faculty Office of the Archbishop of Canterbury at London, 1543–1869,* 83; Lady Eliott-Drake, *The Family and Heirs of Sir Francis Drake,* 2 vols. (1911), 2: 55-56.

2588-2589 *The History of Parliament 1660–1690,* 3: 592-95; *The Complete Baronetage,* 2: 43; *Parish Church of Berry-Pomeroy register transcripts, 1596–1837* Family History Library film 0916,810.

2590-2591 *The visitations of the county of Devon,* 466; *Alumni Oxonienses: The members of the University of Oxford, 1500–1714,* 1-2: 690.

2592-2593   *The Complete Peerage,* 9: 294-96; *The Scots Peerage,* 6: 375-77.

2594-2595   *The Complete Baronetage,* 2: 412.

2596-2597   George Lipscomb, *The History and Antiquities of the County of Buckingham,* 4 vols. (1847), 3: 221; *The Victoria History of the County of Buckingham,* 4 vols. (1905-28), 3: 175; *Publications of the Harleian Society, Visitation Series,* vol. 13, Walter C. Metcalfe, ed., *The Visitations of Essex by Hawley, 1552, Hervey 1558, Cooke 1570, Raven 1612 and Owen and Lilly, 1634, to which are added Miscellaneous Essex Pedigrees from various Harleian Manuscripts and an appendix containing Berry's Essex Pedigrees,* 495, and vol. 58, W. Harry Rylands, ed., *The Visitation of the County of Buckingham Made in 1634 by John Philipot, Esq., Somerset Herald, and William Ryley, Bluemantle Pursuivant, Marshals and Deputies to Sir Richard St. George, Knight, Clarenceux, and Sir John Borough, Knight, Garter, who visited as Norroy by mutual agreement; Including the Church Notes then taken, together with Pedigrees from the Visitation Made In 1566 by William Harvey, Esq., Clarenceux and some Pedigrees from other sources, Being a Transcript of MS. Eng. Misc. CM in the Bodleian Library, Oxford, with additions,* 54; Will of William Adderly or Adderley, Gentleman of Colney Hatch, Middlesex 5 March 1663/64, Proved 20 July 1666 PROB 11/321.

2600-2601   *Visitation of England and Wales, Notes,* 7: 141; Evelyn Dawsonne Heathcote, *An Account of some of the families bearing the name of Heathcote* (1899), 65-67.

2602-2603   *Visitation of England and Wales, Notes,* 7: 141; *The Registers of Allhallows, Bread Street, 1538 to 1892, and St. John The Evangelist, Friday Street, London, 1653 to 1822,* 43: 199, 201; Will of Christopher Rayner, Haberdasher of London 21 March 1662, Proved at London P.C.C. 6 April 1664 PROB 11/313; Will of Frances Rayner, Widow of London 3 July 1681, Proved at London P.C.C. 4 Aug. 1681 PROB 11/367.

2604-2605   *The History of Parliament 1690–1715,* 5: 849-50; *The History of Parliament 1660–1690,* 3: 705-6; Alfred T. Butler, *A Genealogical and Heraldic Dictionary of the Peerage and Baronetage* (1926), 2373.

2606-2607   *The History of Parliament 1690–1715,* 5: 611-12; *Familiae Minorum Gentium,* 38: 578.

2608-2609   *The History of Parliament 1660–1690,* 2: 711; *Pedigrees of the County Families of Yorkshire,* 1: Lascelles.

2610-2611   *The Visitation of London begun in 1687,* 16: 232; *Publications of the Harleian Society, Register Series,* vol. 32, W. Bruce Bannerman, *The Registers of St. Martin Outwich, London, 1670 to 1873,* 101, 108, 110; *Publications of the Harleian Society, Visitation Series,* vol. 23, Joseph Lemuel Chester and George J. Armytage, *Allegations for Marriage Licences issued by the Dean and Chapter of Westminster, 1558–1699; Also for those issued by the Vicar-General of the Archbishop of Canterbury, 1660–1679,* 219; *Register of Stainton, near Yarm, Cleveland: Christenings, marriages and burials, 1551–1837* Family History Library film 0551,576; Will of Edward Lascelles, Citizen and Grocer of London 5 March 1699, Proved at London P.C.C. 20 Sept. 1700 PROB 11/457.

2614-2615   James C. Brandow, *Genealogies of Barbados Families: from* Caribbeana *and* The Journal of the Barbados Museum and Historical Society (1983), 143, 646; Joanne McRee Sanders, *Barbados Records: Marriages 1643–1800,* 2 vols. (1982), 1: 61.

2616-2617   *Dugdale's Visitation of Yorkshire in 1665–6,* 2: 233; *Alumni Oxonienses: The members of the University of Oxford, 1500–1714,* 1-2: 256; *The register booke of Inglebye iuxta Grenhow since 1539* Family History Library film 0599,156, item 3.

2618-2619 *The History of Parliament 1690–1715*, 3: 280-81; *The History and Antiquities of the County Palatine of Durham*, 4: 108; *The Knights of England*, 2: 259; *Chapelry of Barnard-Castle (Durhamshire) register transcripts, 1609–1812* Family History Library film 0091,081.

2620-2621 Llewellynn Frederick William Jewitt, ed., *The Reliquary and illustrated archæologist*, 34 vols. (1860-94), 8: 47-48; *Bishops' Transcripts Parish of Leek, Staffordshire: Baptisms, marriages, and burials 1662–1740* Family History Library film 0421,562.

2624-2625 *The Complete Peerage*, 2: 79-80; *The Registers of St. Bene't and St. Peter, Paul's Wharf, London, 1607 to 1837*, 39: 22.

2626-2627 *Oxford Dictionary of National Biography*, 60: 527-30; *The Complete Peerage*, 12: 1: 131-34; *The Marriage, Baptismal and Burial Registers of the Collegiate Church or Abbey of St. Peter, Westminster*, 10: 201; Michael Jaffé, "Van Dyck Studies II: 'La belle & vertueuse Huguenotte,'" *The Burlington Magazine* 126 [1984]: 603.

2628-2629 Richard Evans, "Jeffrey Howland, Citizen and Grocer of London," *The New England Historical and Genealogical Register* 152 [1998]: 460.

2630-2631 *The History of Parliament 1660–1690*, 2: 57-58; *The Complete Baronetage*, 4: 106-7; W. P. W. Phillimore et al., eds., *Hampshire Parish Registers*, 16 vols. (1899-1914), 10: 9. See also 1102-1103.

2632-2633 *The Complete Baronetage*, 1: 147; *The History of Parliament 1690–1715*, 4: 622-23; *The visitations of Cornwall, comprising the Heralds' visitations of 1530, 1573, & 1620*, 195; *Parish Church of Kilkhampton (Cornwall) register, 1539–1839* Family History Library film 0897,356.

2634-2635 *The History of Parliament 1690–1690*, 3: 14-16; *The Complete Peerage*, 11: 264-66; *Publications of the Harleian Society, Register Series*, vol. 16, F. N. MacNamara and A. Story-Maskelyne, *The Parish Register of Kensington, Co. Middlesex, 1539 to 1675*, 43.

2636-2637 *Publications of the Harleian Society, New Series*, vol. 5, G. D. Squibb, ed., *The Visitation of Nottinghamshire begun in 1662 and finished in 1664 made by William Dugdale, Norroy King of Arms*, 56; Cecil George Savile Foljambe, Earl of Liverpool, *Evelyn Pedigrees and Memoranda* (1893), 56; *The Complete Peerage*, 4: 406, 7: 305-6.

2638-2639 *The Complete Peerage*, 4: 180.

2640-2641 W. J. d'Ablaing van Giessenburg, *De Ridderschap van Veluwe of Geschiedenis der Veluwsche Jonkers: opgeluisterd door hunne acht stamdeelen, huwelijken, kinderen en wapens, hoofdzakelijk getrokken uit de verzameling van handschriften van wijlen den Rijks-Vrijheer W. A. van Spaen* (1859), 246; W. J. Baron d'Ablaing van Giessenburg, *Bannerheeren en Ridderschap van Zutphen: van den aanvang der beroerten in de 16e eeuw tot het jaar 1795* (1877), 131, 149.

2642-2643 H. H. Röell, "Geldersche Geslachten. Bijdrage tot de genealogie van Lintelo," *De Nederlandsche Leeuw* 57 [1939]: 112-13.

2644-2645 *Nederland's Adelsboek*, vol. 11, 239; Abraham Ferwerda, *Adelyk en Aanzienelyk wapen-boek van de zeven provincien; waar by gevoegt zyn een groot aantal genealogien van voornaame Adelyke en Aanzienelyke familien, etc.*, 2 vols. in 3 (1760-81), 2: 10th generation: Genealogie van het Geslagte van der Duyn.

2646-2647 Pieter Dignus de Vos, *De Vroedschap van Zierikzee: van de tweede helft der 16de eeuw tot 1795* (1931), 231.

2648-2649 See 2192-2193.

2650-2651 Anselm de Saint-Marie and M. du Fourny, *Histoire de la Maison Royale de France Anciens Barons du Royaume: et des Grands Officiers de la Couronne*, 3rd ed., 9 vols. (1726–33), 5: 918.

2652-2655 See 1440-1443.

2656-2657 *The Complete Peerage*, 6: 681-82. See also 8122-8123.

2658-2659 *The Complete Peerage*, 9: 627-28; *Burke's Genealogical and Heraldic History of the Peerage and Baronetage* (1953), 1568.

2660-2661 See 524-525.

2662-2663 *Oxford Dictionary of National Biography*, 20: 719; *The Complete Baronetage*, 4: 293; *Familiae Minorum Gentium*, 40: 1296; *Publications of the Harleian Society, Visitation Series*, vol. 42, Robert Hovenden, ed., *The Visitation of Kent Taken in the Years 1619–1621 by John Philipot, Rouge Dragon, Marshal and Deputy to William Camden, Clarenceux*, 19; Will of Dudley Wylde of Bishops Palace, Canterbury, Kent 15 July 1653, Proved 8 Sept. 1653 PROB 11/227.

2664-2665 *The Scots Peerage*, 1: 86-87; *The Complete Baronetage*, 2: 451.

2666-2667 Simon F. Macdonald Lockhart, *Seven Centuries: A History of the Lockharts of Lee and Carnwath* (1978), 32; *The Scots Peerage*, 1: 89.

2668-2669 *Oxford Dictionary of National Biography*, 39: 943-46; *The Complete Peerage*, 1: 315-16; *The Scots Peerage*, 1: 473-75.

2670-2671 *Oxford Dictionary of National Biography*, 24: 764-65, 915-18; *The Complete Peerage*, 6: 264-66; *The Scots Peerage*, 4: 381-82.

2672-2673 Margaret D. Young, *The Parliaments of Scotland: burgh and shire commissioners*, 2 vols. (1992-93), 2: 479; *The Complete Baronetage*, 4: 311; Sir William Fraser, *The Book of Carlaverock: Memoirs of the Maxwells, Earls of Nithsdale, Lords Maxwell and Herries*, 2 vols. (1873), 1: 598.

2674-2675 *Oxford Dictionary of National Biography*, 24: 840; *The Complete Baronetage*, 3: 341; *Burke's Genealogical and Heraldic History of the Peerage and Baronetage* (1953), 1025; *Parish Church of Hamilton registers, 1645–1868* Family History Library film 1066,593.

2676-2677 *The Complete Peerage*, 5: 22; *The Scots Peerage*, 3: 452-54; *Dugdale's Visitation of Yorkshire in 1665–6*, 3: 189; *Allegations for Marriage Licences issued by the Dean and Chapter of Westminster, 1558–1699; Also for those issued by the Vicar-General of the Archbishop of Canterbury, 1660–1679*, 23: 47; *Parish Register of St. Peter-Le-Poer, London, Baptisms, marriages 1561–1904 Burials 1561–1853 Banns 1755–1817* Family History Library film 0374,993.

2678-2679 *The Complete Peerage*, 4: 526-27; *The Scots Peerage*, 3: 350.

2680-2681 *The Parliaments of Scotland*, 2: 611; Keith Stanley Malcolm Scott, *Scott 1118–1923: being a collection of "Scott" pedigrees containing all known male descendants from Buccleuch, Sinton, Harden, Balweary, etc.* (1923), 254; George Robertson, *Topographical Description of Ayrshire: more particularly of Cunningham, together with a genealogical account of the principal families in that Bailiwick* (1820), 241.

2682-2683 *Northern notes and queries, or, The Scottish antiquary* 3 [1889]: 51; *The Knights of England*, 2: 222; *The Complete Baronetage*, 2: 304.

2688-2689 *Visitations of England and Wales, Notes*, 5: 95; *The History and Antiquities of the County of Leicestershire*, 3: 394.

2690-2691 *Oxford Dictionary of National Biography*, 14: 174-75; *The Complete Peerage*, 3: 532; *The Knights of England*, 2: 183; Walter C. Metcalfe, ed., *The Visitations of Northamptonshire Made in 1564 and 1618–9: With Northamptonshire Pedigrees from Various Harleian Mss.* (1887), 176; *The History and Antiquities of the County of Surrey*, 1: 523.

2692-2693 *The Victoria History of the County of Buckingham*, 4 vols. (1905-28), 2: 356; *Suffolk Manorial Families*, 1: 358; *The Visitation of the County of Buckingham Made in 1634*, 58: 98; Will of Dame Susan Drewry or Drury, Widow of Temple Boulstred, Buckinghamshire 28 March 1639, Proved at London P.C.C. 25 Feb. 1641 PROB 11/185.

2694-2695 *The Aldermen of the City of London*, 2: 77; W. H. Shawcross alias Shallcross, *Shallcross Pedigrees* (1908), lxvii; *The Register of St. Martin-in-the-Fields, London 1619–1636*, 66: 143; *Publications of the Harleian Society, Visitation Series*, vol. 17, Joseph J. Howard and Joseph Lemuel Chester, eds., *The Visitation of London Anno Domini 1633, 1634 and 1635: Made by Sr Henry St George, Kt, Richmond Herald, and Deputy and Marshal to Sr Richard St George, Kt, Clarencieux King of Armes*, 26; Will of Humphrey Shalcrosse of Digswell, Hertfordshire 24 Dec. 1664, Proved 17 Feb. 1666 PROB 11/319.

2696-2697 Edward Baines and W. R. Whatton, *History of the County Palatine and Duchy of Lancaster*. New, Revised and Enlarged [3rd] ed., 5 vols. (1888–93), 2: 397; *Dugdale's Visitation of Yorkshire in 1665–6*, 1: 76; *Lancashire Parish Register Society*, vol. 12, Giles Shaw, trans., *The Registers of the Parish Church of Middleton in the County of Lancaster: Christenings, Burials, and Weddings 1541–1663*, 33-34.

2698-2699 *The Complete Baronetage*, 1: 149; *History of the County Palatine and Duchy of Lancaster*, 3: 393; *The registers of the parish church of Padiham in the county of Lancashire, 1573–1653* Family History Library film 0459,650.

2700-2701 *Pedigrees of the County Families of Yorkshire*, 1: Vavasour.

2702-2703 Ralph Thoresby, *Ducatus Leodiensis: or, the Topography of the Ancient and Populous Town and Parish of Leedes, and Parts Adjacent, in the West-Riding of the County of York, with the Pedigrees of Many of the Nobility and Gentry, and Other Matters Relating to those Parts; Extracted from Records, Original Evidence, and Manuscripts* (1816), 222, 225; *The Visitation of Nottinghamshire begun in 1662 and finished in 1664 made by William Dugdale, Norroy King of Arms*, 5: 91; *Hunter's Pedigrees*, 88: 43; *Lincolnshire Pedigrees*, 52: 1017; *The Knights of England*, 2: 162; Joseph Foster, *The Visitation of Yorkshire, made in the years 1584/5, by Robert Glover, Somerset herald; to which is added the subsequent visitation made in 1612, by Richard St. George, Norroy king of arms, with several additional pedigrees, including "The arms taken out of churches and houses at Yorkshire visitation, 1584/5," "Sir William Fayrfax' booke of arms" and other heraldic lists, with copious indices* (1875), 572; *Familiae Minorum Gentium*, 38: 583.

2704-2705 *The History and Antiquities of the County of Buckingham*, 4: 341; *Alumni Oxonienses: The members of the University of Oxford, 1500–1714*, 1-2: 644; *The History of the County Palatine and City of Chester*, 1: 574; *Collections for a History of Staffordshire*, vol. 5, part 2, H. Sydney Grazebrook, ed., *The Heraldic Visitations of Staffordshire Made by Sir Richard St. George, Norroy, in 1614, and by Sir William Dugdale in the Years 1663 and 1664*, 275.

2706-2707 *The History of Parliament 1660–1690*, 2: 44-46; *Oxford Dictionary of National Biography*, 11: 188-90; Frederick Arthur Crisp, *Fragmenta Genealogica*, 14 vols. in 2 series (1897-1910), New Series, 1: 83; *The Complete Baronetage*, 4: 141-42.

2708-2709 William Harrison, Thomas Harrison, and George Willis, *The great Jennens case: being an epitome of the history of the Jennens family* (1879), 4, 29, 32.

2710-2711 *The History of Parliament 1660–1690*, 3: 68; Caroline Robbins, *The diary of John Milward, esq., member of Parliament for Derbyshire, September 1666 to May 1668* (1938), xxiii; *The Heraldic Visitations of Staffordshire Made by Sir Richard St. George, Norroy, in 1614, and by Sir William Dugdale in the Years 1663 and 1664*, 5: 2: 304.

2712-2715 See 2708-2711.

2716-2717 *The Complete Baronetage*, 1: 119; *Oxford Dictionary of National Biography*, 57: 168-69.

2718-2719 *The Visitation of Nottinghamshire begun in 1662 and finished in 1664 made by William Dugdale, Norroy King of Arms*, 5: 22; *The Visitation of London Anno Domini 1633, 1634 and 1635*, 15: 246; *Mortlake parish register, 1599–1678* Family History Library film 0814,225, item 2.

2720-2721 *The Complete Baronetage*, 3: 123; *The History and Antiquities of the County of Hertford*, 1: 479; *Visitation of England and Wales, Notes*, 13: 95.

2722-2723 *The Complete Peerage*, 11: 550-52; *The parish registers of Hunsdon Co. Hertford, 1546–1837* Family History Library film 0496,822, item 2.

2724-2725 *Visitation of England and Wales, Notes*, 7: 21.

2726-2727 *The Complete Peerage*, 2: 516, 105, note c; *Publications of the Harleian Society, Visitation Series*, vol. 73, W. Harry Rylands and W. Bruce Bannerman, eds., *The Visitation of the County of Rutland, begun by Fran. Burghill, Somerset and Gregory King, Rougedragon in Trinity Vacation 1681, carried on and finished by Tho. May, Chester Herald and the said Rougedragon Pursuivt in Hilary and Trinity Vacation 1682 by Virtue of several deputa ons from Sr Henry St George Kt, Clarenceux King of Arms*, 3. See also 5270-5271.

2728-2729 Eduard Georg Ludwig William Howe Graf von Kielmansegg and Erich Friedrich Christian Ludwig Graf von Kielmansegg, *Familien-Chronik der Herren Freiherren und Grafen von Kielmansegg* (1872), Tafel III; *Danmarks Adels Aarbog*, 97 vols. to date (1884-), 40: 478.

2730-2731 *Danmarks Adels Aarbog 1982–84* (1982-84): 617-18.

2732-2733 F. von der Decken, *Das Leben Georg von Braunschweig* (1833-34); Detlev Schwennicke, ed., *Europäische Stammtafeln: Stammtafeln zur Geschichte der Europäischen Staaten*, Neue Folge, 21 vols. (1978-2001), 1: 1: 25.

2734-2735 *Ahnentafeln berühmter Deutscher*, vol. 9, Ernst Freiherr von Obernitz, "256stellige Ahnentafel des Dichters August von Platen-Hallermund 1796-1835," 265.

2736-2737 *The History of Parliament 1660–1690*, 2: 503; *The History and Antiquities of the County of Leicestershire*, 2: 1: 267, 285; Thomas Blore, *The History and Antiquities of the County of Rutland: Compiled from the Works of the Most Approved Historians, National Records and Other Authentic Documents, Public and Private* (1811), 128; *Alumni Cantabrigienses*, 2: 321; *The Knights of England*, 2: 186; W. L. Hutton, "Pedigree of Hopton of Suffolk and Somerset," *Miscellanea Genealogica et Heraldica*, 3rd series, 3 [1900]: 11-12; *The Visitation of London begun in 1687*, 16: 266; Will of Sir Thomas Hartopp or Hartop of Normanton, Rutland 15 Oct. 1661, Proved at London P.C.C. 23 Nov. 1661 PROB 11/306; Will of Dame Mary Hartop, Widow of Stamford Barron, Northamptonshire 28 Sept. 1692, Proved at London P.C.C. 30 May 1693 PROB 11/414.

Both *The Complete Baronetage*, 1: 122, and *The Complete Peerage*, 6: 577-78, note c, confuse the order of Mary Hopton's husbands, and Nichols' *History and Antiquities of the County of*

Leicestershire omits her marriage to Sir Thomas Hartopp entirely. Nichols states that after his first wife's death Sir Thomas Hartopp married Arabella Bennett, daughter of George Bennett [No. 2740] and Hon. Elizabeth St. John [No. 2741], but as George Bennett was a generation younger than Sir Thomas the chronology is suspect. Lady Hartopp's will discusses her first husband and their children, but does not mention her Hartopp husband.

2738-2739   *Lincolnshire Pedigrees,* 51: 596; *Alumni Oxonienses: The members of the University of Oxford, 1500–1714,* 3-4: 918; *The History and Antiquities of the County of Leicestershire,* 2: 1: 376; *The Temple Memoirs,* 49; *The Knights of England,* 2: 188; *Parish registers for St. Bride Fleet Street, 1274–1939* Family History Library film 0380,154. See also 2062-2063.

2740-2741   *The History and Antiquities of the County of Leicestershire,* 2: 1: 285; Will of George Benett of Welby, Leicestershire 1 March 1655/56, Proved at London P.C.C. 14 March 1655/56 PROB 11/254.

2742-2743   George E. Cokayne, *Some Account of the Lord Mayors and Sheriffs of the City of London during the first quarter of the seventeenth century 1601 to 1625* (1897), 63; *The Complete Baronetage,* 3: 75; *The History of Parliament 1660–1690,* 3: 124; G. Milner-Gibson-Cullum, "Middleton or Myddelton of Chirk Castle, Denbigh, Stanstead Mountfichet, Essex, and other places," *Miscellanea Genealogica et Heraldica,* 3rd series, 2 [1898]: 227; John Edwards Griffith, *Pedigrees of Anglesey and Carnarvonshire families* (1914), 254.

2744-2745   *The History and Antiquities of the County of Leicestershire,* 3: 394; *West Leake Baptisms, Marriages and Burials 1622–1812* Family History Library film 0503,787; *The Visitation of Nottinghamshire begun in 1662 and finished in 1664 made by William Dugdale, Norroy King of Arms,* 5: 89; *Alumni Oxonienses: The members of the University of Oxford, 1500–1714,* 3-4: 968.

Thomas Mansfield's mother was Joyce, daughter of Thomas Paget of Barwell, and this first marriage, described in Nichols but not found in the *Visitation,* might be to a cousin or may be an error.

2746-2747   *The Complete Peerage,* 3: 489; *The Knights of England,* 2: 191; *The Register of St. Martin-in-the-Fields, London 1619–1636,* 66: 139; *Parish registers of St. Lawrence Pountney, 1530–1812* Family History Library film 0374,466.

2752-2753   "Annotations to the Heraldic Visitation of London, 1633. Gore: wills and administrations," *Miscellanea Genealogica et Heraldica,* 2nd series, 2 [1888]: 349, 3 [1890]: 116, 246; Joseph Foster, *Peerage, baronetage, and knightage of the British empire for 1883,* 2 vols. (1883), 1: 30; Joseph Foster, *The Visitation of Middlesex, began in the year 1663, by William Ryley, esq., Lancaster, and Henry Dethick, Rouge croix, marshalls and deputies to Sir Edward Bysshe, Clarencieux. As recorded in the College of arms* (1887), 39; *The Registers of St. Mary Magdalen Milk Street, London and St. Michael Bassishaw, London, 1558 to 1892,* 72: 6, 50.

2754-2755   *The Knights of England,* 1: 162; *The History and Antiquities of the County of Hertford,* 2: 477; *Bishop's transcripts for Offley, 1604–1864* Family History Library film 0569,751, item 2.

2756-2757   *The Complete Baronetage,* 1: 233-34.

2758-2759   *The Scots Peerage,* 1: 45.

2760-2761   *Oxford Dictionary of National Biography,* 35: 425, 430; *The History of Parliament 1660–1690,* 3: 13; *Publications of the Harleian Society, Visitation Series,* vol. 59, Sir George J. Armytage, Bart., and John Paul Rylands, eds., *Pedigrees Made at the Visitation of Cheshire 1613* *taken by Richard St. George, Esq., Norroy King of Arms and Henry St. George, Gent., Bluemantle Pursuivant of Arms; and some other Contemporary Pedigrees,* 164.

2762-2763 *Oxford Dictionary of National Biography,* 16: 569-71; *The Marriage, Baptismal and Burial Registers of the Collegiate Church or Abbey of St. Peter, Westminster,* 10: 143; *The Dictionary of National Biography,* 5: 1147-49.

2766-2767 *Publications of the Harleian Society, New Series,* vol. 17, T. C. Wales et al., eds., *The Visitation of London begun in 1687,* 499; *Publications of the Harleian Society, Visitation Series,* vols. 105-6, G. D. Squibb, ed., *Wiltshire Visitation Pedigrees, 1623 with Additional Pedigrees and Arms Collected by Thomas Lyte of Lyte's Cary, co. Somerset, 1628,* 129; Le *Neve's Pedigrees,* 8: 299; *A history of Northumberland,* 11: 402.

2784-2785 *Publications of the Harleian Society, Visitation Series,* vol. 87, H. Isham Longden, ed., *The Visitation of the County of Northampton in the Year 1681,* 142; *Alumni Cantabrigienses,* 3: 201; *Wiltshire Visitation Pedigrees, 1623,* 105-6: 16; Public Record Office, comp., *Return of Members of Parliament, Part 1, Parliaments of England, 1213–1702* (1878-91; reprinted 1989), 476; "Pedigree of Montagu, of Lackham," *Wiltshire Archeological and Natural History Magazine* 3 [1857]: between 86 and 87.

2786-2787 *Wiltshire Visitation Pedigrees, 1623,* 105-6: 93; John Hutchinson, *A Catalogue of Notable Middle Templars: with brief biographical notices* (1902), 129; *Publications of the Harleian Society, Visitation Series,* vol. 5, William Henry Turner, ed., *The Visitations of the County of Oxford taken in the years 1566 by William Harvey, Clarencieux, 1574 by Richard Lee, Portcullis, Deputy of Robert Cooke, Clarencieux, and in 1634 by John Philipott, Somerset and William Ryley, Bluemantle, Deputies of Sir John Borough, Knt., Garter and Richard St. George, knt., Clarencieux; Together with the gatherings of Oxfordshire Collected by Richard Lee in 1574,* 259.

2788-2789 *The History of Parliament 1660–1690,* 2: 285; Will of John Eyles, senior, Merchant of Devizes, Wiltshire 16 Nov. 1660, codicil 17 June 1662, Proved 13 Nov. 1662 PROB 11/309.

2792-2793 *The bishop's transcripts and parish registers of Wilcot, baptisms, marriages & burials, 1812–1842* Family History Library film 1279,437; W.S. Sykes, "Notes on Wilcot and Families" (a manuscript at the Wiltshire Archaelogical Society, Devizes); *Wiltshire Visitation Pedigrees, 1623,* 105-6: 220; *The Knights of England,* 2: 169.

"Lady Anne Wroughton, wife of Sir George Wroughton, knight," died at least nineteen years before the birth of George Wroughton [No. 1396], the youngest son of Sir George. There were at least three children born to Anne (Gibbes), Lady Wroughton, and her son Francis Wroughton inherited Wilcot. "Lady Martha Wroughton" (as she appears in the Wilcot parish registers) is the second wife of Sir George Wroughton and the mother of George Wroughton. She would not be described as "Lady Martha" if she were, as stated by Sykes, the wife of George Wroughton, son of Sir George Wroughton.

2794-2795 *St. Ann Blackfriars Church (London) Parish registers, 1560–1849* Family History Library film 0374,416; *Publications of the Harleian Society, New Series,* vol. 11, G. D. Squibb, ed., *The Visitation of Somerset and the City of Bristol 1672 made by Sir Edward Bysshe, Knight, Clarenceux King of Arms,* 108; Will of George Farewell of Saint Margaret Westminster, Middlesex 9 Feb. 1690, Proved at London P.C.C. 26 March 1691 PROB 11/404.

2796-2797 Peter Townend et al., eds., *Burke's Genealogical and Heraldic History of the Landed Gentry,* 3 vols. (1965-72), 3: 787.

2798-2799 *Parish registers, Church of Aldenham (Hertfordshire) 1559–1812* Family History Library film 1040,851; *The Registers of St. Stephen, Walbrook, and St. Benet Sherehog, London,*

1716 to 1860, 49: 113, 170; Will of John Brisco, Grocer of St. Stephen Walbrook, City of London 6 Jan. 1687, Proved at London 1 Oct. 1689 PROB 11/396.

Beatrix (———) Briscoe's burial record states that she was buried in the vault of St. Stephen Walbrook "from Putney," where she probably died.

2800-2807 See 2792-2799.

2816-2819 See 1056-1059.

2824-2831 See 1064-1071.

2848-2849 *The Complete Peerage,* 5: 264.

2850-2851 J.P. Earwaker, *East Cheshire, Past and Present, or, a History of the Hundred of Macclesfield in the County Palatine of Chester—from Original Records,* 2 vols. (1877-80), 2: 444.

2852-2853 *Publications of the Harleian Society, Visitation Series,* vol. 89, A. W. Hughes Clarke, ed., *The Visitation of Sussex Anno Domini 1662,* 51; *The Complete Baronetage,* 1: 194-95; Will of Sir Thomas Gage of Firle, Sussex, Proved 31 Oct. 1654 PROB 11/234.

2854-2855 W. P. W. Phillimore and W. F. Carter, *Some Account of the Family of Middlemore, of Warwickshire and Worcestershire* (1901), Pedigree C, 68-69; *The visitations of Cornwall,* 300.

2856-2857 G. Dashwood, *Pedigrees selected from the Visitation of the County of Warwick, begun by Thomas May, Chester, and Gregory King, Rouge Dragon, in Hillary Vacac n, 1682, etc., etc.* (1859), Betham; *Some Account of the Family of Middlemore,* Pedigree C.

2858-2859 *The Four Visitations of Berkshire,* 56: 146, 315; J. Renton Dunlop, "The Family of Fettiplace," *Miscellanea Genealogica et Heraldica,* 5th series, 2 [1918]: 242.

2862-2863 *The Heraldic Visitations of Staffordshire Made by Sir Richard St. George, Norroy, in 1614, and by Sir William Dugdale in the Years 1663 and 1664,* 5: 2: 136.

2872-2873 *The History of Parliament 1660–1690,* 2: 100; *The History and Antiquities of the County of Northampton,* 1: 141; *Familiae Minorum Gentium,* 38: 573; *Shropshire Genealogies,* 6: 208.

2874-2875 *The Complete Baronetage,* 1: 196.

2876-2877 See 2542-2543.

2878-2879 *The History and gazetteer of the county of Derby,* 2: 159; *Allegations for Marriage Licences issued by the Faculty Office of the Archbishop of Canterbury at London, 1543–1869,* 24: 80, 141, 195; *Allegations for Marriage Licences issued by the Dean and Chapter of Westminster, 1558–1699; Also for those issued by the Vicar-General of the Archbishop of Canterbury, 1660–1679,* 23: 155; *The visitations of Cornwall,* 601; *The Registers of St. Stephen, Walbrook, and St. Benet Sherehog, London, 1716 to 1860,* 49: 110, 124; *The Complete Baronetage,* 4: 176, 3: 178; *The Visitation of Middlesex, began in the year 1663,* 58; Will of Isaac Meynell, Goldsmith of St. Mary Woolnoth, Lombard Street, London 2 Nov. 1675, Proved at Theobald's, Herts P.C.C. 1 July 1676 PROB 11/352; Will of Dame Elizabeth Norris of St. Ann Westminster, Middlesex 12 July 1712, Proved at London P.C.C. 8 April 1713 PROB 11/532.

2880-2881 Joan Wake, *The Brudenells of Deene* (1953):102-24; *The Complete Peerage,* 3: 13.

2882-2883 *Oxford Dictionary of National Biography,* 49: 67-68; *The Complete Peerage,* 11: 458.

2884-2885 *Oxford Dictionary of National Biography,* 49: 122-23; *The Complete Peerage,* 11: 459-61; *The History of Parliament 1558–1603,* 3: 351-52.

2886-2887 *Oxford Dictionary of National Biography*, 56: 481-82; *The Complete Peerage*, 1: 122-23.

2888-2889 *The History of Parliament 1660–1690*, 1: 736; *The Complete Peerage*, 5: 41-42; *Allegations for Marriage Licences issued by the Bishop of London*, 26: 113.

2890-2891 *Oxford Dictionary of National Biography*, 23: 849-51; *The Complete Peerage*, 12: 1: 217-19; *Allegations for Marriage Licences issued by the Bishop of London*, 26: 89.

2892-2893 *Oxford Dictionary of National Biography*, 49: 899-901; *The Complete Peerage*, 12: 2: 69-73; *The Knights of England*, 1: 159.

2894-2895 See 2202-2203.

2896-2897 *The Complete Baronetage*, 1: 156, 194; *Alumni Oxonienses: The members of the University of Oxford, 1500–1714*, 1-2: 129; *The History of Parliament 1660–1690*, 2: 420-21; *Parish Register of St. Bride Fleet Street: Baptisms, marriages 1587–1653* Family History Library film 0574,353.

2898-2899 *The Victoria History of the County of Oxford*, 13 vols. to date (1907-), 7: 32; *Alumni Oxonienses: The members of the University of Oxford, 1500–1714*, 1-2: 219; *The Visitation of the County of Buckingham Made in 1634*, 58: 48; Anthony A. Wood, *Oxfordshire Monumental Inscriptions* (1825), 88.

2900-2901 *The Complete Peerage*, 2: 436-37; *The Complete Baronetage*, 3: 7; B. W. Greenfield, "Pedigree of Dunch of Little Wittenham, Berks.," *Miscellanea Genealogica et Heraldica*, 3rd series, 2 [1898]: 45; *Parish Church of Little Wittenham (Berkshire) registers, 1538–1992* Family History Library film 0088,309.

2902-2903 *Oxoniensia: a journal dealing with the archaeology, history, and architecture of Oxford and its neighborhood*, vols. 11-12, Michael Maclagan, "Family of Dormer in Oxfordshire and Buckinghamshire," 99; *The History and Antiquities of the County of Buckingham*, 3: 182; Frederick George Lee, *The History, Description and Antiquities of the Prebendal Church of the Blessed Virgin Mary of Thame in the County and Diocese of Oxford, including a transcript of all the monumental inscriptions remaining therein: extracts from the registers and churchwardens' books, together with divers original pedigrees, copious antiquarian, architectural, personal and genealogical notes and appendices, relating to, and illustrative of, the town, its history, and inhabitants, in which is included some account of the Abbey of Thame Park, the grammar school, and the ancient chapelries of Towersey, Tettesworth, Sydenham, North Weston, and Rycott* (1883), 509.

2904-2905 *The visitations of Cornwall*, 47; *Alumni Oxonienses: The members of the University of Oxford, 1500–1714*, 1-2: 152; *The visitations of the county of Devon*, 654; *Registers of St. Michael, Penkivel, Cornwall: Christenings, 1547–1958* Family History Library film 0226,184.

2906-2907 *The visitations of Cornwall*, 184; *Alumni Oxonienses: The members of the University of Oxford, 1500–1714*, 1-2: 577; *The History of Parliament 1660–1690*, 2: 404-5.

2908-2909 *The History of Parliament 1660–1690*, 2: 402; Will of Colonel Francis Godfry or Godfrey of Little Chelsea, Middlesex 25 Feb. 1687/88, Proved at London 5 April 1688 PROB 11/391.

2910-2911 See 1028-1029.

2916-2917 *History of Hertfordshire*, 1: 2: 196; "Inquisitiones Post Mortem *temp.* Henry VIII to Charles I," *The Genealogist*, New Series, 30 [1917]: 66; Jacob Youde William Lloyd, *The History of the Princes, the Lords Marcher and the Ancient Nobility of Powys Fadog and the Ancient Lords of Arwystli, Cedewen and Meirionydd*, 6 vols. (1881-87), 2: 162.

2918-2919   *Registers of St. Matthew, Friday Street, London, 1538 to 1812, and the United Parishes of St. Matthew and St. Peter, Cheap, 1754 to 1812, 63:* 22; *The Registers of Allhallows, Bread Street, 1538 to 1892, and St. John The Evangelist, Friday Street, London, 1653 to 1822,* 43: 110; *The Registers St. Vedast, Foster Lane, 1558 to 1836, and St. Michael Le Quern, 1558 to 1837,* 30: 214.

2920-2921   *The Complete Baronetage,* 1: 75; Charles Humble Dudley Ward, *The family of Twysden and Twisden; their history and archives from an original by Sir John Ramskill Twisden, 12th baronet of Bradbourne* (1939), 140-43.

2922-2923   *The family of Twysden and Twisden,* 181; *Allegations for Marriage Licences issued by the Faculty Office of the Archbishop of Canterbury at London, 1543–1869,* 24: 88; Will of Frances Crosse, Widow of Wood Street, City of London 27 May 1710, Proved at London P.C.C. 3 Dec. 1711 PROB 11/524.

2924-2925   *The History of Parliament 1660–1690,* 3: 784; *Hasted's history of Kent,* 1: 195.

2926-2927   *The Complete Baronetage,* 4: 6, 1: 194; Joseph Foster, *London Marriage Licences, 1521–1869* (1887), 569; *Publications of the Harleian Society, Visitation Series,* vol. 53, W. Bruce Bannerman, ed., The *Visitations of the County of Sussex, Made and Taken in the years 1530 by Thomas Benolte, Clarenceux King of Arms; and 1633–4 by John Philipot, Somerset Herald, and George Owen, York Herald, for Sir John Burroughs, Garter and Sir Richard St. George, Clarenceux,* 46; *The History of Parliament 1660–1690,* 2: 420-21.

2928-2929   *The Complete Baronetage,* 3: 59, 8: 235; *The Registers of St. Olave, Hart Street, London, 1563 to 1700,* 46: 27; John Frederick Dorman, *Adventurers of Purse and Person, Virginia, 1607–1624/5,* 4th ed., 3 vols. (2004-7), 3: 114-17; *Sussex Archeological Collections,* vol. 42, J. H. Cooper, "Cuckfield Familes," pedigree opposite 32.
   Sir William Bowyer, 1st Baronet, was an uncle of siblings John Clayton, Attorney General of Virginia, and Charlotte Clayton, wife of John Lovelace, 4th Baron Lovelace, Governor of New York.

2930-2931   *The Complete Peerage,* 11: 406-7; Duncan Warrand, *Hertfordshire Families* (1907), 117; *Alumni Cantabrigienses,* 1: 312; *The Knights of England,* 1: 160; *Allegations for Marriage Licences issued by the Bishop of London,* 26: 241.

2932-2933   *The History of Parliament 1660–1690,* 3: 205; *The Visitations of the County of Sussex,* 53: 23.

2934-2935   Henry Fitz-Gilbert Waters, *Genealogical Gleanings in England: Abstracts of Wills Relating to Early American Families, with Genealogical Notes and Pedigrees Constructed from the Wills and from Other Records,* 2 vols. (1885–1901), 2: 944-46; *The Visitation of Middlesex, began in the year 1663,* 2; Will of Robert Chilcott of Islesworth, Middlesex 21 July 1688, Proved at London P.C.C. 13 Nov. 1688 PROB 11/393; Will of Robert Newman, Merchant Tailor of London 6 March 1650/51, Proved at London P.C.C. 3 April 1651 PROB 11/216.

2936-2939   See 2264-2267.

2940-2941   *History of Hertfordshire,* 2: 52; *The Complete Baronetage,* 4: 132; A. W. Cornelius Hallen, *The Registers of St. Botolph, Bishopsgate, London,* 3 vols. (1889-93), 2: 239, 427; Will of Dame Margaret Dashwood, Widow of St. Andrew, Holborn, Middlesex 19 Jan. 1713/14, codicil 28 Jan. 1713/14, Proved at London P.C.C. 12 May 1714 PROB 11/540.

2942-2943   *The Complete Baronetage,* 2: 206; *Publications of the Harleian Society, Register Series,* vol. 3, Joseph Lemuel Chester, *The Register Book of St. Dionis Backchurch Parish (City of*

London), 1538 to 1754, 33; Harry Tapley-Soper, *The register of Ottery-St. Mary, Devon, 1601–1837,* 2 parts (1908-29), 1: 257.

2944-2945 See 2192-2193.

2946-2947 See 2650-2651.

2948-2951 See 1440-1443.

2952-2953 Peter Townend, ed., *Burke's Genealogical and Heraldic History of the Peerage, Baronetage and Knightage* (1970), 443.

2954-2955 *Oxford Dictionary of National Biography,* 56: 977-79; *The Knights of England,* 2: 196; *The Dictionary of National Biography,* 20: 584-86; "Pedigree of Dowdall," Society of Genealogists MS pedigree X.A.12:441 (at the Society of Genealogists, London).

2956-2957 K. van de Sigtenhorst, "Lady Diana Spencer," *Gens Nostra: Ons Geslacht, Maanblad der Nederlandse Genealogische Vereniging* 36 [1981]: 230; Johan Engelbert Elias, *De Vroederschap van Amsterdam 1578–1795; met een inleidend woord van den archivaris der stad Amsterdam W. R. Veder,* 2 vols. (1903-5; reprinted in 1963), 2: 626.

2958-2959 *De Vroederschap van Amsterdam 1578–1795,* 2: 549.

2960-2961 *Oxford Dictionary of National Biography,* 36: 421-22; *The Complete Peerage,* 8: 149-51.

2962-2963 *The Complete Peerage,* 1: 204; *The Scots Peerage,* 1: 353-54.

2964-2965 *The Parliaments of Scotland,* 2: 543; Leslie G. Pine, ed., *Burke's Genealogical and Heraldic History of the Landed Gentry* (1952), 1890; *The Complete Baronetage,* 4: 392.

2966-2967 *The Complete Baronetage,* 2: 424.

2968-2969 *The History of Parliament 1660–1690,* 2: 190-91; *The Complete Peerage,* 6: 536; *Allegations for Marriage Licences issued by the Faculty Office of the Archbishop of Canterbury at London, 1543–1869,* 24: 44; *A True Register of all the Christenings, Marriages and Burials in the Parish of St. James, Clerkenwell, 1551 to 1754,* 13: 84; *The Marriage, Baptismal and Burial Registers of the Collegiate Church or Abbey of St. Peter, Westminster,* 10: 201; *The Register of St. Martin-in-the-Fields, London 1619–1636,* 66: 27.

2970-2971 *Oxford Dictionary of National Biography,* 53: 403; *The Complete Peerage,* 7: 626-27; *Alumni Cantabrigienses,* 4: 187; *A True Register of all the Christenings, Marriages and Burials in the Parish of St. James, Clerkenwell, 1551 to 1754,* 13: 106.

2972-2973 *Oxford Dictionary of National Biography,* 49: 244-49; *The Complete Peerage,* 11: 522-26; Walther Möller, *Stammtafeln westdeutscher Adels-Geschlechter im Mittelalter,* 5 vols. in 2 series (1922-51), 1: 93-99, Tafel 25.

2974-2975 *The Complete Peerage,* 11: 529, note b; *Europäische Stammtafeln, Neue Folge,* 1: 1: 95; *Neue Deutsche Biographie,* vol. 11, 246-49; *The Knights of England,* 1: 32.

2976-3003 See 2656-2683.

3008-3009 John Edwards Griffith, *Pedigrees of Anglesey and Carnarvonshire families* (1914), 57; Philip Henry Dudley Bagenal, *Vicissitudes of an Irish Family 1530–1800: a story of Irish romance and tragedy* (1925), 66; *Alumni Oxonienses: The members of the University of Oxford, 1500–1714,* 1-2: 91.

3012-3013 *The Complete Peerage,* 3: 117, 11: 36.

3014-3015 Sir Arthur Vicars, *Index to Prerogative Wills of Ireland 1536–1810* (1897), 109.

3016-3017 *The Complete Peerage,* 10: 284-85; *The Parish Register of Kensington, Co. Middlesex, 1539 to 1675,* 16: 70; *The Knights of England,* 1: 161.

3018-3019 *The Complete Baronetage,* 5: 352, note a.

3020-3021 Joseph Jackson Howard, ed., *The Visitation of the County of Essex, Begun A.D. MDCLXIIII, Finished A.D. MDCLXVIII by Sir Edward Bysshe, Knt., Clarenceux King of Arms* (1888), 100; Arthur Meredyth Burke, *Memorials of St. Margaret's church, Westminster, comprising the parish registers, 1539–1660, and the churchwardens' accounts 1460–1603* (1914), 53; *The Visitations of Essex by Hawley, 1552, Hervey 1558, Cooke 1570, Raven 1612 and Owen and Lilly, 1634,* 13: 521; *The Visitation of London Anno Domini 1633, 1634 and 1635,* 15: 410; Will of Peter Whetcombe of Margaretting, Essex 31 Jan. 1666/67, Proved 25 Nov. 1667 PROB 11/325.

3022-3023 *The History and Antiquities of the County of Leicestershire,* 2: 1: 353; *Publications of the Harleian Society, New Series,* vol. 15, Michael Powell Siddons, ed., *The Visitation of Herefordshire 1634,* 159; *North Witham Bishops' Transcripts* Family History Library film 0436,048, item 5; *St. Margaret Patten's Church (London) registers, 1506–1952* Family History Library film 0374,474.

3024-3025 Joseph Nadaud, *Nobiliaire du diocèse et de la généralité de Limoges,* 4 vols. (1863-82), 4: 29; Charles E. Lart, *Huguenot Pedigrees,* 2 vols. (1924-25), 1: 75.

3026-3027 *Europäische Stammtafeln, Neue Folge,* 10: 50; *Huguenot Pedigrees,* 1: 72; David C.A. Agnew, *Protestant exiles from France in the reign of Louis XIV; or, The Huguenot refugees and their descendants in Great Britain and Ireland,* 3 vols. (1871-74), 2: 125; François-Alexandre Aubert de la Chesnaye-Desbois et Badier, *Dictionnaire de la Noblesse, contenant les généalogies, l'histoire & la chronologie des familles nobles de la France, l'explication de leurs armes et l'état des grandes Terres du Royaume, possédées à titre de Principautés, Duchés, Marquisats, Comtés, Vicomtés, Baronies, &c., par création héritages, alliances, donations, substitutions, mutations, achats ou autrement. On a joint à ce dictionnaire le tableau généalogique et historique des maisons souveraines de l'Europe et une notice des familles étrangères, les plus anciennes, les plus nobles et les plus illustres,* 19 vols., 3rd ed. (1863-76), 17: 387.

Schwennicke identifies the wife of Josias de Robillard, Seigneur de Champagné, as Marie de la Rochefoucauld [No. 1513], daughter of Casimir Jean Charles de la Rochefoucauld, Seigneur de Fontpastour [No. 3026], and Marie Françoise de Maizières [No. 3027]. Agnew identifies Marie de la Rochefoucauld's father as No. 3026, the second son of François de la Rochefoucauld, Seigneur de Fontpastour [No. 6052], but is silent regarding her mother. On the other hand, Lart provides baptismal records for the children of Charles Casimir de la Rochefoucauld (nephew of No. 3026) and makes him husband of Marie Françoise de Maizières (seemingly No. 3027), but according to Chesnaye-Desbois she is Françoise, youngest daughter of Daniel de Maizières, Seigneur du Passage [No. 6054], and Elisabeth de Sainte-Hermine [No. 6055]. It is possible that Marie Françoise de Maizières [No. 3027] could be the eldest daughter of Nos. 6054 and 6055. Charles Casimir de la Rochefoucauld, Seigneur de Fontpastour, died 11 Jan. 1679 aged 28 (Parish Register, Dompierre et Bourgneuf), and his children were baptized between 1672 and 1678. Thus, he was too young to be the father of No. 1513, whose son was born in 1673. Lart mentions the marriage of Marie de la Rochefoucauld [No. 1513], but does not identify her parents. It should be noted that the godparents named at the baptisms of Charles Casimir's five children were often kin to Marie Françoise de Maizières: her father, her mother, or other relatives.

3028-3029 A. Alistair N. Tayler and H. A. Henrietta Tayler, *The House of Forbes* (1937), 330; *The Complete Peerage,* 6: 54-55; *The Complete Baronetage,* 1: 251-52.

3030-3031 *The Complete Baronetage,* 4: 14-15; *The Peerage of Ireland,* 3: 105.

3032-3033 Sheelah Ruggles-Brise, "Spencer and Other Pedigrees," *Notes and Queries* 186 [1944]: 22.

3040-3041 *The Complete Peerage,* 7: 88; *Burke's Genealogical and Heraldic History of the Peerage and Baronetage* (1953), 1145; *The Marriage, Baptismal and Burial Registers of the Collegiate Church or Abbey of St. Peter, Westminster,* 10: 65, 223-24; *The Knights of England,* 2: 254; P. R. Newman, *Royalist Officers in England and Wales, 1642–1660* (1981), 391; *Publications of the Harleian Society, Register Series,* vol. 35, William H. Hunt, *The Registers of St. Paul's Church, Covent Garden, London, 1653 to 1853,* 4.

3042-3043 *The History of Parliament 1660–1690,* 2: 57.

3044-3045 *The History of Parliament 1660–1690,* 2: 538; Edmund Horace Fellowes, *The Family of Frederick* (1932), 10-25; *The East Anglian; or, Notes and queries on subjects connected with the counties of Suffolk, Cambridge, Essex and Norfolk,* vol. 4, George W. Marshall, "Pedigree of the Hernes, of Tibenham, co. Norfolk," 123; *The Aldermen of the City of London,* 2: 107.

3046-3047 *The History of Parliament 1660–1690,* 2: 746; *The Visitation of the County of Northampton in the Year 1681,* 87: 123; *Alumni Oxonienses: The members of the University of Oxford, 1500–1714,* 1-2: 917; *Allegations for Marriage Licences issued by the Bishop of London,* 26: 288.

3048-3049 *The Complete Peerage,* 2: 312; *A True Register of all the Christenings, Marriages and Burials in the Parish of St. James, Clerkenwell, 1551 to 1754,* 13: 73; *Allegations for Marriage Licences issued by the Bishop of London,* 26: 259-60.

3050-3051 *The History of Parliament 1660–1690,* 2: 276-78; *The Complete Peerage,* 2: 210-11; *The Register Book of St. Dionis Backchurch Parish (City of London), 1538 to 1754,* 3: 30; *Burke's Genealogical and Heraldic History of the Peerage and Baronetage* (1953), 2252-53.

3052-3055 See 1028-1031.

3056-3059 See 2920-2923.

3060-3061 *The family of Twysden and Twisden,* 350-68; *The Judges of England,* 7: 179-84; *The Complete Baronetage,* 4: 81.

3062-3063 *The family of Twysden and Twisden,* 373-74; *The Visitation of London Anno Domini 1633, 1634 and 1635,* 17: 60.

3064-3065 Edith Mary Johnston-Liik, *History of the Irish Parliament 1692–1800: commons, constituencies and statutes,* 6 vols. (2002), 3: 376.

3070-3071 *History of the Irish Parliament 1692–1800,* 6: 35; *The Visitation of Middlesex,* 94; Will of Edward Pearce, Gentleman of Witlingham, Norfolk 11 Nov. 1682, codicil 14 April 1683, Proved P.C.C. 10 Nov. 1683 PROB 11/374.

3076-3077 Walter Arthur Copinger, *History of the Copingers or Coppingers of the County of Cork, Ireland, and the Counties of Suffolk and Kent, England* (1884), 167-73.

3078-3079 *History of the Copingers or Coppingers of the County of Cork, Ireland,* 34, 402.

3184-3187 *Burke's Irish Family Records,* 906.

3200-3201 *Burke's Genealogical and Heraldic History of the Peerage, Baronetage and Knightage* (1970), 305; *The History and Antiquities of the County of Leicestershire,* 4: 177; *Visitations of*

England and Wales, Notes, 5: 95; "The Family of Boothby," *Miscellanea Genealogica et Heraldica,* 5th series, 1 [1916]: 130.

3202-3203 *The Complete Baronetage,* 2: 150; *The History and Antiquities of the County of Leicestershire,* 2: 2: 874; John Burke and John Bernard Burke, *A Genealogical and Heraldic History of the Extinct and Dormant Baronetcies of England, Ireland, and Scotland,* 2nd ed. (1844), 238; *Lincolnshire Pedigrees,* 51: 436.

3296-3299 Noel Currer-Briggs and Royston Gambier, *Huguenot Ancestry* (1985), pedigree.

3312-3315 Henry Wagner, "Huguenot Refugee family of Yvonnet," *The Genealogist,* New Series, 28 [1912]: 88.

3408-3411 Gary Boyd Roberts and William Addams Reitwiesner, *American Ancestors and Cousins of The Princess of Wales* (1984), 73-74, 76.

3520-3521 *American Ancestors and Cousins of The Princess of Wales,* 29; Mary Lovering Holman and Winifred Lovering Holman, *Ancestry of Colonel John Harrington Stevens and his wife, Frances Helen Miller: compiled for Helen Pendleton (Winston) Pillsbury,* 2 vols. (1948-52), 1: 349-53; Mary Walton Ferris, *Dawes-Gates Ancestral Lines: A Memorial Volume Containing the American Ancestry of Rufus B. Dawes, Volume I; Dawes and Allied Families; A Memorial Volume Containing the Ancestry of Mary Beman (Gates) Dawes, Volume II, Gates and Allied Families,* 2 vols. (1931-43), 1: 301; Benjamin W. Dwight, *The History of the Descendants of Elder John Strong of Northampton, Mass.,* 2 vols. (1871), 1: 14-19.

3522-3523 *American Ancestors and Cousins of The Princess of Wales,* 29; *Ancestry of Colonel John Harrington Stevens and his wife, Frances Helen Miller,* 390; Rev. Edward Payson Holton and Harriet Scofield, *A Genealogy of the Descendants in America of William Holton (1610–1691) of Hartford, Conn., and Northampton, Mass.,* 2nd ed. (1965), 1-12; Zelinda Makepeace Douhan, ed., *The Ancestry of Russell Makepeace of Marion, Massachusetts 1904–1986: A Descendant of Thomas Makepeace of Dorchester, Massachusetts* (2005), 177-82.

3524-3525 *American Ancestors and Cousins of The Princess of Wales,* 29; Donald Lines Jacobus and Edgar Francis Waterman, *Hale, House and related families: mainly of the Connecticut River Valley* (1952), 447-49; Robert Charles Anderson, *The Great Migration Begins: Immigrants to New England 1620–1633,* 3 vols. (1995), 2: 1038.

3526-3527 *American Ancestors and Cousins of The Princess of Wales,* 29; Penny G. Douglass and Robert Charles Anderson, "The English Origin of Robert Blott of Charlestown and Boston, Mass.," *The American Genealogist* 68 [1992]: 65-67, and Penny G. Douglass and Robert Charles Anderson, "John Black of Charlestown Was Really Robert Blott," 68: 67-68; *Hale, House and related families,* 808-9; *Ancestry of Colonel John Harrington Stevens and his wife, Frances Helen Miller,* 407-10; *The Great Migration Begins: Immigrants to New England 1620–1633,* 3: 2057-60.

3528-3529 See 3520-3521.

3530-3531 *American Ancestors and Cousins of The Princess of Wales,* 29; *Ancestry of Colonel John Harrington Stevens and his wife, Frances Helen Miller,* 400-2; Thomas R. Steadman and Norma Slater Woodward, *Descendants of Richard, Nathaniel, Robert, and Henry Woodward of New England, 1589–1996,* Revised Edition (1996), 575-77; W. M. Bollenbach, Jr., *The New England Ancestry of Alice Everett Johnson 1899–1986* (2003), 400-1.

3534-3535 *American Ancestors and Cousins of The Princess of Wales,* 29; Leonard Lee and Sarah Fiske Lee, *John Lee of Farmington, Hartford co. Connecticut and His Descendants, 1634–1897: con-*

taining over 4,000 names, with much miscellaneous history of the family, brief notes of other Lee families of New England, biographical notices, valuable data collected by William Wallace Lee, military records, to which is added a "roll of honor" of two hundred who have served in the various wars of the country (1897), 44-47; Alfred Andrews, *Genealogical History of Deacon Stephen Hart and His Descendants, 1632–1875, with an introduction of miscellaneous Harts and their progenitors, as far as is known; to which is added a list of all the clergy of the name found, all the physicians, all the lawyers, the authors and soldiers* (1875), 39-41; *The Great Migration Begins: Immigrants to Mew England 1620–1633*, 2: 869-73.

3536-3537 *American Ancestors and Cousins of The Princess of Wales*, 29; Donald Lines Jacobus and Edgar Francis Waterman, *The Granberry Family and allied families: including the ancestry of Helen (Woodward) Granberry* (1945), 169-70.

3538-3539 *American Ancestors and Cousins of The Princess of Wales*, 29; *The Granberry Family and allied families*, 199-200, 250-51; Robert Charles Anderson et al., *The Great Migration: Immigrants to New England 1634–1635*, 4 vols. to date (1999-), 2: 138-39.

3540-3541 *American Ancestors and Cousins of The Princess of Wales*, 30; *The Granberry Family and allied families*, 216-17.

3542-3543 *American Ancestors and Cousins of The Princess of Wales*, 30; McClure Meredith Howland, "English Background of three New England Families," *The New England Historical and Genealogical Register* 115 [1961]: 253-54; *The Granberry Family and allied families*, 223-24; *The Great Migration Begins: Immigrants to New England 1620–1633*, 2: 723; *The New England Ancestry of Alice Everett Johnson 1899–1986*, 145.

3544-3545 *American Ancestors and Cousins of The Princess of Wales*, 30; Edith Bartlett Sumner, *Descendants of Thomas Farr of Harpswell, Maine, and ninety allied families* (1959), 165, 192; Augustus George Hibbard, *Genealogy of the Hibbard Family Who are Descendants of Robert Hibbard of Salem, Massachusetts* (1901), 11-16.

3546-3547 *American Ancestors and Cousins of The Princess of Wales*, 30; *Descendants of Thomas Farr of Harpswell, Maine*, 303; *Records and Files of the Quarterly Courts of Essex County, Massachusetts*, 9 vols. (1911-21), 4: 416; *The New England Ancestry of Alice Everett Johnson 1899–1986*, 360.

3548-3549 *American Ancestors and Cousins of The Princess of Wales*, 30; *The Granberry Family and allied families*, 282.

3550-3551 *American Ancestors and Cousins of The Princess of Wales*, 30; Ruby Parke Anderson and Elizabeth Miller Hunter Ruppert, *The Parke Scrapbook...*, 3 vols. (1965-66), 2: 24; *The Granberry Family and allied families*, 287-88; S. W. McArthur, *McArthur-Barnes Ancestral Lines* (1964), 100-1.

3872-3873 Charles John Guthrie, *Genealogy of the descendants of Reverend Thomas Guthrie, D. D., and Mrs. Anne Burns or Guthrie: connected chiefly with the families of Chalmers and Trail, to which Mrs. Guthrie belonged through her mother, Mrs. Christina Chalmers or Burns, and her great-grandmother, Mrs. Susannah Trail or Chalmers; also incidental references to the families of Guthrie and Burns* (1902), 31.

3874-3875 *Genealogy of the descendants of Reverend Thomas Guthrie, D.D., and Mrs. Anne Burns or Guthrie*, 30.

3876-3877 See 3872-3873.

3878-3879 *The House of Forbes,* 416–19.

3880-3881 *Genealogy of the descendants of Reverend Thomas Guthrie, D. D., and Mrs. Anne Burns or Guthrie,* 42.

3882-3883 *Genealogy of the descendants of Reverend Thomas Guthrie, D. D., and Mrs. Anne Burns or Guthrie,* 42; George Hamilton, *A History of the House of Hamilton* (1933), 969.

3884-3885 "St. Nicholas (Aberdeen) Churchyard Inscriptions," *Scottish Notes and Queries* 2 [1889]: 183; Alexander MacDonald Munro, *Memorials of the Aldermen, Provosts and Lord Provosts of Aberdeen 1272–1895* (1897), 197.

3888-3889 A. Dingwall-Fordyce, *Addenda to the Family Records of Dingwall-Fordyce* (1888), l; "Pedigree of Douglas of Tilquhilly or Tilwhilly, co. Kincardine," *The Genealogist* 5 [1881]: 194.

3896-3897 *The House of Forbes,* 461; G. F. Browne, *Echt-Forbes family charters 1345–1727, records of the Forest of Birse Notarial Signs 926–1786* (1923).

3898-3899 *The Scots Peerage,* 7: 256; *The Complete Baronetage,* 2: 281.

3904-3905 *The Publications of the Yorkshire Parish Register Society,* vol. 78, Edith Horsfall, ed., *The Parish Registers of Heptonstall, in the County of York, 1593–1660,* 7, 85.

3906-3907 *The Registers of the Parish Church of Methley in the County of York, from 1560 to 1812,* 9, 44, 73, 80.

3936-3937 Vere Langford Oliver, "Pedigree of the family of Dingwall of Brucklay," *Miscellanea Genealogica et Heraldica,* 4th series, 5 [1914]: 3.

3938-3939 J. Forbes Leslie, *The Irvines of Drum and collateral branches* (1909), 177; "Pedigree of the family of Dingwall of Brucklay," 13; H. A. Henrietta Tayler, *History of the Family of Urquhart* (1946), 10.

3942-3943 "Pedigree of the family of Dingwall of Brucklay," 3.

3948-3949 "Pedigree of the family of Dingwall of Brucklay," 12; Alexander Dingwall Fordyce, *Family Records of the Name of Dingwall Fordyce in Aberdeenshire* (1885), 183.

3950-3951 "Pedigree of the family of Dingwall of Brucklay," 12.

3960-3961 William Temple, *The Thanage of Fermartyn including the district commonly called Formartine, its proprietors: with genealogical deductions, its parishes, ministers, churches, churchyards, antiquities, &c* (1894), 683.

4016-4019 *The Thanage of Fermartyn,* 624.

4032-4033 *The House of Forbes,* 302; *The Family of Burnett of Leys, with colateral branches: from the mss. of the late George Burnett* (1901), 62; *The Complete Baronetage,* 2: 305.

4034-4035 *Notes and Queries,* 3rd series, 9 [1866]: 389; Thomas Falconer, *The Family of Dalmahoy of Dalmahoy, Ratho, County Edinburgh* (1870), 7; *Publications of the Harleian Society, Visitation Series,* vol. 93, Arthur Adams, ed., *Cheshire Visitation Pedigrees, 1663,* 122.

4036-4037 *The Thanage of Fermartyn,* 154.

4038-4039 *History of the Family of Urquhart,* 10.

4044-4045 *The House of Forbes,* 340.

4046-4047 Alexander Fraser, 17th Lord Saltoun, *The Frasers of Philorth,* 3 vols. (1879), 2: 163.

4048-4051 See 4036-4039.

4052-4053 *The Complete Baronetage,* 4: 288-89.

4054-4055 *The House of Forbes,* 302; *The Complete Baronetage,* 2: 305. See also 2016-2017.

4056-4057 *Burke's Genealogical and Heraldic History of the Landed Gentry* (1952), 702; A. Alistair N. Tayler and H. A. Henrietta Tayler, *The Book of the Duffs,* 2 vols. (1914), 1: 354-59; *Inverness Parish Registers — Marriages vol. viii 1649–1818* Family History Library film 0990,669.

4058-4059 *The Book of the Duffs,* 1: 344-45.

4060-4061 *The Complete Baronetage,* 4: 344; *The Scots Peerage,* 1: 126.

4062-4063 *The Complete Peerage,* 11: 421-22; *The Scots Peerage,* 7: 444-45.

Twelfth Generation

4096-4097 P. W. Hasler, *The History of Parliament: The House of Commons 1558–1603,* 3 vols. (1981), 3: 426; George E. Cokayne et al., *The Complete Peerage,* 14 vols. in 15 (1910-98), 12: 2: 159-60.

4098-4099 *Oxford Dictionary of National Biography,* 60 vols. (2004), 60: 515-20; *The Complete Peerage,* 12: 1: 128-30; *Shropshire Parish Registers: Lichfield Diocese,* vol. 11, *Registers of Hodnet with Wroxeter,* 2.

4100-4101 *Oxford Dictionary of National Biography,* 50: 570-72, 544-45; *The History of Parliament 1558–1603,* 3: 384-87; *The Complete Peerage,* 7: 553-54; "Some Herefordshire Pedigrees," *Miscellanea Genealogica et Heraldica,* 5th series, 8 [1932-34]: 208; *Publications of the Harleian Society, Register Series,* vol. 72, A. W. Hughes Clarke, *The Registers of St. Mary Magdalen Milk Street, London and St. Michael Bassishaw, London, 1558 to 1892,* 102, 164, 180; *Publications of the Harleian Society, Visitation Series,* vol. 96, J. W. Walker, ed., *Yorkshire Pedigrees,* 391.

4102-4103 *Oxford Dictionary of National Biography,* 13: 711-13; *The Complete Peerage,* 9: 732-35.

4104-4105 *The History of Parliament 1558–1603,* 2: 35-36; *Norfolk Archeology: or, Miscellaneous Tracts Relating to the Antiquities of the County of Norfolk,* vol. 3, Joseph Hunter, "The history and topography of Ketteringham, in the County of Norfolk," opposite 284.

4106-4107 *The History of Parliament 1558–1603,* 3: 562-63; *Shropshire Parish Registers: Lichfield Diocese,* vol. 13, *Registers of Ludlow,* 4, 62, 64, 66; John Paul Rylands et al., "Pedigrees from the Visitation of Dorset 1623. Walcot," *Miscellanea Genealogica et Heraldica,* 2nd series, 2 [1888]: 121; *Registers of Ludlow 1558–1812* Family History Library film 0599,486.

4108-4109 *The History of Parliament 1558–1603,* 3: 310-12; *The Complete Peerage,* 11: 239-40; Jeremiah Holmes Wiffen, *Historical memoirs of the house of Russell: from the time of the Norman Conquest,* 2 vols. (1833), 1: 506; *Publications of the Harleian Society, Visitation Series,* vol. 25, Joseph Lemuel Chester and George J. Armytage, *Allegations for Marriage Licences issued by the Bishop of London,* 137.

4110-4111 *The Complete Peerage,* 3: 126-27; *The History of Parliament 1558–1603,* 1: 508.

Frances (Clinton), Baroness Chandos, was the great-aunt of Lady Arbella Clinton, wife of Isaac Johnson, for whom the *Arbella* (of the 1630 Winthrop Fleet) was named.

4112-4113 P. N. Dawe, "The Dorset Churchills," *Notes & Queries for Somerset and Dorset* 27 [1958]: 186, 191.

4114-4115 "The Dorset Churchills," 191; W. Bruce Bannerman, "Wynston Pedigree," *Miscellanea Genealogica et Heraldica,* 3rd series, 4 [1902]: 21; John Hutchins, *The History and*

Antiquities of the County of Dorset: Compiled from the Best and Most Ancient Historians, Inquisitions Post Mortem, and Other Valuable Records and Mss. in the Public Offices and Libraries, and in Private Hands. With a Copy of Domesday Book and the Inquisitio Gheldi for the County: Interspersed with Some Remarkable Particulars of Natural History; and Adorned with a Correct Map of the County, and Views of Antiquities, Seats of the Nobility and Gentry, &c., 3rd ed., corrected, augmented and improved, 4 vols. (1861-70), 4: 127; William A. Shaw, *The Knights of England*, 2 vols. (1906), 2: 90; *Publications of the Harleian Society, Register Series*, vol. 49, W. Bruce Bannerman et al., *The Registers of St. Stephen, Walbrook, and St. Benet Sherehog, London, 1716 to 1860*, 3.

4116-4117 J. L. Vivian, *The visitations of the county of Devon, comprising the heralds' visitations of 1531, 1564, & 1620* (1895), 297; *Publications of the Harleian Society, Visitation Series*, vols. 105-6, G. D. Squibb, ed., *Wiltshire Visitation Pedigrees, 1623 with Additional Pedigrees and Arms Collected by Thomas Lyte of Lyte's Cary, co. Somerset, 1628*, 33.

4118-4119 *The Complete Peerage*, 2: 229; Robert Clutterbuck, *The History and Antiquities of the County of Hertford: Compiled from the Best Printed Authorities and Original Records, Preserved in Public Repositories and Private Collections: Embellished with Views of the Most Curious Monuments of Antiquity, and Illustrated with a Map of the County*, 3 vols. (1815-27), 2: 46; Robert Edmond Chester Waters, *Genealogical Memoirs of the Extinct Family of Chester of Chicheley: their Ancestors and Descendants*, 2 vols. (1878), 1: 143-46.

4120-4121 Herbert C. Andrews, "Notes on the Rowlett and Jennings families," *Miscellanea Genealogica et Heraldica*, 5th series, 8 [1932-34]: 90, 106; *Wiltshire Visitation Pedigrees, 1623*, 105-6: 32; *The Knights of England*, 2: 107; Sentence of Sir John Jennyns or Jenins Dated 22 Nov. 1611 PROB 11/118.

4122-4123 *The History of Parliament 1558–1603*, 3: 425-26; *The History and Antiquities of the County of Hertford*, 2: 361; *The Knights of England*, 2: 104; John Venn and John Archibald Venn, *Alumni Cantabrigienses; A biographical list of all known students, graduates and holders of office at the University of Cambridge, from the earliest times to 1900*, 10 vols. (1922-54), 4: 133.

4124-4125 George E. Cokayne, *The Complete Baronetage, 1611–1880*, 5 vols. (1900-6), 1: 212; *Proceedings of the Somersetshire Archaeological and Natural History Society*, vol. 38, part 2, Henry C. Maxwell Lyte, "Lytes of Lytescary," pedigree; *The History and Antiquities of the County of Dorset*, 1: 437; *Publications of the Harleian Society, Visitation Series*, vol. 117, G. D. Squibb, ed., *The Visitation of Dorset 1677 Made by Sir Edward Bysshe, Knight, Clarenceux King of Arms*, 67-68; Edward Hasted, *The History and Topographical Survey of the County of Kent*, 12 vols. (1797-1801), 3: 487; *Archæologia Cantiana: Being Transactions of the Kent Archæological Society*, vol. 53, C. R. Councer, "Heraldic Notices of the Church of St. Martin, Herne," 94; *The parish registers of St. Peter's Beaksbourne, Kent, 1558–1812* Family History Library film 0924,121, item 3; Will of Sir Stephen Thornhurst of Fulham, Middlesex 31 July 1616, Proved at London P.C.C. 16 Nov. 1616 PROB 11/128.

4126-4127 John Alexander Temple and Harald Markham Temple, *The Temple Memoirs: an account of this historic family and its demesnes; with biographical sketches, anecdotes & legends from Saxon times to the present day* (1925), 48; *Archæologia Cantiana*, vol. 11, Rev. Edward Hawkins, "Notes on some monuments in Rochester Cathedral," 7-9; George Lipscomb, *The History and Antiquities of the County of Buckingham*, 4 vols. (1847), 3: 86; *The Knights of England*, 2: 91; Public Record Office, comp., *Return of Members of Parliament, Part 1, Parliaments of England, 1213–1702* (1878-91; reprinted 1989), 472.

4128-4129 Leslie G. Pine, ed., *Burke's Genealogical and Heraldic History of the Landed Gentry including American Families with British Ancestry* (1939), 593; James Bertrand Payne, *Armorials* *of Jersey: being an account, heraldic and antiquarian, of its chief native families, with pedigrees, biographical notices, and illustrative data; to which are added a brief history of heraldry, and remarks on the mediaeval antiquities of the island* (1860), 118.

4130-4131   *Oxford Dictionary of National Biography*, 10: 388; *Burke's Genealogical and Heraldic History of the Landed Gentry including American Families with British Ancestry* (1939), 593; *The Knights of England*, 2: 161; *Armorials of Jersey*, 81-83; *The Dictionary of National Biography, founded in 1882 by George Smith, edited by Sir Leslie Stephen and Sir Sidney Lee*, 2nd ed., 22 vols. (1885–1901; reprinted 1908-9), 3: 1124-25; Gary Boyd Roberts, *The Royal Descents of 600 Immigrants to the American Colonies or the United States: Who Were Themselves Notable or Left Descendants Notable in American History* (2004; revised and reissued 2006), 311.

Sir Philip de Carteret and Anne Dowse were great-grandparents of Philip Dumaresq of Massachusetts.

4132-4133   *The History of Parliament 1558–1603*, 3: 71; Edwin Chappell, *Eight Generations of the Pepys Family 1500–1800* (1936), 31; *Publications of the Harleian Society, Visitation Series*, vol. 87, H. Isham Longden, ed., *The Visitation of the County of Northampton in the Year 1681*, 141; *Alumni Cantabrigienses*, 3: 202; *The Knights of England*, 2: 159.

4134-4135   *Oxford Dictionary of National Biography*, 14: 164-65; *The Complete Peerage*, 3: 532-33; Joseph Foster, *Alumni Oxonienses: The members of the University of Oxford, 1500–1714: their parentage, birthplace, and year of birth, with a record of their degrees. Being the matriculation register of the University, alphabetically arranged, revised and annotated*, 4 vols. (1891–92), 1-2: 349.

4136-4137   J. L. Vivian, *The visitations of Cornwall, comprising the Heralds' visitations of 1530, 1573, & 1620* (1887), 192; *The Knights of England*, 2: 146; *Alumni Oxonienses: The members of the University of Oxford, 1500–1714*, 1-2: 604.

4138-4139   Arthur M. Smith, *Some Account of the Smiths of Exeter and their descendants* (1896), pedigree; *The visitations of the county of Devon*, 692; *The Knights of England*, 2: 133.

4140-4141   Sir Richard Colt Hoare, Bt., *The History of Modern Wiltshire*, 14 parts in 6 vols. (1822-44), 5: 2: 29; *Publications of the Harleian Society, Register Series*, vol. 69, A. W. Hughes Clarke et al., *Registers of St. Dunstan in the East, 1558 to 1766*, 102, 181, 192; *The Royal Descents of 600 Immigrants to the American Colonies or the United States*, 526-27.

Richard Wyche and Elizabeth Saltonstall were grandparents of Henry Wyche of Virginia. Elizabeth (Saltonstall) Wyche was a first cousin of Sir Richard Saltonstall, a founder of the Massachusetts Bay Colony.

4142-4143   *The History of Parliament 1558–1603*, 3: 42; Jacob Youde William Lloyd, *The History of the Princes, the Lords Marcher and the Ancient Nobility of Powys Fadog and the Ancient Lords of Arwystli, Cedewen and Meirionydd*, 6 vols. (1881-87), 3: 82; *Publications of the Harleian Society, Visitation Series*, vol. 54, Sir George J. Armytage, Bart., ed., *The Visitation of Kent Begun Anno Dni 1663 Finished Anno Dni 1668 by Sir Edward Bysshe, Knt., Clarenceux King of Armes*, 114; *The Complete Baronetage*, 1: 209; *Heraldic Visitations of Wales and Part of the Marches Between the Years 1586 and 1613 by Lewys Dwnn*, 2 vols. (1846), 2: 357; *Dictionary of Welsh Biography Down to 1940* (1959), 995; *Calendar of Patent Rolls, Preserved in the Public Record Office, Edward VI*, 1547-48: 11, 280, 360, *Edward VI*, 1553: 388 and appendix, *Elizabeth I*, 1563-66: 524-25; *Archeologia Cambriensis* 87 [1932]: 240, 243.

4144-4145   *The Complete Baronetage*, 1: 66; Will of Frances Worsley of Newport, Isle of Wight, Hampshire 18 Oct. 1659, Proved at London P.C.C. 27 May 1661 PROB 11/304.

4146-4147 Vernon James Watney, *The Wallop Family and Their Ancestry*, 4 vols. (1928), 1: xlviii, 9; *The Knights of England*, 2: 97.

4148-4149 *Oxford Dictionary of National Biography*, 26: 714-20; *The Complete Peerage*, 10: 415-19; B. D. Henning, *The History of Parliament: The House of Commons 1660–1690*, 3 vols. (1983), 2: 534; *Publications of the Harleian Society, Visitation Series*, vol. 10, Joseph Lemuel Chester, ed., *The Marriage, Baptismal and Burial Registers of the Collegiate Church or Abbey of St. Peter, Westminster*, 128.

4150-4151 *Alumni Oxonienses: The members of the University of Oxford, 1500–1714*, 3-4: 1400; *The Knights of England*, 2: 179; *Publications of the Harleian Society, Visitation Series*, vol. 65, Sir George J. Armytage, Bart., ed., *Middlesex Pedigrees as Collected by Richard Mundy in Harleian MS. No. 1551*, 109; Frederick George Lee, *The History, Description and Antiquities of the Prebendal Church of the Blessed Virgin Mary of Thame in the County and Diocese of Oxford, including a transcript of all the monumental inscriptions remaining therein: extracts from the registers and churchwardens' books, together with divers original pedigrees, copious antiquarian, architectural, personal and genealogical notes and appendices, relating to, and illustrative of, the town, its history, and inhabitants, in which is included some account of the Abbey of Thame Park, the grammar school, and the ancient chapelries of Towersey, Tettesworth, Sydenham, North Weston, and Rycott* (1883), 509.

4152-4153 *The Complete Peerage*, 6: 584, note c; *The History of Parliament 1558–1603*, 3: 508; J. Paul Rylands, "A Vellum Pedigree-Roll of the family of Touchet, of Nether Whitley and Buglawton, Co. Chester, and Touchet, Baron Audley Heleigh, Co. Stafford," *The Genealogist: A Quarterly Magazine of Genealogical, Antiquarian, Topographical and Heraldic Research*, New Series, 36 [1920]: 17; "Lytes of Lytescary," 38: pedigree; *Alumni Oxonienses: The members of the University of Oxford, 1500–1714*, 3-4: 1485; *The Knights of England*, 2: 135.

4154-4155 *The Complete Peerage*, 3: 476-77.

4156-4157 *The Complete Peerage*, 12: 2: 776.

4158-4159 See 2892-2893.

4160-4161 John Maclean, *Historical and Genealogical Memoir of the Family of Poyntz, or, Eight Centuries of an English House* (1886), 156; S. T. Bindoff, *The History of Parliament: the House of Commons 1509–1558*, 3 vols. (1982), 3: 147-48; Douglas Richardson, *Plantagenet Ancestry: A Study in Medieval and Colonial Families* (2004), 785.

4162-4163 *Historical and Genealogical Memoir of the Family of Poyntz*, 156; *Publications of the Harleian Society, Visitation Series*, vol. 43, W. Bruce Bannerman, ed., *The Visitations of the County of Surrey Made and Taken in the years 1530 by Thomas Benolte, Clarenceux King of Arms; 1572 by Robert Cooke, Clarenceux King of Arms; and 1623 by Samuel Thompson, Windsor Herald, and Augustin Vincent, Rouge Croix Pursuivant, marshals and deputies to William Camden, Clarenceux King of Arms*, 27; *Plantagenet Ancestry*, 560.

4164-4165 George F. Sydenham, *The History of the Sydenham Family: Collected from Family Documents, Pedigrees, Deeds, and Copious Memoranda* (1928), 117-18; *The History of Parliament 1509–1558*, 3-4: 414-15; *Plantagenet Ancestry*, 699.

4166-4167 *The History of Parliament 1558–1603*, 3: 243; *The Knights of England*, 1: 153; *Historical and Genealogical Memoir of the Family of Poyntz*, 96; *Pedigrees of the county families of England, comp. by Joseph Foster and authenticated by the members of each family. The heraldic illustrations by J. Forbes-Nixon. Vol. 1– Lancashire* (1873), Stanley pedigree; *Camden Society Series*, vol. 56, John Bruce, ed., *Letters and papers of the Verney family down to the end of the year 1639,* pedigree; *Plantagenet Ancestry,* 596.

4168-4169 *The History of Parliament 1558–1603,* 3: 176; *Publications of the Harleian Society, Visitation Series,* vol. 52, A. R. Maddison, *Lincolnshire Pedigrees,* 759; Robert Thoroton, *Thoroton's History of Nottinghamshire: Republished, with Large Additions, by John Throsby, and Embellished with Picturesque and Select Views of Seats of the Nobility and Gentry, Towns, Village Churches and Ruins,* 3 vols. (1790), 1: 89.

4170-4171 Llewellynn Frederick William Jewitt, ed., *The Reliquary and illustrated archæologist,* 34 vols. (1860-94), 9: pedigree opposite 177; "Pedigrees contained in the Visitations of Derbyshire, 1569 and 1611," *The Genealogist,* New Series, 8 [1891]: 74.

4184-4185 Henry Fitz-Gilbert Waters, "Genealogical Gleanings in England," *The New England Historical and Genealogical Register* 48 [1894]: 110; *Oxford Dictionary of National Biography,* 15: 63.

4186-4187 *Historical and Genealogical Memoir of the Family of Poyntz,* 293; John Bridges, *The History and Antiquities of Northamptonshire,* 2 vols. (1791), 2: 26.

4188-4189 *Historical and Genealogical Memoir of the Family of Poyntz,* 293.

4190-4191 Joseph James Muskett, *Suffolk Manorial Families: Being the County Visitations and Other Pedigrees,* 3 vols. (1900-8), 2: 311.

4192-4193 *The History of Parliament 1558–1603,* 3: 76-77; *The Complete Peerage,* 9: 196; *The Knights of England,* 2: 73.

4194-4195 *The History of Parliament 1558–1603,* 1: 635-36 *The Complete Peerage,* 3: 390, 9: 677; Will of Henry Lord Compton, 17 May 1589, Probated 22 Nov. 1589, Chancery Inquisitions Post Mortem, Series II, 224/37.

4196-4197 *The History of Parliament 1558–1603,* 2: 344-45; *The Complete Peerage,* 9: 782-87.

4198-4199 *The History of Parliament 1558–1603,* 3: 322; *The Complete Peerage,* 11: 335; *The Marriage, Baptismal and Burial Registers of the Collegiate Church or Abbey of St. Peter, Westminster,* 10: 111-12.

4200-4201 *The Complete Peerage,* 6: 627-29; *Oxford Dictionary of National Biography,* 10: 74-79; *The History of Parliament 1509–1558,* 1: 582-83; Sir Joseph Alfred Bradney, *A History of Monmouthshire from the coming of the Normans into Wales down to the present time,* 5 vols. in 13 (1907-93), 1: 278; *Publications of the Harleian Society, New Series,* vol. 14, Michael Powell Siddons, ed., *Visitations by the Heralds in Wales,* 91; *Publications of the Harleian Society, Visitation Series,* vol. 24, Joseph Lemuel Chester and George J. Armytage, *Allegations for Marriage Licences issued by the Faculty Office of the Archbishop of Canterbury at London, 1543–1869,* 4; Anthony Hoskins, "Mary Boleyn Carey's Children – Offspring of King Henry VIII?," *The Genealogists' Magazine: Official Organ of the Society of Genealogists* 25 [1997]: 345-52.

4202-4203 *The visitations of Cornwall,* 501; *A History of Monmouthshire,* 1: 278; Charles James Feret, *Fulham Old and New being an exhaustive history of the ancient parish of Fulham,* 3 vols. (1900), 1: 217.

4204-4205 *The History of Parliament 1558–1603,* 3: 399; *Publications of the Harleian Society, Visitation Series,* vol. 57, W. Harry Rylands, ed., *The Four Visitations of Berkshire Made and Taken by Thomas Benolte, Clarenceux, Anno 1532, By William Harvey, Clarenceux, Anno 1566, By*

Henry Chitting, Chester Herald, and John Philipott, Rouge Dragon, for William Camden, Clarenceux, Anno 1623, and by Elias Ashmole, Windsor Herald, for Sir Edward Bysshe, Clarenceux, Anno 1665–66, 76; Fulham Old and New, 2: 135; Camden Society Series, vol. 44, Sir Henry Ellis, Obituary of Richard Smyth, secondary of the Poultry Compter, London: being a catalogue of all such persons as he knew in their life: Extending from A.D. 1627 to A.D. 1674, xi, 7.

4206-4207   The Complete Peerage, 3: 127; The History of Parliament 1558–1603, 1: 510.

4216-4217   "Pedigree of the family of Lunsford, of Lunsford and Wilegh, co. Sussex," Collectanea Topographica et Genealogica 4 [1837]: 141; Plantagenet Ancestry, 481.

4218-4219   The History of Parliament 1558–1603, 2: 143-44; Publications of the Harleian Society, Visitation Series, vol. 75, W. Bruce Bannerman, The Visitations of Kent Taken in the Years 1530–1 by Thomas Benolte, Clarenceux, and 1574 by Robert Cooke, Clarenceux, and 1592 by Robert Cooke, Clarenceux, 99; The Knights of England, 2: 87.

4220-4221   Oxford Dictionary of National Biography, 40: 498-99; The History of Parliament 1558–1603, 3: 122-23; The Four Visitations of Berkshire, 56: 250; The Knights of England, 2: 92.

4222-4223   The History of Parliament 1558–1603, 3: 403-4; Archæologia Cantiana, vol. 20, John J. Stocker, "Pedigree of Smythe of Ostenhanger, Kent; of Smythe of Bidborough and Sutton-at-Hone, Kent; and of the Smythes, Viscounts of Strangford, of Dromore, Ireland," 76-77; Plantagenet Ancestry, 481.

4224-4225   The History and Antiquities of the County of Dorset, 4: 374, 3: 723.

4226-4227   The History and Antiquities of the County of Dorset, 2: 582; Publications of the Harleian Society, Visitation Series, vol. 64, W. Harry Rylands, ed., Pedigrees from the Visitation of Hampshire Made by Thomas Benolte, Clarenceulx, Ao 1530; Enlarged with the Vissitation of the same county made by Robert Cooke, Clarenceulx, Anno 1575, Both wch are continued wth the Visitation made by John Phillipott, Somersett (for William Camden, Clarenceux) in Ao 1622 most part then don(e) & finished in Ao 1634, as collected by Richard Mundy in Harleian MS. No. 1544, 27.

4232-4233   The History of Parliament 1509–1558, 2: 648; G. Milner-Gibson-Cullum, "Middleton or Myddelton of Chirk Castle, Denbigh, Stanstead Mountfichet, Essex, and other places," Miscellanea Genealogica et Heraldica, 3rd series, 2 [1898]: 214.

4234-4235   "Middleton or Myddelton of Chirk Castle, Denbigh, Stanstead Mountfichet, Essex, and other places," 220; George E. Cokayne, Some Account of the Lord Mayors and Sheriffs of the City of London during the first quarter of the seventeenth century 1601 to 1625 (1897), 60-62.

4236-4237   The Complete Baronetage, 1: 216.

4238-4239   George Morris, Shropshire Genealogies: Shewing the Descent of the principal landed proprietors of the County of Salop from the time of William the Conqueror to the present time; compiled from Heraldic Visitations, public records, chartularies, family documents, parish registers and other sources, 8 vols. (ca. 1836), 5: 475; Publications of the Harleian Society, Visitation Series, vol. 28, George Grazebrook and John Paul Rylands, eds., The Visitation of Shropshire Taken in the year 1623 by Robert Tresswell, Somerset Herald, and Augustine Vincent, Rouge Croix Pursuivant of Arms, Marshals and deputies to William Camden, Clarenceux King of Arms. With Additions from the Pedigrees of Shropshire Gentry Taken by the Heralds in the years 1569 and 1584, and other sources, 281, 29: 391.

4264-4265 Owen Manning and William Bray, *The History and Antiquities of the County of Surrey: Compiled from the Best and Most Authentic Historians, Valuable Records, and Manuscripts in the Public Offices and Libraries, and in Private Hands; with a Facsimile Copy of Domesday, Engraved on Thirteen Plates*, 3 vols. (1804–14), 3: 29.

4266-4267 *The Visitations of the County of Surrey*, 43: 22.

4272-4273 *Journal of the County Kildare Archaeological Society*, vol. 4, Lord Walter FitzGerald, "Patrick Sarsfield, Earl of Lucan, with an account of his family and their connection with Lucan and Tully," 118.

4274-4275 *The Complete Peerage*, 3: 224.

4276-4277 *Journal of the County Kildare Archaeological Society*, vol. 6, Lord Walter FitzGerald, "Pedigree of the O'Mores of Leix, and of Ballina, co. Kildare," xii, pedigree c.

4278-4279 *The Complete Peerage*, 1: 427; *The Knights of England*, 2: 84.

4280-4281 *Journal of the County Louth Archaeological Society*, vol. 8, "Will of father James Hussey, Smarmore, 1635: The Taaffes," 307; "Taaffe Pedigrees," *Herald & Genealogist* 3 [1864]: 471; Karl Taaffe, *Memoirs of the Family of Taaffe* (1856), pedigree; *The Complete Peerage*, 12: 1: 595; *The Knights of England*, 2: 131.

4282-4283 *The Complete Peerage*, 4: 357.

4284-4285 Lord George Scott, *Lucy Walter, Wife or Mistress* (1947), 36; *Heraldic Visitations of Wales and Part of the Marches Between the Years 1586 and 1613 by Lewys Dwnn*, 1: 228.

4286-4287 *Lucy Walter, Wife or Mistress*, 36.

4352-4353 *The Complete Baronetage*, 1: 33; *The History of Parliament 1558–1603*, 3: 369.

4354-4355 *The History of Parliament 1558–1603*, 2: 394; Amos C. Miller, *Sir Henry Killigrew, Elizabethan soldier and diplomat* (1963); *The Knights of England*, 2: 88.

4356-4357 Joseph Jackson Howard and Frederick Arthur Crisp, *Visitation of England and Wales, Notes*, 14 vols. (1896-1921), 2: 165; Frederic William Weaver, ed., *The Visitations of the County of Somerset in the Years 1531 and 1573, together with Additional Pedigrees, Chiefly from the Visitation of 1591* (1885), 88.

4358-4359 *The History of Parliament 1558–1603*, 2: 190; *Wiltshire Visitation Pedigrees, 1623*, 105-6: 32; *Pedigrees from the Visitation of Hampshire*, 64: 17; Herbert C. Andrews, "Notes on the Rowlett and Jennings families," *Miscellanea Genealogica et Heraldica*, 5th series, 8 [1932-34]: 106; *Proceedings of the Hampshire Field Club and Archæological Society* 9 [1920-25]: 11-12.

4360-4361 *The History of Parliament 1558–1603*, 3: 234-36; *Alumni Oxonienses: The members of the University of Oxford, 1500–1714*, 3-4: 1182; *The Knights of England*, 2: 90; Peter C. Bartrum, *Welsh Genealogies AD 1400–1500*, 18 vols. (1983), 2: 223; *The Royal Descents of 600 Immigrants to the American Colonies or the United States*, 171-72.

Sir John Popham was an uncle of George Popham of Maine and a great-uncle of William and Elizabeth Poole of Massachusetts.

4362-4363 *The History of Parliament 1558–1603*, 2: 60-61; *Collections for a History of Staffordshire*, vol. 9, H. Sydney Grazebrook, "The Barons of Dudley," 4-5; *Allegations for Marriage Licences issued by the Bishop of London*, 25: 111; *Publications of the Harleian Society, Register Series*, vol. 18, Francis Collins, *The Registers and Monumental Inscriptions of Charterhouse Chapel, 1671 to 1890*, 81.

4364-4365 "Kerr of Ancrum, Earl of Ancrum, Earl and Marquis of Lothian," *The Genealogist* 2 [1878]: 290; Sir William Fraser, *The Douglas Book: Memoirs of the House of Douglas and Angus,* 4 vols. (1885), 2: 169.

William Kerr and Margaret Dundas were the grandparents of William Kerr, 1st Earl of Lothian [No. 5920].

4366-4367 "Notes on the family of Kerr in Scotland. VIII. Ker of Dolphinstoun, Hirsell, and Littledean," *Herald & Genealogist* 7 [1873]: 513-15.

4368-4369 *Publications of the Harleian Society, Visitation Series,* vol. 92, J. B. Whitmore, ed., *London Visitation Pedigrees, 1664,* 124.

4370-4371 John Roger Woodhead, *The rulers of London 1660–1689: a biographical record of the aldermen and common councilmen of the City of London* (1965), 149; Will of Richard Forbaunche, Gentleman of Ripley, Surrey 19 Jan. 1619/20, Proved at London P.C.C. 19 June 1620 PROB 11/136.

4372-4373 Henry Brierley, ed., *The Registers of Crosthwaite,* 2 vols. (1928-30), 2: 163.

4376-4377 *The History of Parliament 1558–1603,* 3: 217; *The Complete Baronetage,* 1: 176; *Heraldic Visitations of Wales and Part of the Marches Between the Years 1586 and 1613 by Lewys Dwnn,* 1: 115.

4378-4379 *The Complete Baronetage,* 1: 128; Gary Boyd Roberts, *Notable Kin: An Anthology of Columns First Published in the NEHGS NEXUS, 1986–1995, Volume Two … with contributions by John Anderson Brayton and Richard E. Brenneman* (1999), 192, 203, 216-19, 221-22; *The Royal Descents of 600 Immigrants to the American Colonies or the United States,* 278-81; *Plantagenet Ancestry,* 202-3.

Sir Erasmus Dryden, 1st Baronet, and Frances Wilkes were the grandparents of John Dryden, the poet. Sir Erasmus was an uncle of Anne (Marbury) Hutchinson and Katherine (Marbury) Scott of Rhode Island, and a great-uncle of Kenelm Cheseldine, Attorney General of Maryland.

4380-4381 *Alumni Oxonienses: The members of the University of Oxford, 1500–1714,* 1-2: 372; *The Victoria History of the County of Lancaster,* 8 vols. (1906-14), 4: 327; *Journal of the Derbyshire Archæological and Natural History Society,* vol. 6, "Pedigree of the heirs of Sir Ralph Longford, of Longford, co. Derby," opposite 1.

4382-4383 *The Complete Peerage,* 3: 180.

4384-4385 *Oxford Dictionary of National Biography,* 29: 628-57; William Brown Patterson, *King James VI and I and the reunion of Christendom* (1997); Caroline Bingham, *James VI of Scotland* (1979); John Leeds Barroll, *Anna of Denmark, queen of England: a cultural biography* (2001); *The Marriage, Baptismal and Burial Registers of the Collegiate Church or Abbey of St. Peter, Westminster,* 10: 124, 115; Neil D. Thompson and Col. Charles M. Hansen, "A Medieval Heritage: The Ancestry of Charles II, King of England," *The Genealogist* 2 [1981]: 161-62.

4386-4387 Duc de Lévis Mirepoix de l'Académie Française, *Henri IV Roi de France et de Navarre* (1971); Nicola Mary Sutherland, *Henry IV of France and the Politics of Religion 1572–1596* (2002); George Slocombe, *The White Plumed Henry King of France* (1931); *Encyclopaedia Britannica,* 32 vols. (1911), 13: 292; "A Medieval Heritage: The Ancestry of Charles II, King of England," 162-63.

4388-4389 *Oxford Dictionary of National Biography*, 56: 482-83; *The Complete Peerage*, 6: 74-75; Leslie G. Pine, *Burke's Genealogical and Heraldic History of the Peerage and Baronetage* (1953), 1145; *Alumni Cantabrigienses*, 4: 302; *The Knights of England*, 2: 159; Henry F. Waters, "Genealogical Gleanings in England," *The New England Historical and Genealogical Register* 43 [1889]: 403; *The Marriage, Baptismal and Burial Registers of the Collegiate Church or Abbey of St. Peter, Westminster*, 10: 178; Will of Sir Edward Villiers, knt., Lord President of the Province of Munster in the Realm of Ireland 31 Aug. 1625, Probated 2 Feb. 1626[/27] (P.C.C. 20 Skynner).

4390-4391 *The Complete Baronetage*, 1: 81; *The Complete Peerage*, 2: 37, 4: 408-9; *Publications of the Harleian Society, Register Series*, vol. 46, W. Bruce Bannerman, *The Registers of St. Olave, Hart Street, London, 1563 to 1700*, 13, 163.

4392-4393 *The History of Parliament 1558–1603*, 1: 428; *The Dictionary of National Biography*, 2: 233-35; *Alumni Oxonienses: The members of the University of Oxford, 1500–1714*, 1-2: 106; *The visitations of Cornwall*, 27; *The Knights of England*, 2: 113.

4394-4395 John Gage, *History of the Antiquities of Suffolk, Thingoe Hundred* (1838), 134; Walter C. Metcalfe, ed., *The Visitations of Suffolk made by Hervey, Clarenceux, 1561, Cooke, Clarenceux, 1577 and Raven, Richmond Herald, 1612 with notes and an appendix of Additional Suffolk Pedigrees* (1882), 90; *The History of Parliament 1558–1603*, 1: 675; John Comber, *Sussex Genealogies*, 3 vols. (1931-33), 3: 258-59; *The Knights of England*, 2: 97.

4396-4397 Adriaan Willem Eliza Dek, *Van Het Vorstenhuis Nassau* (1970), 77, 146.

4398-4399 Detlev Schwennicke, ed., *Europäische Stammtafeln: Stammtafeln zur Geschichte der Europäischen Staaten*, Neue Folge, 21 vols. (1978-2001), 18: 65.

4400-4401 *The Complete Peerage*, 12: 2: 857-63.

4402-4403 *The Complete Peerage*, 4: 412; *The History, Description and Antiquities of the Prebendal Church of the Blessed Virgin Mary of Thame*, 513-14; *The History and Antiquities of the County of Hertford*, 1: 495.

4404-4405 Duncan Warrand, *Hertfordshire Families* (1907), 92; *The Visitation of the County of Northampton in the Year 1681*, 87: 137; *The History of Parliament 1558–1603*, 3: 68-69; *Some Account of the Lord Mayors and Sheriffs of the City of London during the first quarter of the seventeenth century*, 20; *The Visitations of Kent Taken in the Years 1530–1*, 74: 52; *The History and Antiquities of the County of Hertford*, 3: 132; *The Knights of England*, 2: 104. See also 5080-5081.

4406-4407 *The Complete Baronetage*, 1: 71, 199; *The History and Antiquities of the County of Hertford*, 1: 238; *The Knights of England*, 1: 155; *The History and Antiquities of the County of Dorset*, 3: 595; *The Registers of St. Mary Magdalen Milk Street, London and St. Michael Bassishaw, London, 1558 to 1892*, 72: 22.

4412-4413 *London Visitation Pedigrees, 1664*, 92: 10.

4414-4415 *London Visitation Pedigrees, 1664*, 92: 11.

4416-4417 *The Complete Baronetage*, 2: 213; Henry Foley, *Records of the English Province of the Society of Jesus: historic facts illustrative of the labours and sufferings of its members in the sixteenth and seventeenth centuries*, 7 vols. in 8 (1877-83), 1: pedigree.

4418-4419 *Transactions of the Bristol and Gloucestershire Archeological Society*, vol. 76, J. N. Langston, "The Pastons of Horton," 107; "Fenns Manuscripts of Suffolk and Norfolk" (manuscripts in the Norman Collection, Salford, Lancashire), 208; *Publications of the*

Harleian Society, Visitation Series, vol. 86, A. W. Hughes Clarke and Arthur Campling, *The Visitation of Norfolk Anno Domini 1664 made by Sir Edward Bysshe, Knt., Clarenceux King of Arms,* 159.

4420-4421 *The Complete Baronetage,* 1: 91; *Publications of the Harleian Society, Register Series,* vol. 59, W. Bruce Bannerman, *Registers of St. Mary Somerset, London, 1557 to 1853,* 190.

4422-4423 John Nichols, *The History and Antiquities of the County of Leicestershire: Compiled from the Best and Most Ancient Historians; Inquisitions Post Mortem, and Other Valuable Records; Including Also Mr. Burton's Description of the County, Published in 1622; and the Later Collections of Mr. Stavely, Mr. Carte, Mr. Peck, and Sir Thomas Cave,* 4 vols. in 8 (1795-1815), 3: 406; *Publications of the Harleian Society, Visitation Series,* vol. 13, Walter C. Metcalfe, ed., *The Visitations of Essex by Hawley, 1552, Hervey 1558, Cooke 1570, Raven 1612 and Owen and Lilly, 1634, to which are added Miscellaneous Essex Pedigrees from various Harleian Manuscripts and an appendix containing Berry's Essex Pedigrees,* 324, 528.

4424-4427 See 4384-4387.

4428-4431 See 2056-2059.

4432-4433 *The History and Antiquities of the County of Dorset,* 3: 298; *The History of Modern Wiltshire,* 3: 5: 20; *The Complete Baronetage,* 2: 220; *Publications of the Northamptonshire Record Society,* vol. 19, Mary E. Finch, "The Wealth of Five Northamptonshire Families 1540-1640," 78-80; *The Knights of England,* 2: 130.

4434-4435 *Sussex Archeological Collections: Illustrating the History and Antiquities of the County,* vol. 33, "Warnham: Its Church, Monuments, Registers, and Vicars," 177-78; Dudley George Cary Elwes, *A history of the Castles and Mansions in Western Sussex* (1876), Caryll pedigree; *Sussex Genealogies,* 1: 48; *The Knights of England,* 2: 112.

4436-4437 *The Victoria History of the County of Gloucester,* 7 vols. to date. (1907-), 7: 89; *Publications of the Harleian Society, Visitation Series,* vol. 21, Sir John Maclean and W. C. Heane, *The Visitation of the County of Gloucester Taken in the year 1623, by Henry Chitty and John Phillipot as Deputies to William Camden, Clarenceaux King of Arms, with Pedigrees from the Herald's Visitations of 1569 and 1582-3, and Sundry Miscellaneous Pedigrees,* 21-22.

4438-4439 *The Complete Peerage,* 7: 100.

4440-4441 *The Knights of England,* 2: 101; *The Complete Baronetage,* 1: 43; Robert Surtees, *The History and Antiquities of the County Palatine of Durham: Compiled from Original Records, Preserved in Public Repositories and Private Collections, and Illustrated by Engravings of Architectural and Monumental Antiquities, Portraits of Eminent Persons &c., &c.,* 4 vols. (1816-40), 1: 203; *Pedigrees of the County Families of Yorkshire, comp. by Joseph Foster and authenticated by the members of each family,* 2 vols. (1874), 2: Belasyse pedigree.

4442-4443 *The Knights of England,* 2: 101; *Pedigrees of the County Families of Yorkshire,* 2: Cholmley pedigree.

4444-4445 *The Complete Peerage,* 12: 2: 765-66; Egerton Brydges, *Collins's Peerage of England, Genealogical, Biographical, and Historical, Greatly Augmented, and Continued to the Present Time,* 9 vols. (1812), 2: 375-76; *Publications of the Harleian Society, Register Series,* vol. 25, Thomas Mason, *A Register of Baptisms, Marriages and Burials in the Parish of St. Martin in the Fields, in the County of Middlesex 1550 to 1619,* 74; *Publications of the Harleian Society, Visitation Series,* vol. 23, Joseph Lemuel Chester and George J. Armytage, *Allegations for Marriage Licences issued by the Dean and Chapter of Westminster, 1558–1699; Also for those issued* by the Vicar-General of the Archbishop of Canterbury, 1660–1679, 9; *The Marriage, Baptismal and Burial Registers of the Collegiate Church or Abbey of St. Peter, Westminster*, 10: 111.

4446-4447 *The Complete Peerage*, 2: 230-31, 7: 553, note b; David Starkey, *Rivals in Power* (1990), 203-29. See also 5786-5787.

4448-4449 George Henry Dashwood et al., eds., *The Visitation of Norfolk in the Year 1563, taken by William Harvey, Clarenceux King of Arms*, 2 vols. (1878-95), 1: 367; *Some Account of the Lord Mayors and Sheriffs of the City of London during the first quarter of the seventeenth century*, 93-94; *Alumni Cantabrigienses*, 4: 325.

4450-4451 *The Complete Baronetage*, 2: 15; *The Knights of England*, 2: 137; William Sumner Appleton, *Memorials of the Cranes of Chilton: with a pedigree of the family and the life of the last representative* (1868), 62; *Parish Church of Horseheath (Cambridgeshire) registers, 1558–1876* Family History Library film 1040,532.

4452-4453 *Publications of the Harleian Society, Visitation Series*, vol. 8, George W. Marshall, ed., *Le Neve's Pedigrees of the Knights made by King Charles II, King James II, King William III and Queen Mary, King William alone, and Queen Anne*, 165; *Parish Registers of Woodbridge 1545–1910* Family History Library film 0919,635; *Rougham Parish Register 1565–1837* Family History Library film 0991,971.

4454-4455 Robert Battle, "English Ancestry of Anne (Derehaugh) Stratton of Salem, Massachusetts," *The New England Historical and Genealogical Register* 156 [2002]: 43; *The Visitations of Suffolk made by Hervey, Clarenceux, 1561, Cooke, Clarenceux, 1577 and Raven, Richmond Herald, 1612*, 189; *Publications of the Harleian Society, Visitation Series*, vol. 32, Walter Rye, ed., *The Visitacion of Norffolk Made and Taken by William Hervey, Clarencieux King of Arms, Anno 1563, Enlarged with another Visitacion Made by Clarenceux Cooke, with many other descents and also the Visitation Made by John Raven, Richmond, Anno 1613*, 248, 210.

Thomas Derehaugh was a brother of Anne (Derehaugh) Stratton of Massachusetts.

4456-4463 See 2184-2191.

4480-4481 William Betham, *The Baronetage of England, or, the History of the English Baronets, and Such Baronets of Scotland, as Are of English Families: With Genealogical Tables, and Engravings of Their Armorial Bearings; Collected from the Present Baronetages, Approved Historians, Public Records, Authentic Manuscripts, Well Attested Pedigrees, and Personal Information*, 5 vols. (1801-5), 4: 108.

4512-4513 Leslie G. Pine, ed., *Burke's Genealogical and Heraldic History of the Peerage, Baronetage and Knightage* (1956), 2202.

4528-4529 *The Complete Baronetage*, 2: 36-37; *Allegations for Marriage Licences issued by the Bishop of London*, 25: 199.

4530-4531 *The History of Parliament 1558–1603*, 2: 490-91; *The Complete Peerage*, 7: 229-31; *British Record Society*, vol. 36, George S. Fry, Sidney J. Madge and Edw. Alex. Fry, eds., *Abstracts of Inquisitiones Post Mortem Relating to the City of London*, 200.

4532-4533 *The Complete Baronetage*, 2: 134; "Pedigrees and heraldic notes of Gregory King: Briggs of Ernestree and Haughton, Salop," *Miscellanea Genealogica et Heraldica*, 5th series, 9 [1932]: 150.

4534-4535 "Pedigrees and heraldic notes of Gregory King: Briggs of Ernestree and Haughton, Salop," 150; *Shropshire Genealogies*, 6: 282; *Collections for a History of Staffordshire*, vol. 5, part 2, H. Sydney Grazebrook, ed., *The Heraldic Visitations of Staffordshire Made by Sir Richard St. George, Norroy, in 1614, and by Sir William Dugdale in the Years 1663 and 1664*, 216.

4536-4537 John William Clay, ed., *Dugdale's Visitation of Yorkshire in 1665–6, with additions*, 3 vols. (1899-1917), 3: 276; *Publications of the Harleian Society, Visitation Series*, vol. 39, John W. Clay, ed., *Familiae Minorum Gentium. Diligentiâ Josephi Hunter, Sheffieldiensis, S.A.S.*, 975, 978.

4538-4539 *Publications of the Harleian Society, Register Series*, vol. 5, Joseph Lemuel Chester, *The Registers of St. Mary Aldermary, London, 1558 to 1754*, 9; *Publications of the Harleian Society, Visitation Series*, vol. 12, John Fetherston, ed., *The Visitation of the County of Warwick in the year 1619 Taken by William Camden, Clarenceaux King of Arms (Harl. Mss. 1167)*, 398.

4544-4545 *Heraldic Visitations of Wales and Part of the Marches Between the Years 1586 and 1613 by Lewys Dwnn*, 1: 50, 88; *Dictionary of Welsh Biography Down to 1940*, 999.

4546-4547 *Heraldic Visitations of Wales and Part of the Marches Between the Years 1586 and 1613 by Lewys Dwnn*, 1: 19.

4548-4549 *The rulers of London 1660–1689*, 92.

4550-4551 Walter Arthur Copinger, *History of the Copingers or Coppingers of the County of Cork, Ireland, and the Counties of Suffolk and Kent, England* (1884), pedigree; Robert Eden, "Pedigree of the Lords Burgh of Gainsborough," *The Genealogist*, New Series, 12 [1896]: 234.

4552-4553 *Oxford Dictionary of National Biography*, 59: 453-55; *The Complete Peerage*, 12: 2: 719-21; *Some Account of the Lord Mayors and Sheriffs of the City of London during the first quarter of the seventeenth century*, 89; *Registers of St. Olave Old Jewry, London: Baptisms, burials 1538–1629 Marriages 1538–1637* Family History Library film 0380,325; *A Register of Baptisms, Marriages and Burials in the Parish of St. Martin in the Fields, in the County of Middlesex 1550 to 1619*, 25: 171. See also 4904-4905.

4554-4555 *Wiltshire Visitation Pedigrees, 1623*, 105-6: 75; A. W. Hughes Clarke, ed., *London Pedigrees and Coats of Arms, reprinted from* Miscellanea Genealogica et Heraldica (1935), 129; *The Complete Baronetage*, 1: 24; Oswald Barron, "The Wild Wilmots," *The Ancestor* 11 [1904]: 22; Will of Sir John Saint John of Lydiard Tregoze, Wiltshire 3 July 1645, Proved at London P.C.C. 20 Sept. 1648 PROB 11/205.

According to Barron, the mother of Anne (St. John), Countess of Rochester, was Lucy Hungerford [No. 8779], not Anne Leighton. However, this identification appears chronologically impossible, since Lucy Hungerford died 16 years before Anne St. John's birth. Furthermore, the will of Sir John St. John, Bt., names his grandchildren Sir Henry Lee and Francis Henry Lee, sons of Sir Henry Francis Lee, Bt., and the testator's daughter Anne (the future Lady Rochester).

4556-4557 Arthur Malet, *Notices of an English branch of the Malet family* (1885), 47-48; *Alumni Oxonienses: The members of the University of Oxford, 1500–1714*, 3-4: 962; *Publications of the Harleian Society, Register Series*, vol. 28, Arthur J. Jewers, *The Registers of The Abbey Church of SS. Peter & Paul, Bath, 1569 to 1800*, 363.

4558-4559 *The Complete Peerage*, 6: 418; Charles E. H. Chadwyck-Healey, *The History of the Part of West Somerset Comprising the Parishes of Luccombe, Selworthy, Stoke, Pero, Porlock, Culbone and Oare* (1901), 111; *The Royal Descents of 600 Immigrants to the American Colonies or the United States*, 535-37.

Jane (Gibbes), Baroness Hawley, was an aunt of Robert Gibbs of Massachusetts.

4576-4577 Northumberland County History Commission, *A history of Northumberland*, 15 vols. (1893-1940), 13: 222; *The History and Antiquities of the County Palatine of Durham*, 3: 294.

4578-4579 *A history of Northumberland*, 7: 322; *Publications of the Surtees Society*, vol. 142, H. M. Wood, ed., *Wills and Inventories from the Registry at Durham*, 177.

4580-4581 Percy W. Hedley, *Northumberland Families*, 2 vols. (1968), 2: 130-32.

4582-4583 *The Complete Peerage*, 5: 229.

4584-4585 *Dugdale's Visitation of Yorkshire in 1665–6*, 2: 351.

4586-4587 Joseph Nicolson and Richard Burn. *The History and Antiquities of the Counties of Westmorland and Cumberland*, 2 vols. (1777), 1: 205; *The Knights of England*, 2: 100.

4588-4589 *The History of Parliament 1558–1603*, 3: 350-51, 480-1; *Dugdale's Visitation of Yorkshire in 1665–6*, 1: 335; *The Visitations of Essex by Hawley, 1552, Hervey 1558, Cooke 1570, Raven 1612 and Owen and Lilly, 1634*, 13: 319; Alfred Rudulph Justice, "Genealogical Research in England: Clarke: Addendum, The Weston Family," *The New England Historical and Genealogical Register* 74 [1920]: 137.

4590-4591 *Oxford Dictionary of National Biography*, 21: 574-76; *The Dictionary of National Biography*, 7: 891-93; *London Pedigrees and Coats of Arms*, 24; *Publications of the Harleian Society, Visitation Series*, vol. 15, Joseph J. Howard and Joseph Lemuel Chester, eds., *The Visitation of London Anno Domini 1633, 1634 and 1635: Made by Sr Henry St George, Kt, Richmond Herald, and Deputy and Marshal to Sr Richard St George, Kt, Clarencieux King of Armes*, 304; *The Knights of England*, 2: 207; Alfred Beaven, *The Aldermen of the City of London Temp. Henry III–1908 with Notes on the Parliamentary Representation of the City, the Aldermen and the Livery Companies, the Aldermanic Veto, Aldermanic Baronets and Knights, etc.*, 2 vols. (1908-13), 2: 60.

4608-4609 Thomas George Baring, Earl of Northbrook, et al., eds., *Journals and correspondence from 1808 to 1852, of Sir Francis Thornhill Baring afterwards Lord Northbrook, compiled and edited by his son Thomas George, Earl of Northbrook* (1905), 271; *Deutsches Geschlechterbuch (Genealogisches Handbuch Bürgerlicher Familien)*, vol. 102, "Baring, v. Baring, Baring v. Wallerode: Freiherr v. Baring, Baring-Gould, Baring Baronet of Larkbear, Baring Baronet of Nubia House, Baring Baron of Hillburton, Baring Baron Viscount und Earl of Cromer, Viscount Errington, Baring Baron Viscount und Earl of Northbrook, Baring Baron Revelstoke, aus Groningen in Friesland," 12.

4688-4689 Will of John Watlyngton or Watlington, Yeoman of Natley Scuers, Hampshire 10 Nov. 1558, Proved at London 9 Dec. 1558 PROB 11/42A.

4712-4713 *Archæologia Æliana, or, Miscellaneous Tracts Relating to Antiquity*, New Series, vol. 5, James A. Raine, "Marske," pedigree after 48; *Dugdale's Visitation of Yorkshire in 1665–6*, 1: 284.

4714-4715 See 4582-4583.

4716-4717 *Publications of the Harleian Society, New Series*, vol. 5, G. D. Squibb, ed., *The Visitation of Nottinghamshire begun in 1662 and finished in 1664 made by William Dugdale, Norroy King of Arms*, 118; *Publications of the Harleian Society, Visitation Series*, vol. 88, J. W. Walker, ed., *Hunter's Pedigrees: A Continuation of Familiae Minorum Gentium, Diligentiâ Josephi Hunter, Sheffieldiensis, S.A.S.*, 138; *The History and Antiquities of the County of Leicestershire*, 2: 1: 267.

4718-4719 *Lincolnshire Pedigrees*, 52: 911; *The History and Antiquities of the County of Leicestershire*, 2: 1: 128, note 4.

4728-4731 *Publications of the Surtees Society,* vol. 36, Robert Davies, ed., *The Visitation of the County of Yorke, Began in Ao Dñi MDCLXV and Finished Ao Dñi MDCLXVI, by William Dugdale, Esqr, Norroy King of Armes,* 82; *Dugdale's Visitation of Yorkshire in 1665–6,* 3: 509.

4736-4737 *Visitation of England and Wales, Notes,* 5: 4; Sir Algernon Tudor Tudor-Craig, *The romance of Melusine and de Lusignan: together with genealogical notes and pedigrees of Lovekyn of London, Lovekyn of Lovekynsmede, and of Luckyn of Little Waltham, and Lukyn of Mashbery, all in the county of Essex, and of Lukin of Felbrigg, co. Norfolk* (1932), 17; A. W. Cornelius Hallen, *The Registers of St. Botolph, Bishopsgate, London,* 3 vols. (1889-93), 1: 12.

4744-4745 Algernon Tudor Craig, "Lane of Campsea Ash, co. Suffolk," *Miscellanea Genealogica et Heraldica,* 5th series, 2 [1918]: 58; *Norfolk Genealogy,* vol. 17, Patrick Palgrave-Moore, ed., "A Selection of Revised and Unpublished Norfolk Pedigrees, Part Four," 79.

4746-4747 *Publications of the Harleian Society, Visitation Series,* vol. 61, W. Harry Rylands, ed., A *Visitation of the County of Suffolk Begun Anno Dni 1664 and finished Anno Dni 1668 by Sir Edward Bysshe, Kt., Clarenceux King of Arms,* 48; Walter Arthur Copinger, *The Manors of Suffolk: Notes on Their History and Devolution, with Some Illustrations of the Old Manor Houses,* 7 vols. (1905-11), 2: 187; *The Royal Descents of 600 Immigrants to the American Colonies or the United States,* 182-83.

Edmund Bohun and Dorothy Baxter were grandparents of Edmund Bohun, Chief Justice of South Carolina.

4748-4749 *Rayne, Essex, Christenings, Burials & Marriages, 1558–1664* Family History Library film 1472,666, item 20.

4764-4765 *Panfield, Essex, Christenings, Burials & Marriages, 1569–1711* Family History Library film 1472,590, item 23; Will of Robert Howchin the elder of Panfield, Essex 1 Sept. 1647, Proved at Dunmow 13 Nov. 1647 E.R.O. D/A BW60/63.

4766-4767 *Panfield, Essex, Christenings, Burials & Marriages, 1569–1711* Family History Library film 1472,590, item 23.

4768-4769 G. H. Holley, "Pedigrees compiled from the parish registers, wills, monumental inscriptions, court records, etc., Norfolk County, England" (a 7 vol. manuscript at the Family History Library, Salt Lake City, Utah), 2: 107.

4770-4771 Percy Millican, *A History of Horstead and Stanninghall, Norfolk* (1937), 130; *Lincolnshire Pedigrees,* 51: 693.

4772-4773 "Pedigrees compiled from the parish registers, wills, monumental inscriptions, court records, etc., Norfolk County, England," 3: 75; *The Visitation of Norfolk Anno Domini 1664 made by Sir Edward Bysshe, Knt.,* 86: 131.

4774-4775 *The Visitation of Norfolk Anno Domini 1664 made by Sir Edward Bysshe, Knt.,* 85: 27.

4776-4777 "Pedigrees compiled from the parish registers, wills, monumental inscriptions, court records, etc., Norfolk County, England," 2: 106; *The Visitations of Essex by Hawley, 1552, Hervey 1558, Cooke 1570, Raven 1612 and Owen and Lilly, 1634,* 13: 431; *The Visitacion of Norffolk Made and Taken by William Hervey, Clarencieux King of Arms, Anno 1563,* 32: 199.

4780-4783 "Pedigrees compiled from the parish registers, wills, monumental inscriptions, court records, etc., Norfolk County, England," 5: 24; *The Visitation of Norfolk Anno Domini 1664 made by Sir Edward Bysshe, Knt.,* 86: 161.

4800-4801 *Visitations of England and Wales, Notes,* 11: 107; Gabriel Girod de l'Ain, *Les Thellusson histoire d'une famille* (1977), 26.

4802-4803 *Visitations of England and Wales, Notes,* 11: 107; *Les Thellusson histoire d'une famille,* 30; Anselm de Saint-Marie and M. du Fourny, *Histoire de la Maison Royale de France Anciens Barons du Royaume: et des Grands Officiers de la Couronne,* 3rd ed., 9 vols. (1726-33), 2: 376; *http://www.huguenots-france.org/sites/galiffe/pag0.htm#11,* accessed 22 Feb. 2007.

4804-4805 *http://www.huguenots-france.org/english/lyon/lyon17/dat15.htm#6,* accessed 22 Feb. 2007.

4806-4807 *Visitations of England and Wales, Notes,* 11: 107; J.-A. Galiffe, *Généalogiques sur les familles genevoises, depuis les premiers temps jusqu'à nos jours* (1831), 386; *http://homepages .rootsweb.com/~vfarch/genealogy-data/wc02_150.htm,* accessed 23 April 2007.

4808-4809 *http://www.huguenots-france.org/english/lyon/lyon17/dat6.htm#2,* accessed 22 Feb. 2007.

4810-4811 *http://www.huguenots-france.org/english/lyon/lyon17/dat48.htm#12,* accessed 22 Feb. 2007.

4812-4813 *http://www.huguenots-france.org/english/lyon/lyon17/dat54.htm#12,* accessed 22 Feb. 2007.

4814-4815 *http://www.huguenots-france.org/english/lyon/lyon17/dat55.htm#7,* accessed 22 Feb. 2007.

4852-4853 "Genealogical Gleanings in England," 48: 505-6; *Familiae Minorum Gentium,* 38: 639; Philip Morant, *The History and Antiquities of the County of Essex: Compiled from the Best and Most Ancient Historians: from Domesday-Book, Inquisitiones Post Mortem and Other the Most Valuable Records and Mss. &c, the Whole Digested, Improved, Perfected and Brought Down to the Present Time,* 2 vols. (1768), 1: 101; George Baker, *The History and Antiquities of the County of Northampton,* 2 vols. (1822-41), 1: 527; *The Royal Descents of 600 Immigrants to the American Colonies or the United States,* 289-90, 526-27; *Plantagenet Ancestry,* 102-3, 636.

Sir Richard Saltonstall was a first cousin of (another) Sir Richard Saltonstall, a founder of the Massachusetts Bay Colony. Jane (Bernard), Lady Saltonstall, was an aunt of Colonel William Bernard and Richard Bernard of Virginia, and a great-great-aunt of Sir Francis Bernard, 1st Baronet, Governor of New Jersey and Massachusetts.

4854-4855 *The History of Parliament 1558-1603,* 3: 171; *The Visitations of Suffolk made by Hervey, Clarenceux, 1561, Cooke, Clarenceux, 1577 and Raven, Richmond Herald, 1612,* 156; *The Knights of England,* 2: 122; "Genealogical Gleanings in England," *The New England Historical and Genealogical Register* 49 [1894]: 107-8.

4864-4865 Vivien Allen, *The Bulteels: The Story of a Huguenot Family* (2004), 14-21; Colonel de Lannoy, "La Famille Bulteel ou Bulteau à Tournai et à Anvers au XVI siècle," *Le Parchemin: bulletin belge héraldique, généalogique, onomastique, 1982,* 459-64, *1984,* 81 (question), *1985,* 76 (response); Alfons K. L. Thijs, "Antwerpse Scharlakenververs," *Vlaamse Stam, Tidschrift voor Familiegeschiedenis,* 4 [1969]: 449-51, 454; *The Visitation of London Anno Domini 1633, 1634 and 1635,* 15: 118; Will of Gyles Bulteel, Proved at London P.C.C. 16 May 1603 PROB 11/101; Will of Mary Brontin alias Bulteel, Widow 15 April 1611, Proved at London P.C.C. 28 June 1611 PROB 11/117.

4866-4867 Charles Edward Pitman, *History and pedigree of the family of Pitman of Dunchideock, Exeter, and their collaterals, and of the Pitmans of Alphington, Norfolk and Edinburgh:*

with part pedigrees and acccounts of families connected by marriage (1920), 59; *Publications of the Harleian Society, Visitation Series*, vol. 6, Frederic Thomas Colby, ed., *The Visitation of the County of Devon in the year 1620*, 330; *Barnstaple parish register of baptisms, marriages, and burials 1538 A.D. to 1812 A.D.* Family History Library film number 0962,417; Vivien Allen, *The Bulteels: The Story of a Huguenot Family* (2004), 36; Will of John Peard, Gentleman of Barnstaple, Devon 20 Oct. 1631, Proved 20 Jan. 1632 PROB 11/161.

4868-4869 *The visitations of Cornwall*, 254, 184, 549.

4870-4871 *The visitations of Cornwall*, 95; *The visitations of the county of Devon*, 722.

4880-4881 "The family of Croker," *Herald & Genealogist* 8 [1874]: 380; *The visitations of the county of Devon*, 254; 103; *The Royal Descents of 600 Immigrants to the American Colonies or the United States*, 354.

Hugh Crocker and Agnes Bonville were great-great-grandparents of Mary (Fox) Ellicott of Pennsylvania.

4884-4885 *The History of Parliament 1558–1603*, 3: 228, 209; *The Complete Baronetage*, 2: 57; *Publications of the Harleian Society, Visitation Series*, vol. 11, Frederic Thomas Colby, ed., *The Visitation of the County of Somerset in the year 1623*, 110; *The Knights of England*, 2: 141, *The visitations of the county of Devon*, 603; "Genealogical Gleanings in England," *The New England Historical and Genealogical Register* 48 [1894]: 490, 492; *The Royal Descents of 600 Immigrants to the American Colonies or the United States*, 171-72; *Plantagenet Ancestry*, 81-82. See also 4886-4887.

Sir William Pole and Mary Periam were the parents of William and Elizabeth Poole of Massachusetts. Sir William's first cousins included George Popham of Maine.

4886-4887 *The Complete Baronetage*, 2: 57; *The Visitation of the County of Somerset in the year 1623*, 11: 110; *The History of Parliament 1558–1603*, 3: 228; *The Visitations of the County of Somerset in the Years 1531 and 1573*, 33; *The Registers of St. Mary Magdalen Milk Street, London and St. Michael Bassishaw, London, 1558 to 1892*, 72: 171; Will of Roger Howe, Mercer of London 16 July 1606, codicil 21 July 1606, Proved at London P.C.C. 6 Nov. 1606 PROB 11/108. See also 4884-4885.

4888-4889 *The visitations of the county of Devon*, 163, 470.

4890-4891 *The visitations of the county of Devon*, 447.

4892-4893 *Publications of the Harleian Society, Visitation Series*, vol. 66, W. Harry Rylands, ed., *Grantees of Arms Named in Docquets and Patents to the End of the Seventeenth Century, in the Manuscripts preserved in the British Museum, The Bodleian Library, Oxford, Queen's College, Oxford, Gonville and Caius College, Cambridge, and Elsewhere, alphabetically Arranged by The Late Joseph Foster and Contained in the Additional Ms. No. 37,147 in the British Museum*, 184; *The History of Parliament 1660–1690*, 3: 164-65.

4894-4895 *The visitations of Cornwall*, 229, 553.

4896-4897 *The Complete Peerage*, 4: 471; *The Scots Peerage*, 7: 47.

4898-4901 *The Complete Peerage*, 11: 215-18; *Oxford Dictionary of National Biography*, 31: 390-92; *The Scots Peerage*, 7: 341-43.

4902-4903 *The Complete Peerage*, 5: 98.

4904-4905 *Oxford Dictionary of National Biography*, 38: 929; *The Complete Peerage*, 4: 462. See also 4552-4553.

4906-4907   *The Complete Peerage,* 5: 63-64.

4908-4911   See 4096-4099.

4992-4993   *A history of Northumberland,* 2: 351.

4994-4995   *A history of Northumberland,* 13: 362, 193; *Archæologia Æliana,* 3rd series, vol. 18, Alan Fenwick Radcliffe, "Notes on the Fenwicks of Radcliffe," 66-81.

4996-4997   *A history of Northumberland,* 7: 258.

4998-4999   *A history of Northumberland,* 1: 228, 14: opposite page 328.

5024-5025   *The History and Antiquities of the County Palatine of Durham,* 2: 14; *Lincolnshire Pedigrees,* 50: 19; James Raine, *The History and Antiquities of North Durham, as Subdivided into the Shires of Norham, Island and Bedlington, which from the Saxon Period until the Year 1844, Constituted Parcels of the County Palatine of Durham, but Are Now United to the County of Northumberland* (1852), 184.

5026-5027   *Dugdale's Visitation of Yorkshire in 1665–6,* 1: 286; *Yorkshire Pedigrees,* 95: 337.

5028-5029   *The Dictionary of National Biography,* 3: 1286; *Alumni Cantabrigienses,* 1: 311; *Melton Mowbray Parish Registers: Baptisms, marriages and burials 1547–1718* Family History Library film 0588,441.

5032-5033   *Northumberland Families,* 1: 172; *A history of Northumberland,* 13: 222; *St. Nicholas' Church (Newcastle-upon-Tyne) parish register transcripts, 1558–1837* Family History Library film 0095,017.

5034-5035   *The History and Antiquities of the County Palatine of Durham,* 2: 135; *Publications of the Surtees Society,* vol. 38, "Wills and Inventories from the Registry at Durham, part II," 177-83.

5036-5037   *Visitation of England and Wales, Notes,* 6: 196; *The History and Antiquities of the County Palatine of Durham,* 2: 78, 3: 355.

5038-5039   Joseph Foster, *Pedigrees Recorded at the Visitations of the county palatine of Durham* (1887), 215; *The History and Antiquities of the County Palatine of Durham,* 2: 54; *Antiquities of Sunderland and its vicinity,* vol. 22, H. L. Robson, "George Lilburne, Mayor of Sunderland," 86-132; *The Publications of the Durham and Northumberland Parish Register Society,* vol. 10, Herbert Maxwell Wood, "The registers of Whitburn, in the county of Durham," 92, 143; Gary Boyd Roberts, *Ancestors of American Presidents, First Authoritative Edition … with charts drawn by Julie Helen Otto* (1995), 7-9, 142-43.

George Lilburn and Eleanor Hickes were great-grandparents of Jane (Rogers) Randolph of Virginia, the maternal grandmother of President Thomas Jefferson.

5040-5041   Henry A. Ogle, *Ogle and Bothal: Or, A History of the Baronies of Ogle, Bothal, and Hepple, and of the Families of Ogle and Bertram, Who Held Possession of Those Baronies and Other Property in the County of Northumberland and Elsewhere; Showing Also How the Property Descended into Other Hands: To Which Is Added Accounts of Several Branches of Families Bearing the Name of Ogle Settled in Other Counties and Countries; with Appendices and Illustrations Compiled from Ancient Records and Other Sources* (1902), 117-18; *Archæologia Æliana,* 3rd series, J. E. Hodgson, "Notes on the Manor and Tower of Bitchfield," 18: 106.

5042-5043   *Ogle and Bothal,* 120, xlv.

5046-5047   *A history of Northumberland,* 5: 288.

5048-5049 *A history of Northumberland,* 6: 257, 9: 65.

5052-5053 *A history of Northumberland,* 13: 247; *The History and Antiquities of the County Palatine of Durham,* 3: 322. See also 5054-5055.

5054-5055 *The History and Antiquities of the County Palatine of Durham,* 3: 294, 2: 343; *A history of Northumberland,* 13: 223-24, 247, 249. See also 5052-5053.

5056-5057 *Burke's Genealogical and Heraldic History of the Peerage and Baronetage* (1953), 196.

5058-5059 *The Complete Peerage,* 5: 543; Gary Boyd Roberts, "Lygon Descendants in England and Europe, Part 1," *NEHGS NEXUS* 16 [1999]: 156-59.
Henry Folliott, 1st Baron Folliott, was an uncle of the Rev. Edward Foliot of Virginia and first cousin of Sir Ferdinando Gorges, Lord Proprietor of Maine.

5060-5061 See 2452-2453.

5062-5063 *The Complete Peerage,* 8: 612-13.

5064-5065 H. Loftus Tottenham, "James Margetson, Archbishop of Armagh," *Notes and Queries: A Medium of Inter-Communication for Literary Men, Artists, Antiquaries, Genealogists, etc.,* 8th series, vol. 6 [1894]: 1; William Berry, *County Genealogies: Pedigrees of Surrey Families* (1837), 14.

5068-5069 *The Complete Peerage,* 3: 135; Mervyn Archdall, *The Peerage of Ireland; or, a genealogical history of the present nobility of that kingdom with Engravings of their Paternal Coats of Arms. Collected from public records, authentic Manuscripts, approved Historians, well-attested Pedigrees, and Personal Information, by John Lodge,* 2nd ed. Revised, enlarged and continued to the Present Time, 7 vols. (1789), 3: 218.

5070-5071 See 2452-2453.

5072-5073 *The Complete Peerage,* 4: 341; *Allegations for Marriage Licences issued by the Bishop of London,* 26: 241; *The Marriage, Baptismal and Burial Registers of the Collegiate Church or Abbey of St. Peter, Westminster,* 10: 225.

5074-5075 *Oxford Dictionary of National Biography,* 9: 153-63, 130-31; *The Complete Peerage,* 10: 149-54; *The Knights of England,* 1: 34.

5076-5079 See 2624-2627.

5080-5081 *Publications of the Harleian Society, Visitation Series,* vols. 109-10, H. Stanford London and Sophia W. Rawlins, eds., *Visitation of London, 1568, with Additional Pedigrees 1569–90, The Arms of the City Companies and a London Subsidy Roll, 1589,* 34; "Inquisitiones Post Mortem *temp.* Henry VIII to Charles I," *The Genealogist,* New Series, 29 [1913]: 193; *Le Neve's Pedigrees,* 8: 215; *Hertfordshire Families,* 92; Will of Dame Dorothy Capell, Widow of North Ockendon, Essex 16 Jan. 1650, codicil 30 Nov. 1651, Proved 2 Feb. 1651/52 PROB 11/220. See also 4404-4405.

5082-5083 *The History and Antiquities of the County of Hertford,* 3: 132; *The Registers of St. Stephen, Walbrook, and St. Benet Sherehog, London, 1716 to 1860,* 49: 5; *Registers of St. Olave Old Jewry, London: Baptisms, burials 1538–1629 Marriages 1538–1637* Family History Library film 0380,325; Will of William Hale or Hales of Kings Walden, Hertfordshire Proved 3 Oct. 1634 PROB 11/166.

5084-5085 *The History and Antiquities of the County of Hertford,* 3: 132; *Parish Register of St. Peter-Le-Poer, London, Baptisms, marriages 1561–1904 Burials 1561–1853 Banns 1755–1817*

Family History Library film 0374,993; Will of Rowland Hale of Kings Walden, Hertfordshire Proved 15 April 1669 PROB 11/329.

5086-5087 Oswald Barron, ed., *Northamptonshire Families* (1906), 74; *The Royal Descents of 600 Immigrants to the American Colonies or the United States*, 488; Gary Boyd Roberts, "Gerald Paget, *The Lineage and Ancestry of H.R.H. Prince Charles, Prince of Wales* (A Review and General Essay)," *The Genealogist* 1 [1980]: 115.

Mary (Morley) Elwes was a niece of Robert Drake of Virginia.

5088-5089 *Visitation of England and Wales, Notes*, 4: 113; *Burke's Genealogical and Heraldic History of the Peerage and Baronetage* (1953), 1469.

5090-5091 *The History of Parliament 1558–1603*, 3: 169-70, 2: 474; *Pedigrees of the County Families of Yorkshire*, pedigree of Palmes of Naburne; *Alumni Oxonienses: The members of the University of Oxford, 1500–1714*, 3-4: 1111; *The Knights of England*, 2: 99.

5092-5093 Sir Arthur Vicars, *Index to Prerogative Wills of Ireland 1536–1810* (1897), 71; Francis Elrington Ball, *The Judges in Ireland 1221–1921*, 2 vols. (1927), 1: 344; Colm Lennon, *The Lords of Dublin in the Age of Reformation* (1989), 251.

5094-5095 Leslie G. Pine, *Burke's Genealogical and Heraldic History of the Landed Gentry of Ireland* (1958), 252; John Burke, *A Genealogical and Heraldic History of the Commoners of Great Britain and Ireland Enjoying Territorial Possessions or High Official Rank but uninvested with Heritable Honours*, 4 vols. (1836-37), 4: 753; *Index to Prerogative Wills of Ireland 1536–1810*, 152.

5096-5097 *Alumni Cantabrigienses*, 1: 393; *The Complete Baronetage*, 1: 226; *Publications of the Harleian Society, Visitation Series*, vol. 4, George W. Marshall, ed., *The Visitations of the County of Nottingham in the years 1569 and 1614, with many other descents of the same County*, 140; *The Visitacion of Norffolk Made and Taken by William Hervey, Clarencieux King of Arms, Anno 1563*, 32: 83; *The Knights of England*, 2: 117.

5098-5099 *The Peerage of Ireland*, 2: 67-68.

5100-5101 Sir John St. George, "Pedigree of the family of St. George," *Miscellanea Genealogica et Heraldica*, New Series, 3 [1882]: 78; *Publications of the Harleian Society, Visitation Series*, vol. 41, John W. Clay, ed., *The Visitation of Cambridge Made in Ao [1575], Continued and Enlarged wth the Vissitation of the Same County Made by Henery St. George, Richmond-Herald, Marshall and Deputy to Willm. Camden, Clarenceulx in Ao 1619 wth Many Other Descents Added thereto*, 91; *Chetham Society Series: Remains, Historical and Literary, Connected with the Palatine Counties of Lancaster and Chester*, vol. 82, F. R. Raines, ed., *The Visitation of the County Palatine of Lancaster made in the year 1613, by Richard St. George, Esq., Norroy King of Arms*, xii-xiii.

5102-5103 *The Complete Peerage*, 3: 416; *The Complete Baronetage*, 3: 130; Thomas Barrett Lennard, *An account of the families of Lennard and Barrett, compiled largely from original documents* (1908), 404; *Publications of the Harleian Society, New Series*, vol. 2, Joan Corder, ed., *The Visitation of Suffolk 1561 made by William Hervy, Clarenceux King of Arms*, 136; *The History, Description and Antiquities of the Prebendal Church of the Blessed Virgin Mary of Thame*, 441-42.

5104-5105 Hugh Montgomery-Massingberd, *Burke's Irish Family Records* (1976), 1156.

5106-5107 William Berry, *County Genealogies: Pedigrees of the Families in the County of Hants, Collected from the Heraldic Visitations and Other Authentic Manuscripts in the British Museum and in the Possession of Private Individuals, and from Information of the Present Resident Families*

(1833), 4; *Burke's Irish Family Records,* 1158; Walter Goodwin Davis, *Massachusetts and Maine Families in the Ancestry of Walter Goodwin Davis (1885–1966): A Reprinting in Alphabetical Order by Surname of the Sixteen Multi-Ancestor Compendia (plus* Thomas Haley of Winter Harbor and His Descendants*) compiled by Maine's Foremost Genealogist, 1916–1983,* 3 vols. (1996), 3: 376; *Wiltshire Visitation Pedigrees, 1623,* 105-6: 167; *The Royal Descents of 600 Immigrants to the American Colonies or the United States,* 407.

Captain George St. Barbe was a kinsman (but not a great-uncle) of Christopher Batt of Massachusetts.

5120-5121   *The Scots Peerage,* 1: 52-53; *The Complete Baronetage,* 3: 305, 356-57.

5122-5123   *The Complete Peerage,* 3: 363-64; *Sussex Archeological Collections,* vol. 47, F. W. T. Attree and J. H. L. Booker, "The Sussex Colepepers," 65-66; *The Registers of St. Botolph Bishopsgate,* 1: 76; *The Royal Descents of 600 Immigrants to the American Colonies or the United States,* 56-58, 535-37.

Lord and Lady Colepeper were the parents of Thomas Colepeper, 2nd Baron Colepeper, Governor of Virginia, and great-grandparents of Thomas Fairfax, 6th Lord Fairfax, proprietor of the Northern Neck of Virginia.

5126-5127   *The Complete Baronetage,* 2: 372.

5128-5129   *The Four Visitations of Berkshire,* 56: 70, 262; John Edwin Cussans, *History of Hertfordshire, Containing an Account of the Descents of the Various Manors, Pedigrees of Families Connected with the County, Antiquities, Local Customs, &c., &c.: Chiefly Compiled from Original Mss., in the Record Office and British Museum, Parochial Registers, Local Archives and Collections in the Possession of Private Families,* 8 parts in 3 vols. (1870-81), 1: 1: 141; *The History and Antiquities of the County of Hertford,* 3: 171; Will of John Plummer, Gentleman of Saint Gregory, City of London 8 June 1607, codicil 28 July 1608, Proved at London P.C.C. 17 Oct. 1608 PROB 11/112.

5130-5131   *Middlesex Pedigrees,* 65: 20; *Alumni Cantabrigienses,* 2: 207; Will of Phillipp Gerard of Grays Inn, Middlesex 27 March 1635, Proved at London P.C.C. 27 Feb. 1637 PROB 11/173.

5132-5135   See 5084-5087.

5136-5137   Henry Holman Drake, *Hasted's history of Kent: corrected, enlarged and continued to the present time, from the manuscript collections of the late Rev. Thomas Streatfield and the late Rev. Lambert Blackwell Larking, the public records, and other sources. pt. 1. The hundred of Blackheath* (1886), 138; Albert W. Woods, "Report on the Pedigree of the family of the Right Honourable James Craggs, Postmaster General, the father of the Right Honourable James Craggs, secretary of state in the reign of King George the First," *Miscellanea Genealogica et Heraldica* 2 [1876]: 34.

5138-5139   *The History and Antiquities of the County Palatine of Durham,* 3: 415.

5140-5141   "Report on the Pedigree of the family of the Right Honourable James Craggs, Postmaster General, the father of the Right Honourable James Craggs, secretary of state in the reign of King George the First," 34.

5152-5153   Arthur Stephens Dyer, "Pedigree of Moyle of Bake, St. Germans, Cornwall," *Miscellanea Genealogica et Heraldica,* 5th series, 9 [1932]: 347; *London Pedigrees and Coats of Arms,* 111.

5154-5155   *The Complete Baronetage,* 1: 200; *The visitations of the county of Devon,* 621, 174, 623.

5156-5157 *The visitations of Cornwall,* 611; *The History of Parliament 1660–1690,* 3: 101-2; *Alumni Oxonienses: The members of the University of Oxford, 1500–1714,* 3-4: 1034; *A Genealogical and Heraldic History of the Commoners of Great Britain and Ireland,* 3: 234.

5158-5159 *The visitations of Cornwall,* 611.

5160-5161 *Dugdale's Visitation of Yorkshire in 1665–6,* 2: 52.

5162-5163 *The Visitations of Essex by Hawley, 1552, Hervey 1558, Cooke 1570, Raven 1612 and Owen and Lilly, 1634,* 14: 724.

5164-5165 William Valentine Lloyd, *The Sheriffs of Montgomeryshire: with their armorial bearings, and notices, genealogical & biographical, of their families from 1540 to 1639* (1876), 488; *Heraldic Visitations of Wales and Part of the Marches Between the Years 1586 and 1613 by Lewys Dwnn,* 1: 290.

5166-5167 *The Sheriffs of Montgomeryshire,* 489; *Heraldic Visitations of Wales and Part of the Marches Between the Years 1586 and 1613 by Lewys Dwnn,* 1: 294; "The Pedigree of the Ancient Family of the Palmers of Sussex, 1672," *Miscellanea Genealogica et Heraldica* 1 [1868]: 109; *The Knights of England,* 2: 172; *The Complete Baronetage,* 3: 90.

5168-5169 *The visitations of Cornwall,* 57; *The History of Parliament 1660–1690,* 1: 748; Will of Francis Buller of Kingston upon Thames, Surrey 7 Dec. 1672, codicil 12 June 1677, Proved 22 Nov. 1677 PROB 11/355; Will of Thomazin Buller, Widow of Ospringe, Kent 3 Dec. 1677, Proved 17 Jan. 1677/78 PROB 11/356.

5170-5171 *The visitations of Cornwall,* 95, 20; *Publications of the Harleian Society, Visitation Series,* vol. 9, Lt.-Col. John L. Vivian and Henry H. Drake, eds., *The Visitation of the County of Cornwall in the year 1620,* 6; *The visitations of the county of Devon,* 49.

5172-5173 *The History of Parliament 1660–1690,* 3: 259-61; *The visitations of the county of Devon,* 803, 601; Lady Eliott-Drake, *The Family and Heirs of Sir Francis Drake,* 2 vols. (1911), 2: 59.

5174-5175 *The History and Antiquities of the County of Surrey,* 2: facing 127; *Allegations for Marriage Licences issued by the Bishop of London,* 24: 252; *Alumni Oxonienses: The members of the University of Oxford, 1500–1714,* 1-2: 432.

5176-5177 *The Complete Baronetage,* 2: 43; *The visitations of Cornwall,* 576.

5178-5179 See 2176-2177.

5180-5181 *The visitations of the county of Devon,* 466; *Alumni Oxonienses: The members of the University of Oxford, 1500–1714,* 1-2: 689.

5182-5183 *The visitations of the county of Devon,* 440, 707.

5184-5185 *The Scots Peerage,* 6: 375; *The Complete Peerage,* 9: 294.

5186-5187 *The Complete Peerage,* 8: 479-81; *The Scots Peerage,* 6: 51-53.

5188-5189 *The Complete Baronetage,* 2: 412.

5194-5195 *The History and Antiquities of the County of Buckingham,* 3: 221; *Allegations for Marriage Licences issued by the Bishop of London,* 25: 285; *The Victoria History of the County of Buckingham,* 4 vols. (1905-28), 3: 175; *The Visitations of Essex by Hawley, 1552, Hervey 1558, Cooke 1570, Raven 1612 and Owen and Lilly, 1634,* 13: 495; *Publications of the Harleian Society, Visitation Series,* vol. 58, W. Harry Rylands, ed., *The Visitation of the County of Buckingham Made* *in 1634 by John Philipot, Esq., Somerset Herald, and William Ryley, Bluemantle Pursuivant, Marshals and Deputies to Sir Richard St. George, Knight, Clarenceux, and Sir John Borough, Knight, Garter, who visited as Norroy by mutual agreement; Including the Church Notes then taken, together with Pedigrees from the Visitation Made In 1566 by William Harvey, Esq., Clarenceux and some Pedigrees from other sources, Being a Transcript of MS. Eng. Misc. CM in the Bodleian Library, Oxford, with additions,* 54.

5200-5203   *Visitation of England and Wales, Notes,* 7: 141; Evelyn Dawsonne Heathcote, *An Account of some of the families bearing the name of Heathcote* (1899), 62-65.

5208-5209   Alfred T. Butler, *A Genealogical and Heraldic Dictionary of the Peerage and Baronetage* (1926), 2373; *The History and Antiquities of the County of Leicestershire,* 2: 1: 128.

5210-5211   *The Complete Baronetage,* 2: 179; *The History and Antiquities of the County of Hertford,* 3: 132.

5212-5213   Eveline Cruickshanks, Stuart Handley and David Hayton, *The History of Parliament: The House of Commons 1690–1715,* 5 vols. (2002), 5: 611; *Familiae Minorum Gentium,* 38: 578, 40: 1260.

5214-5215   *The History of Parliament 1660–1690,* 2: 697-98; *Dugdale's Visitation of Yorkshire in 1665–6,* 1: 10; *Familiae Minorum Gentium,* 40: 1181; *The parish register of Sessay, near Thirsk, Yorkshire 1600–1812* Family History Library film 0844,559, item 5.

5216-5217   *Pedigrees of the County Families of Yorkshire,* 1: Lascelles pedigree.

5218-5219   *Dugdale's Visitation of Yorkshire in 1665–6,* 3: 189, 2: 426; *The Complete Baronetage,* 2: 161-62.

5220-5221   *Alumni Cantabrigienses,* 3: 48; *Publications of the Harleian Society, New Series,* vol. 16, T. C. Wales et al., eds., *The Visitation of London begun in 1687,* 231-32; *Pedigrees of the County Families of Yorkshire,* 1: Lascelles pedigree.

5232-5233   *Dugdale's Visitation of Yorkshire in 1665–6,* 2: 232; *The History and Antiquities of the County of Buckingham,* 2: 169; *Pedigrees of the County Families of Yorkshire,* 2: Chaloner pedigree.

5234-5235   *The History of Parliament 1660–1690,* 2: 349-50; *Dugdale's Visitation of Yorkshire in 1665–6,* 1: 148-49; *The Complete Baronetage,* 1: 135; Sir Bernard Burke, *Royal Descents and Pedigrees of Founders Kin* (1864), pedigree vii; *Publications of the Harleian Society, Register Series,* vol. 35, William H. Hunt, *The Registers of St. Paul's Church, Covent Garden, London, 1653 to 1853,* 7.

5236-5237   *The History and Antiquities of the County Palatine of Durham,* 4: 108, 2: 280; Margaret Ethel Kington Blair Oliphant Maxtone-Graham, *The Maxtones of Cultoquhey* (1935), pedigree.

5238-5239   *The History and Antiquities of the County Palatine of Durham,* 2: 255; *The Complete Baronetage,* 2: 188.

5240-5241   *The Reliquary and illustrated archæologist,* 8: 47-48; *Familiae Minorum Gentium,* 38: 478.

5242-5243   *The Reliquary and illustrated archæologist,* 8: 48.

5248-5249   See 2054-2055.

5250-5251   Sir James Balfour Paul, *The Scots Peerage,* 9 vols. (1904-14), 5: 79; *The Complete Peerage,* 12: 1: 66-68; Philip Gibbs, *The King's Favourite; the love story of Robert Carr and Lady Essex* (1909); *The Knights of England,* 1: 154, 2: 144, 30; Raleigh Trevelyan, *Sir Walter Raleigh*

(2002), 421, 432; Sir Edward Abbott Parry, *The Overbury Mystery; a chronicle of fact and drama of the law* (1925).

5252-5253   See 4098-4099.

5254-5255   Charles E. Lart, *Huguenot Pedigrees,* 2 vols. (1924-25), 1: 76.

5256-5257   Richard Evans, "Jeffrey Howland, Citizen and Grocer of London," *The New England Historical and Genealogical Register* 152 [1998]: 460; *Essex Record Office Publications,* vol. 137, Frederick George Emmison, *Essex Wills Commissary Court — Original Wills 1587–1599,* 129.

5258-5259   "Langley Pedigree," *Miscellanea Genealogica et Heraldica,* 2nd series, 3 [1890]: 169; *The Complete Baronetage,* 2: 49; *Publications of the Harleian Society, Register Series,* vol. 1, Granville Leveson-Gower, *The Registers of Christening, Burials and Weddings within the Parish of St. Peter's upon Cornhill, London, 1538 to 1666,* 198; Will of John Langley of London Proved 12 Dec. 1639 PROB 11/181.

5260-5261   See 2204-2205.

5262-5263   *The History of Parliament 1660–1690,* 2: 57; *Allegations for Marriage Licences issued by the Bishop of London,* 26: 244; Will of Edward Boate of Portsmouth, Hampshire 29 March 1650, Proved at London P.C.C. 10 June 1650 PROB 11/212.

5264-5265   *The History of Parliament 1660–1690,* 2: 425-27; *The Complete Baronetage,* 1: 147; Stebbing Shaw, *The History and Antiquities of Staffordshire: Compiled from the Manuscripts of Huntback, Loxdale, Bishop Lyttleton, and Other Collections of Dr. Wilkes,* 2 vols. (1798–1801), 2: 169.

5266-5267   See 1034-1035.

5268-5269   *The Complete Peerage,* 1: 263-64.

5270-5271   *The Complete Peerage,* 2: 516. See also 2726-2727.

5272-5273   *Oxford Dictionary of National Biography,* 44: 264-66; *The History of Parliament 1660–90,* 3: 243-44; *The Visitation of Nottinghamshire begun in 1662 and finished in 1664 made by William Dugdale, Norroy King of Arms,* 5: 56.

5274-5275   *Oxford Dictionary of National Biography,* 18: 770; *The History of Parliament 1660–1690,* 2: 281; Cecil George Savile Foljambe, Earl of Liverpool, *Evelyn Pedigrees and Memoranda* (1893), 56; *The Knights of England,* 2: 182.

5276-5277   *The Complete Peerage,* 4: 257-58; *Publications of the Harleian Society, Register Series,* vol. 16, F. N. MacNamara and A. Story-Maskelyne, *The Parish Register of Kensington, Co. Middlesex, 1539 to 1675,* 18; *The Registers of Christening, Burials and Weddings within the Parish of St. Peter's upon Cornhill, London, 1538 to 1666,* 1: 253.

5278-5279   *Oxford Dictionary of National Biography,* 31: 669-70; *The Complete Peerage,* 7: 297, 12: 2: 743; *Burke's Genealogical and Heraldic History of the Peerage and Baronetage* (1953), 1189; *The Knights of England,* 2: 177; *The Peerage of Ireland,* 3: 225.

5280-5281   J. R. van Keppel, *Genealogische tabellen van het geslacht van Keppel* (1912), Tabel XIV; W. J. Baron d'Ablaing van Giessenburg, *Bannerheeren en Ridderschap van Zutphen: van den aanvang der beroerten in de 16e eeuw tot het jaar 1795* (1877), 78, 131.

5282-5283   W. J. d'Ablaing van Giessenburg, *De Ridderschap van Veluwe of Geschiedenis der Veluwsche Jonkers: opgeluisterd door hunne acht stamdeelen, huwelijken, kinderen en wapens, hoofdzakelijk getrokken uit de verzameling van handschriften van wijlen den Rijks-Vrijheer W. A. van Spaen.*

(1859), 246; *Bannerheeren en Ridderschap van Zutphen: van den aanvang der beroerten in de 16e eeuw tot het jaar 1795*, 131.

5284-5285 H. H. Röell, "Geldersche Geslachten. Bijdrage tot de genealogie van Lintelo," *De Nederlandsche Leeuw* 57 [1939]: 57.

5286-5287 Anton Fahne, *Geschichte der Westphälischen Geschlechter unter besonderer Berück-sichtigung ihrer Uebersiedelung nach Preussen, Curland und Liefland. / Von A. Fahne von Roland. Mit fast 1200 Wappen und mehr als 1300 Familien* (1858), 349; *Bannerheeren en Ridderschap van Zutphen: van den aanvang der beroerten in de 16e eeuw tot het jaar 1795*, 135; "Geldersche Geslachten. Bijdrage tot de genealogie van Lintelo," 112-13; *http://lehre.hki.uni-koeln.de/ schele/*, accessed 11 May 2007.

5288-5289 *Nederland's Adelsboek 1913* (1913), 238; Simon van Leeuwen, *Batavia illustrate* (1685), 1111.

5290-5291 *De Nederlandsche Leeuw* 81 [1964]: 142; *Batavia illustrate*, 882.

5292-5293 Pieter Dignus de Vos, *De Vroedschap van Zierikzee: van de tweede helft der 16de eeuw tot 1795* (1931), 151-52, 231; *De Nederlandsche Leeuw* 9 [1886]: 35.

5294-5295 *Nederland's Adelsboek 1907* (1907), 118.

5296-5299 See 4384-4387.

5300-5301 *Histoire de la Maison Royale de France Anciens Barons du Royaume: et des Grands Officiers de la Couronne*, 5: 918.

5302-5303 *Héraldique et généalogie: bulletin de la Fédération des sociétés françaises de généalogie, d'héraldique et de sigillographie* 22 [1991]: 13; François-Alexandre Aubert de la Chesnaye-Desbois et Badier, *Dictionnaire de la Noblesse, contenant les généalogies, l'histoire & la chronologie des familles nobles de la France, l'explication de leurs armes et l'état des grandes Terres du Royaume, possédées à titre de Principautés, Duchés, Marquisats, Comtés, Vicomtés, Baronies, &c., par création héritages, alliances, donations, substitutions, mutations, achats ou autrement. On a joint à ce diction-naire le tableau généalogique et historique des maisons souveraines de l'Europe et une notice des familles étrangères, les plus anciennes, les plus nobles et les plus illustres*, 19 vols., 3rd ed. (1863-76), 15: 954; *Histoire de la Maison Royale de France Anciens Barons du Royaume: et des Grands Officiers de la Couronne*, 6: 773; *Cahiers de Saint-Louis*, 29 parts (1979-2002), 7: 491; Marie Antoinette d'Andigné, *Généalogie de la Maison d'Andigné* (1971), 29; *The Royal Descents of 600 Immigrants to the American Colonies or the United States*, 106, 819-20.

5304-5311 See 2880-2887.

5312-5313 *The Complete Peerage*, 6: 681.

5314-5315 Patrick Grant, Lord Strathspey, *A History of the Clan Grant* (1983), 107; *The Scots Peerage*, 7: 469.

5316-5317 *The Complete Peerage*, 1: 258.

5318-5319 See 2200-2201.

5320-5323 See 1048-1051.

5324-5325 A. Alistair N. Tayler and H. A. Henrietta Tayler, *The Book of the Duffs*, 2 vols. (1914), 1: 342; Walter MacFarlane, *Genealogical collections concerning families in Scotland, made by W. Macfarlane, 1750–1751. Edited from the original manuscripts in the Advocates' Library, by James Toshach Clark, keeper of the library*, 2 vols. (1900), 2: 323.

5326-5327   *The visitations of the county of Devon,* 154, 156; *Dugdale's Visitation of Yorkshire in 1665–6,* 3: 375; *The Visitation of the County of Yorke,* 36: 84; *Miscellanea Genealogica et Heraldica,* 5th series, 9 [1932]: 129.

5328-5329   *The Scots Peerage,* 1: 86; D.M. Rose, "The Bannermans of Elsick and Watertown," *Scottish Notes and Queries,* 2nd series, 2 [1901]: 18; Sir Robert Douglas, *The Baronage of Scotland: containing an historical and genealogical account of the gentry of that kingdom* (1798), 37.

5330-5331   A. Alistair N. Tayler and H. A. Henrietta Tayler, *The House of Forbes* (1937), 396; *The Royal Descents of 600 Immigrants to the American Colonies or the United States,* 105 (for President Theodore Roosevelt's descent from this couple via John Irvine of Georgia).

5332-5333   Peter Townend et al., eds., *Burke's Genealogical and Heraldic History of the Landed Gentry,* 3 vols. (1965-72), 3: 547.

5334-5335   *Oxford Dictionary of National Biography,* 52: 244-45; Simon F. Macdonald Lockhart, *Seven Centuries: A History of the Lockharts of Lee and Carnwath* (1978), chart; Sir William Fraser, *The Douglas Book: Memoirs of the House of Douglas and Angus,* 4 vols. (1885), 2: 169; Margaret D. Young, *The Parliaments of Scotland: burgh and shire commissioners,* 2 vols. (1992-93), 2: 435-36.

5336-5337   *The Complete Peerage,* 1: 315; *The Scots Peerage,* 1: 472-73.

5338-5339   *Oxford Dictionary of National Biography,* 52: 171-74, 222-25; *The Complete Peerage,* 4: 214-15; *Collins's Peerage of England,* 3: 83-93.

5340-5341   *The Complete Peerage,* 4: 437; *The Scots Peerage,* 1: 302-4.

5342-5343   *The Complete Peerage,* 6: 259-61; *The Scots Peerage,* 4: 376-78; *The Marriage, Baptismal and Burial Registers of the Collegiate Church or Abbey of St. Peter, Westminster,* 10: 133.

5344-5345   Sir William Fraser, *The Book of Carlaverock: Memoirs of the Maxwells, Earls of Nithsdale, Lords Maxwell and Herries,* 2 vols. (1873), 1: 597.

5346-5347   *The Parliaments of Scotland,* 2: 448; *The Book of Carlaverock,* 1: 598.

5348-5349   *Burke's Genealogical and Heraldic History of the Peerage and Baronetage* (1953), 1025.

5350-5351   *Oxford Dictionary of National Biography,* 24: 840; *Burke's Genealogical and Heraldic History of the Peerage and Baronetage* (1953), 1025. See also 5342-5343.

5352-5353   *The Complete Peerage,* 5: 21-22; *The Scots Peerage,* 3: 450-51.

5354-5355   *The Complete Peerage,* 4: 500.

5356-5357   *The Complete Peerage,* 4: 526; *The Scots Peerage,* 3: 344-46.

5358-5359   *The Complete Peerage,* 3: 76-77; *The Scots Peerage,* 2: 477-81. See also 2450-2451.

5360-5361   Keith Stanley Malcolm Scott, *Scott 1118–1923: being a collection of "Scott" pedigrees containing all known male descendants from Buccleuch, Sinton, Harden, Balweary, etc.* (1923), 253.

5362-5363   Thomas Falconer, *The Family of Dalmahoy of Dalmahoy, Ratho, County Edinburgh* (1870), 7; *The Baronage of Scotland,* 550.

5364-5365   *Northern notes and queries, or, The Scottish antiquary* 3 [1889]: 51.

5376-5377 *Visitations of England and Wales, Notes,* 5: 95; *The Visitation of Shropshire Taken in the year 1623,* 29: 471-72.

5378-5379 *The History and Antiquities of the County of Leicestershire,* 3: 394.

5380-5381 George Ormerod, *The History of the County Palatine and City of Chester: Compiled from Original Evidences in Public Offices, the Harleian and Cottonian Mss., Parochial Registers, Private Muniments, Unpublished Mss., Collections of Successive Cheshire Antiquaries, and a Personal Survey of Every Township in the County, Incorporated with a Republication of King's Vale Royal and Leycester's Cheshire Antiquities. Also known as: The King's Vale Royal, The Vale Royall of England and Cheshire Antiquities,* 2nd ed. Revised and enlarged by Thomas Helsby, 3 vols. in 6 (1882), 3: 314; *The Complete Peerage,* 3: 532, note i.

5382-5383 *The History and Antiquities of the County of Surrey,* 1: 523.

5384-5385 *The Victoria History of the County of Buckingham,* 3: 237; P. S. P. Conner, "The Descent of William Penn from the Penns of Penn, co. Bucks," *Notes and Queries,* 5th series, 1 [1874]: 265-66; *Records of the English Province of the Society of Jesus,* 1: pedigree of Poulton or Pulton family of Desborough, co. Northampton; *The Visitation of the County of Buckingham Made in 1634,* 58: 98.

5386-5387 *Suffolk Manorial Families,* 1: 358; *The Knights of England,* 2: 111; Will of Dame Susan Drewry or Drury, Widow of Temple Boulstred, Buckinghamshire 28 March 1639, Proved at London P.C.C. 25 Feb. 1641 PROB 11/185.

5388-5389 W. H. Shawcross alias Shallcross, *Shallcross Pedigrees* (1908), lxvi.

5390-5391 *The Visitation of London Anno Domini 1633, 1634 and 1635,* 17: 26; Will of Francis Kempe, Gentleman, of Cliffords Inn, Middlesex 26 Jan. 1649/50, Proved at London P.C.C. 7 Feb. 1649/50 PROB 11/211.

5392-5393 Edward Baines and W. R. Whatton, *History of the County Palatine and Duchy of Lancaster.* New, Revised and Enlarged [3rd] ed., 5 vols. (1888–93), 2: 397; *Publications of the Harleian Society, Visitation Series,* vol. 59, Sir George J. Armytage, Bart., and John Paul Rylands, eds., *Pedigrees Made at the Visitation of Cheshire 1613 taken by Richard St. George, Esq., Norroy King of Arms and Henry St. George, Gent., Bluemantle Pursuivant of Arms; and some other Contemporary Pedigrees,* 241.

5394-5395 *Dugdale's Visitation of Yorkshire in 1665–6,* 1: 76; *The Complete Baronetage,* 2: 156.

5396-5397 *The Complete Baronetage,* 1: 149; Charles P. Hampson, *The Book of the Radclyffes: being an account of the main descents of this illustrious family from its origin to the present day, compiled from a variety of sources, including public records and private evidences* (1940), 122, 268; *The Visitation of the County Palatine of Lancaster, Made in the Year 1664–5,* 84: 10; *History of the County Palatine and Duchy of Lancaster,* 2: 390; *Dugdale's Visitation of Yorkshire in 1665–6,* 2: 83; John Burke and John Bernard Burke. *A Genealogical and Heraldic History of the Extinct and Dormant Baronetcies of England, Ireland, and Scotland,* 2nd ed. (1844), 19.

5398-5399 See 4586-4587.

5400-5401 *Pedigrees of the County Families of Yorkshire,* 1: Vavasour pedigree; *Dugdale's Visitation of Yorkshire in 1665–6,* 3: 311, 355; *The Knights of England,* 2: 162.

5402-5403 Joseph Foster, *The Visitation of Yorkshire, made in the years 1584/5, by Robert Glover, Somerset herald; to which is added the subsequent visitation made in 1612, by Richard St.*

George, Norroy king of arms, with several additional pedigrees, including "The arms taken out of churches and houses at Yorkshire visitation, 1584/5," "Sir William Fayrfax' booke of arms," and other heraldic lists, with copious indices (1875), 226; *The Complete Baronetage,* 1: 147; *The History and Antiquities of Staffordshire,* 2: 169.

5404-5405 Ralph Thoresby, *Ducatus Leodiensis: or, the Topography of the Ancient and Populous Town and Parish of Leedes, and Parts Adjacent, in the West-Riding of the County of York, with the Pedigrees of Many of the Nobility and Gentry, and Other Matters Relating to those Parts; Extracted from Records, Original Evidence, and Manuscripts,* 2nd ed., With notes and additions by Thomas Dunham Whitaker (1816), 221.

5406-5407 *Ducatus Leodiensis,* 225; *Hunter's Pedigrees,* 88: 43.

5408-5409 *The History and Antiquities of the County of Buckingham,* 4: 341; *Heraldic Visitations of Wales and Part of the Marches Between the Years 1586 and 1613 by Lewys Dwnn,* 2: 313; "Funeral certificate of Mary Puleston, nee Bostock," *Miscellanea Genealogica et Heraldica,* 5th series, 8 [1932-34]: 250; Will of Thomas Hanmer of Fenns, Flintshire 3 Feb. 1624/25, Proved at London 17 May 1625 PROB 11/145.

5410-5411 *The Complete Baronetage,* 3: 66; *Publications of the Harleian Society, Visitation Series,* vol. 93, Arthur Adams, ed., *Cheshire Visitation Pedigrees, 1663,* 116; *Pedigrees Made at the Visitation of Cheshire 1613,* 59: 246; *The History of the County Palatine and City of Chester,* 1: 574.

5412-5413 *The History of Parliament 1660–1690,* 2: 44; *The History and Antiquities of the County of Northampton,* 2: 19; *Registers of St. Dunstan in the East, 1558 to 1766,* 69: 32, 53, 59, 60, 63, 66, 68, 70, 76, 191, 212, 214; *The Visitation of London Anno Domini 1633, 1634 and 1635,* 15:155; *The Royal Descents of 600 Immigrants to the American Colonies or the United States,* 160-62; Will of Robert Charlton of Whitton, Shropshire 12 May 1668, Proved 13 May 1670 PROB 11/332.

Robert Charlton and Emma Harby were great-grandparents of John Coke of Virginia; Emma (Harby) Charlton was an aunt of Rev. John Oxenbridge of Massachusetts.

5414-5415 Frederick Arthur Crisp, *Fragmenta Genealogica,* 14 vols. in 2 series (1897-1910), New Series, 1: 83, 62; *The Visitation of Shropshire Taken in the year 1623,* 28: 50.

5416-5417 William Harrison, Thomas Harrison, and George Willis, *The great Jennens case: being an epitome of the history of the Jennens family* (1879), 4, 22, 23, 32; *The History and Antiquities of the County of Leicestershire,* 4: 859.

5418-5419 *The great Jennens case,* 4, 8.

5420-5421 Caroline Robbins, *The diary of John Milward, esq., member of Parliament for Derbyshire, September 1666 to May 1668* (1938), xxiii.

5422-5423 *The Heraldic Visitations of Staffordshire Made by Sir Richard St. George, Norroy, in 1614, and by Sir William Dugdale in the Years 1663 and 1664,* 5: 2: 304.

5424-5431 See 5416-5423.

5432-5433 *The Complete Baronetage,* 1: 119; "Pedigrees contained in the Visitations of Derbyshire, 1569 and 1611," *The Genealogist,* New Series, 7 [1890]: 135.

5434-5435 *Oxford Dictionary of National Biography,* 57: 168-69; *The Knights of England,* 2: 171; *The Dictionary of National Biography,* 20: 704-5; G. C. Bower and H. W. F. Harwood, "Pedigree of Offley," *The Genealogist,* New Series, 20 [1904]: 51.

5436-5437   *The Visitation of Nottinghamshire begun in 1662 and finished in 1664 made by William Dugdale, Norroy King of Arms*, 5: 22.

5438-5439   *The Visitation of Nottinghamshire begun in 1662 and finished in 1664 made by William Dugdale, Norroy King of Arms*, 5: 21; *The History and Antiquities of the County of Leicestershire*, 3: 882; W. P. W. Phillimore et al., eds., *Nottingham Parish Registers*, 22 vols. (1898-1938), 5: 16.

5440-5441   *Visitation of England and Wales, Notes*, 13: 94; *The Complete Baronetage*, 3: 123; *The History and Antiquities of the County of Hertford*, 1: 479; *Wiltshire Visitation Pedigrees, 1623*, 105-6: 75.

5442-5443   T. Fitz-Roy Fenwick and Walter C. Metcalfe, eds., *The Visitation of the county of Gloucester begun by Thomas May, Chester, and Gregory King, Rouge Dragon, in Trinity Vacacon, 1682 and finished by Henry Dethick, Richmond, and the said Rouge Dragon, Pursuivant, in Trinity Vacacon, 1683, by virtue of several deputations from Sir Henry St. George, Clarenceux Kinge of Armes* (1884), 142; *The Royal Descents of 600 Immigrants to the American Colonies or the United States*, 567.

Thomas Rich and Anne Bourchier were the maternal grandparents of Lancelot Bathurst of Virginia.

5444-5445   *The History of Parliament 1558–1603*, 3: 360-61; *The Complete Peerage*, 11: 549-50.

5448-5449   *Visitation of England and Wales, Notes*, 7: 16; *The Knights of England*, 2: 105.

5450-5451   *The Complete Baronetage*, 1: 18; *The Knights of England*, 2: 105.

5452-5453   *The History of Parliament 1558–1603*, 3: 134; *The Complete Peerage*, 3: 515-16; *The Knights of England*, 2: 100.

5454-5455   *The Complete Peerage*, 12: 2: 867-68; *The Knights of England*, 2: 145.

5456-5457   Eduard Georg Ludwig William Howe Graf von Kielmansegg and Erich Friedrich Christian Ludwig Graf von Kielmansegg, *Familien-Chronik der Herren Freiherren und Grafen von Kielmansegg* (1872), Tafel III; *Gothaisches Genealogisches Taschenbuch der Gräflichen Häuser*, 42: 414; *Danmarks Adels Aarbog 1923* (1923), 478.

5458-5459   *Danmarks Adels Aarbog 1922* (1922), 488.

5460-5461   *Danmarks Adels Aarbog 1982–84* (1982-84), 616, 600-1.

5462-5463   *Danmarks Adels Aarbog 1930* (1930), 112, *1931* (1931), 58.

5464-5465   *Europäische Stammtafeln*, Neue Folge, 1: 1: 25; George Wentworth Watson, "The 4096 Quartiers of the Prince of Wales," *The Genealogist*, New Series, 17 [1901]: 138.

5466-5467   *Europäische Stammtafeln*, Neue Folge, 1: 2: 248; "The 4096 Quartiers of the Prince of Wales," 136.

5468-5471   *Ahnentafeln berühmter Deutscher*, vol. 9, Ernst Freiherr von Obernitz, "256stellige Ahnentafel des Dichters August von Platen-Hallermund 1796-1835," 265.

5472-5473   *The History and Antiquities of the County of Leicestershire*, 2: 1: 267; *Alumni Cantabrigienses*, 2: 321; *Publications of the Harleian Society, Visitation Series*, vol. 42, Robert Hovenden, ed., *The Visitation of Kent Taken in the Years 1619–1621 by John Philipot, Rouge Dragon, Marshal and Deputy to William Camden, Clarenceux*, 196; Will of Sir William Hartopp of Burton Lazars, Leicestershire 17 Jan. 1622/23, Proved at London P.C.C. 13 May 1623 PROB 11/141.

5474-5475 *The Complete Baronetage,* 1: 63; *The History and Antiquities of the County of Essex,* 2: 351.

5476-5477 *Pedigrees of the County Families of Yorkshire,* 1: Lister pedigree.

5478-5479 *The Complete Peerage,* 12: 2: 489-90; *The History, Description and Antiquities of the Prebendal Church of the Blessed Virgin Mary of Thame,* 432-40; *The History and Antiquities of the County of Buckingham,* 3: 131-32; *The Knights of England,* 2: 93.

5480-5481 *The History and Antiquities of the County of Leicestershire,* 2: 1: 285; *Publications of the Harleian Society, Register Series,* vol. 3, Joseph Lemuel Chester, *The Register Book of St. Dionis Backchurch Parish (City of London), 1538 to 1754,* 22; Sentence of George Benett of Welby, Lincolnshire Dated 23 Nov. 1633 PROB 11/164.

5482-5483 *The Complete Peerage,* 2: 204.

5484-5485 *Some Account of the Lord Mayors and Sheriffs of the City of London during the first quarter of the seventeenth century,* 63; *The History of Parliament 1660–1690,* 3: 124; "Middleton or Myddelton of Chirk Castle, Denbigh, Stanstead Mountfichet, Essex, and other places," *Miscellanea Genealogica et Heraldica,* 3rd series, 2 [1898]: 227; John William Clay, "The Savile Family," *Yorkshire Archaeological Journal* 25 [1920]: 44.

5486-5487 *The History of the County Palatine and City of Chester,* 2: 157, 3: 341; *Cheshire Visitation Pedigrees, 1663,* 93: 27.

5488-5489 *The Visitation of Nottinghamshire begun in 1662 and finished in 1664 made by William Dugdale, Norroy King of Arms,* 5: 89.

5490-5491 *The History and Antiquities of the County of Leicestershire,* 3: 394.

5492-5493 *The Complete Peerage,* 3: 489-90; *The Knights of England,* 2: 176; *The Complete Baronetage,* 1: 146; *The Royal Descents of 600 Immigrants to the American Colonies or the United States,* 203-4.

Sir Thomas Richardson and Ursula Southwell were the matrilineal great-grandparents of Robert Peyton of Virginia.

5494-5495 *The Complete Peerage,* 3: 490; *The Knights of England,* 2: 140; *The Complete Baronetage,* 3: 89; *The Visitations of Essex by Hawley, 1552, Hervey 1558, Cooke 1570, Raven 1612 and Owen and Lilly, 1634,* 13: 324-25; *Parish registers for St. Martin-in-the-Fields, 1550–1653* Family History Library film 0560,369; Will of Sir William Hewitt of St. Martin in the Fields, Middlesex 3 May 1636, codicil 25 April 1637, Proved at London P.C.C. 26 Oct. 1637 PROB 11/575.

5504-5505 *The Aldermen of the City of London,* 2: 39; *Some Account of the Lord Mayors and Sheriffs of the City of London during the first quarter of the seventeenth century,* 73; *Publications of the Harleian Society, Register Series,* vol. 43, W. Bruce Bannerman, *The Registers of Allhallows, Bread Street, 1538 to 1892, and St. John The Evangelist, Friday Street, London, 1653 to 1822,* 96; "Annotations to the Heraldic Visitation of London, 1633. Gore: wills and administrations," *Miscellanea Genealogica et Heraldica,* 2nd series, 2 [1888]: 225, 347; *The Registers of St. Mary Magdalen Milk Street, London and St. Michael Bassishaw, London, 1558 to 1892,* 72: 45.

5506-5507 Joseph Foster, *Peerage, baronetage, and knightage of the British empire for 1883,* 2 vols. (1883), 1: 30; Joseph Foster, *The Visitation of Middlesex, began in the year 1663, by William Ryley, esq., Lancaster, and Henry Dethick, Rouge croix, marshalls and deputies to Sir Edward Bysshe, Clarencieux. As recorded in the College of arms* (1887), 39.

5508-5509 *The History and Antiquities of the County of Hertford,* 2: 477; *The Complete Peerage,* 7: 239; *The Knights of England,* 2: 85; *The Royal Descents of 600 Immigrants to the American Colonies or the United States,* 154-57; *Plantagenet Ancestry,* 404-6, 573-74.

Sir Philip Boteler and Catherine Knollys were great-grandparents of Anne Boteler, wife of Lionel Copley, Governor of Maryland. Catherine (Knollys), Lady Boteler, was an aunt of Robert Devereux, 2nd Earl of Essex [No. 5786]; Lettice Knollys [No. 6033]; and the brothers Thomas West, 3rd Baron de la Warr [Delaware], Hon. Francis West, and Hon. John West, all of whom served as Governors of Virginia. Lady Boteler was a great-aunt of siblings Herbert Pelham, first Treasurer of Harvard College, and Penelope Pelham, wife of Richard Bellingham, Governor of Massachusetts, and (through the West family) a great-great-aunt of Anne Humphrey of Massachusetts, wife of William Palmes and the Rev. John Myles.

5510-5511 See 4122-4123.

5512-5513 *The Complete Baronetage,* 1: 233.

5514-5515 See 5068-5069.

5516-5517 *The Scots Peerage,* 1: 43-44.

5518-5519 *The Complete Peerage,* 12: 1: 318-19; *The Scots Peerage,* 1: 49-50.

5520-5521 *Pedigrees Made at the Visitation of Cheshire 1613,* 59: 164; *Publications of the Harleian Society, Visitation Series,* vol. 18, John Paul Rylands, ed., *The Visitation of Cheshire in 1580 made by Robert Glover, Somerset Herald, for William Flower, Norroy King of Arms, with numerous additions and continuations, including those from the Visitations of Cheshire made in the year 1566 by the same herald with an appendix, containing the Visitation of a part of Cheshire in the year 1533 Made by William Fellows, Lancaster Herald, for Thomas Benolte, Clarenceux King of Arms, and a fragment of the Visitation of the City of Chester in the year 1591 Made by Thomas Chaloner, Deputy to the office of Arms,* 163; *The History of the County Palatine and City of Chester,* 2: 106, 861.

5522-5523 *The Visitation of Shropshire Taken in the year 1623,* 29: 330.

5524-5525 *Oxford Dictionary of National Biography,* 16: 569; Edward Peacock, "Isaac Dorislaus," *Notes and Queries,* 4th series, 4 [1869]: 40.

5532-5533 *The Visitation of London begun in 1687,* 17: 499; *Le Neve's Pedigrees,* 8: 299; *The Registers of St. Paul's Church, Covent Garden, London, 1653 to 1853,* 36: 19, 48.

5534-5535 *Wiltshire Visitation Pedigrees, 1623,* 105-6: 128.

5568-5569 *The Complete Peerage,* 8: 365-68; *The History and Antiquities of the County of Hertford,* 3: 429; *The Aldermen of the City of London,* 2: 45 *The Registers of St. Mary Magdalen Milk Street, London and St. Michael Bassishaw, London, 1558 to 1892,* 72: 125.

5570-5571 *Wiltshire Visitation Pedigrees, 1623,* 105-6: 15; *The Knights of England,* 2: 170; "Pedigree of Montagu, of Lackham," *Wiltshire Archeological and Natural History Magazine* 3 [1857]: between 86 and 87; *Parish registers for St. Luke's Church, Chelsea, 1559–1875* Family History Library film 0585,471.

5572-5573 *The History of Parliament 1558–1603,* 2: 353; *Wiltshire Visitation Pedigrees, 1623,* 105-6: 93, 91; *The Knights of England,* 2: 144; *Publications of the Harleian Society, Visitation Series,* vol. 5, William Henry Turner, ed., *The Visitations of the County of Oxford taken in the years 1566 by William Harvey, Clarencieux, 1574 by Richard Lee, Portcullis, Deputy of Robert*

Cooke, Clarencieux, and in 1634 by John Philipott, Somerset and William Ryley, Bluemantle, Deputies of Sir John Borough, Knt., Garter and Richard St. George, knt., Clarencieux; Together with the gatherings of Oxfordshire Collected by Richard Lee in 1574, 259.

5574-5575 *The Visitations of the County of Oxford taken in the years 1566 by William Harvey, Clarencieux, 1574 by Richard Lee, Portcullis, Deputy of Robert Cooke, Clarencieux, and in 1634 by John Philipott, Somerset and William Ryley, Bluemantle,* 5: 292; *Publications of the Harleian Society, New Series,* vol. 12, G. D. Squibb, ed., *The Visitation of Oxfordshire 1669 and 1675 made by Sir Edward Bysshe, Knight, Clarenceux King of Arms,* 93; W. L. Rutton, "Pedigree of Hopton of Suffolk and Somerset," *Miscellanea Genealogica et Heraldica,* 3rd series, 3 [1900]: 11, and J. Renton Dunlop, "The Family of Fettiplace," 5th series, 2 [1918]: 245-46.

5584-5585 *Wiltshire Visitation Pedigrees, 1623,* 105-6: 220; W.S. Sykes, "Notes on Wilcot and Families" (a manuscript at the Wiltshire Archaelogical Society, Devizes); *The Knights of England,* 2: 76.

5588-5589 John Collinson, *The history and antiquities of the county of Somerset: collected from authentick records, and an actual survey made by the late Mr. Edmund Rack; adorned with a map of the county and engravings of Roman or other reliques, town-seals, baths, churches, and gentlemen's seats,* 3 vols. (1791), 3: 255; *Publications of the Harleian Society, New Series,* vol. 11, G. D. Squibb, ed., *The Visitation of Somerset and the City of Bristol 1672 made by Sir Edward Bysshe, Knight, Clarenceux King of Arms,* 108; *The visitations of the county of Devon,* 703; Will of Sir George Farewell of Bishops Hull, Somerset 25 July 1645, Proved at London P.C.C. 17 Nov. 1647 PROB 11/202; Will of Mary Farewell 29 March 1656, Proved at London P.C.C. 22 Jan. 1662 PROB 11/307.

5592-5593 *Wiltshire Visitation Pedigrees, 1623,* 105-6: 62; William Chauncey Fowler, *Memorials of the Chaunceys* (1858), 30-31, chart between 36 and 37.

Thomas Eyre was an uncle of Catherine Eyre of Massachusetts, wife of Rev. Charles Chauncy, second president of Harvard College.

5596-5597 *Parish registers, Church of Aldenham (Hertfordshire) 1559–1812* Family History Library film 1040,851.

5600-5615 See 5584-5599.

5632-5695 See 2112-2175.

5696-5697 See 2220-2221.

5698-5699 *History of the County Palatine and Duchy of Lancaster,* 3: 157; *The Visitations of the County of Nottingham in the years 1569 and 1614,* 4: 102; C. E. L., "Pedigree of Dabridge-court, of Stratfield Say, co. Hants.," *Topographer & Genealogist* 1 [1846]: 198.

5700-5701 J. P. Earwaker, *East Cheshire, Past and Present, or, a History of the Hundred of Macclesfield in the County Palatine of Chester—from Original Records,* 2 vols. (1877-80), 2: 444; *The Knights of England,* 2: 184.

5702-5703 *East Cheshire, Past and Present,* 2: 444.

5704-5705 *The Complete Baronetage,* 1: 193; *The History of Parliament 1558–1603,* 3: 527; Joseph Jackson Howard, ed., *The Visitation of Suffolke, Made by William Hervey, Clarenceaux King of Arms, 1561: With Additions from Family Documents, Original Wills, Jermyn, Davy, and Other Mss., &c.,* 2 vols. (1866-71), 2: 195.

5706-5707 *La Société Guernesiaise, formerly the Guernsey Society of Natural Science and Local Research: Report and Transactions,* vol. 16, part 2, A. H. Ewen, "Essex Castle and the Chamberlain Family," 234; *The Visitations of the County of Oxford taken in the years 1566 by William Harvey, Clarencieux, 1574 by Richard Lee, Portcullis, Deputy of Robert Cooke, Clarencieux, and in 1634 by John Philipott, Somerset and William Ryley, Bluemantle,* 5: 272.

5708-5709 W. P. W. Phillimore and W. F. Carter, *Some Account of the Family of Middlemore, of Warwickshire and Worcestershire* (1901), Pedigree C.

5710-5711 *The visitations of Cornwall,* 300; Will of Sir Maurice Drumond, Gentleman Usher of His Majesty's Privy Chamber 20 April 1640, Proved at London P.C.C. 13 May 1642 PROB 11/189; Will of Dame Dorothea Drumond, Widow of St. Giles in the Fields, Middlesex 16 Jan. 1677/78, codicil 17 Sept. 1679, Proved at London P.C.C. 16 Dec. 1679 PROB 11/361.

5712-5713 *The Visitation of the County of Warwick in the year 1619 Taken by William Camden, Clarenceaux King of Arms,* 12: 215; *Publications of the Harleian Society, Visitation Series,* vol. 62, W. Harry Rylands, ed., *The Visitation of the County of Warwick begun by Thomas May, Chester, and Gregory King, Rouge Dragon, in Hilary Vacation 1682. Reviewing them in the Trinity Vacation following, and Finished by Henry Dethick, Richmond, and the said Rouge Dragon Pursuivant in Trinity Vacation 1683, by virtue of several deputations from Sir Henry St. George, Clarenceux King of Arms,* 44; G. Dashwood, *Pedigrees selected from the Visitation of the County of Warwick, begun by Thomas May, Chester, and Gregory King, Rouge Dragon, in Hillary Vacac n, 1682, etc., etc.* (1859), Betham.

5714-5715 *Some Account of the Family of Middlemore, of Warwickshire and Worcestershire,* Pedigree C.

5716-5717 *The Four Visitations of Berkshire,* 56: 146, 150.

5718-5719 "The Family of Fettiplace," *Miscellanea Genealogica et Heraldica,* 5th series, 2 [1918]: 205, 242.

5724-5725 *The Heraldic Visitations of Staffordshire Made by Sir Richard St. George, Norroy, in 1614, and by Sir William Dugdale in the Years 1663 and 1664,* 5: 2: 137; *Familiae Minorum Gentium,* 38: 562.

5726-5727 *The Complete Peerage,* 1: 285; *The Complete Baronetage,* 1: 24; *The Heraldic Visitations of Staffordshire Made by Sir Richard St. George, Norroy, in 1614, and by Sir William Dugdale in the Years 1663 and 1664,* 5: 2: 19; "Pedigrees and heraldic notes of Gregory King: Sadler," *Miscellanea Genealogica et Heraldica,* 5th series, 9 [1932]: 124.

5744-5745 *Oxford Dictionary of National Biography,* 12: 465-68; *The Dictionary of National Biography,* 11: 244-45; *Some Account of the Lord Mayors and Sheriffs of the City of London during the first quarter of the seventeenth century,* 73; *Familiae Minorum Gentium,* 38: 573; *The Knights of England,* 2: 187.

5746-5747 *Shropshire Genealogies,* 6: 208.

5748-5749 *The Complete Baronetage,* 1: 196; *Visitation of England and Wales, Notes,* 7: 18.

5750-5751 *The Complete Baronetage,* 1: 197; *The History of Parliament 1558–1603,* 2: 104-5; "Pedigree of Smythe of Ostenhanger, Kent; of Smythe of Bidborough and Sutton-at-Hone, Kent; and of the Smythes, Viscounts of Strangford, of Dromore, Ireland," *Archæologia Cantiana* 20: 79.

5752-5755 See 5084-5087.

5756-5757 Stephen Glover, *The History and gazetteer of the county of Derby: drawn up from actual observation and from the best authorities: containing a variety of geological, mineralogical, commercial and statistical information*, 2 vols. in 3 (1831-33), 2: 159; "Pedigrees contained in the Visitations of Derbyshire, 1569 and 1611," *The Genealogist*, New Series, 8 [1891]: 178; Will of Godfrey Meynell, Gentleman of Meynell Langley, Derbyshire 16 April 1667, Proved at The Strand, Middlesex P.C.C. 20 Dec. 1667 PROB 11/32.

5758-5759 *Allegations for Marriage Licences issued by the Dean and Chapter of Westminster, 1558-1699; Also for those issued by the Vicar-General of the Archbishop of Canterbury, 1660-1679*, 23: 270.

5760-5761 Joan Wake, *The Brudenells of Deene* (1953), 47, 102; Peter Alfred Taylor, *Some Account of the Taylor Family (originally Tayland)*, 2 vols. (1875), 2: 690; *The parish register of Rushton, Northamptonshire, 1538-1837* Family History Library film 1441,052, item 4.

5762-5763 *Publications of the Northamptonshire Record Society*, 19: 75-79; *The Knights of England*, 2: 76; *The History and Antiquities of the County of Buckingham*, 4: 401.

5764-5765 *The Complete Baronetage*, 1: 27; *Visitation of England and Wales, Notes*, 7: 23.

5766-5767 *The Complete Peerage*, 4: 79.

5768-5769 *Oxford Dictionary of National Biography*, 49: 97; *The Complete Peerage*, 11: 459; *Lincolnshire Pedigrees*, 51: 528, 52: 957; *The Knights of England*, 2: 82; *Dugdale's Visitation of Yorkshire in 1665-6*, 1: 155-56.

5770-5771 *The History of Parliament 1558-1603*, 1: 545-46; *The Knights of England*, 2: 85; *The visitations of the county of Devon*, 154.

5772-5773 *The Complete Peerage*, 2: 391-92; "Pedigree of Saunders from the Visitation of Northamptonshire 1618," *Miscellanea Genealogica et Heraldica* 1 [1868]: 159; Walter C. Metcalfe, ed., *The Visitations of Northamptonshire Made in 1564 and 1618-9: With Northamptonshire Pedigrees from Various Harleian Mss.* (1887), 45; *The History and Antiquities of the County of Leicestershire*, 3: 197, 4: 621; *Lincolnshire Pedigrees*, 50: 43; *Alumni Cantabrigienses*, 4: 302; *The Knights of England*, 2: 90.

5774-5775 *The Complete Peerage*, 1: 123.

5776-5777 *Oxford Dictionary of National Biography*, 8: 292-93; *The Complete Peerage*, 2: 350-51; *The Scots Peerage*, 3: 474-77; *The Marriage, Baptismal and Burial Registers of the Collegiate Church or Abbey of St. Peter, Westminster*, 10: 129.

5778-5779 *The visitations of Cornwall*, 229; *The visitations of the county of Devon*, 174.

5780-5781 *The History of Parliament 1558-1603*, 2: 223-24; *The Complete Peerage*, 6: 136.

5782-5783 *The History of Parliament 1558-1603*, 1: 581-82; *The Complete Peerage*, 5: 218; *The Knights of England*, 2: 100; *Northamptonshire Families*, 29-30; George Ravenscroft Dennis, *The House of Cecil* (1914), 121-24; *The Marriage, Baptismal and Burial Registers of the Collegiate Church or Abbey of St. Peter, Westminster*, 10: 134; *Nottingham Parish Registers*, 3: 89.

5784-5785 *Oxford Dictionary of National Biography*, 49: 870-71; *The Complete Peerage*, 6: 507.

5786-5787 *Rivals in Power*, 270-83; Robert Lacey, *Robert, Earl of Essex: an Elizabethan Icarus* (1971); Lytton Strachey, *Elizabeth and Essex* (1928); *The Complete Peerage*, 5: 141-42. See also 4446-4447.

5788-5791 See 4404-4407.

5792-5793 *The Complete Baronetage,* 1: 156; *The History of Parliament 1558–1603,* 1: 439.

5794-5795 *The History of Parliament 1558–1603,* 3: 532-33; *The Complete Peerage,* 12: 1: 690-91.

5796-5797 Anthony A. Wood, *Oxfordshire Monumental Inscriptions* (1825), 87; *Middlesex Pedigrees,* 65: 59.

5798-5799 *The Visitation of the County of Buckingham Made in 1634,* 58: 47; *Alumni Oxonienses: The members of the University of Oxford, 1500–1714,* 1-2: 432; Will of Thomas Duncombe of Broughton, Buckinghamshire 6 May 1632, codicils 8 and 10 May 1632, Proved 17 May 1632 PROB 11/161; Will of Sarah Duncombe, Widow of Islington, Middlesex 14 Feb. 1653, Proved 26 Feb. 1654 PROB 11/239.

5800-5801 B. W. Greenfield, "Pedigree of Dunch of Little Wittenham, Berks.," *Miscellanea Genealogica et Heraldica,* 3rd series, 2 [1898]: 45; *The Knights of England,* 2: 111.

5802-5803 *Wiltshire Visitation Pedigrees, 1623,* 105-6: 93; *The Knights of England,* 2: 141; *Registers of the Parish Church of Hungerford (Berkshire) 1559–1813* Family History Library film 0088,273.

5804-5805 *Oxoniensia: a journal dealing with the archaeology, history, and architecture of Oxford and its neighborhood,* vols. 11-12, Michael Maclagan, "Family of Dormer in Oxfordshire and Buckinghamshire," pedigree and 101, note 7; *The History, Description and Antiquities of the Prebendal Church of the Blessed Virgin Mary of Thame,* 509.

5806-5807 *Oxford Dictionary of National Biography,* 56: 971-77; *The History of Parliament 1660–1690,* 3: 653; *The History and Antiquities of the County of Buckingham,* 3: 182; Arthur Meredyth Burke, *Memorials of St. Margaret's church, Westminster, comprising the parish registers, 1539–1660, and the churchwardens' accounts 1460–1603* (1914), 339.

5808-5809 *The visitations of Cornwall,* 47.

5810-5811 *The visitations of the county of Devon,* 654, 464.

5812-5813 *The visitations of Cornwall,* 184; *The Gentleman's Magazine* 102 [1832]: 214; Francis Blomefield and Charles Parkin, *An Essay Towards a Topographical History of the County of Norfolk, a Description of the Towns, Villages, and Hamlets, with the Foundations of Monasteries, Churches, Chapels, Chantries, and Other Religious Buildings: Also an Account of the Ancient and Present State of All the Rectories, Vicarages, Donatives, and Impropriations, Their Former and Present Patrons and Incumbents, with Their Several Valuations in the King's Book, Whether Discharged or Not: Likewise an Historical Account of the Castles, Seats, and Manors, Their Present and Antient Owners, Together with the Most Remarkable Epitaphs, Inscriptions and Arms, in All the Parish Churches and Chapels; with Several Draughts of Churches, Monuments, Arms, Antient Ruins, and Other Relicts of Antiquity: Collected Out of Ledger-Books, Registers, Records, Evidences, Deeds, Court-Rolls, and Other Authentic Memorials,* 2nd ed., 11 vols. (1805-10), 5: 883; *The Knights of England,* 2: 96.

5814-5815 *Visitations of England and Wales, Notes,* 9: 156; "Visitation of Berkshire, 1666," *The Genealogist* 6 [1882]: 66; *The Knights of England,* 2: 147; "Lygon Descendants in England and Europe, Part 1," *NEHGS NEXUS* 16 [1999]: 156-57.

Sir Henry Berkeley was the uncle of Sir William Berkeley, Governor of Virginia, and a first cousin of Sir Ferdinando Gorges, Lord Proprietor of Maine.

5820-5823 See 2056-2059.

5832-5833 *Shropshire Genealogies,* 8: 135; "Inquisitiones Post Mortem *temp.* Henry VIII to Charles I," *The Genealogist,* New Series, 30 [1917]: 66; Will of Thomas Jennynge of Ellesmere, Shropshire 29 April 1640, Proved 4 July 1640 PROB 11/183.

5834-5835 Jacob Youde William Lloyd, *The History of the Princes, the Lords Marcher and the Ancient Nobility of Powys Fadog and the Ancient Lords of Arwystli, Cedewen and Meirionydd,* 6 vols. (1881-87), 2: 161-62; 328; Will of Sir Gerard Eyton of Eyton, Denbighshire 14 Jan. 1650/51, Proved P.C.C. 23 May 1653 PROB 11/229.

5840-5841 *The Complete Baronetage,* 1: 75; Charles Humble Dudley Ward, *The family of Twysden and Twisden; their history and archives from an original by Sir John Ramskill Twisden, 12th baronet of Bradbourne* (1939), 106.

5842-5843 *The History of Parliament 1558–1603,* 3: 345-46, 1: 450; *The family of Twysden and Twisden,* 140; "Extract from the pedigree of the family of Saunders of Ewell in the County of Surrey," *Miscellanea Genealogica et Heraldica,* 5th series, 8 [1918]: 111; *The History and Antiquities of the County of Surrey,* 1: 459; *The Visitations of the County of Surrey,* 43: 69.

5846-5847 *The Complete Baronetage,* 1: 188, 219; *Some Account of the Lord Mayors and Sheriffs of the City of London during the first quarter of the seventeenth century,* 7, 25; *The Registers of St. Mary Aldermary, London, 1558 to 1754,* 5: 12; *The Royal Descents of 600 Immigrants to the American Colonies or the United States,* 363-64; *Plantagenet Ancestry,* 412-13; Will of Sir John Garrard of Lamer, Hertfordshire 25 May 1637, Proved P.C.C. 21 June 1637 PROB 11/174.

Elizabeth (Barkham), Lady Garrard, was a great-aunt of Edmund Jennings, acting Governor of Virginia, and a great-great-aunt of Sir Marmaduke Beckwith, 3rd Baronet, also of Virginia.

5848-5849 *The Dictionary of National Biography,* 21: 1191; *Hasted's history of Kent,* 1: 195; *The Visitation of Kent Taken in the Years 1619–1621,* 42: 188, 192; *The Knights of England,* 2: 122.

5850-5851 *Hasted's history of Kent,* 1: 195.

5852-5853 *A Genealogical and Heraldic History of the Extinct and Dormant Baronetcies of England, Ireland, and Scotland,* 519; William Berry, *County Genealogies: Pedigrees of the Families of the County of Kent, Collected from the Heraldic Visitations and Other Authentic Manuscripts in the British Museum, and in the Possession of Private Individuals, and from the Information of the Present Resident Families* (1830), 162, 175, 226; *The Visitation of Kent Taken in the Years 1619–1621,* 42: 69; *Sussex Archeological Collections,* vol. 42, J. H. Cooper, "Cuckfield Familes," 49-50.

5854-5855 *County Genealogies: Pedigrees of the Families of the County of Kent,* 162; *The Complete Baronetage,* 4: 6.

5856-5857 "Cuckfield Familes," 42: 34; *The Complete Baronetage,* 3: 58; *The Knights of England,* 2: 149; *The Visitations of Essex by Hawley, 1552, Hervey 1558, Cooke 1570, Raven 1612 and Owen and Lilly, 1634,* 13: 213; "Pedigree of Smythe of Ostenhanger, Kent; of Smythe of Bidborough and Sutton-at-Hone, Kent; and of the Smythes, Viscounts of Strangford, of Dromore, Ireland," *Archæologia Cantiana* 20: 79; *Publications of the Harleian Society, Register Series,* vol. 61, W. Bruce Bannerman et al., *The Registers of St. Mary The Virgin, Aldermanbury, London, 1538 to 1859,* 62; *The Registers of St. Olave, Hart Street, London, 1563 to 1700,* 46: 259, 269; *Allegations for Marriage Licences issued by the Bishop of London,* 26: 30.

5858-5859 G. E. Adams, "Genealogical Memoranda Relating to the Fox and Weld Families," *Miscellanea Genealogica et Heraldica,* New Series, 1 [1878]: 113; *Middlesex Pedigrees,*

65: 36; *Pedigrees of the county families of England*, 1: Weld pedigree; *London Pedigrees*, 129; *The History and Antiquities of the County of Dorset*, 3: 371; *The Knights of England*, 2: 167.

5860-5861 *Oxford Dictionary of National Biography*, 10: 796-97; *The Complete Peerage*, 11: 404-6; *The Knights of England*, 1: 157; 133; *Hertfordshire Families*, 114-15.

5862-5863 *The Complete Peerage*, 4: 286-87; *The Scots Peerage*, 3: 129-31.

5864-5865 *The History of Parliament 1660–1690*, 3: 205; *An account of the families of Lennard and Barrett, compiled largely from original documents*, 243; *Publications of the Harleian Society, Visitation Series*, vol. 53, W. Bruce Bannerman, ed., The *Visitations of the County of Sussex, Made and Taken in the years 1530 by Thomas Benolte, Clarenceux King of Arms; and 1633–4 by John Philipot, Somerset Herald, and George Owen, York Herald, for Sir John Burroughs, Garter and Sir Richard St. George, Clarenceux*, 22; *The Knights of England*, 2: 167.

5866-5867 *Oxford Dictionary of National Biography*, 40: 612-13; *The History of Parliament 1660–1690*, 3: 133; *The Complete Baronetage*, 4: 89; *The Royal Descents of 600 Immigrants to the American Colonies or the United States*, 328-29.

Sir Richard Newdigate, 1st Baronet, and Juliana Leigh were grandparents of Mary Newdigate, wife of William Stephens, Governor of Georgia.

5868-5869 Henry Fitz-Gilbert Waters, *Genealogical Gleanings in England: Abstracts of Wills Relating to Early American Families, with Genealogical Notes and Pedigrees Constructed from the Wills and from Other Records*, 2 vols. (1885–1901), 2: 944-46; *The Visitation of Middlesex, began in the year 1663*, 2; Will of Robert Comyn alias Chilcott or Chilcot, Merchant of London 25 Aug. 1609, Proved at London P.C.C. 8 Sept. 1609 PROB 11/114.

5870-5871 *The Visitation of Middlesex, began in the year 1663*, 2; *Publications of the Harleian Society, Visitation Series*, vol. 22, Walter C. Metcalfe, ed., *The Visitations of Hertfordshire, Made by Robert Cooke, Esq., Clarencieux in 1572, and Sir Richard St. George, kt., Clarencieux in 1634, with Hertfordshire Pedigrees from Harleian Mss. 6147 and 1546*, 76; Will of Robert Newman, Merchant Tailor of London 6 March 1650/51, Proved at London P.C.C. 3 April 1651 PROB 11/216; Will of George Monnoxe or Monnox, Haberdasher of Saint Giles Cripplegate, City of London 1 March 1637/38, codicil 12 June 1638, Proved at London P.C.C. 18 July 1638 PROB 11/177.

5872-5879 See 4528-4535.

5880-5883 *History of Hertfordshire*, 2: Dashwood pedigree.

5884-5885 *The Visitation of Oxfordshire 1669 and 1675 made by Sir Edward Bysshe*, 12: 71; *The Complete Baronetage*, 2: 206.

5886-5887 *The Complete Baronetage*, 3: 6; *The visitations of the county of Devon*, 621; *The Visitation of the County of Somerset in the year 1623*, 11: 35.

5888-5591 See 4384-4387.

5892-5895 See 5300-5303.

5896-5903 See 2880-2887.

5904-5905 Peter Townend, ed., *Burke's Genealogical and Heraldic History of the Peerage, Baronetage and Knightage* (1970), 443.

5908-5909 *Hasted's history of Kent*, 1: xxv; *The Visitations of Kent Taken in the Years 1530–1*, 75: 130.

5910-5911 "Pedigree of Dowdall," Society of Genealogists MS pedigree X.A.12: 441 (at the Society of Genealogists, London); *The Visitation of Norfolk in the Year 1563*, 1: 128; *The Knights of England*, 2: 167.

5912-5913 K. van de Sigtenhorst, "Lady Diana Spencer," *Gens Nostra: Ons Geslacht, Maanblad der Nederlandse Genealogische Vereniging* 36 [1981]: 230; Johan Engelbert Elias, *De Vroederschap van Amsterdam 1578–1795; met een inleidend woord van den archivaris der stad Amsterdam W. R. Veder*, 2 vols. (1903-5; reprinted in 1963), 2: 625.

5914-5915 "Lady Diana Spencer," 230; *De Vroederschap van Amsterdam 1578–1795*, 1: 352-53.

5916-5917 "Lady Diana Spencer," 231; P. W. Klein, *De Trippen in de 17e Eeuw; een studie over het ondernemersgedrag op de Hollandse stapelmarkt* (1965), 32-33; *De Vroederschap van Amsterdam 1578–1795*, 2: 548.

5918-5919 Gisela Jongbloet-van Hoette, *Brieven en Andere Bescheiden Betreffende Daniel van der Meulen 1584–1600* (1986), cxxx; "Lady Diana Spencer," 231; Jean le Carpentier, *Histoire généalogique des Païs-Bas, ou, Histoire de Cambray, et du Cambresis, contenant ce qui s'y est passe sous les empereurs, & les rois de France & d'Espagne; enrichie des genealogies, eloges, & armes des comtes, ducs, evesques, & archevesques, & presque de quatre mille familles nobles, tant des XVII. provinces que de France ... Le tout divise en IV. Parties*, 2 vols. (1663-64), 2: 618.

5920-5921 *Oxford Dictionary of National Biography*, 31: 427-29; *The Complete Peerage*, 8: 147-49.

5922-5925 *The Complete Peerage*, 1: 203-4; *The Scots Peerage*, 1: 351-52.

5926-5927 *The Complete Peerage*, 9: 187; *The Scots Peerage*, 6: 321.

5928-5929 Leslie G. Pine, ed., *Burke's Genealogical and Heraldic History of the Landed Gentry* (1952), 1890; Cavendish D. Abercromby, *The Family of Abercromby* (1927), 64, 57.

5932-5933 *The Parliaments of Scotland*, 2: 542; *The Complete Baronetage*, 2: 424.

5934-5935 *The Complete Peerage*, 8: 27-28; Edwin Brockholst Livingston, *The Livingstons of Callendar, and their principal cadets : the history of an old Stirlingshire family* (1920), 110-14.

5936-5937 *The Complete Peerage*, 4: 70, 6: 535; *Dugdale's Visitation of Yorkshire in 1665–6*, 2: 29, 83.

5938-5939 *The Complete Peerage*, 2: 150; *The Marriage, Baptismal and Burial Registers of the Collegiate Church or Abbey of St. Peter, Westminster*, 10: 170, 177.

5940-5941 *The Complete Peerage*, 7: 626, note a; *The Visitations of the County of Nottingham in the years 1569 and 1614*, 4: 143; *Lincolnshire Pedigrees*, 50: 263; *Alumni Cantabrigienses*, 4: 188; *The Knights of England*, 2: 102; *The Royal Descents of 600 Immigrants to the American Colonies or the United States*, 366-67.

Sir William Sutton and Susan Cony were great-great-grandparents of James Edward Oglethorpe, founder of Georgia.

5942-5943 Moya Frenz St. Leger, *St. Leger: The Family and the Race* (1986), 34; *Sussex Genealogies*, 3: 261; *The Complete Peerage*, 7: 627; Melville Amadeus Henry Douglas, 9th Marquis of Ruvigny and Raineval, *The Plantagenet roll of the blood royal: being a complete table of all the descendants now living of Edward III., king of England: the Mortimer-Percy volume, containing the descendants of Lady Elizabeth Percy, née Mortimer, with supplements to the Exeter and*

Essex volumes (1911), 30; "Pedigrees and heraldic notes of Gregory King: Mayny of Kent," *Miscellanea Genealogica et Heraldica,* 5th series, 9 [1932]: 120; *Alumni Cantabrigienses,* 4: 6; *The Knights of England,* 2: 213; Charles Wykeham Martin, *The History and Description of Leeds Castle, Kent* (1869), St. Leger pedigree; *The Registers of Christening, Burials and Weddings within the Parish of St. Peter's upon Cornhill, London, 1538 to 1666,* 1: 253; John Frederick Dorman, *Adventurers of Purse and Person, Virginia, 1607–1624/5,* 4th ed., 3 vols. (2004-7), 3: 103-8; *The Royal Descents of 600 Immigrants to the American Colonies or the United States,* 176-77; *Plantagenet Ancestry,* 630-32.

Sir Anthony St. Leger was a brother of Katherine (St. Leger) Colepepper, and an uncle of Colonel Warham Horsmanden (grandfather of the diarist William Byrd II of Westover) and St. Leger Codd, all of Virginia.

5944-5945 *Europäische Stammtafeln,* Neue Folge, 10: 28; *The Complete Peerage,* 11: 522-23; Mary Anne Everett Green, *Elizabeth, electress palatine and queen of Bohemia* (1909), 9, 107-8.

5946-5947 *Europäische Stammtafeln,* Neue Folge, 10: 28.

5948-5949 *Oxford Dictionary of National Biography,* 17: 85-92; *Neue Deutsche Biographie,* vol. 5, 535-56; *Elizabeth, electress palatine and queen of Bohemia.*

5950-5951 Edmund von der Becke-Klüchtzner, *Stamm-Tafeln des Adels Grossherzogthums des Baden: ein neu bearbeitetes Adelsbuch* (1886), 108; Friedrich Gaisberg-Schöckingen, *Das Könighaus und der Adel von Württemberg* (1908), 558.

5952-6005 See 5312-5365.

6018-6019 *The History of Parliament 1558–1603,* 1: 383-84; John Edwards Griffith, *Pedigrees of Anglesey and Carnarvonshire families* (1914), 57; Philip Henry Dudley Bagenal, *Vicissitudes of an Irish Family 1530–1800: a story of Irish romance and tragedy* (1925), 65-66, pedigree; *The Knights of England,* 2: 78.

6024-6025 Sir Edmund T. Bewley, "An Irish branch of the Fleetwood family," *The Genealogist,* New Series, 24 [1908]: 226; *The Complete Peerage,* 3: 116-17; *The Knights of England,* 2: 92; *The Marriage, Baptismal and Burial Registers of the Collegiate Church or Abbey of St. Peter, Westminster,* 10: 115.

6026-6027 *The Complete Peerage,* 11: 36; *The visitations of Cornwall,* 217; *The Knights of England,* 2: 160; *The Complete Baronetage,* 1: 169; Brandon Fradd, "Ancestry of Thomas Thorne, Grandfather of Thomas[1] Dudley," *The Genealogist* 19 [2005]: 123, 125, and "Additions and Corrections to *The Genealogist*: Thorne," 19: 250.

Frances (Hender), Baroness Robartes, was a first cousin of Thomas Dudley, Governor of Massachusetts Bay Colony.

6032-6033 *The Complete Peerage,* 10: 283-84; Gary Boyd Roberts, *Notable Kin: An Anthology of Columns First Published in the* NEHGS NEXUS, *1986–1995, Volume One … with contributions by David Curtis Dearborn, Julie Helen Otto, Michael J. Wood, and David Allen Lambert* (1998), 48, 50-51.

6034-6035 *The Complete Peerage,* 6: 538-40.

6038-6039 *The Complete Baronetage,* 5: 352, note a; *A Genealogical and Heraldic History of the Commoners of Great Britain and Ireland,* 4: 494.

6040-6041 Joseph Jackson Howard, ed., *The Visitation of the County of Essex, Begun A.D. MDCLXIIII, Finished A.D. MDCLXVIII by Sir Edward Bysshe, Knt., Clarenceux King of Arms*

(1888), 100; *The Visitations of Essex by Hawley, 1552, Hervey 1558, Cooke 1570, Raven 1612 and Owen and Lilly, 1634*, 13: 320, 518, 521; *Memorials of St. Margaret's church, Westminster, comprising the parish registers, 1539–1600, and the churchwardens' accounts 1460–1603*, 299.

6042-6043 *The Visitation of the County of Essex, Begun A.D. MDCLXIIII*, 100; *The Visitation of London Anno Domini 1633, 1634 and 1635*, 15: 410; *The Four Visitations of Berkshire*, 57: 159; *The History of Parliament 1558–1603*, 1: 341.

6044-6045 *North Witham Bishops' Transcripts* Family History Library film 0436,048, item 6; *The History and Antiquities of the County of Leicestershire*, 2: 1: 353, 343; *Lincolnshire Pedigrees*, 50: 189.

6046-6047 *Publications of the Harleian Society, New Series*, vol. 15, Michael Powell Siddons, ed., *The Visitation of Herefordshire 1634*, 159; *Shobdon Parish Register* Family History Library film 1040,024, item 16.

6048-6049 Joseph Nadaud, *Nobiliaire du diocèse et de la généralité de Limoges*, 4 vols. (1863-82), 4: 29.

6052-6053 *Europäische Stammtafeln*, Neue Folge, 10: 50; *Huguenot Pedigrees*, 1: 71; *Histoire de la Maison Royale de France*, 4: 457; *Dictionnaire de la Noblesse, contenant les généalogies, l'histoire & la chronologie des familles nobles de la France*, 17: 387.

6054-6055 *Europäische Stammtafeln*, Neue Folge, 10: 50.

6056-6057 *The House of Forbes*, 316, 329; *The Complete Baronetage*, 2: 360.

6058-6059 *The Complete Baronetage*, 1: 255; W. H. Whelply, "Boleyn", *Notes and Queries* 197 [1952]: 91.

6060-6061 *Camden Society Series*, vol. 85, Robert Davies, ed., *The Life of Marmaduke Rawdon of York*, xi; Sir Thomas Selby Lawson-Tancred, *Records of a Yorkshire Manor* (1937), 137.

6062-6063 *The Complete Peerage*, 3: 400-1; *The Knights of England*, 2: 168.

6080-6081 See 4388-4389.

6082-6083 *The Complete Peerage*, 12: 1: 466-67, 4: 511, note d; John Malcolm Bulloch, *House of Gordon*, 3 vols. (1903-12), 1: 194.

6084-6085 *The History of Parliament 1660–1690*, 2: 57.

6088-6089 *The East Anglian; or, Notes and queries on subjects connected with the counties of Suffolk, Cambridge, Essex and Norfolk*, vol. 4, George W. Marshall, "Pedigree of the Hernes, of Tibenham, co. Norfolk," 123; *Some Account of the Lord Mayors and Sheriffs of the City of London during the first quarter of the seventeenth century*, 82; *The History and Antiquities of the County of Dorset*, 2: 282; *The History of Parliament 1660–1690*, 2: 537; *Allegations for Marriage Licences issued by the Bishop of London*, 26: 23.

6090-6091 *The History of Parliament 1660–1690*, 2: 363-65; Edmund Horace Fellowes, *The Family of Frederick* (1932), 10-25; *The rulers of London 1660–1689*, 73; *The Aldermen of the City of London Temp. Henry III–1908*, 2: 83; *Publications of the Harleian Society, Register Series*, vol. 31, W. Bruce Bannerman, *The Registers of St. Helen's, Bishopsgate, London, 1575 to 1837*, 135.

6092-6093 *The History of Parliament 1660–1690*, 2: 746; *The Visitation of the County of Northampton in the Year 1681*, 87: 123; *The History and Antiquities of the County of Northampton*, 1: 612, 2: 45; *Obituary of Richard Smyth*, 50.

6094-6095 *The Visitation of the County of Northampton in the Year 1681,* 87: 123; *The History of Parliament 1660–1690,* 2: 746; *Alumni Cantabrigienses,* 1: 60.

6096-6097 *The Complete Peerage,* 2: 311-12; *The History of Parliament 1558–1603,* 2: 79-80.

6098-6099 *The Complete Peerage,* 1: 521-26; Sir Charles Harding Firth, ed., *The Life of William Cavendish, Duke of Newcastle, to which is added the true relation of my birth, breeding and life, by Margaret, Duchess of Newcastle* (1906); *The Marriage, Baptismal and Burial Registers of the Collegiate Church or Abbey of St. Peter, Westminster,* 10: 190, 182.

6100-6101 *The Complete Peerage,* 12: 2: 767-69; *Allegations for Marriage Licences issued by the Bishop of London,* 26: 118. See also 2222-2223.

6102-6103 See 2722-2723.

6104-6111 See 2056-2063.

6112-6121 See 5840-5847.

6122-6123 *The Visitation of the County of Yorke,* 36: 66; *Dugdale's Visitation of Yorkshire in 1665–6,* 1: 202; *Familiae Minorum Gentium,* 37: 419; *The Publications of the Yorkshire Parish Register Society,* vol. 41, Robert Beilby Cook, ed., *The Parish Registers of Holy Trinity Church, Goodramgate, York, 1573–1812,* 39.

6124-6125 *The family of Twysden and Twisden,* 374; *The Visitation of London Anno Domini 1633, 1634 and 1635,* 17: 60.

6140-6141 *The Visitation of Middlesex, began in the year 1663,* 94; *Transcripts of parish registers of London, St. Bartholomew the Less, London, Marriages 1558–1706* Family History Library film 0416,713.

6142-6143 *The Visitations of the County of Oxford taken in the years 1566 by William Harvey, Clarencieux, 1574 by Richard Lee, Portcullis, Deputy of Robert Cooke, Clarencieux, and in 1634 by John Philipott, Somerset and William Ryley, Bluemantle,* 5: 124; *Allegations for Marriage Licences issued by the Faculty Office of the Archbishop of Canterbury at London, 1543–1869,* 24: 26; *The Knights of England,* 2: 197; *A Genealogical and Heraldic History of the Commoners of Great Britain and Ireland,* 3: 260; *The Visitation of Middlesex, began in the year 1663,* 94; *The Marriage, Baptismal and Burial Registers of the Collegiate Church or Abbey of St. Peter, Westminster,* 10: 282; *Publications of the Harleian Society, Register Series,* vol. 17, Robert Hovenden, *A True Register of all the Christenings, Marriages and Burials in the Parish of St. James, Clerkenwell, 1551 to 1754,* 298.

6158-6159 *History of the Copingers or Coppingers of the County of Cork, Ireland, and the Counties of Suffolk and Kent, England,* pedigree.

6368-6369 *Burke's Irish Family Records,* 906.

6370-6371 *Burke's Irish Family Records,* 906; Mary Frances Cusack, *A History of the city and county of Cork* (1875), pedigree.

6400-6401 *Burke's Genealogical and Heraldic History of the Peerage, Baronetage and Knightage* (1970), 305; *The History and Antiquities of the County of Leicestershire,* 4: 177; *The History of Parliament 1558–1603,* 1: 655; *Staffordshire Parish Registers Society,* vol. 10, "Bushbury Parish Register," 11; "The Family of Boothby," *Miscellanea Genealogica et Heraldica,* 5th series, 1 [1916]: 8.

6402-6403 See 2688-2689.

6404-6405 *The Complete Baronetage,* 2: 150; *The History and Antiquities of the County of Leicestershire,* 2: 2: 874.

6406-6407 *Lincolnshire Pedigrees,* 51: 436; Alfred W. Gibbons, *Notes on the Visitation of Lincoln 1634* (1898), 22.

6592-6595 Noel Currer-Briggs and Royston Gambier, *Huguenot Ancestry* (1985), pedigree.

6816-6817 Gary Boyd Roberts and William Addams Reitwiesner, *American Ancestors and Cousins of The Princess of Wales* (1984), 76.

7040-7041 *American Ancestors and Cousins of The Princess of Wales,* 29; Mary Lovering Holman and Winifred Lovering Holman, *Ancestry of Colonel John Harrington Stevens and his wife, Frances Helen Miller: compiled for Helen Pendleton (Winston) Pillsbury,* 2 vols. (1948-52), 1: 348-49; Burton W. Spear, *Search for the Passengers of the Mary & John, 1630,* 27 vols. (1985-99), 27: 102-11.

7042-7043 *American Ancestors and Cousins of The Princess of Wales,* 30; *Ancestry of Colonel John Harrington Stevens and his wife, Frances Helen Miller,* 1: 354-55; *Search for the Passengers of the Mary & John, 1630,* 18: 37-39, 48-53; Robert Charles Anderson, *The Great Migration Begins: Immigrants to New England 1620–1633,* 3 vols. (1995), 1: 688-90.

7044-7045 *American Ancestors and Cousins of The Princess of Wales,* 29; Zelinda Makepeace Douhan, ed., *The Ancestry of Russell Makepeace of Marion, Massachusetts 1904–1986: A Descendant of Thomas Makepeace of Dorchester, Massachusetts* (2005), 177.

7054-7055 Penny G. Douglass and Robert Charles Anderson, "The English Origin of Robert Blott of Charlestown and Boston, Mass.," *The American Genealogist* 68 [1992]: 65-67, and "John Black of Charlestown Was Really Robert Blott," 68: 67-68; *American Ancestors and Cousins of The Princess of Wales,* 30; Donald Lines Jacobus and Edgar Francis Waterman, *Hale, House and related families: mainly of the Connecticut River Valley* (1952), 480-82; *Ancestry of Colonel John Harrington Stevens and his wife,* 1: 411-12; Frank Farnsworth Starr, *Various Ancestral Lines of James Goodwin and Lucy (Morgan) Goodwin of Hartford, Connecticut,* 2 vols. (1915), 2: 193-201; Robert Charles Anderson et al., *The Great Migration: Immigrants to New England 1634–1635,* 5 vols. to date (1999-), 1: 334-38.

7056-7059 See 7040-7043.

7060-7061 *American Ancestors and Cousins of The Princess of Wales,* 29; Mary Walton Ferris, *Dawes-Gates Ancestral Lines: A Memorial Volume Containing the American Ancestry of Rufus B. Dawes, Volume I; Dawes and Allied Families; A Memorial Volume Containing the Ancestry of Mary Beman (Gates) Dawes, Volume II, Gates and Allied Families,* 2 vols. (1931-43), 2: 840-49; W. M. Bollenbach, Jr., *The New England Ancestry of Alice Everett Johnson 1899–1986* (2003), 400.

7068-7069 *American Ancestors and Cousins of The Princess of Wales,* 29; Ernest Flagg, *Genealogical Notes on the Founding of New England: My Ancestors' Part in that Undertaking* (1926; reprinted 1973), 258.

7076-7077 *American Ancestors and Cousins of The Princess of Wales,* 30-31; *Dawes-Gates Ancestral Lines,* 1: 188-89; E. O. Jameson, *The Cogswells in America* (1884), xv, 1-7; *The Great Migration: Immigrants to New England 1634–1635,* 2: 137-40.

7078-7079 *American Ancestors and Cousins of The Princess of Wales,* 31; Ethel Farrington Smith, *Adam Hawkes of Saugus, Massachusetts 1605–1672: The First Six Generations in America*

(1980), 1-28; G. Andrews Moriarty, "Gleanings from English Records: Browne," *The New England Historical and Genealogical Register* 103 [1949]: 182; *The Great Migration: Immigrants to New England 1634–1635*, 3: 253-57.

7082-7083 John B. Threlfall, "Smedley-Mitchell Clues from Amsterdam," *The American Genealogist* 56 [1980]: 97-98; *American Ancestors and Cousins of The Princess of Wales*, 31.

7084-7085 *American Ancestors and Cousins of The Princess of Wales*, 31; Donald Lines Jacobus and Edgar Francis Waterman, *The Granberry Family and allied families: including the ancestry of Helen (Woodward) Granberry* (1945), 223; *The Great Migration Begins: Immigrants to New England 1620–1633*, 2: 723-24; *The New England Ancestry of Alice Everett Johnson 1899–1986*, 143-44.

7086-7087 *American Ancestors and Cousins of The Princess of Wales*, 31; McClure Meredith Howland, "English Background of three New England Families," *The New England Historical and Genealogical Register* 115 [1961]: 253-54, 256.

7088-7089 *American Ancestors and Cousins of The Princess of Wales*, 30; Edith Bartlett Sumner, *Descendants of Thomas Farr of Harpswell, Maine, and ninety allied families* (1959), 165; Augustus George Hibbard, *Genealogy of the Hibbard Family Who are Descendants of Robert Hibbard of Salem, Massachusetts* (1901), 8-9; *The New England Ancestry of Alice Everett Johnson 1899–1986*, 185.

7090-7091 *American Ancestors and Cousins of The Princess of Wales*, 31; *Descendants of Thomas Farr of Harpswell, Maine*, 192-93; *The Great Migration: Immigrants to New England 1634–1635*, 4: 359-61; *The New England Ancestry of Alice Everett Johnson 1899–1986*, 244.

In treating John Luff, Anderson argues (in *The Great Migration: Immigrants to New England*) that Luff's wife, a widow Bridget ——, was either the mother or the mother-in-law of Robert Hibbard, and that John and Bridget (——) Luff left no children.

7100-7101 *American Ancestors and Cousins of The Princess of Wales*, 31; Ruby Parke Anderson and Elizabeth Miller Hunter Ruppert, *The Parke Scrapbook…*, 3 vols. (1965-66), 1: 1-2; *The Granberry Family and allied families*, 285-86; S. W. McArthur, *McArthur-Barnes Ancestral Lines* (1964), 98-99. See also 7102-7103.

7102-7103 *American Ancestors and Cousins of The Princess of Wales*, 31; *The Granberry Family and allied families*, 333; Clarence Almon Torrey, "Alice (Freeman) (Tompson) Parke," *The American Genealogist* 13 [1936]: 1-8, and Clarence Almon Torrey, "John Tomson of Little Preston, Northamptonshire, England," 14 [1938]: 145-46; David L. Greene, "Mary, Wife of Rev. Richard Blinman of Marshfield, Gloucester, and New London," *The Genealogist* 4 [1983]: 178-82, 184-86. See also 7100-7101.

7744-7745 Charles John Guthrie, *Genealogy of the descendants of Reverend Thomas Guthrie, D. D., and Mrs. Anne Burns or Guthrie: connected chiefly with the families of Chalmers and Trail, to which Mrs. Guthrie belonged through her mother, Mrs. Christina Chalmers or Burns, and her great-grandmother, Mrs. Susannah Trail or Chalmers; also incidental references to the families of Guthrie and Burns* (1902), 32; William Temple, *The Thanage of Fermartyn including the district commonly called Formartine, its proprietors: with genealogical deductions, its parishes, ministers, churches, churchyards, antiquities, &c* (1894), 87.

7752-7753 See 7744-7745.

7756-7757 *The House of Forbes*, 416-17; *The Baronage of Scotland*, 34.

7758-7759 See 2664-2665.

7760-7761 *Genealogy of the descendants of Reverend Thomas Guthrie, D. D., and Mrs. Anne Burns or Guthrie,* 45.

7762-7763 John Burke and John Bernard Burke, *A Genealogical and Heraldic Dictionary of the Landed Gentry of Great Britain and Ireland, a Companion to the Baronetage and Knightage.* With Supplement, Addenda, Corrigenda and Index, 3 vols. (1843-49), 1: 18; *The Thanage of Fermartyn,* 510-11; *The Scots Peerage,* 7: 440.

7764-7765 See 7760-7761.

7766-7767 George Hamilton, *A History of the House of Hamilton* (1933), 968; *The Peerage of Ireland,* 5: 270.

7776-7777 "Pedigree of Douglas of Tilquhilly or Tilwhilly, co. Kincardine," *The Genealogist* 5 [1881]: 194; A. Dingwall-Fordyce, *Addenda to the Family Records of Dingwall-Fordyce* (1888), xlvi-xlvii.

7778-7779 *The Complete Baronetage,* 2: 301; *The Baronage of Scotland,* 34.

7792-7793 *The House of Forbes,* 461; G. F. Browne, *Echt-Forbes family charters 1345–1727, records of the Forest of Birse Notarial Signs 926–1786* (1923).

7794-7795 *Echt-Forbes Charters 1345–1727,* pedigree.

7796-7797 *The Complete Baronetage,* 2: 280-81.

7798-7799 *The Complete Peerage,* 11: 159-60; *The Scots Peerage,* 7: 255.

7814-7815 *Publications of the Thoresby Society,* vol. 12, George Denison Lumb, ed., *The Registers of the Parish Church of Methley in the County of York, from 1560 to 1812,* 9, 61, 71.

7876-7877 J. Forbes Leslie, *The Irvines of Drum and collateral branches* (1909), 177; Vere Langford Oliver, "Pedigree of the family of Dingwall of Brucklay," *Miscellanea Genealogica et Heraldica,* 4th series, 5 [1914]: 13.

7878-7879 H. A. Henrietta Tayler, *History of the Family of Urquhart* (1946), 9-10.

7896-7897 "Pedigree of the family of Dingwall of Brucklay," *Miscellanea Genealogica et Heraldica,* 4th series, 3 [1900]: 12.

7920-7921 *The Thanage of Fermartyn,* 683.

8032-8035 *The Thanage of Fermartyn,* 624.

8064-8065 *The Complete Baronetage,* 2: 305.

8066-8067 *The Complete Baronetage,* 2: 308; *The Royal Descents of 600 Immigrants to the American Colonies or the United States,* 121.
    Sir Thomas Burnett, 1st Baronet, and Margaret Douglas were the maternal grandparents of Thomas Gordon, Chief Justice of New Jersey.

8068-8069 See 5362-5363.

8070-8071 *Cheshire Visitation Pedigrees, 1663,* 93: 122; *The Visitation of Shropshire Taken in the year 1623,* 28: 124.

8076-8077 See 7878-7879.

8078-8079 *The Scots Peerage,* 3: 541-42.

8088-8089 *The House of Forbes,* 340.

8090–8091   A. Alistair N. Tayler and H. A. Henrietta Tayler, *The valuation of the county of Aberdeen for the year 1667* (1933), 92.

8100–8101   See 7878–7879.

8102–8103   See 8078–8079.

8104–8105   *The Thanage of Fermartyn*, 451–52.

8106–8107   *The Thanage of Fermartyn*, 312; *The Irvines of Drum*, 204–5.

8108–8109   See 4032–4033.

8110–8111   *The Complete Peerage*, 1: 184; *The Scots Peerage*, 1: 304–5.

8112–8113   *The Book of the Duffs*, 1: 38–39; *House of Gordon*, 2: 177–78.

8114–8115   *Burke's Genealogical and Heraldic History of the Landed Gentry* (1952), 702; *The Book of the Duffs*, 1: 354–59.

8116–8117   *The Book of the Duffs*, 1: 343–44.

8118–8119   *The Family of Abercromby*, 61.
   John Abercromby and Katherine Gordon were great-grandparents of Major General James Abercromby, British commander in North America 1758–59, who was defeated at the Battle of Fort Ticonderoga.

8120–8121   *The Thanage of Fermartyn*, 222; *The Royal Descents of 600 Immigrants to the American Colonies or the United States*, 133–34.

8122–8123   *The Complete Peerage*, 1: 72; *The Scots Peerage*, 1: 125–26. See also 2656–2657.

8124–8125   *The Complete Peerage*, 11: 421; *The Scots Peerage*, 7: 443–44.

8126–8127   *Oxford Dictionary of National Biography*, 50: 19–22; *Northern notes and queries, or The Scottish Antiquary* 3 [1889]: 162.

BIBLIOGRAPHY

Books and Manuscripts
(see also Serials)

Cavendish D. Abercromby, *The Family of Abercromby* (1927)

David C. A. Agnew, *Protestant exiles from France in the reign of Louis XIV; or, The Huguenot refugees and their descendants in Great Britain and Ireland,* 3 vols. (1871-74)

Vivien Allen, *The Bulteels: The Story of a Huguenot Family* (2004)

Marie Antoinette d'Andigné, *Généalogie de la Maison d'Andigné* (1971)

Peter John Anderson, ed., *Fasti Academiae Mariscallanae* (1889)

Robert Charles Anderson, *The Great Migration Begins: Immigrants to New England 1620–1633,* 3 vols. (1995)

Robert Charles Anderson et al., *The Great Migration: Immigrants to New England 1634–1635,* 5 vols. to date (1999-)

Ruby Parke Anderson and Elizabeth Miller Hunter Ruppert, *The Parke Scrapbook...,* 3 vols. (1965-66)

Alfred Andrews, *Genealogical History of Deacon Stephen Hart and His Descendants, 1632–1875, with an introduction of miscellaneous Harts and their progenitors, as far as is known; to which is added a list of all the clergy of the name found, all the physicians, all the lawyers, the authors and soldiers* (1875)

William Sumner Appleton, *Memorials of the Cranes of Chilton: with a pedigree of the family and the life of the last representative* (1868)

Mervyn Archdall, *The Peerage of Ireland; or, a genealogical history of the present nobility of that kingdom with Engravings of their Paternal Coats of Arms. Collected from public records, authentic Manuscripts, approved Historians, well-attested Pedigrees, and Personal Information, by John Lodge,* 2nd ed. Revised, enlarged and continued to the Present Time, 7 vols. (1789)

R. A. Austen-Leigh, *The Eton College Register 1698–1752* (1927)

Philip Henry Dudley Bagenal, *Vicissitudes of an Irish Family 1530–1800: a story of Irish romance and tragedy* (1925)

W. Paley Baildon, *Baildon and the Baildons: A History of a Yorkshire Manor and Family,* 3 vols. (1912–26)

Edward Baines and W. R. Whatton, *History of the County Palatine and Duchy of Lancaster.* New, Revised and Enlarged [3rd] ed., 5 vols. (1888–93)

George Baker, *The History and Antiquities of the County of Northampton,* 2 vols. (1822-41)

Francis Elrington Ball, *The Judges in Ireland 1221–1921,* 2 vols. (1927)

Thomas George Baring, Earl of Northbrook, et al., eds., *Journals and correspondence from 1808 to 1852, of Sir Francis Thornhill Baring afterwards Lord Northbrook, compiled and edited by his son Thomas George, Earl of Northbrook* (1905)

G. F. Russell Barker and Alan H. Stenning, *The Record of Old Westminsters…,* 2 vols. (1928)

John Leeds Barroll, *Anna of Denmark, queen of England: a cultural biography* (2001)

Oswald Barron, ed., *Northamptonshire Families* (1906)

Peter C. Bartrum, *Welsh Genealogies AD 1400–1500,* 18 vols. (1983)

John Batten, *Historical and Topographical Collections Relating to the Early History of Parts of South Somerset* (1894)

Alfred Beaven, *The Aldermen of the City of London Temp. Henry III–1908 with Notes on the Parliamentary Representation of the City, the Aldermen and the Livery Companies, the Aldermanic Veto, Aldermanic Baronets and Knights, etc.,* 2 vols. (1908-13)

Edmund von der Becke-Klüchtzner, *Stamm-Tafeln des Adels Grossherzogthums des Baden: ein neu bearbeitetes Adelsbuch* (1886)

William Berry, *County Genealogies: Pedigrees of Berkshire Families* (1837)

William Berry, *County Genealogies: Pedigrees of the Families in the County of Hants, Collected from the Heraldic Visitations and Other Authentic Manuscripts in the British Museum and in the Possession of Private Individuals, and from Information of the Present Resident Families* (1833)

William Berry, *County Genealogies: Pedigrees of Hertfordshire Families* (1837)

William Berry, *County Genealogies: Pedigrees of the Families of the County of Kent, Collected from the Heraldic Visitations and Other Authentic Manuscripts in the British Museum, and in the Possession of Private Individuals, and from the Information of the Present Resident Families* (1830)

William Berry, *County Genealogies: Pedigrees of Surrey Families* (1837)

William Berry, *County Genealogies: Pedigrees of the Families in the County of Sussex: Collected from the Heraldic Visitations and Other Authentic Manuscripts in the British Museum, and in the Possession of Private Individuals, and from the Information of the Present Resident Families* (1830)

William Betham, *The Baronetage of England, or, the History of the English Baronets, and Such Baronets of Scotland, as Are of English Families: With Genealogical Tables, and Engravings of Their Armorial Bearings; Collected from the Present Baronetages, Approved Historians, Public Records, Authentic Manuscripts, Well Attested Pedigrees, and Personal Information,* 5 vols. (1801-5)

S. T. Bindoff, *The History of Parliament: the House of Commons 1509–1558,* 3 vols. (1982)

Caroline Bingham, *James VI of Scotland* (1979)

Francis Blomefield and Charles Parkin, *An Essay Towards a Topographical History of the County of Norfolk, a Description of the Towns, Villages, and Hamlets, with the Foundations of Monasteries, Churches, Chapels, Chantries, and Other Religious Buildings: Also an Account of the Ancient and Present State of All the Rectories, Vicarages, Donatives, and Impropriations, Their*

Former and Present Patrons and Incumbents, with Their Several Valuations in the King's Book, Whether Discharged or Not: Likewise an Historical Account of the Castles, Seats, and Manors, Their Present and Antient Owners, Together with the Most Remarkable Epitaphs, Inscriptions and Arms, in All the Parish Churches and Chapels; with Several Draughts of Churches, Monuments, Arms, Antient Ruins, and Other Relicts of Antiquity: Collected Out of Ledger-Books, Registers, Records, Evidences, Deeds, Court-Rolls, and Other Authentic Memorials, 2nd ed., 11 vols. (1805-10)

Thomas Blore, *The History and Antiquities of the County of Rutland: Compiled from the Works of the Most Approved Historians, National Records and Other Authentic Documents, Public and Private* (1811)

Louis Bobé, *Slaegten Ahlefeldts Historie,* 6 vols. (1897-1912)

W. M. Bollenbach, Jr., *The New England Ancestry of Alice Everett Johnson 1899–1986* (2003)

L. H. Bouwens and B. G. Bouwens, *A Thousand Ancestors* (1935)

Abel Boyer et al., eds., *Political State of Great Britain,* 60 vols. (1711-40)

E. M. Boyle, *Sixty-Four "Quartiers" of Major Gerald Edmund Boyle, and his brothers and sister* (1882)

Sir Joseph Alfred Bradney, *A History of Monmouthshire from the coming of the Normans into Wales down to the present time,* 5 vols. in 13 (1907-93)

James C. Brandow, *Genealogies of Barbados Families: from* Caribbeana *and* The Journal of the Barbados Museum and Historical Society (1983)

John Bridges, *The History and Antiquities of Northamptonshire,* 2 vols. (1791)

Henry Brierley, ed., *The Registers of Crosthwaite,* 2 vols. (1928-30)

Lindsay L. Brook, ed., *Studies in Genealogy and Family History in Tribute to Charles Evans on the Occasion of His Eightieth Birthday.* Association for the Promotion of Scholarship in Genealogy, Occasional Publication, No. 2 (1989)

G. F. Browne, *Echt-Forbes family charters 1345–1727, records of the Forest of Birse Notarial Signs 926–1786* (1923)

Arthur Bryant, *King Charles II* (1931)

Egerton Brydges, *Collins's Peerage of England, Genealogical, Biographical, and Historical, Greatly Augmented, and Continued to the Present Time,* 9 vols. (1812)

John Malcolm Bulloch, *House of Gordon,* 3 vols. (1903-12)

Arthur Meredyth Burke, *Memorials of St. Margaret's church, Westminster, comprising the parish registers, 1539–1660, and the churchwardens' accounts 1460-1603* (1914)

Ashworth P. Burke, *A Genealogical and Heraldic History of the Landed Gentry of Ireland* (1899)

Sir Bernard Burke, *A Genealogical and Heraldic Dictionary of the Peerage and Baronetage* (1879)

Sir Bernard Burke, *A Genealogical and Heraldic Dictionary of the Peerage and Baronetage* (1881)

Sir Bernard Burke, *A Genealogical History of the Dormant, Abeyant, Forfeited and Extinct Peerages of the British Empire* (1883)

Sir Bernard Burke, *Royal Descents and Pedigrees of Founders Kin* (1864)

Sir Bernard Burke and Ashworth Peter Burke, *A Genealogical and Heraldic Dictionary of the Peerage and Baronetage* (1913)

John Burke, *A Genealogical and Heraldic History of the Commoners of Great Britain and Ireland Enjoying Territorial Possessions or High Official Rank but uninvested with Heritable Honours,* 4 vols. (1836–37)

John Burke and John Bernard Burke, *A Genealogical and Heraldic Dictionary of the Landed Gentry of Great Britain and Ireland, a Companion to the Baronetage and Knightage.* With Supplement, Addenda, Corrigenda and Index, 3 vols. (1843–49)

John Burke and John Bernard Burke, *A Genealogical and Heraldic History of the Extinct and Dormant Baronetcies of England, Ireland, and Scotland,* 2nd ed. (1844)

BURKE. A. C. Fox-Davies, *A Genealogical and Heraldic History of the Landed Gentry of Ireland by Sir Bernard Burke* (1912)

BURKE. Hugh Montgomery-Massingberd, *Burke's Irish Family Records* (1976)

BURKE. Charles Mosley, ed., *Burke's Genealogical and Heraldic History of the Peerage and Baronetage,* 2 vols. (1999)

BURKE. Charles Mosley, ed., *Burke's Peerage Baronetage & Knightage, Clan Chiefs, Scottish Feudal Barons,* 3 vols. (2003)

BURKE. Leslie G. Pine, ed., *Burke's Genealogical and Heraldic History of the Landed Gentry including American Families with British Ancestry* (1939)

BURKE. Leslie G. Pine, ed., *Burke's Genealogical and Heraldic History of the Landed Gentry* (1952)

BURKE. Peter Townend et al., eds., *Burke's Genealogical and Heraldic History of the Landed Gentry,* 3 vols. (1965–72)

BURKE. Leslie G. Pine, *Burke's Genealogical and Heraldic History of the Landed Gentry of Ireland* (1958)

BURKE. Leslie G. Pine, *Burke's Genealogical and Heraldic History of the Peerage and Baronetage* (1953)

BURKE. Leslie G. Pine, ed., *Burke's Genealogical and Heraldic History of the Peerage, Baronetage and Knightage* (1956)

BURKE. Peter Townend, ed., *Burke's Genealogical and Heraldic History of the Peerage, Baronetage and Knightage* (1970)

BURNETT. *The Family of Burnett of Leys, with colateral branches: from the mss. of the late George Burnett* (1901)

George Dames Burtchaell and Thomas Ulick Sadleir, eds., *Alumni Dublinenses; a register of the students, graduates, professors and provosts of Trinity college in the University of Dublin (1593–1860)* (1935)

Alfred T. Butler, *A Genealogical and Heraldic Dictionary of the Peerage and Baronetage* (1926)

Cahiers de Saint-Louis, 29 parts (1979–2002)

Calendar of Patent Rolls, Preserved in the Public Record Office. Henry III. 6 vols. London: H.M.S.O., 1901–13. Edward I. 4 vols. London: H.M.S.O., 1893–1901. Edward II. 5 vols.

London: H.M.S.O., 1894–1904. Edward III. 16 vols. London: H.M.S.O., 1891–1916. Richard II. 7 vols. London: H.M.S.O., 1895–1976. Henry IV. 4 vols. London: H.M.S.O., 1903–9. Henry V. 2 vols. London: H.M.S.O., 1910–11. Henry VI. 6 vols. London: H.M.S.O., 1901–10. Edward IV: A.D. 1461–1467. London: H.M.S.O., 1897. Edward IV, Henry VI: A.D. 1467–1477. London: H.M.S.O., 1900. Edward IV, Edward V, Richard III: A.D. 1476–1485. London: H.M.S.O., 1901. Henry VII. 2 vols. London: H.M.S.O., 1914–16. Edward VI. 5 vols. and index. London: H.M.S.O., 1924–29. Philip and Mary. 4 vols. London: H.M.S.O., 1936–39. Elizabeth I. 9 vols. London: H.M.S.O., 1939–86.

Arthur Campling, *The History of the Family of Drury in the Counties of Suffolk and Norfolk from the Conquest: Compiled from Pedigrees in the Possession of F. S. E. Drury, Now Senior Respresentative of the Family, and Other Sources* (1937)

Charles Carlton, *Charles I: The Personal Monarch* (1983)

Jean le Carpentier, *Histoire généalogique des Païs-Bas, ou, Histoire de Cambray, et du Cambresis, contenant ce qui s'y est passé sous les empereurs, & les rois de France & d'Espagne; enrichie des genealogies, eloges, & armes des comtes, ducs, evesques, & archevesques, & presque de quatre mille familles nobles, tant des XVII. provinces que de France … Le tout divise en IV. Parties*, 2 vols. (1663-64)

Nigel Cawthorne, *Sex Lives of the Kings and Queens of England* (1994)

Charles E. H. Chadwyck-Healey, *The History of the Part of West Somerset Comprising the Parishes of Luccombe, Selworthy, Stoke, Pero, Porlock, Culbone and Oare* (1901)

Edwin Chappell, *Eight Generations of the Pepys Family 1500–1800* (1936)

Henry Chauncy, *The Historical Antiquities of Hertfordshire: With the Original of Counties, Hundreds or Wapentakes, Boroughs, Corporations, Towns, Parishes, Villages, and Hamlets; the Foundation and Origin of Monasteries, Churches, Advowsons, Tythes, Rectories, Impropriations and Vicarages, in General; Describing Those of This County in Particular: As Also the Several Honors, Mannors, Castles, Seats, and Parks of the Nobility and Gentry; and the Succession of the Lords of Each Mannor Therein: Also the Characters of the Abbots of St. Albans, Faithfully Collected from Public Records, Leiger Books, Ancient Manuscripts, Charters, Evidences, and Other Select Authorities, Together with an Exact Transcript of Domesday-Book, so far as Concerns This Shire, and the Translation Thereof in English, to which are Added the Epitaphs and Memorable Inscriptions, in All the Parishes, and Likewise the Blazon of the Coats of Arms of the Several Noblemen, and Gentlemen, Proprietors in the Same, Illustrated with a Large Map of the County; a Prospect of Hertford; the Ichnography of St. Albans and Hitchin; and many Sculptures of Principal Edifices and Monuments* (1826)

François-Alexandre Aubert de la Chesnaye-Desbois et Badier, *Dictionnaire de la Noblesse, contenant les généalogies, l'histoire & la chronologie des familles nobles de la France, l'explication de leurs armes et l'état des grandes Terres du Royaume, possédées à titre de Principautés, Duchés, Marquisats, Comtés, Vicomtés, Baronies, &c., par création héritages, alliances, donations, substitutions, mutations, achats ou autrement. On a joint à ce dictionnaire le tableau généalogique et historique des maisons souveraines de l'Europe et une notice des familles étrangères, les plus anciennes, les plus nobles et les plus illustres*, 19 vols., 3rd ed. (1863-76)

Sir Winston Spencer Churchill, *History of the English-Speaking Peoples* (1956-58; reprinted 1995)

Winston Spencer Churchill, *Marlborough, his Life and Times,* 7 vols. (1933-38)

John William Clay, ed., *Dugdale's Visitation of Yorkshire in 1665–6, with additions,* 3 vols. (1899-1917)

Robert Clutterbuck, *The History and Antiquities of the County of Hertford: Compiled from the Best Printed Authorities and Original Records, Preserved in Public Repositories and Private Collections: Embellished with Views of the Most Curious Monuments of Antiquity, and Illustrated with a Map of the County*, 3 vols. (1815-27)

George E. Cokayne, *The Complete Baronetage, 1611–1880*, 5 vols. (1900-6)

George E. Cokayne, *Some Account of the Lord Mayors and Sheriffs of the City of London during the first quarter of the seventeenth century 1601 to 1625* (1897)

George E. Cokayne et al., *The Complete Peerage*, 14 vols. in 15 (1910-98)

John Collinson, *The history and antiquities of the county of Somerset: collected from authentick records, and an actual survey made by the late Mr. Edmund Rack; adorned with a map of the county and engravings of Roman or other reliques, town-seals, baths, churches, and gentlemen's seats*, 3 vols. (1791)

John Comber, *Sussex Genealogies*, 3 vols. (1931-33)

Walter Arthur Copinger, *History of the Copingers or Coppingers of the County of Cork, Ireland, and the Counties of Suffolk and Kent, England* (1884)

Walter Arthur Copinger, *The Manors of Suffolk: Notes on Their History and Devolution, with Some Illustrations of the Old Manor Houses*, 7 vols. (1905-11)

Frederick Arthur Crisp, *Fragmenta Genealogica*, 14 vols. in 2 series (1897-1910)

Eveline Cruickshanks, Stuart Handley and David Hayton, *The History of Parliament: The House of Commons 1690–1715*, 5 vols. (2002)

Helen Van Uxem Cubberley, *Newbold Family Notes* (1937)

Louis M. Cullen, *The Irish Brandy Houses of Eighteenth-Century France* (2000)

Frank Cundall, *The Governors of Jamaica in the First Half of the Eighteenth Century* (1937)

Noel Currer-Briggs and Royston Gambier, *Huguenot Ancestry* (1985)

Mary Frances Cusack, *A History of the city and county of Cork* (1875)

John Edwin Cussans, *History of Hertfordshire, Containing an Account of the Descents of the Various Manors, Pedigrees of Families Connected with the County, Antiquities, Local Customs, &c., &c.: Chiefly Compiled from Original Mss., in the Record Office and British Museum, Parochial Registers, Local Archives and Collections in the Possession of Private Families*, 8 parts in 3 vols. (1870-81)

W. J. d'Ablaing van Giessenburg, *De Ridderschap van Veluwe of Geschiedenis der Veluwsche Jonkers: opgeluisterd door hunne acht stamdeelen, huwelijken, kinderen en wapens, hoofdzakelijk getrokken uit de verzameling van handschriften van wijlen den Rijks-Vrijheer W. A. van Spaen* (1859)

W. J. Baron d'Ablaing van Giessenburg, *Bannerheeren en Ridderschap van Zutphen: van den aanvang der beroerten in de 16e eeuw tot het jaar 1795* (1877)

G. Dashwood, *Pedigrees selected from the Visitation of the County of Warwick, begun by Thomas May, Chester, and Gregory King, Rouge Dragon, in Hillary Vacačon, 1682, etc., etc.* (1859)

George Henry Dashwood et al., eds., *The Visitation of Norfolk in the Year 1563, taken by William Harvey, Clarenceux King of Arms*, 2 vols. (1878-95)

M. G. Dauglish and P. G. Stephenson, eds., *Harrow School Register 1800–1911* (1911)

Walter Goodwin Davis, *Massachusetts and Maine Families in the Ancestry of Walter Goodwin Davis (1885–1966): A Reprinting in Alphabetical Order by Surname of the Sixteen Multi-Ancestor Compendia (plus* Thomas Haley of Winter Harbor and His Descendants*) compiled by Maine's Foremost Genealogist, 1916–1983,* 3 vols. (1996)

DEBRETT. Jean Goodman and David Williamson, *Debrett's Book of the Royal Engagement* (1986)

Adriaan Willem Eliza Dek, *Van Het Vorstenhuis Nassau* (1970)

F. von der Decken, *Das Leben Georg von Braunschweig* (1833-34)

George Ravenscroft Dennis, *The House of Cecil* (1914)

Franklin Bowditch Dexter, *Biographical Sketches of Graduates of Yale College: with annals of the college history,* 6 vols. (1885-1912)

The Dictionary of National Biography, founded in 1882 by George Smith, edited by Sir Leslie Stephen and Sir Sidney Lee, 2nd ed., 22 vols. (1885–1901; reprinted 1908-9)

Dictionary of Welsh Biography Down to 1940 (1959)

A. Dingwall-Fordyce, *Addenda to the Family Records of Dingwall-Fordyce* (1888)

Alexander Dingwall Fordyce, *Family Records of the Name of Dingwall Fordyce in Aberdeenshire* (1885)

John Frederick Dorman, *Adventurers of Purse and Person, Virginia, 1607–1624/5,* 4th ed., 3 vols. (2004-7)

Sir Robert Douglas, *The Baronage of Scotland: containing an historical and genealogical account of the gentry of that kingdom* (1798)

Zelinda Makepeace Douhan, ed., *The Ancestry of Russell Makepeace of Marion, Massachusetts 1904–1986: A Descendant of Thomas Makepeace of Dorchester, Massachusetts* (2005)

"Pedigree of Dowdall," Society of Genealogists MS pedigree X.A.12:441 (at the Society of Genealogists, London)

Henry Holman Drake, *Hasted's history of Kent: corrected, enlarged and continued to the present time, from the manuscript collections of the late Rev. Thomas Streatfield and the late Rev. Lambert Blackwell Larking, the public records, and other sources. pt. 1. The hundred of Blackheath* (1886)

P. Draper, *The House of Stanley* (1864)

Benjamin W. Dwight, *The History of the Descendants of Elder John Strong of Northampton, Mass.,* 2 vols. (1871)

DWNN. *Heraldic Visitations of Wales and Part of the Marches Between the Years 1586 and 1613 by Lewys Dwnn,* 2 vols. (1846)

J. P. Earwaker, *East Cheshire, Past and Present, or, a History of the Hundred of Macclesfield in the County Palatine of Chester—from Original Records,* 2 vols. (1877-80)

Johan Engelbert Elias, *De Vroederschap van Amsterdam 1578–1795; met een inleidend woord van den archivaris der stad Amsterdam W. R. Veder,* 2 vols. (1903-5; reprinted in 1963)

Lady Eliott-Drake, *The Family and Heirs of Sir Francis Drake,* 2 vols. (1911)

Dudley George Cary Elwes, *A history of the Castles and Mansions in Western Sussex* (1876)

F. G. Emmison, *Bedfordshire Parish Registers*, 43 vols. (1931–52)

Encyclopaedia Britannica, 32 vols. (1911)

Anton Fahne, *Geschichte der Westphälischen Geschlechter unter besonderer Berücksichtigung ihrer Uebersiedelung nach Preussen, Curland und Liefland. / Von A. Fahne von Roland. Mit fast 1200 Wappen und mehr als 1300 Familien* (1858)

Thomas Falconer, *The Family of Dalmahoy of Dalmahoy, Ratho, County Edinburgh* (1870)

Edmund Horace Fellowes, *The Family of Frederick* (1932)

"Fenns Manuscripts of Suffolk and Norfolk" (manuscripts in the Norman Collection, Salford, Lancashire)

T. Fitz-Roy Fenwick and Walter C. Metcalfe, eds., *The Visitation of the county of Gloucester begun by Thomas May, Chester, and Gregory King, Rouge Dragon, in Trinity Vacacon, 1682 and finished by Henry Dethick, Richmond, and the said Rouge Dragon, Pursuivant, in Trinity Vacacon, 1683, by virtue of several deputations from Sir Henry St. George, Clarenceux Kinge of Armes* (1884)

Charles James Feret, *Fulham Old and New being an exhaustive history of the ancient parish of Fulham*, 3 vols. (1900)

Mary Walton Ferris, *Dawes-Gates Ancestral Lines: A Memorial Volume Containing the American Ancestry of Rufus B. Dawes, Volume I; Dawes and Allied Families; A Memorial Volume Containing the Ancestry of Mary Beman (Gates) Dawes, Volume II, Gates and Allied Families*, 2 vols. (1931–43)

Abraham Ferwerda, *Adelyk en Aanzienelyk wapen-boek van de zeven provincien; waar by gevoegt zyn een groot aantal genealogien van voornaame Adelyke en Aanzienelyke familien, etc.*, 2 vols. in 3 (1760–81)

Ophelia Field, *Sarah Churchill, Duchess of Marlborough, The Queen's Favourite* (2003)

Sir Charles Harding Firth, ed., *The Life of William Cavendish, Duke of Newcastle, to which is added the true relation of my birth, breeding and life, by Margaret, Duchess of Newcastle* (1906)

Ernest Flagg, *Genealogical Notes on the Founding of New England: My Ancestors' Part in that Undertaking* (1926; reprinted 1973)

Henry Foley, *Records of the English Province of the Society of Jesus: historic facts illustrative of the labours and sufferings of its members in the sixteenth and seventeenth centuries*, 7 vols. in 8 (1877–83)

Cecil George Savile Foljambe, Earl of Liverpool, *Evelyn Pedigrees and Memoranda* (1893)

Henri Forneron, *Louise de Kéroualle, duchesse de Portsmouth, 1649–1734: society in the court of Charles II. Compiled from state papers preserved in the archives of the French foreign office, by H. Forneron. With portraits, facsimile letter, etc., and a preface by Mrs. G. M. Crawford* (1888)

Edward Foss, *The Judges of England with Sketches of Their Lives and Miscellaneous Notices Connected with the Courts at Westminster, from the Time of the Conquest*, 9 vols. (1848–64)

Joseph Foster, *Alumni Oxonienses: The members of the University of Oxford, 1715–1886: their parentage, birthplace, and year of birth, with a record of their degrees. Being the matriculation register of the University, alphabetically arranged, revised and annotated*, 4 vols. (1887–88)

Joseph Foster, *Alumni Oxonienses: The members of the University of Oxford, 1500–1714: their parentage, birthplace, and year of birth, with a record of their degrees. Being the matriculation register of the University, alphabetically arranged, revised and annotated*, 4 vols. (1891-92)

Joseph Foster, *London Marriage Licences, 1521–1869* (1887)

Joseph Foster, *Pedigrees Recorded at the Heralds' Visitations of the Counties of Cumberland and Westmorland made by Richard St. George, Norroy King of Arms in 1615, and by William Dugdale, Norroy King of Arms in 1666* (1891)

Joseph Foster, *Pedigrees Recorded at the Visitations of the county palatine of Durham* (1887)

Joseph Foster, *Pedigrees Recorded at the Heralds' Visitations of the county of Northumberland, made by Richard St. George, Norroy, king of arms in 1615, and by William Dugdale, Norroy, King of Arms in 1666* (1891)

Joseph Foster, *Peerage, baronetage, and knightage of the British empire* (1881)

Joseph Foster, *Peerage, baronetage, and knightage of the British empire for 1883*, 2 vols. (1883)

Joseph Foster, *The Visitation of Middlesex, began in the year 1663, by William Ryley, esq., Lancaster, and Henry Dethick, Rouge croix, marshalls and deputies to Sir Edward Bysshe, Clarencieux. As recorded in the College of arms* (1887)

Joseph Foster, *The Visitation of Yorkshire, made in the years 1584/5, by Robert Glover, Somerset herald; to which is added the subsequent visitation made in 1612, by Richard St. George, Norroy king of arms, with several additional pedigrees, including "The arms taken out of churches and houses at Yorkshire visitation, 1584/5," "Sir William Fayrfax' booke of arms," and other heraldic lists, with copious indices* (1875)

FOSTER. *Pedigrees of the county families of England, comp. by Joseph Foster and authenticated by the members of each family. The heraldic illustrations by J. Forbes-Nixon. Vol. 1– Lancashire* (1873)

FOSTER. *Pedigrees of the County Families of Yorkshire, comp. by Joseph Foster and authenticated by the members of each family*, 2 vols. (1874)

William Chauncey Fowler, *Memorials of the Chaunceys* (1858)

Alexander Fraser, 17th Lord Saltoun, *The Frasers of Philorth*, 3 vols. (1879)

Antonia Fraser, *Royal Charles* (1979)

Sir William Fraser, *The Book of Carlaverock: Memoirs of the Maxwells, Earls of Nithsdale, Lords Maxwell and Herries*, 2 vols. (1873)

Sir William Fraser, *The Douglas Book: Memoirs of the House of Douglas and Angus*, 4 vols. (1885)

Edwin Freshfield, *The register book of the parish of St. Christopher-le-Stocks, in the city of London*, 3 vols. (1882)

John Gage, *History of the Antiquities of Suffolk, Thingoe Hundred* (1838)

Friedrich Gaisberg-Schöckingen, *Das Könighaus und der Adel von Württemberg* (1908)

Alfred W. Gibbons, *Notes on the Visitation of Lincoln 1634* (1898)

Philip Gibbs, *The King's Favourite; the love story of Robert Carr and Lady Essex* (1909)

Reginald Morshead Glencross, ed., "Parish registers of Bodmin, Cornwall," 2 vols. in 4 (undated, unpaginated, at the Family History Library, Salt Lake City, Utah)

Stephen Glover, *The History and gazetteer of the county of Derby: drawn up from actual observation and from the best authorities: containing a variety of geological, mineralogical, commercial and statistical information,* 2 vols. in 3 (1831-33)

Gothaisches Genealogisches Taschenbuch der Gräflichen Häuser, 115 vols. (1826-1942)

Patrick Grant, Lord Strathspey, *A History of the Clan Grant* (1983)

Mary Anne Everett Green, *Elizabeth, electress palatine and queen of Bohemia* (1909)

John Edwards Griffith, *Pedigrees of Anglesey and Carnarvonshire families* (1914)

Charles John Guthrie, *Genealogy of the descendants of Reverend Thomas Guthrie, D. D., and Mrs. Anne Burns or Guthrie: connected chiefly with the families of Chalmers and Trail, to which Mrs. Guthrie belonged through her mother, Mrs. Christina Chalmers or Burns, and her great-grandmother, Mrs. Susannah Trail or Chalmers; also incidental references to the families of Guthrie and Burns* (1902)

A. W. Cornelius Hallen, *The Registers of St. Botolph, Bishopsgate, London,* 3 vols. (1889-93)

Robert Halstead (Henry Mordaunt, Earl of Peterborough), *Succinct Genealogies of the Noble and Ancient Houses of Mordaunt of Turvey* (1685)

George Hamilton, *A History of the House of Hamilton* (1933)

Charles P. Hampson, *The Book of the Radclyffes: being an account of the main descents of this illustrious family from its origin to the present day, compiled from a variety of sources, including public records and private evidences* (1940)

Hanmer Parish Registers 1563–1899, 8 vols. in 10 parts (1992-2000)

Calvert Hanmer, *The Hanmers of Marton and Montford, Salop* (1916)

William Harrison, Thomas Harrison, and George Willis, *The great Jennens case: being an epitome of the history of the Jennens family* (1879)

P. W. Hasler, *The History of Parliament: The House of Commons 1558–1603,* 3 vols. (1981)

Edward Hasted, *The History and Topographical Survey of the County of Kent,* 12 vols. (1797-1801)

Jock Haswell, *James II: soldier and sailor* (1972)

Ragnhild Marie Hatton, *George I, elector and king* (1978)

Evelyn Dawsonne Heathcote, *An Account of some of the families bearing the name of Heathcote* (1899)

Percy W. Hedley, *Northumberland Families,* 2 vols. (1968)

B. D. Henning, *The History of Parliament: The House of Commons 1660–1690,* 3 vols. (1983)

Augustus George Hibbard, *Genealogy of the Hibbard Family Who are Descendants of Robert Hibbard of Salem, Massachusetts* (1901)

Christopher Hibbert, *Charles I* (1968)

Sir Richard Colt Hoare, Bt., *The History of Modern Wiltshire,* 14 parts in 6 vols. (1822-44)

O. F. G. Hogg, *Further Light on the Ancestry of William Penn* (1964)

G. H. Holley, "Pedigrees compiled from the parish registers, wills, monumental inscriptions, court records, etc., Norfolk County England" (a 7 vol. manuscript at the Family History Library, Salt Lake City, Utah)

Martin E. Hollick, *New Englanders in the 1600s: A Guide to Genealogical Research Published Between 1980 and 2005* (2006)

Mary Lovering Holman and Winifred Lovering Holman, *Ancestry of Colonel John Harrington Stevens and his wife, Frances Helen Miller: compiled for Helen Pendleton (Winston) Pillsbury*, 2 vols. (1948-52)

Rev. Edward Payson Holton and Harriet Scofield, *A Genealogy of the Descendants in America of William Holton (1610–1691) of Hartford, Conn., and Northampton, Mass.*, 2nd ed. (1965)

Joseph Jackson Howard, ed., *The Visitation of the County of Essex, Begun A.D. MDCLXIIII, Finished A.D. MDCLXVIII by Sir Edward Bysshe, Knt., Clarenceux King of Arms* (1888)

Joseph Jackson Howard, ed., *The Visitation of Suffolke, Made by William Hervey, Clarenceaux King of Arms, 1561: With Additions from Family Documents, Original Wills, Jermyn, Davy, and Other Mss., &c.*, 2 vols. (1866-71)

Joseph Jackson Howard et al., eds., *Visitation of England and Wales*, 21 vols. (1893-1921)

Joseph Jackson Howard and Frederick Arthur Crisp, *Visitation of England and Wales, Notes*, 14 vols. (1896-1921)

A. W. Hughes Clarke, ed., *London Pedigrees and Coats of Arms, reprinted from* Miscellanea Genealogica et Heraldica (1935)

John Hutchins, *The History and Antiquities of the County of Dorset: Compiled from the Best and Most Ancient Historians, Inquisitions Post Mortem, and Other Valuable Records and Mss. in the Public Offices and Libraries, and in Private Hands. With a Copy of Domesday Book and the Inquisitio Gheldi for the County: Interspersed with Some Remarkable Particulars of Natural History; and Adorned with a Correct Map of the County, and Views of Antiquities, Seats of the Nobility and Gentry, &c.*, 3rd ed., corrected, augmented and improved, 4 vols. (1861-70)

John Hutchinson, *A Catalogue of Notable Middle Templars: with brief biographical notices* (1902)

C. J. Davison Ingledew, *The History and Antiquities of North Allerton, in the County of York* (1858)

Donald Lines Jacobus and Edgar Francis Waterman, *The Granberry Family and allied families: including the ancestry of Helen (Woodward) Granberry* (1945)

Donald Lines Jacobus and Edgar Francis Waterman, *Hale, House and related families: mainly of the Connecticut River Valley* (1952)

E. O. Jameson, *The Cogswells in America* (1884)

Llewellynn Frederick William Jewitt, ed., *The Reliquary and illustrated archæologist*, 34 vols. in 2 series (1860-94)

Edith Mary Johnston-Liik, *History of the Irish Parliament 1692–1800: commons, constituencies and statutes*, 6 vols. (2002)

Gisela Jongbloet-van Hoette, *Brieven en Andere Bescheiden Betreffende Daniel van der Meulen 1584–1600* (1986)

J. R. van Keppel, *Genealogische tabellen van het geslacht van Keppel* (1912)

R. Wyndham Ketton-Cremer, *Felbrigg, the Story of a House* (1962)

Eduard Georg Ludwig William Howe Graf von Kielmansegg and Erich Friedrich Christian Ludwig Graf von Kielmansegg, *Familien-Chronik der Herren Freiherren und Grafen von Kielmansegg* (1872)

P. W. Klein, *De Trippen in de 17e Eeuw; een studie over het ondernemersgedrag op de Hollandse stapelmarkt* (1965)

Kwartierstatenboek: verzameling kwartierstaten bijeengebracht ter gelegenheid van de herdenking van het 100–jarig bestaan van het Koninklijk Nederlandsch Genootschap voor Geslacht-en Wapenkunde, 1883–1983 (1983)

Robert Lacey, *Robert, Earl of Essex: an Elizabethan Icarus* (1971)

Gabriel Girod de l'Ain, *Les Thellusson histoire d'une famille* (1977)

Charles E. Lart, *Huguenot Pedigrees,* 2 vols. (1924-25)

Sir Thomas Selby Lawson-Tancred, *Records of a Yorkshire Manor* (1937)

Frederick George Lee, *The History, Description and Antiquities of the Prebendal Church of the Blessed Virgin Mary of Thame in the County and Diocese of Oxford, including a transcript of all the monumental inscriptions remaining therein: extracts from the registers and churchwardens' books, together with divers original pedigrees, copious antiquarian, architectural, personal and genealogical notes and appendices, relating to, and illustrative of, the town, its history, and inhabitants, in which is included some account of the Abbey of Thame Park, the grammar school, and the ancient chapelries of Towersey, Tettesworth, Sydenham, North Weston, and Rycott* (1883)

Leonard Lee and Sarah Fiske Lee, *John Lee of Farmington, Hartford co., Connecticut and His Descendants, 1634–1897: containing over 4,000 names, with much miscellaneous history of the family, brief notes of other Lee families of New England, biographical notices, valuable data collected by William Wallace Lee, military records, to which is added a "roll of honor" of two hundred who have served in the various wars of the country* (1897)

Thomas Barrett Lennard, *An account of the families of Lennard and Barrett, compiled largely from original documents* (1908)

Colm Lennon, *The Lords of Dublin in the Age of Reformation* (1989)

J. Forbes Leslie, *The Irvines of Drum and collateral branches* (1909)

Duc de Lévis Mirepoix de l'Académie Française, *Henri IV Roi de France et de Navarre* (1971)

George Lipscomb, *The History and Antiquities of the County of Buckingham,* 4 vols. (1847)

Edwin Brockholst Livingston, *The Livingstons of Callendar, and their principal cadets: the history of an old Stirlingshire family* (1920)

Jacob Youde William Lloyd, *The History of the Princes, the Lords Marcher and the Ancient Nobility of Powys Fadog and the Ancient Lords of Arwystli, Cedewen and Meirionydd,* 6 vols. (1881-87)

William Valentine Lloyd, *The Sheriffs of Montgomeryshire: with their armorial bearings, and notices, genealogical & biographical, of their families from 1540 to 1639* (1876)

Amy Audrey Locke, *The Seymour family, history and romance* (1911)

Simon F. Macdonald Lockhart, *Seven Centuries: A History of the Lockharts of Lee and Carnwath* (1978)

Herbert Lüthy, *La banque protestante en France, de la révocation de l'Édit de Nantes à la Révolution* (1959)

Walter MacFarlane, *Genealogical collections concerning families in Scotland, made by W. Macfarlane, 1750–1751. Edited from the original manuscripts in the Advocates' Library, by James Toshach Clark, keeper of the library*, 2 vols. (1900)

John Maclean, *Historical and Genealogical Memoir of the Family of Poyntz, or, Eight Centuries of an English House* (1886)

William Dunn Macray, *The history of the rebellion and civil wars in England begun in the year 1641: by Edward, Earl of Clarendon; re-edited from a fresh collation of the original ms. in the Bodleian Library with marginal dates and occasional notes by W. Dunn Macray*, 6 vols. (1992)

Arthur Malet, *Notices of an English branch of the Malet family* (1885)

Owen Manning and William Bray, *The History and Antiquities of the County of Surrey: Compiled from the Best and Most Authentic Historians, Valuable Records, and Manuscripts in the Public Offices and Libraries, and in Private Hands; with a Facsimile Copy of Domesday, Engraved on Thirteen Plates*, 3 vols. (1804–14)

Joyce Marlow, *The Life and Times of George I* (1973)

Charles Wykeham Martin, *The History and Description of Leeds Castle, Kent* (1869)

Margaret Ethel Kington Blair Oliphant Maxtone-Graham, *The Maxtones of Cultoquhey* (1935)

S. W. McArthur, *McArthur-Barnes Ancestral Lines* (1964)

Walter C. Metcalfe, ed., *The Visitations of Northamptonshire Made in 1564 and 1618–9: With Northamptonshire Pedigrees from Various Harleian Mss.* (1887)

Walter C. Metcalfe, ed., *The Visitations of Suffolk made by Hervey, Clarenceux, 1561, Cooke, Clarenceux, 1577 and Raven, Richmond Herald, 1612 with notes and an appendix of Additional Suffolk Pedigrees* (1882)

Amos C. Miller, *Sir Henry Killigrew, Elizabethan soldier and diplomat* (1963)

Percy Millican, *A History of Horstead and Stanninghall, Norfolk* (1937)

Walther Möller, *Stammtafeln westdeutscher Adels-Geschlechter im Mittelalter*, 5 vols. in 2 series (1922-51)

Philip Morant, *The History and Antiquities of the County of Essex: Compiled from the Best and Most Ancient Historians: from Domesday-Book, Inquisitiones Post Mortem and Other the Most Valuable Records and Mss. &c, the Whole Digested, Improved, Perfected and Brought Down to the Present Time*, 2 vols. (1768)

George Morris, *Shropshire Genealogies: Shewing the Descent of the principal landed proprietors of the County of Salop from the time of William the Conqueror to the present time; compiled from Heraldic Visitations, public records, chartularies, family documents, parish registers and other sources*, 8 vols. (ca. 1836)

Andrew Morton, *Diana: Her True Story* (1998)

Alexander MacDonald Munro, *Memorials of the Aldermen, Provosts and Lord Provosts of Aberdeen 1272–1895* (1897)

Joseph James Muskett, *Suffolk Manorial Families: Being the County Visitations and Other Pedigrees*, 3 vols. (1900-8)

Joseph Nadaud, *Nobiliaire du diocèse et de la généralité de Limoges*, 4 vols. (1878-82)

Sir Lewis Namier and John Brooke, *The History of Parliament: The House of Commons 1754–1790*, 3 vols. (1964; reprinted 1985)

P. R. Newman, *Royalist Officers in England and Wales, 1642–1660* (1981)

John Nichols, *The History and Antiquities of the County of Leicestershire: Compiled from the Best and Most Ancient Historians; Inquisitions Post Mortem, and Other Valuable Records; Including Also Mr. Burton's Description of the County, Published in 1622; and the Later Collections of Mr. Stavely, Mr. Carte, Mr. Peck, and Sir Thomas Cave*, 4 vols. in 8 (1795-1815)

Joseph Nicolson and Richard Burn, *The History and Antiquities of the Counties of Westmorland and Cumberland*, 2 vols. (1777)

Northumberland County History Commission, *A history of Northumberland*, 15 vols. (1893-1940)

Obituaries from The Times *1971–1975* (1976)

Henry A. Ogle, *Ogle and Bothal: Or, A History of the Baronies of Ogle, Bothal, and Hepple, and of the Families of Ogle and Bertram, Who Held Possession of Those Baronies and Other Property in the County of Northumberland and Elsewhere; Showing Also How the Property Descended into Other Hands: To Which Is Added Accounts of Several Branches of Families Bearing the Name of Ogle Settled in Other Counties and Countries; with Appendices and Illustrations Compiled from Ancient Records and Other Sources* (1902)

George Ormerod, *The History of the County Palatine and City of Chester: Compiled from Original Evidences in Public Offices, the Harleian and Cottonian Mss., Parochial Registers, Private Muniments, Unpublished Mss., Collections of Successive Cheshire Antiquaries, and a Personal Survey of Every Township in the County, Incorporated with a Republication of King's Vale Royal and Leycester's Cheshire Antiquities. Also known as: The King's Vale Royal, The Vale Royall of England and Cheshire Antiquities*, 2nd ed. Revised and enlarged by Thomas Helsby, 3 vols. in 6 (1882)

Roger Owen, *Lord Cromer: Victorian Imperialist, Edwardian Proconsul* (2004)

Oxford Dictionary of National Biography, 60 vols. (2004)

Gerald Paget, *The Lineage and Ancestry of H. R. H. Prince Charles, Prince of Wales*, 2 vols. (1977)

Sir Edward Abbott Parry, *The Overbury Mystery; a chronicle of fact and drama of the law* (1925)

Sir James Balfour Paul, *The Scots Peerage*, 9 vols. (1904-14)

James Paterson, *History of the County of Ayr with a Genealogical Account of the families of Ayrshire*, 2 vols. (1847-52)

William Brown Patterson, *King James VI and I and the reunion of Christendom* (1997)

James Bertrand Payne, *Armorials of Jersey: being an account, heraldic and antiquarian, of its chief native families, with pedigrees, biographical notices, and illustrative data; to which are added a brief history of heraldry, and remarks on the mediaeval antiquities of the island* (1860)

W. P. W. Phillimore et al., eds., *Cambridgeshire Parish Registers*, 8 vols. (1907-27)

W. P. W. Phillimore and Ll. Ll. Simpson, eds., *Derbyshire Parish Registers*, 15 vols. (1906-22)

W. P. W. Phillimore et al., eds., *Hampshire Parish Registers*, 16 vols. (1899-1914)

W. P. W. Phillimore and G. E. Cokayne, *London Parish registers, Marriages at St. James' Duke's Place*, 4 vols. (1900-2)

W. P. W. Phillimore et al., eds., *Nottingham Parish Registers*, 22 vols. (1898-1938)

W. P. W. Phillimore and W. F. Carter, *Some Account of the Family of Middlemore, of Warwickshire and Worcestershire* (1901)

Charles Edward Pitman, *History and pedigree of the family of Pitman of Dunchideock, Exeter, and their collaterals, and of the Pitmans of Alphington, Norfolk and Edinburgh: with part pedigrees and acccounts of families connected by marriage* (1920)

Charles Platt, Jr., *Newbold Genealogy in America: The Line of Michael Newbold, who arrived in Burlington County, New Jersey, about 1680, and Other Newbold Lines, including that of Thomas Newbold, who arrived in Somerset County, Maryland about 1665* (1964)

Major-General Sir John Ponsonby, *The Ponsonby Family* (1929)

Public Record Office, comp., *Return of Members of Parliament, Part 1, Parliaments of England, 1213–1702* (1878-91; reprinted 1989)

James Raine, *The History and Antiquities of North Durham, as Subdivided into the Shires of Norham, Island and Bedlington, which from the Saxon Period until the Year 1844, Constituted Parcels of the County Palatine of Durham, but Are Now United to the County of Northumberland* (1852)

James Ralfe, *The naval biography of Great Britain: consisting of historical memoirs of those officers of the British Navy who distinguished themselves during the reign of His Majesty George III*, 4 vols. (1828)

Records and Files of the Quarterly Courts of Essex County, Massachusetts, 9 vols. (1911-21)

Douglas Richardson, *Plantagenet Ancestry: A Study in Medieval and Colonial Families* (2004)

Max Riddington and Gavan Naden, *Frances: The Remarkable Story of Princess Diana's Mother* (2004)

Caroline Robbins, *The diary of John Milward, esq., member of Parliament for Derbyshire, September 1666 to May 1668* (1938)

Gary Boyd Roberts, *Ancestors of American Presidents, First Authoritative Edition … with charts drawn by Julie Helen Otto* (1995)

Gary Boyd Roberts, *Notable Kin: An Anthology of Columns First Published in the* NEHGS NEXUS, *1986–1995, Volume One … with contributions by David Curtis Dearborn, Julie Helen Otto, Michael J. Wood, and David Allen Lambert* (1998)

Gary Boyd Roberts, *Notable Kin: An Anthology of Columns First Published in the* NEHGS NEXUS, *1986–1995, Volume Two … with contributions by John Anderson Brayton and Richard E. Brenneman* (1999)

Gary Boyd Roberts, *The Royal Descents of 600 Immigrants to the American Colonies or the United States: Who Were Themselves Notable or Left Descendants Notable in American History* (2004; revised and reissued 2006)

Gary Boyd Roberts and William Addams Reitwiesner, *American Ancestors and Cousins of The Princess of Wales* (1984)

George Robertson, *Topographical Description of Ayrshire: more particularly of Cunningham, together with a genealogical account of the principal families in that Bailiwick* (1820)

John Horace Round, *Family Origins* (1930)

Margery M. Rowe, *Exeter Freemen 1266–1967* (1973)

A.L. Rowse, *The Churchills, The Story of a Family* (1956)

Melville Amadeus Henry Douglas, 9th Marquis of Ruvigny and Raineval, *The Plantagenet roll of the blood royal: being a complete table of all the descendants now living of Edward III, king of England: the Mortimer-Percy volume, containing the descendants of Lady Elizabeth Percy, née Mortimer, with supplements to the Exeter and Essex volumes* (1911)

"St. Germans Parish Register, 1590-1837," 2 vols. (1938-39; unpaginated manuscript at the Devon and Cornwall Record Society, Exeter)

Moya Frenz St. Leger, *St. Leger: The Family and the Race* (1986)

Anselm de Saint-Marie and M. du Fourny, *Histoire de la Maison Royale de France Anciens Barons du Royaume: et des Grands Officiers de la Couronne*, 3rd ed., 9 vols. (1726-33)

Joanne McRee Sanders, *Barbados records: baptisms, 1643–1800* (1984)

Joanne McRee Sanders, *Barbados Records: Marriages 1643–1800*, 2 vols. (1982)

Joanne McRee Sanders, *Barbados records: wills and administrations*, 3 vols. (1979-81)

Detlev Schwennicke, ed., *Europäische Stammtafeln: Stammtafeln zur Geschichte der Europäischen Staaten*, Neue Folge, 21 vols. (1978-2001)

Lord George Scott, *Lucy Walter, Wife or Mistress* (1947)

Keith Stanley Malcolm Scott, *Scott 1118–1923: being a collection of "Scott" pedigrees containing all known male descendants from Buccleuch, Sinton, Harden, Balweary, etc.* (1923)

Romney Sedgwick, *The History of Parliament: The House of Commons 1715–1754*, 2 vols. (1971)

Stebbing Shaw, *The History and Antiquities of Staffordshire: Compiled from the Manuscripts of Huntback, Loxdale, Bishop Lyttleton, and Other Collections of Dr. Wilkes*, 2 vols. (1798–1801)

William A. Shaw, *The Knights of England*, 2 vols. (1906)

W. H. Shawcross alias Shallcross, *Shallcross Pedigrees* (1908)

John Langdon Sibley et al., *Biographical Sketches of Graduates of Harvard University in Cambridge, Massachusetts*, 18 vols. to date (1873-)

Llewellyn Lloyd Simpson, *The parish registers of S. James' Church, Norton, Co. Derby, 1559–1812* (1908)

George Slocombe, *The White Plumed Henry King of France* (1931)

Arthur M. Smith, *Some Account of the Smiths of Exeter and their descendants* (1896)

Ethel Farrington Smith, *Adam Hawkes of Saugus, Massachusetts 1605–1672: The First Six Generations in America* (1980)

John Smyth, *The Berkeley Manuscripts: The Lives of the Berkeleys, Lords of the Honour, Castle and Manor of Berkeley, in the County of Gloucester, from 1066 to 1618, with a Description of the Hundred of Berkeley and of Its Inhabitants*, 3 vols. (1883–85)

Burton W. Spear, *Search for the Passengers of the Mary & John, 1630*, 27 vols. (1985-99)

Charles Spencer, Earl Spencer, *The Spencer Family: A Personal History of an English Family* (2003)

David Starkey, *Rivals in Power* (1990)

Frank Farnsworth Starr, *Various Ancestral Lines of James Goodwin & Lucy (Morgan) Goodwin of Hartford, Connecticut*, 2 vols. (1915)

Thomas R. Steadman and Norma Slater Woodward, *Descendants of Richard, Nathaniel, Robert, and Henry Woodward of New England, 1589–1996*, Revised Edition (1996)

George Steinman Steinman, *A history of Croydon* (1834)

Michael Stenton, *Who's Who of British Members of Parliament, Volume 1: 1832–1885* (1976)

Lytton Strachey, *Elizabeth and Essex* (1928)

Edith Bartlett Sumner, *Descendants of Thomas Farr of Harpswell, Maine, and ninety allied families* (1959)

Robert Surtees, *The History and Antiquities of the County Palatine of Durham: Compiled from Original Records, Preserved in Public Repositories and Private Collections, and Illustrated by Engravings of Architectural and Monumental Antiquities, Portraits of Eminent Persons &c., &c.*, 4 vols. (1816-40)

Nicola Mary Sutherland, *Henry IV of France and the Politics of Religion 1572–1596* (2002)

George F. Sydenham, *The History of the Sydenham Family: Collected from Family Documents, Pedigrees, Deeds, and Copious Memoranda* (1928)

W. S. Sykes, "Notes on Wilcot and Families" (a manuscript at the Wiltshire Archaeological Society, Devizes)

Marguerite Syvret and Joan Stevens, *Balleine's History of Jersey* (1981)

Karl Taaffe, *Memoirs of the Family of Taaffe* (1856)

Harry Tapley-Soper, *The register of Ottery-St. Mary, Devon, 1601–1837*, 2 parts (1908-29)

A. Alistair N. Tayler and H. A. Henrietta Tayler, *The valuation of the county of Aberdeen for the year 1667* (1933)

A. Alistair N. Tayler and H. A. Henrietta Tayler, *The Book of the Duffs*, 2 vols. (1914)

A. Alistair N. Tayler and H. A. Henrietta Tayler, *The House of Forbes* (1937)

H. A. Henrietta Tayler, *History of the Family of Urquhart* (1946)

Peter Alfred Taylor, *Some Account of the Taylor Family (originally Taylard)*, 2 vols. (1875)

John Alexander Temple and Harald Markham Temple, *The Temple Memoirs: an account of this historic family and its demesnes; with biographical sketches, anecdotes & legends from Saxon times to the present day* (1925)

William Temple, *The Thanage of Fermartyn including the district commonly called Formartine, its proprietors: with genealogical deductions, its parishes, ministers, churches, churchyards, antiquities, &c* (1894)

Ralph Thoresby, *Ducatus Leodiensis: or, the Topography of the Ancient and Populous Town and Parish of Leedes, and Parts Adjacent, in the West-Riding of the County of York, with the Pedigrees of Many of the Nobility and Gentry, and Other Matters Relating to those Parts; Extracted from Records, Original Evidence, and Manuscripts,* 2nd ed., With notes and additions by Thomas Dunham Whitaker (1816)

R. G. Thorne, *The History of Parliament: The House of Commons 1790–1820,* 5 vols. (1986)

Robert Thoroton, *Thoroton's History of Nottinghamshire: Republished, with Large Additions, by John Throsby, and Embellished with Picturesque and Select Views of Seats of the Nobility and Gentry, Towns, Village Churches and Ruins,* 3 vols. (1790)

Raleigh Trevelyan, *Sir Walter Raleigh* (2002)

Meriol Trevor, *The shadow of a crown: the life story of James II of England and VII of Scotland* (1988)

Hugh Rewald Trevor-Roper, *The Trial and Execution of Charles I* (1966)

Sir Algernon Tudor Tudor-Craig, *The romance of Melusine and de Lusignan: together with genealogical notes and pedigrees of Lovekyn of London, Lovekyn of Lovekynsmede, and of Luckyn of Little Waltham, and Lukyn of Mashbery, all in the county of Essex, and of Lukin of Felbrigg, co. Norfolk* (1932)

Simon van Leeuwen, *Batavia illustrate* (1685)

John Venn and John Archibald Venn, *Alumni Cantabrigienses; A biographical list of all known students, graduates and holders of office at the University of Cambridge, from the earliest times to 1900,* 10 vols. (1922-54)

Sir Arthur Vicars, *Index to Prerogative Wills of Ireland 1536–1810* (1897)

Vital Records of Norwich 1659–1848, 2 vols. (1913)

J. L. Vivian, *The visitations of Cornwall, comprising the Heralds' visitations of 1530, 1573, & 1620* (1887)

J. L. Vivian, *The visitations of the county of Devon, comprising the heralds' visitations of 1531, 1564, & 1620* (1895)

Pieter Dignus de Vos, *De Vroedschap van Zierikzee: van de tweede helft der 16de eeuw tot 1795* (1931)

Joan Wake, *The Brudenells of Deene* (1953)

The Yale Edition of Horace Walpole's Correspondence, 48 vols. (1937-83)

Charles Humble Dudley Ward, *The family of Twysden and Twisden; their history and archives from an original by Sir John Ramskill Twisden, 12th baronet of Bradbourne* (1939)

Duncan Warrand, *Hertfordshire Families* (1907)

Henry Fitz-Gilbert Waters, *Genealogical Gleanings in England: Abstracts of Wills Relating to Early American Families, with Genealogical Notes and Pedigrees Constructed from the Wills and from Other Records,* 2 vols. (1885-1901)

Robert Edmond Chester Waters, *Genealogical Memoirs of the Extinct Family of Chester of Chicheley: their Ancestors and Descendants,* 2 vols. (1878)

Vernon James Watney, *The Wallop Family and Their Ancestry,* 4 vols. (1928)

Frederic William Weaver, ed., *The Visitations of the County of Somerset in the Years 1531 and 1573, together with Additional Pedigrees, Chiefly from the Visitation of 1591* (1885)

Alison Weir, *Britain's Royal Families: The Complete Genealogy* (1989)

Jeremiah Holmes Wiffen, *Historical memoirs of the house of Russell: from the time of the Norman Conquest,* 2 vols. (1833)

Who was Who 1951–60 (1961)

Anthony A. Wood, *Oxfordshire Monumental Inscriptions* (1825)

John Roger Woodhead, *The rulers of London 1660–1689: a biographical record of the aldermen and common councilmen of the City of London* (1965)

Margaret D. Young, *The Parliaments of Scotland: burgh and shire commissioners,* 2 vols. (1992-93)

Serials

(see also Books and Manuscripts)

Ahnentafeln berühmter Deutscher, 23 vols. in 6 series (1929-44)
    Volume 9 (1929), Ernst Freiherr von Obernitz, "256stellige Ahnentafel des Dichters August von Platen-Hallermund 1796-1835"

Antiquities of Sunderland and its vicinity, 24 vols. (1902-69)
    Volume 22 (1960), H. L. Robson, "George Lilburne, Mayor of Sunderland"

Archæologia Æliana, or, Miscellaneous Tracts Relating to Antiquity, 130 vols. to date in 5 series (1822-)
    New Series, 5 (1861), James A. Raine, "Marske"
    3rd series, 18 (1921), Alan Fenwick Radcliffe, "Notes on the Fenwicks of Radcliffe"
    3rd series, 18 (1921), J. E. Hodgson, "Notes on the Manor and Tower of Bitchfield"

Archæologia Cambrensis: A Record of the Antiquities of Wales and Its Marches, and the Journal of the Cambrian Archæological Association, 152 vols. to date in seven series (1846-)

Archæologia Cantiana: Being Transactions of the Kent Archæological Society, 121 vols. to date (1858-)
    Volume 11 (1877), Rev. Edward Hawkins, "Notes on Some Monuments in Rochester Cathedral"
    Volume 20 (1893), John J. Stocker, "Pedigree of Smythe of Ostenhanger, Kent; of Smythe of Bidborough and Sutton-at-Hone, Kent; and of the Smythes, Viscounts of Strangford, of Dromore, Ireland"
    Volume 53 (1940), C. R. Councer, "Heraldic Notices of the Church of St. Martin, Herne"

Association for the Promotion of Scholarship in Genealogy, Ltd., Occasional Publication No. 2, Lindsay L. Brook, ed., *Studies in Genealogy & Family History in Tribute to Charles Evans on the Occasion of his Eightieth Birthday* (1989)
    George E. McCracken, "The Vassalls of London & Jamaica"

Transactions of the Bristol and Gloucestershire Archeological Society, 121 vols. to date (1876-)
Volume 76 (1958), J. N. Langston, "The Pastons of Horton"

British Record Society, 119 vols. to date (1888-); see also *The Index Library*
Volumes 15, 26, and 36 (1896-1908), George S. Fry, Sidney J. Madge and Edw. Alex. Fry, eds., *Abstracts of Inquisitiones Post Mortem Relating to the City of London*

Buckinghamshire Record Society, 27 vols. (1937-91)

Cambridge Antiquarian Society Publications, 57 vols. in 2 series (1840-1942)

Camden Society Series, 315 vols. in 5 series to date (1838-)
Volume 43 (1849), Sir Henry Ellis, ed., *The Visitation of the County of Huntingdon under the authority of William Camden, Clarenceux King of Arms by his deputy Nicholas Charles, Lancaster Herald A.D. 1613*
Volume 44 (1849), Sir Henry Ellis, *Obituary of Richard Smyth, secondary of the Poultry Compter, London: being a catalogue of all such persons as he knew in their life: Extending from A.D. 1627 to A.D. 1674*
Volume 56 (1853), John Bruce, ed., *Letters and papers of the Verney family down to the end of the year 1639*
Volume 85 (1863), Robert Davies, ed., *The Life of Marmaduke Rawdon of York*

Chetham Society Series: Remains, Historical and Literary, Connected with the Palatine Counties of Lancaster and Chester, 268 vols. to date in 3 series (1844-)
Volume 81 (1870), F. R. Raines, ed., *The Visitation of the County Palatine of Lancaster, Made in the Year 1567, by William Flower, Esq., Norroy King of Arms*
Volume 82 (1871), F. R. Raines, ed., *The Visitation of the County Palatine of Lancaster made in the year 1613, by Richard St. George, Esq., Norroy King of Arms*
Volumes 84-85 and 88 (1872-73), *The Visitation of the County Palatine of Lancaster, Made in the Year 1664-5, by Sir William Dugdale, Knight, Norroy King of Arms*

Journal of the Cork Historical & Archaeological Society, 95 vols. (1892-1990)
2nd series, volume 30 (1925), George Berkeley, "History of the Lavallins"

Danmarks Adels Aarbog, 97 vols. to date (1884-)

Journal of the Derbyshire Archæological and Natural History Society, 124 vols. to date (1879-)
Volume 6 (1884), "Pedigree of the heirs of Sir Ralph Longford, of Longford, co. Derby"

Deutsches Geschlechterbuch (Genealogisches Handbuch Bürgerlicher Familien), 218 vols. to date (1888-)
Volume 102 (1938), "Baring, v. Baring, Baring v. Wallerode: Freiherr v. Baring, Baring-Gould, Baring Baronet of Larkbear, Baring Baronet of Nubia House, Baring Baron of Hillburton, Baring Baron Viscount und Earl of Cromer, Viscount Errington, Baring Baron Viscount und Earl of Northbrook, Baring Baron Revelstoke, aus Groningen in Friesland"

Parish Register Society of Dublin, 12 vols. (1906-15)
Volume 3 (1907), Henry F. Berry, *The Registers of the church of St. Michan, Dublin, 1636 to 1685*

The Publications of the Durham and Northumberland Parish Register Society, 36 vols. (1898-1926)
Volume 6 (1902), Johnson Baily, *The registers of Ryton: marriages, 1581–1812*
Volume 10 (1900), Herbert Maxwell Wood, "The registers of Whitburn, in the county of Durham"

The East Anglian; or, Notes and queries on subjects connected with the counties of Suffolk, Cambridge, Essex and Norfolk, 17 vols. in 2 series (1858-1900)

Volume 4 (1869), George W. Marshall, "Pedigree of the Hernes, of Tibenham, co. Norfolk"

Essex Record Office Publications, 147 vols. to date (1946-)

Volume 137 (1998), Frederick George Emmison, *Essex Wills Commissary Court - Original Wills 1587–1599*

La Société Guernesiaise, formerly the Guernsey Society of Natural Science and Local Research: Report and Transactions, 26 vols. to date (1922-)

Volume 16, part 2 (1957), A. H. Ewen, "Essex Castle and the Chamberlain Family"

Proceedings of the Hampshire Field Club and Archæological Society, 50 vols. (1885-1995)

Publications of the Harleian Society, New Series, 17 vols. to date (1979-)

Volume 1 (1979), G. D. Squibb, ed., *The Register of the Temple Church, London Baptisms 1629–1853; Marriages 1628–1760*

Volumes 2 and 3 (1981-84), Joan Corder, ed., *The Visitation of Suffolk 1561 made by William Hervy, Clarenceux King of Arms*

Volume 5 (1986), G. D. Squibb, ed., *The Visitation of Nottinghamshire begun in 1662 and finished in 1664 made by William Dugdale, Norroy King of Arms*

Volume 8 (1989), G. D. Squibb, ed., *The Visitation of Derbyshire begun in 1662 and finished in 1664 made by William Dugdale, Norroy King of Arms*

Volume 10 (1991), G. D. Squibb, ed., *The Visitation of Hampshire and the Isle of Wight 1686 made by Sir Henry St. George, Knight, Clarenceux King of Arms*

Volume 11 (1992), G. D. Squibb, ed., *The Visitation of Somerset and the City of Bristol 1672 made by Sir Edward Bysshe, Knight, Clarenceux King of Arms*

Volume 12 (1993), G. D. Squibb, ed., *The Visitation of Oxfordshire 1669 and 1675 made by Sir Edward Bysshe, Knight, Clarenceux King of Arms*

Volume 14 (1996), Michael Powell Siddons, ed., *Visitations by the Heralds in Wales*

Volume 15 (2002), Michael Powell Siddons, ed., *The Visitation of Herefordshire 1634*

Volumes 16 and 17 (2004), T. C. Wales et al., eds., *The Visitation of London begun in 1687*

Publications of the Harleian Society, Register Series, 89 vols. (1877-1953)

Volume 1 (1877), Granville Leveson-Gower, *The Registers of Christening, Burials and Weddings within the Parish of St. Peter's upon Cornhill, London, 1538 to 1666*

Volume 3 (1878), Joseph Lemuel Chester, *The Register Book of St. Dionis Backchurch Parish (City of London), 1538 to 1754*

Volume 5 (1880), Joseph Lemuel Chester, *The Registers of St. Mary Aldermary, London, 1558 to 1754*

Volume 7 (1882), Joseph Lemuel Chester, *The Parish Registers of St. Michael, Cornhill, London, 1546 to 1754*

Volume 8 (1883), Joseph Lemuel Chester and George J. Armytage, *The Parish Registers of St. Antholin, Budge Row, London, 1538 to 1754; and St. John Baptist on Wallbrook, London, 1682 to 1754*

Volumes 9-10, 13, 17, and 19-20 (1884-94), Robert Hovenden, *A True Register of all the Christenings, Marriages and Burials in the Parish of St. James, Clerkenwell, 1551 to 1754*

Volumes 11, 14, 22, and 24 (1886-97), John H. Chapman, ed., *The Register Book of Marriages Belonging to the Parish of St. George, Hanover Square, in the County of Middlesex, 1725 to 1837*

Volume 16 (1890), F. N. MacNamara and A. Story-Maskelyne, *The Parish Register of Kensington, Co. Middlesex, 1539 to 1675*

Volume 18 (1892), Francis Collins, *The Registers and Monumental Inscriptions of Charterhouse Chapel, 1671 to 1890*

Volume 25 (1898), Thomas Mason, *A Register of Baptisms, Marriages and Burials in the Parish of St. Martin in the Fields, in the County of Middlesex, 1550 to 1619*

Volume 26 (1899), John W. Clay, *The Registers of St. Paul's Cathedral, 1697 to 1899*

Volumes 27 and 28 (1900-1), Arthur J. Jewers, *The Registers of The Abbey Church of SS. Peter & Paul, Bath, 1569 to 1800*

Volumes 29 and 30 (1902-3), Willoughby A. Littledale, *The Registers St. Vedast, Foster Lane, 1558 to 1836, and St. Michael Le Quern, 1558 to 1837*

Volume 31 (1904), W. Bruce Bannerman, *The Registers of St. Helen's, Bishopsgate, London, 1575 to 1837*

Volume 32 (1905), W. Bruce Bannerman, *The Registers of St. Martin Outwich, London, 1670 to 1873*

Volumes 33-37 (1906-9), William H. Hunt, *The Registers of St. Paul's Church, Covent Garden, London, 1653 to 1853*

Volumes 38-41 (1909-12), Willoughby Littledale, *The Registers of St. Bene't and St. Peter, Paul's Wharf, London, 1607 to 1837*

Volume 42 (1912), W. Bruce Bannerman, *The Registers of St. Mildred, Bread Street, 1658 to 1853, and St. Margaret Moses, Friday Street, London, 1558 to 1850*

Volume 43 (1913), W. Bruce Bannerman, *The Registers of Allhallows, Bread Street, 1538 to 1892, and St. John The Evangelist, Friday Street, London, 1653 to 1822*

Volume 45 (1915), W. Bruce Bannerman, ed., *The Registers of St. Mary le Bowe, Cheapside, All Hallows, Honey Lane, and of St. Pancras, Soper Lane, London, 1538–1837*

Volume 46 (1916), W. Bruce Bannerman, *The Registers of St. Olave, Hart Street, London, 1563 to 1700*

Volumes 47-48 and 51-57 (1917-27), W. Bruce Bannerman et al., *The Registers of Marriages of St. Mary le Bone, Middlesex, 1668–1812, and Oxford Chapel, Vere Street, St. Marylebone, 1736–1754*

Volumes 49 and 50 (1919-20), W. Bruce Bannerman et al., *The Registers of St. Stephen, Walbrook, and St. Benet Sherehog, London, 1716 to 1860*

Volumes 59 and 60 (1929-30), W. Bruce Bannerman, *Registers of St. Mary Somerset, London, 1557 to 1853*

Volumes 61-62 and 65 (1931-35), W. Bruce Bannerman et al., *The Registers of St. Mary The Virgin, Aldermanbury, London, 1538 to 1859*

Volume 63 (1933), W. Bruce Bannerman, *Registers of St. Matthew, Friday Street, London, 1538 to 1812, and the United Parishes of St. Matthew and St. Peter, Cheap, 1754 to 1812*

Volumes 64 and 86-89 (1934-77), Herbert F. Westlake et al., *The Register of St. Margaret's, Westminster, 1660 to 1699*

Volume 66 (1936), J. V. Kitto, *The Register of St. Martin-in-the-Fields, London 1619–1636*

Volumes 67 and 68 (1937-38), A. W. Hughes Clarke, *The Register of St. Clement, Eastcheap and St. Martin Orgar, 1539 to 1839*

Volumes 69 and 84-87 (1939-57), A. W. Hughes Clarke et al., *Registers of St. Dunstan in the East, 1558 to 1766*

Volumes 70 and 71 (1940-41), A. W. Hughes Clarke, *The Register of St. Lawrence Jewry and St. Mary Magdalen Milk Street, London, 1538 to 1812*

Volumes 72-74 (1942-44), A. W. Hughes Clarke, *The Registers of St. Mary Magdalen Milk Street, London and St. Michael Bassishaw, London, 1558 to 1892*

Volumes 75-81 (1945-52), A. W. Hughes Clarke et al., *The Registers of St. Katherine by the Tower, London, 1584 to 1695*

Publications of the Harleian Society, Visitation Series, 117 vols. (1869-1977)

Volume 1 (1869), Joseph J. Howard and George J. Armytage, eds., *The Visitation of London in the Year 1568 Taken by Robert Cooke, Clarenceaux King of Arms and since augmented with both descents and arms*

Volume 2 (1870), John Fetherston, ed., *The Visitation of the County of Leicester in the Year 1619 Taken by William Camden, Clarenceaux King of Arms*

Volume 3 (1870), George J. Armytage, *The Visitation of the County of Rutland in the Year 1618–19 Taken by William Camden, Clarenceaux King of Arms; and other descents of families not in the Visitation*

Volume 4 (1871), George W. Marshall, ed., *The Visitations of the County of Nottingham in the years 1569 and 1614, with many other descents of the same County*

Volume 5 (1871), William Henry Turner, ed., *The Visitations of the County of Oxford taken in the years 1566 by William Harvey, Clarencieux, 1574 by Richard Lee, Portcullis, Deputy of Robert Cooke, Clarencieux, and in 1634 by John Philipott, Somerset and William Ryley, Bluemantle, Deputies of Sir John Borough, Knt., Garter and Richard St. George, knt., Clarencieux; Together with the gatherings of Oxfordshire. Collected by Richard Lee in 1574*

Volume 6 (1872), Frederic Thomas Colby, ed., *The Visitation of the County of Devon in the year 1620*

Volume 7 (1872), John Fetherston, ed., *The Visitation of the County of Cumberland in the year 1615 Taken by Richard St. George, Norroy King of Arms*

Volume 8 (1873), George W. Marshall, ed., *Le Neve's Pedigrees of the Knights made by King Charles II, King James II, King William III and Queen Mary, King William alone, and Queen Anne*

Volume 9 (1874), Lt.-Col. John L. Vivian and Henry H. Drake, eds., *The Visitation of the County of Cornwall in the year 1620*

Volume 10 (1875), Joseph Lemuel Chester, ed., *The Marriage, Baptismal and Burial Registers of the Collegiate Church or Abbey of St. Peter, Westminster*

Volume 11 (1876), Frederic Thomas Colby, ed., *The Visitation of the County of Somerset in the year 1623*

Volume 12 (1877), John Fetherston, ed., *The Visitation of the County of Warwick in the year 1619 Taken by William Camden, Clarenceaux King of Arms (Harl. Mss. 1167)*

Volumes 13 and 14 (1878-79), Walter C. Metcalfe, ed., *The Visitations of Essex by Hawley, 1552, Hervey 1558, Cooke 1570, Raven 1612 and Owen and Lilly, 1634, to which are added Miscellaneous Essex Pedigrees from various Harleian Manuscripts and an appendix containing Berry's Essex Pedigrees*

Volumes 15 and 17 (1880-83), Joseph J. Howard and Joseph Lemuel Chester, eds., *The Visitation of London Anno Domini 1633, 1634 and 1635: Made by Sr Henry St George, Kt, Richmond Herald, and Deputy and Marshal to Sr Richard St George, Kt, Clarencieux King of Armes*

Volume 16 (1881), Charles Best Norcliffe, ed., *The Visitation of Yorkshire in the years 1563 and 1564 Made by William Flower, Esquire, Norroy King of Arms*

Volume 18 (1882), John Paul Rylands, ed., *The Visitation of Cheshire in 1580 made by Robert Glover, Somerset Herald, for William Flower, Norroy King of Arms, with numerous additions and continuations, including those from the Visitations of Cheshire made in the year 1566 by the same herald with an appendix, containing the Visitation of a part of Cheshire in the year 1533*

Made by William Fellows, Lancaster Herald, for Thomas Bertolte, Clarenceux King of Arms, and a fragment of the Visitation of the City of Chester in the year 1591 Made by Thomas Chaloner, Deputy to the office of Arms

Volume 19 (1884), Frederic Augustus Blaydes, ed., *The Visitations of Bedfordshire, annis Domini 1566, 1582, and 1634; Made by William Harvey, esq., Clarencieulx king of arms, Robert Cooke, esq., Clarencieulx king of arms, and George Owen, esq., York herald, as deputy for Sir Richard St. George, kt., Clarencieulx king of arms; Together with additional pedigrees, chiefly from Harleian MS. 1531; and an appendix, containing a list of Pedigrees Entered at the Visitation of 1669; also lists of Bedfordshire Knights and Gentry taken from Landsdowne ms. 877*

Volume 20 (1885), John Paul Rylands, ed., *The Visitation of the County of Dorset Taken in the year 1623 by Henry St. George, Richmond Herald, and Sampson Lennard, Bluemantle Pursuivant, Marshals and deputies to William Camden, Clarenceaux King of Arms*

Volume 21 (1885), Sir John Maclean and W. C. Heane, *The Visitation of the County of Gloucester Taken in the year 1623, by Henry Chitty and John Phillipot as Deputies to William Camden, Clarenceaux King of Arms, with Pedigrees from the Herald's Visitations of 1569 and 1582–3, and Sundry Miscellaneous Pedigrees*

Volume 22 (1886), Walter C. Metcalfe, ed., *The Visitations of Hertfordshire, Made by Robert Cooke, Esq., Clarencieux in 1572, and Sir Richard St. George, kt., Clarencieux in 1634, with Hertfordshire Pedigrees from Harleian Mss. 6147 and 1546*

Volume 23 (1886), Joseph Lemuel Chester and George J. Armytage, *Allegations for Marriage Licences issued by the Dean and Chapter of Westminster, 1558–1699; Also for those issued by the Vicar-General of the Archbishop of Canterbury, 1660–1679*

Volume 24 (1886), Joseph Lemuel Chester and George J. Armytage, *Allegations for Marriage Licences issued by the Faculty Office of the Archbishop of Canterbury at London, 1543–1869*

Volumes 25 and 26 (1887), Joseph Lemuel Chester and George J. Armytage, *Allegations for Marriage Licences issued by the Bishop of London*

Volume 27 (1888), W. P. W. Phillimore, ed., *The Visitation of the County of Worcester Made in the year 1569 with Other Pedigrees Relating to that County from Richard Mundy's Collection*

Volumes 28 and 29 (1889), George Grazebrook and John Paul Rylands, eds., *The Visitation of Shropshire Taken in the year 1623 by Robert Tresswell, Somerset Herald, and Augustine Vincent, Rouge Croix Pursuivant of Arms, Marshals and deputies to William Camden, Clarenceux King of Arms. With Additions from the Pedigrees of Shropshire Gentry Taken by the Heralds in the years 1569 and 1584, and other sources*

Volumes 30-31 and 33-34 (1890-92), George J. Armytage, *Allegations for Marriage Licences issued by the Vicar-General of the Archbishop of Canterbury*

Volume 32 (1891), Walter Rye, ed., *The Visitacion of Norffolk Made and Taken by William Hervey, Clarencieux King of Arms, Anno 1563, Enlarged with another Visitacion Made by Clarenceux Cooke, with many other descents and also the Visitation Made by John Raven, Richmond, Anno 1613*

Volumes 37-40 (1894-96), John W. Clay, ed., *Familiae Minorum Gentium. Diligentiâ Josephi Hunter, Sheffieldiensis, S.A.S.*

Volume 41 (1897), John W. Clay, ed., *The Visitation of Cambridge Made in Ao [1575], Continued and Enlarged wth the Vissitation of the Same County Made by Henery St. George, Richmond-Herald, Marshall and Deputy to Willm. Camden, Clarenceulx in Ao 1619 wth Many Other Descents Added thereto*

Volume 42 (1898), Robert Hovenden, ed., *The Visitation of Kent Taken in the Years 1619–1621 by John Philipot, Rouge Dragon, Marshal and Deputy to William Camden, Clarenceux*

Volume 43 (1899), W. Bruce Bannerman, ed., *The Visitations of the County of Surrey Made and Taken in the years 1530 by Thomas Benolte, Clarenceux King of Arms; 1572 by Robert Cooke, Clarenceux King of Arms; and 1623 by Samuel Thompson, Windsor Herald, and Augustin Vincent, Rouge Croix Pursuivant, marshals and deputies to William Camden, Clarenceux King of Arms*

Volumes 44-49 (1899-1901), Sir George J. Armytage, Bart., ed., *Obituary Prior to 1800 (as far as relates to England, Scotland, and Ireland), Compiled by Sir William Musgrave, 6th Bart. of Hayton Castle, co. Cumberland, and entitled by him "A General Nomenclator and Obituary, with reference to the books where the persons are mentioned, and where some account of their character is to be found"*

Volumes 50-52 and 55 (1902-6), A. R. Maddison, *Lincolnshire Pedigrees*

Volume 53 (1905), W. Bruce Bannerman, ed., The *Visitations of the County of Sussex, Made and Taken in the years 1530 by Thomas Benolte, Clarenceux King of Arms; and 1633–4 by John Philipot, Somerset Herald, and George Owen, York Herald, for Sir John Burroughs, Garter and Sir Richard St. George, Clarenceux*

Volume 54 (1906), Sir George J. Armytage, Bart., ed., *The Visitation of Kent Begun Anno Dni 1663 Finished Anno Dni 1668 by Sir Edward Bysshe, Knt., Clarenceux King of Armes*

Volumes 56 and 57 (1907-8), W. Harry Rylands, ed., *The Four Visitations of Berkshire Made and Taken by Thomas Benolte, Clarenceux, Anno 1532, By William Harvey, Clarenceux, Anno 1566, By Henry Chitting, Chester Herald, and John Philipott, Rouge Dragon, for William Camden, Clarenceux, Anno 1623, and by Elias Ashmole, Windsor Herald, for Sir Edward Bysshe, Clarenceux, Anno 1665–66*

Volume 58 (1909), W. Harry Rylands, ed., *The Visitation of the County of Buckingham Made in 1634 by John Philipot, Esq., Somerset Herald, and William Ryley, Bluemantle Pursuivant, Marshals and Deputies to Sir Richard St. George, Knight, Clarenceux, and Sir John Borough, Knight, Garter, who visited as Norroy by mutual agreement; Including the Church Notes then taken, together with Pedigrees from the Visitation Made In 1566 by William Harvey, Esq., Clarenceux and some Pedigrees from other sources, Being a Transcript of MS. Eng. Misc. CM in the Bodleian Library, Oxford, with additions*

Volume 59 (1909), Sir George J. Armytage, Bart., and John Paul Rylands, eds., *Pedigrees Made at the Visitation of Cheshire 1613 taken by Richard St. George, Esq., Norroy King of Arms and Henry St. George, Gent., Bluemantle Pursuivant of Arms; and some other Contemporary Pedigrees*

Volume 60 (1910), Sir George J. Armytage, Bart., ed., *A Visitation of the County of Surrey Begun Anno Dni 1662 and finished Anno Dni 1668*

Volume 61 (1910), W. Harry Rylands, ed., *A Visitation of the County of Suffolk Begun Anno Dni 1664 and finished Anno Dni 1668 by Sir Edward Bysshe, Kt., Clarenceux King of Arms*

Volume 62 (1911), W. Harry Rylands, ed., *The Visitation of the County of Warwick begun by Thomas May, Chester, and Gregory King, Rouge Dragon, in Hilary Vacation 1682. Reviewing them in the Trinity Vacation following, and Finished by Henry Dethick, Richmond, and the said Rouge Dragon Pursuivant in Trinity Vacation 1683, by virtue of several deputations from Sir Henry St. George, Clarenceux King of Arms*

Volume 63 (1912), Sir George J. Armytage, Bart., and W. Harry Rylands, ed., *Staffordshire Pedigrees, Based upon the Visitation of that county made by Sir William Dugdale, Esquire, Norroy King of Arms in the Years 1663–1664, from the original manuscript written by Gregory King, (Successively Rouge Dragon and Lancaster Herald) during the years 1680 to 1700*

Volume 64 (1913), W. Harry Rylands, ed., *Pedigrees from the Visitation of Hampshire Made by Thomas Benolte, Clarenceulx, Ao 1530; Enlarged with the Vissitation of the same county made by Robert Cooke, Clarenceulx, Anno 1575, Both wch are continued wth the Visitation made* by John Phillipott, Somersett (for William Camden, Clarenceux) in Ao 1622 most part then don(e) & finished in Ao 1634, as collected by Richard Mundy in Harleian MS. No. 1544

Volume 65 (1914), Sir George J. Armytage, Bart., ed., *Middlesex Pedigrees as Collected by Richard Mundy in Harleian MS. No. 1551*

Volume 66 (1915), W. Harry Rylands, ed., *Grantees of Arms Named in Docquets and Patents to the End of the Seventeenth Century, in the Manuscripts preserved in the British Museum, The Bodleian Library, Oxford, Queen's College, Oxford, Gonville and Caius College, Cambridge, and Elsewhere, alphabetically Arranged by The Late Joseph Foster and Contained in the Additional Ms. No. 37,147 in the British Museum*

Volumes 67 and 68 (1916-17), W. Harry Rylands, ed., *Grantees of Arms Named in Docquets and Patents Between the Years 1687 and 1898 Preserved in Various Manuscripts Collected and Alphabetically Arranged by the Late Joseph Foster, Hon. A.M. Oxon., and Contained in the Additional Ms. No. 37,149 in the British Museum*

Volume 73 (1922), W. Harry Rylands and W. Bruce Bannerman, eds., *The Visitation of the County of Rutland, begun by Fran. Burghill, Somerset and Gregory King, Rougedragon in Trinity Vacation 1681, carried on and finished by Tho. May, Chester Herald and the said Rougedragon Pursuivt in Hilary and Trinity Vacation 1682 by Virtue of several deputaćons from Sr Henry St George Kt, Clarenceux King of Arms*

Volumes 74 and 75 (1923-24), W. Bruce Bannerman, *The Visitations of Kent Taken in the Years 1530–1 by Thomas Benolte, Clarenceux, and 1574 by Robert Cooke, Clarenceux, and 1592 by Robert Cooke, Clarenceux*

Volumes 85 and 86 (1933-34), A.W. Hughes Clarke and Arthur Campling, *The Visitation of Norfolk Anno Domini 1664 made by Sir Edward Bysshe, Knt., Clarenceux King of Arms*

Volume 87 (1935), H. Isham Longden, ed., *The Visitation of the County of Northampton in the Year 1681*

Volume 88 (1936), J. W. Walker, ed., *Hunter's Pedigrees: A Continuation of Familiae Minorum Gentium, Diligentiâ Josephi Hunter, Sheffieldiensis, S.A.S.*

Volume 89 (1937), A. W. Hughes Clarke, ed., *The Visitation of Sussex Anno Domini 1662*

Volume 90 (1938), A. T. Butler, *The Visitation of Worcestershire 1634*

Volume 92 (1940), J. B. Whitmore, ed., *London Visitation Pedigrees, 1664*

Volume 93 (1941), Arthur Adams, ed., *Cheshire Visitation Pedigrees, 1663*

Volumes 94-96 (1942-44), J. W. Walker, ed., *Yorkshire Pedigrees*

Volumes 105-6 (1954), G. D. Squibb, ed., *Wiltshire Visitation Pedigrees, 1623 with Additional Pedigrees and Arms Collected by Thomas Lyte of Lyte's Cary, co. Somerset, 1628*

Volumes 109-10 (1963), H. Stanford London and Sophia W. Rawlins, eds., *Visitation of London, 1568, with Additional Pedigrees 1569–90, The Arms of the City Companies and a London Subsidy Roll, 1589*

Volume 117 (1977), G. D. Squibb, ed., *The Visitation of Dorset 1677 Made by Sir Edward Bysshe, Knight, Clarenceux King of Arms*

Historical Register, 25 vols. (1714-38). Note: The *Historical Register Chronicle* is the chronological diary of the *Historical Register*.

Publications of the Huguenot Society of London, 47 vols. (1887-1961)

Volume 19 (1908), Thomas Philip Le Fanu, ed., "Registers of the French Church of Portarlington, Ireland"

Volume 41 (1946), Thomas Philip Le Fanu et al., eds., "Dublin and Portarlington veterans: King William III's Huguenot army"

The Index Library (British Record Society), 119 vols. to date. (1888-); see also *British Record Society*
>Volumes 58 and 60 (1948-50), Thomas Mathews Blagg and F. Arthur Wadsworth, eds., *Abstracts of Nottinghamshire marriage licences*

Journal of the County Kildare Archaeological Society, 18 vols. to date (1891-)
>Volume 1 (1894), Lord Walter FitzGerald, "The FitzGeralds of Lackagh"
>Volume 4 (1903), Lord Walter FitzGerald, "Patrick Sarsfield, Earl of Lucan, with an account of his family and their connection with Lucan and Tully"
>Volume 6 (1909), Lord Walter FitzGerald, "Pedigree of the O'Mores of Leix, and of Ballina, co. Kildare"

Lancashire and Cheshire Record Society, 128 vols. to date (1879-)
>Volumes 24, 26, 29, 36, 72, 95, and 96 (1891-1942), J. H. Stanning and John Brownbill, eds. *The Royalist Compostition Papers: Being the Proceedings of the Committee for Compounding, A.D. 1643–1660, so far as They Relate to the County of Lancaster, Extracted from the Records Preserved in the Public Record Office, London*

Lancashire Parish Register Society, 159 vols. to date (1898-)
>Volume 12 (1902), Giles Shaw, trans., *The Registers of the Parish Church of Middleton in the County of Lancaster: Christenings, Burials, and Weddings 1541–1663*
>Volume 18 (1902), Giles Shaw, trans., *The Registers of the Parish Church of Middleton in the County of Lancaster: Christenings, Burials, and Weddings 1653–1729*

Survey of London, 45 vols. to date (1900-)
>Volume 41 (1983), F. H. W. Sheppard, ed., *Brompton*

Journal of the County Louth Archaeological Society, 26 vols. to date (1904-)
>Volume 8 (1936), "Will of father James Hussey, Smarmore, 1635: The Taaffes"

Publications of the Navy Records Society, 149 vols. to date (1894-)
>Volumes 13, 30, 37, 41, and 46 (1899-1913), Samuel Rawson Gardiner and C. T. Atkinson, *Letters and Papers relating to the First Dutch War 1652–1654*

Nederland's Adelsboek, 83 vols. (1903-95)

Neue Deutsche Biographie, 23 vols. to date (1953-)

Norfolk Archeology: or, Miscellaneous Tracts Relating to the Antiquities of the County of Norfolk, 45 vols. to date (1847-)
>Volume 3 (1852), Joseph Hunter, "The history and topography of Ketteringham, in the County of Norfolk"

Norfolk Genealogy, 24 vols. (1969-92)
>Volume 17 (1985), Patrick Palgrave-Moore, ed., "A Selection of Revised and Unpublished Norfolk Pedigrees, Part Four"

Publications of the Northamptonshire Record Society, 40 vols. to date (1924-)
>Volume 19 (1956), Mary E. Finch, "The Wealth of Five Northamptonshire Families 1540-1640"
>Volume 31 (1986), Peter Gordon, ed., *The Red Earl: The Papers of the Fifth Earl Spencer 1885–1910*

Oxoniensia: a journal dealing with the archaeology, history, and architecture of Oxford and its neighborhood, 70 vols. to date (1936-)

Volumes 11-12 (1946-47), Michael Maclagan, "Family of Dormer in Oxfordshire and Buckinghamshire"

Le Parchemin: bulletin belge héraldique, généalogique, onomastique, 71 vols. to date (1936-)
(1982), Colonel de Lannoy, "La Famille Bulteel ou Bulteau à Tournai et à Anvers au XVI siècle"
(1984), response

Shropshire Parish Registers: Lichfield Diocese, 21 vols. (1899-1942)
Volume 11 (1911), *Registers of Hodnet with Wroxeter*
Volume 13 (1912), *Registers of Ludlow*

Proceedings of the Somersetshire Archaeological and Natural History Society, 149 vols. to date (1851)
Volume 38, part 2 (1892), Henry C. Maxwell Lyte, "Lytes of Lytescary"

Collections for a History of Staffordshire, 83 vols. to date in 4 series (1880-); see also *William Salt Archæological Society*
Volume 3, Part 2 (1883), H. Sydney Grazebrook, ed., *The Visitacion of Staffordshire Made by Robert Glover, Al's Somerset Herald, Mareschall to William Flower, Al's Norroy Kinge of Arms, Anno D'ni 1583*
Volume 5, Part 2 (1885), H. Sydney Grazebrook, ed., *The Heraldic Visitations of Staffordshire Made by Sir Richard St. George, Norroy, in 1614, and by Sir William Dugdale in the Years 1663 and 1664*
Volume 9 (1888), H. Sydney Grazebrook, "The Barons of Dudley"
3rd series, volume 25 (1925), W. Fowler Carter, "Notes on Staffordshire Families"

Staffordshire Parish Registers Society, 105 vols. to date (1902-)
Volume 10 (1900), "Bushbury Parish Register"

Suffolk Green Books, 20 vols. in 24 (1894-1924)
Volume 4 (1900), S. H. A. H[ervey], ed., *Horringer Parish Registers. Baptisms, Marriages, and Burials, with appendixes and biographical notes (1558–1850)*

Publications of the Surtees Society, 210 vols. to date (1835-)
Volume 36 (1859), Robert Davies, ed., *The Visitation of the County of Yorke, Began in Ao Dñi MDCLXV and Finished Ao Dñi MDCLXVI, by William Dugdale, Esqr, Norroy King of Armes*
Volume 38 (1860), "Wills and Inventories from the Registry at Durham, part II"
Volumes 122, 133, 144, and 146 (1912-32), F. W. Dendy and C. H. Hunter Blair, eds., *Visitations of the North, or, Some Early Heraldic Visitations of, and Collections of Pedigrees Relating to, the North of England*
Volume 142 (1929), H. M. Wood, ed., *Wills and Inventories from the Registry at Durham*

Sussex Archeological Collections: Illustrating the History and Antiquities of the County, 140 vols. to date (1848-)
Volume 33 (1880), "Warnham: Its Church, Monuments, Registers, and Vicars"
Volume 42 (1899), J. H. Cooper, "Cuckfield Familes"
Volume 47 (1904), F. W. T. Attree and J. H. L. Booker, "The Sussex Colepepers"

Publications of the Thoresby Society, 59 vols. (1891–1986)
Volume 12 (1902), George Denison Lumb, ed., *The Registers of the Parish Church of Methley in the County of York, from 1560 to 1812*

Transactions of the Thoroton Society, 106 vols. to date (1897-)
Volume 49 (1945), G. Ellis Flack, "Sir Thomas Parkyns of Bunny"

The Victoria History of the Counties of England
> *The Victoria History of the County of Bedford,* 3 vols. (1904-14)
> *The Victoria History of Berkshire,* 4 vols. (1906-27)
> *The Victoria History of the County of Buckingham,* 4 vols. (1905-28)
> *The Victoria History of the County of Cambridge and the Isle of Ely,* 10 vols. (1938-2002)
> *A History of the County of Chester,* 3 vols. to date (1987-)
> *The Victoria History of the County of Cornwall,* 2 vols. to date (1906-)
> *The Victoria History of the County of Cumberland,* 2 vols. to date (1901-)
> *The Victoria History of the County of Derby,* 2 vols. to date (1905-)
> *The Victoria History of the County of Devon,* 1 vol. to date (1906-)
> *The Victoria History of the County of Dorset,* 2 vols. to date (1908-)
> *The Victoria History of the County of Durham,* 3 vols. to date (1908-)
> *The Victoria History of the County of Essex,* 9 vols. to date (1903-)
> *The Victoria History of the County of Gloucester,* 7 vols. to date (1907-)
> *The Victoria History of Hampshire and the Isle of Wright,* 5 vols. (1900-14)
> *The Victoria History of the County of Hereford,* 1 vol. (1908)
> *The Victoria History of the County of Hertford,* 4 vols. (1902-12)
> *The Victoria History of the County of Huntingdon,* 4 vols. (1926-38)
> *The Victoria History of the County of Kent,* 3 vols. to date (1908-)
> *The Victoria History of the County of Lancaster,* 8 vols. (1906-14)
> *The Victoria History of the County of Leicester,* 5 vols. (1907-64)
> *The Victoria History of the County of Lincoln,* 1 vol. (1906)
> *The Victoria History of London,* 1 vol. (1909)
> *The Victoria History of the County of Middlesex,* 10 vols. to date (1911-)
> *The Victoria History of the County of Norfolk,* 2 vols. to date (1901-)
> *The Victoria History of the County of Northampton,* 4 vols. to date (1902-)
> *The Victoria History of the County of Nottingham,* 2 vols. to date (1906-)
> *The Victoria History of the County of Oxford,* 13 vols. to date (1907-)
> *The Victoria History of the County of Rutland,* 2 vols. (1908-36)
> *The Victoria History of Shropshire,* 6 vols. to date (1908-)
> *The Victoria History of the County of Somerset,* 6 vols. to date (1906-)
> *The Victoria History of the County of Stafford,* 11 vols. to date (1908-)
> *The Victoria History of the County of Suffolk,* 2 vols. to date (1907-)
> *The Victoria History of the County of Surrey,* 4 vols. (1902-12)
> *The Victoria History of the County of Sussex,* 7 vols. in 9 to date (1905-)
> *The Victoria History of the County of Warwick,* 8 vols. (1904-69)
> *[The Victoria] History of Wiltshire,* 15 vols. in 16 to date (1953-)
> *The Victoria History of the County of Worcester,* 4 vols. (1901-26)
> *The Victoria History of the County of York,* 3 vols. (1907-25)
> *[The Victoria] History of the County of York, East Riding,* 7 vols. to date (1969-)
> *The Victoria History of the County of York, North Riding,* 2 vols. (1914-25)
> *[The Victoria] History of Yorkshire: The City of York* (1961)

Wiltshire Family History Society
> 1999-2000 volume, *The bishop's transcripts and parish registers of Wilcot, baptisms & burials, 1564–1837 and Huish, baptisms & burials, 1603–1837*

William Salt Archæological Society; see also *Collections for a History of Staffordshire*

Yorkshire Archæological Society, Parish Register Series, 166 vols. to date (1899-)

Yorkshire Archæological Society, Record Series, 152 vols. to date (1885–)

The Publications of the Yorkshire Parish Register Society, 168 vols. to date (1899–)
    Volume 27 (1906), George Denison Lumb, ed., *The Registers of the Parish Church of Rothwell, Co. York*
    Volume 41 (1911), Robert Beilby Cook, ed., *The Parish Registers of Holy Trinity Church, Goodramgate, York, 1573–1812*
    Volume 78 (1925), Edith Horsfall, ed., *The Parish Registers of Heptonstall, in the County of York, 1593–1660*

Journals

The American Genealogist, 81 vols. to date (1922–)
    Volume 13 (1936): 1-8, Clarence Almon Torrey, "Alice (Freeman) (Tompson) Parke"
    Volume 14 (1938): 145-46, Clarence Almon Torrey, "John Tomson of Little Preston, Northamptonshire, England"
    Volume 21 (1945): 169-77, Donald Lines Jacobus, "The Darcy Ancestry of Mrs. John Sherman"
    Volume 29 (1952): 215-18, Robert L. Steenrod, "Alice (Freeman) (Tompson) Parke"
    Volume 56 (1980): 97-98, John B. Threlfall, "Smedley-Mitchell Clues from Amsterdam"
    Volume 58 (1982): 115-16, Mary Ann Nicholson, "Recent Gleaning from English Quaker Records"
    Volume 58 (1982): 242, 246, Gary Boyd Roberts, "Clayton of New Jersey to Prince William of Wales"
    Volume 68 (1992): 65-67, Penny G. Douglass and Robert Charles Anderson, "The English Origin of Robert Blott of Charlestown and Boston, Mass."
    Volume 68 (1992): 67-68, Penny G. Douglass and Robert Charles Anderson, "John Black of Charlestown Was Really Robert Blott"

The Ancestor, 12 vols. (1902-5)
    Volume 11 (1904): 22, Oswald Barron, "The Wild Wilmots"

The Burlington Magazine, 149 vols. to date (1903–)
    Volume 126 (1984): 603, Michael Jaffé, "Van Dyck Studies II: 'La belle & vertueuse Huguenotte'"

Collectanea Topographica et Genealogica, 8 vols. (1834-43)
    Volume 4 (1837): 142, "Pedigree of the family of Lunsford, of Lunsford and Wilegh, co. Sussex"
    Volume 7 (1841): 193, Charles George Young, "The Earldom of Glamorgan: Addendum for Dugdale"

The Genealogist, 20 vols. to date (1980–)
    Volume 1 (1980): 106-27, Gary Boyd Roberts, "Gerald Paget, *The Lineage and Ancestry of H.R.H. Prince Charles, Prince of Wales* (A Review and General Essay)"
    Volume 2 (1981): 71-114, Francis James Dallett, "The Inter-Colonial Grimstone Boude and his family"
    Volume 2 (1981): 161-63, Neil D. Thompson and Col. Charles M. Hansen, "A Medieval Heritage: The Ancestry of Charles II, King of England"
    Volume 4 (1983): 173-86, David L. Greene, "Mary, wife of the Rev. Richard Blinman of Marshfield, Gloucester, and New London: An Unresolved Problem"

The Genealogist: A Quarterly Magazine of Genealogical, Antiquarian, Topographical and Heraldic Research, 45 vols. in 2 series (1877-1922)

Volume 2 (1878): 282-89, "Kerr of Fernihirst, Baron Jedburgh"

Volume 2 (1878): 289-93, "Kerr of Ancrum, Earl of Ancrum, Earl and Marquis of Lothian"

Volume 5 (1881): 193-203, Pedigree of Douglas of Tilquhilly or Tilwhilly, co. Kincardine

Volume 6 (1882), "Visitation of Berkshire, 1666"

New series, volume 7 (1890): 1-16, 65-80, 129-44, 225-32, "Pedigrees contained in the Visitations of Derbyshire, 1569 and 1611"

New series, volume 8 (1891): 17-24, "Pedigrees contained in the Visitations of Derbyshire, 1569 and 1611"

New series, volume 10 (1894): 57-60, 122-24, 186-88, "Inquisitiones Post Mortem *temp.* Henry VIII to Charles I"

New series, volume 12 (1896): 233-35, Robert Eden, "Pedigree of the Lords Burgh of Gainsborough"

New series, volume 16 (1900): 98-104, 187-92, 255-62, George Wentworth Watson, "The 4096 Quartiers of the Prince of Wales"

New series, volume 17 (1901): 44-50, 135-40, 193-98, 267-72, George Wentworth Watson, "The 4096 Quartiers of the Prince of Wales"

New series, volume 18 (1902): 52-56, 104-9, 196-203, 268-73, George Wentworth Watson, "The 4096 Quartiers of the Prince of Wales"

New series, volume 19 (1903): 51-58, 127-34, 174-81, 262-70, George Wentworth Watson, "The 4096 Quartiers of the Prince of Wales"

New series, volume 19 (1903): 217-31, G. C. Bower and H. W. F. Harwood, "Pedigree of Offley"

New series, volume 20 (1904): 40-48, 114-22, 189-96, 261-68, George Wentworth Watson, "The 4096 Quartiers of the Prince of Wales"

New series, volume 20 (1904): 49-56, 78-86, 197-99, 268-73, G. C. Bower and H. W. F. Harwood, "Pedigree of Offley"

New series, volume 24 (1908): 217-41, Sir Edmund T. Bewley, "An Irish branch of the Fleetwood family"

New series, volume 28 (1912): 88, Henry Wagner, "Huguenot Refugee family of Yvonnet"

New series, volume 29 (1913): 56-60, 122-24, 193-96, 265-69, "Inquisitiones Post Mortem *temp.* Henry VIII to Charles I"

New series, volume 30 (1914): 64-67, 140-42, 253-57, "Inquisitiones Post Mortem *temp.* Henry VIII to Charles I"

New series, volume 33 (1917): 59-64, 184-88, 266-70, "Extracts from a Seventeenth Century Note-book"

New series, volume 36 (1920): 9-21, J. Paul Rylands, "A Vellum Pedigree-Roll of the family of Touchet, of Nether Whitley and Buglawton, Co. Chester, and Touchet, Baron Audley of Heleigh, Co. Stafford"

The Genealogists' Magazine: Official Organ of the Society of Genealogists, 27 vols. to date (1924-)

Volume 20 (1980-82): 192-97, 281-82, David Williamson, "The Ancestry of Lady Diana Spencer"

Volume 22 (1986-88): 244-48, Peter Hall, "Charles II's Noble Descendants"

Volume 25 (1997): 345-52, Anthony Hoskins, "Mary Boleyn Carey's Children – Offspring of King Henry VIII?"

Gens Nostra: Ons Geslacht, Maanblad der Nederlandse Genealogische Vereniging, 61 vols. to date (1946-)
> Volume 36 (1981): 213-37, K. van de Sigtenhorst, "Lady Diana Spencer."

The Gentleman's Magazine, 302 vols. (1731–1868). Note: Vols. 1-5 (1731-35) with subtitle *Or, Monthly Intelligencer;* vols. 6-151 (1736-1832) with subtitle *And Historical Chronicle;* and vols. 201-4 (1856-68) with subtitle *And Historical Review.* New series begin with volumes 103, 155, 201, 220 and 225 though volumes are traditionally numbered consecutively.

Herald & Genealogist, 8 vols. (1863-74)
> Volume 3 (1864): 371, "Taaffe Pedigrees"
> Volume 7 (1873): 512-15, "Notes on the family of Kerr in Scotland. VIII. Ker of Dolphinstoun, Hirsell, and Littledean"
> Volume 8 (1874): 377-85, "The family of Croker"

Héraldique et généalogie: bulletin de la Fédération des sociétés françaises de généalogie, d'héraldique et de sigillographie, 38 vols. to date (1969-)
> Volume 22 (1991): 13, response to query

Miscellanea Genealogica et Heraldica, 31 vols. in 6 series (1868-1938)
> Volume 1 (1868): 105-22, "The Pedigree of the Ancient Family of the Palmers of Sussex, 1672"
> Volume 1 (1868): 159, "Pedigree of Saunders from the Visitation of Northamptonshire 1618"
> Volume 2 (1876): 34-35, Albert W. Woods, "Report on the Pedigree of the family of the Right Honourable James Craggs, Postmaster General, the father of the Right Honourable James Craggs, secretary of state in the reign of King George the First"
> New series, volume 1 (1878): 113-14, G. E. Adams, "Genealogical Memoranda Relating to the Fox and Weld Families"
> New series, volume 3 (1882): 77-81, Sir John St. George, "Pedigree of the family of St. George"
> New series, volume 4 (1884): 244, P. D. Vigors, "Gore"
> 2nd series, volume 2 (1888): 120-21, John Paul Rylands et al., "Pedigrees from the Visitation of Dorset 1623. Walcot"
> 2nd series, volume 2 (1888): 347-50, "Annotations to the Heraldic Visitation of London, 1633. Gore: wills and administrations"
> 2nd series, volume 3 (1890): 169-72, "Langley Pedigree"
> 2nd series, volume 3 (1890): 116-18, 151-53, "Annotations to the Heraldic Visitation of London, 1633. Gore"
> 2nd series, volume 4 (1892): 173-74, 152, "Family of Cooke," "Pedigree of Cooke"
> 3rd series, volume 1 (1896): 41-46, 76-80, 102-5, 149-52, 172-76, 194-96, 246-53, George Edward Cokayne, "Skinner's Company Apprentices"
> 3rd series, volume 2 (1898): 43-48, B. W. Greenfield, "Pedigree of Dunch of Little Wittenham, Berks."
> 3rd series, volume 2 (1898): 213-35, 261-79, G. Milner-Gibson-Cullum, "Middleton or Myddelton of Chirk Castle, Denbigh, Stanstead Mountfichet, Essex, and other places"
> 3rd series, volume 3 (1900): 9-12, 49-53, 81-86, W. L. Rutton, "Pedigree of Hopton of Suffolk and Somerset"
> 3rd series, volume 4 (1902): 16-21, W. Bruce Bannerman, "Wynston Pedigree"
> 4th series, volume 4 (1912): 270-71, Henry Wagner, "Pedigree of Guinand."
> 4th series, volume 5 (1914): 3-9, Vere Langford Oliver, "Pedigree of the family of Dingwall of Brucklay"

4th series, volume 5 (1914): 105-13, Everard Green et al., "Pedigree of James and Gervis-James of Ightham Mote, Kent"

5th series, volume 1 (1916): 8, 130, "The Family of Boothby"

5th series, volume 2 (1918): 57-59, Algernon Tudor Craig, "Lane of Campsea Ash, co. Suffolk"

5th series, volume 2 (1918): 93-100, 131-33, 183-92, 202-10, 242-49, 282-89, J. Renton Dunlop, "The Family of Fettiplace"

5th series, volume 8 (1932-34): 88-108, Herbert C. Andrews, "Notes on the Rowlett and Jennings families"

5th series, volume 8 (1932-34): 109-13, "Extract from the pedigree of the family of Saunders of Ewell in the County of Surrey"

5th series, volume 8 (1932-34): 250, "Funeral certificate of Mary Puleston, nee Bostock"

5th series, volume 8 (1932-34): 152-54, 176-78, 207-9, 251-53, 266-69, 294-95, 327, 332, "Some Herefordshire Pedigrees"

5th series, volume 9 (1932): 344-56, Arthur Stephens Dyer, "Pedigree of Moyle of Bake, St. Germans, Cornwall"

5th series, volume 9 (1932): 118-21, "Pedigrees and heraldic notes of Gregory King: Mayny of Kent"

5th series, volume 9 (1932): 124-25, "Pedigrees and heraldic notes of Gregory King: Sadler"

5th series, volume 9 (1932): 150-51, "Pedigrees and heraldic notes of Gregory King: Briggs of Ernestree and Haughton, Salop"

De Nederlandsche Leeuw: Maandblad van het Koninklijk Nederlandsch Genootschap voor Geslacht-en Wapenkunde, 123 vols. to date (1883-)

Volume 4 (1886): 35, J. C. v. d. M., "Genootschap in Het Hertogdom Limburg – Pieterson"

Volume 57 (1939): 53-63, 112-20, H. H. Röell, "Geldersche Geslachten. Bijdrage tot de genealogie van Lintelo"

Volume 81 (1964): 117-44, W. W. van Valkenburg, "Voorouders van Z. K. H. Carlos Hugo Prins van Bourbon-Parma"

Volume 87 (1970): 202, Ir. J. C. Deknatel, "le Boullenger-van Roubais"

NEHGS NEXUS, 16 vols. (1983-99)

Volume 13 (1996): 156-59, Gary Boyd Roberts, "Lygon Descendants in England and Europe, Part 1"

Volume 13 (1996): 167-72, Scott C. Steward, "Six Generations of the Anglo-American Ancestry of Sir Winston Churchill"

Volume 13 (1996): 205-6, Gary Boyd Roberts, "Royally Descended Immigrant Kin and Presidential Cousins of Sir Winston Churchill"

Volume 14 (1997): 65-68, Scott C. Steward, "The Eighth-Generation Ancestry of Sir Winston Churchill"

Volume 14 (1997): 70-73, Gary Boyd Roberts, "The Leveson-Gower Progeny: Our 'Whig Cousinage'"

Volume 16 (1999): 116-19, Gary Boyd Roberts, "Royal Descents and American Cousins of Sophie Helen Rhys-Jones"

The New England Historical and Genealogical Register, 161 vols. to date (1847-)

Volume 43 (1889): 403, Henry F. Waters, "Genealogical Gleanings in England"

Volume 44 (1890): 194-95, Henry Fitz-Gilbert Waters, "Genealogical Gleanings in England," note to editor

Volume 48 (1894): 489-95, Henry Fitz-Gilbert Waters, "Genealogical Gleanings in England"

Volume 49 (1895): 107-8, 122, Henry Fitz-Gilbert Waters, "Genealogical Gleanings in England"

Volume 74 (1920): 137, Alfred Rudulph Justice, "Clarke, Addendum: The Weston Family"

Volume 103 (1949): 182, G. Andrews Moriarty, "Gleanings from English Records: Browne"

Volume 115 (1961): 253-54, McClure Meredith Howland, "English Background of three New England Families"

Volume 152 (1998): 453-64, Richard Evans, "Jeffrey Howland, Citizen and Grocer of London"

Volume 155 (2001): 367-90, Robert Battle, "English Ancestry of Anne (Derehaugh) Stratton of Salem, Massachusetts"

Volume 156 (2002): 39-61, Robert Battle, "English Ancestry of Anne (Derehaugh) Stratton of Salem, Massachusetts"

Northern notes and queries, or, The Scottish antiquary, 17 vols. (1888-1903); see also *The Scottish antiquary, or, Northern notes and queries*

Notes and Queries: A Medium of Inter-Communication for Literary Men, Artists, Antiquaries, Genealogists, etc., 228 vols. in 14 series to date (1849-)

3rd series, volume 9 (1866): 389, note on Dalmahoy

4th series, volume 4 (1869): 40, Edward Peacock, "Isaac Dorislaus"

5th series, volume 1 (1874): 266, P. S. P. Conner, "The Descent of William Penn from the Penns of Penn, co. Bucks"

7th series, volume 10 (1890): 383-84, "Penn Family"

8th series, volume 6 (1894): 1, H. Loftus Tottenham, "James Margetson, Archbishop of Armagh"

Volume 186 (1944): 22, Sheelah Ruggles-Brise, "Spencer and Other Pedigrees"

Volume 197 (1952): 91, W. H. Whelply, "Boleyn"

Notes & Queries for Somerset and Dorset, 36 vols. to date (1890-)

Volume 27 (1958): 185-92, P. N. Dawe, "The Dorset Churchills"

The Pennsylvania Genealogical Magazine, 44 vols. to date (1895-)

Volume 33 (1984): 180-203, Francis James Dallett, "Captain Peter Young and Descendants: Further Philadelphia Roots of the Princess of Wales"

Scottish Notes and Queries, 33 vols. in 3 series (1887-1935)

Volume 2 (1889): 183, "St. Nicholas (Aberdeen) Churchyard Inscriptions"

2nd series, volume 2 (1901): 18, D. M. Rose, "The Bannermans of Elsick and Watertown"

Time, 20 April 1981

Topographer & Genealogist, 3 vols. (1846-58)

Volume 1 (1846): 197-207, C. E. L., "Pedigree of Dabridgecourt, of Stratfield Say, co. Hants."

Vlaamse Stam, Tidschrift voor Familiegescheidenis, 40 vols. to date (1965-)
  Volume 4 (1969): 449-51, 454, Alfons K. L. Thijs, "Antwerpse Scharlakenververs"

Virginia Magazine of History and Biography, 115 vols. to date (1894-)
  Volume 17 (1909): 26-35, "Note: Sir Thomas Lunsford"

William & Mary Quarterly, 63 vols. to date (1892-)
  1st series, volume 8 (1900): 183-86, "Sir Thomas Lunsford"

Wiltshire Archeological and Natural History Magazine, 58 vols. (1854-1962)
  Volume 3 (1857): between 86 and 87, "Pedigree of Montagu, of Lackham"

Wiltshire Notes & Queries, 8 vols. (1893-1916)
  Volume 2 (1897): 207-18, M. E. Light, "Hedington and the Child family"

The Yale Journal of Biology and Medicine, 80 vols. to date (1928-)
  Volume 13 (1941): 429-50, Lockwood Barr, "Biography of Dr. Joseph Strong"

Yorkshire Archæological Journal, 73 vols. to date (1870-)
  Volume 25 (1920): 1-47, John William Clay, "The Savile Family"

Newspapers

The New York Times, 26 Sept. 1880; 4 March 1891; 16 July 1906; 17 July 1906; 2 Nov. 1906; 17 March 1911; 18 Sept. 1931; 7 Feb. 1936; 13 March 1936; 27 Jan. 1947; 15 Nov. 1948; 15 Dec. 1948; 2 June 1954; 9 July 1955; 30 July 1981; 8 July 1993; 29 Aug. 1996; 1 Sept. 1997

The Oakland Tribune, 8 Sept. 1907

The Sunday Times, London, 11 July 1993

The Sunday Times Magazine, London, 26 July 1981

The Times, London, 18 Aug. 1897; 27 Sept. 1922; 14 May 1924; 28 April 1925; 10 Sept. 1929; 14 Sept. 1953; 30 March 1992; 8 July 1993; 3 June 2004

Hibernian Chronicle, Cork, 11 Jan. 1798; 1 Nov. 1798

Microforms

Parish Church of Aberdour (Aberdeenshire) Registers, 1698–1854 Family History Library film 0091,252

Parish registers, Church of Aldenham (Hertfordshire) 1559–1812 Family History Library film 1040,851

Bishop's transcripts for Antony (Cornwall), 1677–1772 Family History Library film 0090,239

Bishops' Transcripts, parish church of Ardeley, Herts: Marriages 1604–1850 Family History Library film 0569,700

Parish Register of Baldock, Herts: Baptisms and burials 1710–1792 Family History Library film 0991,305

Chapelry of Barnard-Castle (Durhamshire) register transcripts, 1609–1812 Family History Library film 0091,081

Barnstaple parish register of baptisms, marriages, and burials 1538 A.D. to 1812 A.D. Family History Library film number 0962,417

Parish Church of Bartlow (Cambridgeshire) registers, 1573–1876 Family History Library film 1040,366

Parish Church of Berry-Pomeroy register transcripts, 1596–1837 Family History Library film 0916,810

Parish Church of Berwick-upon-Tweed (Northumberland) Register Transcripts, 1573–1812 Family History Library film 0094,987

Berwick-upon-Tweed Parish Register Transcripts 1573–1812 Family History Library film 0094,988

Bishop's transcripts of Bolingbroke, 1562–1831 Family History Library film 0421,928

Parish Church of Branston (Leicestershire) registers, 1591–1975 Family History Library film 0811,942

Parish registers for Breage, 1559–1995 Family History Library film 0254,175

The parish register of Bubwith, 1600–1753 Family History Library film 0599,998

Chichester: All Saints Parish Registers 1563–1812 Family History Library film 0504,430

Parish Church of Coleshill (Warwickshire) registers, 1538–1956 Family History Library film 0229,158

The parish registers of Coxwold, 1583–1666 Family History Library film 0844,560, item 4

Parish register transcripts, Church of Crediton, Devon 1558–1843 Family History Library film 0917,184

Dulwich College Church (Comberwell [sic]) Parish register transcripts, 1616–1837 Family History Library film 0434,254

Parish registers of Easebourne, 1538–1901 Family History Library film 0918,250

Parish registers of Echt, Aberdeen 1648–1854 Family History Library film 0993,524

Bishops' transcripts, 1662–1848 Parish registers of Edensor Family History Library film 0428,909

Old parochial registers for Edinburgh, 1595–1860 Family History Library films 1066,663

Old parochial registers for Edinburgh, 1595–1860 Family History Library film 1066,689

Old Parochial Registers for Edinburgh 1595–1860 Family History Library film 1066,690

Bishops' transcripts, 1604–1869 Parish of Essendon, Hertfordshire, Family History Library film 0569,718

Parish Church of Forgue 1684–1854 Family History Library film 0993,183

Parish Church of Fyvie 1685–1854 Family History Library film 0993,186

Parish Registers of Great Witley 1538–1968 Family History Library film 0596,845

A transcript of the early registers of the parish of Guiseley in the county of York, 1584–1720 Family History Library film 6035,726

Parish Church of Hamilton registers, 1645–1868 Family History Library film 1066,593

Parish Church of Heavitree (Devonshire) register transcripts, 1653–1837 Family History Library film 0917,199

Bishops' transcripts, Parish Church of Holbeton 1620–1850 Family History Library film 0917,144

Parish Church of Holme-upon-Spalding-Moor (Yorkshire) register transcripts, 1559–1650 Family History Library film 0098,534, item 3

Bishops' Transcripts, Holy Trinity Micklegate, York 1601–1864 Family History Library film 0990,869

Parish Church of Horseheath (Cambridgeshire) registers, 1558–1876 Family History Library film 1040,532

Parish Church of Howick Register Transcripts, 1678–1812 Family History Library film 0094,970

Registers of the Parish Church of Hungerford (Berkshire) 1559–1813 Family History Library film 0088,273

The parish registers of Hunsdon Co. Hertford, 1546–1837 Family History Library film 0496,822, item 2

The register booke of Inglebye iuxta Grenhow since 1539 Family History Library film 0599,156, item 3

Inverness Parish Registers — Marriages vol. viii 1649–1818 Family History Library film 0990,669

Parish registers of Kemnay, 1660–1854 Family History Library film 0993,195

Parish registers of Kildrummy 1678–1854 Family History Library film 0993,195

Parish Church of Kilkhampton (Cornwall) register, 1539–1839 Family History Library film 0897,356

Bishop's transcripts for Kings-Walden, 1604–1855 Family History Library film 0569,765

Parish registers of Kings-Walden, 1557–1951 Hertfordshire Record Office: D/P 112 1/18–19 Family History Library film 0991,340

Parish Church of Kingsteignton register transcripts, 1606–1837 Family History Library film 0916,852

Parish Church of Kintore 1717–1854 Family History Library film 0993,336

Parish Church of Lanchester (Durhamshire) Register Transcripts Family History Library film 0091,099

The Registers of the parish church of Leeds Family History Library film 0599,919

Bishops' Transcripts Parish of Leek, Staffordshire: Baptisms, marriages, and burials 1662–1740 Family History Library film 0421,562

Parish Church of Lincoln's Inn Registers, 1695–1842 Family History Library film 0823,848, item 3

Registers of Little Hadham, Hertfordshire 1559–1812 Family History Library film 0477,641

Little Saxham parish registers, 1559–1850 Family History Library film 0496,951

Parish Church of Little Wittenham (Berkshire) registers, 1538–1992 Family History Library film 0088,309

Parish Church of Ludford (Shropshire) register transcripts, 1643–1838 Family History Library film 0510,667

Registers of Ludlow 1558–1812 Family History Library film 0599,486

Parish Church of Mamhead registers and bishops' transcripts, 1549–1837 Family History Library film 0916,857, item 1

Parish Registers of Marnoch 1676–1854 Family History Library film 0990,988

Melton Mowbray Parish Registers: Baptisms, marriages and burials 1547–1718 Family History Library film 0588,441

Methley, Yorkshire Bishop's transcripts, 1598–1845 Family History Library film 0990,707

Parish register transcripts, Modbury, Devon, Baptisms 1599–1837 Family History Library film 0916,861

Parish register transcripts Modbury, Devon, Marriages 1553–1565, 1601–1837 Family History Library film 0916,862

Parish register of Monquhitter, Aberdeenshire: vol. i. Baptisms, 1670–1771 Family History Library film 0993,345

Parish Registers of Montrose — Baptisms v. 3 1697–1732 Family History Library film 0993,496

Mortlake parish register, 1599–1678 Family History Library film 0814,225, item 2

Parish Church of Morval (Cornwall) register transcripts 1538–1837 Family History Library film 0916,952

Parish Registers of New Machar: vol. 1. Baptisms, 1676–1699, 1713–1819; marriages, 1676–1698, 1717–1819; burials, 1738–1820 Family History Library film 0993,349

All Saints Church (Newcastle-upon-Tyne, Northumberland) register transcripts, 1600–1720 Family History Library film 0095,005

Parish register transcripts for Newlyn (near St. Columb-Major), 1559–1837 Family History Library film 0916,981

Parish Church of Norham (Northumberland) Transcripts 1654–1812 Family History Library film 0090,787

Parish Church of North Lydbury registers, 1563–1812 Family History Library film 0510,668

North Witham Bishops' Transcripts Family History Library film 0436,048

Archdeaconry wills for the deaneries of Nottingham & Bingham 1698–1712 Family History Library film 1278,629

Bishop's transcripts for Offley, 1604–1864 Family History Library film 0569,751, item 2

Old Machar parish registers — Baptisms vol. iv 1763–1792 Family History Library film 0991,206

Parish Registers of Old Machar — Baptisms vol. iii 1721–1763 Family History Library film 0991,206

Old Machar parish registers — Marriages vol. vii, 1722–1783 Family History Library film 0991,141

Parish registers of Old Meldrum, Aberdeen 1713–1854 Family History Library film 0993,351

Parish Register of Oving, Sussex 1561–1876 Family History Library film 0918,463

The registers of the parish church of Padiham in the county of Lancashire, 1573–1653 Family History Library film 0459,650

Panfield, Essex, Christenings, Burials & Marriages, 1569–1711 Family History Library film 1472,590, item 23

Parish registers for Peebles, 1622–1854 Family History Library film 1067,919

Parish Church of Pelynt (Cornwall) transcripts and bishops' transcripts 1641–1837 Family History Library film 0916,953

Parish Registers of Peterculter 1643–1854 Family History Library film 0993,352

Parish Registers of Radley, Berkshire 1599–1837 Family History Library film 1040,564

Baptisms, Parish Registers of Rayne, Essex, 1558–1663 Family History Library film 1472,666, item 20

Rayne, Essex, Christenings, Burials & Marriages, 1558–1664 Family History Library film 1472,666, item 20

Bishops' transcripts of Rotherham, 1600–1837 Family History Library film 0919,315

Parish registers of Rothwell, Yorkshire 1599–1780 Family History Library film 0990,764

Rougham Parish Register 1565–1837 Family History Library film 0991,971

The parish register of Rushton, Northamptonshire, 1538–1837 Family History Library film 1441,052, item 4

St. Andrew's Church (Enfield, Middlesex) registers, 1550–1928 Family History Library film 0585,397

St. Andrew, Holborn, Middlesex Parish registers, 1556–1934 Family History Library film 0374,349

Parish registers of St. Andrew, Holborn: Baptisms 1693–1704 Family History Library film 0374,351

Parish registers of St. Andrew Hubbard Church, London, 1538–1846 Family History Library film 0374,407

St. Andrew Undershaft Church (London) Registers 1558–1901 Family History Library film 0374,408

St. Ann Blackfriars Church (London) Parish registers, 1560–1849 Family History Library film 0374,416

St. Anne's Church (Soho, Westminster) Parish Registers 1686–1931 Family History Library film 0918,606

Parish registers St. Anne's Soho, 1686–1931 Family History Library film 0918,609

St. Bartholomew by the Exchange Parish Registers 1558–1840 Family History Library film 0374,424

Transcripts of parish registers of London, St. Bartholomew the Less, London, Marriages 1558–1706 Family History Library film 0416,713

Parish registers for St. Bride Fleet Street, 1274–1939 Family History Library film 0380,154

Parish Register of St. Bride Fleet Street: Baptisms, marriages 1587–1653 Family History Library film 0574,353

St. Giles Cripplegate Church (London) Registers, 1559–1936 Family History Library film 0380,199

Parish registers of St. Gregory by St. Paul's Church, 1559–1853 Family History Library film 0375,028

Parish registers for St. James' Church, Westminster, 1685–1881 Family History Library film 1042,307, items 2-3

Parish Registers for St. James's Church, Westminster, 1685–1881 Family History Library film 1042,313

Parish Registers for St. James's Church, Westminster 1685–1881 Family History Library film 1042,320

Scotch Church, 1750–1840 St. James, Westminster Family History Library film 0596,973

St. John's Church (Hackney) Parish register transcripts, 1540–1812 Family History Library film 0569,924

St. John's Church (Newcastle-upon-Tyne, Northumberland) parish register transcripts, 1587–1812 Family History Library film 009,5014

Parish registers of St. Lawrence Pountney, 1530–1812 Family History Library film 0374,466

Parish registers for St. Luke's Church, Chelsea, 1559–1875 Family History Library film 0585,471

Memorials of St. Margaret's church, Westminster: comprising the parish registers, 1539–1660 Family History Library film 0908,519, item 1

Parish registers for St. Margaret Lothbury, London Family History Library film 0374,471

St. Margaret Patten's Church (London) registers, 1506–1952 Family History Library film 0374,474

Parish registers of St. Martin's-in-the-Fields, Westminster, Marriages 1658–1757 Family History Library film 0561,155

Parish registers for St. Martin-in-the-Fields, 1550–1653 Family History Library film 0560,369

Parish Registers for St. Martin-in-the-Fields 1550–1926 Family History Library film 0560,371

Parish Registers for St. Martin-in-the-Fields 1550–1926 Family History Library film 0560,372

Parish Registers, St. Martin Ludgate, London 1646–1654 Family History Library film 0374,476

Bishops' Transcripts of St. Martin-Micklegate-with-St. Gregory's Church, York Family History Library film 0990,875

St. Mary at Hill's Church (London) parish registers 1560–1812 Family History Library film 0374,485

Parish registers of St. Mary Cray, 1579–1916 Family History Library film 1042,461

St. Mary's, Southampton parish register transcripts, 1675–1837 Family History Library film 1595,861

St. Mary's Church (Stoke-Newington) parish register transcripts, 1559–1812 Family History Library film 0094,717

St. Mary's Church (Watford, Hertfordshire) parish registers and miscellaneous public records, 1539–1932 Family History Library film 0991,355

Parish Registers of St. Mary Magdalen Old Fish Street Church: marriages, 1664–1754 Family History Library film 0374,490

Parish register transcripts, St. Mary Major Church (Exeter) 1561–1837 Family History Library film 0917,103

Registers of St. Michael, Penkivel, Cornwall: Christenings, 1547–1958 Family History Library film 0226,184

The registers of St. Michael-le-Belfry, York, 1565–1778 Family History Library film 0496,806

St. Nicholas, Aberdeen parish registers — Baptisms vol. iv 1647–72 Family History Library film 0991,134

St. Nicholas, Aberdeen parish registers —Baptisms vol. vi 1688–1704 Family History Library film 0991,135

Parish registers of St. Nicholas, Aberdeen: Baptisms vol. vii 1704–1734 Family History Library film 0991,136

Parish Registers of St. Nicholas, Aberdeen: Baptisms 1771–1820 Family History Library film 0991,137

Parish Registers of St. Nicholas, Aberdeen — Marriages vol. xiii 1695–1776 Family History Library film 0991,138

St. Nicholas Aberdeen, Baptisms Family History Library film 0991,199

Parish registers, St. Nicholas, Aberdeen — Marriages vol. xxviii 1820–1831 Family History Library film 0991,201

Parish Registers of St. Nicholas, Aberdeen: Marriages 1820–1854 Family History Library film 0991,202

St. Nicholas' Church (Newcastle-upon-Tyne) parish register transcripts, 1558–1837 Family History Library film 0095,017

Bishops' transcripts St. Nicholas' Church Nottingham, 1601–1877 Family History Library film 0503,803

Registers of St. Olave's Hart Street, London: Baptisms, 1631–1812 Family History Library film 0557,012

Registers of St. Olave Old Jewry, London: Baptisms, burials 1538–1629 Marriages 1538–1637 Family History Library film 0380,325

Parish registers of St. Pancras Old Church (London), Marriages, 1794–1811, Family History Library film 0598,179

The registers of St. Paul's Church, Covent Garden, London 1653–1837 Family History Library film 0845,241

The parish registers of St. Peter's Beaksbourne, Kent, 1558–1812 Family History Library film 0924,121, item 3

Parish Register of St. Peter-Le-Poer, London, Baptisms, marriages 1561–1904 Burials 1561–1853 Banns 1755–1817 Family History Library film 0374,993

Parish Registers of Chichester, St. Peter the Great: 1679–1812 Family History Library film 0504,431

Exeter St. Petrock's Parish Register 1538–1837 Family History Library film 0916,838

Registers of St. Swithin Stone Church, London Family History Library film 0375,020

St. Thomas the Apostle's Church (Exeter) Register Transcripts, 1554–1837 Family History Library film 0916,843

Sandon, Essex, Christenings, Burials & Marriages, 1554–1740 Family History Library film 1472,680, item 24

The parish register of Sessay, near Thirsk, Yorkshire 1600–1812 Family History Library film 0844,559

Shobdon Parish Register Family History Library film 1040,024

Parish register transcripts, Parish Church of Silkstone 1557–1784 Family History Library film 0098,538

South Ockendon Register 1538–1783 Family History Library film 1472,589

Parish Church of Speymouth (Morayshire) Registers, 1651–1854 Family History Library film 0990,811

Register of Stainton, near Yarm, Cleveland: Christenings, marriages and burials, 1551–1837 Family History Library film 0551,576

Parish Registers of the Stepney parish church, 1568–1929 Family History Library film 0595,417

Parish Church of Stoke-Poges (Buckinghamshire) Registers 1563–1753 Family History Library film 0924,121

Parish Church of Sunbury (Middlesex) registers, 1565–1875 Family History Library film 0577,573

Parish Church of Taplow (Buckinghamshire) 1710–1897 Family History Library film 0919,250

Parish registers 1695–1854 Tarves parish, Aberdeen Family History Library film 0993,301

Parish Church of Turriff (Aberdeenshire) Registers, 1696–1769 Family History Library film 0993,303

Turriff parish registers — marriages, 1783–1820 Family History Library film 0993,304

Parish registers of Tyrie, 1710–1854 Family History Library film 0993,305

Registers of Walkern, Herts: Baptisms 1559–1812 Family History Library film 1040,799

Parish registers of Waltham-St. Lawrence, 1559–1845 Family History Library film 0088,466

Parish registers for Walton-upon-Thames, 1639–1918 Family History Library film 1041,721

West Leake Baptisms, Marriages and Burials 1622–1812 Family History Library film 0503,787

Registers of the Parish Church of Westbury, Wiltshire Family History Library film 1279,369

Parish registers of Westmill church, Herts, 1562–1947 Family History Library film 0991,401

The Parish Register of Whitby, 1600–1676 Family History Library film 0599,996, item 6

The bishop's transcripts and parish registers of Wilcot, baptisms, marriages & burials, 1812–1842 Family History Library film 1279,437

Parish Registers of Woodbridge 1545–1910 Family History Library film 0919,635

Parish registers of the Church of Wymering, 1653–1875 (including Widley parish) Family History Library film 0918,878

Parish register transcripts of Yealmpton (Devonshire), 1600–1850 Family History Library film 0917,560

Original wills transcribed by the author

Will of Gregory Ballard, Batchelor of Laws of University of Oxford, Oxfordshire 22 Dec. 1664, Proved at London P.C.C. 6 April 1665 PROB 11/316

Will of Edward Boate of Portsmouth, Hampshire 29 March 1650, Proved at London P.C.C. 10 June 1650 PROB 11/212

Will of Reverend Ralph Brideoake, Archdeacon of Winchester and Rector of the Church of St. Maries near Southampton of Hampshire 9 Nov. 1742, Proved 17 May 1743 PROB 11/726

Will of John Brisco, Grocer of Saint Stephen Walbrook, City of London 6 Jan. 1687, Proved 1 Oct. 1689 PROB 11/396

Will of John Buller of Morval, Cornwall 21 Nov. 1714, codicils 24 Jan. 1714/15, 1 Sept. 1715, and 4 Nov. 1715, Proved at London P.C.C. 13 April 1716 PROB 11/552

Will of James Bulteel, Merchant of Barnstaple, Devon, Proved at London P.C.C. 30 Oct. 1632 PROB 11/162

Will of Sir Dudley Carleton of the City of London, Proved P.C.C. 22 March 1654 PROB 11/239

Will of Robert Charlton of Whitton, Shropshire 12 May 1668, Proved 13 May 1670 PROB 11/332

Will of Richard Childe or Child, Weaver of London 8 Sept. 1638, codicils 13 March 1638/39 and 5 May 1639, Proved 25 May 1639 PROB 11/180

Will of The Honorable Thomas Collier, Colonel of Jersey, 8 Feb. 1714/15, codicil 16 June 1715, Proved 2 Nov. 1715 PROB 11/5

Will of Henry Lord Compton, 17 May 1589, Probated 22 Nov. 1589, Chancery Inquisitions Post Mortem, Series II, 224/37

Will of Sir Joseph Copley heretofore Joseph Moyle and afterwards Joseph Copley of Southampton, Hampshire, Proved at London P.C.C. 27 April 1781 PROB 11/1076

Will of Dame Mary Copley, Widow of Princes Street, Cavendish Square, Middlesex, Proved at London 20 March 1787 PROB 11/1151

Will of Frances Crosse, Widow of Wood Street, City of London 27 May 1710, Proved at London P.C.C. 3 Dec. 1711 PROB 11/524

Will of The Right Honourable John Earl of Darnley [I] and Baron Clifton of Leighton of Bromwold, Huntingdonshire made at Dublin 21 Aug. 1767, codicils dated 29 June 1774 and 6 Oct. 1778, Proved at London P.C.C. 6 Sept. 1781 PROB 11/1081

Will of Thomas Dillingham, Clerk of Over Dean, Bedfordshire 1 Dec. 1647, Proved at London P.C.C. 28 Jan. 1648 PROB 11/203

Testament Testamentar and Inventory of Arthur Dingwall of Brownhill 18 Dec. 1729 Aberdeen Commissary Court CC1/6/10

Testament Testamentar and Inventory of Jean Chalmers, relict of Arthur Dingwall, sometime of Brownhill 8 Feb. 1750 Aberdeen Commissary Court CC1/6/31A

Will of Robert Doughty of Hanworth, Norfolk 25 Sept. 1756, Proved at London P.C.C. 12 Jan. 1759 PROB 11/843

Will of Sir John Drake of Ash, Devon 8 Aug. 1636, Proved 26 Jan. 1636/37 PROB 11/173

Will of Dame Dorothea Drumond, Widow of St. Giles in the Fields, Middlesex 16 Jan. 1677/78, codicil 17 Sept. 1679, Proved at London P.C.C. 16 Dec. 1679 PROB 11/361

Will of Sir Maurice Drumond, Gentleman Usher of His Majesty's Privy Chamber 20 April 1640, Proved at London P.C.C. 13 May 1642 PROB 11/189

Will of Dame Susan Drewry or Drury, Widow of Temple Boulstred, Buckinghamshire 28 March 1639, Proved at London P.C.C. 25 Feb. 1641 PROB 11/185

Testament Dative of John Duff of Culbin 29 Oct. 1747 Inverness Commissary Court CC11/1/5

Will of Henry Dunch of Newington, Oxfordshire 8 Oct. 1686, Proved at London P.C.C. 4 Nov. 1686 PROB 11/385

Will of Sarah Duncombe, Widow of Islington, Middlesex 14 Feb. 1653, Proved 26 Feb. 1654 PROB 11/239

Will of Thomas Duncombe of Broughton, Buckinghamshire 6 May 1632, codicils 8 and 10 May 1632, Proved 17 May 1632 PROB 11/161

Will of John Eyles, senior, Merchant of Devizes, Wiltshire 16 Nov. 1660, codicil 17 June 1662, Proved 13 Nov. 1662 PROB 11/309

Will of Robert Eyre, Citizen and Grocer of London, 7 Aug. 1718, Proved at London P.C.C. 24 Sept. 1718 PROB 11/565

Will of Sir Gerard Eyton of Eyton, Denbighshire 14 Jan. 1650, Proved P.C.C. 23 May 1653 PROB 11/229

Will of Sir George Farewell of Bishops Hull, Somerset 25 July 1645, Proved at London P.C.C. 17 Nov. 1647 PROB 11/202

Will of George Farewell of Saint Margaret Westminster, Middlesex 9 Feb. 1690, Proved at London P.C.C. 26 March 1691 PROB 11/404

Will of Mary Farewell 29 March 1656, Proved at London P.C.C. 22 Jan. 1662 PROB 11/307

Testament Testamentar and Inventory of George Forbes of Upper Boyndlie 30 Dec. 1794 Aberdeen Commissary Court CC1/6/57

Will of Sir Thomas Gage of Firle, Sussex, Proved 31 Oct. 1654 PROB 11/234

Will of Sir John Garrard of Lamer, Hertfordshire 25 May 1637, Proved at London P.C.C. 21 June 1637 PROB 11/174

Will of Phillipp Gerard of Grays Inn, Middlesex 27 March 1635, Proved at London P.C.C. 27 Feb. 1636/37 PROB 11/173

Will of Elizabeth Grey, Widow of Fallodon, Northumberland 1 April 1801, codicil 25 March 1803, Proved at London P.C.C. 6 April 1807 PROB 11/1459

Will of Rowland Hale of Kings Walden, Hertfordshire Proved 15 April 1669 PROB 11/329

Will of William Hale or Hales of Kings Walden, Hertfordshire Proved 3 Oct. 1634 PROB 11/166

Will of William Hale of King's Walden, Hertfordshire Proved 4 July 1688 PROB 11/392

Will of Isaac Hamon of Portarlington, Queens County, Ireland 19 May 1753, codicil 12 Aug. 1754, Proved 4 April 1755 PROB 11/815

Will of Elizabeth Hanmer, of Iscoyd, Flintshire 16 Oct. 1773, Proved 4 Nov. 1777 PROB 11/1036

Will of Esther Hanmer, Widow of Bettisfield, Flintshire 2 Oct. 1754, Proved at London P.C.C. 2 Aug. 1770 PROB 11/959

Will of Thomas Hanmer of Fenns, Flintshire 3 Feb. 1624/25, Proved at London 17 May 1625 PROB 11/145

Will of William Hanmer of Fenns, Flintshire 14 June 1746, codicil (as of Iscoyd) 9 Feb. 1754, Proved at London P.C.C. 30 April 1754 PROB 11/808

Will of Dame Mary Hartop, Widow of Stamford Barron, Northamptonshire 28 Sept. 1692, Proved at London P.C.C. 30 May 1693 PROB 11/414

Will of Gerrard Herring, Draper of Cambridge, Cambridgeshire 8 Aug. 1701, Proved at London P.C.C. 2 May 1704 PROB 11/476

Will of John Herring, Draper of Cambridge, Cambridgeshire 20 Aug. 1674, codicil 17 Sept. 1674, Proved 13 Nov. 1674 PROB 11/346

Will of Mary Herring, Widow of Cambridge, Cambridgeshire 15 Jan. 1714/15, Proved at London P.C.C. 24 May 1715 PROB 11/546

Will of Samuel Herring, Merchant Taylor of Lambeth, Surrey, esquire 18 Oct. 1756, codicil 19 Oct. 1756, Proved 13 Oct. 1757 PROB 11/833

Will of William Herring, Woollen Draper of Cambridge 22 Nov. 1721, Proved 20 Sept. 1722 PROB 11/587

Will of William Herring of Croydon, Surrey 1 Feb. 1801, Proved at London P.C.C. 6 Nov. 1801 PROB 11/1365

Will of Charles Hoskins of Oxted, Surrey 8 July 1657, nuncupative codicil 26 Aug. 1657, Proved at London P.C.C. 6 Nov. 1657 PROB 11/269

Will of John Hoskins of Oxted, Surrey 25 March 1713, Proved at London P.C.C. 3 June 1717 PROB 11/558

Will of Robert Howchin the elder of Panfield, Essex 1 Sept. 1647, Proved at Dunmow 13 Nov. 1647 E.R.O. D/A BW60/63

Will of Roger Howe, Mercer of London 16 July 1606, codicil 21 July 1606, Proved 6 Nov. 1606 PROB 11/108

Will of Robert Hutchin of Rayne, Essex 22 Jan. 1690/91, Proved 2 May 1692 E.R.O. D/A MR8/24

Sentence of Sir John Jennyns or Jenins Dated 22 Nov. 1611 PROB 11/118

Will of Sir John Jennyns of St. Albans, Hertfordshire 21 March 1638/39, Proved at London P.C.C. 9 Aug. 1642 PROB 11/190

Will of John Langley of London, Proved 12 Dec. 1639 PROB 11/181

Will of Edward Lascelles, Citizen and Grocer of London 5 March 1699, Proved 20 Sept. 1700 PROB 11/457

Will of Weyman Lee of the Inner Temple, Middlesex 10 June 1765, Proved at London P.C.C. 26 Nov. 1765 PROB 11/913

Will of The Right Honorable Lady Louisa Mary Lennox, Widow of Funtington, Sussex 10 Sept. 1829, Proved 1 Feb. 1831 PROB 11/1781

Testament Testamentar and Inventory of Patrick Littlejohn, merchant of Old Meldrum 7 Jan. 1738, registered 8 June 1738, inventory 22 Feb. 1740 Aberdeen Commissary Court CC1/6/21

Will of Godfrey Meynell, Gentleman of Meynell Langley, Derbyshire 16 April 1667, Proved at The Strand, Middlesex P.C.C. 20 Dec. 1667 PROB 11/325

Will of Isaac Meynell, Goldsmith of St. Mary Woolnoth, Lombard Street, London 2 Nov. 1675, Proved at Theobald's, Herts P.C.C. 1 July 1676 PROB 11/352

Will of Stephen Monteage, Merchant of All Hallows on the Wall, City of London 26 June 1685, Proved 26 Nov. 1687 PROB 11/389

Testament Dative and Inventory of Alexander Morison of Bognie 30 May 1809 Aberdeen Commissary Court CC1/6/72

Will of Catherine Moyle, Widow of Southampton, Hampshire 22 April 1748, Proved at London P.C.C. 20 March 1775 PROB

Will of John Moyle of Buke, Cornwall 7 April 1744, Proved at London P.C.C. 18 April 1748 PROB 11/761

Will of Joseph Moyle of Southampton, Hampshire 13 April 1741, Proved at London P.C.C. 14 April 1742 PROB 11/717

Will of Susanna Moyle of Bath, Somerset 14 Feb. 1760, Proved at London P.C.C. 10 April 1760 PROB 11/855

Will of Valentine Munbee of Horningsheath, Suffolk 14 Nov. 1741, Proved at London P.C.C. 1 Feb. 1750/51 PROB 11/786

Will of Dame Elizabeth Norris of St. Ann Westminster, Middlesex 12 July 1712, Proved at London P.C.C. 8 April 1713 PROB 11/532

Will of Elizabeth Ogle, Widow of Kirkley, Northumberland, Proved 25 May 1751 PROB 11/788

Will of Thomas Paske, Doctor in Divinity and Rector of Much Hadham, Hertfordshire 12 Sept. 1662, Proved at London P.C.C. 19 Nov. 1662 PROB 11/309

Will of Edward Pearce, Gentleman of Witlingham, Norfolk 11 Nov. 1682, codicil 14 April 1683, Proved at London P.C.C. 10 Nov. 1683 PROB 11/374

Will of Sarah Penn, Widow of Penn, Buckinghamshire 5 Dec. 1698, Proved at London P.C.C. 10 Jan. 1698/99 PROB 11/449

Will of William Penn the younger of Penn Place, Buckinghamshire 8 July 1686, Proved at London P.C.C. 15 June 1696 PROB 11/432

Will of Philip Perring, Clothier of Modbury, Devon 23 Feb. 1764, Proved at London P.C.C. 11 Sept. 1771 PROB 11/971

Will of John Plumer, Gentleman of New Windsor, Berkshire 15 March 1668, Proved at London P.C.C. 9 Oct. 1672 PROB 11/340

Will of John Plummer, Gentleman of Saint Gregory, City of London 8 June 1607, codicil 28 July 1608, Proved P.C.C. 17 Oct. 1608 PROB 11/112

Will of Christopher Rayner, Haberdasher of London 21 March 1662, Proved at London P.C.C. 6 April 1664 PROB 11/313

Will of Frances Rayner, Widow of London 3 July 1681, Proved at London P.C.C. 4 Aug. 1681 PROB 11/367

Will of Jacob Richards, Salter of London 5 Nov 1675, Proved at London P.C.C. 17 Dec. 1675 P.C.C. PROB 11/349

Will of Jacob Richards, Gentleman of Saint Martin in the Fields, Middlesex 16 April 1692, Proved 1 Aug. 1701 PROB 11/461

Will of Dame Mary Saltonstall of South Ockendon, Essex 11 Nov. 1651, Proved at London P.C.C. 21 May 1662 PROB 11/308

Will of Sir Richard Saltonstall of South Ockenden, Essex 16 Feb. 1649, Proved at London P.C.C. 6 March 1649/50 PROB 11/211

Will of Humphrey Shalcrosse of Digswell, Hertfordshire 24 Dec. 1664, Proved 17 Feb. 1666 PROB 11/319

Will of Thomas Sherer, Gentleman of Chichester, Sussex 31 Jan. 1706, Proved at London P.C.C. 8 Sept. 1707 PROB 11/496

Testament Dative and Inventory of Alexander Tait, Merchant in Edinburgh, residenter in South Leith 23 March 1716 Edinburgh Commissary Court CC8/8/86

Will of Susanna Vansittart, Widow of Ormond Street, St. Andrew Holborn, Middlesex 13 April 1725, Proved at London P.C.C. 4 April 1726 PROB 11/608

Will of John Vowler of Exeter, Devon 14 April 1747, Proved at London P.C.C. 4 June 1748 PROB 11/763

Will of Dame Catherine Waldegrave Proved 4 April 1695 PROB 11/425

Will of Isaac Watlington of Cambridge, Cambridgeshire 1 Jan. 1699, Proved at London P.C.C. 10 Feb. 1701 PROB 11/459

Will of Peter Whetcombe of Margaretting, Essex 31 Jan. 1666/67, Proved 25 Nov. 1667 PROB 11/325

Will of Peter Whitcomb or Whitcombe of Great Bransted, Essex, Proved 12 Sept. 1704 PROB 11/478

Will of Francis Worsley of Newport, Isle of Wight, Hampshire 18 Oct. 1659, Proved at London P.C.C. 27 May 1661 PROB 11/304

Will of Ann Wroughton, Widow of Bath, Somerset 14 May 1760, Proved at London P.C.C. 15 May 1761 PROB 11/866

Will of Francis Wroughton, Gentleman of Wilcot , Wiltshire, Proved 3 Oct. 1722 PROB 11/587

Will of George Wroughton of Shercott in the parish of Pewsey, Wiltshire 14 Nov. 1691, Proved at London P.C.C. 29 March 1698 PROB 11/444

Will of George Wroughton of Wilcot, Wiltshire 6 May 1702, Proved P.C.C. 7 May 1703 PROB 11/471

Will of George Wroughton 16 June 1779, Proved at London P.C.C. 2 Aug. 1779 PROB 11/1056

Will of James Wroughton of Wilcot, Wiltshire 10 May 1745, codicil 26 June 1745, Proved at London P.C.C. 13 Jan. 1745/46 PROB 11/744

Will of Susanna Wroughton, Widow of Wilcot House, Wiltshire 16 Dec. 1815, codicil 13 Jan. 1816, Proved at London P.C.C. 6 April 1816 PROB 11/1579

Will of Dudley Wylde of Bishops Palace, Canterbury, Kent 15 July 1653, Proved 8 Sept. 1653 PROB 11/227

British Censuses

1851 England Census, HO107, Folio 187: 22

1851 England Census, HO107, Folio 386: 27

1851 England Census, HO107, Folio 415: 13

1851 Scotland Census, CSSCT1851_41, parish # 168B, E.D. # 6: 49

1851 Scotland Census, CSSCT1851_49, parish # 227, E.D. # 3: 4

1851 Scotland Census, CSSCT1851_52, parish # 243, E.D. # 12, household # 54

1851 Scotland Census, CSSCT1851_80, parish # 387, E.D. # 5: 11

1861 Scotland Census, CSSCT1861_33, parish # 243, E.D. # 11: 1

1861 Scotland Census, CSSCT1861_33, parish # 249, E.D. # 4: 4

1871 England Census, RG10, Folio 38: 27

1871 England Census, RG10, Folio 57: 47

1871 England Census, RG10, Folio 64: 18

INDEX

A note on the Index: Names with particles are generally indexed under the surname, not the particle. For example, Daniel de Robillard will be found under Robillard, and Claus von Ahlefeldt-Gjelting will be found under Ahlefeldt-Gjelting. Compound names, such as Velez de Guevara, are found under the first name in the compound. Long compound names with particles follow both these rules: Louise Renée de Penancoët de Kerouallé is found under Penancoët. Monarchs are indexed under the country or countries. Nobles and other titled people are indexed twice: by their given names and by their titles — for example, James Hamilton, 1st Duke of Abercorn, will be found under both Abercorn and Hamilton.

A

ABERCORN
James Hamilton, 1st Duke of, 16, 17
James Hamilton, 2nd Duke of, 11
James Hamilton, 1st Earl of, 294
James Hamilton, 6th Earl of, 122
James Hamilton, 7th Earl of, 78
James Albert Edward Hamilton, 3rd Duke of, 9
John James Hamilton, 1st Marquess of, 34
Louisa Jane (Russell), Duchess of, 16,17, 342
ABERCROMBY
Anne, 221
Elizabeth, 315
Major General James, 460
John, 337, 460
ABERDEEN
George Gordon, 1st Earl of, 127, 129, 140
George Gordon, 4th Earl of, 23
William Gordon, 2nd Earl of, 82, 89
ABERNETHY
Alexander, 149
Thomas, 149
ABRAHAM
Frances, 49
Robert, 71
ACLAND
———, 312
Margaret, 141
ACUÑA
Diego Sarmiento de, Count of Gondomar, 240
ADAMS
Amy, 235
Thomas, 328
ADCOCK
Eleanor, 255
ADDERLEY
Frances, 79

William, 124, 182
ADDINGTON
Henry, 24
ADELMANN VON ADELMANNSFELDEN
Anna Maria, 317
AHLEFELDT
Marie Elisabeth Christine von, 131
AHLEFELDT-GJELTING
Claus von, 290
Major Claus von, 193
AHLEFELDT-STUBBE
Adelheid von, 290
AILESBURY
Robert Bruce, 1st Earl of, 136, 185
Thomas Bruce, 2nd Earl of, 87
AIRLIE
James Ogilvy, 1st Earl of, 337
James Ogilvy, 2nd Earl of, 187, 337
ALBEMARLE
Arnold Joost van Keppel, 1st Earl of, 80, 81
George Monck, 1st Duke of, 105, 106
William Anne Keppel, 2nd Earl of, 53
ALBERT
Margaret, 60
ALBRET
Jeanne III d', *see* Jeanne III d'Albret, Queen of Navarre
ALDBOROUGH
Dorothy, 323
ALDERSEY
Dorothy, 246, 267
Elizabeth, 228
ALENÇON
François de Valois, Duke of, 156
ALFORD
Sir Richard, 247
ALINGTON
Dorothy, 301
Sir Giles, 250, 289, 301
Hon. Juliana, 83

Lady Jane, 177
Sarah, 332
BRACEY
Mary, 307
BRADFORD
Beatrice, 254
Grace, 302
BRADLEY
——, 274
Nathan, 145
BRADSHAW
Jane, 288
John, 288
BRAGANÇA
Infanta Doña Catarina Henriqueta de, *see*
Catherine (of Bragança), Queen of England
and Scotland
Dom João IV de, King of Portugal, 103
BRAITHWAITE
Mary, 177
BRANDENBURG
Johann Georg, Elector of, 291
Magdalene Markgräfin von, 291
BRANSBY
Sarah, 257
BRAUNSCHWEIG *see* BRUNSWICK
BRAUWE
Anna, Vrouwe tot Camp en Dijckhuis,
279
Herman, 279
BRAY
Reginald, 285
Temperance, 189
BREBNER
Isobel, 148
BREDERODE
Floris van, 246
BRERETON
Hon. Mary, 164
William, 1st Baron Brereton, 164
BRETT
Margaret, 234
BRIDEOAK
Rev. John, 76
Mary, 50
Right Rev. Dr. Ralph, Bishop of Chichester,
118
Richard, 173
BRIDGES
Catherine, 141
John, 141
BRIDGEWATER
John Egerton, 1st Earl of, 292
John Egerton, 2nd Earl of, 211
John Egerton, 3rd Earl of, 142
Scroop Egerton, 1st Duke of, 90
BRIGGES/BRIGGS
John, 216
Martha, 113, 138
Sir Moreton, 1st Baronet, 251, 311
Robert, 167, 204

BRISCOE
Anne, 133, 134
Beatrix (——), 408
Dorothy, 177
John, 177, 196, 197
Thomas, 296, 297
BRISTOL
George Digby, 2nd Earl of, 97
John Digby, 1st Earl of, 151
BROCKETT
Helen, 225, 293
BROKESBY
William, 248
BROME
Constance, 229
Mary, 131
Thomas, 131
BROMFIELD
Elizabeth, 309
BRONTIN
Marie, 259
BROOKE
Hon. Margaret, 136
Priscilla, 300
William, 10th Baron Cobham, 136
BROOKSBY
Winifred, 161
BROUNCKER
Anne, 225
Susan, 235
BROWN/BROWNE
Anne, 196
Anthony Joseph, 7th Viscount Montagu, 11,
15
Anthony Maria, 2nd Viscount Montagu, 248
Elizabeth, 228
Hon. Elizabeth Mary, 11, 15
Hon. Frances, 161
Jane, 247
John, 257
Katherine, 129, 140
Mabel, 293
Sir Matthew, 229
Sarah, 41
Captain Thomas, 50
Sir Thomas, 2nd Baronet, 207
BROWNELL
Ann, 27
John, 39
BROWNLOW
Elizabeth, 322
BRUCE
Lady Diana, 185
Edward, 1st Lord Bruce, 303
Lady Elizabeth, 56
Lady Marie Thérèse Charlotte, 366
Robert, 2nd Earl of Elgin and 1st Earl of
Ailesbury, 136, 185
Thomas, 1st Earl of Elgin, 200
Thomas, 3rd Earl of Elgin and 2nd Earl of
Ailesbury, 87, 366

H

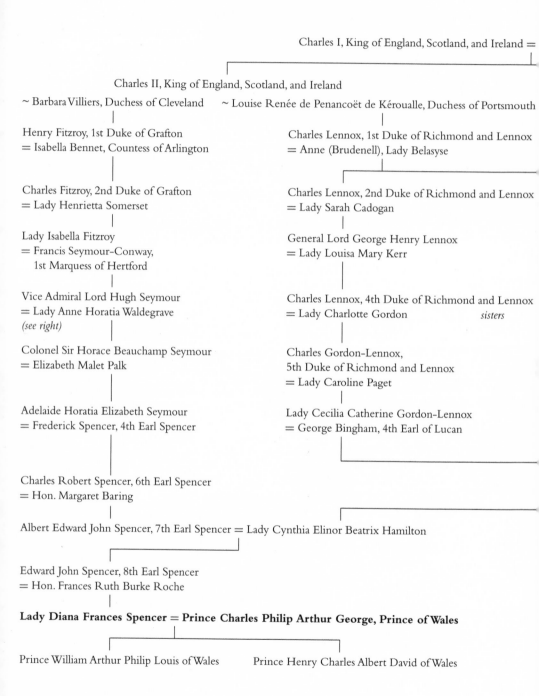

Charles I, King of England, Scotland, and Ireland =

Charles II, King of England, Scotland, and Ireland

~ Barbara Villiers, Duchess of Cleveland   ~ Louise Renée de Penancoët de Kéroualle, Duchess of Portsmouth

Henry Fitzroy, 1st Duke of Grafton   Charles Lennox, 1st Duke of Richmond and Lennox
= Isabella Bennet, Countess of Arlington   = Anne (Brudenell), Lady Belasyse

Charles Fitzroy, 2nd Duke of Grafton   Charles Lennox, 2nd Duke of Richmond and Lennox
= Lady Henrietta Somerset   = Lady Sarah Cadogan

Lady Isabella Fitzroy   General Lord George Henry Lennox
= Francis Seymour-Conway,   = Lady Louisa Mary Kerr
   1st Marquess of Hertford

Vice Admiral Lord Hugh Seymour   Charles Lennox, 4th Duke of Richmond and Lennox
= Lady Anne Horatia Waldegrave   = Lady Charlotte Gordon   *sisters*
(see right)

Colonel Sir Horace Beauchamp Seymour   Charles Gordon-Lennox,
= Elizabeth Malet Palk   5th Duke of Richmond and Lennox
                                                                            = Lady Caroline Paget

Adelaide Horatia Elizabeth Seymour   Lady Cecilia Catherine Gordon-Lennox
= Frederick Spencer, 4th Earl Spencer   = George Bingham, 4th Earl of Lucan

Charles Robert Spencer, 6th Earl Spencer
= Hon. Margaret Baring

Albert Edward John Spencer, 7th Earl Spencer = Lady Cynthia Elinor Beatrix Hamilton

Edward John Spencer, 8th Earl Spencer
= Hon. Frances Ruth Burke Roche

Lady Diana Frances Spencer = Prince Charles Philip Arthur George, Prince of Wales

Prince William Arthur Philip Louis of Wales   Prince Henry Charles Albert David of Wales